RELIGIOUS FREEDOM, LGBT RIGHTS, AND THE PROSPECTS FOR COMMON GROUND

The rights of lesbian, gay, bisexual, and transgender persons (LGBT) are strongly contested by certain faith communities, and this confrontation has become increasingly pronounced following the adjudication of a number of legal cases. As the strident arguments of both sides enter a heated political arena, many wonder whether there is any possibility of both communities' contested positions being reconciled under the same law. This volume assembles impactful voices from the faith, LGBT advocacy, legal, and academic communities – from the Human Rights Campaign and ACLU to the National Association of Evangelicals and Catholic and LDS churches. The contributors offer a 360-degree view of culture-war conflicts around faith and sexuality – from *Obergefell* to *Masterpiece Cakeshop* – and explore whether communities with such profound differences in belief are able to reach mutually acceptable solutions in order to live with integrity.

WILLIAM N. ESKRIDGE, JR. is the John A. Garver Professor of Jurisprudence at Yale Law School. A renowned scholar of statutory interpretation and legislation, in 1990–95, Professor Eskridge represented a gay couple suing for recognition of their same-sex marriage. He has published a field-establishing casebook, three monographs, and dozens of articles articulating a legal and political framework for proper state treatment of sexual and gender minorities. Historical materials in *Gaylaw* formed the basis for an *amicus* brief filed by the Cato Institute and much of the US Supreme Court's (and the dissenting opinion's) analysis in *Lawrence v. Texas* (2003), invalidating consensual sodomy laws.

ROBIN FRETWELL WILSON is the Roger and Stephany Joslin Professor of Law at the University of Illinois College of Law. Professor Wilson assisted the Utah legislature as it enacted landmark legislation balancing religious freedom and LGBT nondiscrimination protections. She also founded and directs the Fairness for All Initiative, which provides tangible support to legislators seeking to enact laws protecting both communities. A member of the American Law Institute, she is the author, coauthor, or editor of eleven books, including *Same-Sex Marriage and Religious Liberty* and *The Contested Place of Religion in Family Law*. In 2018, she received the Thomas L. Kane Religious Freedom Award.

Religious Freedom, LGBT Rights, and the Prospects for Common Ground

Edited by

WILLIAM N. ESKRIDGE, JR.

Yale University

ROBIN FRETWELL WILSON

University of Illinois Urbana-Champaign

CAMBRIDGE
UNIVERSITY PRESS

CAMBRIDGE
UNIVERSITY PRESS

University Printing House, Cambridge CB2 8BS, United Kingdom

One Liberty Plaza, 20th Floor, New York, NY 10006, USA

477 Williamstown Road, Port Melbourne, VIC 3207, Australia

314-321, 3rd Floor, Plot 3, Splendor Forum, Jasola District Centre, New Delhi - 110025, India

79 Anson Road, #06-04/06, Singapore 079906

Cambridge University Press is part of the University of Cambridge.

It furthers the University's mission by disseminating knowledge in the pursuit of
education, learning and research at the highest international levels of excellence.

www.cambridge.org
Information on this title: www.cambridge.org/9781108454582
DOI: 10.1017/9781316999752

First published 2019
First paperback edition 2019

A catalogue record for this publication is available from the British Library

Library of Congress Cataloging in Publication data
NAMES: Eskridge, William N., Jr., 1951-, editor. | Wilson, Robin Fretwell, editor.
TITLE: Religious freedom, LGBT rights, and the prospects for common ground /
Edited by William N. Eskridge Jr., Yale University, Connecticut, Robin Fretwell Wilson,
University of Illinois Urbana-Champaign.
DESCRIPTION: New York : Cambridge University Press, 2018. | Includes bibliographical
references and index.
IDENTIFIERS: LCCN 2018024259 | ISBN 9781108470155 (hardback : alk. paper) |
ISBN 9781108454582 (pbk. : alk. paper)
SUBJECTS: LCSH: Freedom of religion–United States. | Sexual minorities–Civil rights–United States. |
Discrimination–Religious aspects. | Civil rights–Religious aspects.
CLASSIFICATION: LCC KF4783 .R429 2018 | DDC 342.7308/52–dc23
LC record available at https://lccn.loc.gov/2018024259

ISBN 978-1-108-47015-5 Hardback
ISBN 978-1-108-45458-2 Paperback

To Elder Von G. Keetch, the moral and intellectual soul of fairness for all. You will be sorely missed.

Contents

Contributors

EDITORS

William N. Eskridge, Jr., John A. Garver Professor of Jurisprudence, Yale Law School. Professor Eskridge's primary legal academic interest has been statutory interpretation. Together with Professor Philip Frickey, he developed an innovative casebook on legislation. In 1990–95, Professor Eskridge represented a gay couple suing for recognition of their same-sex marriage. Since then, he has published a field-establishing casebook, three monographs, and dozens of law review articles articulating a legal and political framework for proper state treatment of sexual and gender minorities. The historical materials in his book, *Gaylaw*, formed the basis for an *amicus* brief he drafted for the Cato Institute and for much of the Court's (and the dissenting opinion's) analysis in *Lawrence v. Texas* (2003), which invalidated consensual sodomy laws.

Robin Fretwell Wilson, Roger and Stephany Joslin Professor of Law, University of Illinois College of Law. Professor Wilson founded and directs the Fairness for All Initiative at the University of Illinois, which provides tangible support and advice to legislators seeking to balance religious freedom and LGBT nondiscrimination protections. She also founded the Tolerance Means Dialogues, public discussions designed to bring together leading thought leaders and members of the community to discuss whether there are more constructive approaches to living together in a plural society. A member of the American Law Institute, she is the author, coauthor, or editor of eleven books, including *Same-Sex Marriage and Religious Liberty* (2008, with Douglas Laycock and Anthony Picarello, eds.) and *The Contested Place of Religion in Family Law* (Robin Fretwell Wilson, ed., Cambridge University Press, 2018). Professor Wilson assisted the Utah legislature as it enacted the Utah Compromise and has worked with the United Arab Emirates' Judicial Department to permit expatriates to resolve family law matters using the laws of their home country or of their faith traditions. In February 2018, she was awarded the Thomas L. Kane Religious Freedom Award by the J. Reuben Clark Law Society.

CONTRIBUTORS

Senator J. Stuart Adams, Majority Whip, Utah State Senate. Senator Adams has served as the senator for Utah's 22nd District since 2009, previously serving in the Utah State House of Representatives from 2002 to 2006. Senator Adams is a former chairman of both the Utah State Transportation Commission and the Military Installation Development Authority. Senator Adams is a business owner. He received a B.A. in business finance from the University of Utah. He sponsored the legislation now colloquially known as the Utah Compromise.

Leith Anderson, President, National Association of Evangelicals. Anderson has served as president of the National Association of Evangelicals since 2006 and was the senior pastor of Wooddale Church in Eden Prairie, Minnesota, for thirty-five years. He regularly teaches in seminaries, addresses evangelical concerns with elected officials, and provides theological and cultural commentary to leading news outlets. He has been published in many periodicals and has written over twenty books. Anderson has a D.Min. from Fuller Theological Seminary and is a graduate of Moody Bible Institute, Bradley University, and Denver Seminary.

Ryan T. Anderson, William E. Simon Senior Research Fellow, the Heritage Foundation. Anderson is the author of *When Harry Became Sally: Responding to the Transgender Moment* and *Truth Overruled: The Future of Marriage and Religious Freedom*, and he is the coauthor of *What Is Marriage? Man and Woman: A Defense* and *Debating Religious Liberty and Discrimination*. Anderson's research has been cited by two US Supreme Court justices in two Supreme Court cases. He received his B.A. from Princeton University, graduating Phi Beta Kappa and magna cum laude, and his Ph.D. in political philosophy from the University of Notre Dame. His dissertation was titled: "Neither Liberal Nor Libertarian: A Natural Law Approach to Social Justice and Economic Rights."

Thomas C. Berg, James L. Oberstar Professor of Law and Public Policy at the University of St. Thomas School of Law (Minnesota). Professor Berg is the author of four books (including a leading casebook), more than 100 scholarly and popular articles, and more than fifty briefs in the Supreme Court and other courts on freedom of religion and expression. He also founded and supervises students in St. Thomas's religious-liberty appellate clinic, and he writes on intellectual property, social justice, and development. He codirected St. Thomas's Murphy Institute for Catholic Thought, Law, and Public Policy; he serves on the board of Democrats for Life of America; and he contributes to Mirror of Justice, SCOTUS Blog, and other weblogs. He has degrees from the University of Chicago, the University of Oxford, and Northwestern University. He practiced law with Mayer Brown in Chicago and clerked for Judge Alvin Rubin on the US Court of Appeals for the Fifth Circuit.

Alan Brownstein, Professor of Law Emeritus, University of California, Davis, School of Law. Professor Brownstein has been a constitutional law scholar and teacher at the University of California, Davis, School of Law for more than thirty-five years. While the primary focus of his scholarship relates to church-state issues and free exercise and establishment clause doctrine, he has also written extensively on freedom of speech, privacy and autonomy rights, and other constitutional law subjects. Before retiring to emeritus status, he held the Boochever and Bird Chair for the Study and Teaching of Freedom and Equality. Brownstein received the UC Davis School of Law's Distinguished Teaching Award in 1995 and the UC Davis Distinguished Scholarly Public Service Award in 2008. He is a member of the American Law Institute. A graduate of Antioch College and Harvard Law School, he clerked for the Honorable Frank M. Coffin, Chief Judge of the US Court of Appeals for the First Circuit.

Brad Crofford, Legislative Assistant, Council for Christian Colleges & Universities (CCCU). Crofford assists the CCCU's government relations efforts in Washington, DC. A Gilman Scholar, he holds an M.A. in international studies from the University of Oklahoma and a B.A. and B.S. in communications and politics from CCCU member institution Southern Nazarene University. His academic articles and book reviews have been published in *Political Studies Review*, *African Studies Quarterly*, *The Journal of Retracing Africa*, *International Affairs Review*, and *The Journal of Global Affairs*.

Marc O. DeGirolami, Professor of Law and Associate Director, Center for Law and Religion, St. John's University School of Law. Professor DeGirolami's scholarship focuses on law and religion, constitutional law, and criminal law. His book, *The Tragedy of Religious Freedom*, was published in 2013. His papers have been published in various law journals including the *Notre Dame Law Review*, *Stanford Law and Policy Review*, *Constitutional Commentary*, *Legal Theory*, *Ohio State Journal of Criminal Law*, *Boston College Law Review*, *San Diego Law Review*, *Alabama Law Review*, and *St. John's Law Review*, among others. He has written for *The New Republic*, *First Things*, *The Weekly Standard*, *Commonweal*, and *The Library of Law and Liberty*.

Sister Jeannine Gramick, Cofounder, New Ways Ministry. Sister Jeannine Gramick, a Roman Catholic nun, helped to begin three organizations for Catholic lesbian and gay people. In addition, she cofounded New Ways Ministry, a Catholic social justice center working for the reconciliation of lesbian, gay, bisexual, and transgender people and the church. Sister Gramick holds a Ph.D. in mathematics education from the University of Pennsylvania and an M.S. in mathematics from the University of Notre Dame. She served on the national boards of the National

Assembly of Religious Women, the Religious Network of Equality for Women, the Lambda Legal Defense and Education Fund, and the Women's Ordination Conference. She is currently Executive Codirector of the National Coalition of American Nuns. She is strongly committed to justice and peace for humanity.

Kent Greenawalt, University Professor, Columbia Law School. Professor Greenawalt's interests include constitutional law and jurisprudence, with special emphases on church and state, freedom of speech, legal interpretation, and criminal responsibility. Greenawalt was the deputy US solicitor general from 1971 to 1972. He was law clerk to Justice John M. Harlan when he served on the US Supreme Court, and, subsequently spent part of a summer as an attorney with the Lawyers Committee for Civil Rights in Jackson, MS. From 1966 to 1969, Greenawalt served on the New York City Bar Association's civil rights committee. He has been a fellow several times at Clare Hall, University of Cambridge; All Souls College, University of Oxford; and the American Academy of Arts and Sciences.

Michael A. Helfand, Ph.D., Associate Dean for Faculty and Research and Professor of Law, Pepperdine University School of Law and Codirector, Diane and Guilford Glazer Institute for Jewish Studies, Pepperdine University. Professor Helfand is an expert on religious law and religious liberty, focusing on how US law treats religious law, custom, and practice. His articles have appeared in numerous law journals, including the *Yale Law Journal*, *New York University Law Review*, and *Duke Law Journal*, as well as in various general audience publications, including the *Wall Street Journal*, *Los Angeles Times*, and *USA Today*. He received his J.D. from Yale Law School and his Ph.D. in political science from Yale University.

B. Jessie Hill, Associate Dean for Academic Affairs and Judge Ben C. Green Professor of Law, Case Western Reserve University School of Law. Professor Hill's teaching focuses on constitutional law, health law, civil rights, reproductive rights, and law and religion. Her scholarship has been published in the *Michigan Law Review*, *Duke Law Journal*, *Columbia Journal of Gender and Law*, and the *Texas Law Review*, among others. Prior to teaching, she worked at the national ACLU Reproductive Freedom Project in New York and then practiced First Amendment and civil rights law with a small law firm in Cleveland. She presents, litigates, and consults frequently on health law, constitutional law, and civil rights issues.

Dennis P. Hollinger, President and Colman M. Mockler Distinguished Professor of Christian Ethics, Gordon-Conwell Theological Seminary. President Hollinger leads Gordon-Conwell Theological Seminary, in South Hamilton, MA, the seventh largest seminary in the United States. Prior to this position, he was President and Professor of Christian Ethics at Evangelical Theological Seminary, Vice Provost at Messiah College, Pastor of the Washington Community Fellowship on Capitol Hill, and Associate Professor at Alliance Theological Seminary. He has served as an adjunct or visiting professor at Moscow Theological Seminary in Russia, Union

Biblical Seminary in India, the Eastern European Seminary for Evangelical Leadership in Ukraine, and Trinity International University. President Hollinger received his B.A. from Elizabethtown College, his M.Div. from Trinity Evangelical Divinity School, and his M.Phil. and Ph.D. from Drew University, and did postdoctoral studies at the University of Oxford.

Holly Hollman, General Counsel and Associate Executive Director, Baptist Joint Committee for Religious Liberty, Adjunct Professor of Law, Georgetown University Law Center. Hollman's work includes providing legal analysis and insight on church-state issues that arise before Congress, the courts, and administrative agencies. She leads the Baptist Joint Committee's involvement in legal cases through friend-of-the-court briefs, and her tenure includes dozens of briefs filed by the BJC, including more than twenty at the US Supreme Court. She consults regularly with churches, individuals, and organizations about religious liberty issues and writes a column for the BJC's magazine, *Report from the Capital*. She teaches the Church-State Law Seminar as an adjunct professor at the Georgetown University Law Center. Prior to her work at the BJC, Hollman was an attorney in private practice specializing in employment law and litigation in Nashville, TN, and in the District of Columbia. Hollman earned a B.A. in politics from Wake Forest University and a J.D. from the University of Tennessee College of Law.

Shirley V. Hoogstra, President, Council For Christian Colleges & Universities. In September 2014, Hoogstra became the seventh president of the Council for Christian Colleges & Universities, an organization founded in 1976 representing 181 Christian faith-related institutions worldwide. Having received a B.A. in education at Calvin College in Grand Rapids, MI, and a J.D., with honors, from the University of Connecticut School of Law, Hoogstra spent more than a decade practicing law as a partner at a New Haven, CT firm that specialized in litigation. She was the youngest president of the New Haven County Bar Association and Foundation and a founding board member and officer of the Bridgeport Rescue Mission. She became the vice president for student life at Calvin College in July 1999, a role she served in until she became president of CCCU.

Elder Von G. Keetch, General Authority Seventy, The Church of Jesus Christ of Latter-day Saints. The late Elder Keetch was sustained as General Authority Seventy of The Church of Jesus Christ of Latter-day Saints on April 4, 2015. At the time of his call, he had been serving as chief outside counsel to the Church. Among other ecclesiastical duties, he served as Executive Director of the Public Affairs Department. Elder Keetch was a graduate of Brigham Young University, where he received both his B.A. in political science and his J.D. He served as a judicial clerk to Judge George C. Pratt of the US Court of Appeals for the Second Circuit and to Chief Justice Warren E. Burger and Justice Antonin Scalia of the US Supreme Court. He practiced law in Salt Lake City at Kirton McConkie from 1990 to 2015. Elder Keetch was involved in defending and advancing religious liberty issues for his entire career and testified before Congress on several occasions. His responsibilities with the Church included oversight of all legislative and policy efforts to strengthen religious liberty here in the United States and throughout the world. He died unexpectedly on January 26, 2018, at age fifty-seven of complications incident to cancer.

Andrew Koppelman, John Paul Stevens Professor of Law, Northwestern Pritzker School of Law. Professor Koppelman received Northwestern University's 2015 Walder Award for Research Excellence. His scholarship focuses on issues at the intersection of law and political philosophy. His latest books are *The Tough Luck Constitution and the Assault on Health Care Reform* (2013) and *Defending American Religious Neutrality* (2013). He has also published more than 100 articles in books and scholarly journals. He is an occasional contributor to the Balkinization blog.

Ronald J. Krotoszynski, Jr., John S. Stone Chairholder of Law and Director of Faculty Research, University of Alabama School of Law. Professor Krotoszynski earned his B.A. and M.A. from Emory University and his J.D. and LL.M. from Duke University. He clerked for the Honorable Frank M. Johnson, Jr., of the US Court of Appeals for the Eleventh Circuit before working as an associate with Covington & Burling, Washington, DC. Professor Krotoszynski served on the law faculties at Washington and Lee University and the Indiana University School of Law-Indianapolis and as a visiting professor at the Washington and Lee University School of Law, the Marshall-Wythe School of Law at the College of William and Mary, Florida State University College of Law, and Brooklyn Law School.

Douglas Laycock, Robert E. Scott Distinguished Professor of Law and Professor of Religious Studies, University of Virginia, and Alice McKean Young Regents Chair in Law Emeritus, University of Texas. Professor Laycock is one of the nation's leading authorities on the law of religious liberty and the law of remedies. He has taught and written about these topics for four decades at the University of Chicago, the University of Texas, the University of Michigan, and now the University of Virginia. Laycock has testified frequently before Congress and has argued many religious freedom cases in the courts, including the US Supreme Court. Laycock is the vice president of the American Law Institute and a fellow of the American Academy of Arts and Sciences. He earned his B.A. from Michigan State University and his J.D. from the University of Chicago Law School.

Governor Michael O. Leavitt was elected governor of Utah three times, from 1993 to 2003. He occupied two roles in the cabinet of President George W. Bush, first as Administrator of the Environmental Protection Agency (2003–05) and then as Secretary of the Department of Health and Human Services (2005–09). Since leaving government, he has been devoted to improving the American health-care system and serving as a lay member of the Public Affairs Committee of The Church of Jesus Christ of Latter-day Saints.

Shapri D. LoMaglio, Vice President for Government and External Relations, Council for Christian Colleges & Universities (CCCU). LoMaglio leads the CCCU's response to legislative, legal, and regulatory matters on behalf of its more than 180 institutions of Christ-centered higher education. She advocates on their behalf in Washington, DC on a wide range of policy issues rooted in their shared faith. She also leads the external relations team of the CCCU, making the case for Christian higher education by promoting its valuable contributions to society and the academy. LoMaglio is a graduate of CCCU member-institution Gordon College (Wenham, MA) and earned her J.D. from the University of Arizona (Tucson). She is licensed to practice law in the state of Arizona. Prior to the CCCU, she served as a legal fellow in the US Senate.

Archbishop William E. Lori, Archbishop of Baltimore, past Chairman, Ad Hoc Committee for Religious Liberty, US Conference of Catholic Bishops. The Most Reverend William Edward Lori, S.T.D., was installed as the Sixteenth Archbishop of the Archdiocese of Baltimore on May 16, 2012. He obtained a B.A. from the Seminary of Saint Pius X in Erlanger, KY, in 1973, an M.A. from Mount Saint Mary's Seminary in Emmitsburg, MD, in 1977, and his Ph.D. in sacred theology from the Catholic University of America in 1982. He was appointed to the US Conference of Catholic Bishops' Ad Hoc Committee on Sexual Abuse, which drafted the Charter for the Protection of Children and Young People. He is Supreme Chaplain of the Knights of Columbus.

Linda C. McClain, Professor of Law and Paul M. Siskind Research Scholar, Boston University School of Law. Professor McClain teaches family law, gender and the law, and feminist legal theory, as well as an undergraduate seminar on Marriage, Families, and Gender in BU's Kilachand Honors College. In 2016–17, she was a Laurance S. Rockefeller Visiting Faculty Fellow at Princeton University's University Center for Human Values, where she worked on her book *Bigotry, Conscience, and Marriage* (forthcoming), which examines the rhetoric of bigotry and conscience in controversies over same-sex, interracial, and interfaith marriage and religious exemptions from antidiscrimination laws. Her most recent books are *Ordered Liberty: Rights, Responsibilities and Virtues* (2013, with James E. Fleming) and *Gay Rights and the Constitution* (2016, with Jim Fleming, Sotirios Barber, and Steve Macedo). McClain earned her B.A. from Oberlin College (with High Honors in religion), and has an M.A. in religious studies from the University of Chicago Divinity School and law degrees from Georgetown (J.D.) and NYU (LL.M.). She is a member of the American Law Institute.

Michael W. McConnell, Richard and Frances Mallery Professor of Law, Director, Stanford Constitutional Law Center, Stanford Law School. Professor McConnell is a senior fellow at the Hoover Institution in addition to his roles at Stanford Law School. From 2002 to 2009, he served as a circuit judge on the US Court of Appeals for the Tenth Circuit. McConnell has held chaired professorships at the University of Chicago and the University of Utah, and visited at Harvard University and NYU. In the past decade, his work has been cited in opinions of the US Supreme Court second most often of any legal scholar. McConnell has argued fifteen cases in the Supreme Court. He served as law clerk to Justice William J. Brennan, Jr. and is of counsel to Kirkland & Ellis.

Louise Melling, Deputy Legal Director and Director of the Center for Liberty, American Civil Liberties Union. Melling directs the ACLU's work on reproductive freedom, women's rights, lesbian, gay, bisexual, and transgender rights, disability rights, and freedom of religion and belief. In this role, she leads the work of the ACLU to address the intersection of religious freedom and equal treatment, among other issues. Before becoming deputy legal director in 2010, Melling was director of the ACLU Reproductive Freedom Project, in which capacity she oversaw nation-wide litigation, communications research, public education campaigns, and advocacy efforts in the state legislatures. An attorney with the ACLU since 1992, she is a graduate of Yale Law School and clerked for Judge Morris Lasker of the US District Court for the Southern District of New York.

Shannon Price Minter, Legal Director, National Center for Lesbian Rights (NCLR). Minter, a transgender man, was lead counsel for same-sex couples in the landmark California marriage equality case, which held that same-sex couples have the fundamental right to marry and that laws that discriminate based on sexual orientation are inherently discriminatory and subject to the highest level of constitutional scrutiny. Minter was counsel in other successful challenges to state marriage bans in Alabama, Florida, Idaho, New Mexico, North Dakota, South Dakota, and Wyoming. He represented married same-sex couples from Tennessee in *Obergefell v. Hodges*, the 2015 Supreme Court decision striking down state laws barring same-sex couples from marriage. In 2011, Minter was also NCLR's lead attorney in *Christian Legal Society v. Martinez*, a US Supreme Court decision upholding student group policies prohibiting discrimination based on sexual orientation and gender identity, and rejecting the argument that such policies violated a student group's rights to freedom of speech, religion, and association. NCLR represented Hastings Outlaw, an LGBT student group that intervened to help defend the nondiscrimination policy.

Jason R. Moyer, Associate Professor of Communication Arts, Malone University. Professor Moyer writes and teaches about religious language in presidential rhetoric. He serves his denomination, Mennonite Church USA, and preaches at his local congregation. Recently, he published the essay "Turning the Prophetic into Civil Religion: Barack Obama's March 4, 2007 Sermon in Selma, Alabama." He holds a Ph.D. in communication from the University of Iowa. He received the top dissertation of the year award from the Religious Communication Association for his thesis,

"Not Just Civil Religion: Theology in the Cases of Woodrow Wilson, John Kennedy, and Barack Obama."

Douglas NeJaime, Professor of Law, Yale Law School. Professor NeJaime joined the faculty at Yale Law School in 2017 and teaches in the areas of family law, legal ethics, law and sexuality, and constitutional law. In fall 2016, he was the Martin R. Flug Visiting Professor of Law at Yale. Before joining the Yale faculty, NeJaime was Professor of Law at UCLA School of Law, where he served as Faculty Director of the Williams Institute, a research institute on sexual orientation and gender identity law and public policy. He has also served on the faculties at UC Irvine School of Law and Loyola Law School in Los Angeles, and was Visiting Professor of Law at Harvard Law School in Spring 2017. NeJaime is the coauthor of *Cases and Materials on Sexuality, Gender Identity, and the Law* (with Carlos Ball, Jane Schacter, and William Rubenstein) and *Ethical Lawyering: Legal and Professional Responsibilities in the Practice of Law* (with Paul Hayden). His recent scholarship includes "The Nature of Parenthood," 126 *Yale Law Journal* 2260 (2017); "Marriage Equality and the New Parenthood," 129 *Harvard Law Review* 1185 (2016); "Conscience Wars: Complicity-Based Conscience Claims in Religion and Politics," 124 *Yale Law Journal* 2516 (2015), with Reva B. Siegel; and "Before Marriage: The Unexplored History of Nonmarital Recognition and Its Relationship to Marriage," 102 *California Law Review* 87 (2014). NeJaime has twice received the Dukeminier Award, which recognizes the best sexual orientation legal scholarship published in the previous year, and has also been the recipient of UCI Law's Professor of the Year Award and Loyola Law School's Excellence in Teaching Award.

Michael J. Perry, Robert W. Woodruff Professor of Law, Emory University School of Law. Professor Perry is Senior Fellow at Emory University's Center for the Study of Law and Religion and a coeditor of the *Journal of Law and Religion*. He taught at Northwestern University, Wake Forest University, and the Ohio State University College of Law and has visited at Yale, Tulane, New York Law School, the University of Tokyo, the University of Alabama, the University of Western Ontario, Canada, the University of Dayton, and the University of San Diego. He received his A.B. from Georgetown University and his J.D. from Columbia University. He clerked for US District Judge Jack B. Weinstein and US Circuit Judge Shirley M. Hufstedler of the United States Court of Appeals for the Ninth Circuit. Perry is the author of thirteen books, most recently, *A Global Political Morality: Human Rights, Democracy, and Constitutionalism* (Cambridge University Press 2017).

Jennifer C. Pizer, Senior Counsel and Director of Law and Policy, Lambda Legal. Jennifer C. Pizer was cocounsel in the litigation that won marriage for same-sex couples in California in 2008 and in Arizona in 2014. From 2011 to 2012, she was Legal Director of the Williams Institute at UCLA School of Law. Before joining the Williams Institute, she directed Lambda Legal's Marriage Project. Pizer has served as an adjunct professor of law at University of Southern California School of Law, Loyola Law School, and Whittier Law School. Before joining Lambda Legal, she practiced business litigation with a national law firm, was legal director of the National Abortion Rights Action League, and clerked for the Honorable Ann Aldrich of the US District Court for the Northern District of Ohio. She is a graduate of NYU School of Law and Harvard College.

Intisar A. Rabb, Professor of Law, Harvard Law School, and Director, Islamic Legal Studies Program; Professor of History, Harvard University. Professor Rabb also holds an appointment as Professor of Law at Harvard Law School, Professor of History at Harvard University Faculty of Arts and Sciences, and as a Susan S. and Kenneth L. Wallach Professor at the Radcliffe Institute for Advanced Study. She previously served as Associate Professor at NYU Department of Middle Eastern and Islamic Studies and at NYU Law School and as Assistant Professor at Boston College Law School. She also served as a law clerk for Judge Thomas L. Ambro of the US Court of Appeals for the Third Circuit, as a Temple Bar Fellow in London with the American Inns of Court, and as a Carnegie Scholar.

Rabbi David N. Saperstein, Adjunct Professor of Church-State Law, Georgetown University. Rabbi Saperstein was Ambassador-at-Large for International Religious Freedom from 2015 to 2017. By law, the ambassador is a principal advisor to the president and secretary of state, serves as the United States' chief diplomat on issues of religious freedom worldwide, and heads the Office of International Religious Freedom in the Bureau of Democracy, Human Rights, and Labor. Ambassador Saperstein previously served for forty years as Director of the Religious Action Center of Reform Judaism (RAC), overseeing the national social justice programming for the largest segment of American Jewry. A rabbi and an attorney, for thirty-five years Saperstein taught seminars in First Amendment Church-State Law and in Jewish Law at the Georgetown University Law Center. During his tenure at the helm of the RAC, Ambassador Saperstein has headed several national religious coalitions, including the Coalition to Protect Religious Liberty. He has served on the boards of numerous national organizations including the NAACP (and most recently chaired its national Religious Affairs Committee), the National Religious Partnership on the Environment, and the World Bank's "World Faiths Development Dialogue." In 1999, Ambassador Saperstein served as the first chair of the US Commission on International Religious Freedom. In 2009, he was appointed by President Obama as a member of the first White House Council on Faith-Based and Neighborhood Partnerships. His articles have been published in the *Washington Post*, the *New York Times*, and the *Harvard Law Review*. His latest book is *Jewish Dimensions of Social Justice: Tough Moral Choices of Our Time*.

Reva B. Siegel, Nicholas deB. Katzenbach Professor of Law at Yale Law School. Professor Siegel's recent publications include *Community in Conflict: Same-Sex*

Marriage and Backlash, 64 U.C.L.A. L. Rev. 1728 (2017); *The Difference a Whole Woman Makes: Protection for the Abortion Right After Whole Woman's Health*, 126 Yale L.J. F. 149 (2016) (with Linda Greenhouse), and *Conscience Wars: Complicity-Based Conscience Claims in Religion and Politics*, 124 Yale L.J. (2015) (with Douglas NeJaime), as well as *Processes of Constitutional Decisionmaking* (with Paul Brest, Sanford Levinson, Jack M. Balkin, and Akhil Reed Amar, 2018). Professor Siegel is a fellow of the American Academy of Arts and Sciences and an honorary fellow of the American Society for Legal History. She serves on the Board of Advisors of the American Constitution Society and on the General Council of the International Society of Public Law.

Steven D. Smith, Warren Distinguished Professor of Law, University of San Diego College of Law. Steven D. Smith (J.D. Yale, B.A. Brigham Young) is a Warren Distinguished Professor of Law at the University of San Diego and Codirector of the Institute for Law and Religion. His writings include *Pagans and Christians in the City* (forthcoming), *The Rise and Decline of American Religious Freedom* (2014), *The Disenchantment of Secular Discourse* (2010), and *Foreordained Failure: The Quest for a Constitutional Principle of Religious Freedom* (1995).

Sarah Warbelow, Legal Director, Human Rights Campaign (HRC). Warbelow leads HRC's team of lawyers and fellows focused on federal, state, and municipal policy. She also coordinates HRC's advocacy efforts as *amicus curiae* (friend of the court) in litigation affecting the lesbian, gay, bisexual, transgender, and queer community. As part of her public education efforts on the laws, legislation, and policies affecting the LGBTQ community, Warbelow regularly appears on national television and contributes to media outlets such as the *New York Times*, NPR, the *Washington Post*, the *Wall Street Journal*, and *Time* magazine. She was previously HRC senior counsel for special projects and Justice for All fellow from January 2008 to September 2009 and State Legislative Director through April 2014. Warbelow is an affiliated professor at George Washington University and George Mason Law School, teaching courses on civil rights law and public policy. Prior to joining HRC, Warbelow served as the program manager for the American Association of University Women Foundation Legal Advocacy Fund. She received her M.A. in public policy and law degree from the University of Michigan.

Acknowledgments

We are grateful to Yale Law School for hosting the conference "Faith, Sexuality, and the Meaning of Freedom" that preceded this book. Special thanks to the Family Law and Policy Program at the University of Illinois College of Law and to the First Amendment Partnership for supporting that conference, out of which came the corpus of this volume.

We are especially grateful to our contributors for their insight, professionalism, and goodwill. Special thanks to Senator Orrin Hatch who made every effort to be with us at Yale, and to Senator J. Stuart Adams, Governor Michael O. Leavitt, and the advocates and litigators at the forefront of the religious liberty and non-discrimination struggles – Louise Melling, Sister Jeannine Gramick, Holly Hollman, Shannon Price Minter, Ryan T. Anderson, Jennifer C. Pizer, and Sarah Warbelow – for making time in busy schedules to ground this dialogue with real-world perspectives. We're especially grateful to the late Elder Von G. Keetch for assisting us to reach out to thought leaders in the faith community who have contributed: Leith Anderson, Archbishop William P. Lori, Rabbi David N. Saperstein, Dennis P. Hollinger, Shirley V. Hoogstra, Shapri D. LoMaglio, and Brad Crofford.

Special thanks to the University of Illinois College of Law's Law Library for partnering to produce timely, relevant scholarship. Thanks to Stephanie Davidson for painstaking work on the index. Tanner Bean assisted with research on generalized religious protections in the fifty states.

Most, we are grateful to Carla Gall, Tanner Bean, Pamela Melton, and William Duncan for pouring themselves into refining the final manuscript, and to Robin's research assistants for extensive citation work, legal research, and generally making all of us look good: Blake Gibney (J.D. expected May 2019), Dmitri Kachan (J.D. 2018), Kamron Kompani (J.D. 2018), Vaughn Olson (J.D. expected May 2019), Brianna Richardson (J.D. 2018), Jessica Roberts (J.D. expected May 2020), James Schmidt

(J.D. 2018), Jason Shultz (J.D. expected May 2019), Breanna Taylor (J.D. 2017), and Daniel Wille (J.D. 2018). The book is so much better for all your hard work.

Finally, we are thankful for John Berger's advice in the formative stages of this project and for Niranjana Harikrishnan's and Wendy Nardi's careful, thoughtful copyediting.

Prospects for Common Ground

Introduction

William N. Eskridge, Jr. and Robin Fretwell Wilson

Religious Freedom, LGBT Rights, and the Prospects for Common Ground explores the deeply contested question of whether respect for the lesbian, gay, bisexual, and transgender (LGBT) and faith communities can be reconciled in the law. This book brings into deliberate dialogue leading voices in the faith and LGBT advocacy communities, together with equality and religious liberty scholars, to explore the interests at stake when two communities that sometimes have "profound differences in belief" (Chapter 2) live together in society, each striving to be true to the things most core to them. It examines whether, through dialogue and negotiation, these communities can reach mutually acceptable laws. Our authors give voice to first principles that would, or should, guide any attempt to bridge differences between communities. And many charged with protecting the interests of faith communities or LGBT persons articulate their fears for their community members about staking out common ground. Because the dialectic between religious liberty and nondiscrimination norms is as difficult as it is important, this book comprehensively assembles some of the most impactful voices in these fields.

The result is a rich set of thirty-five crisp, consciously accessible thought pieces. Together, contributors unpack the thorny questions at the intersection of religious liberty and nondiscrimination law. Should religious organizations that partner with the state to provide adoption and foster care placement services receive public funds, or even licenses to operate, when making placements consistent with their faith tenets (Chapters 8, 19, 24, 32)?

Should nonprofit universities that oppose same-sex marriage be at risk of losing their tax-exempt status – and is that a real risk given the structure of our laws (Chapters 22, 25)? Should any religious organizations guided by faith in their missions benefit from government funds, and should governments wield that spending power in ways that leave people of faith and religious organizations little viable recourse other than closure or repeatedly violating the law? Should nondiscrimination law stop at the door of houses of worship – or the entrance to bakeries operated by religious owners so that these wedding vendors have the ability to live out their faith in the public square? And how is it that LGBT persons have no guarantee across much of America of securing jobs and housing without discrimination, let alone being served in restaurants, bars, and hotels?

This dialogue comes at an important moment, as the vital gains that the LGBT community made under the Obama administration are being recalibrated in real time.[1] President Trump's 2017 announcement that transgender persons may no longer serve in the military is but one instance of this phenomenon.[2] While it remains to be seen to what degree the Trump administration will reexamine, and perhaps uproot, Obama-era protections, the administration has struck a troubling tone, naming polarizing figures on civil rights to key positions tasked with enforcing nondiscrimination protections – as one example, the Patient Protection and Affordable Care Act's ban on sex discrimination, which expanded access to gender reassignment surgery.[3] *Religious Freedom, LGBT Rights, and the Prospects for Common Ground* is the first forward-looking examination in the Trump era of the push-and-pull over nondiscrimination and religious liberty values and their relative weighting in government policy.

This nascent retrenchment is taking place against the background of rapidly changing public opinion about the meaning of bigotry, tolerance, and the morality of religious and LGBT conduct. A high-profile clash of views has unfolded over whether it is possible to protect LGBT individuals from discrimination without harming faith communities – and whether that possibility should even be the goal.[4]

---

[1]   Jacklyn Wille, *After Military Ban, Are Transgender Health Protections Next?*, BLOOMBERG LAW (July 27, 2017).

[2]   John Bowden, *Mattis Appalled by Trump Tweets Announcing Transgender Ban: Report*, THE HILL (July 28, 2017), https://perma.cc/8LZT-HLVA ("After consultation with my generals and military experts, please be advised that the United States government will not accept or allow transgender individuals to serve in any capacity in the U.S. Military. Our military must be focused on decisive and overwhelming victory and cannot be burdened with the tremendous medical costs and disruption that transgender in the military would entail."). President Trump later dialed back the ban in an official memorandum that was challenged in federal court. *See Presidential Memorandum for the Secretary of Defense and the Secretary of Homeland Security*, WHITE HOUSE (Aug. 25, 2017), https://perma.cc/8LZT-HLVA; *After Court Ruling, Military Will Accept Openly Transgender Recruits As of Jan. 1*, NPR (Dec. 11, 2017), https://perma.cc/X4P3-KK59. Lawsuits challenging the ban are still proceeding, as Warbelow explains in Chapter 31; implementation of Trump's policy has been enjoined since December 2017. Karnoski v. Trump, 2:17-cv-01297-MJP (W.D. Wash. 2018).

[3]   Emma Green, *The Man Behind Trump's Religious-Freedom Agenda for Health Care*, THE ATLANTIC (June 7, 2017), https://perma.cc/SD2K-FEP9; Robert Pear, *Foes of Obama-Era Rule Work to Undo Birth Control Mandate*, N.Y. TIMES (July 10, 2017), https://perma.cc/B2KY-9ZNR.

[4]   *Compare, e.g.*, Jonathan Rauch, *Nondiscrimination for All*, NAT'L AFFAIRS 99 (Summer 2017); Jonathan Merritt, *3 Reasons Conservatives Will Lose the Transgender Debate*, RELIGION NEWS SERVICE (May 14, 2016); George M. Marsden, *A More Inclusive Pluralism*, FIRST THINGS (Feb. 2015); John Inazu, *Pluralism Doesn't Mean Relativism*, CHRISTIANITY TODAY (Apr. 6, 2015); Tim Keller & John Inazu, *How Christians Can Bear Gospel Witness in an Anxious Age*,

In September 2016, in a 306-page report entitled *Peaceful Coexistence: Reconciling Non-Discrimination Principles with Civil Liberties*, the US Commission on Civil Rights reached the damning conclusion that religious protections in nondiscrimination laws "significantly infringe upon these civil rights."[5] In the words of Commission Chairman Martin Castro, religious accommodations are "code words for discrimination."[6] That view fractured the Commission and precipitated sharp dissents from two commissioners.[7] The majority's dim view of the desirability of leaving room for people of faith was not a foregone conclusion. Three of our contributors, Professors Alan Brownstein, Marc O. DeGirolami, and Michael A. Helfand, testified before the Commission.

Even to moderate voices outside the Commission process, the report was jarring. It represented the first time an instrumentality of the US government had said, "Our first freedom is first no more."[8]

The Commission's grim appraisal of the need to respect, and protect, both the LGBT and the faith communities was met with an equally hard-line stance from social conservatives and some faith leaders. In December 2016, seventy-five religious leaders and commentators – including two contributors to this volume, the Most Rev. William E. Lori, Archbishop of Baltimore, and commentator Ryan Anderson – declared that sexual orientation and gender identity (SOGI) nondiscrimination laws are "unnecessary" and threaten "fundamental freedoms," no matter how "narrowly crafted."[9] All "ostensible protections for religious liberty," these critics of SOGI laws said, "are inherently inadequate and unstable."

The Commission's report and its terse rejoinder are not the last words – far from it. New nondiscrimination laws that reconcile religious liberty concerns with LGBT nondiscrimination protections were enacted in Utah in 2015[10] and are now being proposed in less monolithic "purple" states.[11] But, as Utah Senator Stuart Adams explains in this volume, new laws protecting LGBT people against discrimination in

---

CHRISTIANITY TODAY (June 20, 2016); Dennis P. Hollinger, *Religious Freedom, Civil Rights and Sexuality: A Christian Ethicist's View of Fairness for All*, ADVANCE 27 (Spring 2017) *with* J.C. Derrick, *Fair or Foul?*, WORLD MAG. (Dec. 31, 2016), https://perma.cc/5GRD-DADP; Sarah Kramer, *The Unfairness of "Fairness for All" Legislation*, ALLIANCE DEFENDING FREEDOM (June 8, 2017), https://perma.cc/KH7Y-PFYZ.

[5] U.S. COMMISSION ON CIVIL RIGHTS, PEACEFUL COEXISTENCE: RECONCILING NONDISCRIMINATION PRINCIPLES WITH CIVIL LIBERTIES 25 (2016).

[6] *Id.* at 29.

[7] *Id.* at 42 (2016) (Commissioner Peter Kirsanow's rebuttal); *id.* at 115 (Commissioner Gail Heriot's rebuttal).

[8] Charles C. Haynes, *The Deeply Troubling Federal Report Targeting Religious Freedom*, WASH. POST (Sept. 16, 2016), https://perma.cc/UG53-5YPJ.

[9] Colson Center, *Preserve Freedom, Reject Coercion* (Dec. 2016), https://perma.cc/YMK2-QWKK.

[10] *See* S.B. 297, 2015 Utah Laws Ch. 46; S.B. 296, 2015 Utah Laws Ch. 13.

[11] Bruce Ledewitz, *Religion and Gay Rights Need Not Be at Loggerheads*, PITTSBURGH POST-GAZETTE (July 23, 2017), https://perma.cc/Y8UV-9EXE (making the case that compromise addresses real fears in the LGBT community).

workplaces, housing, and public accommodations may not currently be possible across much of America without holding religious communities harmless or finding reasonable accommodations for religious practice.

Federally, progressive and conservative legislators alike have proposed win-lose approaches in this realm. The Equality Act would protect the LGBT community from discrimination but makes no concessions for faith communities.[12] The First Amendment Defense Act (FADA), on the other hand, authorizes a host of religiously motivated refusals, with scant precautions to ensure that LGBT individuals, or others, are not harmed.[13] FADA was reintroduced in the 115th Congress in March 2018.[14] These policy proposals, however, have little prospect for enactment, despite their vocal supporters.[15]

As lawmakers haltingly engage what arguably is the defining civil rights question of our time,[16] the US Supreme Court and federal and state courts are left to fill in key terms of the debate.

The day after the Supreme Court decided *Obergefell v. Hodges*, former Solicitor General Ted Olson cued up the one issue left unresolved by the Court in its June 2018 decision in *Masterpiece Cakeshop v. Colorado Civil Rights Commission*: whether "being asked to participate in a wedding, to perform a wedding, to sing in a wedding, to ... be a wedding planner" is different than "walk[ing] into a bakery on the street and want[ing] to buy a pie or a doughnut." "People," Olson said, "have the right to refuse personal services with respect to [participating in a wedding] on a religious basis."[17]

In *Masterpiece Cakeshop*, shop owner and baker Jack Phillips declined on religious grounds to decorate a cake "honoring the wedding of a same-sex couple,"[18] despite Colorado's public accommodations SOGI nondiscrimination law. In a 7-2 decision, the Court found for Phillips, erasing the penalties Colorado had imposed upon him, which included comprehensive staff training, a change in his business practices, and quarterly compliance reports for two years.[19] Writing for the majority,

---

[12] Equality Act, S. 1006, 115th Congress (introduced May 2, 2017), https://perma.cc/DSD5-826N; H.R. 2282, 115th Congress (introduced May 2, 2017), https://perma.cc/PN4U-63VQ.

[13] First Amendment Defense Act, H.R. 2802, 114th Congress (introduced June 17, 2015), https://perma.cc/8TB6-VDAC.

[14] S. 2525, 115th Congress (2nd Sess. 2018), https://www.congress.gov/bill/115th-congress/senate-bill/2525/text.

[15] David Blankenhorn, *A Way Forward for LGBT and Religious Liberty Rights*, Time (Aug. 10, 2015), https://perma.cc/HJD6-KYF4.

[16] Jaime Fuller, *Holder Calls LGBT Rights One of the "Civil Rights Challenges of Our Time,"* Wash. Post (Feb. 4, 2014), https://perma.cc/ES3G-J5WQ.

[17] Melanie Hunter, *Ted Olson: "Not Illegal" for Bakery to Refuse to Take Part in Gay Wedding Under SCOTUS Ruling*, CNS News (June 29, 2015), https://perma.cc/2LCU-CMKR.

[18] No. 16–111 (2017); *see also* Craig v. Masterpiece Cakeshop, Inc., 2015 COA 115 (Colo. App. 2015).

[19] Masterpiece Cakeshop, Ltd. v. Colorado Civil Rights Comm'n, No. 16–111, slip op. at 8 (U.S. June 4, 2018).

Justice Anthony Kennedy latched onto damning statements made by one commissioner, unrebutted by the others, that the baker's religious explanation for declining to serve the couple – that marriage is between one man and one woman – was a "despicable piece[] of rhetoric," no different than justifying the Holocaust or slavery.[20] The government should never suggest whether religious grounds for "conscience-based objection[s] [are] legitimate or illegitimate."[21] Seven justices agreed that Colorado violated its constitutional duty to administer laws without "hostility to a religion or religious viewpoint."[22]

Although staking out little new ground, *Masterpiece* stands as a call for greater respect for one another, a thicker pluralism where all can be true to who they are. Justice Kennedy explained, "these disputes must be resolved with tolerance, without undue disrespect to sincere religious beliefs, and without subjecting gay persons to indignities when they seek goods and services in an open market."[23] Indeed, LGBT persons must not be treated as "social outcasts or as inferior in dignity and worth"[24] and the government must not "act in a manner that passes judgment upon or presupposes the illegitimacy of religious beliefs and practices."[25] In many ways, Kennedy sketches the outer boundaries of an acceptable legislative compromise.

Left unanswered by *Masterpiece Cakeshop* is what would have happened if state officials had weighed the state's interest in shielding "gay persons [from] indignities when they seek goods and services in an open market" against the baker's "sincere religious objections" in a neutral way, as free exercise guarantees demand.[26] On June 25, 2018, the Court remanded for reconsideration in light of *Masterpiece Cakeshop* another high-profile refusal, the case of Barronelle Stutzman, a Washington florist who declined to arrange flowers for a same-sex wedding.[27]

As a decision largely limited to Phillips himself, *Masterpiece Cakeshop* does not resolve the universe of competing claims, especially as to the borders of public accommodations laws. Phillips had claimed the First Amendment bars being forced to endorse a message with which he did not agree, but the Court skirted this claim.

Even if the Court had embraced the compelled speech claim, the paradigm of compelled speech will not insulate all who have, for religious reasons, asked to step aside from facilitating weddings. The caterer who delivers food,[28] farm owners asked

---

[20] *Id.* at 13.
[21] *Id.* at 17.
[22] *Id.*
[23] *Id.* at 18.
[24] *Id.* at 9.
[25] *Id.* at 17.
[26] *Id.* at 18.
[27] Order List, 585 U.S. __ (June 25, 2018), https://perma.cc/3X9Z-ADQQ.
[28] *See* Tom Coyne, *Memories Pizza Reopens After Gay Wedding Comments Flap*, WASH. TIMES (Apr. 9, 2015), https://perma.cc/Z3FQ-226E.

to host a wedding reception,[29] and sundry others presumably add little creative or expressive value to the day's celebration, but may nonetheless feel complicit in facilitating or honoring certain marriages they cannot recognize for religious reasons. Our contributors who (with the exception of the Afterword) wrote before the Supreme Court's opinion in *Masterpiece Cakeshop* had been handed down, probe the need for and limits of any concessions made for religious belief in the public square, surveying the scope of public accommodations laws across the nation and surfacing norms developed around racial nondiscrimination laws. They argue the merits of core nondiscrimination and religious liberty principles. Many make poignant cases for the dignitary interests of either LGBT persons, religious observers or, as is often the case, both. Indeed, some of our contributors have deep connections to both communities; some point to religious commitments to embrace and protect LGBT persons in the law; others to equality and liberty norms requiring us to embrace and protect religious practices with which others may disagree.

In these swirling cross-currents around faith and sexuality, this volume starts fresh. It asks whether it is possible for the state to honor the parallel claims of the LGBT and faith communities to, as Professor Douglas Laycock urges, not interfere with conduct essential to each community's identity – and, if so, when the state should honor those requests.

In January 2017, ecclesiastical leaders, LGBT rights advocates, sitting seminary presidents, theologians, grassroots activists, social commentators, scholars of major faith traditions, lobbyists for the faith and LGBT communities, and leading religious liberty and equality scholars gathered for two days at Yale Law School to engage in an open dialogue on exactly these questions. The lively discourse and constructive feedback sharpened positions articulated here. Among the resulting chapters are those that anchor the poles in this debate – that is, authors who believe that LGBT rights and religious liberty cannot be reconciled; rather, one should take precedence over the other. However, the vast majority of the volume's thirty-five contributors see possibilities for reconciliation, although the authors would draw lines in different places.

Importantly, religious leaders speak in their own voices in this book about the demands of faith – voices not filtered by interests that benefit from continued conflict. Unlike the black-and-white response to the Commission report described earlier, this set of chapters signal an openness to exploring how to reconcile faith and sexuality in a diverse, pluralistic, inclusive society.

Even within these chapters, there is diversity of opinion and approach. Sister Jeannine Gramick reminds us not only that religions are not monolithic on questions of sexuality but also that within a given faith tradition there may be cross-currents between teachings on sexual ethics and teachings on social justice. Further, while some contributors argue that the demands of faith mean special solicitude, including access to funding, is needed in the law, Holly Hollman of the Baptist Joint

---

[29] Gifford v. McCarthy, 520410 (N.Y. App. 2016), https://perma.cc/TTN5-H4WY.

Committee contends that religious communities are corrupted by money. Both as a matter of constitutional concern and sound public policy, Hollman argues that avoiding government-funded religion is a fundamental good.

The range of perspectives from those aligned with faith communities on whether competing interests should be given respect or reconciled in laws is mirrored in the chapters written by LGBT advocates and attorneys. Some challenge the supposition that ending discrimination will be possible if society accommodates religious differences. Louise Melling of the ACLU argues that harm to the promise of equality, questions about exemptions' limits, and the probability that exemptions will thwart additional progress coalesce to make allowances for religious belief bad policy in this arena. Others, such as Shannon Minter, argue for giving religious communities space in the law to integrate LGBT persons, including children, on their own terms.

Like these stakeholders, the equality and religious liberty scholars writing for the volume engage in a point and counterpoint with one another through extensive cross talk between the chapters. For example, Professor Jessie Hill tackles questions raised by religious education, proposing a framework for answering the question of which universities should qualify as "religious" and therefore be treated differently under nondiscrimination laws. Taking a different tack, Professor Michael Helfand contends that when it is obvious to employees that a business, nonprofit or for-profit, is organized around a core religious mission, special accommodation in the law should follow because employees have impliedly consented to the religious organization's imposition of its values. Both identify devices for muting harms to others from efforts to protect specific interests.

The dialogue in this volume proceeds at both the general and the specific levels. A number of contributors develop the parallelism of claims made upon society by both LGBT persons and religious believers. Professor Alan Brownstein, for example, argues that both communities claim a right to act wrongly in the eyes of others: "the right to express the wrong ideas, to worship the wrong gods, or the right God in the wrong way, and to marry the wrong partner." Other contributors advance specific approaches to reconciling plural interests or tests for when governments should seek to accommodate religious or "conscience-based" objections. Professor Michael Perry, for example, draws the line at conscience-based objections that presuppose or assert the moral inferiority of any human being, which governments should not accommodate.

Unlike most other academic volumes, *Religious Freedom, LGBT Rights, and the Prospects for Common Ground* contains the perspectives of legislators and policymakers charged with resolving these tensions in practice. They include Senator Adams, who shepherded to enactment Utah's landmark law combining LGBT nondiscrimination protections with religious liberty protections; former Utah governor Michael Leavitt, who headed both the federal Environmental Protection Agency and the Department of Health and Human Services; and rabbi and former ambassador David Saperstein, the Obama administration's Ambassador-at-Large for

Religious Freedom and a longtime advocate for religious freedom. These statesmen, old hands at taking "brave gambles," as Governor Leavitt describes them, point to the possibility of finding politically acceptable, livable solutions to even these divisive problems.

Together, our contributors offer a 360-degree vantage point on the questions raised by the intersection of faith and sexuality, a panoramic view essential to charting a path forward.

As the list of contributors makes clear, this volume represents an honest attempt to give parity of treatment between communities and ideas without prejudging the outcome. Our contributors are especially suited to open this dialogue. All have written extensively about LGBT rights, same-sex marriage, or religious liberty. Many have long had a foot in the policy and legislative worlds and so bring a healthy respect for how difficult that task may be. All approach the subject with good will and a recognition that these are hard issues that go to who we are as individuals and as a people. To enhance the cohesion of the book, the editors have added references throughout the chapters to other chapters. As you read the volume, we hope you will share our optimism that people of good will can forge new ways to reconcile the needs of the faith and LGBT communities.

Readers almost certainly will disagree with something in this volume. But whatever policy prescription Americans ultimately embrace, it is essential to develop a public understanding of what is at stake.

This volume begins a long overdue conversation about whether we must remain divided as a nation over matters at the intersection of faith and sexuality. It could not be more timely.

PART I

The Search for Common Ground

Framing the Dialogue

Choosing among Non-Negotiated Surrender, Negotiated Protection of Liberty and Equality, or Learning and Earning Empathy

Alan Brownstein

It is worth our collective efforts to develop accommodations for religious objectors to same-sex marriage that are respectful of the dignity and needs of the people on both sides of these disputes. However, there is every reason to be discouraged about the prospects of having a meaningful dialogue on this issue, much less reaching political compromise. In 2016, the Pew Research Center conducted a study to determine public attitudes on the question of whether businesses should be required to provide wedding-related services to same-sex couples – even if the owners have religious reasons for refusing to do so.[1]

The public was pretty evenly split on the issue.[2] Most problematic, people on each side of this debate overwhelmingly indicated that they had virtually no sympathy for people on the other side.[3]

With this kind of polarization, it is tempting to conclude that dialogue and compromises are impossible. In this view, conflicts will only be resolved when one side obtains enough political power to force the other side to submit to the victorious side's decisions. There is no basis for noncoercive negotiation. The only things to talk about are the terms of surrender of the defeated constituency. True, this is certainly one possible outcome of these conflicts.

But, there are other possible approaches to resolving these conflicts. These approaches emphasize greater dialogue between the opposing sides and greater

---

[1] *Where the Public Stands on Religious Liberty vs. Nondiscrimination*, Pew Res. Ctr. (Sept. 28, 2016), http://www.pewforum.org/2016/09/28/where-the-public-stands-on-religious-liberty-vs-non discrimination/.

[2] *Id.* (reporting that 48% favored a business's ability to refuse and 49% favored requiring the business to provide the services).

[3] *Id.* ("Just 18% say they have at least some sympathy for both sides, while an additional 15% sympathize with *neither* side.").

tolerance for the needs and interests of both the LGBT community and those religious communities opposed to same-sex marriage.[4]

Under this engagement model, compromises can be negotiated. Daunting difficulties exist, but they can be confronted and resolved. Indeed, for people who are committed to both the liberty and equality rights of the LGBT community and to religious liberty for people of all faiths, there really is no choice but to pursue negotiated compromises, even if doing so sometimes appears to be futile.[5]

The first step is to recognize the conflict for what it is. Here, how one defines and identifies the problem can itself be contentious. Let's start with some facts. Millions of devout religious people in the United States believe in traditional marriage and consider same-sex marriage to be sinful and unacceptable.[6] These people are not going to go away or immediately change their beliefs. Further, they have countless relatives, colleagues, neighbors, co-congregants and friends who are committed to protecting their religious liberty.

There are millions of LGBT people in the United States.[7] Many of them are in loving, long-term relationships and have joined together in same-sex marriages.[8] Others hope to form such relationships and to have the opportunity to marry, just as many heterosexuals hope to form loving relationships and marry. This community is not going to go away or change their identity and relationships. Further, they have countless relatives, colleagues, neighbors, co-congregants and friends who are committed to protecting their liberty and equality rights.

Both sides in this conflict are motivated in part by fear. The fears of the LGBT community are grounded in history. Gays and lesbians[9] have been subject to

---

[4] Millions of religious Americans believe that same-sex marriages are consistent with their religious beliefs. *See, e.g.,* David Masci & Michael Lipka, *Where Christian Churches, Other Religions Stand on Gay Marriage,* PEW RES. CTR., http://www.pewresearch.or/fact-tank/2015/12/21/where-christian-churches-stand-on-gay-marriages/ (indicating the following religions sanction same-sex marriage: Conservative Jewish Movement, Episcopal Church, Evangelical Lutheran Church in America, Presbyterian Church (U.S.A.), Reform Jewish Movement, Society of Friends (Quaker), Unitarian Universalist Association of Churches, and United Church of Christ); Robert P. Jones et al., *Beyond Same-Sex Marriage: Attitudes on LGBT Discrimination Laws and Religious Exemptions,* PUB. RES. RELIGION INST., 5–6 (Feb. 18, 2016), https://www.prri.org/research/poll-same-sex-gay-marriage-lgbt-nondiscrimination-religious-liberty/.

[5] For an example of where this worked, see Adams, Chapter 32.

[6] *See supra* note 4.

[7] Gary J. Gates, *In U.S., More Adults Identifying as LGBT,* GALLUP NEWS (Jan. 11, 2017), http://news.gallup.com/poll/201731/lgbt-identification-rises.aspx (finding 4.1% of the U.S. population, or 10 million Americans, identify as LGBT). *See also* Robin Fretwell Wilson, *Being Transgender in the Era of Trump: Compassion Should Pick Up Where Science Leaves Off,* 7 UC IRVINE L. REV. (forthcoming 2017).

[8] Jeffrey M. Jones, *Same-Sex Marriages Up One Year After Supreme Court Verdict,* GALLUP NEWS (June 22, 2016), http://news.gallup.com/poll/193055/sex-marriages-one-year-supreme-court-verdict.aspx?g_source=position2&g_medium=related&g_campaign=tiles.

[9] In this chapter, gays and lesbians is used as shorthand to refer to the LGBT community. This is not meant to overlook or ignore bisexual and transgender individuals. In fact, bisexuals have

virulent prejudice and pervasive discrimination in the United States.[10] Not long ago, the law essentially required members of the LGBT community to be celibate and childless.[11] Until recently, same-sex couples were denied the legal benefits and cultural status of marriage.[12]

Prejudice against the LGBT community continues today, manifested in part by ongoing discrimination in public accommodations, housing, and employment.[13] While there has been considerable cultural change over the last two decades,[14] the history of other victimized groups demonstrates that neither prejudice nor discrimination dissipates quickly. Few would argue today that because of changes in public attitudes neither African Americans nor Jews need the protection of civil rights laws.[15] Yet in many states, the LGBT community still remains vulnerable to limitless discrimination in employment, housing, and public accommodations.[16]

Unlike the LGBT community, the fears of the religious community are grounded in the present and in the future, not the past. Religious groups worry that government through civil rights laws or other regulations will coerce religious individuals and institutions to violate their religious convictions. They point to clashes described across this volume from religious bakers forced to sell wedding cakes to adoption

---

been reported to make up the largest portion of the LGBT community. Anna Brown, 5 *Key Findings About LGBT Americans*, PEW RES. CTR. (June 13, 2017), http://www.pewresearch.org/fact-tank/2017/06/13/5-key-findings-about-lgbt-americans/.

[10] Courts evaluating bans on same-sex marriage review this grim treatment, see, e.g., Windsor v. United States, 699 F.3d 169, 182 (2d Cir. 2012) (concluding that the history of prejudice and discrimination against gays and lesbians in the United States was not open to serious debate); Pedersen v. Office of Personnel Management, 881 F. Supp. 294, 316–18 (D. Conn. 2012); Campaign for Southern Equality v. Bryant, 64 F. Supp. 3d 906, 930–37 (S.D. Miss. 2014).

[11] *See, e.g.*, TEX. PENAL CODE ANN. § 21.06 (West 1974).

[12] *See, e.g.*, Obergefell v. Hodges, 135 S. Ct. 2584 (2015).

[13] For empirical support for this commonsense observation, see, e.g., Brad Sears and Christy Mallory, EMPLOYMENT DISCRIMINATION AGAINST LGBT PEOPLE: EXISTENCE AND IMPACT, *in* GENDER IDENTITY AND SEXUAL ORIENTATION DISCRIMINATION IN THE WORKPLACE: A PRACTICAL GUIDE (Christine Michelle Duffy and Denise M. Visconti eds., Bloomberg BNA 2014), https://williamsinstitute.law.ucla.edu/wp-content/uploads/CH40-Discrimination-Against-LGBT-People-Sears-Mallory.pdf (explaining employment discrimination); Christy Mallory and Brad Sears, *Evidence of Discrimination in Public Accommodations Based on Sexual Orientation and Gender Identity: An Analysis of Complaints Filed with State Enforcement Agencies, 2008–2014*, WILLIAMS INST. (2016), https://williamsinstitute.law.ucla.edu/wp-content/uploads/Public-Accommodations-Discrimination-Complaints-2008–2014.pdf (explaining public accommodations discrimination).

[14] A 2017 Pew Research Center public opinion poll identified changing attitudes. *Changing Attitudes on Gay Marriage*, PEW RES. CTR. (June 26, 2017), http://www.pewforum.org/fact-sheet/changing-attitudes-on-gay-marriage/ (finding 74% of Millennials (those born after 1981), 65% of Generation X (those born between 1965 and 1980), 56% of Baby Boomers (those born between 1946 and 1964), and 41% of the Silent Generation (those born between 1928 and 1945) favor same-sex marriage).

[15] *See, e.g.*, Emma Green, *Why Attacks on Jewish Cemeteries Provoke Particular Fear*, THE ATLANTIC (Feb. 27, 2017), https://www.theatlantic.com/politics/archive/2017/02/jewish-cemeteries-destruction/518040/.

[16] For a list of these states, see *Introduction*, Chapter 1.

agencies closing when accommodations were not forthcoming to efforts to link state grants for college to how religious colleges treated gender identity and sexual orientation.[17] They seek exemptions from civil rights laws protecting the LGBT community in order to obey the dictates of their faith. The number of disputes being actively contested may be relatively small, but the range of conflicts is broad and varied, as this volume illustrates. Some highly publicized disputes involve wedding photographers, florists, and bakers who assert that it would violate their religious convictions to provide certain goods or services to a same-sex wedding.[18]

Other conflicts extend far beyond the provision of goods and services for wedding ceremonies.[19] Landlords may decline to rent accommodations to same-sex couples.[20] Or disputes may involve religiously affiliated institutions. Religious hospitals may refuse to recognize that a same-sex spouse is entitled to a range of privileges to be afforded to marital partners. Religious adoption agencies may not place children for adoption with same-sex families, who are able to adopt in every state in America but would be forced to seek another provider. Religious colleges may deny a same-sex couple's access to married student housing.[21] A religious school may refuse to hire individuals in a same-sex marital relationship as employees.[22] A marriage counselor may refuse to accept and treat same-sex couples as clients.[23]

The LGBT community fears that religious exemptions from nondiscrimination regulations reinforce prejudice against its members.[24] Permitting discrimination against same-sex couples denies them the equal status in public life that civil rights protections are intended to provide.[25] Many who hold this view believe legal regimes generally receptive to such accommodations will license broad-based discrimination, in important matters, against same-sex couples and single LGBT people in ways that will be difficult to limit or contain.

Given these starting positions, no dialogue or compromise in this area is possible without each side acknowledging the legitimacy of the experience and fears of the other side. The unwillingness to do so ends any attempt at meaningful discussion.

---

[17] *See* Berg, Chapter 24; Hoogstra et al., Chapter 25; McConnell, Chapter 28.

[18] *See* State v. Arlene's Flowers, Inc., 389 P. 3d 543 (Wash. 2017), *vacated*, 138 S. Ct. 2671 (2018); Craig v. Masterpiece Cakeshop, Inc., 370 P. 3d 272 (Colo. App. 2015); Elane Photography, LLC v. Willock, 309 P.3d 53 (N.M. 2013), *cert denied*, 134 S. Ct. 1787 (2014).

[19] *See generally* Elizabeth Sepper, *Doctoring Discrimination in the Same-Sex Marriage Debate*, 89 INDIANA L. REV. 703, 712–13 (2014).

[20] *See* Adams, Chapter 32.

[21] A major question here is whether and to what extent the government funding of religious institutions should influence the debate. If a religious organization operates a government-funded program, may it discriminate against gays and lesbians or same-sex couples in hiring staff or providing state-subsidized services?

[22] *See generally* Robin Fretwell Wilson, *Squaring Faith and Sexuality: Religious Institutions and the Unique Challenge of Sports*, 34 LAW & INEQ. 385 (2016).

[23] *See* Ward v. Polite, 667 F.3d 727 (2012); Keeton v. Anderson-Wiley, 664 F.3d 865 (2011).

[24] *See* Melling, Chapter 19.

[25] *See* NeJaime & Siegel, Chapter 6; Wilson, Chapter 30.

Arguing about the exact number of religious individuals and institutions burdened by government actions promoting LGBT rights or the exact number of same-sex couples and members of the LGBT community subject to discrimination is a tangent and a distraction. There are enough instances of substantial burdens and discrimination for each side to experience and express cognizable concerns.

Without the protection of civil rights laws and other forms of government intervention, same-sex couples and members of the LGBT community will suffer discrimination in housing, employment, and access to goods and services. Religious exemptions and accommodations will impose real costs and burdens on the LGBT community including tangible disadvantages, loss of status, and emotional distress. Those who have never experienced the denial of equal access to goods, services, jobs, or apartments may not grasp this harm. When a group of persons can be denied such things for no reason other than who they are, their equal status in the community has been collectively disparaged and denied.

Without exemptions and accommodations, religious individuals and institutions will be burdened. Some individuals will risk losing their jobs or their businesses because of their adherence to their faith. Others are burdened if they are denied access to vocations and professions because they cannot agree to provide services in violation of their religious beliefs about same-sex relationships. Institutions risk penalties or other burdens if they obey and enforce the dictates of their religion.

A second barrier to serious negotiation to be overcome is the aspiration that constitutional law or general religious liberty statutes can solve the problem for us. This is a false and errant hope. We cannot avoid the hard work of negotiated compromise by passing the buck to the courts.

For the most part, existing law provides uncertain or problematic solutions to these conflicts. Constitutional law is largely, although not entirely, silent on these matters. Even if the US Supreme Court determined that LGBT people are a suspect class, the Equal Protection Clause of the Fourteenth Amendment would not protect the LGBT community from discrimination in most of these disputes because most employers, landlords, and providers of goods and services are not state actors. Similarly, it would be a rare case in which the Free Exercise Clause of the First Amendment provided protection to religious employers, landlords, or business owners. In 1990, the Supreme Court decided that, with very narrow exceptions, the Free Exercise Clause provides no protection against neutral laws of general applicability that do not single out religion for discriminatory treatment.[26] Civil rights laws are neutral laws of general applicability. Absent evidence that a law

---

[26] Employment Division v. Smith, 494 U.S. 872 (1990); Hosanna-Tabor Evangelical Lutheran Church and School v. EEOC, 565 U.S. 171 (2012) (recognizing constitutional protection against nondiscrimination claims for certain "ministerial" positions, but limiting the holding to employment discrimination.).

somehow targeted religious actors, the Free Exercise Clause will not provide protection against its enforcement.

Free speech doctrine prohibiting the government from forcing a person to express the government's or another person's message may have some applicability to a narrow class of public accommodations disputes. Here the argument would be that services, such as those of a wedding photographer, are sufficiently creative and expressive in nature that requiring the photographer to take pictures at a same-sex wedding or reception would constitute government compelled speech prohibited by the First Amendment. The merits of these claims are sharply contested.[27] Even if claims of creative expression are upheld, there is little reason to believe that constitutional restrictions on compelled speech will govern any significant number of conflicts between religious liberty and the rights of the LGBT community. As Robin Fretwell Wilson notes elsewhere, framing protections in terms of creative expression overlooks the broader set of requests not to facilitate same-sex marriages.[28]

Unlike free exercise doctrine, general religious liberty statutes such as the federal Religious Freedom Restoration Act (RFRA) and state RFRAs do protect religious exercise against neutral laws of general applicability.[29] The extent to which they support religious claims against nondiscrimination laws remains clouded in uncertainty, however. As Senator J. Stuart Adams notes in Chapter 32, RFRA has been used successfully only once to defend against a duty not to discriminate – in the Michigan funeral home case involving a transgender receptionist.[30] That case is on appeal.[31] Indeed, the application of RFRA laws to religious liberty challenges to civil rights laws may produce inconsistent results that are likely to ignore the interests of one side of the conflict or the other.[32]

The Supreme Court's decision in *Burwell v. Hobby Lobby* supports the conclusion that civil rights laws may substantially burden religious liberty rights protected by RFRA in some cases.[33] But a finding of substantial burden only requires that that government justify its regulation under rigorous review.[34] It does not predict or control whether the government can satisfy that standard. On this question, the *Hobby Lobby* decision provides little guidance as to how courts should adjudicate RFRA cases challenging the application of nondiscrimination laws.

The Court in *Hobby Lobby* upheld the plaintiffs' claims for an exemption from the "contraceptive mandate" required by federal regulations because it determined

---

[27] Most courts have rejected these compelled speech arguments. *See, e.g.*, Elane Photography, *supra* note 18 at 63–71.

[28] *See* Wilson, Chapter 30.

[29] *See, e.g.*, 42 USC § 2000bb (2012).

[30] *See* Adams, Chapter 32.

[31] E.E.O.C. v. R.G. & G.R. Harris Funeral Homes, Inc., 201 F. Supp. 3d 837 (2016).

[32] For a compendium of RFRA law in all the states, see Appendix, Chapter 35.

[33] 134 S. Ct. 2751 (2015).

[34] 42 USC § 2000bb (2012) ("[G]overnments should not substantially burden religious exercise without compelling justification.").

that a less restrictive alternative was available that would enable the government to meet its public health goals[35] without burdening religious employers who argued that complying with the contraceptive mandate would violate their religious convictions.[36] By shifting the cost of insurance coverage for medical contraceptives from objecting religious employers to insurance companies, as the Obama administration had done for religious nonprofits, the government could exempt religious objectors from the contraceptive mandate and still fully accomplish the government's purpose.

No such existing or obvious less restrictive alternatives exist to enable governments to achieve their equal opportunity goals in housing, employment, or public accommodations if exemptions are granted to religious objectors to nondiscrimination laws. Governments cannot provide comparable jobs, housing, or goods and services to same-sex couples or LGBT persons who are denied access to these basic goods as a result of exemptions from civil rights laws. Courts will have to balance the competing liberty and equality interests at stake in these disputes, and no one knows with any certainty how they would do so.

Uncertainty is a major problem with relying on RFRA laws to deal with these disputes. Conflicts are stoked when neither side knows what their rights are until a case is adjudicated. But uncertainty is not the only problem. Judicial decisions are more likely to provide too little or too much protection to one side or the other than they are to promote or reflect reasoned compromises. If courts generally reject RFRA claims against civil rights laws, religious objectors will certainly feel their rights are neither protected nor respected. If courts uphold these claims and conclude that the government can grant religious exemptions without seriously interfering with the goals of nondiscrimination regulations, it is difficult to see how these holdings could be limited to discrimination against same-sex couples. Laws protecting racial, ethnic, and religious minorities would be equally subject to challenge, as would laws prohibiting discrimination on the basis of gender or sexual orientation.[37]

These limits of RFRA and federal doctrine demonstrate that the conflicts between religious liberty and the liberty and equality rights of the LGBT community – including disputes about accommodations for religious objectors to same-sex

---

[35] The Court did not focus on gender equality in its opinion, despite the fact that the justification for contraceptive coverage was premised both on women's equal participation in the workplace and on public health. *See* Robin Fretwell Wilson, *The Calculus of Accommodation: Contraception, Abortion, Same-Sex Marriage, and Other Clashes Between Religion and the State*, 53 B.C. L. Rev. 1417 (2012).

[36] *Hobby Lobby*, 134 S. Ct. at 2782.

[37] Put another way, if the availability of goods and services from alternative providers justifies exemptions from civil rights laws prohibiting discrimination on the basis of sexual orientation, the same analysis would justify exemptions from civil rights laws prohibiting discrimination on the basis of race, religion, or gender.

marriage – cannot be resolved through constitutional adjudication and statutory interpretation. The hard work of political deliberation is unavoidable.

A third impediment to meaningful political negotiations is the concern that any potential compromise will require either side to abandon its core beliefs or identity. Yet, no such abandonment of principle is required. Negotiations can proceed with the understanding that some religious individuals and clergy and some members and supporters of the LGBT community consider the views and the conduct of the other side to be immoral and wrongful. The predicate for such negotiations is the recognition by both sides that this is part of the social contract in a free democratic society. The essence of liberty in a free society is the right to act wrongfully in the eyes of others. Liberty means the right to express the wrong ideas, to worship the wrong gods, or the right G-d in the wrong way, and to marry the wrong partner.[38]

Concededly, this is very much a rights-based approach. When society acknowledges the right of individuals to speak or to exercise religion it does not suggest that society agrees with what every individual says or affirms their beliefs. This freedom does recognize, at least implicitly, that the speech and faith of others – as immoral and false as one may think those messages and beliefs may be – are as important and deserving of protection as our own speech and beliefs are to us.

Although the struggle has been long – and it is certainly not entirely over – many adherents of traditional religious faiths have come to terms with this understanding of liberty regarding the free exercise of religion. These traditionalists accept that believers in "false faiths" have the right to exercise and espouse their errant religious beliefs.[39] Under a regime committed to religious liberty and equality, government protects all faiths equally and does not elevate preferred religions over others.

This freedom does not come without costs. Rights are often expensive political goods. To the minds of some, false faiths and secular ideologies can lead people away from a true understanding of G-d and toward eternal damnation.[40] Yet many traditional religious adherents are committed to religious liberty for all. Possible political compromises between religious liberty and the liberty and equality rights of the LGBT community will be facilitated if traditionalists can extend their understanding of liberty to include not only the right to worship wrongly, but the right to marry wrongly. Same-sex couples have the right to marry even if traditional religious faiths deem their behavior to be errant and sinful.

Similarly, the possibility of political compromise will be enhanced if proponents of same-sex marriage and the liberty and equality rights of the LGBT community, can accept the universality of rights of religious conscience. Religious conscience is like speech. We protect it not because we agree with the way that it is being

---

[38] Alan Brownstein, *Gays, Jews, and Other Strangers in a Strange Land: The Case for Reciprocal Accommodation of Religious Liberty and the Right of Same-Sex Couples to Marry*, 45 U.S.F. L. Rev. 389, 406 (2010) [hereinafter *Strangers in a Strange Land*].

[39] *Id.* at 406–07.

[40] *Id.* at 406.

exercised, but because of our commitment to the right itself. And we protect rights of conscience and speech even though we recognize that the cost of doing so is sometimes high and painful.

Because religious liberty claims in recent times often involve issues relating to gender and sexuality and resonate with what are generally considered to be conservative political values (opposition to abortion, same-sex marriage, and LGBT rights), progressives may sometimes have lost sight of this understanding of rights of conscience. The utility of religious liberty to protect progressive acts of conscience seemed limited to hypotheticals. Thus, instead of a pharmacist objecting on religious grounds to selling a drug deemed to be an abortifacient,[41] one might offer the analogy of a pharmacist religiously opposed to selling a drug manufactured in a third-world country by workers who were treated only marginally better than slaves.

Today, however, arguments about universal respect for claims of religious conscience are no longer limited to hypotheticals.[42] Progressives find themselves supporting the religious liberty claims of Muslims whose rights are under attack.[43] An even stronger moral imperative grounded in faith can be asserted to challenge the current administration's immigration and deportation policies.[44] As it is so often repeated in the Jewish Bible, "You shall not wrong a stranger or oppress him, for you were strangers in the land of Egypt."[45]

These arguments can be countered by rejoinders from both sides that religious liberty accommodations for discriminatory conduct and the right of same-sex couples to marry are sufficiently distinct interests that no useful analogies can be employed to form the basis for meaningful discourse, negotiation, and compromise. These distinctions are substantially overstated. There are parallel identity claims in this conflict. Serious liberty and equality interests are at stake on both sides of these disputes.

When same-sex couples make a lifelong commitment to be responsible for each other and to love one another (including sexual intimacy), that is not a lifestyle

---

[41] Stormans Inc. v. Wiesman, 794 F.3d 1064 (9th Cir. 2015), *cert. denied* 136 S. Ct. 2433 (2016).

[42] Sanford Levinson, *The New (Religious) Face of Civil Disobedience: A Resurgent Sanctuary Movement May Complicate the Precepts of the Christian Right*, ALJAZEERA AM. (Sept. 7, 2014), http://america.aljazeera.com/opinions/2014/9/religion-sanctuarymovementimmigrationrefugee spoverty.html.

[43] *See, e.g.,* Carolyn Davis & Lauren Kokum, *Addressing Challenges to Progressive Religious Liberty in Michigan*, CTR. AM. PROGRESS (May 12, 2016), https://www.americanprogress.org/ issues/religion/reports/2016/05/12/137320/addressing-challenges-to-progressive-religious-liberty-in-michigan.

[44] *See, e.g.,* Donald J. Trump, *Presidential Proclamation Enhancing Vetting Capabilities and Processes for Detecting Attempted Entry into the United States by Terrorists or Other Public-Safety Threats*, WHITEHOUSE.GOV (Sept. 24, 2017), https://www.whitehouse.gov/the-press-office/ 2017/09/24/enhancing-vetting-capabilities-and-processes-detecting-attempted-entry.

[45] THE JEWISH BIBLE: TANAKH: THE HOLY SCRIPTURES – THE NEW JPS TRANSLATION ACCORDING TO THE TRADITIONAL HEBREW TEXT (Jewish Publication Society ed., 1985), *Exodus* 22:20. *See also Leviticus* 19:33.

choice. That is a life-defining decision that serves as the foundation on which they will live the rest of their lives. Their right to make that decision deserves great respect.

For devout individuals, religion is not a lifestyle choice either. An individual's decision to accept the duties that arise out of his or her relationship to God is central to human dignity and defines that person's identity.[46] The right to make that decision deserves great respect as well.[47]

Indeed, if we look at the language Justice Anthony M. Kennedy used to describe the meaning of marriage in *Obergefell v. Hodges*,[48] we can see a common theme of personal autonomy and dignity that serves as the foundation for both religious liberty and the liberty and equality rights of the LGBT community.[49] Justice Kennedy emphasizes the nobility and dignity of marriage. He describes how the bond of marriage enables "expression, intimacy, and spirituality."[50] Kennedy argues that the liberty that the Constitution protects includes "personal choices central to individual dignity and autonomy."[51] And he movingly acknowledges "the universal fear that a lonely person might call out only to find no one there."[52]

Defenders of religious liberty could embrace these core principles and insist that they apply as meaningfully and forcefully to individuals seeking to adhere to their religious beliefs, identity, and community as they do to individuals joining together in marriage. Religious liberty is grounded in human dignity and personal autonomy. Membership in a religious community enables "expression, intimacy, and spirituality" in ways that may transcend what an individual can do alone. Faith and religion also respond to the "universal fear" that we may call out in need and receive no response.[53]

This rights-based foundation for negotiated compromises only carries us so far. There is an additional approach to addressing the conflict between religious liberty and the rights and interests of the LGBT community. This aspiration can be described as learning and earning empathy – for in today's world it surely is no more than that. In addition to the acceptance of rights of others for the purpose of political compromise, it involves some empathy for the individual exercising his or her rights. This requires that we see the other as a whole person and do not just define them by one aspect of their identity.

Empathy rejects defining individuals or groups on the basis of one attribute alone. It means accepting that traditional religions are a lot more than one discriminatory

---

[46] Alan E. Brownstein, *Perception and Reality*, LIBERTY MAG. (Nov./Dec. 2015), http://libertyma gazine.org/article/perception-and-reality.
[47] *See Strangers in a Strange Land, supra* note 38, at 400–08.
[48] Obergefell v. Hodges, 135 S. Ct. 2584, 2599–2600 (2015).
[49] *Id.*
[50] *Id.* at 2599.
[51] *Id.* at 2597.
[52] *Id.* at 2600; *see also Strangers in a Strange Land, supra* note 38.
[53] *Id.*

belief, and LGBT families are a lot more than their sexual orientation. It reflects a basic idea underlying civil rights law that part of what makes discrimination against a vulnerable class so unacceptable is the demeaning falsehood that we can sort human beings and determine how they should be treated by reference to only one personal characteristic, be it race, gender, religion, or sexual orientation.

Achieving this kind of empathy is very hard to do – but it may be harder to do in the abstract than in real life. We do it all the time when we live and work together with people with whom we strongly disagree. But, there are limits. A Jewish person cannot develop empathy for a virulent anti-Semite. But they may work with and have strong bonds of empathy with some people who may think their religious beliefs are false, that they are forever alienated from G-d because they are a Jew, or that they must be crazy because they take religion seriously.

How do we move away from an unconditional surrender mentality toward negotiated compromise or even some degree of empathy? There are ways to lower the temperature in the room and to begin to incrementally bridge the gap between the opposing sides in these conflicts.

Both sides can look for some things to take off the table. Gay rights advocates can agree that no attempts will be made to deny tax exempt status to religious organizations that do not recognize same-sex marriages. The Bob Jones University case[54] was the exception, not the rule. Tax exemption is like police protection and sidewalks – a general benefit available to all nonprofits. It exists to facilitate the range of private charity, education, and religion beyond what the government determines to be of value.[55] Taking tax exemptions off the table removes a major concern for religious opponents of same-sex marriage.

Religious liberty proponents can agree to accept the constitutional decision declaring the right of same-sex couples to marry. This will not be an issue like the right to have an abortion that will be endlessly re-litigated.

Both sides can put some things on the table. Gay rights advocates can support laws that demonstrate to the other side that they value religious liberty – even though they think it can be outweighed in some cases by sufficiently important equality rights. This could include supporting religious liberty statutes with civil rights and equality carve-outs such as the Workplace Religious Freedom Act enacted in California in 2012 which requires greater accommodations of religious employees by their employers.[56] They could also support state RFRA statutes with appropriate exclusions for civil rights laws. Exhibiting a willingness to protect religious liberty in circumstances when important LGBT rights (or other core equality rights) are not at risk creates a less mistrustful environment for simultaneous and ongoing negotiations over exemptions from nondiscrimination laws.

[54] Bob Jones University v. United States, 461 U.S. 574 (1983).
[55] *Id.* at 608–10 (Powell, J., concurring).
[56] CAL. GOV'T CODE §§ 12926(q), 12926(u) (2012).

Proponents of religious liberty accommodations could agree to support civil rights laws protecting LGBT people against discrimination in employment, housing, and public accommodations by for-profit businesses in the numerous circumstances in which religious liberty is not at issue while negotiating the contours of exemptions from civil rights laws. They could also agree to demonstrate concern for the LGBT community in other areas, such as assisting undocumented members of the LGBT community who are at risk of being deported to countries where they will be subject to persecution and violence.

Both sides could begin to discuss the hard issues by identifying cases where compromise may be most possible. For example, there are some, limited personal professional services where the religious beliefs of the provider cannot be isolated from the personal empathy and support needed to achieve quality services. Here, the value or utility of the service to same-sex couples and other clients is substantially diminished if the professionals are required to provide the services, notwithstanding their religious beliefs.

Some services are necessarily of limited value if they are provided under compulsion. That is part of the reason why some "personal" employment contracts cannot be meaningfully subject to specific performance in contract law.[57]

Assume there is a devoutly religious marriage counselor whose faith rejects same-sex marriages. Most of the counselor's clients are also devoutly religious. They believe that only a counselor who can positively empathize with their religious beliefs can be helpful to them and create an effective therapeutic setting for the successful resolution of their marital problems.

This counselor believes that because of her religious beliefs she will not be able to provide the empathy and psychological support necessary for a successful therapeutic relationship if she counsels same-sex couples. Could there be an agreement to exempt such professionals from nondiscrimination laws requiring them to accept clients, such as same-sex couples, where the counselor's religion limits her ability to provide effective services?[58]

---

[57] *See, e.g.*, E. ALLAN FARNSWORTH, FARNSWORTH ON CONTRACTS (3d ed. 2004) Sec. 12.7, 185–86 (explaining judicial reluctance to grant specific performance for personal service contracts because of the difficulty of evaluating the quality of the services and the undesirability of requiring performance where confidence in the loyalty of the provider is in doubt).

[58] Providing exemptions to marriage counselors is a seriously contested issue. *See, e.g.*, Emma Green, *When Doctors Refuse to Treat LGBT Patients*, THE ATLANTIC (Apr. 19, 2016), https:// www.theatlantic.com/health/archice/2016/04/medical-religious-exemptions-doctors-therapists-mississippi-tennessee/478797/; Laurie Meyers, *License to Deny Services*, COUNSELING TODAY (June 27, 2016), http://ct.counseling.org/2016/06/license-deny-services; James N. Sells & W. Bryce Hagedorn, *CACREP Accreditation, Ethics, and the Affirmation of Both Religious and Sexual Identities: A Response to Smith and Okech*, 94 J. COUNSELING & DEV. 265 (2016); Lance C. Smith & Jane E. Atieno Okech, *Ethical Issues Raised by CACREP Accreditation of Programs Within Institutions That Disaffirm or Disallow Diverse Sexual Orientations*, 94 J. COUNSELING & DEV. 252 (2016).

The way both sides talk at or to each other can change to promote dialogue. Advocates from both sides of this conflict should shift the discussion away from partisan politics. They should recognize that there are people of good faith and bad faith on both sides. The model to be followed is more like deal-making than litigation. In litigation, one side wins and the other loses. In deal-making, both sides lose if the deal falls through or if the agreement ends up being litigated.

Representatives of both sides need to demonstrate that they understand the deeply felt needs and concerns of the other side. They should try to discuss their own side's interests in terms that are applicable to and can be heard by the opposing side.

Finally, those seeking a negotiated solution need to acknowledge that we should ask others to accept only the kinds of burdens that we are willing to bear ourselves. If religious accommodations permit discrimination against LGBT people, the accommodation should apply broadly and also permit discrimination on the basis of religion. If we are going to ask the LGBT community to accept religious accommodations that permit businesses to discriminate against their families, we should also be willing to accept accommodations that permit discrimination against people because they are Jews or Christians or Muslims, or persons of another faith.[59]

---

[59] *Strangers in a Strange Land, supra* note 38, at 339 n. 22.

3

Liberty and Justice for All

Douglas Laycock

We teach our children that America offers "liberty and justice for all." But we aren't doing so well on the part about "for all." Americans tend to have an expansive vision of liberty and justice for themselves and for people they sympathize with on their side of the culture wars – and a minimalist vision of liberty and justice for people on the other side.

A 2016 poll by the Pew Research Center asked how much people sympathized with businesses seeking religious exemptions from assisting with same-sex weddings.[1] Nearly half sympathized "some" or "a lot." Just over half sympathized "some" or "a lot" with those who would refuse exemptions.

So each side elicits at least "some" sympathy from about half the population – and only half. How many people expressed at least "some" sympathy for both sides? Only 18 percent. More than 80 percent of the population expressed no or "not much" sympathy for the people they disagreed with. And 15 percent could not muster even "some" sympathy for either side.

These are not people looking for a way to balance conflicting rights and protect as much as possible for both sides. The great bulk of the population, on both sides of the issue, says, in effect, "This is an easy choice and I have little or no sympathy for the other side." These are not Americans committed to "liberty and justice for all"; these are two sides determined to crush each other.

On the policy choice here, 48 percent supported religious exemptions in the wedding cases and 49 percent opposed exemptions.[2] The precise question asked was: "If you had to choose, which comes closest to your view? Business owners with

---

[1] *Americans Divided over Whether Wedding-Related Businesses Should Be Required to Serve Same-Sex Couples*, Pew Res. Ctr. (Sept. 28, 2016), http://www.pewforum.org/2016/09/28/2-americans-divided-over-whether-wedding-related-businesses-should-be-required-to-serve-same-sex-couples/ [https://perma.cc/2354-WLAJ].

[2] *Id.*

religious objections to homosexuality should be [required to provide services OR able to refuse services OR no answer] to same-sex couples."

So suppose Americans were seriously interested in liberty and justice for all – for both sides of the culture wars. Could American law protect the essential rights of same-sex couples, and also protect the essential rights of conscientious objectors, with only modest sacrifice or accommodation by each side? For the most part, it could, if we cared to do so. Only occasionally are solutions impossible, and there is ample reason to pursue the solutions that are available. This chapter elaborates on these points.

I THE INTERESTS AT STAKE

Same-sex civil marriage is a great advance for human liberty. Marriage has long been recognized as a fundamental human right.[3] The choice of whom to marry is one of the most intimate and personal decisions that any human being can make. Government should not interfere with that choice without a very important reason. Nor should government leave a substantial class of people with no one, on any realistic view of the matter, whom they can legally marry.

The gain for human liberty will be severely compromised if same-sex couples now force religious dissenters to violate their consciences in the same way that those dissenters, when they had the power to do so, used to force same-sex couples to live in the closet. We appeared to be headed towards that outcome until the 2016 election. And in the long run, the social forces increasing support for gay rights are probably unstoppable.[4] But in the near and intermediate term, I now worry as much about LGBT progress being stopped or reversed as about religious dissenters being crushed.[5] The near and intermediate future appears to be religious dissenters getting crushed in blue states and gays and lesbians still discriminated against and denied protection in federal law and in red states.[6] As the gay-rights side likes to point out, in much of the country you can legally get married on Saturday and legally get fired for it on Monday.[7]

---

3   See Zablocki v. Redhail, 434 U.S. 374, 383 (1978); Loving v. Virginia, 388 U.S. 1, 12 (1967); Griswold v. Connecticut, 381 U.S. 479, 486 (1965); Skinner v. Oklahoma, 316 U.S. 535, 541 (1942); Meyer v. Nebraska, 262 U.S. 390, 399 (1923).
4   For views, see Brownstein, Chapter 2; Greenawalt, Chapter 8.
5   See *Introduction*, Chapter 1.
6   See *Non-Discrimination Laws*, MOVEMENT ADVANCEMENT PROJECT, http://www.lgbtmap.org/equality-maps/non_discrimination_laws [https://perma.cc/R2MS-63C3] (identifying states with and without laws prohibiting employment discrimination on the basis of sexual orientation or gender identity).
7   Gene Robinson, *State of LGBT Rights: Married on Sunday, but Fired on Monday*, DAILY BEAST (Dec. 14, 2014), https://www.thedailybeast.com/state-of-lgbt-rights-married-on-sunday-but-fired-on-Monday [https://perma.cc/2YXH-V5PK].

In the worst-case scenario for gay rights, some recalcitrant state will reenact its ban on same-sex marriage and try to persuade the conservative justices, with Trump-appointed reinforcements, to overrule the marriage decisions.[8] One can only hope that some of these justices understand the chaos and disruption that could ensue from removing constitutional protection from more than half a million same-sex marriages across the country.[9] What would happen when existing marriages suddenly became illegal? *Obergefell* is the law of the land, and one can hope that everyone understands that it is too late to roll it back.

Assuming that *Obergefell* holds, the prospect remains that blue states will oppress religious conservatives with respect to same-sex marriage – leaving no room to step aside from facilitating or assisting with same-sex wedding celebrations – and that red states will oppress same-sex couples – leaving them unprotected from discrimination with respect to anything except marriage, which is all that federal law reaches. That is a very bad outcome in both places.

There is a sad irony to the bitter conflict between the supporters of same-sex civil marriage and the religious dissenters. Sexual minorities and religious minorities make essentially parallel claims on the larger society. Thomas Berg has elaborated on these parallel claims, and William Eskridge wrote about some of these parallels twenty years ago.[10]

First, both same-sex couples and committed religious believers argue that some aspects of human identity are so fundamental that they should be left to each individual, free of all nonessential regulation, even when manifested in conduct.

Second, no person who wants to enter a same-sex marriage can change his sexual orientation by any act of will, and no religious believer can change his understanding of divine command by any act of will. Both religious beliefs and sexual orientation can change over time.[11] But these things do not change because government says they must, or because an individual decides they should; for most people, one's sexual orientation and one's understanding of what God commands are experienced as involuntary, beyond individual control.

Third, both religious and sexual minorities face the argument that their conduct is separable from any claim of protected legal rights, and thus subject to regulation

---

[8] Obergefell v. Hodges, 135 S. Ct. 2584 (2015); United States v. Windsor, 570 U.S. 744 (2013).

[9] The Gallup Poll estimated that there were 491,000 same-sex marriages in the United States as of early summer 2016, and the number was growing rapidly. Jeffrey M. Jones, *Same-Sex Marriages Up One Year After Supreme Court Verdict*, GALLUP NEWS (June 22, 2016), http://news.gallup.com/poll/193055/sex-marriages-one-year-supreme-court-verdict.aspx?g_source=Social%20Issues&g_medium=newsfeed&g_campaign=tiles [https://perma.cc/RN4E-FWNJ].

[10] *See* Thomas C. Berg, *What Same-Sex-Marriage and Religious-Liberty Claimants Have in Common*, 5 NW. J.L. & SOC. POL'Y 206, 212–26 (2010); William N. Eskridge, Jr., *A Jurisprudence of "Coming Out": Religion, Homosexuality, and Collisions of Liberty and Equality in America*, 106 YALE L.J. 2411, 2416–30 (1997).

[11] For data, *see* Steven E. Mock & Richard P. Eibach, *Stability and Change in Sexual Orientation Identity over a 10-Year Period in Adulthood*, 41 ARCH. SEX. BEHAV. 641 (2012).

with few limits. Courts rejected a distinction between sexual orientation and sexual conduct because they correctly found that both the orientation and the conduct that follows from that orientation are central to a person's identity.[12] Religious believers face similar attempts to distinguish their religious beliefs from the conduct based on those beliefs. This is the premise of *Employment Division v. Smith*,[13] refusing to protect religiously motivated conduct from burdens imposed by generally applicable laws. But believers cannot fail to act on God's will, and it is no more reasonable for the state to demand that they do so than for the state to demand celibacy of all gays and lesbians.

Fourth, both same-sex couples and religious dissenters seek to live out their identities in ways that are publicly visible and socially acknowledged. Same-sex couples claim the right to participate in the social institution of civil marriage and to live their lives as couples in public as well as in private.[14] Religious believers likewise claim a right to follow their faith not just in worship services, but also in the charitable works of their religious organizations, in their daily lives, and in their professions and occupations.[15]

Finally, both same-sex couples and religious dissenters face the problem that what they experience as among the highest virtues is condemned by others as a grave evil. Where same-sex couples see loving commitments of mutual care and support, many religious believers see disordered conduct that violates natural law and scriptural command. And where those religious believers see obedience to a loving God who undoubtedly knows best when he lays down rules for human conduct, many supporters of gay rights see intolerance, bigotry, and hate. Because gays, lesbians, and religious conservatives are each viewed as evil by a substantial portion of the population,[16] each is subject to substantial risks of intolerant and unjustifiably burdensome regulation.

The two sides have very different understandings of what it is they are disagreeing about. Marriage is a legal relationship, a deeply personal human relationship, and for many people, also a religious relationship. The secular side sees the legal and personal relationships as primary. Committed religious believers see the religious relationship as primary, and they see same-sex marriage as the state interfering with the sacred, changing a religious institution. In their view, the legal institution of

---

[12] *See, e.g.,* In re Marriage Cases, 183 P.3d 384, 442–43 (Cal. 2008); Kerrigan v. Comm'r of Pub. Health, 957 A.2d 407, 438 (Conn. 2008); Varnum v. Brien, 763 N.W.2d 862, 885, 893 (Iowa 2009).

[13] Employment Div., Dept. of Human Resources of Oregon v. Smith, 494 U.S. 872 (1990).

[14] *See, e.g.,* Pizer, Chapter 29; Berg, *supra* note 10, at 217.

[15] *See e.g.,* Leith Anderson, Chapter 12; Lori, Chapter 13; Hoogstra et al., Chapter 25; Berg, *supra* note 10, at 217–18.

[16] *See* Douglas Laycock, *Religious Liberty and the Culture Wars*, 2014 U. Ill. L. Rev. 839, 869–71; Douglas Laycock, *Sex, Atheism, and Religious Liberty*, 88 U. Det. Mercy L. Rev. 404, 414–17 (2011).

marriage is based on the religious institution. In the most succinct formulation, the state can *recognize* marriage, but it cannot *redefine* marriage.[17]

Of course, conservative believers are wrong about that. Civil marriage is a legal institution, defined by law, and there was never a guarantee that traditionalists would always control the law. Voters, legislatures, and sometimes courts can change the law and redefine civil marriage. And they have repeatedly done so. No-fault divorce brought a huge change to the meaning of civil marriage. The end of coverture had brought a bigger change. The husband no longer controls his wife, her property, and her earnings; he is no longer legally entitled to beat her "within reasonable bounds."[18] Same-sex marriage is another substantial change, but unlike no-fault divorce and the end of coverture, it does not change opposite-sex marriages. In that sense, it is a smaller change than those that came before.

Government can change the legal institution of civil marriage, but it cannot change religious marriage. Churches do not have to perform or recognize marriages that they believe to be religiously invalid. This much seems implicit in the rule that government cannot interfere in the internal affairs of churches.[19] It is at least common ground that clergy do not have to perform weddings against their will.[20] But in other contexts, there are active attacks on exemptions even for religious nonprofits.[21]

The religious liberty claim of the wedding vendors is closely related to the same understanding that protects the clergy and places of worship: that marriage is an inherently religious relationship and that a wedding is therefore an inherently religious ceremony.[22] Even if the couple understands their marriage in wholly secular terms, many religious believers will understand it in religious terms, because for them, civil marriage simply implements the underlying religious institution.[23] These conscientious objectors refuse to facilitate a relationship that in their view is

---

[17] R. R. Reno, *Government Marriage*, First Things (Dec. 2014), at 3, 4.

[18] *See* William Blackstone, 1 Commentaries on the Laws of England 430–33 (1765) (Univ. of Chicago facsimile ed., 1979); Nancy Cott, Public Vows: A History of Marriage and the Nation 11–12 (2000).

[19] Hosanna-Tabor Evangelical Church & Sch. v. Equal Empl. Opportunity Comm'n, 565 U.S. 171, 188–90 (2012).

[20] *See, e.g.*, Pizer, Chapter 29.

[21] See *infra* notes 67–73 and accompanying text.

[22] *See, e.g.*, J.A. at 157–58, Masterpiece Cakeshop, Ltd. v. Colo. Civil Rights Comm'n, No. 16–111, 2017 WL 4232758 (U.S. Aug. 31, 2017) (setting out the individual petitioner's religious understanding of marriage); *id.* at 167 (stating that his refusal to assist with same-sex weddings "*has everything to do with the nature of the wedding ceremony itself*, and about my religious belief about what marriage is and whether God will be pleased with me and my work") (emphasis added).

[23] R. R. Reno, *supra* note 17, at 4 (stating with approval that in "the past, government *recognized* marriage," and complaining that now "the courts have *redefined* rather than recognized marriage" (emphasis added)).

both inherently religious and religiously prohibited. People should at least be able to practice their religion in religious contexts, and a wedding is a religious context.

The job of the wedding planner, photographer, or caterer is to make each wedding the best and most memorable it can be. They are promoting it. And some of them say they cannot do that. This creative and promotional role is narrower for bakers and florists, but they too are promoting the wedding, doing their part to make this wedding better and more memorable.

I would not grant exemptions for refusing to serve gays and lesbians in contexts not directly related to the wedding or the marriage.[24] Exemptions should not be extended to large and impersonal businesses even in the wedding context. But for very small businesses, where the owner is likely to be personally involved in providing any services, we should exempt wedding vendors so long as another vendor is available without hardship to the same-sex couple.[25]

The law should also exempt marriage and relationship counselors. It does no good for either side to pair a same-sex couple with a religiously conservative counselor who thinks that the very existence of their relationship defies God's law. Complaints about counselors seek to drive religious conservatives from the helping professions.[26] They are not about obtaining counseling for anyone.

II BALANCING COMPETING HARMS

Even in the typical case where another vendor is immediately available, same-sex couples complain of the insult and dignitary harm of being turned away because of the first vendor's moral disapproval.[27] That can be a serious emotional harm for some couples. But it cannot be considered in isolation; there is also dignitary and emotional harm on the religious side.

Those seeking exemption believe that they are being asked to defy God's will, disrupting the most important relationship in their lives, a relationship with an

---

[24] For the somewhat different view that society should reject refusals to serve same-sex couples separated in time from the wedding celebration, see Greenawalt, Chapter 8. I would focus more on the purpose of the event than on the elapsed time. The difference is illustrated by the facts of *Masterpiece Cakeshop*, where the couple's wedding reception was separated in time and space from the wedding. But the whole purpose of the reception was to celebrate the wedding and the marriage. For an alternative proposal in which businesses are regulated but given the flexibility to staff with subcontractors, see Wilson, Chapter 30.

[25] For a case affirming a baker's right to refuse to create a wedding cake for a lesbian couple that the baker referred to another baker who had agreed to create the cake, see Dep't of Fair Empt. and Hous. v. Cathy's Creations, Inc., BCV-17-102855 (Cal. Super. Ct. of Kern Cty.) (Feb. 5, 2018) ("Ruling on Order to Show Cause in re: Preliminary Injunction"), https://globalfreedomofexpression.columbia.edu/cases/department-fair-employment-housing-v-cathys-creations/ [https://perma.cc/WC5X-LA24].

[26] *See, e.g.*, Ward v. Polite, 667 F.3d 727 (6th Cir. 2012).

[27] Douglas NeJaime & Reva B. Siegel, *Conscience Wars: Complicity-Based Conscience Claims in Religion and Politics*, 124 YALE L.J. 2516, 2574–78 (2015); Pizer, Chapter 29.

omnipotent being who controls their fates.[28] They believe that they are being asked to do serious wrong that will torment their conscience for a long time after. These are among the harms religious liberty is intended to prevent, and an expressive harm on the other side cannot justify inflicting such harms. Viewed in purely secular terms, there are intangible emotional harms on both sides of the balance. The emotional harm to potential customers cannot compellingly outweigh the emotional harm to believers.[29] Reciprocal moral disapproval is inherent in a pluralistic society; the desire of same-sex couples never to encounter such disapproval is not a sufficient reason to deprive others of religious liberty.

The argument from dignitary harm to individuals is, at bottom, an argument that these religious practices must be suppressed because they offend the customer who is turned away. That argument is at odds with the whole First Amendment tradition. It is settled that offensiveness is not a compelling interest than can justify suppressing speech.[30]

Now it is true that the wedding-vendor cases involve conduct, and not just speech. But these cases arise in a context where conduct is legally protected, usually under a compelling-interest test, by state Religious Freedom Restoration Acts (RFRAs) or state constitutions.[31] Offensiveness or insult cannot satisfy that test. The speech cases say that preventing such harm is not a compelling interest. It is no more compelling when invoked in response to a state RFRA or constitution that protects religiously motivated conduct with a compelling-interest test.

But there is more. In one important respect, the balance of hardships clearly and unambiguously tilts in favor of the religious objectors. The offended gay couples who get referred to another florist or wedding planner still get to live their own lives by their own values. They will still love each other; they will still be married; and they will still have their occupations or professions.

The conscientious objector who is forced to close her business or to assist with same-sex marriages does not get to live her own life by her own values. She is forced to repeatedly violate her conscience and disrupt her relationship with God, every time a same-sex couple asks, or she is forced to abandon her occupation. The harm of regulation on the religious side is permanent loss of identity or permanent loss of

---

[28] See, e.g., *supra* note 22, where the baker in *Masterpiece Cakeshop* emphasizes his concern about "whether God will be pleased with me and my work."

[29] This chapter is not discussing race discrimination, which differs from the wedding cases in many ways. *See* Douglas Laycock, *The Campaign Against Religious Liberty*, *in* THE RISE OF CORPORATE RELIGIOUS LIBERTY 231, 252–53 (Micah Schwartzman et al. eds., 2016) (summarizing some of those ways). For a useful distinction between religious objections to same-sex marriage and to interracial marriage, see Perry, Chapter 20.

[30] *See, e.g.*, McCullen v. Coakley, 134 S. Ct. 2518, 2531–32 (2014) (abortion counseling); Texas v. Johnson, 491 U.S. 397, 414 (1989) (flag burning); Hustler Magazine, Inc. v. Falwell, 485 U.S. 46, 50–57 (1988) (intentional infliction of emotional distress); Cohen v. California, 403 U.S. 15, 18–26 (1971) (profanity).

[31] See Appendix, Chapter 35, for state constitutional and statutory protections.

occupation; that harm is greater than the onetime dignitary or insult harm on the couple's side. And because the exemptions proposed here are narrowly confined, they do not expose same-sex couples to the continuing risk of legally protected discrimination in all their other transactions.

So is there a way legally and politically to reach a compromise that protects both sides and involves only modest sacrifice or accommodation by each side? In theory we can protect both sides. We can have employment, housing, and marriage equality for gays and lesbians, while also protecting the consciences of religious conservatives in all but the hardest cases. This is legally and conceptually possible, but it increasingly appears to be politically impossible.

The compelling-interest test in state constitutions and RFRAs has so far failed to protect in these cases.[32] State RFRAs and state constitutions have the great advantage of universal scope., and the corresponding disadvantage of enacting a quite general standard that does not resolve specific cases. They are valuable principally for relatively uncontroversial cases with no organized interest group opposed to the religious-liberty claim.

The sponsors of new state RFRA bills hope for the best, and are usually disappointed. The opponents fear the worst. Misunderstanding, miscommunication, and deliberate misinformation have made state RFRAs all but impossible to enact.[33]

The other solution is specific exemptions in specific legislation. When a legislature enacts a gay-rights law, it can specify who is to be exempt and under what circumstances.[34] If the exemptions are sufficiently specific, both sides can know what they are enacting. Religious objectors can be much more confident of being protected, and gays and lesbians need not fear that runaway judges might invoke general language to create overly broad exemptions. The disadvantage in this approach is that these deals are hard to negotiate, and they have become even harder as we became more polarized. Supporters of gay rights increasingly believed that they could get a total win without agreeing to any more exemptions. But the 2016 election has cast doubt on that expectation.

Most existing gay-rights laws that apply to the private sector have some level of exemption for religious organizations.[35] Such exemptions are universal in

---

[32] State v. Arlene's Flowers, Inc., 389 P.3d 543 (Wash. 2017) (state constitution), *vacated*, 138 S. Ct. 2671 (2018); Elane Photography, LLC v. Willock, 309 P.3d 53 (N.M. 2013) (state RFRA). Dep't of Fair Empt. and Hous. v. Cathy's Creations, Inc., BCV-17–102855 (Cal. Super. Ct. of Kern Cty.) (Feb. 5, 2018) ("Ruling on Order to Show Cause in re: Preliminary Injunction"), https:// globalfreedomofexpression.columbia.edu/cases/department-fair-employment-housing-v-cathys-creations/ [https://perma.cc/WC5X-LA24], the California trial court decision, seems highly likely to be reversed. *See* Catholic Charities of Sacramento, Inc. v. Sup'r Ct., 85 P.3d 67 (Cal. 2004); Smith v. Fair Empt. & Hous. Comm'n, 913 P.2d 909 (Cal. 1996).

[33] *See* Laycock, *The Campaign Against Religious Liberty, supra* note 29, at 248–50.

[34] For one example, Utah's, see Adams, Chapter 32.

[35] Center for American Progress Action Fund, *A State-by-State Examination of Nondiscrimination Laws and Policies* 3–4 (2012), https://www.americanprogress.org/wp-content/uploads/issues/2012/06/pdf/state_nondiscrimination.pdf [https://perma.cc/H4XA-7PKQ].

state employment-discrimination laws.[36] All the legislation providing for same-sex marriage in blue states has explicit exemptions, always confined to non-profit religious organizations.[37] In most of these states, the religious exemptions made the difference; marriage equality could not have been enacted without them.[38]

Nor should we assume that the Supreme Court would have acted if the legislatures had not. Without those legislative enactments, *United States v. Windsor*[39] would have looked very different to the Court, It was surely easier for the Court to require the federal government to recognize same-sex marriages authorized by a democratic vote of state legislatures than to require recognition of marriages authorized only by controversial judicial decisions in a handful of states. And without *Windsor*, there would have been no *Obergefell*[40] – or at least the wait for a decision recognizing same-sex marriage would have been much longer.

It is too late to enact compromises that protect both sides in the blue states. Religious conservatives have nothing left to give, so they have no bargaining leverage. Their last chance to strike a deal was when marriage equality still hung in the balance. But there are obvious deals to be done in Congress and in red states. Enacting gay-rights laws in Congress or red states will require religious exemptions. That is why the gay-rights side has tried to bypass the legislative process by reinterpreting Title VII[41] and Title IX[42] to apply not only to sex discrimination but to sexual-orientation and gender-identity discrimination as well.[43] This would require

---

[36] *Id.*

[37] *See* Nelson Tebbe, *Religion and Marriage Equality Statutes*, 9 HARV. L. & POL'Y REV. 25, 31–33 (2015).

[38] *See* Robin Fretwell Wilson, *Marriage of Necessity: Same-Sex Marriage and Religious Liberty Protections*, 64 CASE W. RES. L. REV. 1161 (2014).

[39] 570 U.S. 744 (2013)

[40] Obergefell v. Hodges, 135 S. Ct. 2584 (2015).

[41] 42 U.S.C. §§ 2000e–2000e-17 (2012 & Supp. V 2017) (prohibiting sex discrimination in employment).

[42] 20 U.S.C. §§ 1681–1688 (2012 & Supp. V 2017) (prohibiting sex discrimination in federally assisted education).

[43] *See* EEOC v. R.G. & G.R. Harris Funeral Homes, Inc., 884 F.3d 560 (6th Cir. 2018) (holding that Title VII protects against gender-identity discrimination); Zarda v. Altitude Express, 883 F.3d 100 (2d Cir. 2018) (en banc) (holding that Title VII protects against sexual-orientation discrimination); Whitaker v. Kenosha Unified Sch. Dist. No. 1, 858 F.3d 1037 (7th Cir. 2017) (holding that Title IX protects against gender-identity discrimination), *cert. dis'd*, 138 S. Ct. 1260 (2018); Hively v. Ivy Tech Cmty. Coll. of Ind., 853 F.3d 339 (7th Cir. 2017) (en banc) (holding that Title VII protects against sexual-orientation discrimination); Christiansen v. Omnicom Group, Inc., 852 F.3d 195 (2d Cir. 2017) (holding that Title VII does not protect against sexual-orientation discrimination, but that a gay plaintiff had sufficiently alleged claim of gender stereotyping); Evans v. Ga. Reg'l Hosp., 850 F.3d 1248, 1273 (11th Cir. 2017) (holding that Title VII does not protect against sexual-orientation discrimination), *cert. denied*, 138 S. Ct. 557 (2017); G.G. by Grimm v. Gloucester Cty. Sch. Bd., 822 F.3d 709 (4th Cir. 2016) (deferring to agency interpretation, since withdrawn, that Title IX prohibits discrimination based on claimant's preferred gender, without regard to biological sex), *vacated and remanded*, 137 S. Ct. 1239 (2017). For implications, see Hill, Chapter 26.

overruling many cases in the Courts of Appeals,[44] but none in the Supreme Court, which has never addressed the issue. The great advantage is that such a reinterpretation would provide federal protection for LGBT people; the great disadvantage is that it would make religious-liberty protections through legislation politically impossible at the federal level – and legally impossible at the state level, because states cannot create exemptions to federal law.

The same interpretive choices are not available for public accommodations, which means that no amount of litigation will secure this protection.[45] The federal public-accommodations law does not apply to most wedding vendors and does not prohibit sex discrimination.[46] Legislation will be required. So the more alluring possibility is a statewide or nationwide grand bargain: religious conservatives will vote to prohibit discrimination against LGBT persons if the bill contains adequate exemptions for religious objectors. The problem is the problem with all compromise: Republicans oppose the nondiscrimination law, and Democrats oppose the religious exemptions.[47]

Professor Robin Wilson and Senator Stuart Adams report progress in some states.[48] There are bitter opponents of compromise on both sides, but the opposition to compromise is not so nearly unanimous as it once was. Religious conservatives now face many local ordinances with no religious liberty protections;[49] a statewide nondiscrimination law with religious exemptions and preemptive effect is more appealing. Incentives have changed less substantially on the gay-rights side, but the Trump election has clouded the horizon and made at least some groups more open to compromise.

Utah is the shining example here, but the Utah compromise addressed only part of the problem and was immediately denounced by many gay-rights supporters. Utah, one of the reddest of red states, now prohibits discrimination on the basis of sexual orientation and gender identity in employment and housing, but not in public accommodations.[50] Religious organizations are exempt, and the

---

[44] *See Hively*, 853 F.3d at 341–42 (collecting cases).

[45] *See* Pizer, Chapter 29.

[46] *See* 42 U.S.C. § 2000a (2012) (prohibiting discrimination on the basis of race, color, religion, or national origin in hotels, restaurants, gas stations, and theaters, stadiums, and similar entertainment venues).

[47] Charles C. Haynes, *Republicans, Democrats and the Stakes for Religious Freedom*, Newseum Inst. (Aug. 4, 2016), http://www.newseuminstitute.org/2016/08/04/republicans-democrats-and-the-stakes-for-religious-freedom/ [https://perma.cc/Y84N-4W8Y].

[48] *See* Wilson, Chapter 30; Adams, Chapter 32.

[49] *See Municipal Equality Index: A Nationwide Evaluation of Municipal Law*, Human Rights Campaign (2013), http://www.hrc.org/files/assets/resources/MEI_2013_report.pdf [https://perma.cc/2BKU-8YF7]; *MEI 2017: See Your City's Score*, Human Rights Campaign, https://www.hrc.org/resources/mei-2017-see-your-citys-score [https://perma.cc/3U46-XT6H].

[50] 2015 Utah L., ch. 13, codified in various sections of the Utah Antidiscrimination Act (Utah Code, Title 34A, § 5), and the Utah Fair Housing Act (Utah Code, Title 57, ch. 21). As Senator

law does not apply to employers with fewer than fifteen employees. Critics immediately said that this compromise is only for Utah and is not a model for anywhere else.[51]

On the other side, the 2016 election emboldened Republicans in Congress. In the wake of the election, they announced plans to move forward with one of the broadest versions of the proposed First Amendment Defense Act, or FADA.[52] FADA would provide absolute protection, with no exception for compelling interests or anything else, in contexts far beyond those few religious environments, such as houses of worship, in which absolute protection might plausibly be justified.[53] Unless the Senate abolishes the legislative filibuster, this bill is going nowhere. But the widespread support for FADA illustrates the difficulty of reaching any sensible compromise.

Another argument against protecting wedding vendors is that these cases arise in the commercial sector.[54] Of course, the *Hobby Lobby* case also involved a business in the commercial sector.[55] Many opponents of religious liberty say that is disqualifying – that American law simply does not protect the religious-liberty rights of businesses, especially not of corporations.[56] But that is not true.

Businesses have principally secular motivations and rarely file religious-liberty claims. When such claims arose in the past, the Court had decided them on the merits, and the businesses had lost. *Hobby Lobby* is fully consistent with that history.[57] The Court did not say that the commercial context was irrelevant or that businesses would now win many claims. It said that a business won the claim in *Hobby Lobby*.

Legislators have enacted specific religious-liberty protections for businesses. Abortion-conscience legislation protects for-profit medical practices, even if incorporated, as most of them are, and for-profit hospitals, if they have a religious

---

Adams notes in Chapter 32, no Utah municipality had banned discrimination in public accommodations on the basis of sexual orientation or gender identity.

[51] *See, e.g.*, Nelson Tebbe et al., *Utah "Compromise" to Protect LGBT Citizens from Discrimination Is No Model for the Nation*, SLATE (Mar. 1, 2015), http://www.slate.com/blogs/outward/2015/03/18/gay_rights_the_utah_compromise_is_no_model_for_the_nation.html [https://perma.cc/U5Y9-XEK9].

[52] Mary Emily, *First Amendment Defense Act Looms Over Sessions' Confirmation Vote*, NBC NEWS (Jan. 30, 2017), https://www.nbcnews.com/feature/nbc-out/first-amendment-defense-act-looms-over-sessions-confirmation-vote-n714226 [https://perma.cc/YHM3-9TLA]. The bill is S. 2525 in the 115th Congress.

[53] S. 2525 in the 115th Cong. (2018).

[54] *See* Melling, Chapter 19; Pizer, Chapter 29.

[55] Burwell v. Hobby Lobby Stores, Inc., 134 S. Ct. 2751 (2014).

[56] Brief for the Petitioners at 16–20, Burwell v. Hobby Lobby Stores, Inc., 134 S. Ct. 2751 (2014) (No. 13–354), 2014 WL 173486. Perhaps the most extreme version of this argument, at least so far, is Elizabeth Sepper, *Free Exercise Lochnerism*, 115 COLUM. L. REV. 1453 (2015).

[57] *See Hobby Lobby*, 134 S. Ct. at 2767–73.

or moral objection.[58] The conscience provisions of assisted-suicide laws cover for-profit doctors, hospitals, nursing homes, and hospices.[59] For-profit kosher slaughterhouses have long been exempt from rules requiring nonkosher methods of slaughter.[60]

The Supreme Court in *Hobby Lobby* correctly interpreted the federal RFRA to protect the owners of incorporated businesses.[61] That is what the statutory text said; RFRA protects "person[s],"[62] and "person" is a defined term in the United States Code.[63] The plain meaning of the text is supported by the drafting history and by the shared understanding that RFRA would apply one universal standard to all religious-liberty claims.[64] And this plain meaning is how both sides in Congress understood the statutory text in a fierce debate over whether to exclude most civil-rights claims against businesses from substantially identical language in the proposed Religious Liberty Protection Act.[65] Both sides in this debate thought it was important to protect corporations, but they disagreed over how far that protection should extend with respect to civil-rights claims. This debate led to amendments that strengthened RFRA, and those amendments were applied to the language that everyone understood to protect corporations – language that was left unchanged.[66]

In any event, the attack on exemptions for business owners is just one piece of a much broader attack. The assault on religious exemptions even for religious non-profits is widespread and vigorous. It appears in the intense opposition to *Hosanna-Tabor* and the ministerial exception.[67] It appeared in the *Zubik* litigation, better

---

[58] See 42 U.S.C. § 238n (2012) (protecting "any health care entity"); 42 U.S.C. § 300a-7 (2012) (protecting "any individual or entity"); Robin Fretwell Wilson, *Matters of Conscience: Lessons for Same-Sex Marriage from the Healthcare Context, in* SAME-SEX MARRIAGE AND RELIGIOUS LIBERTY: EMERGING CONFLICTS 77, 299–310 (Douglas Laycock et al., eds., 2008) (collecting similar state statutes).

[59] *See* CAL. HEALTH & SAFETY CODE § 443.15 (2016) (protecting any "health care provider"); OR. REV. STAT. § 127.885(4), (5)(a) (West 2016) (same); VT. STAT. ANN. tit. 18 § 5286 (West 2016) (protecting any "health care facility"); WASH. REV. CODE § 70.245.190(1)(d) (2016) (protecting any "health care provider").

[60] 7 U.S.C. § 1906 (2012).

[61] Hobby Lobby, 134 S. Ct. at 2767–69.

[62] 42 U.S.C. § 2000bb-1(b) (2012).

[63] 1 U.S.C. § 1 (2012).

[64] Hobby Lobby Brief of Christian Legal Society, in Douglas Laycock, *Religious Liberty Volume 3: Religious Freedom Restoration Acts, Same-Sex Marriage Legislation, and the Culture Wars* 412–15 (2018).

[65] *Id.* at 10–34, *Religious Liberty Volume 3* at 415–28.

[66] *See* Religious Land Use and Institutionalized Persons Act, §§ 7(a)(1) and (2), 7(b), 114 STAT. 803, 806 (2000), as codified in Religious Freedom Restoration Act, 42 U.S.C. §§ 2000bb-2(1), (2), and 2000bb-3(a) (2012).

[67] *Hosanna-Tabor*, 565 U.S. 171. For the critics, see, e.g., Caroline Mala Corbin, *The Irony of Hosanna-Tabor Evangelical Lutheran Church and School v. EEOC*, 106 Nw. U.L. REV. 951 (2012); Frederick Mark Gedicks, *Narrative Pluralism and Doctrinal Incoherence in Hosanna-Tabor*, 64 MERCER L. REV. 405 (2013); Leslie C. Griffin, *The Sins of Hosanna-Tabor*, 88 IND. L.J. 981 (2013).

known as the case about the Little Sisters of the Poor. I think that this was an exemption claim that should have been denied.[68] The religious organizations in the *Zubik* cases were not required to provide or pay for anything they objected to; they were really seeking exemptions for their secular insurers.[69] But the reasons that matter to me do not matter to the groups opposed to exemptions; they were and are just opposed.

The unfettered opposition to exemptions even for religious nonprofits is evident in scholarly attacks on the Utah compromise.[70] It is evident in religious adoption agencies forced to close because they would not place children with same-sex couples.[71] It is evident in litigation about nonprofit participation in other government programs and benefits.[72] It was evident in President Obama's threat to veto the defense appropriation bill if it included an exemption for religious organizations with government contracts.[73] There the argument is that a group forfeits its rights if it accepts government funds. Religious exemptions are in danger even for religious organizations.

III CONCLUSION

The central problem in the search for common ground is that what each side claims as a fundamental human right, the other side sees as a grave evil. One side sees sin; the other sees bigotry. And we have to live with each other. Opinions are changing rapidly on gay rights and marriage. Resistance will eventually fade, but the transition will be full of conflict. On abortion and related issues, the pro-life side sees wholly innocent victims; on those issues, resistance will not fade.[74] And still, we have to live with each other.

If one takes seriously America's professed commitment to liberty and justice for all, then we have to get past the intransigence and take the core needs of each side seriously. If we are to continue living with each other in relative peace and equality,

---

[68] Zubik v. Burwell, 136 S. Ct. 1557 (2016) (vacating for further negotiations between government and religious nonprofits).

[69] Brief of Baptist Joint Committee for Religious Liberty as Amicus Curiae in Support of Respondents at 7–28, Zubik v. Burwell, 136 S. Ct. 1557 (No. 14–1418), 2016 WL 692850 (2016).

[70] *See supra* note 51 and accompanying text.

[71] Laurie Goodstein, *Illinois Bishops Drop Program over Bias Rule*, N.Y. Times (Dec. 29, 2011), at A16.

[72] *See, e.g.*, Christian Legal Soc'y v. Martinez, 561 U.S. 661 (2010); Marc D. Stern, *Same-Sex Marriage and the Churches*, in Same-Sex Marriage and Religious Liberty, *supra* note 58, at 1; Jonathan Turley, *An Unholy Union: Same-Sex Marriage and the Use of Governmental Programs to Penalize Religious Groups with Unpopular Practices*, in Same-Sex Marriage and Religious Liberty, *supra* note 58, at 59.

[73] *Democrats Draw Line over LGBT Provision in Defense Authorization Bill*, Roll Call (Oct. 25, 2016), https://www.rollcall.com/policy/democrats-draw-line-lgbt-provision-defense-authorization-bill [https://perma.cc/D7LC-8H3Y].

[74] *See* Greenawalt, Chapter 8, for commentary on the splintering of views on abortion.

then we must find solutions that give LGBT persons the rights to employment, housing, access to public accommodations, and marriage with as fancy a wedding as they desire, and that, to the maximum extent possible, spare conscientious objectors from violating their deeply held religious commitments. Such solutions are possible. Americans can have liberty and justice for all. What is needed to make that possibility a reality is mutual tolerance and political will.

4

Belief and Belonging

Reconciling Legal Protections for Religious Liberty and LGBT Youth

Shannon Price Minter

The perceived conflict between religious liberty and protections for LGBT youth is one of the most important issues facing the LGBT movement. It is one that also matters deeply to communities of faith and, ultimately, to our entire country, which has become increasingly polarized around seemingly intractable divisions between those who support and those who oppose legal protections for LGBT people.

Most discussions of religious liberty and LGBT rights conceptualize the communities involved as separate groups whose interests are entirely distinct. While conservative religious communities seek the freedom to define and practice their own religious beliefs, LGBT people seek the right to be treated equally in all aspects of society, including in schools, workplaces, businesses, and health care settings. This chapter shines a light on a group often ignored by both sides in these cultural and legal battles: LGBT youth who are growing up in conservative religious communities. Many LGBT children are born into conservative faiths or conservative parts of the country; however, neither LGBT advocates nor conservative communities are providing resources to these young people and their families. Neither are providing hope to LGBT youth struggling to reconcile both aspects of their lives.

For LGBT youth and their families, the costs of that failure have been high, as Section I shows. Both the LGBT movement and the broader society have failed to respond to the grim prospects facing many LGBT children and young adults with an appropriate level of concern about the suffering they endure as a result of family rejection, which is often fueled by religious beliefs. Instead of squarely confronting that reality, most discussions about religious liberty and LGBT rights have focused on the need for faith communities and LGBT people to find a means of peaceful coexistence. Perhaps because the issues seem so intractable, political and legal debates have fallen into an uneasy stalemate between LGBT advocates on the one hand – always pushing for greater legal protections against anti-LGBT discrimination – and conservative religious groups on the other, insisting on their right to maintain traditional religious beliefs that reject "homosexuality" and transgender identity.[1] Section II documents the shortcomings of that polarized framework. In particular, as Section III explores, many LGBT young people in conservative communities deeply value their families, cultures, and faiths, but neither they nor their families have constructive ways to understand or navigate their place in those communities. In part because many adult LGBT advocates have been alienated from religion by their own painful childhood experiences, the LGBT movement has done a poor job of supporting these young people and their families. Advocacy for these youth has focused much more on the message that youth can escape their conservative families and communities when they turn eighteen than on creating resources and support for conservative communities to develop organic ways of learning how to support their own LGBT children. Despite this historical failure, there are burgeoning signs of hope. Research has shown that relatively modest changes in family behavior can significantly mitigate the negative health impacts of family rejection. Among other things, this means that conservative faith traditions have ample room to help families and religious schools develop new ways to support LGBT children. In Section IV, I share my personal story of coming of age as a transgender man growing up in a religious home as an example of a particularly important point: religious communities need not change their traditional religious doctrines in order to support these young people and protect them from serious risks to their long-term health and well-being. Section V highlights some recent examples of such change. Section VI examines how centering the interests of LGBT youth might lead both LGBT advocates and religious advocates to some new approaches to advocacy in the specific contexts of laws relating to religious schools and conversion therapy.

The purpose of this chapter is to break through the current stalemate between LGBT advocates and conservative religious groups to make an essential, and yet consistently overlooked, point: we cannot begin to think meaningfully about how to protect LGBT youth from the serious harms caused by religiously based family rejection without coming to a different understanding about the perceived clash between religious liberty and LGBT rights.

I THE UNTOLD COSTS TO LGBT YOUTH

Our nation is paying a high cost for failing to address the challenges faced by LGBT youth and their families. As has been well documented, LGBT young people are dramatically overrepresented among the universe of all youth who are not able to live at home. Nearly 20 percent of children who are in state custody, including both the foster care and juvenile justice systems, are LGBT.[2]

---

[1] *See Introduction* (for instances of these polar positions).
[2] Ctr. for Am. Progress et al., Unjust: LGBTQ Youth Incarcerated in the Juvenile Justice System 2 (2017).

And LGBT youth account for at least 40 percent of homeless youth living on our city's streets.[3]

This grim picture has remained unchanged over decades, as have related data showing that, as a group, lesbian, gay, and bisexual (LGB)[4] youth are four to five times more likely to attempt suicide than other youth.[5] They are also significantly more likely to experience serious depression, substance abuse, HIV infection, and dropping out of school.[6] While data on transgender youth is sparser, emerging research indicates that these youth are even more vulnerable, particularly with respect to suicide.[7]

II PITTING FAITH AGAINST LGBT IDENTITY

Throughout the history of the LGBT movement, cases have pitted religious liberty against LGBT rights.[8] Now that same-sex couples have won the right to marry in the US Supreme Court, these tensions have become even more salient and intense. In recent years, state legislatures have introduced dozens of bills seeking to create new religious exemptions for those who disagree with the Supreme Court's decision in *Obergefell v. Hodges*,[9] or who do not want to accommodate transgender people.[10]

Congress has considered federal legislation that would do the same, and the national press has reported rumors of a possible federal executive order that would create broad new religious exemptions to federal nondiscrimination policies for LGBT people.[11] In May 2017, President Trump ordered all federal agencies "to

---

[3] Laura E. Durso & Gary J. Gates, Serving Our Youth: Findings from a National Survey of Service Providers Working with Lesbian, Gay, Bisexual, and Transgender Youth who are Homeless or At Risk of Becoming Homeless 3 (2012).

[4] This chapter uses LGB when discussing studies or data that are particular only to the lesbian, gay, and bisexual populations.

[5] U.S. Dep't of Health & Human Servs., Ctrs. for Disease Control & Prevention, Sexual Identity, Sex of Sexual Contacts, and Health-Related Behaviors Among Students in Grades 9–12 – United States and Selected Sites, 2015 (2016), at 2, 20.

[6] See Jaime M. Grant et al., Injustice at Every Turn: A Report of the National Transgender Discrimination Survey 33 (2011); see also Robin Wilson, *Being Transgender in the Era of Trump: Compassion Should Pick Up Where Science Leaves Off*, U.C. Irvine L. Rev. (forthcoming 2018), https://papers.ssrn.com/sol3/papers.cfm?abstract_id=3055888) [hereinafter *Being Transgender*].

[7] See Richard T. Liu & Brian Mustanski, *Suicidal Ideation and Self-Harm in Lesbian, Gay, Bisexual, and Transgender Youth*. 42 Am. J. Preventive Med. 221 (2012); Sandy E. James et al., The Report of the 2015 U.S. Transgender Survey 106, 112–13 (2016).

[8] See, e.g., Gay Rights Coalition of Georgetown University Law Center v. Georgetown University, 536 A.2d 1 (D.C. 1987).

[9] See, e.g., H.B. 1523, Reg. Sess. (Miss. 2016); Emma Green, *Can States Protect LGBT Rights Without Compromising Religious Freedom?*, The Atlantic (Jan. 6, 2016), https://perma.cc/E3Z4-V84T.

[10] See Wilson, *Being Transgender, supra* note 6.

[11] First Amendment Defense Act, H.R. 2802, 114th Cong. (2015); *Legislation Affecting LGBT Rights Across the Country*, ACLU, https://perma.cc/BV2V-Z3DU; Ian Lovett, Jacob Gershman

vigorously enforce Federal law's robust protections for religious freedom."[12] Attorney General Jeff Sessions issued guidance under President Trump's May 4, 2017 executive order purporting to give faith communities greater latitude to follow their convictions,[13] although the impact on nondiscrimination protections around gender identity and sexual orientation is unclear.[14] In December 2017, the US Supreme Court heard a case addressing an asserted conflict between religious liberty and state laws prohibiting discrimination based on sexual orientation.[15] The case, which involved a Christian bakery that refused to make a wedding cake for a gay couple, attracted dozens of *amicus* briefs on both sides.[16] And there is an ever-growing body of legal scholarship addressing the relationship between religious liberty and LGBT rights, not least of which is this volume and the prior scholarship of the editors and contributors.

In these cases and discussions, both sides tend to assume that the conflicts between religious liberty and LGBT rights arise between two separate groups: LGBT people on one side and conservative religious individuals on the other. That assumption drives many proposals about how to resolve these conflicts. In particular, one of the most common tropes is that of "peaceful coexistence," which reflects the notion that legislatures and courts must appropriately balance these competing concerns and allow both camps to maintain their separate identities and live alongside one another in peace.

The problem with that metaphor for many LGBT children and young people, however, is that their core identities and allegiances straddle both camps. Many are born into and grow up within conservative religious families and communities while also struggling to come to terms with being gay or transgender.[17] LGBT adults and adults who embrace conservative religious faiths may indeed have the freedom to live in two relatively separate worlds. But many LGBT children and young people have no such choice.

& Louise Radnofsky, *Trump Draft Order Would Expand Religious Rights, Could Allow Denial of Services to Gays*, WALL ST. J. (Feb. 5, 2017), https://perma.cc/KLQ3-XNSQ.

[12] *See* Exec. Order No. 13798, 82 FR 21675 (2017); Exec. Order No. 13672, 79 FR 42971 (2014). To date, President Trump's executive orders have not rolled back President Obama's orders regarding sexual orientation and gender identity nondiscrimination protections for employees of federal contractors and subcontractors.

[13] Memorandum from Attorney General Jeff Sessions on Implementation of Memorandum on Federal Law Protections for Religious Liberty (Oct. 6, 2017), https://perma.cc/6FCS-27QJ.

[14] Rachel Zoll et al., *AG Directive Protects Religious Objectors to LGBT Rights*, CHI. TRIB. (Oct. 7, 2017), https://perma.cc/V5DK-A3LL.

[15] Masterpiece Cakeshop, Ltd. v. Colo. Civil Rights Comm'n, No. 16–111, slip op. (U.S. June 4, 2018).

[16] *See Masterpiece Cakeshop v. Colorado Civil Rights Commission*, ACLU, https://perma.cc/HDX2-SBCE (providing links to all *amicus* briefs filed in the case).

[17] PEW RESEARCH CTR., A SURVEY OF LGBT AMERICANS: ATTITUDES, EXPERIENCES AND VALUES IN CHANGING TIMES 91 (2013) [hereinafter PEW 2013 REPORT].

Neither LGBT advocates nor religious liberty advocates have fully acknowledged or come to grips with that reality. Instead, when LGBT advocates consider these young people, they tend to think of them as temporary hostages across enemy lines, just waiting for the day when they can escape from what are presumed to be hostile and dangerous places.[18] That tendency is exacerbated by the fact that many LGBT advocates, particularly at the national level, are not themselves religious. As commentator Eliel Cruz observed, "Many queer people have left spiritually abusive households and don't want anything to do with religion. Some of the loudest LGBT pundits are atheist and are critical of LGBT people who adhere to religions that, at least formally, condemn same-sex relationships."[19]

In that respect, however, those leading the movement are not representative of LGBT people as a whole. While the percentage of Americans who identify with a particular religious faith tradition is decreasing,[20] the percentage of LGB people who do so appears to be on the rise. According to the Pew Research Center, the percentage of Americans who identify as Christian dropped from 78.4 percent in 2007 to 70.6 percent in 2014. In contrast, the percentage of LGB persons identifying as Christian increased from 42 percent in 2013 to 48 percent in 2014.[21] Eleven percent of LGB respondents identified as Jewish, Muslim, Buddhist, or Hindu, which is a higher percentage than the overall population.[22] In total, 59 percent of the LGB respondents identified as people of faith.[23]

This dual membership in faith and LGBT communities is all the more remarkable considering that the 2013 Pew Survey of LGBT Americans found that many LGBT adults regard major faith groups as "unfriendly" to their community.[24] Large majorities perceived Islam and The Church of Jesus Christ of Latter-day Saints, also known as the Mormon Church, as unfriendly to LGBT people – 84 percent and 83 percent, respectively.[25] Likewise, 79 percent saw the Catholic Church as unfriendly, and 73 percent had the same view of evangelical churches.[26] This distrust and concern about faith communities by LGBT persons underscores the importance of this volume's search for common ground.

---

[18] *See infra*, Section III.

[19] Eliel Cruz, *LGBT People of Faith: Why Are They Staying?*, THE ADVOCATE (Sept. 17, 2015), https://perma.cc/3YDL-PNQT.

[20] *See* PEW RESEARCH CTR., "NONES" ON THE RISE: ONE-IN-FIVE ADULTS HAVE NO RELIGIOUS AFFILIATION (2012).

[21] *See* PEW RESEARCH CTR., AMERICA'S CHANGING RELIGIOUS LANDSCAPE 20, 87 (2015) [hereinafter PEW 2015 REPORT]; PEW 2013 REPORT, *supra* note 17, at 91 (also noting, "About half of LGBT respondents describe[d] themselves as atheist, agnostic or having no particular religion (48%) – more than double the portion of the general public that is religiously unaffiliated (20%).").

[22] *See* PEW 2015 REPORT, *supra* note 21, at 87.

[23] *Id.*

[24] *See* PEW 2013 REPORT, *supra* note 17, at 90, 100.

[25] *Id.* at 100.

[26] *Id.*

So long as debates about religious liberty and LGBT rights ignore these complex dynamics, LGBT youth and their families will continue to pay a high price. Currently, however, both sides face internal obstacles to acknowledging that complexity. In the LGBT movement, there is a disconnect between the reality that many LGBT youth are growing up in religiously affiliated families and communities, and the fact that most adult advocates are not religious and may even be somewhat hostile to religion. One result is that within the LGBT movement, "[h]istorically, families were seen as rejecting and incapable of supporting their LGBT children."[27]

Likewise, religious conservatives who advocate for greater religious autonomy often fail to acknowledge the LGBT youth in their midst at all.[28] Instead, these advocates typically stress the importance of freedom of choice and association – the right of those who share particular religious beliefs to join together to create separate spaces and institutions.[29] Certainly, the protection of these associational rights is an important foundation of religious liberty and, in some respects, captures the very essence of religious pluralism.[30] The beauty and strength of our constitutional system owes much to its recognition of the value of religious diversity.

But the framework of voluntary association has limited utility in addressing the situation of children born into religious families. No one comes into the world full-blown as an adult. Some individuals convert to a chosen faith as adults, but most of us are born not only into a particular family and community, but into a faith, if we have one.[31] These realities, though often ignored, are critical for understanding the place of LGBT children in conservative religious communities.

Human beings are hardwired – some would say created – for connection and relationships.[32] We are intensely, innately interdependent. Isolation from others is debilitating. That is why, historically, banishment was considered to be among the most terrible and severe punishments.[33] And that is why solitary confinement is profoundly damaging.[34]

---

[27] Caitlin Ryan, *Helping Religious Families Support Their Children*, INTERFAITH OBSERVER (July 15, 2013), https://perma.cc/Q94A-JSRF.

[28] *See* Tom Gjelten, *In Religious Freedom Debate, 2 American Values Clash*, NPR (Feb. 28, 2017), https://perma.cc/J9KV-ZK5J.

[29] *See id.* See also Helfand, Chapter 11 (discussing notions of implied consent to accept the values of religious communities when one takes employment with a religious employer); Hoogstra et al., Chapter 25 (discussing the need and value of religious educational institutions to fashion deliberate communities of believers).

[30] JOHN D. INAZU, CONFIDENT PLURALISM (2016); FREEDOM OF ASSOCIATION (Amy Gutmann ed., 1998).

[31] *See* PEW RES. CTR., FAITH IN FLUX (2011).

[32] *See, e.g.*, MATTHEW D. LIEBERMAN, SOCIAL: WHY OUR BRAINS ARE WIRED TO CONNECT (2013).

[33] *See* Michael F. Armstrong, *Banishment: Cruel and Unusual Punishment*, 111 U. PA. L. REV. 758 (1963).

[34] Eli Hager & Gerald Rich, *Shifting Away from Solitary*, MARSHALL PROJECT (Dec. 23, 2014), https://perma.cc/23AV-JDCQ.

That hardwired need for connection is especially significant for children, who are completely dependent on parents and other adults. In order to develop into healthy adults who are capable of caring for themselves and others, children must be guided by parents or other caregivers.[35] Few things are more distressing to any feeling adult than the thought of a child on his or her own, separated from any family or community support.

And yet that continues to be the experience of many LGBT children and youth. One might expect that our society's progress in securing increased legal protections for LGBT people[36] would reduce the number of families who reject their LGBT children. In the long run, that likely will be true. In the short run, however, LGBT children are more likely to experience family rejection today because they are more likely to openly discuss their sexual orientation and gender identity with their families at younger ages, long before becoming independent adults.[37]

In the past, very few adolescents, much less younger children, came out to their families or told others they were gay or transgender.[38] Most people waited until they were adults. Today, with greater access to information and resources and with the increased visibility of LGBT people in the media, young people are coming out at much younger ages, as young as nine or ten for LGB youth and, in some cases, even younger for transgender youth.[39] As a result, these young people must navigate an extended window of vulnerability and dependence. These children are coming out and living in families that, in many cases, are completely unequipped to understand or deal with them.[40] This important shift in our culture has spurred a resurgence of conversion therapy targeted at young people, because this situation has created a ready-made market of parents who are vulnerable to being told that their children can be fixed.[41]

---

[35] *See, e.g.,* Michael D. Resnick et al., *Protecting Adolescents from Harm. Findings from the National Longitudinal Study on Adolescent Health*, 278 J. Am. Med. Assoc. 823 (1997).

[36] *See* Wilson, Chapter 30 (for a discussion of state laws). *See generally* William N. Eskridge, Jr. & Chris Riano, From Outlaws to Inlaws: Marriage Equality in America (2018).

[37] LGBT youth are also more likely to experience social rejection and trauma, including "bullying, harassment, traumatic loss, intimate partner violence, and physical and sexual abuse, as well as traumatic forms of societal stigma, bias and rejection." *LGBTQ Issues and Child Trauma*, Nat'l Child Traumatic Stress Network, https://perma.cc/V58W-EDNF.

[38] Williams Institute, Sexual Minorities in the 2008 General Social Survey: Coming Out and Demographic Characteristics (2010).

[39] *See* Ritch C. Savin-Williams & Lisa M. Diamond, *Sexual Identity Trajectories Among Sexual-Minority Youths: Gender Comparisons*, 29 Arch. Sexual Behav. 607 (2000).

[40] There are a number of theological and social science resources about transgender identity that can be a resource for religious conservatives. *See* Hoogstra et al., Chapter 25 (citing Mark A. Yarhouse, Understanding Gender Dysphoria: Navigating Transgender Issues in a Changing Culture (2015)).

[41] *See, e.g.,* Am. Psychol. Ass'n, Appropriate Therapeutic Responses to Sexual Orientation, 12 (2009) (noting that starting in the early 1990s, "some APA began to express concerns about the resurgence of individuals and organizations that actively promoted the idea of homosexuality as a developmental defect or a spiritual and moral failing and that advocated

Especially in light of these realities, the burgeoning body of research on how family rejection affects LGBT youth is particularly valuable. The leading study by Dr. Caitlin Ryan examined more than 200 families and measured the impact of more than 100 specific rejecting behaviors on the long-term health and well-being of LGB and gender-nonconforming youth.[42] The study found that youth in highly rejecting families were more than 8 times more likely to attempt suicide, nearly 6 times more likely to be seriously depressed, and 3.4 times more likely to use drugs and have unprotected sex – all findings that were statistically significant.[43] Patently, these are serious negative health consequences.[44]

In many cases, parents reject their children based upon their religious beliefs, which have taught them that being gay or transgender is a sin. Often, "religious families feel that they must choose between their LGBT child and their religious beliefs."[45] These families genuinely love their children and want to help them, but by pressuring their children to change or to view themselves as broken and defective, they are causing serious harms. "Being valued by their parents and family helps children learn to value and care about themselves. But hearing that they are bad or sinful sends a deep message that they are not a good person," which "increases risky behaviors, such as risk for HIV or substance abuse," "affects their ability to plan for

---

psychotherapy and religious ministry to alter homosexual feelings and behaviors"). Contributing to this resurgence are controversial "review articles" that advocate positions on conversion therapy that do not have wide support in the academy. *Compare* Lawrence S. Mayer & Paul R. McHugh, *Sexuality & Gender: Findings from the Biological, Psychological, and Social Sciences*, THE NEW ATLANTIS 1, 2 (2016) *with* Chris Beyrer et al., *Hopkins Faculty Disavow "Troubling" Report on Gender and Sexuality*, BALT. SUN (Sept. 28, 2016), https://perma.cc/76Y7-G5F2 ("We also vigorously support the right to academic freedom and scientific disagreement and debate. Indeed, debates are the very basis of the scientific method. That same commitment to scientific debate means we must engage the dialogue in a circumstance such as this, and not stand silently by."). For a review and critique of the controversy, see Wilson, *Being Transgender*, *supra* note 6; B. Anton, *Proceedings of the American Psychological Association for the Legislative Year 2009: Minutes of the Annual Meeting of the Council of Representatives and Minutes of the Meetings of the Board of Directors*, 65 AM. PSYCHOL., 385 (2010). *See generally* Jack Drescher et al., *The Growing Regulation of Conversion Therapy*, 102 J. MED. REGUL. 7 (2017).

[42] Caitlin Ryan et al., *Family Rejection as a Predictor of Negative Health Outcomes in White and Latino Lesbian, Gay, and Bisexual Young Adults*, 123 PEDIATRICS 346 (2009).

[43] *Id.*

[44] For transgender youth in particular, these negative health consequences may be exacerbated by a lack of access to competent medical care and health insurance coverage. A study by Dr. William Padula looked at the cost of insurance for transgender individuals and the cost of denying insurance to this population. William V. Padula et al., *Societal Implications of Health Insurance Coverage for Medically Necessary Services in the U.S. Transgender Population: A Cost Effectiveness Analysis*, 31 J. GEN. INTERN MED. 394 (2016). Removing insurance barriers would be one part of improving the life chances of transgender people. *Id.* at 400.

[45] Ryan, *supra* note 27. For discussions of strands within Islam and the Christian faith that are more embracing of LGBT youth, see Gramick, Chapter 10; Rabb, Chapter 15; Hoogstra et al., Chapter 25.

the future," and "makes them less likely to have a family or to be parents them-selves."[46] Many LGBT adults who experienced this type of family rejection as children deal with lifelong trauma and associated health problems.[47] And many are alienated from religion, as already noted.

III THE MESSAGE TO LGBT YOUTH: SELF-EXILE

On the whole, the LGBT movement has taken a narrow and, ultimately, largely ineffective approach towards dealing with family rejection of LGBT children. That approach, in many ways, can be summed up in the slogan, "It gets better."[48]

That slogan is the name of a campaign started by gay columnist Dan Savage. As the website of the It Gets Better Project explains:

In September 2010, syndicated columnist and author Dan Savage created a You-Tube video with his partner Terry Miller to inspire hope for young people facing harassment. In response to a number of students taking their own lives after being bullied in school, they wanted to create a personal way for supporters everywhere to tell LGBT youth that, yes, it does indeed get better.

Implicit in the message of this approach is not just that it gets better later, but that it gets better somewhere else. The campaign tells LGBT adolescents that if they can hang on until they reach adulthood, they will be able to leave home, relocate to an LGBT-friendly location, find a partner, make new friends, and have a happy life.

To be clear, Dan Savage deserves great credit for initiating this project. It likely has saved many lives. Nonetheless, the obvious limitations of this approach are a searing indictment of both the LGBT movement *and* the larger society. How can it be that the best we can do for a group of children who are suffering so severely is to urge them to endure as best they can until they are old enough to leave their homes?

Mindy Drucker, sister of LGBT youth advocate and businessman Mitchell Gold, has shared a story that illustrates the terrible inadequacy of this approach. While helping her brother research his groundbreaking book about the childhood trauma experienced by many gay youth,[49] Drucker interviewed a young gay man in rural South Carolina. The young man was fifteen and facing serious problems at school, where he was being harassed, and in his family, who believed that being gay was immoral and sinful. In an effort to be encouraging, Drucker found herself telling him, "Just hang in there, it will

---

[46] Caitlin Ryan, *Helping Families Support Their Lesbian, Gay, Bisexual and Transgender (LGBT) Children*, HELPING FAMILIES SUPPORT LGBT CHILDREN (Fall/Winter 2009), https://perma.cc/9YXZ-GXM7.

[47] *See, e.g.*, Darrell C. Greene & Paula J. Britton, *Predicting Adult LGBTQ Happiness: Impact of Childhood Affirmation, Self-Compassion, and Personal Mastery*, 9 J. LGBT ISSUES IN COUN-SELING 158 (2015); Ryan, *supra* note 42.

[48] *See What Is the It Gets Better Project?*, ITGETSBETTER.ORG, https://perma.cc/45MS-D3WW.

[49] CRISIS: 40 STORIES REVEALING THE PERSONAL, SOCIAL, AND RELIGIOUS PAIN AND TRAUMA OF GROWING UP GAY IN AMERICA (Mitchell Gold & Mindy Drucker eds., 2008).

get better, when you turn 18 you can move to a city, and you will be so much happier and have so many more options." He said to her: "Thank you, ma'am, but I don't want to move to a city. I don't want to leave my family or my church. And when the time comes, I want to sit with my parents and grandparents in heaven."

The truth is a stark one: for the most part, the LGBT movement has nothing helpful to say to that young man or his family. He might as well be speaking a language from another planet. If one were to survey the entire LGBT movement, with all of its organizations and resources, to identify the education, information, or services provided to conservative families raising LGBT children, the answer would be almost none.

That vacuum leaves young people in these families between a rock and a hard place. They are told that in order to have a happy life as LGBT adults, they must leave their family, their culture, and their faith. But faith is a culture – young people who grow up in religious communities can no more simply shed their religious values and beliefs and adopt new ones than they can adopt a new culture. And to the extent that urban gay life acts as a subculture, it does not supplant other ethnic, racial, or religious cultures to which LGBT youth belong.[50]

Moreover, despite increasing geographic mobility, most people today still live close to where they grew up – 54 percent, according to a 2015 poll.[51] That is particularly true for those from rural areas and small towns. For many LGBT youth, the ability to pick and up move to a large gay-friendly city when they turn eighteen is simply not a realistic option.

Attachment to place is the rock. The hard place is that, for these young people, their place within their families and communities is murky. Many cannot see any path forward for themselves because, as they explore their identities, they no longer feel part of any shared cultural stories. And their parents and family members face an equally blank script, in that they literally cannot envision a good or happy future for a child who is gay or transgender.[52]

This is the dynamic that leads to family rejection. In most cases, parents who engage in rejecting behaviors are motivated by wanting to help their children. In particular, parents may believe they are protecting their child through actions such

---

[50] For a discussion of this intersectionality, see Rabb, Chapter 15. *See generally,* Christine Emba, *Intersectionality,* WASH. POST (Sept. 21, 2015), https://perma.cc/8LU8-9Q5B.

[51] Heartland Monitor Poll No. 22, *Americans' Local Experiences,* HEARTLAND MONITOR POLL (2015), https://perma.cc/DPN9-U9GD (surveying 1000 American adults age eighteen or older in a national sample, with 500 reached by landline, 500 by cell). *See also* Gillian B. White, *Staying Close to Home, No Matter What,* THE ATLANTIC (Mar. 18, 2015), https://perma.cc/3M72-BHKU.

[52] *Cf.* David E. Sandberg et al., *Interdisciplinary Care in Disorders/Differences of Sex Development (DSD): The Psychosocial Component of the DSD – Translational Research Network,* 175 AM. J. MED. GENETICS 279, 280 (2017) (discussing post-traumatic stress syndrome among parents of intersex children, "comparable to those reported by caregivers of children diagnosed with cancer").

as isolating the child, withholding affection, or telling a child that they must stop being gay or transgender in order to remain at home.[53] But research also shows that when families learn that actions they see as protecting their children are harming them, parents and caregivers generally modify their behavior.[54] When they "learn that family rejection contributes to serious health risks," "few parents want to contribute to their child's risk for suicide substance, or HIV."[55] As a general rule, parents are receptive to learning that "they can maintain religious values and beliefs while they love and support their LGBT child."[56]

This process is beautifully illustrated in *Families Are Forever*, a film about a Mormon family's evolving reactions after the parents discovered that their thirteen-year-old son was gay.[57] The mother in the film talks poignantly about her feelings of loss and sadness when she discovered that her son was attracted to other boys.

> I felt like what I saw his life would be, what I expected his life to be as a Mormon boy was now gone. I saw him preparing for a mission for our church. Gone. I saw a temple wedding. Gone. I saw him being a father, gone. ... A Mormon boy really has his life kind of laid out for him, and when he saw this big question mark looking into his future, and the plan wasn't laid out, and the things he thought brought happiness were all of a sudden not available to him, he talked several times about suicide. He said, what's the point of my life? I didn't have answers at that point. I thought, I don't know.

The boy's father talks about his realization that he needed to help his son find purpose and meaning in his life:

> You can't just leave some void for a young child, what, God doesn't have a plan for me anymore? I want to make sure he can get to adulthood and not have made huge mistakes that compromise his health and his happiness, and there's a lot of landmines along that road. ... Figuring that out is not easy. But if you take your family support away, I don't know how you do it as a kid.

These responses illustrate one of the unexpected, and yet most hopeful, findings from the family acceptance research. This research shows that nearly all of the negative health impacts caused by family rejection can be alleviated simply by encouraging families to challenge their own initial reactions – to shift from being rejecting to being ambivalent.[58] Importantly, families do not have to move all the

---

[53] Ryan, *supra* note 42.

[54] *See* Anna Paula Pelxoto da Silva, *Supporting Gay and Lesbian Families in the Early Childhood Classroom*, NAEYC Young Children 40 (Sept. 2014).

[55] *Id.*

[56] *Id.*

[57] *See Family Videos*, Family Acceptance Project, https://perma.cc/BJA7-6CN8.

[58] *See* Ryan, *supra* note 42, at 350; Caitlin Ryan, Family Acceptance Project, Supportive Families, Healthy Children: Helping Families with Lesbian, Gay, Bisexual & Transgender Children 6–7 (2009).

way to celebration or unqualified acceptance in order to protect their children.[59] "Parents and caregivers who believe that homosexuality and gender non-conformity are wrong can support their gay or transgender child without accepting an identity they think is wrong or against God's will by modifying or changing rejecting behaviors that increase their LGBT child's risk."[60] To prevent the most serious lifelong harms, families must only learn to stop engaging in the very worst and most damaging behaviors – and society's task is to help these families do that important work.

IV A PAGE FROM MY LIFE

My own story as a transgender man may help illuminate the hopeful aspect of this research. I was born female and raised as a girl. Like a lot of transgender men of my generation, I did not come to terms with being transgender until well into middle age. As a teenager, I initially thought I was a lesbian. I grew up in a conservative religious family in rural east Texas. When my parents discovered that I had a girlfriend, they did exactly all of the things the research summarized earlier counsels families not to do. They isolated me, told me I was disgusting and sinful, forbade me from talking about my identity with anyone else in the family, and conveyed other similarly shaming messages. I now know they were acting out of love, but my experience as a child was that one day my parents loved me, and the next day they did not. The impact was devastating, and I struggled with intense feelings of self-loathing and despair.

But for my fundamentalist Christian evangelical government teacher, Mr. Jackson, I am not sure I would have survived. Mr. Jackson and I were already friends. When I told him that I had come out and how my family reacted, he met with me every morning before class to check in. He told me that the isolation and shame my parents subjected me to was wrong. He wanted me to know that while, from his perspective as a Christian, being gay was sinful, it was no more sinful than a lot of other things, including many things he had done – and that while it might be a failing in him, he especially wanted me to know that he did not find my feelings any way disgusting. And that was enough. Hearing those things from a supportive adult was enough to ensure my survival through a perilous time.

---

[59] *See* Ryan, *supra* note 27 (Family Acceptance Project "research shows that a little change – being a little less rejecting – is related to decreased risk for serious negative health concerns. Reducing family rejection can improve relationships and keep families from fracturing.").

[60] *Id.* These supportive behaviors "include talking with the child about his or her sexual orientation or gender identity, even when this feels uncomfortable; requiring that other family members treat the child with respect, even when they disagree or believe that being gay or transgender is wrong; and standing up for the child when others mistreat him or her because of who he or she is." *Id.*

I share this story because it underscores a point often missed: the kinds of changes society urgently needs, that will enable conservative communities to support LGBT children in ways that maintain their cultural and religious integrity, may bear little resemblance to an idealized secular version of acceptance and support. LGBT advocates often see acceptance only in rainbow flags, pride marches, PFLAG meetings, and other familiar expressions of support. Importantly, however, recognition of a child's needs and struggles need not require conservative religious communities to alter their religious doctrines about marriage, family, or sexual ethics. Relatedly, support for LGBT youth will look very different in different families, localities, racial and ethnic communities, and faith communities. Society has in a sense deprived these racially and religiously diverse cultures of the opportunity to develop their own organic ways to include and support their own children, on their own terms.

V CHANGE FROM WITHIN

Increasingly, the impetus to support LGBT children comes from within faith communities themselves, including from parents who do not want to disown or alienate their LGBT children and from young people who have LGBT friends. The impact of marriage equality and the greater visibility of LGBT people have also helped to bring these issues to the forefront and to rebut many negative stereotypes about LGBT people. As a result, many conservative religious faiths are confronting the issue of how to respond to LGBT children and their families much more directly, and with more compassion, than in the past. Recently, for example, the Mormon Church expressly disavowed conversion therapy, acknowledging that it is harmful and does not work, and expressly counseled Mormon families not to shun or isolate their LGBT children.[61]

Change is underway in other conservative religious communities as well. To cite merely one recent example, Lead Them Home: Loving LGBT People in the Church, is a new initiative in the conservative evangelical community that helps pastors and parents support LGBT young people. It does so in a way that takes into account the family acceptance research, but without challenging traditional Christian doctrines around marriage or sexual ethics.[62] It is quite extraordinary to see these and other similar efforts taking shape.

---

[61] *See, e.g., Human Sexuality Policies for Catholic Schools*, CARDINAL NEWMAN SOC'Y (Mar. 29, 2016), https://perma.cc/8B6N-PU62; Nico Lang, *Mormon Church Comes Out Against LGBT Conversion Therapy in New Website*, THE ADVOCATE (Oct. 26, 2016), https://perma.cc/T8AB-QXFZ; *On Transgender Identity*, SOUTHERN BAPTIST CONVENTION, https://perma.cc/E9FM-9DGD.

[62] LEAD THEM HOME, https://perma.cc/WQN9-39ZE.

VI CHANGE FROM OUTSIDE

So, what does this nascent recognition of the unique challenges faced by LGBT youth in conservative communities mean for the law? How would our strategies for addressing the relationship between religious liberty and LGBT rights change if we were to: (1) stop assuming that the question concerns two entirely separate groups; and (2) prioritize the interests of LGBT children living in conservative religious communities? In answering this question our goal should be to most effectively help these young people. At least two areas implicated by these questions warrant immediate attention: religious schools and conversion therapy.

A *Religious Schools*

One important issue concerns how the law should address discrimination against LGBT students in religious schools. Currently, Title IX provides religious schools with a broad exemption. To opt out of Title IX's prohibition against sex discrimination, a religious school need only assert that complying with Title IX in a particular respect would "not be consistent" with the school's "religious tenets."[63] Nothing further is required. When a school invokes such an exception, there is no meaningful judicial scrutiny.[64] Historically, very few religious schools have claimed that exemption – almost none. But in the past few years, as federal courts and the Department of Education under President Obama began taking the position that Title IX protects LGBT students, and as the federal circuits began to hold that same-sex couples have a right to marry, the number of religious schools claiming the Title IX exemption skyrocketed, from only one school in 2013 to more than forty-three schools in 2015.[65]

According to a summary by the Human Rights Campaign: "There were no requests at all from 2009 through 2011. In 2012 and 2013, only one school requested an exemption each year. In 2014 there were 13 requests, and in 2015 there were at least 43."[66] The Department of Education has never denied a requested waiver.[67]

How should LGBT advocates respond? At one end of the spectrum, advocates could seek to eliminate or narrow Title IX's religious exemption, and in fact some

---

[63] *See* 20 U.S.C. § 1687 (Westlaw through Pub. L. No. 115–61). For a discussion of the regulation implementing the exemption, see Robin Fretwell Wilson, *Squaring Faith and Sexuality: Religious Institutions and the Unique Challenge of Sports*, 34 L. & INEQ. 385 (2016).

[64] Kif Augustine-Adams, *Religious Exemptions to Title IX* (forthcoming 2016) (manuscript at 5–6), http://papers.ssrn.com/sol3/papers.cfm?abstract_id=2735173.

[65] *See* SARAH WARBELOW & REMINGTON GREGG, HUMAN RIGHTS CAMPAIGN, HIDDEN DISCRIMINATION: TITLE IX RELIGIOUS EXEMPTIONS PUTTING LGBT STUDENTS AT RISK 11 (2015).

[66] *Id.*

[67] Augustine-Adams, *supra* note 64, at 3.

are opting for that approach.[68] Certainly, there is a principled position to be taken. If a school is receiving federal funding, there is a sound argument that it should not be allowed to discriminate against any group of students.

Another response – supported by the Human Rights Campaign, GLSEN, and several other groups – is to ask the Department of Education to list schools claiming a religious exemption in a prominent place on the its website, so that at least students can know whether a particular school would protect them or not. The Department of Education under President Obama agreed to do so and made the list readily available on the Department's website.[69] Under President Trump, that list still exists, but now appears only as archived information. Letters for 2017 are not easily located, if they exist on the website at all.

Based on the 2009–16 list, a group called Campus Pride went farther, using that list to mount a public campaign to criticize schools that had invoked a religious exemption. Every year, Campus Pride publishes a list of schools with the most hostile policies and climates for LGBT students. Using the Department of Education list of schools requesting Title IX waivers, Campus Pride repurposed the Department of Education list on its website under the heading: "The Shame List."[70] While some religious schools have reacted negatively to this campaign, the public discussions spurred by these lists likely have also caused some schools to consider the potential harms their policies cause and possible ways to mitigate them.

In California, advocates considered yet another approach: legislation that would have prohibited any state-funded grant money from being used at a school that invoked the Title IX waiver in order to discriminate. Tying LGBT protections to funding has intuitive appeal on one level. While the Title IX exemption exists and schools have a legal right to invoke it, the State of California also has a legal right to determine how it will use its own money and can make the determination that taxpayer funded grants should not go to schools that discriminate against any group of students. Ultimately, however, legislators settled on an approach that favors disclosure.[71]

California's mere consideration of this legislation, despite ultimately opting for a different approach, had serious negative consequences.

Word that California was even contemplating such legislation spread like wildfire through the conservative religious educational community, generating a palpable

---

[68] Cara Duchene, *Rethinking Religious Exemptions from Title IX After Obergefell*, 2017 BYU Educ. & L. J. 249 (2017); Alan Noble, *Keeping Faith Without Hurting LGBT Students*, The Atlantic (Aug. 15, 2016), https://perma.cc/5T8S-R9ZB.

[69] To access the archived link, see *Religious Exemptions Index*, U.S. Dep't of Educ., https://perma.cc/26PM-GGK9.

[70] See *The Shame List: The Absolute Worst Campuses for LGBTQ Youth*, Campus Pride, https://perma.cc/D6ZT-4E6V.

[71] California ultimately passed legislation that simply requires the provision of information about sexual orientation and gender identity policies to faculty and staff, see Hoogstra et al., Chapter 25 (for a discussion of S.B. 1146, which was signed into law in 2016).

degree of fear and panic. In response to an embryonic proposal in a single state that was never enacted or even introduced, many of these schools were genuinely convinced that they were being targeted more broadly, that more states were certainly going to pass bills like the one California had considered, and that it was just a matter of time before their ability to invoke religious exemptions would be effectively nullified by measures that, in their view, punished them for doing so.[72] As a result, many of them became intent upon enacting so-called anti-retaliation laws.

Proposed anti-retaliation laws would create sweeping new religious exemptions that go far beyond those already in place. Dozens of such laws have been proposed at the state level and in the proposed federal so-called First Amendment Defense Act, which would create a free-floating exemption from any federal law for any person who has religious objections to marriage by same-sex couples.[73] By fueling support for these measures, the proposed California bill gave renewed energy to already existing fears and efforts to position religious conservatives as embattled minorities in danger of being coerced by the state to give up their beliefs.

For similar reasons, the proposed California measure made it harder for those working from within conservative religious communities for more supportive policies regarding LGBT youth. Rather than encouraging schools to adopt more supportive policies for LGBT youth, the specter of potentially losing state funding caused anger and fear, leading some conservative religious schools to become more entrenched against considering new approaches to LGBT students. In contrast, many positive developments have emerged as a result of recent explorations seeking common ground. For example, in the past two years, the NCAA has brought together LGBT advocates and athletes with staff from conservative religious schools, simply to meet together and try to learn more about each other's perspectives and concerns.[74] After the first such meeting, a number of the schools that participated have taken proactive steps to reach out to their LGBT students.[75] Similarly, the Council on Christian Colleges and Universities sponsored extensive programming at its annual conference for member schools on how to be supportive of LGBT students.[76]

Some general lessons from these experiences can be drawn. LGBT advocates must recognize that many religious schools are undergoing a process of internal reflection and change. If given the space to evolve, many will. Equally important, what is most helpful to those seeking change from within are more opportunities for

---

[72] To see one response, see Strode, *ERLC-led Coalition Urges Defeat of Calif. Bill*, BAPTIST PRESS (Aug. 9, 2016), https://perma.cc/ZQF7-GQ4W.

[73] For the text of the law, see First Amendment Defense Act, H.R. 2802, 114th Cong. (2015). For a discussion of FADA and Mississippi's similar state law, see Krotoszynski, Chapter 7. For a listing of state laws, see Appendix.

[74] *See Common Ground*, NCAA.ORG, https://perma.cc/5C9H-V5XM.

[75] *See, e.g.,* Natalie Ipson, *NCAA Inclusivity Director Meets with BYU Students and Staff*, BYU NEWS (Apr. 18, 2017), https://perma.cc/6EUV-8W2B.

[76] *See* Hoogstra et al., Chapter 25.

the kind of low-stakes dialogue like that the NCAA facilitated, where both sides can share perspectives and build trust without the pressure of being in a litigation or legislation context.

At the same time, those who hold conservative religious beliefs must recognize that the law should not be used to try to insulate religious schools or communities from ordinary exposure to the evolution of scientific knowledge about sexual orientation and gender identity, or from changing social practices and norms. They should not seek to choke off internal dialogue within their communities. Nor can any religious exemption, no matter how broad, change the reality that religious schools already have, and will have, LGBT children and young people in their midst. As many staff and administrators at these schools already know, there are many different ways to support such students while also maintaining a school's religious values and doctrines. Religious schools should not use legal arguments and defenses as an excuse to justify policies that harm these students or treat them harshly.

B *Conversion Therapy*

A similar dynamic plays out in laws protecting LGBT youth from conversion therapy. In the past ten years, state and local legislatures have passed a growing number of laws that prohibit state-licensed mental health professionals from engaging in conversion therapy with minors.[77] Some LGBT advocates want to go further to ban pastoral counseling that engages in this harmful practice as well. Legally, there would be a plausible argument that, notwithstanding the strong First Amendment protections in this area,[78] the harms are so great that the state has a sufficiently compelling justification to act. In at least some states, it might well be possible to pass such a law. But for reasons similar to those that counsel against laws that seek to deny funding to religious schools that invoke Title IX's religious exemption, legislators should not take that step. Doing so would be viewed by many faith communities as an existential threat – as an attempt not to protect youth from a dangerous practice, but to directly coerce people of faith in their religious beliefs. The backlash caused by such a measure – including the risk of pushing some religious groups to endorse conversion therapy when they might not otherwise do so – would likely far outweigh any benefits.

Conversely, however, it is equally inappropriate for religious groups to claim that states should refrain from regulating licensed professionals simply because some parents or therapists, for religious reasons, believe in conversion therapy and wish to engage in it – given the clear medical and scientific consensus that conversion

---

[77] Drescher, *supra* note 41 (laws passed in: California, Illinois, New Jersey, Oregon, Washington, DC, and the Canadian Province of Ontario).
[78] *See* Laycock, Chapter 3; Krotoszynski, Chapter 7.

therapy is harmful. Yet several laws banning conversion therapy have been challenged on that basis, albeit unsuccessfully thus far. In California and New Jersey, and most recently in Tampa, Florida, conservative Christian legal organizations have argued that requiring licensed mental health professionals to adhere to professional standards that prohibit these practices infringes upon the freedom of religious parents and therapists who disagree.[79] Those challenges are a clear example of religious groups inappropriately trying to muster the power of the State to insulate themselves from ordinary health and safety regulations that reflect well-established scientific knowledge and that protect LGBT young people from serious harms.

VII CONCLUSION

In conclusion, when one acknowledges that many LGBT children are growing up in conservative religious communities, it is no longer possible to maintain the fiction that conflicts between religious liberty and LGBT rights simply pit one set of exclusive interests against another. There can be no "peaceful coexistence" because there is no clear line separating two groups. Instead, both groups have internal divisions that cut both ways. Religious communities include LGBT youth, and the LGBT population includes children who are growing up in conservative communities and who do not want to lose their families, cultures, or faiths. These intersections have caused much trauma and pain, but they also provide a foundation for healing, both for individual families and communities and for our society as a whole. While our differences are real, our common interests are real as well. In particular, both "sides" have a shared interest in the health and well-being of LGBT youth *and* in the ability of conservative faiths to support these young people in ways that maintain their cultural and religious integrity. Conservative religious communities cannot count themselves successful in protecting religious freedom if it comes at the cost of causing grievous harm to vulnerable young people and their families. And the LGBT movement cannot effectively protect LGBT youth until it acknowledges that the LGBT children in those communities need their families and their faiths.

---

[79] *See, e.g.*, Welch v. Brown, 834 F.3d 1031 (9th Cir. 2013) (rejecting free exercise challenge to California conversion therapy law); King v. Christie, 981 F. Supp. 2d 296 (D.N.J. 2013) (rejecting free exercise challenge to New Jersey conversion therapy law), *aff'd*, 767 F.3d 216 (3d Cir. 2014); Xander Peters, *Anti-LGBTQ Group Files Suit Against the City of Tampa for Banning Gay Conversion Therapy*, ORLANDO WEEKLY (Dec. 5, 2017), https://perma.cc/3DK9-36CA.

5

Religious Freedom, Civil Rights, and Sexuality

A *Christian Ethics Perspective*

Dennis P. Hollinger

When approaching any ethical issue, especially those related to sexuality discussions, it is imperative to distinguish religious ethics (in this chapter, Christian ethics) from law and public policy. Religious ethics establishes normative expectations drawn from the particularities of a religious tradition and deeply embedded in the sacred scriptures of that tradition. Within a given society the expectations in both character and actions that scriptures have for adherents are typically more rigorous than expectations for neighbors from other social groups, who are not adherents. Sacred scriptures act as transcendent designs calling for faithfulness to those designs by the members of that tradition.

Public policy and law also embody normative expectations, but from a different framework and grounding. In a society, public policy and legal prescriptions attempt to determine rights, responsibilities, and policies in a pluralistic setting. The moral force of law is regulated by both positive adjudications that engender rights within a society and by punitive actions that protect rights, freedom, and societal order. Generally, public policy and law focus on the right to do something, and religious ethics on the right thing to do from within the framework of a particular religious tradition.

Religious ethics and public policy and law are not totally divorced from each other, but they are not the same realities. They invoke different languages, expectations, and patterns of thought. Frequently, however, the public misunderstands the relationship between the two – believing either that they are the same or that the two inherently stand in opposition to each other. The key question to ask is, can society simultaneously affirm the freedom for religious groups, with their particularistic ethical commitments, and civil rights for all individuals, even when those civil rights support actions that may be at odds with particular religious expectations? This question should be put to both religious communities and to society at large.

As a Christian ethicist from the evangelical wing of the Christian Church, I am committed to protecting both the freedom of religious convictions and actions in my and other communities of faith, along with protecting the civil rights of all individuals, even though their patterns of life may contradict my tradition's ethical convictions. This chapter's approach is a big picture one, basically contending that as a public policy strategy society can make a case for both freedom and rights.

Thus, this chapter takes exception to the verdict of the US Commission on Civil Rights, that "overly-broad religious exemptions unduly burden non-discrimination laws and policies."[1] Specifically, this chapter suggests that from a Christian ethics perspective, specifically the evangelical wing of the Christian Church, there are understandings and frameworks that can enable Christians to affirm a robust freedom of religion with exemptions for churches, religious institutions, and individual believers, *and* at the same time affirm civil rights for the LGBTQ communities. This chapter sets forth three primary understandings to make this case and then it responds to anticipated critiques. First, certain judicial and political actions prioritize secular worldviews over religious beliefs, and therefore enthrone secularism at the expense of religious freedom. Second, Christians generally seek to express their beliefs in communities of faith and are not seeking a privileged establishment of their faith. Third, Christian ethics proceeds from our shared humanity but also rests on a distinction between ethics and public policy; this allows room for secular public policy that may even entail the ability of citizens to act in ways that Christians would see as contrary to Christians' ethical core.

I ETHICAL COMMITMENTS AND ACTIONS FLOW OUT OF A LARGER NARRATIVE OR WORLDVIEW ABOUT GOD, HUMANITY, AND THE WORLD

Worldview commitments are simply the ways by which people put the world together.[2] Worldviews constitute a mental map or grand narrative out of which come ethical obligations in life. Thus for the varied Christian communities and other communities of faith that seek to embody particular practices that run against the grain of prevailing cultural norms, the ethical patterns flow from worldview assumptions about God, human nature, marriage, family, sexuality, and the nature of religious communities. That is, the ethical commitments are not merely arbitrary commands from the Divine but are reflections of larger understandings of reality from the designs of the Divine.

All ethical systems flow from some kind of larger narrative, not just those based on a religious perspective. As the cultural anthropologist Clifford Geertz once noted, there is an interplay between worldview and ethical behavior.[3] Ethics is never

---

[1]   U.S. Comm'n on Civil Rights, Peaceful Coexistence: Reconciling Nondiscrimination Principles with Civil Liberties, Briefing Rep., at 26 (2016).

[2]   Amy Poppinga, *Inside the Bubble: Creating a Nurturing Learning Environment, in* From Bubble to Bridge: Educating Christians for a Multifaith World 75 (2017).

[3]   Clifford Geertz, The Interpretation of Cultures 126 (1973).

divorced from larger perceptions of reality held by groups and individuals. "The source of [a religion's] moral vitality is conceived to lie in the fidelity with which it expresses the fundamental nature of reality. The powerful coercive 'ought' is felt to grow out of a comprehensive factual is." Thus, ethical judgments, including those surrounding sexuality and the nature of gender, flow out of a particular narrative about reality, as the spectrum of views contained in this volume illustrates. The challenge in today's pluralistic world is that multiple worldviews live side by side, leading sometimes to conflicts between ethical expectations derived from differing underlying beliefs.

The US Commission on Civil Rights wants to divide action from belief, when it states "[r]eligious exemptions to nondiscrimination laws and policies should be pursuant to the holdings of *Employment Division v. Smith*, which protect religious belief rather than conduct."[4] The Commission effectively asserts that a person can believe anything, but cannot necessarily live it out.[5] In other words, religious beliefs should be protected, but not the actions stemming from those beliefs, for they are perceived to encroach on civil rights in a pluralistic society. Religious claims to truth and goodness that persons of faith seek to impose upon themselves are thought invariably to lead to political exclusivism that mandates those religious claims for the whole society, thereby limiting the rights of others.[6]

Jean-Jacques Rousseau makes the same fundamental mistake in *The Social Contract*; he contends that "those who distinguish civil intolerance from theological intolerance are ... mistaken. These two kinds of intolerance are inseparable."[7] Rousseau is saying that persons guided strongly by their faith in all aspects of their life are constitutionally unable to be tolerant of others in the public square: "Wherever theological intolerance is allowed, it cannot but have some effect in civil life; and as soon as it has any, the sovereign is no longer sovereign even in secular affairs; from that time the priests are the real masters."[8]

In these renditions religious liberty is limited by a boundary around belief that stops at action. But this division into belief and action encroaches on something at the core of a human being – to limit worldview to expression only of deeply held beliefs without ensuing actions is to strike at the heart of one's own personhood.

---

[4] U.S. COMM'N ON CIVIL RIGHTS, *supra* note 1, at 27.

[5] For critique of *Smith*, see, Brownstein, Chapter 2; Laycock, Chapter 3; Krotoszynski, Chapter 7; Helfand, Chapter 11; Moyer, Chapter 16; Smith, Chapter 18; Berg, Chapter 24; and Hoogstra et al., Chapter 25.

[6] For a helpful description and refutation of this perspective, see MIROSLAV VOLF & TONY BLAIR, FLOURISHING: WHY WE NEED RELIGION IN A GLOBALIZED WORLD 137–60 (2016) (arguing that being guided by strong faith convictions – which they shorthand as religious exclusivism – can be compatible with political pluralism and has been at various points in history and in the contemporary world).

[7] JEAN-JACQUES ROUSSEAU, THE SOCIAL CONTRACT 186 (Maurice Cranston trans., Penguin Classics 1968).

[8] JEAN-JACQUES ROUSSEAU, THE SOCIAL CONTRACT AND DISCOURSE ON THE ORIGIN OF INEQUALITY 162 (Lester G. Crocker ed., Washington Square Press 1989).

Such infringement violates something near and dear to human beings, even if those convictions are not widely accepted in the society.

Note the obvious: limiting religious liberty this way, by parsing action from belief, frequently ends up actually establishing one worldview over others, something the Establishment Clause of the First Amendment teaches us society cannot do in favor of one religion over another or of all religions over none at all.[9] In operation, this approach makes ascendant a secular or naturalistic worldview at the expense of an individual's religious freedom to actualize their worldviews.

More than two decades ago the late Father Richard John Neuhaus lamented what he called the "Naked Public Square," noting that "[w]hen recognizable religion is excluded, the vacuum will be filled by *ersatz* religion, by religion bootlegged into public space under other names."[10] Further, "[b]ecause government cannot help but make moral judgments of an ultimate nature, it must, if it has in principle excluded identifiable religion, make those judgments by 'secular' reasoning that is given the force of religion." This in effect establishes secularism as the dominant worldview or religion, while hobbling others.

This enthronement of secularism at the expense of religious freedom was evident at the European Court of Human Rights (ECHR) in another context recently. A Muslim couple in Basel, Switzerland refused to enroll their daughters in a school's mandatory swimming class in which boys and girls would swim together. School officials fined the couple 1,400 Swiss Francs or roughly $1,380 dollars "for acting in breach of their parental duty," even though their decision was rooted in their religious outlook on life.[11] In January 2017, the ECHR "upheld the Swiss officials' decision, rejecting the parents argument that Swiss authorities had violated the 'freedom of thought, conscience and religion' guaranteed by the European Convention on Human Rights, which the court enforces." The court argued that "the public interest in following the full school curriculum should prevail over the applicants' private interest in obtaining an exemption from mixed swim lessons for their daughters."[12]

This decision not only stifled something at the very core of the couple's being – their practice of modesty and separating the sexes rooted in the couple's religious worldview – it also seemingly establishes a singular secular view as acceptable, much

---

[9] *See generally* Michael A. Helfand, *Litigating Religion*, 93 B.U. L. Rev. 493 (2013).

[10] Richard John Neuhaus, The Naked Public Square: Religion and Democracy in America 80, 82 (2d ed. 1988).

[11] Dan Bilefsky, *Muslim Girls in Switzerland Must Attend Swim Classes with Boys, Courts Says*, N.Y. Times (Jan. 10, 2017), https://www.nytimes.com/2017/01/10/world/europe/swiss-muslim-girls-must-attend-swim-classes-with-boys-court-says.html. For a thoughtful view on the importance of modesty for Muslims, *see* Asma T. Uddin, *Religious Modesty for Women and Girls: A Comparative Analysis of Legal Protections in France and the United States*, in The Contested Place of Religion in Family Law (Robin Fretwell Wilson ed., Cambridge University Press 2018).

[12] Osmanoglu & Kocabas v. Switzerland, No. 29086/12 (Eur. Ct. Hum. Rts. 2017).

as if the state had established secularism as the religion of European societies. And incidentally, in this case no one's civil rights would have been violated by an exemption from the mandatory mixed swimming lessons.

In the midst of recent attempts to curb religious freedom expressions for the sake of civil rights, it should not be forgotten that religious ethics, like all ethics, is ultimately shaped by worldview commitments. To curb those worldview commitments is to strike at the very core of a person's and community's being, thereby violating something fundamental to the human self and the communities attempting to live out their beliefs and commitments. Moreover, such actions privilege one set of worldviews, secular ones, over all others, hence violating the animating principle behind the Establishment Clause of the First Amendment to the US Constitution.[13]

II THE PRIMARY LOCUS OF CHRISTIAN BELIEFS AND ETHICS IS IN THE CHRISTIAN COMMUNITY, NOT IN THE LARGER SOCIETY

Historically, Christians have contended that the primary location of the Christian worldview expression is in the church.[14] This flows naturally and logically out of the observation in Section I that ethics is rooted in worldview. If this is true, then the primary locus for worldview expression in ethical thought and action is in the particular communities of faith that espouse and embody their worldviews – churches and varied religious institutions. Religious educational institutions would be included here in that they play a key role in the socialization and reinforcement of a Christian worldview and ethical commitments.[15]

Christians have a long history that at first blush might seem to contradict this postulate – namely, the Christendom model of Christianity that dominated Europe for over a thousand years and continued in various forms long after the legal separation of church and state.[16] In the Christendom model, Christian freedom was not only vigorously granted, but Christian values and beliefs were legally privileged. At times the church had more political power in society than did the state. Citizens, whatever their worldview and beliefs, were mandated to live by the church's religious ethics expectations.

In the Christendom model, "The position of a king rested on eternal foundations: he was in the strictest sense God's anointed, endowed by God with powers which combined important aspects of the powers of bishops and priests, as well as the

---

[13] This statement obviously assumes a broad definition of religion, one that can include secular understandings and belief systems.

[14] DAVID K. NAUGLE, WORLDVIEW: THE HISTORY OF A CONCEPT (2002).

[15] See Helfand, Chapter 11; Hoogstra, Chapter 25; Hill, Chapter 26.

[16] Richard William Southern, *The Bonds of Christian Society, in* MEDIEVAL SOCIETY: 400–1450, at 85–86 (Norman F. Cantor & Michael S. Werthman eds., 2d ed. 1972).

sanctions of secular rule."[17] Christendom frequently was perceived to be a theocracy, a political rule of God.[18] Sometimes this meant the state took the lead and the emperor was regarded as God's appointee.[19] At other times, a Christian society meant the pope, as leader of the Catholic Church, exerted the greatest civil authority.[20] In Christendom, religious offenses were civil offenses, and civil offenses were religious offenses.[21]

Christendom's history is often cited as the clear reason why religious freedoms must be curtailed so as to not establish one religion over another, and thereby protect civil rights.[22] After all, in nineteenth-century America, there was a kind of Protestant hegemony, which functioned much like Christendom despite legal separation of church and state.[23] Church historian Martin Marty once referred to this as the "Righteous Empire" in that "[t]hey set out consciously to create an empire . . . and, despite their great diversities, knew considerable success. They set out to attract the allegiance of all the people . . . to shape the nation's ethos, mores, manners, and often its laws."[24] Societal reform projects frequently emerged when "the Second Great Awakening not only made evangelical Protestantism the dominant religion in the country but . . . it created a Protestant consensus that set the cultural and social agenda for the rest of the century."[25]

There are, however, clear strands in Christian history and in sacred scripture that would call into question the Christendom model in which Christianity is given a privileged place in the public square. Many would argue that attempting to impose Christianity on the larger culture actually undermines Christian vitality and ethics.[26] The very nature of Christian belief and its derivative ethics is actually weakened by mandates for an entire society that does not embrace those commitments. Indeed, in today's society, Christian growth and vitality are most evident not in places of established privilege but rather in places of overt opposition to the faith, with China and India as prime examples.[27]

---

[17]   *Id.* at 102.
[18]   MEDIEVAL SOCIETY: 400–1450 at 139 (Norman F. Cantor & Michael S. Werthman eds., 2d ed. 1972).
[19]   *Id.* at 208.
[20]   ROLAND HERBERT BAINTON, THE MEDIEVAL CHURCH 48 (1962).
[21]   STEVEN K. GREEN, THE SECOND DISESTABLISHMENT: CHURCH AND STATE IN NINETEENTH-CENTURY AMERICA 161 (2010).
[22]   *Id.* at 115.
[23]   *Id.* at 98.
[24]   MARTIN E. MARTY, RIGHTEOUS EMPIRE: THE PROTESTANT EXPERIENCE IN AMERICA 1 (1970).
[25]   FRANCES FITZGERALD, THE EVANGELICALS: THE STRUGGLE TO SHAPE AMERICA 848–54 (2017).
[26]   *See, e.g.,* Bruce P. Frohnen, *Christianity, Culture, and the Problem of Establishment,* 37 POL. SCI. REVIEWER 276 (Fall 2008), https://isistatic.org/journal-archive/pr/37_01/frohnen.pdf.
[27]   Tom Phillips et al., *China on Course to Become "World's Most Christian Nation" Within 15 Years,* THE TELEGRAPH (Apr. 19, 2014), http://www.telegraph.co.uk/news/worldnews/asia/china/10776023/China-on-course-to-become-worlds-most-Christian-nation-within-15-years.html; Stephanie Parker, *Despite Increased Persecution, Christianity Growing in India,*

Consider the images that Jesus used when talking about Christian influence in the world – they were not metaphors of control or dominance, that is, they were not images of establishment.[28] Rather, they were metaphors of gentle influence from a presence within the culture, images such as salt, light, and leaven.[29] Evangelical Christians emphasize that our way of life and ethics is rooted in a particularistic worldview on the one hand, but also rooted in a very personalized faith centered in Jesus Christ on the other.[30] Centered as it is on the relationship to Christ, the expectations for Christian ethical patterns will be most explicitly found, not in the wider society and its social institutions but in the specific communities of faith that are committed to the worldview and seek to express it through a highly personalized faith.[31] Because the ethical and belief patterns of the faith must be personally appropriated rather than systemically mandated, when the ethic is systemically mandated for a society, it actually undermines the very nature of that ethic. There is always the hope that such beliefs and patterns might influence people and cultural patterns outside the communities of faith – but the clear understanding remains that their primary locus of expression is the church and Christian institutions.

If Christians expect a pluralistic society to grant them the freedom to live out their particularistic beliefs and ethics, it also means that Christians and the Church should not be seeking a privileged establishment of their faith – the Christendom model – in which those beliefs and patterns of life are required for the whole society. Of course, Christians may seek to be a voice in public discourse in society, but with more modest expectations of their ethic in a pluralistic society than was the case during Christendom. In being a voice in the public arena, Christians and other faith communities should not be prohibited from expressing their sentiments in the language of their faith. But they would do well to enter the dialogue with broader language that is accessible to the whole of society.[32]

All of this does not mean that Christians wall off faith from daily lives or privatize their faith, but rather that their expectations for the expression of faith will not be found in the social institutions of a pluralistic society. Rather they seek the freedom to express their faith in the contexts that are most pertinent to their faith – their churches and various institutions.[33]

FAITHWIRE (Dec. 6, 2016), http://www.faithwire.com/2016/12/06/despite-increased-persecution-christianity-growing-in-india/.

[28] *Matthew 5:13–16; Luke 13:20–21.*

[29] *Id.*

[30] THE BOISI CENTER FOR RELIGION AND AMERICAN PUBIC LIFE, AN INTRODUCTION TO CHRISTIAN THEOLOGY, https://www.bc.edu/content/dam/files/centers/boisi/pdf/bc_papers/BCP-Christianity.pdf.

[31] For an explanation of this phenomenon, see Hoogstra et al., Chapter 25.

[32] For a discussion of public reason, see Kent Greenawalt, *On Public Reason*, 69 CHI.-KENT. L. REV. 669 (1994), http://scholarship.kentlaw.iit.edu/cklawreview/vol69/iss3/5.

[33] This of course does not resolve all tensions between religious norms and their implementation. There are still complex issues to navigate, such as how personal religious conscience intersects with the workplace. See Adams, Chapter 32, for constructive approaches.

III HUMAN RIGHTS FLOW FROM A HUMAN DIGNITY SHARED
BY ALL HUMANITY

Classical Christianity holds two fundamental tenets about human nature: we are wonderfully made and terribly fallen.[34] The two must be held together in reflecting on complex societal issues, for the one guards the dignity of all humans and the other reminds us that our best human efforts are frequently inverted and distorted.

The wonderfully made understanding in Judaism and Christianity comes from the biblical story of creation in the image of God. Whatever may be entailed in the *imago dei* doctrine, a clear implication, found in several biblical texts, is the dignity of the human person flowing from the divine image in humans.[35] Historically this human value is deemed to be an intrinsic dignity, not a functional dignity that depends on how a person functions in this world. That is, dignity resides in the human person simply because they are part of the human race. Even when people freely choose paths of life antithetical to perceived biblical teaching and Christian commitments, they nonetheless retain this intrinsic dignity.

The Christian grounding for human rights is premised on human dignity, which clearly played a role in the development of human rights in modern times.[36] People intuitively sense this dignity and the human rights it demands, even if they emerge from other worldviews and frameworks.[37] Thus, while Christians historically have provided a specific grounding for human rights, they have believed that all humans intuit their own and others' dignity, together with the rights that flow from that dignity.[38]

The centrality of dignity runs through the 1948 *Universal Declaration of Human Rights (Declaration)* from the General Assembly of the United Nations.[39] The document begins with "recognition of the inherent dignity and of the equal and inalienable right of all members of the human family" as the foundation of "freedom, justice and peace in the world."[40] Article 1 of the *Declaration* declares: "All human beings are born free and equal in dignity and rights."[41] The various rights spelled out by the *Declaration* are rooted in the concept of the intrinsic dignity of

---

[34] *See Genesis* 1:27. For a similar view, see Perry, Chapter 20.

[35] *Genesis* 1:26–28 gives the story of creation in God's image. The dignity concept is linked to the image in *Genesis* 9:6 as the grounds for protecting human life and in *James* 3:9 in relation to verbal treatment of other humans.

[36] *See, e.g.,* Adrien Katherine Wing, *The South African Constitution as a Role Model for the United States,* 24 HARV. BLACKLETTER L.J. 73 (2008) (discussing the role of dignity in the drafting and adoption of the South African Constitution).

[37] For a discussion of the moral foundations on protections against discrimination, including the role of dignity, see Perry, Chapter 20.

[38] *See, e.g.,* UNDERSTANDING HUMAN DIGNITY (Christopher McCrudden ed., 2014).

[39] Universal Declaration of Human Rights, G.A. Res. 217A, U.N. Doc. A/RES/217A, at 1, 2 (Dec. 10, 1948).

[40] *Id.*

[41] *Id.*

human persons.[42] The language of dignity also found its way into the constitution of numerous countries following the lead of the *Declaration*.[43]

During the *Declaration's* writing, the United Nations Educational, Scientific and Cultural Organization, commonly known as UNESCO, brought together a group of philosophers to explore the theoretical foundations for claims about dignity and human rights.[44] Jacques Maritain, a philosopher participating in the gathering, noted: "At one of the meetings ... where human rights were being discussed, someone expressed astonishment that certain champions of violently opposed ideologies had agreed on a list of those rights. 'Yes,' they said, 'we agree about the rights but on condition that no one asks us why.'"[45] The philosophers could agree on the language of dignity and particular rights, but could not agree on foundations for dignity and rights.[46]

Thus, while Christians typically assert a particular grounding for human rights, they also recognize a broader discernment of those rights. And even when people choose paths of life contrary to Christian faith, there is an affirmation of their human dignity, from which comes basic rights within society. To note the obvious: this puts Christians in the unusual position of affirming that one's rights may even entail a right to take actions that Christians deem contrary to their ethical core. These are not inconsistent positions. One's Christian ethic is not the same as the contours of public policy. Moreover, all of this logically flows from this chapter's first two main points: ethics flow from a worldview and the major locus for that ethic is in the church and its institutions.

Thus, Christians argue for the freedom to practice the peculiarities of their ethic, while asserting a public policy stance that leads to actions not commensurate with specific contours of their ethic. Nonetheless, because their ethic also embodies a commitment to human dignity and its ensuing rights, they live with and affirm the distinction between ethics and public policy.

IV CONCLUSION

All three propositions of this chapter affirm both religious freedom and civil rights: ethics arises from a worldview, the main locus of Christian expression is in its own communities, and human dignity is the grounding of rights for all. This central thesis raises profound critiques for all in this debate. For those principally motivated

---

[42] Erin Daly, Dignity Rights: Courts, Constitutions, and the Worth of the Human Person 83 (Rogers M. Smith & Mary L. Dudziak eds., 2012).

[43] Jacques Maritain, *Introduction, in* Human Rights: Comments and Interpretations: A Symposium edited by UNESCO with an Introduction by Jacques Maritain 9 (1949); Wing, *supra* note 36.

[44] *Id.*

[45] *Id.*

[46] *Id.*

by religious freedom, affirming civil rights for all raises for some the conundrum of moral complicity – to what degree is a person responsible for unethical actions by having some indirect involvement in that action. This is a highly complex debate in ethics that spills over to a wide range of issues: war, bioethics, financial investments, and paying taxes that are used for actions contrary to conscience.[47] In the Christian tradition there is a long history of critiquing moral complicity, stemming primarily from the writings of theologian Thomas Aquinas in the thirteenth century. For Aquinas, one could be ethically culpable for a wide range of actions and nonactions: by command, by counsel, by consent, by flattery, by receiving, by participating, by remaining silent, by not preventing, and by not denouncing.[48]

While Aquinas's account has had significant impact on Christian thinking, particularly within the Roman Catholic tradition, it should be noted that Aquinas was dealing with complicity in relation to a particular ethical issue, namely theft that warranted restitution.[49] Moreover, he noted that complicity (not his term) could only be affirmed when there is clear linkage between a person's nonaction and another's explicit actions.[50] One might even argue that moral complicity is closely linked to the moral actor's proximity, in both time and place, to the actions in question.

Allowing people the freedom to act in ways that are judged as ethically suspect by a religious tradition, but do not threaten the lives of others, is quite common, especially in the realm of more private actions. While most Christians would argue that adultery is a grievous moral action, most would also not want the state to engage in bedroom espionage to curb such actions. Protecting both the dignity and rights of human beings, albeit involving choices deemed morally wrong by the religious tradition, entails an understanding that one is not morally complicit in granting the rights that may lead to freely chosen actions.

For those wanting to affirm civil rights by limiting religious freedom there are also deep challenges – namely, allowing for actions by religious institutions, which would seem at first glance to diminish those rights. For many who give priority to civil rights, the tendency is to see ethical and religious pluralism as requiring a limitation or boundary around them in order to ensure civil rights.

In response to more secular strands of civil rights, Miroslav Wolf argues that "respect for freedom of religion is a form of respect for persons and for their sovereignty in determining their way of life, regardless of whether or not we respect

---

[47] *Compare* Chiara Lepora & Robert Goodin, On Complicity and Compromise (2013) *with* P. Calain, *Response to "On Complicity and Compromise" by Chiara Lepora and Robert Goodin*, 43 J. Med. Ethics 266 (2017).

[48] Saint Thomas Aquinas, Summa Theologiae, Part II–II, Q. 62 (Benziger Bros. ed. 1947), http://dhspriory.org/thomas/summa/SS/SS062.html#SSQ62OUTP1.

[49] *Id.*

[50] *Id.*

that way of life itself."[51] Moreover, he contends, "[r]espect for a religion is respect for that way of life itself and for a set of convictions that undergirds and expresses it." Such respect will not only allow for religious freedom within the confines of the religious institutions, but will effect a true pluralism that allows for expression of all sentiments in the market place of ideas within a society.

What is needed to move society forward in affirming both freedom and rights, and moving beyond the current conflicts over sexuality? Perhaps the solution lies in embracing what some have termed principled pluralism, or as John Inazu of Washington University, terms it, confident pluralism:

> Confident pluralism argues that we can, and we must, learn to live with each other in spite of our deep differences. It requires a tolerance for dissent, a skepticism of government orthodoxy, and a willingness to endure strange and even offensive ways of life. Confident pluralism asks that those charged with enforcing our laws do better in preserving and strengthening our constitutional commitments to voluntary groups, public forums, and certain kinds of generally available funding. It also challenges each of us to live out the aspirations of tolerance, humility, and patience in our civic practices.[52]

And Inazu adds, "Confident pluralism does not give us the American Dream. But it might help us avoid the American nightmare."[53] We have two futures in front of us; we need the wisdom to choose well.

---

[51] Volf, *supra* note 6, at 117.
[52] JOHN D. INAZU, CONFIDENT PLURALISM: SURVIVING AND THRIVING THROUGH DEEP DIFFERENCE 125 (2016).
[53] *Id.*

PART II

Guiding Principles for Mediating Conflicts

6

Religious Accommodation, and Its Limits, in a Pluralist Society

Douglas NeJaime and Reva B. Siegel

For the past several years, we have been writing with a view to reconciling commitments to religious freedom, reproductive rights, and LGBT equality in conflicts that arise when laws of general application constrain religiously motivated conduct.[1] Persons of faith object to laws that require them to participate in conduct they deem sinful – such as performing an abortion or officiating a marriage.[2] They also object to complying with laws such as those requiring businesses not to discriminate or requiring health-care professionals to serve patients, on the grounds that compliance enables *others* to engage in sin or sanctions their wrongdoing.[3] In our writing, we have focused extensively on these complicity-based conscience claims.

High-profile examples have proliferated in recent years. After the US Supreme Court's decision recognizing the right of same-sex couples to marry in *Obergefell v. Hodges*, Kim Davis, a county clerk in Kentucky, claimed that religious conscience prevented her from issuing marriage licenses to same-sex couples or allowing others in her office to do so.[4] In Colorado, Jack Phillips, owner of Masterpiece Cakeshop, sought an exemption from his state's nondiscrimination law on the ground that

---

[1]   For extended treatment of questions of religious accommodation arising in these conflicts, see Douglas NeJaime & Reva Siegel, *Conscience Wars: Complicity-Based Conscience Claims in Religion and Politics*, 124 YALE L.J. 2516 (2015), and Douglas NeJaime & Reva Siegel, *Conscience Wars in Transnational Perspective: Religious Liberty, Third-Party Harm, and Pluralism*, in THE CONSCIENCE WARS: RETHINKING THE BALANCE BETWEEN RELIGION, IDENTITY, AND EQUALITY 187 (Susanna Mancini & Michel Rosenfeld eds., 2018); Douglas NeJaime & Reva Siegel, *Religious Exemptions and Antidiscrimination Law in* Masterpiece Cakeshop, 128 Yale L. J. F. (forthcoming 2018).

[2]   *Conscience Wars supra* note 1, at 2529.

[3]   *See id.* at 2535.

[4]   *See* Appellant Kim Davis's Emergency Motion for Immediate Consideration and Motion for Injunction Pending Appeal at 7–8, Miller v. Davis, No. 15–5961 (6th Cir. Sept. 7, 2015) (claiming that her religious beliefs make her unable "to issue [marriage] licenses" to same-sex couples or to provide "the 'authorization' to marry (even on licenses she does not personally sign)").

making a wedding cake for a same-sex couple would facilitate a marriage he believes is sinful.[5]

Objections of this kind also feature prominently in conflicts over abortion and contraception. In *Burwell v. Hobby Lobby Stores*, owners of a corporation argued that regulations requiring them to include contraception in health insurance benefits for their employees violated the federal Religious Freedom Restoration Act (RFRA).[6] Providing employees insurance that covers contraceptives, the claimants asserted, would make them complicit in conduct they view as sinful.[7] In 2014, the Supreme Court ruled 5–4 in favor of the employers' conscience objections.[8]

This chapter makes three points about claims for religious exemption from laws that protect contraception, abortion, and same-sex relationships. First, claims for religious exemption from laws that protect contraception, abortion, and same-sex relationships differ from accommodation claims involving ritual observance in dress or prayer, most importantly in their capacity to inflict targeted harms on other citizens who do not share the claimant's beliefs. Second, US constitutional and statutory law recognizes concerns about third-party harm as reason for limiting religious accommodation. Third, religious accommodation serves pluralist ends only when the accommodation is structured in such a way that other citizens who do not share the objectors' beliefs are protected from material and dignitary harm.

I HOW RELIGIOUS LIBERTY CLAIMS DIFFER IN FORM, AND WHY IT MATTERS

We assume that religious objections to contraception, abortion, and same-sex marriage are asserted in good faith. Yet these claims differ in *form* from traditional religious liberty claims involving ritual or ceremonial observance – such as wearing a headscarf or observing a Saturday Sabbath.

Consider two Supreme Court cases involving ritual observance. In *Holt v. Hobbs*, a case decided by the Supreme Court in 2015, a prisoner sought a religious exemption from a rule prohibiting prisoners from wearing beards.[9] The Court granted the accommodation, with Justice Ruth Bader Ginsburg pointing out in her concurring opinion that "accommodating petitioner's religious belief in this case would not detrimentally affect others who do not share petitioner's belief."[10] In a ritual observance case such as *Holt*, members of minority sects with little voice in the political

---

[5] *See* Masterpiece Cakeshop, Ltd. v. Colo. Civil Rights Comm'n, 138 S. Ct. 1719 (2018).

[6] Burwell v. Hobby Lobby Stores, Inc., 134 S. Ct. 2751, 2759 (2014) (deciding challenge under RFRA, 42 U.S.C. § 2000bb-1(a) to (b) (2012)).

[7] *Id.* at 2765.

[8] *Id.* at 2785. Opponents of same-sex marriage sought to enact state laws that mirror the federal RFRA. *See, e.g.,* IND. CODE § 34-13-9-0.7 to –11 (2016).

[9] Holt v. Hobbs, 135 S. Ct. 853, 856–57 (2015).

[10] *Id.* at 867 (Ginsburg, J., concurring).

process seek exemptions from laws in order to act in conformity with unconventional beliefs or practices generally not considered by lawmakers when they adopted the challenged laws.[11] The religious practitioners' faith claims are not focused on other citizens; the costs of accommodating their claims are minimal and widely shared.

An earlier, and more controversial, Supreme Court case provides an additional illustration. In *Employment Division v. Smith*, members of the Native American Church were denied unemployment benefits after they were terminated from their jobs for using peyote in ritual ceremonies.[12] In response, they sought an exemption from laws criminalizing possession and use of the drug.[13] The burden of accommodating the religious practitioners would not have fallen on an identified group of citizens.[14] Even so, the Court denied the exemption under the Constitution's Free Exercise Clause.[15]

Contrast these religious liberty claims involving ritual observance with the religious liberty claims asserted in conflicts over contraception, abortion, and same-sex relationships. In these cases, religious claimants seek exemptions from laws that protect women's access to contraception and abortion and from laws that protect LGBT people from discrimination. Accommodating these claims can inflict targeted harms on other citizens and so raises concerns less commonly presented by religious liberty claims involving ritual observance.

These claims differ from ritual observance claims in yet another dimension. In the typical ritual observance case, a member of a *minority* religious sect is challenging a law that comports with the dominant faith traditions of the majority. Yet in the cases involving religious objections to contraception, abortion, and same-sex marriage, it is not entirely clear whether to characterize the religious claimant as a member of a minority religious sect *or* as adhering to the dominant faith traditions of the majority. In cases involving religious objections to contraception, abortion, and same-sex marriage, the religious claimant is condemning a practice that the majority itself long condemned, but now, perhaps through court decision, has come to protect. In seeking an exemption from a law that departs from customary morality, the religious claimant defends customary morality. In this way, religious liberty claims offer a framework for opposing an emergent legal order and the newly recognized rights of those the order protects.

Laws authorizing religious objections of health-care workers – which this chapter terms health-care refusal laws – illustrate this dynamic. After *Roe v. Wade*

---

[11] Employment Division v. Smith, 494 U.S. 872, 874 (1990); Wisconsin v. Yoder, 406 U.S. 205, 209 (1972); Sherbert, 374 U.S. at 409.

[12] Smith, 494 U.S. at 872.

[13] *Id.* at 880.

[14] *Id.* at 911–12, 916 (Blackmun, J., dissenting).

[15] *See infra* text at note 28 and accompanying text.

recognized a constitutional right to abortion,[16] laws were enacted in the United States that authorized doctors with religious or moral objections to refuse to perform abortions or sterilizations, exempting them from duties of care imposed by professional licensing law and tort law.[17] When opponents of abortion rights failed to secure *Roe*'s reversal in 1992,[18] they responded by supporting the enactment of more expansive health-care refusal laws.

The concept of complicity animated this expanded coverage. The more recent health-care refusal laws authorize conscience objections, not only by the doctors and nurses directly involved in the objected-to procedure, but also by others indirectly involved who object on grounds of conscience to being made complicit in the procedure.[19] Today, health-care refusal laws expressly authorize objecting health-care workers *to refuse* to provide counseling or referrals to the patients they turn away that might help those patients find alternative care.[20] Some opponents of abortion and contraception object to referring patients to alternate providers, on the ground that it would make religious health-care professionals complicit in the sins of those they refer.[21]

While health-care refusal laws can facilitate a pluralist regime in which health-care providers and patients with different moral outlooks may coexist, the

[16] 410 U.S. 113, 153 (1973).

[17] The primary example of a health-care refusal law in this early period is the Church Amendment, which was passed as part of the Health Programs Extension Act of 1973, Pub. L. No. 93–45, §401(b)-(c), 87 Stat. 91, 95. It allows health-care providers to object, but only in cases of direct involvement in particular procedures. The statute provides that receipt of federal funds would not furnish a basis for requiring a physician or nurse "*to perform or assist in the performance* of any sterilization procedure or abortion if his performance or assistance in the performance of such procedure or abortion would be contrary to his religious beliefs or moral convictions." 42 U.S.C. § 300a–7(b)(1) (2012) (emphasis added). The legislative debate distinguishes between objections to performing particular procedures and objections based on more remote forms of involvement. See *Conscience Wars: Complicity-Based Conscience Claims in Religion and Politics, supra* note 1, at 2537 & notes 87–88. On the duties of care imposed on health-care providers, see *id.* at 2534–35 n. 72–76.

[18] Planned Parenthood v. Casey, 505 U.S. 833, 855 (1992).

[19] For a more general discussion of the trajectory and expansion of exemption legislation after the Supreme Court's 1992 decision reaffirming *Roe*, see *Conscience Wars: Complicity-Based Conscience Claims in Religion and Politics, supra* note 1, at 2538–39. Notably, health-care refusal laws also expanded in terms of subject matter, from abortion and sterilization to contraception. See, *e.g.*, Act of Mar. 13, 1998, ch. 226, 1998 S.D. Sess. Laws 292, 293 (codified as amended at S.D. CODIFIED LAWS § 36–11–70 (2015)).

[20] See MISS. CODE ANN. § 41–107–3(a) (West 2016); ARK. CODE ANN. § 20–16–304 (West 2015); COLO. REV. STAT. ANN. § 25–6–102 (West 2015); FLA. STAT. ANN. § 381.0051 (West 2016); 745 ILL. COMP. STAT. § 70/4 (2014). Federal legislation allows providers to refuse to refer patients to alternative care. See Omnibus Consolidated Rescissions and Appropriations Act of 1996, Pub. L. No. 104–34, § 245(a), 110 Stat. 1321, 1321–245 (codified as amended at 42 U.S.C. § 238n (a) (2012)).

[21] There is debate among Catholic thinkers regarding the religious constraints on counseling and referral. See *Conscience Wars: Complicity-Based Conscience Claims in Religion and Politics, supra* note 1, at 2570 n. 222.

health-care refusal laws this chapter describes protect conscientious objection on a different model. Such laws provide conscience exemptions without providing for the needs of patients with different beliefs and may be understood as part of an effort to build a legal order that would restrict access to abortion services for all.

In losing the fight over same-sex marriage, conservatives have expressly invoked health-care refusal laws as a model for continuing the fight over same-sex marriage.[22] And political leaders have encouraged the faithful to seek religious exemptions as they mobilize against laws authorizing contraception, abortion, and same-sex marriage.[23]

Through this lens, one can see that in conflicts over abortion, contraception, and same-sex marriage, religious liberty claims offer a way to oppose emergent legal orders and newly protected rights.[24] Some proponents openly discuss the political goals of religious exemption claims. Considering exemptions in the contexts of reproductive health care and LGBT equality, Sherif Girgis explains that "political potency and moral stigma are *part of the point*."[25] Religious objections have grown to be such an integral part of a political debate that the *Washington Post* casually described conscience objections as if they simply expressed political disagreement, referring to "exemptions for religious believers, schools and corporations *to federal laws they disagree with, including LGBT and abortion rights laws*."[26]

Section II next considers how law responds to these claims.

---

[22] *See* Ryan T. Anderson, *Will Marriage Dissidents Be Treated as Bigots or Pro-Lifers?*, THE FEDERALIST (July 14, 2015), http://thefederalist.com/2015/07/14/will-marriage-dissidents-treated-bigots-pro-lifers/.

[23] *See, e.g.*, *Manhattan Declaration: A Call of Christian Conscience*, MANHATTAN DECLARATION (Nov. 2009), http://manhattandeclaration.org/man_dec_resources/Manhattan_Declaration_full_text.pdf. For extended treatment of this mobilization, *see Conscience Wars: Complicity-Based Conscience Claims in Religion and Politics, supra* note 1, at 2544–51.

[24] Those who oppose the law do not seek to engage in civil disobedience – defying the law as an act of political action and accepting the consequences. Rather, some seek conscience exemptions – that is, legal privileges not to comply with the law – as a means of disabling the law that they opposed as a political matter in recent democratic contests. *See* Robert Post, *The Politics of Religion: Afterword, in* THE CONSCIENCE WARS: RETHINKING THE BALANCE BETWEEN RELIGION, IDENTITY, AND EQUALITY (Susanna Mancini & Michel Rosenfeld eds., 2018).

[25] Sherif Girgis, *Nervous Victors, Illiberal Measures: A Response to Douglas NeJaime and Reva Siegel*, 125 YALE L.J. F. 399, 407 (2016), http://www.yalelawjournal.org/forum/nervous-victors-illiberal-measures. *See also* Ryan T. Anderson & Sherif Girgis, *Against the New Puritanism: Empowering All, Encumbering None, in* JOHN CORVINO, RYAN T. ANDERSON & SHERIF GIRGIS, DEBATING RELIGIOUS LIBERTY AND DISCRIMINATION 108, 170–71 (2017).

[26] Sarah Pulliam Bailey, *Many Religious Freedom Advocates Are Actually Disappointed with Trump's Executive Order*, WASH. POST (May 5, 2017) (emphasis added), https://www.washingtonpost.com/news/acts-of-faith/wp/2017/05/05/many-religious-freedom-advocates-are-disappointed-with-trumps-executive-order/?tid=ss_mail&utm_term=.o1d5befecec4.

II ACCOMMODATION AND THIRD-PARTY HARM: THE LAW

US law supports claims to religious accommodation, but imposes limits on such claims when the accommodation would inflict significant targeted harms on other citizens.

For some years, the Supreme Court interpreted the First Amendment's Free Exercise Clause to protect claimants seeking religious exemptions from laws of general application. In *Sherbert v. Verner*, the Court provided free exercise protection to a woman who had been denied unemployment compensation when she refused to accept a job because she observed Sabbath on Saturday.[27] In 1990, in *Smith*, the Court rejected this approach and ruled that a free exercise challenge to a generally applicable law merits only minimal constitutional scrutiny, unless the law targets or singles out religion.[28]

Displeased with the Court's decision to narrow protection for religious liberty, Congress passed RFRA. The statute allows persons to seek an exemption from federal laws that impose a substantial burden on religious exercise, but authorizes courts to reject their claims if judges find that enforcing the law without the sought-after exception is "the least restrictive means of furthering [a] compelling governmental interest."[29] Many states have enacted laws that mirror the federal RFRA.

In 2014, the Court interpreted RFRA expansively in *Hobby Lobby*.[30] Owners of a for-profit corporation sought a religious exemption from a federal law that required employers to include contraception in health insurance benefits for their employees.[31] The employers objected that complying with the law's insurance requirement would burden their religious exercise by making them complicit in their employees' use of contraceptive methods which the Food and Drug Administration (FDA) regulates as "contraception" and "birth control," but the employers' religion leads them to believe are abortifacients.[32] The Court ruled 5–4 in favor of the employers' religious conscience objections.[33]

Hobby Lobby allowed for-profit corporations to make claims for religious exemptions under RFRA and in other ways interpreted RFRA broadly. Even so, both Justice Anthony Kennedy's concurring opinion and the majority opinion in

---

[27] 374 U.S. 398, 403–05 (1963).
[28] 494 U.S. 872, 883–84 (1990).
[29] 42 U.S.C. § 2000bb-1(a) to (b) (2012).
[30] 134 S. Ct. 2751 (2014).
[31] *Id.* at 2754.
[32] *See id.* at 2760 ("The owners of the businesses have religious objections to abortion, and according to their religious beliefs the four contraceptive methods at issue are abortifacients."); *id.* at 2762–63 (discussing FDA regulation of the contraceptive methods as birth control). The dispute has many layers. For some of its legal, religious, scientific, and political dimensions, see *Conscience Wars: Complicity-Based Conscience Claims in Religion and Politics, supra* note 1, at 2582 n. 273.
[33] 134 S. Ct. at 2785.

Hobby Lobby suggest that courts are to consider harms to other citizens in evaluating exemption claims under RFRA.[34] The majority reasoned that because the government could provide the claimants' employees contraception without involving their employer, "[t]he effect of the ... accommodation on the women employed by Hobby Lobby ... would be precisely zero."[35] This concern with third-party harm as a limiting principle on religious accommodation reflected the reasoning of Justice Kennedy, who in a concurring opinion not only credited the government's compelling interest in protecting women's health but also expressed concern with the impact of the sought-after accommodation on female employees.[36]

Even if the Court was incorrect in its assumption that the accommodation would have "precisely zero" effect on Hobby Lobby's employees,[37] its reasoning demonstrates how third-party harm matters in analysis under RFRA. Although RFRA does not speak explicitly in the register of third-party harm, *Hobby Lobby* shows that third-party harm matters in determining whether unobstructed enforcement of the law is, in the language of RFRA, the "least restrictive means" of furthering "a compelling government interest."[38] If the government is pursuing a compelling interest and if religious accommodation would impose material or dignitary harm on the individuals protected by the law or otherwise undermine the societal interests the law promotes, then unimpaired enforcement of the law is likely the least restrictive means of furthering the government's compelling ends.[39]

A concern with third-party harm also shaped the Supreme Court's subsequent decision in *Zubik v. Burwell.*[40] The government had accommodated religiously affiliated nonprofits with religious objections to providing employee insurance benefits that covered contraception; those organizations needed to notify the

---

[34] *Id.* at 2779, 2786–87.

[35] *Id.* at 2760.

[36] *Id.* at 2751, 2787 (Kennedy, J., concurring). For analysis, see *Conscience Wars: Complicity-Based Conscience Claims in Religion and Politics, supra* note 1, at 2530–31.

[37] For commentators questioning the accuracy of the Court's premises, see Frederick Mark Gedicks, *One Cheer for* Hobby Lobby: *Improbable Alternatives, Truly Strict Scrutiny, and Third-Party Employee Burdens,* 38 HARV. J.L. & GENDER 153, 159–62 (2015); Andrew Koppelman & Frederick Mark Gedicks, *Is Hobby Lobby Worse for Religious Liberty Than Smith?,* 9 CATHOLIC ST. THOMAS J.L. & PUB. POL'Y 223, 234–39 (2015).

[38] *See Conscience Wars: Complicity-Based Conscience Claims in Religion and Politics, supra* note 1, at 2580–84.

[39] *See id.* at 2580–81 ("An antidiscrimination law can illustrate. In enacting an antidiscrimination law, legislators seek to provide the citizens the law protects equal access to employment, housing, and public accommodations and to ensure that they are treated with equal respect; legislators also seek to promote the growth of a more integrated and less stratified society. If granting a religious accommodation would harm those protected by the antidiscrimination law or undermine societal values and goals the statute promotes, then unencumbered enforcement of the statute is the least restrictive means of achieving the government's compelling ends. If, however, the government can accommodate the religious claimant in ways that do not impair pursuit of the government's compelling interests in banning discrimination, then RFRA requires the accommodation.").

[40] 136 S. Ct. 1557, 1561 (2016).

government of their objections, thus allowing the government to offer coverage to the organizations' employees through other entities.[41] Religiously affiliated nonprofits challenged this accommodation on grounds that it made them complicit in their employees receiving contraceptive coverage from alternative sources.[42] In essence, they objected to "triggering" an obligation on the government to furnish insurance benefits that included contraceptive coverage to employees.[43] In other words, they objected to the religious accommodation itself as a violation of their religious liberty. Instead, the religiously affiliated nonprofits sought a complete exemption from the health-care regulations. In fact, they argued to the Court that their employees should purchase their own (contraception-specific) insurance in the private market[44] – even though insurance of this kind is not available for purchase in the private market.

In response to these claims, the Court issued a *per curium* order remanding the cases to the lower courts in hopes of reaching a negotiated resolution.[45] In doing so, the Court reiterated *Hobby Lobby*'s concern with third-party harm. The parties, the Court instructed, should have "an opportunity to arrive at an approach going forward that accommodates petitioners' religious exercise while at the same time ensuring that women covered by petitioners' health plans 'receive full and equal health coverage, including contraceptive coverage.'"[46]

As *Hobby Lobby* and *Zubik* demonstrate, accommodation of complicity-based objections raises special concerns about third-party harm. Such accommodation expands the universe of potential objectors, from those directly involved to those who consider themselves indirectly involved in the objected-to conduct. The number of claimants may grow, especially in regions where majorities still oppose recently legalized conduct. Under these circumstances, barriers to access to goods and services may spread, and refusals may demean and stigmatize members of the community. Further, as *Zubik* demonstrates, complicity-based objections may be lodged against efforts to mediate the impact of religious objections on third parties. That is, the logic of complicity offers a ground on which to object to the very principle that limits religious accommodation to prevent third-party harm.

These concerns with third-party harm have intensified in the midst of the Trump administration's efforts to dismantle the Patient Protection and Affordable Care Act. In October 2017, federal agencies issued interim final rules on the coverage of contraception that break with the arrangements that the Court sanctioned in *Hobby*

---

[41] *Id.* at 1559.

[42] *See* Brief for Petitioners at 44, 51 Zubik v. Burwell, 136 S. Ct. 1557 (2016) (No. 15–35), 2016 WL 93988.

[43] *Id.* at 50.

[44] *See id.* at 75–76.

[45] *See* Zubik, 136 S. Ct. at 1559.

[46] 136 S. Ct. at 1560.

Lobby and *Zubik*.[47] In these cases the Court allowed employers religious accommodations under RFRA on the assumption that the government would provide the companies' employees with alternative access to contraception, so that the accommodation would have "zero" effect on the employees.[48] Here, in contrast, the rules proposed by the Trump administration offer objecting employers a complete exemption from the contraceptive requirements while doing nothing to ensure that their employees have access to the contraceptive coverage to which they are entitled.[49] Instead, the government dismissed concerns with third-party harm, asserting that contraception is "readily available" and that "contraceptive coverage may be available through State sources or family plans obtained through non-objecting employers."[50] The government simply assumed that women could gain access to contraception in other ways. This line of reasoning was advanced by the claimants in *Zubik* in their unsuccessful attempt to obtain a complete exemption,[51] and now the Trump administration has adopted it. In doing so, the administration has left women to fend for themselves and thus bear the significant costs of other citizens' religious beliefs – a position US religious liberties law ordinarily does not tolerate and the Court did not sanction under RFRA.[52]

The interim final rules not only furnish exemptions without ensuring that employees have access to contraception; they also allow a much wider range of objections than anything the Court sanctioned in *Hobby Lobby* or *Zubik*. While one rule offers "exemptions ... based on sincerely held religious beliefs,"[53] the other rule extends exemptions to employers with moral, rather than religious, objections.[54] Religious conservatives litigated *Hobby Lobby* and *Zubik* as claims for *religious*

---

[47] Religious Exemptions and Accommodations for Coverage of Certain Preventive Services Under the Affordable Care Act, 82 Fed. Reg. 47,792 (interim final rule Oct. 6, 2017); Moral Exemptions and Accommodations for Coverage of Certain Preventive Services Under the Affordable Care Act, 82 Fed. Reg. 47,838 (interim final rule Oct. 6, 2017).

[48] *See* Burwell v. Hobby Lobby Stores, Inc., 134 S. Ct. 2751, 2760 (2014).

[49] In this way, the new rules follow the model of health-care refusal laws. While a robust religious liberties tradition observed under the Constitution and RFRA (and Title VII) demonstrates concern with third-party harm in deciding whether and how to grant accommodations, health-care refusal laws deviate from this norm and commonly exempt institutions and persons from care obligations without efforts to mediate the impact of refusals on patients. For more on the distinction between these two regimes, see *Conscience Wars: Complicity-Based Conscience Claims in Religion and Politics*, *supra* note 1, at 2524–42.

[50] Religious Exemptions and Accommodations for Coverage of Certain Preventive Services Under the Affordable Care Act, 82 Fed. Reg. 47,792, 47,807 (interim final rule Oct. 6, 2017).

[51] Zubik v. Burwell, 136 S. Ct. 1557 (2016).

[52] The government's action has been challenged in court. *See, e.g.,* Complaint, ACLU v. Wright, Case No. 3:17–CV–05772 (N.D. Cal. 2017).

[53] Religious Exemptions and Accommodations for Coverage of Certain Preventive Services Under the Affordable Care Act, 82 Fed. Reg. 47,792, 47,808 (interim final rule Oct. 6, 2017).

[54] Moral Exemptions and Accommodations for Coverage of Certain Preventive Services Under the Affordable Care Act, 82 Fed. Reg. 47,838, 47,841 (interim final rule Oct. 6, 2017).

exemptions – part of their more general mobilization under the banner of faith.[55] As we have shown, religious arguments for exemptions in the contraceptive coverage setting in fact straddled the line between religion and politics.[56] Now, the interim final rules explicitly cover objections regardless of whether they derive from religious convictions. Those who oppose the contraceptive coverage requirements, even if their opposition does not spring from religious belief, can refuse to comply with the requirements.[57] As a general matter, one might believe that conscience protections should include ethical as well as religious beliefs. But on these facts, what could possibly be the government's interest in countenancing moral objections to women's use of contraception? Further, proceeding down this path undoubtedly expands the universe of potential objectors and, without a mechanism for mitigating third-party effects, is likely to obstruct enforcement of the law.

In accommodating both religious and moral objections and doing nothing to mediate the impact on third parties, the Trump administration's interim final rules follow the logic of the health-care refusals regime that has developed in the last several decades. That regime illustrates the problems that can arise when health-care refusal laws do not honor the principle of *Hobby Lobby* and *Zubik* limiting exemptions that inflict third-party harm. In certain regions of the country, the availability of abortion services is severely restricted and the practice remains stigmatized.[58] It is especially important to notice the material and dignitary harms inflicted by health-care refusal laws given that opponents of same-sex marriage hold up health-care refusals as a model for shaping law in the LGBT context.

III PLURALISM AND THE QUESTION OF CONSCIENCE

A classic justification for providing conscience exemptions is that protecting conscience facilitates a pluralist regime in which those with different moral outlooks may coexist.[59] But as illustrated by health-care refusal laws, as well as the Trump administration's recent action on insurance coverage for contraception, conscience exemptions do not always serve pluralist ends. Conscience exemptions can be deployed to enforce indirect restrictions on access that, for constitutional or political reasons, cannot be enforced directly. Religious claimants may speak as a minority and yet assert what have long been the norms of the majority against those whose rights the law has only recently and fragilely come to protect.

[55] Zubik v. Burwell, 136 S. Ct. 1557 (2016); Burwell v. Hobby Lobby Stores, Inc., 134 S. Ct. 2751 (2014).

[56] See *Conscience Wars: Complicity-Based Conscience Claims in Religion and Politics, supra* note 1, at 2542–65.

[57] Moral Exemptions and Accommodations for Coverage of Certain Preventive Services Under the Affordable Care Act, 82 Fed. Reg. at 47,841.

[58] For evidence of the "climate of extreme hostility to the practice of abortion" prevailing in Alabama, see Planned Parenthood v. Strange, 33 F. Supp. 3d 1330, 1334 (M.D. Ala. 2014).

[59] See, *e.g.*, Anderson & Girgis, *supra* note 25, at 147.

An accommodation regime's pluralism is measured, not only by its treatment of objectors, but also by its attention to protecting other citizens who do not share the objectors' beliefs. Exemption regimes that exhibit indifference to the impact of widespread exemptions on others do not promote pluralism; they sanction and promote the objectors' commitments.

The accommodation of religiously motivated conduct is commonly understood to be part of religious liberty, but in some legal systems, judges understand accommodation to protect the equality of religious practitioners as well as their liberty of conscience.[60] Considerations of equality arise when the polity is divided as to religious affiliation, with some faiths claiming many more members and much greater political authority than others.[61] Judges might ask whether in adopting a law of general application, the government has valued and respected the religious practices of minority faiths in the ways it values and respects the religious practices of majority faiths. In these circumstances, judges may understand religious accommodation as redressing the hostility or indifference of the majority to the minority.

Yet accommodating religion can also entrench inequality between groups. This is especially likely when claimants seek religious exemptions from laws that promote equality for racial minorities and other groups. This of course is the problem raised by claims seeking exemptions from laws that require businesses to serve LGBT individuals on a nondiscriminatory basis. Harm to those individuals protected by the equality mandate – here, LGBT citizens – may be a sufficient reason to deny the sought-after religious exemption. This is also the problem raised by claims seeking exemptions from laws that protect women's reproductive rights. In *Planned Parenthood v. Casey*, the Court recognized that "the ability of women to participate equally in the economic and social life of the Nation has been facilitated by their ability to control their reproductive lives."[62] Opposition to contraception and abortion may reflect traditional views about women's natural and proper role as mothers and can deprive women of control over the timing of motherhood in ways that impair "the ability of women to participate equally in the economic and social life of the Nation."[63]

---

[60] *See, e.g.*, Multani v. Comm'n Scolaire Marguerite-Bourgeoys, [2006] 1 S.C.R. 256, para. 79 (Can.) (ordering accommodation for the practices of a Sikh student, the court explained that "[a] total prohibition against wearing a kirpan to school undermines the value of this religious symbol and sends students the message that some religious practices do not merit the same protection as others," whereas providing an accommodation "demonstrates the importance that our society attaches to protecting freedom of religion and to showing respect for its minorities").

[61] *Cf.* Martha C. Nussbaum, Liberty of Conscience: In Defense of America's Tradition of Religious Equality 116 (2008).

[62] Planned Parenthood v. Casey, 505 U.S. 833, 856 (1992).

[63] *See* Neil S. Siegel & Reva B. Siegel, *Contraception as a Sex Equality Right*, 124 Yale L.J. F. 349, 349 (2015), http://www.yalelawjournal.org/forum/contraception-as-a-sex-equality-right; Reva B. Siegel, *Reasoning from the Body: A Historical Perspective on Abortion Regulation and Questions of Equal Protection*, 44 Stan. L. Rev. 261, 376–77 (1992).

IV CONCLUSION

Studying religious liberty claims proliferating in conflicts over reproductive health care and LGBT rights leads us to make a series of practical recommendations for courts and legislatures approaching questions of religious accommodation. First, it is important to take account of differences between religious liberty claims for ceremonial observance and religious liberty claims for exemptions from laws protecting abortion, contraception, and same-sex relationships. In cases of ritual observance, generally the claims do not focus on other citizens, and the costs of accommodation are minimal and spread across society.[64] In contrast, in cases involving reproductive health care and LGBT equality, the claims are focused on specific citizens courts and legislatures have acted to protect; and accommodation of the claims would harm those citizens. These differences are important to consider in deciding whether and how to accommodate the claims.

Second, and more concretely, considerations of third-party harm are critical in deciding whether and how to accommodate religious objections. Harm to other citizens may be a reason to deny religious accommodation. If it is not, it nonetheless should influence the shape of religious accommodation. Accommodations should be designed in ways that mitigate the impact on third parties. Here, both material and dignitary harms are relevant.[65] Citizens should be protected not only from deprivations of goods and services, but also from the stigma that refusals and denials can produce.[66] Put differently, accommodations should be structured in ways that (1) ensure access to goods and services, and (2) shield citizens from stigmatizing encounters.

---

[64] *See, e.g.,* Holt v. Hobbs, 135 S. Ct. 853 (2015); Employment Division v. Smith, 494 U.S. 872, 874 (1990); Sherbert, 374 U.S. at 409.

[65] Some have raised First Amendment objections to limiting religious exemptions based on the dignitary harm refusals inflict on other citizens. But, as Robert Post shows, this argument "would suggest that our entire tradition of antidiscrimination law is suspect under the First Amendment." Robert Post, *RFRA and First Amendment Freedom of Expression*, 125 YALE L.J. F. 387, 396 (2015), http://www.yalelawjournal.org/forum/rfra-and-first-amendment-freedom-of-expression. Post explains:

> A fundamental purpose of antidiscrimination law is to prevent "the deprivation of personal dignity that surely accompanies denials of equal access to public establishments." Because the law commonly conceptualizes the dignity of persons as dependent upon how they are regarded by others, legal efforts to uphold dignity typically have the purpose and effect of regulating conduct that transmits messages of disrespect. That is why antidiscrimination law characteristically prohibits conduct that creates social meanings associated with the stigmatization or stereotyping of protected groups.

Id. at 394 (quoting Heart of Atlanta Motel, Inc. v. United States, 379 U.S. 241, 250 (1964)) (quoting S. REP. No. 88–872, at 16–17 (1964)).

[66] *See* Joseph William Singer, *Religious Liberty and Public Accommodations: What Would Hohfeld Say?*, in WESLEY HOHFELD A CENTURY LATER: EDITED MAJOR WORKS, SELECT PERSONAL PAPERS, AND ORIGINAL COMMENTARIES (Shyam Balganesh et al. eds., forthcoming 2018).

Finally, and more generally, courts and legislatures entertaining claims for religious accommodation should consider whether providing the accommodation will promote equality or perpetuate inequality. Before granting religious objectors exemptions from laws designed to promote equality for groups of citizens who historically have been subject to discrimination, decision-makers must decide whether the exemptions will undermine protections provided by the law and frustrate its aim of bringing into being a more egalitarian society.

7

"The Devil Is in the Details"

On the Central Importance of Distinguishing the Truly Public from the Truly Private in Reconciling Equality and Religious Liberty

Ronald J. Krotoszynski, Jr.

In its 2016 report, *Peaceful Coexistence: Reconciling Nondiscrimination Principles with Civil Liberties*,[1] the US Commission on Civil Rights (Commission) argues, in very strong terms, for the primacy of nondiscrimination rules over religiously motivated conscience claims. The Commission explains that "[c]ivil rights protections ensuring nondiscrimination, as embodied in the Constitution, laws, and policies, are of preeminent importance in American jurisprudence."[2] And the Commission observes that "[r]eligious exemptions to the protections of civil rights based upon classifications such as race, color, national origin, sex, disability status, sexual orientation, and gender identity, when they are permissible, significantly infringe upon these civil rights."[3] These observations will strike many as accurate and unobjectionable – but they tell us little, nothing in fact, about how to go about reconciling the competing fundamental human rights and values of equality and freedom of conscience.

Unfortunately, the Commission does not seem interested in reconciling competing fundamental human rights; it seeks instead to restrict religiously motivated expressive conduct that falls afoul of existing nondiscrimination laws and policies. More specifically, to the extent that the federal Religious Freedom Restoration Act (RFRA) or state-law equivalents might offer a defense against violations of nondiscrimination laws and policies, the Commission asserts that such exemptions should be narrowly construed – or even legislatively abolished – to protect only religious belief rather than conduct. It advocates this approach in order to ensure that such enactments "do not unduly burden civil liberties and civil rights protections against

---

[1] U.S. COMM'N ON CIVIL RIGHTS, PEACEFUL COEXISTENCE: RECONCILING NONDISCRIMINA-TION PRINCIPLES WITH CIVIL LIBERTIES (2016).

[2] *Id.* at 25.

[3] *Id.*

status-based discrimination."[4] The Commission walks very close to the line of arguing that only belief – not conduct – should be protected in the context of public accommodation laws.[5]

Reconciling sincerely held religious convictions with federal, state, and local nondiscrimination laws cannot turn on a simplistic dichotomy between belief and conduct. This distinction has the potential effect of zeroing out protections for religious beliefs in any circumstance where a religious adherent attempts to share a religious belief with others. Taken to its logical conclusion, the belief/conduct dichotomy would permit a state government to punish actions taken to communicate religious belief.

For example, Marie and Gathie Barnette arguably engaged in "conduct" when they declined to participate in the Pledge of Allegiance.[6] West Virginia's Board of Education did not require the Barnette girls to affirm their subjective belief or agreement with the Pledge of Allegiance; it merely required them to say the words as part of a daily morning ritual. So, too, a ban on "covering" in public, so long as the ban applies to all women within the jurisdiction, at least arguably would constitute a regulation of "conduct" rather than "belief." Muslim women would be quite free to maintain the belief that they should cover their heads when in public; they would simply lack the discretion to engage lawfully in conduct consistent with this belief.

If we are intellectually honest, then we have to concede that compelling interests exist on both sides of the ledger when claims of religious freedom come into conflict with public accommodation statutes. Any workable framework for sorting out the relative priority of religious liberty and freedom from status-based forms of discrimination must take this basic fact fully and fairly into account. As Section I explains, the belief/conduct framework constitutes a very poor mechanism for sorting out such claims. A focus on either third-party harm or proportionality analysis also suffers from serious shortcomings.[7] Although no perfect framework exists, the public/private distinction presents the most promising available framing device for resolving these conflicts, as Section II explains. Section III offers preliminary thoughts on how the public/private distinction might be utilized to better resolve conflicts between equality and religious liberty. Section IV concludes.

---

[4] *Id.* at 27.

[5] *See id.* at 25–27; *see also id.* at 29 (Statement of Chairman Martin R. Castro) (positing that "[t]he phrases 'religious liberty' and 'religious freedom' will stand for nothing except hypocrisy so long as they remain code words for discrimination, intolerance, racism, sexism, homophobia, Islamophobia, Christian supremacy or any form of intolerance" and arguing that "[t]his generation of Americans must stand up and speak out to ensure that religion never again be twisted to deny others the full promise of America").

[6] West Virginia State Bd. of Educ. v. Barnette, 319 U.S. 624, 641–42 (1943).

[7] *See infra* notes 20–31 and accompanying text.

I THE SUBSTANTIAL SHORTCOMINGS OF THE BELIEF/CONDUCT, THIRD-PARTY HARM, AND PROPORTIONALITY ANALYSIS FRAMEWORKS

The belief/conduct dichotomy does not do much, if any, real work in separating claims for religious exemptions that possess significant merit from those that do not. Because the expression of religious beliefs will inevitably involve conduct, the use of a belief/conduct dichotomy does not afford much protection to religious belief. Indeed, restricting the scope of religious liberty laws, and even the Free Exercise Clause itself, to privately held beliefs renders them virtually meaningless. Absent an ability to read people's minds, government can never be certain what subjective beliefs a citizen does or does not hold. If religious freedom is limited to the sphere of subjective belief, it will cease to exist.

Consideration of general free speech cases makes this point very clearly – expressive conduct counts as "speech" and may not be regulated freely because it annexes the communication of viewpoints and ideas to action. Thus, in *Texas v. Johnson*, the US Supreme Court had no difficulty in finding that flag burning constitutes "speech" and that a state law ban on flag burning constituted an unconstitutional, viewpoint-based regulation of speech.[8] Justice William J. Brennan, Jr., writing for the majority, observed "that we have had little difficulty identifying an expressive element in conduct relating to flags should not be surprising" because "[t]he very purpose of a national flag is to serve as a symbol of our country."[9] Although Texas characterized the mistreatment of a US flag as conduct and not speech, the Supreme Court emphatically held that burning a flag at a protest plainly constitutes speech[10] and reaffirmed this ruling a year later in *United States v. Eichman*.[11]

Other cases are consistent with this approach. Wearing a jacket emblazoned with "Fuck the Draft" in a public building constitutes speech and not mere conduct.[12] Justice John Marshall Harlan swatted away the argument that Paul Cohen only engaged in conduct when wearing this jacket, wryly observing that "[t]he only 'conduct' which the State sought to punish is the fact of communication."[13] By way of contrast, Justice Harry Blackmun, writing in dissent, attempted to justify Cohen's prosecution and criminal conviction by arguing that "Cohen's absurd and immature antic, in my view, was mainly conduct and little speech."[14] He added, for

---

[8] 491 U.S. 397, 411–13 (1989).
[9] *Id.* at 405.
[10] *See id.* at 420; *see also* Spence v. Washington, 418 U.S. 405, 409–11 (1974).
[11] 496 U.S. 310, 315–18 (1990). On the First Amendment's protection of expressive conduct more generally, see United States v. O'Brien, 391 U.S. 367, 377 (1968).
[12] Cohen v. California, 403 U.S. 15, 16–18 (1971).
[13] *Id.* at 18.
[14] *Id.* at 27 (Blackmun, J., dissenting).

emphasis, that because Cohen engaged solely in unprotected conduct, "this Court's agonizing over First Amendment values seems misplaced and unnecessary."[15]

Individuals telegraph beliefs to others in large and small ways and do so constantly. What is more, individuals do this through conduct – through actions – as well as through words. The First Amendment's protection of expressive conduct as speech means that religiously motivated conduct constitutes an expression of belief.

Covering in order to honor a religious duty constitutes an expression of belief no less than burning a flag to protest the federal government's policies. Moreover, beliefs and actions are inextricably intertwined: Marie and Gathie Barnette not saying the Pledge of Allegiance; NFL 49ers quarterback Colin Kaepernik refusing to stand during the National Anthem and raising a "Black Power" fist after scoring a touchdown.[16] Any public expression of belief will involve conduct of some sort, rendering it potentially unprotected under the First Amendment if government may regulate conduct with a relatively free hand.

Another side of the coin exists, however, and must be taken into account. Any action can be characterized as an expression of belief and therefore beyond the legitimate regulatory power of the state. Civil society simply cannot exist if groups within society, including self-constituted communities of faith, may be essentially self-regulating – and can decide which laws they will observe and which laws they will disregard.[17] A position of absolute accommodation in the context of nondiscrimination laws also fails to credit fully and fairly the government's compelling interest in protecting members of minority groups from overt, often highly public, forms of discrimination.[18] As Justice Brennan explained in *Roberts v. United States Jaycees*, "acts of invidious discrimination in the distribution of publicly available goods, services, and other advantages cause unique evils that government has a compelling interest to prevent – wholly apart from the point of view such conduct may transmit," and, in consequence, "like violence or other types of potentially

---

[15] *Id.*

[16] Valerie Strauss, *A Lesson On The Free-Speech Debate Colin Kaepernick Started*, WASH. POST (Sept. 26, 2017), https://perma.cc/V3RR-TCMH.

[17] *See* Reynolds v. United States, 98 U.S. 145, 166–67 (1878) (observing that excusing a man's practices because they are contrary to his religious belief "would be to make the professed doctrines of religious belief superior to the law of the land, and in effect to permit every citizen to become a law unto himself. Government could exist only in name under such circumstances.").

[18] *See* Roberts v. United States Jaycees, 468 U.S. 609, 623–25, 628–29 (1984) (holding that application of the Minnesota Human Rights Act forbidding discrimination on basis of sex in "places of public accommodation" to the Jaycees, requiring them to admit women to local chapters in Minnesota, did not abridge male members' freedom of intimate or expressive association); Bob Jones Univ. v. United States, 461 U.S. 574, 575, 592–96 (1983) (upholding denial of tax-exempt status to a nonprofit private school that prescribed and enforced racially discriminatory admission standards on the basis of religious doctrine on the grounds that the school did not meet two common-law standards of a charity, "namely, that an institution seeking tax-exempt status must serve a public purpose and not be contrary to established public policy").

expressive activities that produce special harms distinct from their communicative impact, such practices are entitled to no constitutional protection."[19]

Permitting persons of faith to characterize any and all actions as manifestations of belief invites totalizing claims that would potentially render nugatory virtually all major civil rights enactments. For example, had complicity-based exemption claims enjoyed widespread cultural, political, and legal salience in the mid-1960s, Ollie's BBQ, in Birmingham, Alabama, could easily have justified operating its dining room on a racially segregated basis by invoking a religious basis for its racially discriminatory policies.[20] Other businesses across the Deep South would have adopted this strategy in quick succession, thereby utterly defeating Title II of the Civil Rights Act of 1964. Religiously based justifications for segregation were widespread in the South, both before and after the Civil War; indeed, advocates of human chattel slavery routinely justified the practice by invoking biblical references.[21]

In sum, the belief/conduct dichotomy will not provide clear, predictable answers in hard cases – an essential condition for securing peaceful coexistence. The Commission's understanding of "peaceful coexistence" requires unilateral surrender by those who seek to communicate their beliefs to others through their words and actions. At the same time, however, the dissenting commissioners are equally mistaken when they advocate sweeping exemptions to neutral laws of general applicability, notably including public accommodation laws.[22]

Some members of the contemporary Supreme Court have suggested that third-party harm demarks when a generalized protection for religious practice like RFRA should no longer provide a shield against a neutral law of general applicability that advances a compelling government interest.[23] Thoughtful legal academics also have

---

[19] Roberts, 468 U.S. at 628; *see also* Bob Jones Univ., 461 U.S. at 592 (observing that "there can no longer be any doubt that racial discrimination in education violates deeply and widely accepted views of elementary justice").

[20] *See generally* Katzenbach v. McClung, 379 U.S. 294, 296–98 (1964).

[21] *See* ALFRED L. BROPHY, UNIVERSITY, COURT, AND SLAVE: PRO-SLAVERY THOUGHT IN SOUTHERN COLLEGES AND COURTS AND THE COMING OF CIVIL WAR (2016); *see also* William N. Eskridge Jr., *Noah's Curse: How Religion Often Conflates Status, Belief, and Conduct to Resist Antidiscrimination Norms,* 45 GA. L. REV. 657, 665–72 (2011) (tracing the evolution of religious justifications for both slavery and Jim Crow, observing that "religious leaders ... deployed Bible-based arguments to support the notion that the Word of God sanctioned the slavery of Africans," notably including "Noah's Curse," which "provided an authorization for the enslavement of the descendants of Ham (Africans taken to the American colonies) to the descendants of Japheth (the English colonists)"). Professor Eskridge notes that "[e]ven after the Thirteenth Amendment, adopted in 1865, abolished slavery, some religious leaders continued to invoke biblical arguments for slavery, but increasingly, southern religious leaders modernized Noah's Curse to address the post-slavery environment." *Id.* at 669.

[22] U.S. COMM'N ON CIVIL RIGHTS, *supra* note 1, at 42 (Commissioner Peter Kirsanow's rebuttal); *id.* at 115 (Commissioner Gail Heriot's rebuttal).

[23] *See* Hobby Lobby v. Burwell, 134 S. Ct. 2751, 2799–2801 (2014) (Ginsburg, J., dissenting).

endorsed this approach, including Doug NeJaime and Reva Siegel in this volume.[24] Third-party harm is, admittedly, an attractive way of trying to draw the line between valid and invalid claims to religious accommodations. However, third-party harm presents its own pathologies.

As with the belief/conduct dichotomy, third-party harm is potentially a rather esoteric concept. Third-party harm often lies in the eye of the beholder. Virtually any religiously motivated conduct could be characterized as causing, or not causing, third-party harm. This is so because offense can be – and is – characterized as a third-party harm.[25] Justice John Paul Stevens, for example, characterized the profound offense that veterans experience when subjected to flag burning as a third-party harm sufficient to justify criminalizing flag burning.[26] So too, torts such as intentional infliction of emotional distress and intrusion upon seclusion use offense – outrageousness – as a basis for imposing civil liability.[27]

Consider once again a legislative ban on women covering their faces with headscarves. Localities in France that banned "burkinis" did not justify this legislation on the basis of hostility toward Islam, but rather on the basis of a perceived third-party harm.[28] The argument goes something like this: When women cover in public places, such as beaches, they convey a message of self-imposed gender subordination that conflicts with France's public policy of advancing the equality of the sexes; girls who see women covering in public are arguably harmed because they might internalize a message that it is appropriate for women to self-subordinate themselves in public. This concept of speech creating a third-party harm also explains the ban on Confederate battle flags at several SEC university stadiums; university administrators wish to avoid the infliction of third-party harms on those who experience not merely offense, but psychological harm, when exposed to this emblem synonymous with racist white power ideology.[29]

---

[24] *See* NeJaime & Siegel, Chapter 6; Douglas NeJaime & Reva B. Siegel, *Conscience Wars: Complicity-Based Conscience Claims in Religion and Politics*, 124 YALE L.J. 2516 (2015) [hereinafter *Conscience Wars*].

[25] Professors NeJaime and Siegel define "third party" harm in careful terms; this is not to suggest that the concept lacks *any* utility in deciding which claims to religious accommodation should be credited. *See id.* at 2519, 2529–33, 2580–86. Nevertheless, the concept is not self-defining and a broad definition of third-party harm would essentially require the rejection of all claims to accommodations.

[26] Texas v. Johnson, 491 U.S. 397, 437–39 (1989) (Stevens, J., dissenting).

[27] Snyder v. Phelps, 562 U.S. 443, 458–59 (2011); Hustler Magazine, Inc. v. Falwell, 485 U.S. 46, 54–55 (1988); RESTATEMENT (SECOND) OF TORTS § 652B (AM. LAW INST. 1977).

[28] *See generally* Asma T. Uddin, *Religious Modesty for Women and Girls: A Comparative Analysis of Legal Protections in France and the United States, in* THE CONTESTED PLACE OF RELIGION IN FAMILY LAW 308 (Robin Fretwell Wilson ed., 2018).

[29] *See, e.g.*, Bob Carlton, *Former Ole Miss Chancellor Talks About How Confederate Flag Ban Changed a Culture*, AL.COM (Oct. 29, 2013), https://perma.cc/Z3G3-SAVY.

To be sure, the First Amendment imposes limits on the ability of civil juries to impose liability for offensive or outrageous speech.[30] But even pure speech can engender liability without violating the First Amendment – a plaintiff may establish a hostile work environment claim based entirely on speech. To be actionable, the speech must create a pervasively oppressive environment. Nevertheless, speech that creates an environment intolerable to a reasonable woman, person of color, or religious believer may be proscribed.[31]

Because a broad application of a third-party harm doctrine could prohibit the expression of beliefs that are offensive to others, drawing a line using a theory of third-party harm risks providing insufficient protection for the public expression of religious belief. For example, a polity strongly committed to full marriage equality could deem public expressions of support for the traditional, heterosexual nuclear family to constitute impermissible hate speech that produces an unacceptable risk of imposing third-party harm on families helmed by a same-sex couple. If a business posts a sign saying "We Support Traditional Family Values," but also serves all comers on identical terms, liability for a constructive denial of service should not exist. But if the state deems the public expression of support for traditional heterosexual families to demean or marginalize nontraditional families, thereby producing third party harm, a government civil rights agency could impose liability for nothing more than the public expression of a religiously motivated, sincerely held belief.[32]

If third-party harm is to work as a means of cabining the scope of religious accommodations, the universe of harms to be recognized must be limited to avoid potentially creating liability for the public expression of religious ideas and beliefs. The kinds of third-party harm that justify withholding religious accommodations need to be defined with particular care so as to provide sufficient breathing room for speech and expressive conduct. Thus, although plainly preferable to the belief/conduct dichotomy, using third-party harm as a framing device will not reliably produce clear answers in hard cases.

---

[30] *See Snyder*, 562 U.S. at 458–61 (prohibiting liability against the Westboro Baptist Church for outrageously offensive speech involving a targeted funeral protest of a dead soldier killed while on active duty). Justice Samuel Alito would have permitted the civil jury verdict against Westboro Baptist Church to stand. *See id.* at 463 (Alito, J., dissenting).

[31] *See Meritor Savings Bank v. Vinson*, 477 U.S. 57, 64–68, 72 (1986). Some First Amendment scholars object to hostile work environment liability precisely because it can create civil liability for speech alone. Kingsley R. Browne, *Title VII as Censorship: Hostile-Environment Harassment and the First Amendment*, 52 Ohio St. L.J. 481 (1991); Eugene Volokh, *How Harassment Law Violates Free Speech*, 47 Rutgers L. Rev. 563 (1995).

[32] *But cf.* U.S. Comm'n on Civil Rights, *supra* note 1, at 25–27 (proposing a scope of liability under federal and state nondiscrimination laws that would arguably encompass mere statements of religious belief if those statements arguably reflect discriminatory viewpoints); *id.* at 29 (Statement of Chairman Martin R. Castro) (arguing that discriminatory points of view should not be tolerated and that "any form of intolerance" should be subject to government regulation).

Proportionality analysis, a widely adopted device in much of the democratic world, might seem a promising approach to reconciling equality principles with religious liberty.[33] Proportionality analysis requires a rights claimant to invoke the right successfully at step one and then permits the entity violating the right to attempt to justify the burden at step two.[34] If a burden or restriction on the exercise of a right advances sufficiently important goals and objectives, the regulation may be applied even though it burdens a fundamental right (such as freedom of conscience). In Canada, South Africa, and the jurisprudence of the European Court of Human Rights, proportionality analysis is entirely quotidian.[35]

An obvious problem exists with adopting proportionality analysis as a sorting mechanism: proportionality analysis will not produce predictable results across a wide range of disputes. The relative equities of a person seeking to invoke rights of conscience to deny service and a person seeking to obtain services free and clear of targeted discrimination are highly subjective. Within this volume, for example, some would weight the interests of religious objectors more heavily, whereas others would see burdens upon them as in service of more pressing values.[36] This subjectivity has particularly pernicious implications for religious liberty claims because members of unpopular or "oddball" religious sects will find their claims routinely rejected whereas similar claims brought by members of more culturally familiar religions will prevail.[37] Thus, proportionality analysis too often will redound to the detriment of unpopular religious minorities when government agencies and courts seek to reconcile demands for specific accommodations with the imperatives of generally applicable nondiscrimination rules. Further, as Americans increasingly move away from organized religion, even more mainstream sects may find their interests given short shrift.[38] In the end, then, proportionality analysis is too openended and subjective to provide a workable solution.

However, the public/private distinction, the application of which involves a more limited form of proportionality analysis, might provide a workable solution. The analysis would not involve separating belief from conduct, or assessing third-party harm, but rather would seek to disentangle the truly public from the truly private. Self-constituted communities of faith are inherently private in nature and should not be subject to pervasive forms of state regulation – even to advance a cause as

---

[33] *See* Vicki C. Jackson, *Constitutional Law in the Age of Proportionality*, 124 YALE L.J. 3094, 3096 (2015); Vicki C. Jackson, *Being Proportional About Proportionality*, 21 CONST. COMMENT. 803, 804–07 (2004).

[34] *See* R. v. Oakes, [1986] 1 S.C.R. 103, 135–40 (Can.); *see also* DAVID M. BEATTY, THE ULTIMATE RULE OF LAW 163–68 (2004).

[35] RONALD J. KROTOSZYNSKI, JR., PRIVACY REVISITED: A GLOBAL PERSPECTIVE ON THE RIGHT TO BE LEFT ALONE 148–50 (2016).

[36] *See* Laycock, Chapter 3; Smith, Chapter 18; Melling, Chapter 19.

[37] *See* Ronald J. Krotoszynski, Jr., *"If Judges Were Angels": Religious Equality, Free Exercise, and the (Underappreciated) Merits of Smith*, 102 Nw. U.L. REV. 1189, 1235–43, 1261–62 (2008).

[38] *See generally* PEW RESEARCH CTR., AMERICA'S CHANGING RELIGIOUS LANDSCAPE (2015).

important as equality.[39] The structure of the federal Civil Rights Act and state nondiscrimination laws reflect this supposition, routinely leaving aside private clubs and associations.[40] On the other hand, however, status-based denials of service based on one's identity are stigmatizing and degrading; members of minority groups should not be taken by surprise at the grocery store checkout line. This approach, as explained later in this chapter, would involve a careful, contextual analysis of the fundamental nature of the entity seeking an exception from a nondiscrimination law or policy.

II TOWARD A MORE WORKABLE FRAMEWORK BASED ON THE PUBLIC/PRIVATE DISTINCTION

Drawing an effective boundary line requires a framing device that does real work – that permits the predictable sorting of claims that justify an exemption from those that do not. Predictability and ease of application are necessary attributes because in this context, uncertainty will produce severe chilling effects on the expression of religious belief.[41] It also leaves minorities vulnerable to unexpected, and stigmatizing, denials of service at businesses that ostensibly serve all comers. Thus, discretion needs to be constrained in both directions – and constrained in predictable ways.[42] The question then becomes: What means would best permit the sorting of claims in a predictable way?

Case law involving more general freedom of association claims provide a doctrinal framework that could be redeployed in the context of religious accommodation claims – whether brought under the Free Exercise Clause itself or a RFRA-type

---

[39] Hosanna-Tabor Evangelical Lutheran Church & School v. EEOC, 565 U.S. 171, 188–93 (2012); JOHN D. INAZU, LIBERTY'S REFUGE: THE FORGOTTEN FREEDOM OF ASSEMBLY 13, 167–76, 185–86 (2012) (arguing that private, noncommercial self-constituted groups should enjoy a broad freedom to choose their fellow travelers even using discriminatory metrics).

[40] *See, e.g.,* 42 U.S.C. § 12187 (2017); WIS. STAT. § 106.52(3)(e) (2015).

[41] If a reasonable person does not know when she can invoke the First Amendment as a shield against liability for violating a nondiscrimination law, the prudent response would be to self-censor speech and behavior to avoid incurring civil liability. The interest in clear rules that produce predictable results also benefits those protected by nondiscrimination enactments; clear rules would permit members of protected minority groups to avoid the embarrassment or humiliation that accompanies a denial of service based on their identity. Clear rules regarding the scope of exemptions thus redound to the benefit of both religionists and minority group members.

[42] To be sure, predictability is not an absolute value in and of itself – after all, "predictability" could be achieved by adopting a legal rule that ignores either nondiscrimination or religious liberty values by zeroing out completely one interest or the other. This would not constitute a just or reasonable approach – but it would certainly advance the cause of predictability. Nevertheless, in the context of setting a principled and reasonable balance, predictability constitutes a signal virtue (and not a vice) because it permits both religious believers and members of minority communities to make informed decisions about how to live their lives in ways that maximize their autonomy and freedom.

statute. Decisions such as *Roberts v. United States Jaycees*[43] and *New York State Club Association*[44] would parse claims on the basis of the nature of the institutions seeking to claim an accommodation from a generally applicable nondiscrimination rule. Under the constitutional logic of these precedents, institutions that do not hold themselves out as open and available to the general public possess a considerably stronger claim to operate in idiosyncratic ways than institutions (whether religious in character or not) that purport to be open and available to any and all persons.[45] To state the matter in another way, if exclusion is essential to the identity of an institution and to its very *raison d'être*, then its rules and behavior should reflect these facts. A society of cloistered nuns does not typically operate a hamburger stand on the public square – or provide the general public with unfettered access to its convent. A McDonald's restaurant or Walmart store, by way of contrast, goes out of its way to signal "we are open to and will serve anyone who wishes to buy our goods." These, then, constitute the two poles of the truly private (a cloistered convent) and the truly public (a McDonald's restaurant or Walmart store).

The public/private distinction aligns nicely with the animating purposes and goals of nondiscrimination laws. When a religious organization denies nonadherents access to its rites, the exclusion does not impose a dignitarian harm; it does not stigmatize. The fact that exclusion based on nonmembership in a faith community is nontargeted prevents or, at the least, significantly muffles the dignitarian harm; even if all members of a particular minority are excluded from membership in a church, a great number of nonminorities are excluded as well. Sussing out the precise reasons for exclusion involves a considerably more complex analysis than when a store otherwise open to the general public displays a sign stating that it will not serve LGBT persons (where the only explanation can be animus). Alternatively, to the extent that exclusions from membership in a religious community might be stigmatizing in some respects, society reflexively deems the social harm justified in the name of permitting the self-constituted community of faith to maintain the tenets of its faith.[46]

The harms that public accommodation laws seek to forestall are dignitarian in nature, namely the unfair surprise of finding that one's money will not spend in a store otherwise open to everyone else. As Chief Justice Earl Warren explained in *Brown v. Board of Education*,[47] status-based discrimination, in the form of exclusion,

---

[43] 468 U.S. 609, 623–29 (1984).

[44] New York State Club Ass'n, Inc. v. City of New York, 487 U.S. 1, 12–14 (1988).

[45] Of course, one could object that conduct motivated by religious conviction is special and merits a broader scope of protection than conduct motived by an economic, scientific, moral, ideological, or political belief. This objection, however, relates more to the strength of the private interest than to the potential utility of using the public/private distinction as the appropriate doctrinal framework for sorting religious accommodation claims.

[46] *Hosanna-Tabor Evangelical Lutheran Church & School*, 565 U.S. at 188–90, 194–96.

[47] 347 U.S. 483 (1954).

is humiliating and imposes serious psychological harms.[48] Deterring and remediating harms of this sort constitute the lodestar of our nondiscrimination laws.

Denials of service in places and spaces generally open to the public are inherently stigmatizing;[49] on the other hand, however, denials of service by entities that are not generally open to any and all comers are not. Whether framed in terms of a lack of dignitarian harm or in terms of the legitimate autonomy claims of a faith community, the religious group's claim to be free from government regulation trumps the interest of a person excluded based on her identity or beliefs.[50] A concrete example will help to demonstrate the relevant distinction.

If a person applies to teach at a madrassa (or Islamic religious academy), and she is not Muslim, she should not be surprised to have her application for a teaching position rejected. The Court in *Hosanna-Tabor Evangelical Lutheran Church & School v. EEOC* embraced the logic of this position, in the form of a ministerial exemption for instructional staff at a church-operated school.[51] Consistent with an approach that exempts truly private entities from general nondiscrimination laws, an accommodation for employment-related policies should be extended beyond the teaching staff to all positions in the school – even the custodial staff. A community of faith operating a school should be able to employ a staff that shares the faith-commitment that the school exists to inculcate and advance.[52]

Nor should the nature of the screening device – discrimination – matter. When a pervasively religious private entity screens for coreligionists, a wide variety of

[48] *Id.* at 494 ("To separate them from others of similar age and qualifications solely because of their race generates a feeling of inferiority as to their status in the community that may affect their hearts and minds and minds in a way unlikely ever to be undone."); *see* Chai Feldblum, *Moral Conflict and Conflicting Liberties, in* SAME-SEX MARRIAGE AND RELIGIOUS LIBERTY: EMERGING CONFLICTS 123, 153 (Douglas Laycock, et al. eds., 2008) (arguing that status-based denials of service impose significant psychological harms); NeJaime & Siegel, *Conscience Wars, supra* note 24, at 2566–78 (documenting the harms associated with excusing general legal obligations, such as nondiscrimination rules, based on the concept of complicity).

[49] Regents of the Univ. of Cal. v. Bakke, 438 U.S. 265, 324, 361–62, 374 (1978) (Brennan, J., concurring in part and dissenting in part) (arguing that "any statute must be stricken that stigmatizes any group or that singles out those least well represented in the political process," even if the statute was intended to benefit members of minority groups who suffered from legally sanctioned discrimination in the past); United Jewish Orgs. v. Carey, 430 U.S. 144, 173–74 (1977) (Brennan, J., concurring) (positing that when an affirmative action program has the effect of stigmatizing those it seeks to benefit, it violates the Equal Protection Clause).

[50] *See* Ira C. Lupu & Robert W. Tuttle, *The Mystery of Unanimity in* Hosanna-Tabor Evangelical Lutheran Church & School v. EEOC, 20 LEWIS & CLARK L. REV. 1265, 1280–92 (2017).

[51] *Hosanna-Tabor Evangelical Lutheran Church & School*, 565 U.S. at 194–96; *see* Lupu & Tuttle, *supra* note 50, at 1280–84.

[52] Whether Title VII's protections allowing religious employers and universities to hire on the basis of religion authorizes them to legally make religiously based distinctions that implicate collateral protected grounds such as sex, or relatedly, sexual orientation or gender identity, is the subject of considerable debate. *See generally* Robin Fretwell Wilson, *Squaring Faith and Sexuality in Religious Institutions: The Unique Challenge of Sports*, 34 L. & INEQ. 385 (2016).

characteristics and attributes could potentially lead to targeted forms of exclusion – for example, a promiscuous heterosexual lifestyle could be a basis for rejection, just as a total lack of interest in procreative marital sex might be a basis for exclusion from employment. Some forms of exclusion might be based on behavior; others might be based entirely on mere status. For example, if a religious sect took seriously "Noah's Curse,"[53] it might exclude people of color from membership. This would be stigmatizing to those excluded, but the alternative would be for the state to regulate the rules of membership for churches. Such an outcome simply cannot be reconciled with a meaningful commitment to the freedom of religious belief.[54]

Under the logic that the state may extirpate any and all forms of discrimination, religious organizations could be forced to violate core doctrines of the faith – for example, the Roman Catholic Church's absolute reservation of the sacrament of Holy Orders (*i.e.*, consecration as a priest) to men.[55] Such an outcome should be, if not unthinkable, then close to it in a society that purports to enshrine freedom of conscience as a core human rights value.

Accordingly, a self-constituted community of faith, hiring for a church, temple, or mosque, or a school annexed to a church, temple, or mosque, should be able to use religiously motivated metrics to hire and fire its staff. Aren't all religious beliefs entitled to equal respect and concern?[56] To validate some screening rules but not others is to validate some religions but not others. An institutional analysis that asks whether the enterprise is entitled to an exemption from public accommodation laws avoids the embarrassment, and constitutional infirmity, of deciding which religious commitments merit respect and consideration – and which do not.

---

[53] *See* Eskridge, *supra* note 21, at 665–78 (discussing "Noah's Curse" and its commonplace use to defend and support the maintenance of human chattel slavery and also *de jure* and *de facto* forms of racial segregation in the United States).

[54] *See* United States v. Ballard, 322 U.S. 78, 94–95 (1944) (Jackson, J., dissenting) (arguing for absolute constitutional protection for religious beliefs, however benighted or bizarre from the perspective of the dominant religious sects within the community, because freedom of even offensive or outlandish religious belief "is precisely the thing the Constitution put beyond the reach of the prosecutor, for the price of freedom of religion or of speech or of the press is that we must put up with, and even pay for, a good deal of rubbish" and cautioning that an alternative approach, permitting government to regulate religious beliefs, "easily could degenerate into religious persecution").

[55] *See* Ronald J. Krotoszynski, Jr., The First Amendment in Cross-Cultural Perspective: A Comparative Legal Analysis of the Freedom of Speech 99 (2006) (noting that the abolition of the state action doctrine could lead to efforts to enforce the Equal Protection Clause against entities such as the Roman Catholic Church, and federal courts "would be required to weigh [a group] of nuns' interest in being free of gender discrimination against [the local] bishop's interest in enforcing the doctrines of the Roman Catholic Church regarding the sacrament of Holy Orders").

[56] *See Ballard*, 344 U.S. at 93–95 (Jackson, J., dissenting) (arguing for the robust constitutional protection of even highly unorthodox and controversial religious beliefs and positing that under the Free Exercise Clause, the federal courts should scrupulously avoid the "business of judicially examining other people's faiths").

In sum, denials of service by intrinsically and pervasively *private* entities do not demean or stigmatize those denied service in the same way, or to the same degree, as denials of service by entities open to the public. Denials of service by entities that hold themselves out as generally open to any and all persons impose serious dignitarian harms. Thus, the relevant questions that must be asked and answered are: (1) To what extent does the entity or business hold itself out as open to all comers?; and alternatively, (2) To what extent does it telegraph, "We choose our fellow travelers"? An entity that holds itself out as private should be entitled to claim exemptions from public accommodation enactments; by way of contrast, an entity generally open to the public should not.[57]

One should bear in mind that the public or private character of an entity should not be a function of its physical location. Instead, the character or nature of the actor should determine its public or private status. We need to think of "public" and "private" in associational, not physical, terms. For example, a K–12 school operated by a religious community is private, even if the school building sits on the town's main public square. A small bookstore in a Catholic cathedral is private, not public. By way of contrast, a McDonald's fast-food restaurant or Books-A-Million store is public, as are an Olan Mills photography studio and an Arthur Murray dance school.[58]

Of course, hard cases will exist. Could a Catholic hospital refuse to recognize a same-sex couple as the parents of a newborn? Or could the hospital treat a same-sex spouse as a third party for all intents and purposes, including visitation privileges? Refusing to credit a legally valid civil marriage is likely a bridge too far, particularly if the hospital operates an emergency room or participates in preferred provider networks and so receives patients who do not make a conscious choice to patronize

---

[57] Ronald J. Krotoszynski, Jr., *Agora, Dignity, and Discrimination: On the Constitutional Shortcomings of "Conscience" Laws That Promote Inequality in the Public Marketplace*, 20 Lewis & Clark L. Rev. 1221, 1234–39 (2017) [hereinafter *Agora*].

[58] By definition, a business operated on a franchised basis will never possess the characteristics necessary to render it "private." After all, the owners have ceded control over central aspects of the business to a third party, with the expectation that the business will be operated in lockstep fashion with others operating under the same brand name. Ceding control of the manner in which a business operates to a third party severely undermines an owner's (franchisee's) claim that her business operation constitutes an exercise in highly personalized expressive conduct. Even franchise operations, such as Chick-fil-A, that tend to attract co-venturers that maintain a common religious, political, or ideological sensibility, invariably require franchisees to follow a set template for their operations. Moreover, the principal objective is to win sales – rather than converts. *See* Timothy Egan, *Conscience of a Corporation*, N.Y. Times (Apr. 3, 2015), http:// nyti.ms/1MJrdBT (noting that Chick-fil-A has a corporate nondiscrimination policy with respect to sexual orientation that it adopted "[a]fter condemning same-sex marriage and becoming a culture-war battleground"). In this regard, it bears noting the Chick-fil-A corporate policy prohibits status-based discrimination by franchisees; Chick-fil-A serves anyone and everyone with cash in hand to make a purchase. *See* Krotoszynski, *Agora*, *supra* note 57, at 1257–58 n.141. Moreover, "there are no reported incidents of Chick-fil-A seeking to discriminate against LGBT customers or employees." *Id.* at 1258 n.141.

the facility.[59] Moreover, many states regulate the provision of medical services, requiring a certificate of need in order to open a new health care facility. When the state limits market entry, and vests a license with a pervasively discriminatory service provider, the actions have the effect of denying access to goods and services to those the enterprise will not serve.[60]

III SOME PRELIMINARY THOUGHTS ON DEPLOYING THE PUBLIC/ PRIVATE DISTINCTION TO RESOLVE CONFLICTS BETWEEN EQUALITY AND RELIGIOUS LIBERTY

The public/private distinction constitutes the most promising route to peaceful coexistence. It is not possible to work out all the details – the bells and whistles – in this short chapter. Nevertheless, it is possible to sketch out some first principles and to address a few potential objections.

First, religious belief should be vigorously protected, whether as a matter of constitutional or statutory law, and should include conduct intended to convey religious belief. This protection should extend to conduct in public spaces and places. Protection of belief also should require searching consideration of laws and the application of laws potentially motivated by animus toward a faith community.[61]

Second, a McDonald's or Jiffy Lube should not be permitted to post "We Do Not Serve Homosexuals" signs in their businesses even if the owners wish to refuse service to LGBT customers because of a sincerely held religious belief.[62] State "conscience" laws, such as Mississippi's H.B. 1523, would permit businesses open to the public to engage in comprehensive forms of discrimination.[63] Efforts of this sort to attach formal legal sanction to targeted forms of discrimination by businesses open to the public violate the Equal Protection Clause.[64] The state's ability to authorize third-party harms through positive law is not infinite and the state must

---

[59] There is clearly no "implied consent" when a person suffering a medical emergency is transported to a religiously identified trauma center. *Cf.* Helfand, Chapter 11; Michael A. Helfand, *Religious Institutionalism, Implied Consent, and the Value of Voluntarism*, 88 S. Cal. L. Rev. 539 (2015).

[60] Moose Lodge No. 107 v. Irvis, 407 U.S. 163, 182–83 (1972) (Douglas, J., dissenting) (arguing that "state-enforced scarcity of licenses" implicates the Equal Protection Clause when such licenses are vested with discriminatory service providers).

[61] *See generally* Church of the Lukumi Babalu Aye, Inc. v. City of Hialeah, 508 U.S. 520 (1993).

[62] *See* Inazu, *supra* note 39, at 13 (positing that "antidiscrimination norms should typically prevail when applied to commercial entities"). *But cf.* Douglas Laycock, *Afterword, in* Same-Sex Marriage and Religious Liberty, *supra* note 48, at 198–200 (advocating the posting of signs in commercial businesses indicating to the public that a business does not serve LGBT customers).

[63] Krotoszynski, *Agora*, *supra* note 57, at 1225–26, 1239–45.

[64] *Id.* at 1245–49.

not seek to do indirectly that which the Equal Protection Clause forbids it to do directly.[65]

Third, the availability of exemptions for religiously motivated denials of service should depend, at least in part, on the reasonableness of the refusal of service taken in context – much as free association claims turn on the entity that seeks to invoke the First Amendment as a shield clearly establishing a link between the association's core reasons for existing and the exemption it seeks from a nondiscrimination law.[66] To what extent does the entity seeking the exemption telegraph that it picks and chooses those it will serve based on the precepts of a particular faith tradition? The question of surprise – of ambush – should be front and center in this contextual analysis. When a business signals that it is open to any and all persons, it is a "public" enterprise and should be subject to comprehensive regulation that promotes the health, safety, welfare, and morals of the community.[67]

Fourth, and finally, the requisite analytical exercise should bear some resemblance to ferreting out state action. The state action doctrine uses a careful, context-sensitive approach to identify the circumstances that justify treating an ostensibly private entity as the state itself – and imposing constitutional obligations on the entity as a consequence. The federal courts inquire into the nature of the activity at issue (is it an exclusive government function, like conducting elections for public office, that the government has delegated to an ostensibly private entity?), the interrelationship of the government and the ostensibly private entity (a coffee shop operating in a county courthouse building stands on different state action ground than a coffee shop not located in a government edifice), whether the government has encouraged behavior that it cannot directly command via regulation

---

[65] *See* Reitman v. Mulkey, 387 U.S. 369, 372–77, 380–81 (1967); *see also* NeJaime & Siegel, *Conscience Wars, supra* note 24, at 2519 (noting that laws creating broad, complicity-based exemptions "are explicitly oriented toward third parties, [and] they present special concerns about third-party harm").

[66] Boy Scouts of America v. Dale, 530 U.S. 640 (2000); Hurley v. Irish-American Gay, Lesbian & Bisexual Group of Boston, 515 U.S. 557 (1995); New York State Club Ass'n, Inc. v. City of New York, 487 U.S. 1 (1988); *see* INAZU, *supra* note 39, at 175 (arguing that although "there is much to be said for an antidiscrimination norm and the value of equality that underlies it," we must also keep in mind that "our constitutionalism also recognizes values other than equality, including a meaningful pluralism that permits diverse groups to flourish within our polity").

[67] Of course, nothing requires a bakery otherwise open to the public to sell personalized wedding cakes to anyone. If a business owner wishes to limit the goods or services that she offers to the public because of her religious beliefs – and to do so comprehensively – nondiscrimination laws should not come into play. We do not have a legal or social history, save in highly regulated industries, such as health care, of regulating a business's scope of operation. Thus, a photographer could decline to shoot *any* weddings – and such a policy should not run afoul of local, state, or federal nondiscrimination enactments. Similarly, if an adherent of Islam operates a bodega, but declines to stock and sell any pork products, that decision should not be subject to second-guessing by the government. Simply put, not offering a particular good or service to *anyone* is not stigmatizing in the same way as targeted denials of access to goods and services and, therefore, should be entirely lawful even for a business open to the general public.

(for example, encouraging private property owners to discriminate on the basis of race when selling or renting real property), and whether, in the totality of the circumstances, the ostensibly private entity is sufficiently "entwined" with the government to render it an alter ego of the state (does the government have a significant measure of control over the entity and lend it targeted forms of support not typically provided to nongovernmental institutions?).[68]

State action analysis is highly fact-specific and relies on context – including whether a reasonable observer would perceive the ostensibly private entity as an instrument of the state itself.[69] It also bears noting that state action rules, although holistic and highly contextual, are sufficiently clear and predictable that an entity that wishes to avoid the risk of state actor status can easily do so by carefully limiting its connections with the government and avoiding undertaking tasks, such as running a prison or tax collection, that are the exclusive prerogatives of the state.

The state action doctrine exists to ensure that government does not slip the bounds of constitutional constraints, but it also seeks to preserve and protect a sphere of private autonomy, a realm that exists free and clear of the constitutional limitations applicable to the government.[70] In the context of reconciling religious liberty with nondiscrimination principles, the objectives are quite similar, but not identical. The legal system should seek simultaneously to safeguard a realm of private religious autonomy and also to ensure that a dollar may be spent as easily in an LGBT or racial minority person's hands as in anyone else's.

In this regard, it bears noting that complicity claims generally should be rejected when based on religious motives, just as the Supreme Court has rejected them in a more generalized First Amendment context. In *Rumsfeld v. Forum for Academic and*

---

[68] *See* Ronald J. Krotoszynski, Jr., *Back to the Briarpatch: An Argument in Favor of Constitutional Meta-Analysis in State Action Determinations*, 94 MICH. L. REV. 302, 314–21, 337–46 (1995).

[69] *See* Burton v. Wilmington Parking Auth., 365 U.S. 715, 722 (1961) (holding that the federal courts must "sift facts" and "weigh circumstances" in order to ferret out "nonobvious" forms of state action); *see also* Krotoszynski, *supra* note 68, at 334–37, 342 (emphasizing the importance of a searching and contextual analysis when making state action determinations and observing that "[o]nly by expanding the state action inquiry – thereby requiring the lower federal courts to cast their analytical nets more broadly – can actions 'fairly attributable to the State' be identified accurately").

[70] Brentwood Acad. v. Tennessee Secondary Sch. Athletic Ass'n, 531 U.S. 288, 295–96 (2001) (observing that "[w]hat is fairly attributable is a matter of normative judgment, and the criteria lack rigid simplicity" and holding that "no one fact can function as a necessary condition across the board for finding state action; nor is any set of circumstances absolutely sufficient, for there may be some countervailing reason against attributing activity to the government"); *Burton*, 365 U.S. at 722 ("Only by sifting facts and weighing circumstances can the nonobvious involvement of the State in private conduct be attributed its true significance."); *see* Krotoszynski, *supra* note 68, at 335, 346 (noting that the state action doctrine "preserves a sphere of individual freedom of action, a freedom of action that would be reduced significantly were the Supreme Court to jettison the doctrine in favor of some sort of ad hoc rights balancing" and positing that the state action doctrine "permits courts to hold government accountable and protects the freedom of individual citizens to make fundamental decisions about their economic, social, religious, and personal relationships").

Institutional Rights, Inc. (FAIR),[71] the Supreme Court unanimously held that FAIR's claim that permitting military recruiters on campus forced them to be complicit in discrimination against gay and lesbian persons lacked merit.[72] The law schools comprising FAIR had argued that permitting the military to interview on campus, when the "Don't Ask, Don't Tell" policy was in effect, would violate their polices against discrimination based on LGBT status and render them complicit in such discrimination. In this context, however, the deeply held conviction that discrimination against LBGT persons is morally wrong had little, if any, traction. Chief Justice John G. Roberts, Jr., squarely rejected the complicity argument – as did all of the other justices.

The Supreme Court characterized the mandatory access provision as a regulation of conduct and a condition of government largesse – which a university could elect to reject if it wished to avoid the conduct regulation.[73] As Chief Justice Roberts put it, "a law school's decision to allow recruiters on campus is not inherently expressive" because "[a] law school's recruiting services lack the expressive quality of a parade."[74] The law schools had "overstate[d] the expressive nature of their activity" in a failed "attempt[ ] to stretch a number of First Amendment doctrines well beyond the sort of activities these doctrines protect."[75] A law school's accommodation of a military recruiter "is not compelled speech because the accommodation does not sufficiently interfere with any message of the school."[76] The logic of this position seems apropos in the context of commercial businesses – selling a good or service on a nondiscriminatory basis does not constitute forced speech, at least when the regulated enterprise generally holds itself out as open to any and all comers.[77]

Consider, too, that universities, going back to *Keyishian v. Board of Regents*[78] and *Sweezy v. New Hampshire*,[79] enjoy special First Amendment status as institutions; academic freedom is a well-established penumbra of the First Amendment. Thus,

---

[71] 547 U.S. 47 (2006).

[72] *Id.* at 69–70.

[73] *Id.* at 64.

[74] *Id.*

[75] *Id.* at 70.

[76] *Id.* at 64.

[77] Caroline Mala Corbin, *Speech or Conduct? The Free Speech Claims of Wedding Vendors*, 65 Emory L.J. 241, 244–57, 267–74, 297–301 (2015) (arguing that the sale of goods and services constitutes conduct rather than speech and usually lacks significant expressive context or meaning).

[78] 385 U.S. 589, 603 (1967) ("Our Nation is deeply committed to safeguarding academic freedom, which is of transcendent value to all of us and not merely to the teachers concerned. That freedom is therefore a special concern of the First Amendment, which does not tolerate laws that cast a pall of orthodoxy over the classroom.").

[79] 354 U.S. 234, 250 (1957) ("The essentiality of freedom in the community of American universities is almost self-evident. No one should underestimate the vital role in a democracy that is played by those who guide and train our youth.").

although most universities are not religious entities,[80] universities nonetheless possess special First Amendment status as institutions[81] – a point repeatedly recognized in cases such as *Bakke, Southworth,* and *Grutter.*[82] Thus, one cannot simply waive off *FAIR* on the proposed distinction that the belief at issue was not religiously based. Academic freedom, no less than religious freedom, enjoys a zone of enhanced First Amendment protection.[83]

In consequence, crediting "complicity" as a sound legal basis for excusing compliance with a conduct-based rule (*i.e.*, that you cannot refuse service to a person based on their status) in one context, but not in another, constitutes a rather heavy jurisprudential lift. Just as a law school that accepts federal funds must abide by the conditions that attach to receipt of those funds, a business owner that wants the benefit of participating in the public marketplace cannot have its cake and eat it too by refusing to play by the rules that govern the agora.[84] Public accommodation statutes, as Professor Caroline Mala Corbin argues persuasively, regulate conduct, not speech.[85] As such, the holding of *FAIR* ought to be controlling with respect to whether mandatory nondiscrimination rules can be adopted and enforced with respect to commercial businesses open to the public.

To be sure, a balancing exercise is necessary – a balance that involves how exclusionary ("private") the entity in question happens to be and how related the activity is to its core religious activities. We should not be regulating a madrassa's afternoon day care operation because it excludes nonbelievers or sex-segregates its program.[86] But, a Denny's restaurant simply is not the same as a mosque's day care program.

---

[80] Hoogstra et al., Chapter 25, note that roughly one in four colleges and universities is religiously affiliated.

[81] *See* PAUL HORWITZ, FIRST AMENDMENT INSTITUTIONS 86–87, 107–41, 234–35 (2013).

[82] *See, e.g.,* Grutter v. Bollinger, 539 U.S. 306, 329 (2003) ("We have long recognized that, given the important purpose of public education and the expansive freedoms of speech and thought associated with the university environment, universities occupy a special niche in our constitutional tradition.").

[83] *See, e.g.,* Garcetti v. Ceballos, 547 U.S. 410, 425 (2006); *id.* at 438–39 (Souter, J., dissenting).

[84] Krotoszynski, *Agora, supra* note 57, at 1235–40.

[85] *See* Corbin, *supra* note 77, at 273–74 ("In analyzing the conduct versus speech distinction in the context of services provided by a business open to the public, it would appear that conducting a commercial transaction is ultimately conduct."). Professor Corbin's emphasis on "commercial" businesses that are generally "open to the public" demonstrates that the public character of the enterprise is plainly playing an important role in her analysis. *See id.* at 244–57, 267–74, 297–301. Her reliance on the belief/conduct distinction has persuasive force precisely because the kind of business that she describes is not private in character.

[86] The fact that an entity *could* exclude does not mean that it *must* exclude. If an extension of a faith community's religious activities chooses to open itself up to the general public, even absent a legal obligation to do so, it arguably should be subject to government regulations applicable to a "public" entity. For example, a private dining club may operate as a "private" entity and exclude nonmembers. *See* New York State Club Ass'n, Inc. v. City of New York, 487 U.S. 1, 12–14 (1988) (rejecting a facial challenge to the application of New York City's nondiscrimination ordinance to certain large private dining clubs "because of the kind of role

In short, the state ought to be able to require that a business open to the public serve all comers – much as ferries, inns, and toll roads subject to licensure requirements and tariff regulation were required to serve anyone who could pay the posted rate.[87] On the other hand, however, if a ferryman wishes to festoon his ferryboat with an image of the Virgin Mary, or an innkeeper hangs a picture of Dürer's praying hands above the inn's check-in desk, such public expressions of belief should lie beyond the legitimate reach of government regulation. Belief must encompass the ability to communicate religious convictions and commitments to others in the community – even if some find these convictions upsetting, discriminatory, or offensive. This result obtains because the ability to share a belief with others is integral to holding a belief. And, actions motivated by belief do not cease to be beliefs.

IV CONCLUSION

The devil really is in the details. The United States needs clear rules that predictably and reliably reconcile nondiscrimination rules with claims of religious liberty – but clear rules seem highly elusive in this context. The Commission's approach, however, fails to give adequate scope or sweep to "belief" and seeks to subject to pervasive government regulation the expression of sincerely held religious beliefs that happen to occur in public places and spaces. This line of demarcation cuts too deeply into the realm of private religious practice and would subject self-constituted communities of faith to an unacceptably high level of government regulation.[88] A better approach would attempt to create and deploy a legal taxonomy that characterizes particular institutions and enterprises as either public or private in nature and then makes accommodations available to the latter – but not to the former.

To be sure, the public/private distinction is not a perfect solution. Important details will still need to be worked out to operationalize it to separate valid and invalid claims to exemptions from public accommodation laws, whether under statutes, like the RFRA, or directly under the Free Exercise Clause itself. Despite the dichotomy's shortcomings, however, it seems a more promising general framing

that strangers play in their ordinary existence" and the voluntary maintenance of operating practices that belied a plausible constitutional claim that these entities were truly private rather than "nonprivate" in nature). However, if the enterprise seeks to augment its revenue by serving a large number of nonadherents, it risks losing its First Amendment-based shield against pervasive government regulation of its operations. *See id.* at 11–14, 18. In consequence, if the ability to exclude is actually important to the *raison d'être* of a faith community's affiliated enterprise, then that enterprise should exclude nonbelievers and not operate on an open-to-all-comers basis.

[87] *See* The Civil Rights Cases, 109 U.S. 3, 37–43 (1883) (Harlan, J., dissenting).

[88] Inazu, *supra* note 39, at 185–86 (arguing for the protection of self-constituted groups that "com[e] together in a way of life").

device than the belief/conduct dichotomy or a focus on potential third-party harms. In sum, a workable test must provide for a balancing of the relative equities in a context-specific way and the public/private distinction provides a potentially workable framing device for undertaking this analysis.

Aristotle admonishes that virtue often consists of the mean between two extremes.[89] For example, courage constitutes the virtuous mean between the two extremes of being cowardly or foolhardy. So, too, magnanimity represents the virtuous mean between the extremes of being a miser or a spendthrift. Peaceful coexistence can be achieved only if we find and hold the "virtuous mean" between the vicious extremes of unlimited exemptions from nondiscrimination laws and the mindless application of such laws to essentially private activity that bears a close nexus with the existence and maintenance of a self-constituted community of faith.

---

[89] ARISTOTLE, NICOMACHEAN ETHICS 1106a5–1109b (Terence Irwin trans., Hackett Pub. Co. 1985). For a relevant discussion of Aristotle's concept of the virtuous mean, see Dan M. Kahan & Martha C. Nussbaum, *Two Conceptions of Emotion in Criminal Law*, 96 COLUM. L. REV. 269, 286–88 (1996).

8

Mutual Tolerance and Sensible Exemptions

Kent Greenawalt

This chapter focuses on three general themes that bear on the need to understand one another in society and how that understanding bears on appropriate exemptions relating to abortions and same-sex marriage,[1] two questions that continue to divide the American people.[2]

First, there is a need for mutual tolerance toward others who see things differently. Second, a great deal in life is not subject to rational answers. Third, people should generally not be required to do directly what they believe is deeply wrong. However, society can work only if people do not refuse to help those who, they believe, have done something they see as seriously wrong.

Although the moment that life begins is not subject to a rational answer, powerful reasons support both a woman's right to abortion at the early stages of pregnancy and also the interests of doctors and nurses to not participate in or assist with abortion, as Section II notes. Likewise, as Section III explains, in modern culture, powerful reasons support the right of people to marry someone else of the same gender. Yet, there are some people who believe same-sex marriage is contrary to God's will, or fundamentally wrong for some other reason. They should not have to be directly involved in the solemnization or celebration of those marriages. However, people should not be able to refuse general services to same-sex couples in the time that follows.

---

[1] *See generally* KENT GREENAWALT, EXEMPTIONS: NECESSARY, JUSTIFIED OR MISGUIDED? (2016) (analyzing claims for exemptions across a range of contexts and outlining competing positions).

[2] Michael Lipka & John Gramlich, *5 Facts about Abortion*, PEW RES. CTR. (Jan. 26, 2017), https://perma.cc/H9S2-X2H2 (reporting that 59% of adults say that abortions should be legal, while 37% think abortions should be illegal; by comparison, in 2002, only 30% of Americans thought abortion should be legal most of the time and 12% thought abortion should be legal all of the time); *Changing Attitudes on Gay Marriage*, PEW RES. CTR. (June 26, 2017), https://perma.cc/9B35-7GG8 (reporting that in 2017, 62% of Americans favored same-sex marriage, a dramatic leap from when Pew first began polling on the question in 2001, when only 35% supported same-sex marriage).

I MUTUAL TOLERANCE

First and foremost, within society, tolerance for others is a core element of being a good citizen. We live in a liberal democracy in which people are entitled to be equal citizens despite radically different backgrounds, racial characteristics, religious convictions, and other beliefs. Part of being a good citizen in society is respecting and caring for others who see things differently from ourselves, a perspective that should include many with religious convictions, including myself. Even those who have religious outlooks that are more restrictive need to be aware that tolerance is a key element of social and political life. Regrettably, it seems that advances in electronic communications seem to be pushing the American public toward one-sided off-the-cuff, intolerant responses to those whose basic convictions differ from one's own – a coarsening of public dialogue that is met by many Americans with growing alarm.[3] Society desperately needs to understand that the consequences of this phenomenon are deeply regrettable both ethically and politically. For instance, a growing segment of Americans now lack trust in the "institutions that are the backbone of American democracy," whether the media, courts, Congress, or even elections themselves.[4]

II THE LIMITS OF ORDINARY REASON

The need for mutual tolerance, although not directly dependent on the limits of reason, is bolstered by the fact that many questions about life are not subject to simple rational answers. Included among these questions are what life warrants protection and how great should that protection be?[5] Consider two questions that do not concern the beginning of life: (1) how should society treat human beings who will never have even the capacity of ordinary apes and dogs, such as infants who, tragically, are born with anencephaly, and (2) how should society treat those who through age or illness have lost all their capacities and will never recover them?[6] Simple reason – that is, rational analysis that extends beyond cultural assumptions and ideas about what is workable – does not answer these questions. As with the beginning of life, reason cannot define those capacities that mandate serious protections in these instances either. In respect to same-sex marriage, modern

---

[3] *Everything President Trump Has Tweeted (And What It Was About)*, LA TIMES (Nov. 27, 2017), https://perma.cc/HMM5-7KUL.

[4] Jessica Taylor, *Americans Say Civility Has Worsened Under Trump; Trust in Institutions Down*, NPR (July 3, 2017), https://perma.cc/XFX9-XSZB.

[5] *See, e.g.*, Daniel P. Sulmasy, *Preserving Life? The Vatican and PVS*, 134 COMMONWEAL (Dec. 7, 2007), https://perma.cc/BEZ5-ZAJD.

[6] *See, e.g.*, Mary Crossley, *In Re T.A.C.P. and In the Matter of Baby K: Anencephaly and Slippery Slopes*, in HEALTH LAW & BIOETHICS: CASES IN CONTEXT 123 (Sandra H. Johnson et al. eds., 2009) [hereinafter *Health Law & Bioethics*]; Sandra H. Johnson et al. *Beyond the Symbols*, in HEALTH LAW & BIOETHICS 53.

understandings provided powerful rational reasons to support legalizing it.[7] But given cultural traditions and various religious convictions, it is not surprising that that some people see things quite differently.[8]

A word about religious belief is warranted. Although some religious persons will disagree, many religious convictions are based mainly on faith or tradition or both, rather than on simple rational analysis. To be clear, these bases of religion, faith and tradition, are not completely separated. They are often intermingled. Most people will not accept religious premises that they actually see as irrational, but society needs to recognize that some competing perspectives may be equally consistent with ordinary reason. In this respect, Elaine Pagels's *Gnostic Gospels* and her *Beyond Belief* reveal just how diverse views were in the early Christian movement.[9] To take obvious modern differences, reason alone cannot resolve the truth of two Christian premises: whether a loving God exists or the significance of the life of Jesus. And, if one accepts these Christian premises, reason alone cannot tell one whether a Catholic or Protestant view better captures the place of Jesus in the lives of believers.

Given diverse views in a plural society, based partly on the limits of rationality, what should society require people to do? Sections III and IV explore this question in relationship to abortion and same-sex marriage. But first, it is important to posit a fundamental idea, namely, that people should not be required to do directly what they believe is deeply wrong. However, it does not follow that people should treat negatively others who perform acts with which they deeply disagree, especially when that performance is based on an understandable sense of what is right.

III ABORTION

Whether or not the US Supreme Court should have created a constitutional right to have an abortion at the time of *Roe v. Wade* is arguable.[10] But three powerful reasons support not treating abortions at the early stage of pregnancy as criminal.

First, the most obvious reason is that people should generally be free to decide what will happen to their own bodies;[11] pregnancy deeply involves what happens to a prospective mother's body. Second, since there is no obvious rational ground to conclude that an early fetus deserves the protection of a full human being, that conclusion should not be imposed on women or couples who see things differently. Finally, there exists a practical problem with criminalization. Before *Roe v. Wade*,

---

[7] For such a case, see Brownstein, Chapter 2.

[8] *See, e.g.,* Lori, Chapter 13; Ryan Anderson, Chapter 27.

[9] *See generally* Elaine Pagels, THE GNOSTIC GOSPELS (1979) (showing that the Gnostics did not accept the authority of the dominant church and saw a much more significant place for the beliefs of women); Elaine Pagels, BEYOND BELIEF: THE SECRET GOSPEL OF THOMAS (2003).

[10] *See generally* Roe v. Wade, 410 U.S. 113 (1973). For a summary of views on *Roe*, see CAROL SANGER, ABOUT ABORTION: TERMINATING PREGNANCY IN 21ST CENTURY AMERICA (2017); MARY ZIEGLER, AFTER ROE: THE LOST HISTORY OF THE ABORTION DEBATE (2015).

[11] *See* Cruzan v. Director, Missouri Dept. of Health, 497 U.S. 261 (1990).

many women had abortions despite its criminal status in most states.[12] The laws were not effectively enforced and since abortion does not injure anyone who can directly complain, general enforcement is nearly impossible. The difficulty of enforcement, in itself, is not a compelling reason against classifying any act as criminal, but it does push in that direction. Together, these three reasons strongly support allowing women to have abortions during the early stages of pregnancy.

However, as federal law provides, hospitals, individual doctors, nurses, and other workers should not be required to perform or assist with the provision of abortions.[13] The basis for this is simple. If an individual believes that abortions at the early stages of pregnancy amount to the intentional taking of human life,[14] in essence a form of murder, whether the law allows it or not, that person should not have to perform that act or directly assist someone else to do so. The borders of what constitutes assistance are hardly exact, but a nurse handing instruments to a doctor is assisting; a clerk who registers a patient entering the hospital is not.[15]

One question about exemptions is whether they should be left to those with religious convictions or also include people with nonreligious moral convictions.[16] Since individuals may believe early abortions are wrong based on nonreligious grounds for assessing when life deserving protection starts, the exemption should

---

[12] *See generally* Michelle Oberman, Her Body Our Laws chapters 2 and 5 (2017).

[13] 42 U.S.C. § 300a–7 (2012) (known as the Church Amendment, this 1973 law prohibits a court from using receipt of certain federal monies as a basis for making an individual or institution perform an abortion or sterilization contrary to their "religious beliefs or moral convictions"); 20 U.S.C. § 1688 (2012) (known as the Danforth Amendment, this 1988 law provides that no provision of the Labor and Public Health and Welfare codes "shall be construed to require or prohibit any person, or public or private entity, to provide or pay for any benefit or service, including the use of facilities, related to an abortion" and that "[n]othing in this section shall be construed to permit a penalty to be imposed on any person or individual because such person or individual is seeking or has received any benefit or service related to a legal abortion"); 42 U.S.C. § 238n (2012) (enacted as the Coates-Snow Amendment, this 1996 law prohibits federal agencies, and state or local governments receiving federal funds, from "discriminating" against healthcare providers and health training programs because they do not provide abortions or abortion training); Public Law 111–8 § 508(d)(1) (known as the Hyde-Weldon Amendment, this annual appropriations rider since 2004 has forbidden federal funding of government bodies which "discriminate" against health-care providers and insurers for decisions related to abortion.).

The Patient Protection and Affordable Care Act, or ACA, carries forward abortion con-science protections. *See* Pub. L. No. 111–148, § 1303(b)(2)(A), 124 Stat. 119, 171 (2010) ("Nothing in this Act shall be construed to have any effect on Federal laws regarding – (i) conscience protection; (ii) willingness or refusal to provide abortion; and (iii) discrimination on the basis of the willingness or refusal to provide, pay for, cover, or refer for abortion or to provide or participate in training to provide abortion.").

[14] Planned Parenthood v. Casey, 505 U.S. 833 (1992).

[15] For a detailed discussion, see Kent Greenawalt, *Refusals of Conscience: What Are They and When Should They Be Accommodated?*, 9 Ava Maria L. Rev. 47 (2001).

[16] Kent Greenawalt, Religion and the Constitution: Volume 1 Free Exercise and Fairness 49 (2006).

include them.[17] When it comes to hospitals and other institutions, it is dubious whether there are enough nonreligious shared convictions to warrant inclusion in any exemption.

A final question concerns exception to an exemption. Briefly, if a pregnant woman's life is at stake and other medical providers who are willing to do the procedure are not readily available, a doctor or nurse who would otherwise be eligible for an exemption should be under a duty to perform the needed procedure. A hard question about abortion sure to arise in the not-too-distant future concerns the possibility for fetuses to survive and develop outside of a woman's body.[18] Should a woman and her sexual partner be able to terminate the fetus, or should doctors or the law have the right to assure its survival and then make the baby available for adoption? Individual states should be able to decide how to address this possibility since the right answer is far from clear.[19]

IV SAME-SEX MARRIAGE

With respect to same-sex marriage, in more than one way, matters are more complicated than with abortions. First, should there be a right to marry? The answer is clearly "yes," powerfully supported by ordinary reason. On this, society must take account of its place in history and why some people have strong inclinations to sexual relations with someone of the same gender. On the first matter, the stage in history, if marriage were perceived as crucial for the conceiving and raising of children, it could rationally be seen as limited to a union of man and woman.[20] However, given the ability today to conceive children without sexual intercourse, together with the broader sense of marriage's relevance, as well as various legal privileges given to couples who are married, the reasons to extend the legal right to marry to gay couples are very strong.

Importantly, perceptions about what is perceived to be the main determinant of attraction to others of the same gender have shifted.[21] Is same-gender attraction a

---

[17] *See* Michael Lipka & John Gramlich, *5 Facts About Abortion*, PEW RES. CTR. (Jan. 26, 2017), https://perma.cc/K7A9-V7XN; *see* David Masci, *Where Major Religious Groups Stand on Abortion*, PEW RES. CTR. (June 21, 2016), https://perma.cc/AL98-5RHH. For a breakdown of religious versus nonreligious views on abortion, see Hannah Fingerhut, *On Abortion, Persistent Divides Between – and Within – the Two Parties*, PEW RES. CTR (July 7, 2017), https://perma.cc/9TMP-G2WW (reporting, as one contrast, that 53% of Catholics believe abortion should be legal while 80% of those who have no religious affiliation believe abortion should be legal).

[18] For a review of emerging technology assisting premature babies to survive outside to womb, see Lucy Westcott, *Finding That Babies Born at 22 Weeks Can Survive Could Change Abortion Debate*, NEWSWEEK (May 7, 2015).

[19] *See, e.g.,* Planned Parenthood v. Casey, *supra* note 14 (affirming the state's interest in fetal life after viability).

[20] For a recitation of these views, see Lori, Chapter 13; Ryan Anderson, Chapter 27.

[21] Jason Koebler, *Scientists May Have Finally Unlocked the Puzzle of Why People Are Gay*, U.S. NEWS (Dec. 11, 2012).

product of natural inclinations, social circumstances, or some psychological failure that leads to a misconception? Many people, perhaps partly for religious reasons, once saw this attraction as based on some failure within those who experience it. After all, if the great majority of people are attracted to people of the opposite sex, would not opposite-sex attraction essentially be the natural inclination of everyone? The medical assumption now is that most gay people have a natural inclination that is not based on any flaw and is beyond their control.[22] Given this reality, treating same-sex couples worse in respect to a crucial privilege in life does strike one as unfair.

Given the appropriateness of evolutionary constitutional interpretation, the US Supreme Court was right to discern a constitutional right to same-sex marriage,[23] but a constitutional grounding is not crucial for the analysis here, which depends only on the conclusion that same-sex marriage should be legal by one means or another.

Does it follow that no relevant exemptions from equal treatment in access to marriage should be granted? The answer here is definitely "no," but the appropriate exemption is quite limited. Some people believe that if anyone else suffers harm, no exemption from equal treatment is appropriate.[24] This is an oversimplification. In the old days, constitutional rights against the government had little to do with how other individuals could treat each other. Someone exercising a constitutional right to free speech could be fired from a private firm for taking a position the firm did not approve of. What has mainly reached private behavior in the realm of equal treatment laws are nondiscrimination statutes.[25] Formally this kind of restriction on private behavior requires a statute. These statutes typically do create some exemptions, primarily for religious objections.[26] In brief, in some situations individuals do have a right to treat unequally even those who must be treated equally by the government. The focus in this volume is on what is right as a matter of principle, but in those states that do not yet have nondiscrimination laws concerning same-sex marriage, some concessions may be necessary to get the laws passed. Utah is a notable example of where this did occur.[27]

In the public accommodations context, the basic exemption should focus on direct participation in the wedding itself. As with abortion, people should not have to perform or assist with what they believe is deeply wrong. And even if rational bases strongly support such marriage, it should not be assumed that all those opposed to

---

[22] *Id.*

[23] *See generally* Obergefell v. Hodges, 135 S. Ct. 2584 (2015). My developed views about constitutional interpretation are in KENT GREENAWALT, INTERPRETING THE CONSTITUTION (2015).

[24] *See, e.g.,* Melling, Chapter 19.

[25] *See, e.g.,* Americans with Disabilities Act of 1990, 42 U.S.C. § 12101 et seq. (2012); The Age Discrimination in Employment Act of 1967, 29 U.S.C § 623 *et seq.* (2016); Title VII of the Civil Rights Act of 1964, 42 U.S.C. § 2000e (2012); *see generally Obergefell, supra* note 23.

[26] See Hill, Chapter 26, for examples.

[27] *See* Adams, Chapter 32; Laurie Goodstein, *Utah Passes Antidiscrimination Bill Backed by Mormon Leaders,* N. Y. TIMES (Mar. 12, 2015).

same-sex marriage are irrational. Opponents can understand their position as supported by historical culture, religious belief founded on core church doctrine, or an intuition concerning what marriage is fundamentally about. Obviously, the cultural history and a religious upbringing can still influence someone's intuition even if they do not stand in that person's eyes as genuine independent reasons.

Three basic questions about this approach immediately arise: (1) whether drawing a line at direct participation makes sense, (2) whether nonreligious objections should be included, and (3) how does one draw the line itself.

Let's start with the limit to direct participation. No one outside the government should have to perform the marriage itself or be deeply involved in the ceremony. This is not a simple line for all circumstances, but to take the example of *Elane Photography LLC v. Willock*, the role of acting as the main photographer for a ceremony involves taking hundreds of photographs, some of which will be treasured by a couple for their lifetimes.[28] That role is direct enough to warrant an exemption from required involvement.

A related but equally important question is whether limiting the exemption to direct involvement is defensible. This chapter does not address internal organizations within religious bodies, including religious schools and universities, subjects that are dealt with extensively in other chapters in this volume.[29] Instead, the focus here is on ordinary services that are provided to the public in general. Concededly, although my suggestion for a limit on the scope of an exemption to direct involvement is arguable, such a distinction exists in most people's lives. Virtually all of society, including professors and many others, provide services to people who have done things they see as seriously wrong. Restaurants and hotels rarely refuse service to former criminals, to women who have publicly acknowledged having abortions, and to inter-gender couples who are not married. Almost no one refuses to provide spousal insurance for members of a married couple, even if the insurance provider happens to know or guess that one partner did not receive what the provider perceives as a morally acceptable divorce from a prior marriage. If ordinary services are provided to all sorts of people, it is hard to see a powerful argument to allowing ordinary services to be refused for same-sex married couples.

Providing an extensive exemption here would raise the question how often those who insist upon an exemption are really acting out of conscience, as contrasted with seeking to make a political statement or to satisfy constituents who are opposed to such marriage. This point relates to an important general reality about legal norms in many areas. Often it would be nearly impossible for officials, juries, and judges to discern what exactly is going on in someone's mind and to draw sensible distinctions

---

[28] 309 P.3d 53 (N.M. 2013) (fining a New Mexico photographer for refusing on religious grounds to photograph a same-sex commitment ceremony notwithstanding the state's Religious Freedom Restoration Act). See McClain, Chapter 17; Wilson, Chapter 30, for additional detail on lawsuits against wedding vendors.

[29] *See* Berg, Chapter 24; Hoogstra et al., Chapter 25; Hill, Chapter 26.

in actual circumstances. For this reason, the legal standards often need to be somewhat more straightforward than one might think would be ideally correct.

One form of subsequent involvement after the couple marries does involve fairly direct participation in a marriage – namely, putting children up for adoption. Two points are important here. First, this act will seem more direct to those who put their children up for adoption and to religious groups that run adoption agencies. Second, seeing same-sex marriage as in general deserving equal treatment under the law does not mean that gender is irrelevant for adoption. The genders of a child's parents could be viewed, like age and economic status, as relevant to a placement decision although not a general basis for unequal treatment. A couple's gender should be able to count, but agencies should not absolutely exclude same-sex couples.

Finally, should an exemption regarding same-sex marriages be limited to religious convictions? Regarding direct participation, the answer is no. If someone offers a genuine nonreligious conviction that same-sex marriage is deeply wrong, that person should not have to participate directly in it. However, given concerns noted previously that if an exemption is extended more broadly, many individuals and organizations who "object" may be mainly making political statements or attempting to satisfy clients,[30] limiting any exemption to claimed religious convictions would be wise for later, indirect treatment.[31]

What of public employees? Public offices themselves must provide equal treatment if the law calls for that.[32] But, especially as to an individual who has taken a job and did not expected a change in legal marriage rights to encompass same-sex couples, if that individual has a serious objection to participation – and someone else can provide the service without either genuine delay or embarrassment for the couple to be married – excusing that individual from participation can make sense. This staffing-around can be done under some basic standard or by her boss's discretion or a device such as the one Utah adopted to expand the number of authorized celebrants, avoiding the need to override any person's objections. Providing a concession to such individuals is not fundamentally wrong. To take a personal example, when I was a deputy solicitor general, my boss did excuse me from reviewing a brief that asserted a position I saw as deeply unjust. More generally, it is now common in states with capital punishment not to require objecting individual officials to work on briefs arguing for that consequence.[33]

---

[30] *Tennessee Hardware Store Puts Up No Gays Allowed Sign*, USA Today, (July 2015).

[31] For additional development of this point, see Greenawalt, *supra* note 1.

[32] For a discussion of public services and public employees, see Wilson, Chapter 30; Adams, Chapter 32.

[33] *Cf.* Sara Rimer, *Working Death Row: A Special Report*, N.Y. Times (Dec. 17, 2000), https://perma.cc/82RG-N5SA.

V CONCLUSION

Probably everyone will disagree with some of the specific proposals in this chapter, but the main point here is that we need to aim for mutual tolerance in how we think about the interests of groups often seen at odds with one another. Religious believers who feel that God sees genuine marriage as only between men and women must understand why those with strong homosexual inclinations both have a contrary view and care deeply about being respected and treated equally. Those strongly favoring gay marriage need to recognize that people with a powerful contrary religious view are not necessarily bad people who do not care about outsiders. If each side respects the humanity of those with competing views, that can greatly assist reasonable resolutions of what should be legal rights and duties within our shared communities.

9

The Joys of Mutual Contempt

Andrew Koppelman

Religious disagreement sometimes means – when the notion of toleration was developed in the age of religious wars, it did mean – that each side's most basic commitments entail that the other is in error about moral fundamentals, that the other's entire way of life is predicated on that error and ought not to exist.[1]

Such loathing of one another's theologies has gone out of fashion, for the most part. Yet it is back in the divide over religious exemptions from antidiscrimination laws. I'm going to argue that the past success in dealing with religious diversity has several important lessons for how to deal with the present dispute.

I WHY ANTIDISCRIMINATION LAW?

Coexistence has largely been achieved in the religious sphere. The United States, one of the most religiously diverse regimes in the history of the world,[2] is a long-standing counterexample to Jean-Jacques Rousseau's dictum that "[i]t is impossible to live in peace with people whom one believes are damned."[3]

A crucial foundation for this success, already present in John Locke's classic defense of toleration, is private property and freedom of association.[4] The fundamental classical liberal rights are those of bodily integrity, property, and contract: "the business of Laws is not to provide for the Truth of Opinions, but for the Safety

---

[1] Andrew Koppelman, Defending American Religious Neutrality (2013).

[2] For a breakdown of faith traditions in the United States by share of the U.S. population, see Pew Research Ctr. Religion & Pub. Life Project, *America's Changing Religious Landscape*, https://perma.cc/4LWV-3JYZ. For discussion of the rise of the "nones," adults who self-identify as spiritual but affiliate with no organized faith tradition, see Moyer, Chapter 16.

[3] Jean-Jacques Rousseau, On The Social Contract 131 (Roger D. Masters ed., Judith R. Masters trans., 1978) (1762).

[4] John Locke, A Letter Concerning Toleration (James H. Tully ed., 1983) (1689).

and Security of the Commonwealth and of every particular man's Goods and Person."[5] If the classical liberal rights are respected, then conflict is easy to avoid. If all associations must be based on mutual agreement, then in religious matters, "no man will have a Legislator imposed upon him, but whom himself has chosen."[6] Those who find one another's presence unendurable can stay apart. Occasionally we will discover that our fellow citizens hold views we regard as loathsome,[7] but that discovery is not the kind of injury that law needs to remedy.

Nondiscrimination law is inconsistent with these principles, which is why some libertarians find it repugnant.[8] It is nonetheless justified by certain special conditions, pervasive patterns of exclusion with such deep cultural roots that the market is unlikely to remedy them.[9] In such cases, it is appropriate to create a right to be free from discrimination. That is why the Civil Rights Act of 1964 was necessary and why LGBT people should now be protected against discrimination.[10] But notice that these rights are based, not on individual injury, but on the aggregate effects of the prohibited conduct.[11] It is confusing to treat discrimination as though it were an act of violence. Law tolerates idiosyncratic discrimination, even unfair idiosyncratic discrimination, because in a free market it affects no one's life chances. It may be insulting for someone to refuse to hire anyone with large earlobes, but free speech protects insults.[12]

Pervasive prejudice is different. Even libertarians ought to endorse the project of transforming culture to eradicate the notion that some classes of persons are beings of an inferior order who have no rights. Such prejudices have typically meant that the law could not even be relied upon to protect the affected group's minimal rights

---

[5] *Id.* at 46.

[6] *Id.* at 29.

[7] For a discussion of specific views that have divided Americans, such as the belief that another worships the wrong god, or worships the right god in the wrong way, or marries in the wrong way, see Brownstein, Chapter 2.

[8] *See, e.g.,* AYN RAND, THE VIRTUE OF SELFISHNESS: A NEW CONCEPT OF EGOISM 126–34 (1964); Robert Bork, *Civil Rights – A Challenge,* 149 NEW REPUBLIC 21, 22 (1963); RICK PERLSTEIN, BEFORE THE STORM: BARRY GOLDWATER AND THE UNMAKING OF THE AMERICAN CONSENSUS 462 (2001) (quoting a Goldwater speech, which was coauthored by then campaign advisor William Rehnquist and political theorist Harry Jaffa, and which opposed the Civil Rights Act of 1964 because "the freedom to associate means the same thing as the freedom not to associate"). The most prominent contemporary libertarian critique of civil rights laws is RICHARD EPSTEIN, FORBIDDEN GROUNDS: THE CASE AGAINST EMPLOYMENT DISCRIMINATION LAWS (1992). *See generally* Samuel R. Bagenstos, *The Unrelenting Libertarian Challenge to Public Accommodations Law,* 66 STAN. L. REV. 1205 (2014).

[9] Given the tendency of some ethnic groups to violently dominate others, such conditions exist in many parts of the world. *See* TARUNABH KHAITAN, A THEORY OF DISCRIMINATION LAW (2015).

[10] For evidence of discrimination in both contexts, see Melling, Chapter 19; Perry, Chapter 20; Pizer, Chapter 29.

[11] *See* Andrew Koppelman, *Justice for Large Earlobes! A Comment on Richard Arneson's "What Is Wrongful Discrimination?",* 43 SAN DIEGO L. REV. 809 (2006).

[12] *Id.*

of security of person and property. African Americans were lynched; violence against women was casually tolerated; police regarded assaults on gay people with indifference and sometimes perpetrated it themselves. A guarantee of Lockean rights demands a culture that respects those rights.[13]

Pervasive prejudice has to be combated with equally strong cultural forces. This takes us into the realm of pollution and taboo. Liberal theorists are uncomfortable with the invocation of such primitive impulses, but they appear to be an ineradicable part of humanity's moral vocabulary.[14] Racism itself has come to be stigmatized as contaminating. A similar cultural move has happened with prejudice against gay people.[15] As with racism, the stigmatization of gays is so deeply rooted in American culture that it is probably necessary to rely on this kind of countertaboo in order to respond to it.[16] In each case, the aim is to induce citizens to regard the relevant prejudice as itself ritually unclean.

Again, note the tension with the conventional classical liberal answer to religious disagreement. Now, some ideas are regarded as unclean and contaminating. The tensions with free speech are obvious.[17] There is also a tension with religious liberty, because, just as in the bad old days of religious suppression, the state again finds itself in the business of deciding which ideas are so odious as to be intolerable.[18]

II MORAL EQUIVALENCIES?

Much of the debate about exemptions focuses on whether condemnation of homosexual conduct is the moral equivalent of racism.[19] That question is interesting but irrelevant to the exemption question. There are a few kinds of moral equivalence that could matter here. One is whether, in its aggregate operation, condemnation of

---

[13] ANDREW KOPPELMAN, ANTIDISCRIMINATION LAW AND SOCIAL EQUALITY 181–90 (1996).

[14] *See* JONATHAN HAIDT, THE RIGHTEOUS MIND: WHY GOOD PEOPLE ARE DIVIDED BY POLITICS AND RELIGION 170–77 (2012).

[15] On the question whether religiously grounded refusals should be treated as bigotry, see Laycock, Chapter 3; Leith Anderson, Chapter 12; Lori, Chapter 13; Smith, Chapter 18; Melling, Chapter 19; Perry, Chapter 20; Hollman, Chapter 23; Berg, Chapter 24; Ryan Anderson, Chapter 27.

[16] This is not to say that Americans views on LGBT rights have not progressed. *See, e.g.,* William N. Eskridge, Jr. & Chris Riano, FROM OUTLAWS TO INLAWS: MARRIAGE EQUALITY IN AMERICA (forthcoming 2018). For example, support for same-sex marriage has leapt from 35% in 2001 to 62% in 2017. *Changing Attitudes on Gay Marriage,* PEW RES. CTR. (June 26, 2017), https://perma.cc/EU7B-Q989.

[17] *See* Andrew Koppelman, *A Free Speech Response to the Gay Rights/Religious Liberty Conflict,* 110 Nw U. L. REV. 1125 (2016).

[18] *See* Andrew Koppelman, *Gay Rights, Religious Accommodations, and the Purposes of Antidiscrimination Law,* 88 S. CAL. L. REV. 619 (2015).

[19] *See, e.g.,* Smith, Chapter 18; Perry, Chapter 20; Richard Thompson Ford, *Analogy Lesson: Racism Is the Wrong Frame for Understanding the Passage of California's Same-Sex Marriage Ban,* SLATE (Nov. 14, 2008), https://perma.cc/NB3K-TRVF.

homosexuality produces destructive effects in the same way that racism does.[20] That is the right question to ask when society considers whether it is appropriate to ban discrimination in the first place (the answer likely is yes), but it does not tell us whether religious accommodations can be permitted without defeating the purposes of nondiscrimination laws. A second is whether those who oppose gay rights have evil in their hearts – a question that the state is massively incompetent to decide.[21] The countertaboo has important cultural work to do, but it does not need to, and cannot, come from the state. Americans have managed to resist Communism and Nazism without the state hectoring us about them.[22]

A third kind of moral equivalence, one that moves many but which the law absolutely needs to be silent about, is that both homosexuality and religious condemnation of it are moral errors. Slightly less than half of Americans, most of them for religious reasons,[23] think that homosexual sex is never morally acceptable.[24] I think that these people's religious ideas are obviously wrong. But I believe that about an enormous range of beliefs, religious and other. Most Americans surely agree that some religious beliefs are worthless, harmful, weird delusions.[25] They do not agree about which ones. This is nothing new. It is the chronic condition of the United States. The way the American regime has coped with this diversity is to treat religion – understood at such an abstract level as to ignore all doctrinal differences – as a good and to accommodate it where this is possible.[26] There are undoubtedly erroneous religious views. There logically must be, since many of the religious views that citizens hold contradict one another. But the state must not say which ones they are.

---

[20] For views on this question, see Leith Anderson, Chapter 12; Melling, Chapter 19; Ryan Anderson, Chapter 27.

[21] A different and more manageable question is whether a statute on its face reflects animus against an unpopular group. That is a familiar question of statutory purpose, and so the U.S. Supreme Court has managed to address it without attempting to search anyone's heart. *See* Andrew Koppelman, *Beyond Levels of Scrutiny: Windsor and "Bare Desire to Harm,"* 64 Case Western Reserve L. Rev. 1045 (2014); Andrew Koppelman, Romer v. Evans *and Invidious Intent*, 6 Wm. & Mary Bill of Rts. J. 89 (1997).

[22] See Andrew Koppelman, *You're All Individuals: Brettschneider on Free Speech*, 79 Brook. L. Rev. 1023 (2014).

[23] *See* Frank Newport, *Religion Big Factor for Americans Against Same-Sex Marriage*, Gallup (Dec. 5, 2012), https://perma.cc/S4QZ-T9UP (Americans who oppose same-sex marriage are most likely to explain their position on the basis of religious beliefs or interpretation of biblical passages).

[24] In 2013, 41% thought that homosexual sex was not morally acceptable, compared with 60% in 2001. Frank Newport & Igor Himelfarb, *In U.S., Record-High Say Gay, Lesbian Relations Morally OK*, Gallup (May 20, 2013), https://perma.cc/LBA5-BAWQ. In September 2017, Gallup reported that 54% of American adults surveyed believed that gay and lesbian relationships are "morally acceptable." Frank Newport, *On Moral Issues, Not All Protestants Are Created Equal*, Gallup (Sept. 8, 2017).

[25] For general views by Americans of faith traditions, see *How Americans Feel About Religious Groups*, Pew Res. Ctr. (July 16, 2014), https://perma.cc/4HAU-6G3Y.

[26] Andrew Koppelman, Defending American Religious Neutrality 1–119 (2013).

There may be good reasons for nondiscrimination protections for gay people. There may even be good reasons to deny religious exemptions. But treating discrimination as equivalent to violence against the person, or regarding the pertinent attitudes as contaminants that must be eradicated, confuses the issue.

III US CIVIL RIGHTS COMMISSION: BLOCK THAT METAPHOR

The 2016 US Commission on Civil Rights (Commission) report, ironically titled *Peaceful Coexistence*,[27] is full of examples of this kind of confusion. Here is the essence of the Commission's findings:

> Civil rights protections ensuring nondiscrimination, as embodied in the Constitution, laws, and policies, are of preeminent importance in American jurisprudence ... Religious exemptions ... significantly infringe upon these civil rights ... The First Amendment's Establishment Clause constricts the ability of government actors to curtail private citizens' rights to the protections of nondiscrimination laws and policies.[28]

The rights in question are not "of preeminent importance."[29] The ones that are of preeminent importance are the rights to the protection of person and property – rights, once again, that gay people have often been denied. Nondiscrimination rights are contingent and derivative.

Metaphors of violence do a lot of work in the various statements of the commissioners:

> Nondiscrimination laws stand as a bulwark against the assaults of intolerance and animus.[30]

> Religious liberty was never intended to give one religion dominion over others, or a veto power over the civil rights and civil liberties of others. However, today, as in the past, religion is being used as both a weapon and a shield by those seeking to deny others equality.[31]

> The First Amendment is a shield that ensures a diversity of religious views are allowed to flourish in the United States. However, there are some seeking to make the right to exercise their religion a sword that can be used against others who do not conform with their interpretation of their faith.[32]

Commissioner Heriot's response is accurate, albeit incomplete:

---

[27] U.S. COMM'N ON CIVIL RIGHTS, PEACEFUL COEXISTENCE: RECONCILING NONDISCRIMINA-TION PRINCIPLES WITH CIVIL LIBERTIES (2016).
[28] Findings and Recommendations, *in id.* at 25.
[29] *Id.*
[30] *Id.* at 40 (statement of Commissioners Achtenberg, Castro, Kladney, and Yaki).
[31] *Id.* at 29 (statement of Chairman Martin R. Castro).
[32] *Id.* at 41 (statement of Commissioner Karen K. Narasaki).

It is serious error to fail to make a distinction between the desire not to be coerced by the government and the desire to use governmental authority to coerce others. RFRA-style laws are about the former; anti-discrimination laws, especially when enforced with great zeal even against the most trivial of deviation, are about the latter. By declining to listen, a private citizen has not "vetoed" the right of another to speak. By declining to associate, a private citizen has not exercised "dominion" over another's right of association.[33]

The question Heriot raises is how we can know the difference between the appropriate application of nondiscrimination law and the inappropriateness that rises to the level of "great zeal." On that crucial question Heriot is silent. The only commissioner who appears to grasp what is at stake in the precise question the Commission is supposed to be deciding is Commissioner Peter Kirsanow. He casually claims, without citing any evidence, that it "seems unlikely" that there are "large numbers of service providers and business owners who would discriminate against gays and lesbians based purely on their sexual orientation if nondiscrimination laws were not in place."[34] If refusals rarely occurred, it would make the policy question easy: if the law in question were unnecessary, then the exemptions question would not arise.[35] We are where we are because many legislatures have concluded that Kirsanow doesn't understand the daily experience of gay people.

Although doctrinaire libertarianism leaves much to be desired,[36] any case for nondiscrimination law needs to take the libertarian position seriously enough to answer it. Libertarians who address this issue tend to undermine their own credibility by overstating their case, rigidly opposing any protection against discrimination as an intolerable intrusion on liberty.[37] What they offer is, however, the appropriate baseline for regulation. Most of the time, property and markets ameliorate inequality and make everyone better off. Sometimes they fail. Nondiscrimination law is a response to market failure.

---

[33] *Id.* at 123 (statement and rebuttal of Commissioner Gail Heriot).

[34] *Id.* at 66 (statement of Commissioner Peter Kirsanow). The economic consequences of anti-gay discrimination are documented, with citations to the scholarship on the topic, in the report accompanying the Employment Non-Discrimination Act of 2013, S. Rep. No. 113–105, at 14–19 (2013).

[35] For an argument against necessity, see Ryan Anderson, Chapter 27.

[36] Andrew Koppelman, The Tough Luck Constitution and the Assault on Health Care Reform (2013); Andrew Koppelman & Tobias Barrington Wolff, A Right to Discriminate? How the Case of *Boy Scouts of America v. James Dale* Warped the Law of Free Association (2009); Andrew Koppelman, *Feminism and Libertarianism: A Response to Richard Epstein*, 1999 U. of Chicago Legal F. 115; Andrew Koppelman, *Richard Epstein's Imperfect Understanding of Antidiscrimination Law*, Law & Liberty F. (Jan. 12, 2016), https://perma.cc/KX64-S3TR.

[37] A few years ago, I was at a libertarian conference where I discovered, in response to a request for a show of hands, that I was the only one at the table who was entirely confident that the Civil Rights Act of 1964 was not unconstitutional.

The crucial question is whether religious accommodation would defeat the purpose of nondiscrimination laws – a purpose, once more, that is concerned with aggregate effects rather than individual injury. Because nondiscrimination laws' purposes are a response to pervasive discrimination, those purposes are not frustrated by discrimination that is unusual. If gay people are generally protected against discrimination, then a few outliers will not make any difference. Discrimination is also insulting, of course, but the dignitary harm of knowing that some of your fellow citizens condemn your way of life is not one from which the law can or should protect you in a regime of free speech.[38]

So, the exemption question turns on how many people would invoke the accommodation if it were offered. That question is hard, but it is not unique to the gay rights/religious liberty issue. It is presented by every proposed religious accommodation. The decision to accommodate always rests on a guess that society is not opening the floodgates to an unmanageable number of claims. Often the guess is correct: exempting Quakers from the military draft did not make the United States militarily feeble, and allowing sacramental wine did not cripple Prohibition.[39] No one knows how many people would exercise a right of religious exemption from nondiscrimination laws. The range of reasonable guesses is all over the map.[40] If it turns out that more exemptions are invoked than lawmakers expected – if that happens in some geographical areas but not others – lawmakers should have some idea of how the question should be reopened. Those are the conversations we should be having.

Metaphors of violence and contamination merely confuse the issue. Even after we move past our confusion, compromise is impossible if we cannot be sure what we are agreeing to. The religious accommodation most commonly proposed is a state-level Religious Freedom Restoration Act (RFRA), which broadly requires that religious objectors to any law be accommodated unless application of the law to them is necessary to a compelling state interest.[41] Such a law may or may not help

---

[38] Advocates of exemptions have lately been arguing that discrimination is sometimes protected as an exercise of free speech. When this goes beyond the use of language, to a claim that one has a right to the symbolic conduct of discriminating, it quickly becomes incoherent. The murky claims that underlie the case of *Masterpiece Cakeshop v. Colorado*, pending in the Supreme Court as this is written, are an illustration. *See* Andrew Koppelman, *The Gay Wedding-Cake Case Isn't About Free Speech: The Inconvenient Facts of* Masterpiece Cakeshop, AMERICAN PROSPECT (Nov. 27, 2017), https://perma.cc/3SQ3-U7GJ; Andrew Koppelman, *Baking Chaos: Masterpiece Cakeshop Argument Misses the Mark*, AMERICAN PROSPECT (Dec. 6, 2017), https://perma.cc/RJ6J-EP32.

[39] In the last years of the Vietnam War, on the other hand, the broadening of military exemptions did hamstring the draft. *See* ANDREW KOPPELMAN, *The Story of* Welsh v. United States: *Elliott Welsh's Two Religious Tests*, *in* FIRST AMENDMENT STORIES 293 (Richard W. Garnett & Andrew Koppelman eds., 2012).

[40] *See* Koppelman, *supra* note 13, at 639–44.

[41] *Id.* at 629–38. For a discussion of state RFRAs versus specific exemptions in nondiscrimination laws themselves, see Laycock, Chapter 3; Wilson, Chapter 30; Appendix.

the wedding photographers, bakers, and florists who object to facilitating same-sex marriage; that will be up to the courts, which have not been friendly to such claims.[42] No one knows how many such claims would be brought. A model statute tailored to those cases would guarantee accommodation, but it is still impossible to know how often it would be invoked, and its field of application remains uncertain.[43] Each side of the controversy thus has some basis for focusing on its worst-case scenario. It might, thus, be more promising to propose rules rather than standards, for instance exempting businesses of five or fewer employees or exempting married student housing in religious colleges.[44] At least then it would be clear what is at stake.

IV CONCLUSION

Law cannot and should not try to eradicate the view that homosexual conduct is inherently worthless and harmful. That view is too deeply ingrained in religious views that are held by large numbers of Americans. That view is being engaged, but it involves theological questions that are none of the state's business. Diversity of opinion, about matters of significance, is an inevitable consequence of a free society. The best we can hope for is to live peacefully together in mutual contempt.

---

[42] Koppelman, *supra* note 18, at 633.

[43] *Id.* at 638–39. See Wilson, Chapter 30, for the argument that without specific provisions to deal even with rare cases, no new state nondiscrimination laws are politically viable in the near term.

[44] For views on accommodations for religious universities, *see* Helfand, Chapter 11; Hoogstra et al., Chapter 25; Hill, Chapter 26.

10

From Conflict to Coexistence

The Catholic Response to the LGBT Community

Sister Jeannine Gramick

While much of this volume discusses how different parts of society approach the question of the inherent dignity of LGBT persons, this chapter explores a difference in approach within a single faith tradition, the Catholic Church, toward LGBT issues. This chapter shows that representatives of the official Church generally filter questions raised by sexual orientation and gender identity (SOGI) through the lens of sexual ethics. By contrast, rank-and-file Catholics in the parish, who are involved in the day-to-day lives of people, are concerned about the human welfare of LGBT persons, both inside the Church and outside it. These lay members see LGBT people through the lens of social teachings. Can these differences in approach between Church officials and Church members be resolved so the whole Church peacefully coexists?

To frame this question, consider two stories about the call for the Church to pastor its members rather than preach doctrine. First, a couple of years ago, I had a conversation with a bishop about a pastoral visit to members of an organization for LGBT Catholics. The group had invited him to come to their Sunday evening Mass or the social time following Mass. He declined, saying that his presence would validate that Mass's theology, which sanctions sexual expression for lesbian and gay persons who are in a committed, loving relationship. Because of his theological beliefs about sexual ethics, he felt he could not visit the group.

I pointed out to him that this invitation asked for something more pastoral, rather than a theological response. At that point, he became very pensive. He responded that, if he attended the social event following that Mass, it would not be a theological issue, but attending a Mass would be. I asked: "Would he pray about this pastoral visit?" The bishop is a good man with a kind heart who has selflessly devoted his life to the service of the Church. He suggested that the group's leader write him another letter, reiterating the request to stop by for a social visit some Sunday evening after their Mass.

The second story concerns Sandra Worsham, a retired teacher who worshipped at a Catholic church in Milledgeville, Georgia, since 1975.[1] She was in a thirty-five-year celibate relationship with a woman, but after her partner died, Sandra met and fell in love with Letha Hawkins, the daughter of a Baptist minister. Sandra had sung in the choir, been a Eucharistic minister and lector, and the Saturday night organist and cantor for about twenty-five years. Letha, who had a superb voice and church music degree, often sang solos during Communion. Many, perhaps most, people in the parish were very supportive of them as a couple. Some told Sandra that they had family members who were gay or who had died of AIDS and that they had never shared this information with anyone before.

On Valentine's Day 2010, Sandra and Letha were married in Vermont and, upon their return to Georgia, held a private reception in their home. After the celebration, the pastor called Sandra into his office and showed her a copy of the invitation, which a parishioner had shared with him. He told her that the purpose of marriage was procreation and that there was no way two women can have a baby. Sandra wanted to say, "I'm a postmenopausal woman and couldn't have a baby if I were marrying a man." Instead she said, "I didn't send you an invitation because I didn't want you to have to deal with this." After a pause, the pastor said, "What you did wrong here is making it public" and asked for her to resign as the parish organist. He said that she and Letha were welcomed to come to church, but she would not be allowed to receive the Eucharist.

This chapter explores the conflict within a single faith, Catholicism, about what the proper response to Sandra and Letha, and the LGBT Catholic group, should be.

I OFFICIAL CATHOLIC RESPONSE

For about twenty centuries, the magisterium – or teaching authority of the Catholic Church – has treated LGBT persons merely as embodiments of genital acts. This assumes that lesbian or gay persons are sexually active, coloring all discussions or decisions about them.[2] At the end of the nineteenth century, psychiatrists and psychologists started to distinguish sexual orientation from sexual behavior and concluded that homosexual acts, in and of themselves, were inadequate or sometimes confusing in assessing whether or not a person was homosexual. Sexual orientation, the scientists said, was the best indicator of a person's homosexuality. They referred to various sexual orientations as natural to animal species.[3]

---

[1]   Sandra Worsham, Going to Wings 297 (2017).
[2]   For example, when New Ways Ministry sponsored a retreat for celibate lesbian nuns in 1979, the Vatican responded that the word celibate was used as a slogan; i.e., lesbians are sexually active.
[3]   For studies see Minter, Chapter 4; Amber Ruigrok et al., *A Meta-analysis of Sex Differences in Human Brain Structure*, 39 Neuroscience & Biobehavioral Revs. 34 (2014).

Official Catholic sexual ethics did not incorporate the concept of orientation in its discourse until a 1986 Vatican document used the words "homosexual condition or tendency."[4] The document refused to use the scientific words "sexual orientation," prevalent at the time. The Vatican said that an "overly benign interpretation" had been given to this tendency. While scientists thought the orientation was a natural phenomenon, the document called it an "objective disorder," a characterization that was neither good nor even neutral. Homosexual acts, of course, were judged immoral or "intrinsically disordered."

The magisterial teaching on homosexuality is a logical extension of its teaching on Christian marriage and sexual morality. For centuries, Catholic doctrine has maintained that (1) every genital act must be open to procreation in the context of marriage because of the very nature of human sexuality and (2) procreative capacity is part of the natural law that God ordained for the universe.[5] Because contraception and masturbation do not lead to procreation, the teaching says, these acts are also forbidden. Similarly, any heterosexual activity outside of marriage is also forbidden.

The Bible is not the primary basis for the magisterium's opposition to same-sex acts, as it is for some Christian churches. Scriptural texts such as Genesis's account of creation and the heterosexual thrust of the Hebrew and Christian Scriptures are used to support or buttress the traditional argument, which is ultimately based on the natural law and God's purpose for sexuality.

The major architect of the sexual teachings was St. Augustine of Hippo, whose ideas were influenced by the philosophy of Stoicism he encountered in the late fourth and early fifth centuries.[6] Like the Stoics, Augustine was suspicious of any pleasure. Sexual pleasure needed a reasonable justification to make the pleasure morally good. The obvious justification for him: procreation. This logic established the direction of Christian sexual ethics for the next 1,600 years.

Sexual desire, Augustine thought, was an evil, uncontrollable passion, which needed to be ordered rightly and according to reason in order to justify its use in a right and moral way. This ordering could be done only in a heterosexual marriage open to procreation. Any other sexual act, he maintained, was the result of an unnatural or disordered sexual desire. Therefore, anal and oral sex, masturbation, and *coitus interruptus* were unnatural acts because they did not result in procreation. In this logic, incest and rape, although immoral, constituted "natural" acts because they could result in procreation.

---

[4] All cites in the same paragraph are to Letter to the Bishops of the Catholic Church on the Pastoral Care of Homosexual Persons, Congregation For The Doctrine Of The Faith ¶3 (Oct. 1, 1986), https://perma.cc/8KHF-D8EQ. The 1994 *Catechism of the Catholic Church* also described homosexual acts as "acts of grave depravity." Catechism of the Catholic Church ¶ 2357 (1994).

[5] Catechism, *supra* note 4, at ¶2331–2400.

[6] Margaret A. Farley, Just Love: A Framework for Christian Sexual Ethics 38–45 (2006).

Contemporary theologians recognize that our understanding of natural law continues to change.[7] We no longer believe that women are naturally inferior to men or are "misbegotten males," as St. Thomas Aquinas and the Christian Church taught in the thirteenth century. Slavery is no longer considered a natural institution.[8] With knowledge gained from the sciences, society now knows that a homosexual orientation is natural for a minority of the human population. Furthermore, homosexual behavior naturally occurs in other mammalian species.[9]

II THEOLOGIANS

This shift in determining what is natural and what constitutes natural law has brought about a comparable shift among theologians in evaluating sexuality, who have "mov[ed] away from a static, predominantly biological, understanding of natural law to a more dynamic interpretation of it as our participation in God's plan."[10] Most Catholic ethicists do not agree with the traditional, negative moral evaluation of homosexuality. Some take a moderate stance; they maintain that same-sex behavior is morally permissible in the context of a loving, faithful relationship, but that a homosexual orientation is inferior to a heterosexual one. These theologians arrive at their conclusions in various ways. Some maintain that a heterosexual orientation was originally part of God's plan for creation, but because of original sin or some component that went awry, a certain percentage of the population is sexually attracted to their own gender. The Church should not doom these individuals to a lonely life of celibacy, but should advocate a viable option of forming a committed relationship, within which the couple can express their love sexually in a holy and wholesome way. Charles Curran, a world-renowned Catholic moral theologian and leading exponent of the moderate school of thought, applies his theory of compromise to homosexuality along these lines.[11]

Other theologians take a more liberal position.[12] Like the moderates, the progressives maintain that same-sex behavior is morally permissible in the context of a loving, faithful relationship, but they believe that a homosexual orientation is just as good as a heterosexual one; no orientation is inferior or superior to any other. They see sexual orientation as an example of the diversity vital to God's plan for humanity.

---

[7] *Id.*

[8] *Cf.* William N. Eskridge, Jr., *Noah's Curse: How Religion Often Conflates Status, Belief, and Conduct to Resist Antidiscrimination Norms*, 45 GA. L. REV. 657 (2011).

[9] *See* BRUCE BAGEMIHL, BIOLOGICAL EXUBERANCE: ANIMAL HOMOSEXUALITY AND NATURAL DIVERSITY (1999).

[10] ANTHONY KOSNICK, THE CATHOLIC THEOLOGICAL SOCIETY OF AMERICA, HUMAN SEXUALITY, NEW DIRECTIONS IN AMERICAN CATHOLIC THOUGHT 124 (1977).

[11] CHARLES E. CURRAN, A NEW LOOK AT CHRISTIAN MORALITY: CHRISTIAN MORALITY TODAY, II (1968).

[12] *See, e.g.,* FARLEY, *supra* note 6.

Progressive sexual ethicists believe that principles such as partners' free-consent, equality, and sense of commitment provide a better basis for evaluating the good in a partnership than does the procreative norm. Of course, criteria such as mutuality, equality, and commitment can be applied to heterosexual couples as well. The traditional reproductive rule is expanded to a norm of creativity, generativity, or fruitfulness, which values the partners' contributions to the human community as a result of the partners' participating in an intimate relationship. Raising other people's children is one example of a couple's fruitfulness.[13]

Some bishops, particularly in Germany, acknowledge that new insights about human nature and the changing conditions of contemporary society should affect the Church's teaching on sexuality. Johan Bonny, a bishop in Belgium, has advocated that the Church should have some kind of recognition of same-sex relationships.[14] Bishop Geoffrey Robinson of Sydney, Australia, has publicly called for a reexamination of the traditional teachings on sexuality.[15] These bishops are the exception. Most of the world's bishops hold to the traditional procreative ethic.

The Vatican has not embraced any calls for change or reexamination of sexual teachings. In fact, during the papacies of John Paul II and Benedict XVI, many moderate and progressive theologians were sanctioned by the Congregation for the Doctrine of the Faith, the Vatican department formerly known as the Office of the Inquisition. During the papacy of Pope Francis, no theologians have been silenced or punished; this pope has encouraged open debate and discussion. He exhorted the bishops at the two Synods on the Family in 2014 and 2015 to speak their minds, even if they disagreed with him, and some conservative cardinals have. But while he has called for new pastoral approaches to the LGBT community, he has not repudiated traditional sexual ethics.[16]

Yet, as Pope Francis ended his South America trip in 2015, he urged young people to "[m]ake a mess ... (a mess) which gives us a free heart, a mess which gives us solidarity, a mess which gives us hope."[17] A mess happens when there is diversity of thought and opinion, all of which is needed before a theological consensus can develop.

[13] *See id.*
[14] John A. Dick, *Belgian Bishop Advocates Church Recognition of Gay Relationships*, Nat'l Cath. Rep. (Dec. 30, 2014), https://perma.cc/WA25-TTRN.
[15] Bishop Geoffrey Robinson, Confronting Power and Sex in the Catholic Church: Reclaiming the Spirit of Jesus (2007). *See also* Geoffrey James Robinson, The 2015 Synod: The Crucial Questions: Divorce and Homosexuality (2015).
[16] John P. Langan, S.J., *See the Person: Understanding Pope Francis' Statements on Homosexuality*, Am.: The Jesuit Rev. (Feb. 25, 2014), https://perma.cc/GTM5-4KBR.
[17] Philip Pullella & Daniela Desantis, *Pope Closes South America Trip Urging Youths to "Make a Mess,"* Reuters (July 12, 2015). https://perma.cc/HJ45-YJPE.

III THE LAITY

As the story of Sandra and Letha shows, the laity are interested in the person – their feelings and their ability to work together and be good neighbors. They are concerned about the lives, not the sexual behavior of their LGBT friends, relatives, or coworkers, something considered a private matter. The laity instinctively follow the Church's social teachings, which are expressed by Jesus in the Gospels and found in various papal encyclicals and documents from councils and bishops' conferences. Three themes of the social teachings that particularly apply to LGBT people are the dignity of the human person, the option for the poor, and the rights of workers.

A *The Dignity of the Human Person Within Community*

The Catholic Church teaches that each person has a basic dignity because each has been created in the image and likeness of God.[18] Because of human dignity, a person should not be neglected or ignored, made to feel worthless, or treated more as an object than as a person. Dignity means care, self-respect, self-worth, and physical and psychological empowerment. The belief that the dignity of each person is to be honored and respected is the foundation of all the principles of Catholic social teaching and provides a moral vision for the human family. The measure of any institution or state is whether, and how, it protects and enhances the life and dignity of its people.

Respect for the dignity of the human person includes respect for the dignity of LGBT people. This means acknowledging and accepting them fully as human persons with equal human rights in search of a valuable place in society. According to a 2013 survey by the Pew Research Center, there is a great acceptance of lesbian and gay people in some, though not all, countries with a heavily Catholic population.[19] There is a general tolerance in North America, Latin America, and Europe but a strong rejection in the Middle East, Asia, and Africa, although there are exceptions within each of these continents. Homosexuality is punishable by death in ten countries, particularly in Africa and parts of Asia.

Catholic bishops' adherence to sexual teaching becomes a problem when it is used to oppose the rights and dignity of the person. Consider Africa. In 2009, with the support of the bishops, Uganda introduced the Anti-Homosexuality Act, also known as "Kill the Gays Bill," which sought the death penalty for homosexual acts and criminalized the medical treatment of gays with HIV/AIDS.[20] Many people lived in fear and hid from their family, friends, and coworkers. David Cato, a

---

[18] CATECHISM, *supra* note 4, at ¶355.
[19] *See The Global Divide on Homosexuality: Greater Acceptance in More Secular and Affluent Countries*, PEW RES. CTR. (June 4, 2013), https://perma.cc/T6QN-2VPC.
[20] Gregory Warner, *Uganda Passes Anti-Gay Bill that Includes Life in Prison*, NPR (Dec. 20, 2013, 4:01 PM), https://perma.cc/S9HP-995B.

prominent gay activist who spoke about the bill at a United Nations conference, was beaten to death. The initial bill failed and a follow-up bill passed but was later annulled on a technicality. Ugandan LGBT people still face discrimination and worry about a new law. Frank Mugisha, the executive director of Sexual Minorities Uganda, told a Catholic audience about the enormous influence of the Church in enacting the annulled measure because 44 percent of Ugandans are Catholic.[21]

Mugisha also pointed to Tanzania, Rwanda, and Nigeria, where homophobia and transphobia are rampant. In Malawi, merely *being* gay or lesbian is illegal, with a penalty of up to fourteen years of hard labor for men and up to five years imprisonment for women. Even though there is a government moratorium on enforcing these laws, Malawi's bishops encouraged Catholics to support the arrest and imprisonment of lesbian or gay people.[22] In contrast, the Catholic Church in India is speaking out for the rights of LGBT people and has even established a school for transgender people.[23]

Sexual ethics should never trump social ethics. Sexual ethics is culture bound. Civilizations have drawn up their own rules to regulate sexual transactions among their people. What is sexually permissible in one society may not be in another.

By contrast, the universality of social ethics is illustrated in the Universal Declaration of Human Rights adopted in 1948 by the member countries of the General Assembly of the United Nations.[24] The Gospels reveal that, although Jesus alluded briefly to divorce, he was not overly concerned about sexual proscriptions; he was, however, very much concerned about how people treated each other.[25] For the Catholic, social teachings, which are rooted in the Gospel, are basic and fundamental. They apply to the whole human community, regardless of culture. Social teachings transcend sexual ones.

The person is not only a sacred individual but also a social being, who is called to participate in family and various communities. Many Catholics do not believe that LGBT persons should be alienated from their biological families. To counter the alienation that many other Catholic families still experience, Fortunate Families was founded by a husband-wife team who have a gay son. This network of Catholic parents of LGBT sons and daughters works to bring about respect and justice for their children. They provide resources to help Catholic families deal with such concerns as acceptance or rejection in family

[21] Patricia Lefevere, *Frank Mugisha Tells New Ways Ministry of Human Rights Fight*, Nat'l Cath. Rep. (May 5, 2017), https://perma.cc/22V3-JTQ6.

[22] Robert Shine, *Jail LGBT People, Say Malawi's Bishops in New Pastoral Letter on Mercy*, New Ways Ministry (Mar. 28, 2016), https://perma.cc/U5DJ-L8TF.

[23] Shawn Sebastian, *Church Offers Support for Kerala's Transgender People: Priests, Nuns Act to Combat Discrimination, Exploitation of the Community*, UCANews.com (Jan. 3, 2017), https://perma.cc/V8Y2-FQNU.

[24] Universal Declaration of Human Rights, G. A. Res. 217 A (III), UN Doc A/810 (1948).

[25] *See* Matthew 22:35–40 and 25:34–40.

relationships, fear for their child's physical, spiritual, or emotional security, and the response of the institutional church.[26]

Because marriage and family are fundamental social institutions, parents want their gay sons and lesbian daughters to be able to marry and form their own families, just as their heterosexual children can do. Today, 67 percent of US Catholics respond that they support the legalization of same-sex marriage.[27]

B *Option for the Poor and Vulnerable*

Another social teaching of the Church calls for a special outreach to the poor and vulnerable. Poverty is not merely the absence or scarcity of money, material possessions, or property. Although there certainly are LGBT people who are materially destitute, this teaching refers also to those who are poor in more subtle ways. Poverty is associated with a whole range of crucial human features, such as physical and mental health, emotional well-being, and acceptance. Poverty could mean being exposed to greater personal risks, treated as inferior, less able to access life's necessities, or having a poor quality of life.

LGBT people are vulnerable because, if they are not open, they may risk personal blackmail. If they are open about their sexual orientation or gender identity, they are often the victims of bullying.[28] Many feel they need to conceal their identities for fear of being rejected by their families, criminalized by the state, or ostracized by their own social communities. Being in the closet can have devastating consequences, such as low self-esteem, chronic depression, and even self-hatred. Too often LGBT people are socialized into believing they are bad or immoral. Some internalize homophobia or self-loathing.

The effects of being poor and vulnerable can lead LGBT people to substance abuse, addictions, and suicide. Suicide is the second leading cause of death among young people between ten and twenty-four years of age.[29] The rate of attempted suicide is four times greater for lesbian, gay, and bisexual youth than for heterosexual youth.[30]

---

[26] For further information about Fortunate Families, see FORTUNATE FAMILIES: CATHOLIC PARENTS OF LGBT CHILDREN, https://perma.cc/678M-2BWX.

[27] *See Support for Same-Sex Marriage Grows, Even Among Groups That Had Been Skeptical*, PEW RES. CTR. (June 26, 2017), https://perma.cc/QJ47-XEDH.

[28] *See* Minter, Chapter 4; Warbelow, Chapter 31. *See* Ann P. Haas et al., *Suicide Attempts Among Transgender and Gender Non-Conforming Adults*, NAT'L TRANSGENDER DISCRIMINATION SURV. (2014) (reporting that the rate of suicide attempts among trans individuals ranges as high as 41%).

[29] Erin M. Sullivan et al., *Suicide Trends Among Persons Aged 10–24 Years – United States, 1994–2012*, 64 MORB. MORTAL WKLY. REP., no. 8 (Mar. 15, 2015), at 201.

[30] *See* Minter, Chapter 4; Ann P. Haas et al., *Suicide Attempts Among Transgender and Gender Non-Conforming Adults*, NAT'L TRANSGENDER DISCRIMINATION SURV. (2014) (reporting that the rate of suicide attempts among trans individuals ranges as high as 41%). *See generally*

Many Catholic organizations are trying to bring the vulnerability of LGBT people out of the closet and are adding LGBT concerns to their justice agenda.[31] The Global Network of Rainbow Catholics grew out of a meeting before the 2015 Synod on the Family in Rome.[32] This international coalition of LGBT and heterosexual people brings together about fifty organizations from Africa, Asia, Europe, Latin America and the Caribbean, North America, and Oceania.

C The Rights of Workers

The dignity of work and the rights of workers form a major part of Catholic social teaching. Unfortunately, violations of worker rights for LGBT persons, or those associated with them, are widespread. Consider the poignant story of Margie Winters, a long-time religious education director in a Catholic school, who was fired after a disgruntled parent complained about Margie's marriage to another woman. "I still love that community because it's a part of my heart," Winters said. "It was like a death. This kind of firing is a trauma. The sense of exile has been hardest for me."[33] Despite prolonged protests from a majority of her students and their parents, Margie Winters was not reinstated.

Since 2007, in the United States more than fifty employees in Catholic institutions have been fired, forced to resign, or had their jobs threatened because of their orientation, gender identity, or legal marital status – in parts of the country where those firings remain legal.[34] This number omits individuals who never make their cases public. Among the fired are devoted Church musicians, teachers, administrators, and even food service directors. In one case, a woman was fired from a Catholic high school because her lesbian partner was listed in her mother's obituary.[35] In another case, a university rescinded its employment offer because of the candidate's academic research about lesbians.[36]

The Catholic laity have been vocal in objecting to these outcomes, often with public demonstrations or petitions to authorities. A 2014 fact sheet from the Public Religion Research Institute reported that Catholic support for the worker

TREVOR PROJECT, https://perma.cc/DV69-PCLU (leading U.S. crisis intervention and suicide prevention organization serving LGBT youth since 1998).

[31] *See* DIGNITYUSA (founded in 1969), https://perma.cc/89HC-FDWN; NEW WAYS MINISTRY (founded in 1977), https://perma.cc/6ZCK-2FJF.

[32] *See* GLOBAL NETWORK OF RAINBOW CATHOLICS, https://perma.cc/6GZW-7J2F.

[33] John Gehring, *LGBT Catholics & the Francis Papacy: A Complex Conversation*, COMMONWEAL MAG. (May 22, 2017), https://perma.cc/FB5F-3LD9.

[34] For a review of state nondiscrimination laws, see Wilson, Chapter 30.

[35] Francis DeBernardo, *Lesbian Teacher Fired for Listing Her Partner's Name in Her Mother's Obituary*, NEW WAYS MINISTRY (Apr. 17, 2013), https://perma.cc/SY7F-V3UT.

[36] Susan Donaldson James, *Marquette University Hires Lesbian Dean, Then Rescinds Offer*, ABC NEWS (May 26, 2010), https://perma.cc/5YCU-SLZH.

rights of gay and lesbian people is strong – 73 percent favor workplace nondiscrimination laws.[37]

In 2016, the editor-in-chief of *Catholic News Service*, an affiliate of the United States Conference of Catholic Bishops, was forced to resign for tweeting about LGBT issues from his personal account. An institutional paranoia has developed, not only about LGBT people, but also about public discussion of these issues.

At the bottom of all these cases is the concern that LGBT workers are held "to different standards or [are] dismiss[ed] abruptly"[38] for things that can cause scandal. Consider the German bishops' policies, which currently prohibit employees of Catholic institutions from being dismissed because of divorce and remarriage *or* entering same-sex unions. Previously, most divorced and remarried heterosexuals were not dismissed, but married lesbian and gay persons were. To prevent the selective enforcement of a "morals clause," the bishops changed their policies.

Consider these insightful questions regarding the criteria for hiring and firing in Catholic institutions:

> How just is it to fire someone whose life or practices are not in accord with official church teaching? Where do you draw the line? Do you get fired if you have remarried without an annulment? Do you get fired if you don't attend Mass on Sunday regularly? Do you get fired because you are a Protestant who does not recognize the Catholic hierarchical structure? A more theological question is how perfect do all church employees have to be? We are all sinners who fall way short of the mark. Will our church employ only people whose lives are near blameless?[39]

Work means more than just making a living. It gives purpose and dignity to people by enabling them to participate in God's creation. Through work, a person gains a sense of self-esteem and community recognition. Work becomes each person's gift to the community. How much poorer would the human family be without the works of Michelangelo, Tchaikovsky, and Audre Lorde? If the integral value of work and the respect it engenders is to be protected, then the basic rights of workers must be respected, including the right to work of LGBT people.[40]

---

[37] *Fact Sheet: Gay and Lesbian Issues, Spotlight Analysis*, Pub. Religion Research Inst. (June 8, 2014), https://perma.cc/PU6M-6UZR. 61% of Catholics favor allowing gay and lesbian couples to adopt children, which they can do everywhere in America now by law. *See* Appendix.

[38] Editorial, *Unjust Discrimination*, Am. the Jesuit Rev. (Nov. 7, 2016).

[39] Francis DeBernardo, *Church Must Change Its Ideas Toward Gay and Lesbian Employees*, Nat'l Cath. Rep. (May 3, 2012), https://perma.cc/72GT-XAAS.

[40] For an exhaustive treatment of worker rights regarding LGBT individuals in Catholic institutions, together with resource material, see New Ways Ministry: Bondings 2.0, https://perma.cc/NJ4F-N5LG.

IV MUCH-NEEDED CONVERSION

Each previous example illustrates that Catholic laity view LGBT people through the lens of Catholic social teaching, while Catholic bishops reduce LGBT people to their sexual practices. How can this conflict in approach and emphasis be resolved? What responses from the hierarchy and the laity can ameliorate the tensions? Is a peaceful coexistence even possible? This chapter offers a simple suggestion: both parties need to engage in a process of conversion.

A *Conversion of the Hierarchy*

The Catholic Catechism says that lesbian and gay people should be accepted with "respect, compassion, and sensitivity."[41] The conversion of Church leaders can begin by putting these words into practice by following Pope Francis's example. Without changing the Church's traditional teachings on sexual ethics, Pope Francis has called for a new way of treating LGBT people and others on the periphery of the institutional Church – specifically, ending the obsession with issues such as abortion, same-sex marriage, and contraception.

Pope Francis said that the Church sometimes seems locked up "in small-minded rules" and forgets the most important message, proclaiming that Jesus Christ has saved humanity. He warned his ministers of the danger of being too rigorist or too lax. They should be ministers of mercy, accompany people, and heal their wounds.[42]

Catholic doctrine on conscience, rooted in the human person as a free, intelligent, and responsible moral agent, is a primary Church teaching affirmed at the highest level of authority. The teaching about conscience is most sacred because "[e]very one of us will render an account of oneself to God (Rom 14:12), and for this reason each person is bound to obey one's conscience."[43] Commenting on this teaching, Joseph Ratzinger, who later became Pope Benedict XVI, said, "Over the pope as an expression of the binding claim of ecclesiastical authority, there stands one's own conscience, which must be obeyed before all else, even if necessary against the requirement of ecclesiastical authority."[44]

As Pope Francis explained, structural and organizational reforms are needed, but they are less significant than a change of heart, which must come first. The people want and need pastors, not bureaucrats. Pastoral ministry should not be "obsessed

---

[41] CATECHISM, *supra* note 4, at ¶2358.

[42] Eugenio Scalfari, *The Pope: How the Church will Change*, LA REPUBBLICA (Oct. 1, 2013), https://perma.cc/NW83-84ZZ.

[43] *Declaration of Religious Freedom*, in DOCUMENTS OF VATICAN II ¶ 11 (Walter Abbott ed., 1966).

[44] Joseph Ratzinger, *Gaudium et Spes*, in COMMENTARY ON THE DOCUMENTS OF VATICAN II, VOL. V 134 (Herbert Vorgrimler ed., 1967).

with the disjointed transmission of a multitude of doctrines to be insistently imposed."[45] Pope Francis has said that priests and bishops should be shepherds who live with the "smell of the sheep." He sees the Church as a "field hospital" after a battle where ministers care for the wounded with "God's mercy." Pope Francis has returned to these images repeatedly to describe a Church that is mandated to follow in Jesus' footsteps.

In one striking example of caring for the wounded and marginalized, Pope Francis met personally with a transgender man who had been excluded from his parish in Spain. The pope described the man as "he who was she who is he" and used male pronouns, as the man did. "I have also met homosexual persons, accompanied them, brought them closer to the Lord, as an apostle, and I have never abandoned them," he said. "Jesus surely doesn't tell them 'go away because you are homosexual.'"[46]

The Church's ministers are to be "like the good Samaritan, who washes, cleans, and raises up his neighbor." They need to leave no one behind and accept those who have "a flair for finding new paths." In addition to keeping its doors open, Francis advocates that the Church find new roads, step outside itself, and go out to those who no longer come to church or have quit altogether. The Gospel needs to be proclaimed on every street corner. That takes boldness and courage, he says.[47]

About a year after his 2013 election, Francis showed boldness by asking for a meeting with Bishop Jacques Gaillot, who had a flair for finding new paths. Bishop Gaillot was removed from his diocese in Northern France in 1995 for blessing the union of a same-sex couple. According to Gaillot, he told the Pope how he had recently blessed a homosexual couple and a divorced couple, saying of Pope Francis: "he listened, he is open to all those things ... He said that to bless is to speak well of God to people ... what you do (for the downtrodden) is good."[48]

Pope Francis, through an aide, sent his own blessings to a same-sex couple, who were legally married in Brazil. They wrote the Pope about the upcoming baptism of their three adopted children and received a congratulatory letter that said, "Pope Francisco wishes you congratulations, calling for his family abundance of divine graces, to live constantly and faithfully the condition of Christians."[49]

[45] Pope Francis, *Evangelii Gaudium (The Joy of the Gospel)*, Apostolic Exhortation ¶ 35 (2013).

[46] *Pope Francis' In-Flight Press Conference from Azerbaijan*, Cath. News Agency (Oct. 2, 2016, 6:08 PM), https://perma.cc/8A9E-GDDD.

[47] *Id.*

[48] Agence France-Presse, *"Red Cleric" Defends Migrants, Gay Rights in Pope Chat*, Yahoo! (Sept. 1, 2015), https://perma.cc/G5GN-6CWY.

[49] Michael K. Lavers, *Pope Francis Congratulates Gay Couple for Baptizing Children*, Wash. Blade (Aug. 8, 2017), https://perma.cc/F5DG-9KDS. *See also* Francis DeBernardo, *Pope Congratulates, Blesses Gay Couple on the Baptism of Their Adopted Children*, New Ways Ministry (Aug. 9, 2017), https://perma.cc/6LQU-DZPJ.

Pope Francis made a bold statement when he welcomed some fifty LGBT Catholics and their families on pilgrimage with New Ways Ministry. Before an Ash Wednesday audience, papal ushers led the pilgrims through thousands gathered in St. Peter's Square, up the steps of the Basilica, to reserved VIP seats on a platform within twenty-five yards of the Pope's chair. The place of honor represented a striking welcome to *all* LGBT Catholics and their allies.[50]

Some local church leaders have begun to follow his lead. For example, Cardinal Joseph Tobin greeted an LGBT pilgrimage to his cathedral in Newark, New Jersey. "I am Joseph, your brother," the cardinal told the group. "I am your brother, as a disciple of Jesus. I am your brother, as a sinner who finds mercy with the Lord."[51] Bishop John Stowe led prayer at a symposium about LGBT people and has set up an LGBT ministry in his Kentucky diocese.[52] And Bishop Antônio Carlos Cruz Santos of Caicó, Brazil, told his congregation in a homily, "'If [being gay] is not a choice, if it is not a disease, in the perspective of faith it can only be a gift . . . The gospel par excellence is the gospel of inclusion."[53] In his homespun language, poetic metaphors, and concrete witness, Pope Francis is calling Church leaders to a conversion in their approach toward LGBT people and their families. Are the laity called to a similar conversion toward their bishops?

B Conversion of the Laity

Most of the Catholic laity in the United States and Western Europe disagrees with the sexual teachings of their Church.[54] A progressive Catholic publication said it is time for dialogue on sexual ethics, for "[w]ithout a change in the church's teaching on sex and sexuality, can LGBT people ever hope to be treated with equality and justice by the hierarchy?"

The editorial points out the interesting observation that the Church's opposition to same-sex acts camouflages the fact that its sexual teaching is opposed not only to homosexual acts but also to other sexual acts that a majority of Catholics practice, such as nonprocreative sex with contraception and masturbation. These, too, are condemned as intrinsically evil or disordered. In reality, very few Catholics live up to the current sexual norms.

---

[50] David Gibson, *Gay Catholics Find a New Tone Under Pope Francis, and From Their Own Bishops*, Wash. Post (Feb. 16, 2015), https://perma.cc/377Z-JWGX.

[51] Sharon Otterman, *As Church Shifts, a Cardinal Welcomes Gays; They Embrace a "Miracle,"* N.Y. Times (June 13, 2017), https://perma.cc/9DXF-FR5M.

[52] Patricia Lefevere, *Bishop John Stowe Leads Prayer at LGBT Catholic Gathering*, Nat'l Cath. Rep. (May 4, 2017), https://perma.cc/W8YA-NT9W.

[53] Inés San Martin, *Bishop Calls Homosexuality "Gift from God," Seeks to End "Prejudices that Kill,"* Crux (Aug. 9, 2017), https://perma.cc/5MJU-CR8Y.

[54] It should be noted that the official sexual teaching has changed over the centuries, so there is reason to believe that it will continue to evolve.

Importantly, by repeatedly hammering the procreative standard, the Church's guidance in fostering healthy and mature relationships remains underdeveloped. Indeed, if bishops "were more vocal about their opposition to masturbation, in vitro fertilization or vasectomies as they are in their campaign again same-sex marriage, perhaps more Catholics would realize how urgent the need is to rethink the entirety of the Church's sexual ethics."[55]

Many Catholics are frustrated and angered by repeated denunciations of sexual practices. Many stop going to church or stop paying attention to any statements by bishops. What can these Catholics do? What is their call to conversion? It may be a matter of interior spiritual discipline – a compassion toward their leaders. In an attempt to "get inside the other person's skin," they could try to understand where these condemnations are coming from. What is the mind-set or worldview of Church leaders who feel they need to defend orthodoxy, which they often equate with sexual ethics?

V WORLDVIEWS

Most, though not all, of the world's approximately 5,000 bishops were trained in a worldview of "royal consciousness."[56] In this worldview, faith is adherence to a set of doctrines in which the Church representative envisions himself (the person is always a male) as the defender of the faith. Clearly, the institution is free from error because the truth, which is unambiguous and possessed in its entirety, has been divinely communicated to the leaders. The responsibility of religious authorities is to safeguard the truth and to uphold the teachings strictly so that the truth can be handed down in its purity from generation to generation. The members of the religious group are thus freed from confusion and anxiety because they are assured that they possess the truth.

Because authority is divinely ordained, it is not open to criticism. All members need to agree with institutional positions, which maintain the status quo. Dissent only weakens or threatens the truth and opposition undermines authority; therefore, dissenters should be silenced. Obedience to good order and to hierarchical authorities becomes a supreme virtue. Conformity, disguised as unity, must be maintained. Naturally, decisions need to be made for the good working order of the institution, which subsumes the good of the individual member.

Some version of this royal consciousness worldview was routinely taught in most seminaries around the globe since the Reformation and the Council of Trent in the sixteenth century. It became the unarticulated philosophy in the training of future priests until the Second Vatican Council, 1962–65, when another worldview began

---

[55] Editorial, *Time for Dialogue on Sexual Ethics*, Nat'l Cath. Rep. (Aug. 11–24, 2017).
[56] For a biblical treatment of "royal consciousness," see Walter Brueggemann, The Prophetic Imagination 21–38 (2d ed. 2001).

to gain ground. Taking its name from the prophets of the Hebrew Scriptures, the prophetic worldview proclaimed that faith was not so much a strict adherence to formulas or doctrines, but a love relationship with God. Faith was a matter of the heart and not the head. Faith was belief in a Person, not in a set of teachings.

In the prophetic worldview, truth is not static. Through a process of discussion and theological reflection, the community is in a continual search for truth, the fullness of which will be revealed only at the end of earthly time. In this worldview, there is no silencing of dissent. Alternative viewpoints are welcomed so that ideas can be tested. Unity does not mean uniformity. Diversity is respected and accepted because the community believes it is united in what is essential.

Those who embrace a prophetic worldview believe that authority rests in a community of individuals and each person's conscience is to be respected. There are no royal figures or gatekeepers to the divine because the Spirit speaks through all God's people. Because all humans are fallible, authority figures can err. Those who live according to this worldview believe in a servant leadership, where the responsibility of the spiritual leader is to serve others, not oneself, or the institution. Obedience is not the highest virtue, unless it is obedience to the will of God. Love is the supreme virtue because love is the ultimate fulfillment of the will of God.

The Church's teachings represent the community's wisdom gained throughout the ages. As scientific information and human experiences enable the community to grow in knowledge and understanding, the Church gains greater insights into the truth. This process is what has been called development of doctrine.[57]

This prophetic worldview is foreign to most priests and bishops who are caught up in a medieval structure and do not know how to break out of it. The clerical system indoctrinated them into a viewpoint that is static, unbending, and bound by legalism. Too few know the virtues of compassion and flexibility that are learned and needed in pastoral life. The conversion that the laity needs is the grace to be able to put a human face on the institution. The laity needs to appreciate that Church leaders are human and fallible, but good human beings who are committed to the Church and the welfare of the people entrusted to them.

VI COEXISTENCE REQUIRES DIALOGUE

Hopefully, the hierarchy and laity can move from active conflict to peaceful coexistence by means of conversion. Bishops need to stop firing LGBT church workers and practice equal treatment before the law. They need to speak out about the bullying, violence, and repressive laws against LGBT people around the globe. The laity needs to be sympathetic to the weight of centuries of tradition and the cultural norms in diverse parts of the world that Church leaders are contending with.

---

[57] *See* JOHN HENRY NEWMAN, AN ESSAY ON THE DEVELOPMENT OF CHRISTIAN DOCTRINE (1989).

In the midst of this conversion is the need for dialogue. Both parties require a bridge of dialogue to bring them together in a place where they can tell their stories and listen respectfully to one another.[58] The laity have wanted and sought some kind of bridge for a long time and some bishops have already set foot on the bridge.

As they walk on this bridge of dialogue, I hope that Church leaders and laity will recall Jesus' discourse at the Last Supper where he uses the image of the vine and the branches to describe the community's relationship to him and to each other (John 15:1–8). Jesus comforts his disciples by describing himself as a vine, the source and sustenance of life for the branches. The members of the community are the branches that abide in the vine to live and bear fruit. The laity are probably the leftmost branches that hunger for new growth while Church leaders are most likely right-leaning branches that grow in a seemingly ordered way. But all the branches are connected. They are all one because they are all rooted, nourished, and sustained in the vine, which is Christ. As they dialogue on the bridge, may leaders and laity feel that they are truly united in Christ, who mandated his followers to "love one another as I have loved you" (John 15:12).

---

[58] For a good treatment of building bridges, see JAMES MARTIN SJ. BUILDING A BRIDGE: HOW THE CATHOLIC CHURCH AND THE LGBT COMMUNITY CAN ENTER INTO A RELATIONSHIP OF RESPECT, COMPASSION, AND SENSITIVITY (2017).

11

Implied-Consent Religious Institutionalism

Applications and Limits

Michael A. Helfand

What makes religious institutions different? This question stands at the center of numerous contemporary religious liberty debates. Should houses of worship be allowed to make distinctions in the hiring and firing of ministers on the basis of religion or faith tenets? And should religiously motivated business owners be allowed to decline to provide their services at same-sex marriages?

Much of this debate stems from a recent legal puzzle. In 1990, the US Supreme Court held that the Free Exercise Clause did not require the government to provide individuals exemptions from laws so long as those laws do not target or discriminate against religion. Thus, the fact that a law substantially burdens someone's religious exercise does not have constitutional significance so long as the law is facially neutral and generally applicable.[1]

Nonetheless, courts continued to hold that – in some circumstances – religious institutions ought to receive constitutional protections from laws that do not target or discriminate against religion.[2] For example, there is widespread consensus that a Catholic church or an Orthodox synagogue should be *constitutionally* permitted to reject all female applicants for an open priest or rabbi position,[3] even if Title VII of the 1964 Civil Rights Act did not include an exception to the general prohibition against sex discrimination in employment.[4] And this constitutional protection still operates even though the prohibition against sex discrimination in employment does not target religion in any way; it is undeniably a facially neutral and generally applicable law. So why the disparity in outcomes when it comes to laws that do not

---

[1] Emp't Div. v. Smith, 494 U.S. 872, 901–02 (1990).

[2] *See, e.g.*, Hosanna-Tabor Evangelical Lutheran Church & School v. EEOC, 565 U.S. 171 (2012).

[3] The EEOC's attorney in *Hosanna-Tabor* conceded this point during oral argument. *See* Or. Arg. Tr. 32:10–33:18, https://perma.cc/8724-S2CN.

[4] To be sure, Title VII itself does provide potential statutory grounds for exemption in such circumstances. *See, e.g.*, 42 U.S.C. § 2000e-1 (2012).

target religion? Why should individuals be unable to assert religious liberty claims in cases where religious institutions are granted some degree of legal protection?

For some, the distinction itself cannot be justified on religious liberty grounds; they would allow no exceptions for religious organizations or individuals.[5] For others, the reason why religious institutions sometimes receive wider legal protections is because they fall under the broader umbrella of freedom of association.[6] Therefore, a religious institution, like other secular institutions, such as private clubs, ought to be afforded certain protections from neutral and generally applicable laws.

The Supreme Court in *Hosanna-Tabor v. EEOC* rejected this view as "untenable" and "hard to square with the text of the First Amendment itself."[7] The Court did not, however, provide much of a solution, arguing that its reluctance to grant free exercise protections only extended to "government regulation of … outward physical acts," which differed fundamentally from "government interference with an internal church decision that affects the faith and mission of the church itself."[8] To many, this seemed like a distinction without a difference. Furthermore, surely the employment decision at issue in *Hosanna-Tabor* was also an "outward physical act."[9]

To fill this doctrinal void, courts and scholars have provided alternative explanations for the unique legal and constitutional standing of religious institutions. The "sovereigntist approach" views religious institutions as asserting religious liberty claims that are fundamentally different than those of individuals;[10] religious institutions are constitutionally granted inherent sovereignty over their own internal affairs so that they can develop religious doctrine and practice free from government interference and influence.[11]

A second prominent theory contends that the disparate treatment of individual and institutional religious liberty claims is not a function of the fundamental autonomy of religious institutions but exists to ensure that courts do not become

---

[5] *See, e.g.*, NELSON TEBBE, RELIGIOUS FREEDOM IN AN EGALITARIAN AGE 93 (2017); Caroline Mala Corbin, *Above the Law? The Constitutionality of the Ministerial Exemption from Anti-discrimination Law*, 75 FORDHAM L. REV. 1965, 2004–05 (2007).

[6] *See* Or. Arg. Tr., *supra* note 3 at 37:22–25 (statement of the EEOC's attorney describing church autonomy as a "question of freedom of association").

[7] *Hosanna-Tabor*, *supra* note 2, at 189.

[8] *Id.*

[9] *See, e.g.*, Michael Dorf, *Ministers and Peyote*, DORF ON LAW (Jan. 12, 2012), https://perma.cc/SE7X-9LNN.

[10] *See, e.g.*, EEOC v. Catholic Univ. of Am., 83 F.3d 455, 462 (D.C. Cir. 1996).

[11] *See, e.g.*, Richard W. Garnett, *Do Churches Matter? Towards an Institutional Understanding of the Religion Clauses*, 53 VILL. L. REV. 273, 288 (2008); Paul Horwitz, *Churches as First Amendment Institutions: Of Sovereignty and Spheres*, 44 HARV. C.R.-C.L. L. REV. 79, 87 (2009); Thomas Berg et al. *Religious Freedom, Church-State Separation, and the Ministerial Exception*, 106 NW. U. L. REV. COLLOQUY 175 (2011).

embroiled in resolving religious questions in violation of the Establishment Clause.[12] On this theory, most forcefully and thoughtfully advanced by Ira Lupu and Robert Tuttle, religious institutions are not "presumptively autonomous";[13] rather, the autonomy of religious institutions is simply a by-product of courts' "adjudicative disability" – that is, the fact that courts cannot resolve disputes within religious institutions because they lack the constitutional competence to do so.[14]

Both theories have drawbacks. The sovereignty approach appears to place the internal workings of religious organizations beyond the authority of courts, never properly subject to government regulation or legal liability regardless of the circumstances.[15] And the adjudicative disability approach would similarly prohibit courts from addressing claims implicating religious standards – such as the supervision of employees with religious job responsibilities and claims predicated on the organizational structure of religious institutions – regardless of the government interest at stake in a case.[16] The goal of this chapter, therefore, is to briefly summarize my theory of implied-consent institutionalism,[17] explain how it might address these cases involving religious institutions, and respond to some criticism of the theory[18] in the hopes of correcting some of the misconceptions about how the theory works and applies.

I HOW IMPLIED CONSENT WORKS

An implied consent theory contends that religious institutions deserve protection because they are created through the voluntary choices of individuals to join together in the pursuit of collective religious objectives such as faith and salvation. These voluntary choices, however, are inferred implicitly from the decision of individuals to join the institution's membership.

The underlying logic of implied consent institutionalism begins with two basic premises. The first is *voluntarism*, which in this context captures "the freedom to

---

[12] *See* Schleicher v. Salvation Army, 518 F.3d 472, 475 (7th Cir. 2008).

[13] Ira C. Lupu & Robert W. Tuttle, *The Distinctive Place of Religious Entities in Our Constitutional Order*, 47 VILL. L. REV. 37, 78–79 (2002).

[14] Ira C. Lupu & Robert W. Tuttle, *Courts, Clergy, and Congregations*, 7 GEO. J.L. & PUB. POL'Y 119, 122 (2007).

[15] *See, e.g.*, Richard Schragger & Micah Schwartzman, *Against Religious Institutionalism*, 99 VA. L. REV. 917, 946 (2013); Ira C. Lupu & Robert W. Tuttle, *The Mystery of Unanimity in Hosanna-Tabor Evangelical Lutheran Church & School v. EEOC*, 20 LEWIS & CLARK L. REV. 1265, 1298 (2017).

[16] *See, e.g.*, Ira C. Lupu & Robert W. Tuttle, *Sexual Misconduct and Ecclesiastical Immunity*, 2004 BYU L. REV. 1789, 1844–45.

[17] *See* Michael A. Helfand, *Religious Institutionalism, Implied Consent, and the Value of Voluntarism*, 88 S. CAL. L. REV. 539 (2015).

[18] *See* Lupu & Tuttle, *The Mystery of Unanimity*, *supra* note 15, at 1299–1304. For an extended defense of implied consent theory, *see* Michael A. Helfand, *Implied Consent: A Primer and A Defense*, 50 CONN. L. REV. (2018) (forthcoming).

make religious choices for oneself free from governmental compulsion of improper influence."[19] On this approach, religious institutions are valuable because they are born out of members' voluntary choices.[20] Grounding the value of religious institutions in voluntarism entrenches the constitutional protections afforded religious institutions under the umbrella of the Free Exercise Clause. Religious institutions are created through the voluntary decisions of individuals to join together and affirmatively pursue shared religious values.

The second premise is that religion is predominantly experienced as a social or group phenomenon, something both the framers and contemporary observers recognize.[21] As Zoe Robinson has noted "[r]eligion is rarely an individual endeavor." Instead, people come together, bound in collective belief, worship, and related action.[22] Robert Cover famously captured this phenomenon in constitutional terms: "[t]he religion clauses of the Constitution seem to me unique in the clarity with which they presuppose a collective, norm-generating community whose status as a community and whose relationship with the individuals subject to its norms are entitled to constitutional recognition and protection."[23] Religious institutions therefore represent the recurring desire of individuals to pursue religious objectives collectively.

The implied consent framework values religious institutions to the extent they represent the voluntary choices of individuals to join together, form a religious institution, and become members of that institution. Of course, what is unique – and controversial – about the implied consent framework is that it infers – from the act of joining a religious institution – a grant of authority to the institution to make rules and resolve disputes so that the institution can serve as a successful medium for members' pursuit of collective religious aspirations. The argument justifying this inference of implied consent runs as follows.

As a general matter, individuals seek to pursue religious experiences and aspirations as groups. Religious institutions provide the framework to make that collective experience possible. The challenge for religious institutions is that they need some set of rules to make the collective work together in pursuit of these religious objectives. John Locke formulates this need most clearly, explaining that individuals voluntarily join churches to achieve "the salvation of their souls" and that this "hope of salvation" serves as the motivation for "members voluntarily uniting" into a church. However, Locke notes, in order to successfully accomplish such objectives, the church "must be regulated by some laws, and the members all consent to

---

[19] Daniel O. Conkle, Constitutional Law: The Religion Clauses 38 (2003).
[20] For more on this link, see Richard Schragger & Micah Schwartzman, *Against Religious Institutionalism*, 99 Va. L. Rev. 917, 956–62 (2013).
[21] Abner S. Greene, *Conflicting Paradigms of Religious Freedom: Liberty Versus Equality*, 1993 B.Y.U. L. Rev. 7, 24 (1993).
[22] Zoe Robinson, *What Is a Religious Institution?*, 55 B.C. L. Rev. 181, 206 (2014).
[23] Robert M. Cover, *Nomos and Narrative*, 97 Harv. L. Rev. 4, 32 (1982).

observe some order." Without the authority to make religious rules and resolve internal religious disputes, the "church ... will presently dissolve and break in pieces."[24] Locke emphasizes that rules for governing the inner workings of a religious institution could only come from within that institution. They cannot be supplied by civil society, which is geared to "procur[e], preserv[e], and advanc[e] ... civil interests" and "outward things" such as "life, liberty, health ... and the possession of outward things, such as money, land, houses, furniture, and the like." By focusing its energies on "outward things," a civil society avoids taking sides on how its citizens should lead the good life, leaving room for the deep value-pluralism that typifies liberal nation-states.

Because individuals become members of religious institutions to collectively pursue religious objectives – and because religious institutions need to make internal religious rules to pursue those objectives – an implied consent approach concludes that the law can infer from mere membership a grant of authority to the religious institution to make those necessary religious rules.

Importantly, the Supreme Court embraced this framework of implied consent institutionalism in its early decisions addressing the autonomy of religious institution. For example, in 1871, the Court grounded the authority of religious institutions in the voluntary choices of their members, arguing "[t]hat in so far as the law can regard them, the powers of the church judicatories are derived solely from the consent of the members of the church."[25] Similarly, in 1929, the Court held that "the decisions of the proper church tribunals on matters purely ecclesiastical ... are accepted in litigation before the secular courts as conclusive, *because the parties in interest made them so by contract or otherwise.*"[26]

And this consent, according to the Court, could be inferred implicitly: "All who unite themselves to such a body do so with an *implied consent* to this government, and are bound to submit to it." In this way, joining a church or other religious institution entails an implicit consent authorizing the institution to self-govern and resolve internal disputes. As the Court explained, "[i]t is of the essence of these religious unions, and of their right to establish tribunals for the decision of questions arising among themselves, that those decisions should be binding in all cases of ecclesiastical cognizance, subject only to such appeals as the organism itself provides for." Indeed, according the Court, "it would be a vain consent and would lead to the total subversion of such religious bodies, if any one aggrieved by one of their decisions could appeal to the secular courts and have them reversed."[27]

---

[24] John Locke, A *Letter Concerning Toleration, in* A LETTER CONCERNING TOLERATION 20 (John Horton & Susan Mendus eds., 1991) (giving as examples "[p]lace and time of meeting ... rules for admitting and excluding members").

[25] Watson v. Jones, 80 U.S. 679, 710 (1871).

[26] Gonzalez v. Roman Catholic Archbishop, 280 U.S. 1, 16 (1929) (emphasis added).

[27] *Watson, supra* note 25, at 729.

Thus, as outlined by the Court in those early decisions, the reason courts can infer implied consent from the mere act of joining a religious institution is because it tracks individuals' general impulse to pursue religious experiences and objectives collectively – and pursuing those religious experience and objectives are only possible if institutions develop internal religious rules and doctrine to organize members. If institutions could not self-regulate regarding these aspirations, individuals would not be able to join together to achieve these goals. Accordingly, if religious decisions are valued to the extent they are voluntary, and individuals are presumed to desire collective pursuit of religious aspirations, then the law can infer, from the mere act of joining, that individuals implicitly grant the relevant institution the authority and autonomy necessary to enable the collective to reach shared religious goals.

The following section outlines the ramifications of constructing the authority and autonomy of religious institutions on the implied consent of members.

II IMPLICATIONS OF IMPLIED CONSENT

In implied consent institutionalism, the decision to become a member and pursue religious objectives is an implied grant of authority to the institution to make religious rules and resolve religious disputes to facilitate pursuit of religious objectives. This section fleshes out key concepts and implications of the framework.

A *Granting Implied Consent: Membership*

In the implied consent model, membership represents a decision to join together with others in pursuit of religious objectives, such as faith, prayer, and salvation. The paradigm case is undoubtedly joining a house of worship. And what makes that case a useful paradigm example is that the nature of the institution and the nature of the institution's activities together provide a strong basis for presuming that the individual is joining to pursue religious objectives. Put simply, people typically join houses of worship for religious reasons. But how should the implied consent framework apply as the nature of the religious institution and its members change?

The first step removed from membership in a house of worship is its employment of a religious leader. While this case differs from the core case of a pure member, the implied consent rationale still stands on strong footing. In the case of a minister, there is still good reason to presume that in agreeing to become a congregation's religious leader, he or she is implicitly joining that congregation's pursuit of religious objectives. Indeed, this conclusion tracks the core of the ministerial exception, which shields houses of worship from liability under various nondiscrimination statutes in the hiring and firing of ministers. The ministerial exception, according to *Hosanna-Tabor*, draws from both of the religion clauses; and it would allow a religious institution, for example, to hire only male clergy even when doing so might contravene Title VII or terminate clergy even in circumstances that would otherwise violate the Americans with Disabilities Act.[28]

An implied consent approach largely tracks this version of the ministerial exception, although the approach relies more on the Free Exercise Clause than on the Establishment Clause. It grants authority to a religious institution over employment decisions related to a minister because that minister has impliedly granted the religious institution that authority by agreeing to join the institution as its religious leader.[29]

Of course, this logic raises other questions. Should other employees of houses of worship also be viewed similarly as impliedly consenting to the religious institution's authority? Some have approached this question by inquiring whether a particular employee has a sufficient amount of religious responsibilities to make them analogous to a minister.[30] An implied consent approach, by contrast, focuses less on the job's religious content and more directly on whether the circumstances justify an inference of implied consent. Thus, not only might church music directors or communications directors qualify as sufficiently religious to trigger the ministerial exception, but employees with far fewer religious responsibilities would too, *if* there is a sufficient basis to conclude that the employers conveyed their religious expectations and aspirations to them.[31]

For example, consider a general studies teacher at a religious school who is expected to integrate certain religious values into her curriculum and to ensure classroom material conforms to the faith community's religious values.[32] Where those expectations are adequately conveyed to the teacher prior to joining the school, the fact that the teacher has a limited amount of purely religious job tasks would not, without more, undermine an inference of implied consent because the entity's mission is marked by clear and obvious religious characteristics.

To be sure, this analysis may be complex, since employees may not want to join a religious endeavor, but simply need a job. Such considerations surely ought to factor into any evaluation of implied consent – and thereby constrain any inference that the employee has granted the religious institution authority to make religious rules and resolve religious disputes with respect to that employment relationship. But an implied consent framework incorporates these considerations into the overall inquiry; instead of assessing how much religion is enough to trigger doctrines such

---

[28] *See, e.g.*, Hosanna-Tabor, *supra* note 2, at 171.

[29] This is consistent with some early ministerial exception cases. *See, e.g.*, McClure v. Salvation Army, 460 F.2d 553, 560 (5th Cir. 1972); Kedroff v. St. Nicholas Cathedral of Russian Orthodox Church, 344 U.S. 94, 116 (1952).

[30] *See, e.g.*, EEOC v. Roman Catholic Diocese of Raleigh, N.C., 213 F.3d 795, 802–03 (4th Cir. 2000); Alicea-Hernandez v. Catholic Bishop of Chicago, 320 F.3d 698, 704 (7th Cir. 2003).

[31] See Hill, Chapter 26, for a discussion of transparency.

[32] *See, e.g.*, EEOC v. Tree of Life Christian Sch., 751 F. Supp. 700, 706 (S.D. Ohio 1990); Gallo v. Salesian Soc'y, 676 A.2d 580, 590 (N.J. Super. Ct. App. Div. 1996).

as the ministerial exception, an implied consent framework reorients the inquiry towards the expectations and aspirations of the employee.[33]

Line-drawing is complicated not only by the challenges of categorizing the employee as a member but also by deciding which employers should be categorized as religious institutions. This has been a recurring question in religious liberty litigation. For example, in response to the Affordable Care Act's requirement that employers include contraceptive coverage in their employees' health insurance plans, numerous for-profit companies filed lawsuits, claiming that the requirement violated their religious consciences by making them complicit in "sin."[34] A similar claim has been leveled by various businesses that have refused to provide their services at same-sex weddings, despite public accommodation nondiscrimination laws.[35] In each case, the businesses owners asserted religious liberty defenses. Among other issues, such cases highlight the challenges of identifying which institutions might be considered religious institutions entitled to some scope of authority and autonomy. Some scholars have argued that the profit motive and the religious motivation are mutually exclusive,[36] while others have identified more nuanced dividing lines between truly religious institutions and those that do not quite fit into that category.[37]

The implied consent approach focuses on whether the context justifies an inference of implied consent to the authority of the institution and not the religious nature of the organization or whether it is operated for profit. To justify such an inference, the employer must clearly convey to its prospective employees that they are working at an institution geared towards the pursuit of collective religious objectives. Without clearly conveying this collective pursuit, there would be no reason for prospective employees to grant institutions the autonomy and authority to make religious rules and establish methods of religious dispute resolution. If employees do not know of their employer's religious objectives, there

---

[33] For additional discussion, see Michael A. Helfand, *Religion's Footnote Four: Church Autonomy as Arbitration*, 97 MINN. L. REV. 1891, 1952–57 (2013).

[34] For a list, see *HHS Case Database*, BECKET FUND FOR RELIGIOUS LIBERTY, https://perma.cc/5M2L-7UUR.

[35] Mullins v. Masterpiece Cakeshop, Inc., 2015 COA 115 (Colo. Ct. App. 2015) [hereinafter *Masterpiece Cakeshop I*], *cert. granted* Masterpiece Cakeshop v. Colorado Civil Rights Comm'n, 138 S. Ct. 1719 (2018) [hereinafter *Masterpiece Cakeshop II*]; State v. Arlene's Flowers, Inc., 187 Wash. 2d 804 (2017), *vacated*, 138 S. Ct. 2671 (2018); Elane Photography, LLC v. Willock, 309 P.3d 53, 60, 77 (N.M. 2013), *cert. denied*, 134 S. Ct. 1787 (2014). See Wilson, Chapter 30, for state laws.

[36] *See, e.g.,* Caroline Mala Corbin, *Corporate Religious Liberty*, 30 CONST. COMMENTARY 277, 280 (2015); Zoe Robinson, *The Contraception Mandate and the Forgotten Constitutional Question*, 2014 WIS. L. REV. 749, 793.

[37] *See, e.g.,* Bruce N. Bagni, *Discrimination in the Name of the Lord: A Critical Evaluation of Discrimination by Religious Organizations*, 79 COLUM. L. REV. 1514, 1539–40 (1979).

is no reason for them to have impliedly consented to their employer's autonomy or authority.[38]

The standard for knowledge of the employer's religious objectives need not be actual. To justify an inference of implied consent, however, it is not enough simply to impute that knowledge. For example, some cases have focused on the institution's by-laws and whether they evidence the institution's religious character. Thus, if the by-laws required enough board members to have a specified religious affiliation – or other religiously relevant provisions – then, the logic goes, the institution is clearly religious.[39] But from an implied consent perspective, the content of by-laws and other corporate documents provides little insight as to whether the religious mission of the institution was sufficiently conveyed to prospective employees. And without sufficiently conveying the religious objectives and aspirations of the institution, the law ought not to infer that employees have impliedly consented to the institution's authority with respect to religious rule-making and dispute resolution. For this reason, courts would be better served looking to the institution's day-to-day operations to see if its operations sufficiently manifest its religious objectives and aspirations.[40]

At the outer boundary of implied consent cases stand recent cases of religiously motivated businesses, including a florist, a photographer, and a baker, unwilling to provide their services at same-sex wedding ceremonies notwithstanding state laws prohibiting businesses serving the public from discrimination on the basis of sexual orientation.[41] And with the Supreme Court's recent decision in *Masterpiece Cakeshop v. Colorado Civil Rights Commission*,[42] this type of claim is likely to remain in the public's eye for some time. How might the wedding-refusal cases be viewed from an implied consent perspective?

While surely a consumer's decision to enter into a commercial transaction with a business is to some degree voluntary, it seems unlikely that an implied consent approach would conceptualize entering a store as a form of joining the business in a pursuit of collective religious objectives. In such cases, the prospective purchaser and shop owner never enter into any joint pursuit; the business refuses to sell its services to the same-sex couple. Thus, even in circumstances where the business viewed its mission, day in and day out, as pursuing religious objectives with its customers, and it shared those objectives and aspirations with prospective customers, an implied consent model would find it difficult to see the prospective customers as

---

[38] The implied consent framework might have led to a different decision in *Hobby Lobby* depending on the extent to which each of the employers made their religious aspirations widely known. *See* Helfand, *Religious Institutionalism, supra* note 17, at 576.

[39] *See, e.g.,* Scharon v. St. Luke's Episcopal Presbyterian Hosp., 929 F.2d 360, 362 (8th Cir. 1991).

[40] *See, e.g.,* Hollins v. Methodist Healthcare, Inc., 474 F.3d 223, 225–26 (6th Cir. 2007); Shaliehsabou v. Hebrew Home of Greater Wash., Inc., 363 F.3d 299, 310 (4th Cir. 2004).

[41] *See supra* note 35; see also McClain, Chapter 17; McConnell, Chapter 28 for additional detail.

[42] *Masterpiece Cakeshop I & Masterpiece Cakeshop II, supra* note 35.

having joined with the business in the pursuit of those religious objectives. Put differently, the implied consent model, which grounds the rights of religious institutions in notions of collectivity and membership, would be hard pressed to identify a joint enterprise in cases where businesses reject prospective customers on account of the owner's religious commitment that necessitates avoiding participation in a same-sex wedding. Of course, such a business might still be eligible for the standard religious liberty protections afforded individuals,[43] including, for example, a free exercise claim or a claim under Religious Freedom Restoration Act.[44] In that way, there may be circumstances where even without the implied consent architecture, store owners might simply revert to the status of all other individuals with respect to religious liberty claims.

B *Withdrawing Implied Consent: Exit*

The voluntary pursuit of collective religious association underlying the implied consent framework requires not only careful attention to when and how individuals join religious institutions, but also whether they seek to exit the institution's membership. If a member chooses to leave an institution, no longer interested in participating in that collective pursuit, then the institution's claim to prospective authority and autonomy related to that individual must end as well.

This issue arises, for example, in cases where houses of worship employ a practice of "shun[ning] members of their religious communities for failing to abide by shared religious rules of conduct."[45] Such communal shunning typically "involves the complete withdrawal of social, spiritual, and economic contact from a member or former member of a religious group."[46] Can members assert claims of defamation and intentional infliction of emotional distress against an institution based on communal shunning?

As a general matter, courts have been reluctant to allow such claims to go forward,[47] holding that "[c]hurches are afforded great latitude when they impose discipline ... '[R]eligious activities which concern only members of the faith are and ought to be free – as nearly absolutely free as anything can be.'"[48] Many courts have applied constitutional frameworks to these cases that apply irrespective of

---

[43] *See* Arlene's Flowers, Inc., *supra* note 35, at n.20.
[44] 42 U.S.C. §§ 2000bb–2000bb-4 (2012).
[45] Michael A. Helfand, *Fighting for the Debtor's Soul: Regulating Religious Commercial Conduct*, 19 GEO. MASON L. REV. 157, 181 (2011).
[46] Justin K. Miller, *Comment, Damned If You Do, Damned If You Don't: Religious Shunning and the Free Exercise Clause*, 137 U. PA. L. REV. 271, 272 (1988).
[47] *See generally* Annotation, *Suspension or Expulsion from Church or Religious Society and the Remedies Therefor*, 20 A.L.R. 2d 435–36 (1951).
[48] Paul v. Watchtower Bible & Tract Soc., 819 F.2d 875, 883 (9th Cir. 1987) (quoting Prince v. Massachusetts, 321 U.S. 158, 177 (1944) (Jackson, J. concurring)).

whether the plaintiff has withdrawn from the relevant religious community.[49] But if the implied consent framework is to be taken seriously, then exit ought to impose a noteworthy limit on the authority of religious institutions, allowing tort claims to go forward when premised on post-withdrawal conduct. Some courts have taken this approach, limiting the house of worship's shield from liability to only pre-withdrawal conduct.[50]

Sometimes the challenges of exit are more complicated than merely determining whether post-withdrawal tort claims ought to be permitted. Sometimes exit raises more fundamental questions regarding whether membership is indeed voluntary and can be claimed to be so. From an implied consent perspective, where the burdens of exit become sufficiently great, the religious institution can no longer lay claim to authority or autonomy grounded in the implied consent of its members; if members cannot reasonably leave the institution, then their consent is a fiction. Of course, figuring out how significant hurdles to exit must be before they undermine implied consent requires contextual assessment and judicial line-drawing. But ultimately, the successful implementation of an implied consent framework entails courts taking the question of exit seriously.

C Content of Implied Consent: Process, Not Substance

Assessing truly voluntary entrance into and exit from the membership of a religious institution are essential to implementing the implied consent framework. But they gloss over a second and related issue: how can an individual consent to the religious institution's rule-making authority without knowing what rules he or she is signing up for?[51]

True, entering a standard agreement requires certainty about the terms.[52] But an implied consent framework understands this implicit agreement to join with others in the pursuit of religious objectives as an agreement over the *process* of rule-making and dispute resolution as opposed to an agreement over the *substance* of those rules. Indeed, the most natural comparison for the implied consent model of religious institutionalism is arbitration agreements.[53]

When it comes to arbitration, parties frequently do not know the content or specifics of the rules that will be applied to their case[54] – and courts police

---

[49] This is true for a sovereignty approach, *see, e.g.*, Paul, 819 F.2d at 883, as well as an adjudicative disability approach, *see, e.g.*, Anderson v. Watchtower Bible & Tract Soc'y of N.Y., Inc., 2007 Tenn. App. LEXIS 29, 96–97 (Tenn. Ct. App. 2007).

[50] *See, e.g.*, Guinn v. Church of Christ of Collinsville, 775 P.2d 766, 786 (Okla. 1989); Hester v. Barnett, 723 S.W.2d 544, 559 (Mo. Ct. App. 1987).

[51] B. Jessie Hill, *Ties That Bind? The Questionable Consent Justification for Hosanna-Tabor*, 109 Nw. L. Rev. 91, 97 (2014).

[52] Restatement (Second) of Contracts § 33.

[53] *See* Helfand, *Religion's Footnote Four, supra* note 33, at 1943.

[54] *See* Stephen J. Ware, *Default Rules from Mandatory Rules: Privatizing Law Through Arbitration*, 83 Minn. L. Rev. 703, 720–21 (1999).

arbitration awards, not for substantive errors but for procedural misconduct.[55] As a result, when signing up for arbitration, parties agree not necessarily to a particular set of substantive rules but to a process that must be inherently fair if it is to be deemed conclusive and enforceable by civil authorities.[56]

This same arbitration framework animates the implied consent model of religious institutionalism – a parallel that courts have drawn from time to time.[57] Members that implicitly consent to the authority of a religious institution do so without necessarily knowing what rules the institution will issue and what methods of dispute resolution it will adopt. What those members are guaranteed, however, is that the institution will make rules and resolve disputes in ways that will advance the membership's collective religious objectives by enforcing rules fairly, without fraud, self-dealing, or misconduct.

Procedural safeguards are part and parcel of the implied consent framework. Members cede authority to an institution only to the extent that the institution's rules and dispute resolution processes are necessary to pursue collective religious objectives. When religious institutions make rules and resolve disputes for institutional gain – or engage in fraud or misconduct for the personal windfall of religious leaders – those decisions are not granted any degree of legal protection; members have not impliedly consented.

Not surprisingly, when the Supreme Court's implied consent jurisprudence was at its zenith, this focus on procedural safeguards was central to the Court's decisions regarding religious institutional autonomy. Internal religious rule-making and institutions' dispute resolution received "marginal civil court review"[58] for "fraud, collusion or arbitrariness."[59] Although the Court subsequently discarded marginal review as ostensibly unconstitutional,[60] the link between implied consent and civil oversight made perfect sense; members implicitly consent to a religious institution's internal religious rules and decisions because they are necessary to enable the collective to pursue shared religious objectives. However, if those rules are simply a function of self-dealing and fraud – if they fail to facilitate good faith adjudication –

---

[55] *See, e.g.*, 9 U.S.C. § 10 (2012). For examples of recent federal decisions emphasizing this point, see Rainier DSC 1, L.L.C. v. Rainier Capital Mgmt., L.P., 828 F.3d 362, 364 (5th Cir. 2016); Whitehead v. Pullman Grp., LLC, 811 F.3d 116, 120 (3d Cir. 2016).

[56] *Id.*

[57] *See* Trustees of East Norway Lake Norwegian Evangelical Lutheran Church v. Halvorson, 42 Minn. 503, 508 (1890); Elmora Hebrew Ctr. v. Fishman, 593 A.2d 725, 731 (N.J. 1991).

[58] Presbyterian Church in the U.S. v. Mary Elizabeth Blue Hull Mem'l Presbyterian Church, 393 U.S. 440, 447 (1969).

[59] Gonzalez, *supra* note 26, at 16.

[60] *See, e.g.*, Serbian E. Orthodox Diocese v. Milivojevich, 426 U.S. 696, 712 (1976) (concluding that marginal civil court review violated the Establishment Clause by requiring judicial inquiries into religious doctrine).

then the consent of the membership no longer provides a justification for the institution's rule-making authority.[61]

From an implied consent perspective, marginal civil court review – such as a fraud, collusion, and arbitrariness standard – is necessary to adopt a framework geared towards allowing religious institutions the authority to make religious rules and resolve disputes. Without it, there can be no assurance that the processes of rule-making and dispute resolution truly comport with the religious aspirations of the membership. Indeed, before the Supreme Court turned away from the implied consent framework, courts invoked this kind of marginal review of religious institutional decision-making, assessing whether decisions failed to abide by their own institutional rules.[62] An implied consent approach embraces this kind of check on religious institutions as it ensures that religious authority and autonomy are not used as a mere pretext to circumvent the legitimate rights of members who have joined together to pursue collective and authentic religious objectives.[63]

D Limits on Implied Consent: Strict Scrutiny

An implied consent approach to religious institutionalism relocates the doctrinal origins of the authority and autonomy of religious institutions under the Free Exercise Clause as opposed to the Establishment Clause. In this way, religious authority and autonomy is a set of affirmative rights ceded to religious institutions by members.

The central implication of this relocation is that religious institutional authority must, like any other religious liberty right under the Free Exercise Clause, be subjected to strict scrutiny.[64] Accordingly, if the assertion of religious institutional authority threatens a compelling government interest – and withholding that institutional autonomy and authority is the least restrictive means for advancing the compelling government interest – then the rights of a religious institution must cede to the compelling government interest.

This is in stark contrast to theories like the adjudicative disability framework, which highlight the Establishment Clause and see the authority of religious institutions as simply a by-product of the inability of civil courts to resolve religious disputes that implicate religious doctrine.[65] Establishment Clause constraints on government authority are not subject to strict scrutiny; they are structural constraints

---

[61] *See* Ira Mark Ellman, *Driven from the Tribunal: Judicial Resolution of Internal Church Disputes*, 69 CAL. L. REV. 1378, 1391 (1981).

[62] *See* Helfand, *Religion's Footnote Four, supra* note 33.

[63] Marginal review does require a significant loosening of the religious question doctrine. For an argument in favoring of loosening the doctrine, see Michael A. Helfand, *Litigating Religion*, 93 B.U. L. REV. 493 (2012).

[64] *See, e.g.,* Wisconsin v. Yoder, 406 U.S. 205 (1972); Sherbert v. Verner, 374 U.S. 398 (1963).

[65] *See supra* note 16 and accompanying text.

on government authority.[66] Thus, to the extent the claims of religious institutions draw from the Establishment Clause, they could not be overcome in cases where the attempted government regulation was narrowly tailored to advance a compelling government interest. And given the wide range of cases where religious institutions might assert their religious liberty, the unavailability of strict scrutiny review might provide reason to worry.

Of course, this raises another central question for assessing religious institutional claims: what should qualify as a compelling government interest under the Free Exercise Clause? Qualifying as a compelling interest has often been perceived as requiring the interest to clear a relatively high threshold. Indeed, in equal protection contexts, the list of compelling government interests is typically viewed as quite short, where strict scrutiny has been described as "strict in theory, but fatal in fact." But the fact that few interests are viewed as compelling in the equal protection context does not necessarily demand a similar result in the free exercise context. Under the Equal Protection Clause, one of the primary purposes of subjecting racial classifications to strict scrutiny is "to 'smoke out' illegitimate uses of race by assuring that the legislative body is pursuing a goal important enough to warrant use of a highly suspect tool."[67] Using a racial classification where no compelling government interest is at stake indicates that there may be some sort of invidious discriminatory intent behind the statute or regulation under discussion.

By contrast, the compelling government interest test under the Free Exercise Clause has long been conceived of as a balancing of competing legitimate claims and values. In *Wisconsin v. Yoder*, religious liberty's high watermark, the Supreme Court explained the test as follows: "only those interests of the highest order and those not otherwise served can *overbalance* legitimate claims to the free exercise of religion."[68] Similarly, in *McDaniel v. Paty*, the Court referred to the "delicate balancing required" when applying the compelling government interest test under free exercise analysis[69] – a characterization that has continued in subsequent Supreme Court decisions.[70]

This express focus on interest-balancing fits with a voluntarist approach to the claims of religious institutions. Under this approach, religious institutions are afforded constitutional protections because they embody members' voluntary decisions to join together to pursue collective religious objectives. Members' claims represent core and fundamental constitutional values that must be jealously safeguarded.

---

[66] *See generally* Carl H. Esbeck, *The Establishment Clause as a Structural Restraint on Governmental Power*, 84 IOWA L. REV. 1 (1998).

[67] City of Richmond v. J. A. Croson Co., 488 U.S. 469, 493 (1989).

[68] *Yoder, supra* note 64, at 215.

[69] McDaniel v. Paty, 435 U.S. 618, 628 n.8 (1978).

[70] Church of Lukumi Babalu Aye v. City of Hialeah, 508 U.S. 520, 565 (1993); Bowen v. Roy, 476 U.S. 693, 729 (1986).

But that does not mean there are no other vital government objectives that also must be given significant weight. An implied consent framework embraces a doctrine that balances competing interests, recognizing that the free exercise claims of religious institutions must be considered against the potential interests harmed when accommodations are granted.[71]

In this way, an implied consent framework leverages its free exercise origins, providing an important check on the authority and autonomy of religious institutions. And that check draws directly on the other values conflicting with the rights of religious institutions, ensuring that courts can assess and evaluate these competing claims so as to balance the institutional needs of faith communities against other claims central to civil society generally.

III CONCLUSION

An implied consent framework does have its blind spots and drawbacks. But all told, it provides a useful framework for evaluating the claims of religious institutions. It captures the strong impulse of individuals to join together in pursuit of collective religious objectives. It emphasizes the voluntarist impulse embedded in the authority and autonomy of religious institutions – an impulse that has a long history in the US constitutional tradition. And it takes the expectations and aspirations of individuals seriously in identifying where the authority and autonomy of religious institutions starts and ends. With a range of tensions between the objectives of religious institutions and the demands of the law, implied consent religious institutionalism holds out hope for balancing the two, providing institutions with space to advance the religious goals of their membership without running roughshod over other important government interests.

---

[71] Kent Greenawalt, *Should the Religion Clauses of the Constitution Be Amended?*, 32 Loy. L.A. L. Rev. 9, 15, n.25 (1998).

PART III

The Demands of Faith

Perspectives from Select Faith Traditions

12

Christian Identity and Religious Liberty

Leith Anderson

For many, the title of Evangelical is synonymous with a certain set of beliefs that, in the context of LGBT rights, is often seen to place people of faith at odds with the LGBT community. Indeed, this richly illustrates a spectrum of views among both faith communities and LGBT advocates about whether the interest of these two communities must, in fact, be at odds.

This chapter begins from the premise that Evangelicals, and other faith communities, have a great deal in common with the LGBT community.[1] Both communities care deeply about an aspect of their identity that, for them, is nonnegotiable. At various times in history, both communities have found themselves on the outside looking in.[2]

This chapter will share a perspective often missing in the public dialogue: precisely why is it that Evangelicals in particular sometimes fear legal change that protects other communities from discrimination? Just as other communities have been vilified in the past, the fear is that as the views held by Evangelicals and other

---

[1]   For others who have emphasized commonality rather than difference, see Chai R. Feldblum, *Moral Conflict and Conflicting Liberties, in* SAME-SEX MARRIAGE AND RELIGIOUS LIBERTY: EMERGING CONFLICTS 123, 157 (Douglas Laycock et al. eds., 2008) (arguing that the "identity liberty" same-sex couples have in marriage and the "belief liberty" objectors have in their religious tenets are both fundamental values deserving protection); Thomas C. Berg, *What Same-Sex Marriage and Religious-Liberty Claims Have in Common*, 5 Nw. J. L. & Soc. Pol'y 206, 219–20, 230–32 (2010). Douglas Laycock & Thomas C. Berg, *Protecting Same-Sex Marriage and Religious Liberty*, 99 VA. L. REV. BRIEF 1, 7 (2013)(noting that religious liberty advocates and LGBT movement advocates both seek to protect minorities that have been historically oppressed).

[2]   *See* Laycock & Berg, *supra* note 1. For a deeply personal account of the humiliation that LGBT persons have experienced, see Minter, Chapter 4. And for a compelling account that Christians in particular also feel imperiled and subject to ridicule, see Smith, Chapter 18.

persons of faith increasingly become minority views,[3] Evangelicals will be vilified and vilification will become a tool for discriminating against them.

This chapter unfolds as follows. Section I discusses changing perceptions of the word "Evangelical" from a religious identity to a political one. Section II critiques the conventional wisdom in some quarters that respect for religion equates with intolerance, close-mindedness, homophobia, or sexism, and invariably works to discriminate against others or establish the supremacy of one group over another. Ironically, it is this view that portends discrimination against religious individuals. Section III concludes with a simple proposition: society's goal should be to find a solution amenable to all, not one that results in forcing Christians, and many other religious people, to live in ways that deny who they are as persons of faith.

I FAITH, NOT POLITICS

The question most frequently asked of me following the 2016 election, as president of the National Association of Evangelicals, has been: "Should we abandon our Evangelical name?" In part, the question arises after the support many Evangelicals gave to President Donald Trump during the election.[4]

True, President Trump's election set off alarms within the LGBT community.[5] Many Clinton supporters felt lost, "waking up to a whole new world."[6] That deep unease continues unabated from policy announcement to policy announcement.[7]

Just as the LGBT community feared Trump, Evangelicals had their own fears of a Clinton presidency. In 2016, the Pew Research Center reported that 41 percent of Evangelicals felt that it had become more difficult to be an Evangelical Christian in the United States during the end of the Obama administration.[8] They expressed concerns about what was being taught in public schools, the speed with which

---

[3] *See* Kimberly Winston, Religion News Service, *"Christian America" Dwindling, Including White Evangelicals, Study Shows*, St. Louis Post-Dispatch (Sept. 8, 2017), https://perma .cc/MTV2-54BH; *see also* Elizabeth Podrebarac Sciupac et al., *Americans Say Religious Aspects of Christmas Are Declining in Public Life*, Pew Res. Ctr. (Dec. 12, 2017), https://perma.cc/ Y9AW-GUT5.

[4] Exit polls showed that 80% of self-identified Evangelicals voted for Trump. *See* Sarah Pulliam Bailey, *White Evangelicals Voted Overwhelmingly for Donald Trump, Exit Polls Show*, Wash. Post (Nov. 9, 2016), https://perma.cc/2VWS-G3QG.

[5] Some feared that a repeal of the Patient Protection and Affordable Care Act, or "Obamacare," on which Trump and others campaigned would frustrate access to healthcare for transgender people, and that same-sex marriage would be undone by judicial decision if the Supreme Court's composition changed, among other fears. Emanuella Grinberg, *What a Trump Presidency Could Mean for LGBT Americans*, CNN (Dec. 5, 2016), https://perma.cc/2R9P-LPLB.

[6] Matea Gold et al., *"Not My President": Thousands Protest Trump in Rallies Across the U.S.*, Wash. Post (Nov. 11, 2016), https://perma.cc/2BN4-CWZA.

[7] For examples, see Eskridge, Chapter 22; Wilson, Chapter 30.

[8] Michael Lipka, *Evangelicals Increasingly Say It's Becoming Harder for Them in America*, Pew Res. Ctr. (July 14, 2016), https://perma.cc/6AVC-6ADQ.

same-sex marriage was recognized by the courts, and litigation over religious displays on public property.[9] The primary reason for the question about abandoning the term "Evangelical" is that it has become a political term in addition to a faith-identity across many parts of the American culture.[10] This shift is curious in itself because most Evangelicals around the world today and throughout history would never think of themselves primarily in political terms.[11] But this disconnect begs the greater question of whether religious individuals get to define themselves and their identities or if they are defined by others.

The reality that Evangelicals had become a focal point for angst over the election results, and all it signifies for America going forward, was driven home by an experience my wife and I had on a three-day Caribbean cruise. The first night we sat in assigned seats at the dinner table where everyone in the circle was asked to self-introduce and tell why they were there.

The woman seated next to my wife said she took the cruise to rest after an exhausting election season where she gave herself wholeheartedly to fighting Evangelicals and all they stand for. I was next. Needless to say, it did not seem wise to introduce myself just then as president of the National Association of Evangelicals.

The challenge is how to reclaim the older meaning of Evangelical as a faith identity. Consider who are Evangelical Christians. Evangelicals are persons who ascribe to a core set of faith commitments that shape their identity – namely, (1) the belief that the Bible is the highest authority for actions one is called to; (2) the belief that Jesus Christ's death on the cross is the only sacrifice that could remove the penalty of sin; (3) a personal faith in Jesus Christ as Savior; and, (4) a duty to share Christian faith with others.[12] Based on a major recent study by Lifeway Research in Nashville, 30 percent of Americans may be identified as Evangelicals. Especially noteworthy is the breakdown by ethnicity: 44 percent of African Americans are Evangelicals; 30 percent of Hispanics are Evangelicals; 29 percent of whites are Evangelicals.[13] Because there are more white Americans in the United States, there are naturally more white Evangelicals in absolute numbers. But in terms of percentages, African Americans are significantly more evangelical in faith than are whites or Hispanics.

In terms of growth, Hispanics make up the growing edge of American Evangelicalism, with a smaller rate of growth among African Americans and a comparative

---

[9] *Id.*

[10] Jonathan Merritt, *Defining "Evangelical,"* THE ATLANTIC (Dec. 7, 2015), https://perma.cc/FYD3-MNS2.

[11] Neil J. Young, *"Evangelical" Is Not a Political Term*, RELIGION & POL. (July 18, 2017), https://perma.cc/9PCB-TN5X.

[12] *See generally* DANIEL J. TREIER & WALTER A. ELWELL, EVANGELICAL DICTIONARY OF THEOLOGY 35, 42, 148, 774 (3d ed. 2017); *Jesus Christ is the Only Way to God*, https://perma.cc/SRZ2-KZ4V.

[13] Leith Anderson & Ed Stetzer, *Defining Evangelicals in An Election Year*, CHRISTIANITY TODAY (Mar. 2, 2016), at 52–55.

plateau among whites.[14] And the major growth of evangelicalism around the globe is outside of the United States, especially in Africa, Latin America, and parts of Asia.[15] Immigrants to the United States often bring evangelical faith with them or become Evangelicals after they arrive in this country.[16]

II FAITH AND FEARS

So, how does all this connect to the topic of this volume, whether religious freedom and LGBT rights can find common ground, enabling the faith and LGBT communities to peacefully coexist, in the words of the US Commission on Civil Rights? Evangelicals have enjoyed religious liberty in America and perceived themselves as both beneficiaries and supporters of religious liberty. Thus, for Evangelicals, the notion anyone would say that religious freedom and religious liberty "stand for nothing except hypocrisy so long as they remain code words for discrimination, intolerance, racism, sexism, homophobia, Christian supremacy, or any form of intolerance" is stunning and difficult to grasp, and it is all the more unfathomable when those words emanate from the chairman of the US Commission on Civil Rights.[17] The stridency of that view strikes fear into the evangelical community about what new civil rights for the LGBT community may mean in terms of discrimination and law.[18]

2017 marked the 500th anniversary of Martin Luther's Ninety-Five Theses in 1517. In Minnesota and other parts of the country that drew settlers of northern European heritage, especially German and Scandinavian, there have been frequent articles about Luther and Germany.[19] Some depict the impact of Communist discrimination against Christians in the old East Germany where Luther lived and where the

---

[14] Samuel Rodriguez, *The Latino Transformation of American Evangelicalism*, YALE UNIV. REFLECTIONS (2008), https://perma.cc/JYH4-MNZ3.

[15] EVANGELICAL CHRISTIANITY AND DEMOCRACY IN AFRICA 1–3 (Terence O. Ranger ed., 2008); https://perma.cc/8RGN-6V5K; *The Incredible Growth of Africa, Asia, Latin America Evangelicals*, https://perma.cc/GD46-8W96; John L. Allen Jr., *The Dramatic Growth of Evangelicals in Latin America*, NAT'L CATH. REP. (Aug. 18, 2006), https://perma.cc/L4QD-925G.

[16] The Pluralism Project, *Fundamentalism, Evangelicalism, and Pentecostalism*, HARVARD UNIV., https://perma.cc/W9PB-BXQR.

[17] U.S. COMM'N ON CIVIL RIGHTS, PEACEFUL COEXISTENCE: RECONCILING NONDISCRIMINATION PRINCIPLES WITH CIVIL LIBERTIES (2016), https://perma.cc/XLV6-63ET (statement of Chairman Martin Castro).

[18] *See* Smith, Chapter 18; Ryan Anderson, Chapter 27. Even respected constitutional law professors such as Mark Tushnet at Harvard have argued against accommodations. *See* Mark Tushnet, *Abandoning Defensive Crouch Constitutionalism*, BALKINIZATION (May 6, 2016), https://perma.cc/4NYH-DEMP ("My own judgment is that taking a hardline ('You lost, live with it') is better than trying to accommodate the losers.").

[19] *See, e.g., Germany Marks 500th Anniversary of Martin Luther's Challenge*, STARTRIBUNE (Oct. 31, 2017), http://www.startribune.com/germany-marks-500th-anniversary-of-church-s-refor mation/454252973/; *Welcome to Luther's Town*, STARTRIBUNE (July 7, 2017), https://perma.cc/ 7BST-RJME.

Protestant Reformation began.[20] Teachers in schools ridiculed Christian children as "unscientific" and "stupid."[21] Lutherans in eastern Germany grew up being ridiculed and laughed at in classes.[22] Universities excluded Christians from admission because of their beliefs and lifestyles.[23] Persons were denied employment because of their faith.[24] The Communist government strategy actually worked. In 1950, 90 percent of East Germans were Christians. By 1990, that number had dropped to 30 percent. Vilification is often a tool of discrimination and sometimes expungement.

Some would draw no lesson from this history. A natural retort is to cite American exceptionalism;[25] certainly, militant marginalization of faith will not happen in America. That is, it is simply not going to happen in America. Perhaps not. Yet, examples such as these are seared into the minds of believers, who fear the law could become a source of religious discrimination. This fear extends not only to the LGBT context but to other areas that are deeply bound up with religious belief.[26]

Sometimes persons of faith experience limits on their religious freedom as existential threats when the religious practice is one that is identity forming or a badge of membership in the specific community. Sometimes, faith acts as a boundary between the faithful and others in public places. This section describes both phenomena briefly to humanize practices that to outsiders seem strange.

As one example, consider Germany once more. In 2012, a court in Cologne banned male circumcision.[27] The court considered circumcision, even when religiously motivated, a form of involuntary physical mutilation, making it medically unnecessary. At the time, draft federal legislation would have forbidden all circumcisions below the age of fourteen and permitted them after fourteen only with the boy's informed consent.[28] Needless to say, this law would have made illegal the

---

[20] Jean Hopfensperger, *In Eastern Germany, the Land of Luther, Church Pews are Mostly Empty,* StarTribune (Jan. 1, 2017), https://perma.cc/AB5K-PFZM.

[21] *Id. See also* Kenji Yoshino, Covering: The Hidden Assault on Our Civil Rights 26–27 (2007) (discussing passing oneself as white as a coerced conformity and noting that those seen as religious are likely to be discriminated against today).

[22] *See* Hopfensperger, *supra* note 20.

[23] Caroline Ward, *Church and State in East Germany,* 6 Religion in Communist Land 89, 93 (2008), https://perma.cc/SEF6-HZJB.

[24] *Id.*

[25] Classics of American Political and Constitutional Thought: Reconstruction to the Present 818 (Scott J. Hammond et al. eds., 2007) (quoting Ronald Reagan's "City Upon a Hill" speech: "You can call it mysticism if you want to, but I have always believed that there was some divine plan that placed this great continent between two oceans to be sought out by those who were possessed of an abiding love of freedom and a special kind of courage.").

[26] For a review of abortion conscience protections as devices to assure providers that they will never be asked to assist with a procedure they would view as a killing, see Greenawalt, Chapter 8.

[27] Kay-Alexander Scholz, *Circumcision Remains Legal in Germany,* Deutsch Welle (Dec. 12, 2012), https://perma.cc/K3GQ-Q3FV.

[28] *Id.*

millennia-old Jewish practice of circumcising boys when they are eight days old.[29] Circumcision is an essential element of Jewish identity. Ironically, one might think that Germany would be the last place to discriminate against Jews. Remarkably, almost 5 million Muslims live in Germany, and Muslims are by far the largest practitioner of religious male circumcision in the world.[30] The national debate that enveloped the proposed anti-circumcision law was filled with "acrimony, frostiness and at times brutal intolerance."[31] Eventually, the proposed law forbidding male circumcision was defeated by a divided vote in Germany's legislature, the Bundestag.[32]

As religious liberty attorney Eric Rassbach shows in a new volume on *The Contested Place of Religion in Family Law*, the decision acted as a domino:

> opening a space for other European critics of religiously motivated male circumcision to jump into. Shortly after the German decision, hospitals in parts of Austria and Switzerland ceased providing religious circumcision. The Jewish Hospital of Berlin temporarily suspended its circumcision practice because of "the lack of legal clarity." In Norway, the Ombudsman for Children, a government official, stated that religious circumcision should be replaced with a bloodless rite.[33]

Of course, many reflexively assume that nothing akin to Germany's decision to regulate a millennia-old religious rite could occur in America today. That optimism is unwarranted.[34]

Indeed, the New York City Department of Health and Mental Hygiene (Department) regulated a practice related to circumcision in an orthodox Jewish community – namely, cleaning the circumcision wound using oral suction. The Department feared that the practice could spread the herpes virus to infants. However, the Department elected not just to launch a public awareness campaign, but to also force, by regulation, religious figures to ask parents to fill out forms conflicting with the religious figure's religious tradition.[35] Failure to comply would result in a financial penalty.

---

[29] *See* Sara E. Karesh & Mitchell M. Hurvitz, *Brit Milah, in* ENCYCLOPEDIA OF JUDAISM 70–71 (2005).

[30] *See* Conrad Hackett, *5 Facts about the Muslim Population in Europe*, PEW RES. CTR. (Nov. 29, 2017), https://perma.cc/4K67-PE6H; *see also Islam and Male Circumcision*, BBC (Aug. 13, 2009), https://perma.cc/2KMW-GANY.

[31] *See* Scholz, *supra* note 27.

[32] *Id.*

[33] Eric Rassbach, *Coming Soon to a Court Near You: Male Circumcision in Religious Families in Europe and the United States, in* THE CONTESTED PLACE OF RELIGION IN FAMILY LAW 177 (Robin Fretwell Wilson ed., 2018) (citations omitted).

[34] *Id.*

[35] Cent. Rabbinical Cong. of the U.S. and Can. v. N.Y.C. Dep't of Health and Mental Hygiene, 763 F.3d 183, 186 (2d Cir. 2014).

A group of mohels and rabbis sued in federal court, arguing that the regulation violated their rights to the free exercise of religion and freedom of speech.[36] The federal district court ruled against them for two main reasons. First, the court found that the Department's rule was neutral and generally applicable to all circumcisions, not just religiously grounded ones; because the regulation did not target religion, it did not trigger strict scrutiny under the Free Exercise Clause of the First Amendment of the US Constitution, as Doug Laycock explains in Chapter 3. Second, the court concluded that the city's enlisting of the mohels to spread the city's message – a message with which the mohels strongly disagreed – did not trigger strict scrutiny review under the Free Speech Clause of the First Amendment either, according to the court.[37] Applying the more deferential rational basis review, the district court upheld the City's regulation.[38]

The rabbis appealed to the US Court of Appeals for the Second Circuit, which reversed.[39] The Second Circuit found that the city's regulation was not neutral because it singled out a particular Orthodox Jewish practice for regulation, which triggers strict scrutiny of the regulation, making it far less likely to be sustained. The city ultimately settled with the plaintiffs and agreed to rescind the regulation.[40]

New York City has not been an isolated data point. Similar proposals have cropped up and gotten traction in California.[41] A proposed ballot measure in San Francisco sought to criminalize the performance of male circumcision within the city limits, notwithstanding a California Business and Professions Code section allowing circumcision.[42] In 2011, activists proposed a similar ballot measure in Santa Monica, but later abandoned it.[43]

In 2011, the California Legislature barred California municipalities from adopting rules that would prohibit male circumcision.[44] Under that law, medical need, family affiliation, and community affiliation all constitute recognized reasons for the practice of male circumcision.[45]

---

[36] *Id.*

[37] For a discussion of compelled speech as a doctrine, see Chapter 7.

[38] *Cent. Rabbinical Cong.*, 763 F.3d at 192.

[39] *Id.* at 198.

[40] *Id.* at 194 (finding that "the Regulation is neither neutral nor, on this record, generally applicable, and thus must be afforded heightened scrutiny."); Dep't of Health and Mental Hygiene Bd. of Health, *Notice of Adoption of Amendments to the New York City Health Code* (Sept. 9, 2015), https://perma.cc/PSX9-FSNN (stating that §181.21 is repealed).

[41] *See supra* note 33.

[42] Adam Cohen, *San Francisco's Circumcision Ban: An Attack on Religious Freedom?*, TIME (June 13, 2011), https://perma.cc/NU24-HY63; CAL. BUS. & PROF. CODE § 460(b) (West 2018).

[43] *See* Rassbach, *supra* note 33, at 178.

[44] CAL. HEALTH & SAFETY CODE § 125850(b) (2018) (providing that "[n]o city, county, or city and county ordinance, regulation, or administrative action shall prohibit or restrict the practice of male circumcision, or the exercise of a parent's authority to have a child circumcised.").

[45] *Id.* at § 125850(a)(1) (stating that "[m]ale circumcision has a wide array of health and affiliative benefits").

To paraphrase Rassbach, society risks a grave threat to the religious identities of faith communities when it substitutes its judgment for those of parents. Laws such as California's reflect that wisdom.

III MAINTAINING FAITH IN PUBLIC PLACES

The desire to follow one's faith sometimes appears in unexpected places, such as New York City's public swimming pools. For twenty years, city pools offered limited pool hours restricted to women only, until an anonymous inquiry to the New York Human Rights Commission claimed that the practice violated gender-discrimination laws related to public services.[46] The two pools with women-only hours were at the Metropolitan Recreation Center in Williamsburg and the St. John's Recreation Center in Crown Heights – both facilities that serve women in Hasidic Jewish neighborhoods.[47] These Jewish women share a religious identity that forbids mixed-gender swimming. In July 2016, after weeks of deliberation, the city granted an exemption and reinstituted reduced hours for those who identify as female.[48] Explanations of the exemption spoke movingly about cultural differences, sexual violence, sexual abuse, and body-consciousness.

But not everyone saw this as a win–win. Donna Lieberman of the New York Civil Liberties Union called the exemption "deeply troubling."[49] She said "[i]t has all the earmarks of a religious exemption. People have every right to go swimming in a gender-segregated environment pursuant to their religious beliefs, but not on the taxpayer dime." A *New York Times* editorial attacked the city's decision, claiming that during the gender-segregated pool hours, the public pool would be "temporarily unmoored from the laws of New York City and the Constitution, and commonly held principles of fairness and equal access."[50] The *Times* said the religious accommodation reflected "a theocratic view of government services."[51] Consider what this stance entails as a matter of policy. In this view, rules and exemptions from them designed to accommodate our increasingly diverse polity in the public square may be established on a broad variety of criteria *as long as none are religious*.

As this push and pull over the state's regulation of public spaces and religious practices show, the fears expressed by Christians in the run-up to the 2016 elections were not predictions, but narratives, about their palpable concern about losing their religious liberty. The fear may loom larger in the white evangelical community than

---

[46] Eli Rosenberg, *Gender-Segregated Swimming Cut Back at 2 Public Pools Near Brooklyn Hasidic Areas*, N.Y. Times (July 6, 2016), https://perma.cc/7493-W726.
[47] *Id.*
[48] *Id.*
[49] *Id.*
[50] Editorial Board, *Everybody Into the Pool*, N.Y. Times (June 1, 2016), https://perma.cc/U9A4-P7NC.
[51] *Id.*

in the African American and Hispanic evangelical communities. This may be because the white majority has not felt threatened in terms of its liberty until recent years.

This was driven home for me when I asked a prominent African American leader recently what white Christians need to learn from the black church.[52] He said that the black church knows how to live with discrimination and can teach the white church how to live with discrimination. Sadly, neither community should have to accept discrimination, just as LGBT persons and other minorities should not have to accept discrimination – something that I hope the diverse voices collected in these pages can agree upon.

IV EVANGELICALS IN A PLURALISTIC SOCIETY

Evangelical beliefs and practices around human sexuality and marriage are shared with more than 2 billion Christians around the world, including the Roman Catholic Church, the Orthodox churches, and others.[53] These beliefs are part of Christian identity.[54]

Evangelical belief in marriage as a lifelong, exclusive covenant between a man and a woman is based on the teaching of the Bible that is our rule of faith and practice.[55] To ask Christians to change faith and practice is to ask them to jettison their core beliefs and commitments in order to conform to the beliefs and commitments of the government, society, and others. That governments would seek this result is not consistent with religious freedom. Christians should not be expected to sacrifice historic beliefs and practices on the altar of contemporary mandate.

Religious liberty should not be defined as religious worship. It extends beyond gatherings in a church building, synagogue, mosque, or other worship venue to living personal and corporate faith and identity in homes, schools, businesses, prisons, and, yes, public swimming pools.

Does this mean that laws should preserve religious liberty at the cost of legal and societal discrimination against those who disagree? For some Evangelicals, the answer might be yes. But there are many opinions and practices among 100 million people. However, in my own experience and context, it is rare to hear Evangelicals advocate for discrimination against others. Instead, the clarion call is for mutual tolerance in a diverse nation.

So how does the society find a solution amenable to all? It is far from easy, but that vision of a single community where all are respected should be our quest. There is

---

[52] Claude Alexander & Leith Anderson, *What White Christians Need To Know About Black Churches*, NAT'L ASS'N OF EVANGELICALS (Jan. 15, 2017), https://perma.cc/7493-W726.

[53] Mark Galli, *Breaking News: 2 Billion Christians Believe in Traditional Marriage*, CHRISTIANITY TODAY (June 9, 2015), https://perma.cc/YS4U-5F4U.

[54] For an interesting historical examination of Christian identity, see DeGirolami, Chapter 21.

[55] *Id.*

no doubt that like-minded members of the faith community have their work cut out for them in securing agreement in religious communities that all can in fact be respected.

And legal scholars, politicians, and courts have the challenges of writing and enforcing fair laws for everyone.

Emma Green wrote in *The Atlantic* that:

> Legal scholars have no idea how to resolve the government's conflicting obligations to allow free religious exercise and protect minority groups from discrimination. Ultimately, legal language is not sufficient to resolve ultimate conflicts over belief and identity. Legislatures and litigators will have to continue muddling through, finding an imperfect balance between competing cultural norms.[56]

The First Amendment to the US Constitution prioritizes religious freedom, in the Bill of Rights itself. Our laws should prioritize the preservation and protection of religious freedom and seek creative solutions so that the good that governments seek to do – erase discrimination of others – do not become the tools of discrimination against persons of faith, simply because that is the preference of the government.[57]

This is not to say that religious freedom is either absolute or unlimited. It is to say that religious beliefs and practices hold a first priority against the government, that the government seeks respectful solutions when enacting laws. The challenge is great and the stakes are high. Evangelical Christians pray that conversations, considerations, and conclusions will lead to resolutions of the dilemmas described in this volume – with compassion and fairness for all.

[56] Emma Green, *Even the Government's Smartest Lawyers Can't Figure Out Religious Liberty*, THE ATLANTIC (Sept. 14, 2016), https://perma.cc/GQ8E-RH2R.

[57] U.S. CONST. amend. I.

13

The "Demands" of Faith

Archbishop William E. Lori

This volume can contribute to generating a productive and mutually respectful dialogue on the meaning of fundamental freedoms, including religious freedom, at a time when the nation's sexual mores are rapidly changing, especially with the legalization of same-sex marriage and the advent of many sexual orientation and gender identity nondiscrimination laws and policies.[1] This is an endeavor to move beyond mere rhetoric and slogans but instead try to focus on the serious legal and philosophical questions that need to be discussed.

This chapter addresses the "demands" of faith in the current social context. A clarification of the term "demands" is in order. There are three possible meanings, coupled with corresponding responsibilities:

(1) The personal and social imperatives ("demands") that arise from faith itself;

(2) The societal conditions under which people of faith and their ministries flourish, that is, the need to ensure ("demand") that there is ample "room" in society for people of faith, for their institutions and ministries, and for religious concepts and teachings;

(3) The legitimate expectation ("demand") of people of faith that they and their religious institutions will be fully accorded protection of their God-given religious freedoms, guaranteed by the Constitution and the Bill of Rights; and

(4) The responsibilities of people of faith and their institutions and ministries in the exercise of their freedom toward society and the state.

This chapter elaborates on each point.

---

[1] For a review of laws, see Wilson, Chapter 30; Appendix. For critique, see Ryan Anderson, Chapter 27. For public opinion, see Brownstein, Chapter 2; Greenawalt, Chapter 8.

I IMPERATIVES THAT ARISE FROM FAITH ITSELF

The demands that arise from the vast array of world religions vary; these varying demands cannot be addressed in the space of a short chapter.[2] This chapter will address them from the religious tradition I know best, namely, Roman Catholicism.

Society often tends to reduce religious teachings to a series of unpleasant, countercultural moral prohibitions.[3] This may be exemplified by Roman Catholicism. Many identify the Catholic Church solely with bans on abortion, extramarital sex, same-sex marriage, contraception, and so forth.[4] The core in which these teachings are rooted, as well as the Church's social teachings, is all but forgotten or unknown. In today's culture, it is not hard to paint teachings on personal morality as unreasonable, especially when severed from their source. Indeed, many see the Church as the destroyer of *eros*.[5] As Pope Benedict XVI wrote, "Doesn't [the Church] blow the whistle just when the joy of the Creator's gift [of sexuality] offers a happiness which is itself a certain foretaste of the Divine?"[6]

Christianity, however, does not begin with a series of moral prohibitions, nor is it merely coextensive with them. Rather, it is centered on the person of Christ. As Pope Benedict XVI also wrote, "Being Christian is not the result of an ethical choice or a lofty idea, but the encounter with an event, a person, who gives life a new horizon and a decisive direction."[7] Catholic Christians believe that encountering Christ in Scripture, prayer, and the Sacraments leads to the realization that we are loved by God and called to share His friendship – a realization that changes how we think, live, and act.[8] Similarly, Pope Francis stresses that an encounter with the person of Christ gives rise to the dynamism and joy of the Christian faith.[9] This encounter leads to a whole new way of life in which belief, worship, and ethics are intertwined.[10] This new way of life demands a conversion of life – "a new way of

---

[2] For an encyclopedic treatment, see the Encyclopedia of Religion (2d ed., Lindsay Jones ed., 2005).

[3] For attitudes toward religious institutions as forces for good that can "bring people together and strengthen community bonds," a view held by 89% of U.S. adults, with the strongest critique among religiously unaffiliated "nones" being that religious institutions "focus too much on rules" (68%), see Pew Research Ctr. Religion & Pub. Life, U.S. Public Becoming Less Religious chapter 3 (Nov. 3, 2015).

[4] See, e.g., Reva B. Siegel, *Dignity and Sexuality: Claims on Dignity in Transnational Debates Over Abortion and Same-Sex Marriage*, 10 Int'l J. of Const. L. 355, 358 (2012); *The Position of the Church on Artificial Contraception, in* Pro-Life Activist's Encyclopedia (1994), https://www.ewtn.com/library/PROLENC/ENCYC098.HTM.

[5] Pamela Dickey Young, Re-creating the Church Communities of Eros 110 (2000).

[6] Pope Benedict XVI, God is Love Deus Caritas Est 6 (3d. ed. 2007), http://w2.vatican.va/content/benedict-xvi/en/encyclicals/documents/hf_ben-xvi_enc_20051225_deus-caritas-est.html.

[7] *Id.* at 1.

[8] For a similar view from the evangelical tradition, see Leith Anderson, Chapter 12.

[9] Pope Francis, Evangelii Gaudium 7 (2013), http://w2.vatican.va/content/francesco/en/apost_exhortations/documents/papa-francesco_esortazione-ap_20131124_evangelii-gaudium.html.

[10] Pope Benedict XVI, *supra* note 6, at 14.

seeing things centered on Christ."[11] It also demands a moral transformation that responds to God's prior love, a conversion that includes a renunciation of a self-centered way of life, a rejection of sin, and all that substitutes for God. In this moral transformation, love of God and love of neighbor are interwoven.

As the love of Christ takes root in one's heart, there arises a desire to share this experience in the life of the Church and beyond. Included in the conversion or transformation that results from a living encounter with Christ is a *missionary imperative* – a burning desire to share the faith, even when it is costly to do so.[12] This imperative to spread the faith was expressed by St. Paul, who wrote "Woe to me if I do not preach the Gospel" and "The love of Christ impels us."[13]

This is but a thumbnail sketch designed for a limited purpose, namely, to address what history repeatedly demonstrates. In spite of the sinfulness which mars the Church's history, there is an inner dynamism in the life of the Church which takes root in the heart of Christ's disciples and leads to the proclamation of the Gospel, to "worship in spirit and truth," and to a new way of life in imitation of Christ's own gift of love – a love manifested through personal example and through the Church's ministries.[14] These imperatives, arising from the faith itself, asserted themselves in the severe persecutions that marked the early centuries of the Church's history. The Lord predicted that his followers and that the Church herself would suffer persecution and martyrdom.[15] Before his Ascension into heaven, Jesus instructed his Apostles, "you will receive power when the Holy Spirit comes upon you, and you will be my witnesses in Jerusalem, throughout Judea and Samaria, and to the ends of the earth."[16] Surveying the second-century persecution of Christians and the calumnies uttered against them, the author Tertullian wrote, "The blood [of martyrs] is the seed of Christians."[17] That is to say, when one's living and spreading the faith leads to the witness of giving up one's life, then it is that the faith attracts those searching for God; thus the faith spreads. The witness of martyrs animated and energized the entire history of the Church.

Pope Francis has said that in our day there are even more Christian martyrs than in the earliest centuries of the Church.[18] While speaking out against the persecution

---

[11] Pope Francis, Lumen Fidei The Light of Faith 20 (2013), http://w2.vatican.va/content/benedict-xvi/en/encyclicals/documents/hf_ben-xvi_enc_20051225_deus-caritas-est.html.

[12] *See* Pope Francis, *supra* note 9, at 19.

[13] 1 *Corinthians* 9:16 (New International Version); 2 *Corinthians* 5:14 (New American Bible (Rev. Ed.)).

[14] *John* 4:24 (New King James Version); John Paul II, Redemptoris Missio: On the Permanent Validity of the Church's Missionary Mandate 1 (1990), http://w2.vatican.va/content/john-paul-ii/en/encyclicals/documents/hf_jp-ii_enc_07121990_redemptoris-missio.html.

[15] *Matthew* 5:11 (New International Version).

[16] *Acts* 1:8 (New American Bible (Rev. Ed.)).

[17] The Apology of Tertullian 135 (Wm. Reeve, A.M. trans., 1889).

[18] Pope Francis focused his Homily on the Feast of the Roman Martyrs. *See Pope Francis: Church Grows from the Blood of the Martyrs*, Today's Catholic (June 30, 2014), https://satodayscatholic.wordpress.com/2014/06/30/pope-francis-church-grows-from-the-blood-of-the-martyrs/.

of Christians and other religious minorities in the Middle East, Pope Francis also took note of the "polite persecution" of Christians in the West.[19] This ranges from marginalizing believers, to eroding their rights to conscientious objection, and compromising religious freedom by confining it merely to the right to worship in a church.[20] In fact, it should not be surprising that in a hostile environment or culture, the inner demands of Christianity and other religious faiths will assert themselves and that more than a few believers will be willing to advance the faith no matter what the cost personally. This does not absolve believers from dialogue with the ambient culture and the search for common ground and it does not give permission for any form of unjust discrimination against others – though the definition of what constitutes unjust discrimination remains a matter under discussion.[21]

II SOCIETAL CONDITIONS THAT FOSTER RELIGIOUS EXPRESSION

The Church is sometimes described as a ship sailing on the storm-tossed seas of history.[22] Christians believe that the mission entrusted to the Church's care will continue until the end of time.[23] While enduring many things for the sake of the Kingdom, the Church also must seek to help create a just and peaceful society. Fundamental to such a society is the exercise of basic human freedoms such as freedom of speech and assembly as well as freedom of conscience and religion. Fundamental also are a spirit of toleration and a readiness for dialogue, even in the face of seemingly impossible odds of success.

As in much of political theory,[24] the Church's social teaching distinguishes between society and the state. Civil society precedes the state, and the latter is at the service of the former.[25] It is defined as "the sum of relationships and resources, cultural and associative that are relatively independent from the political sphere and the economic sector."[26] At the heart of this distinction is the human person

---

[19] *Pope's Morning Homily: Denial of Conscientious Objection is Persecution*, ZENIT (Apr. 12, 2016), https://zenit.org/articles/popes-morning-homily-denial-of-conscientious-objection-is-persecution/.

[20] *Id.*

[21] For a range of views in this volume, compare Smith, Chapter 18; Perry, Chapter 20; and Ryan Anderson, Chapter 27, with Melling, Chapter 19; Pizer, Chapter 29.

[22] *See, e.g.,* 1 *Peter* 3:20–21; *Mark* 4:35–41; SEPTIMI FLORENTIS DE BAPTISMO xii (J.M. Lupton, M.A. ed., 1908), as well as numerous paintings.

[23] POPE PAUL VI, DOGMATIC CONSTITUTION ON THE CHURCH LUMEN GENTIUM 20 (Nov. 21, 1964).

[24] *See, e.g.,* Brett Bowden, *Civil Society, the State, and the Limits to Global Civil Society,* 20 GLOBAL SOCIETY 155 (2006).

[25] *See* COMPENDIUM OF THE SOCIAL DOCTRINE OF THE CHURCH 417 (2004).

[26] *Id.*

"understood as an autonomous, relational being who is open to the Transcendent."[27] A society marked by a healthy pluralism and by democratic principles is best suited to this understanding of human dignity. Thus, the Church seeks to foster such a society by her social teaching, especially the principles of human dignity, the common good, solidarity, and subsidiarity[28] – teachings backed up by an array of educational and social services to the poor and vulnerable.[29] In contrast to pluralistic democracies, totalitarian states absorb society and subjugate human persons by denying their fundamental and natural freedoms.[30] As persons endowed with inalienable dignity and rights, we are to participate in civil society, seeking our fulfillment and contributing to the common good.

Society and the state are distinct but interconnected. Civil society is not a mere component or extension of the government. Rather, it is or ought to be the case that society gives rise to the state. It is the duty of the state to provide "an adequate legal framework" for the exercise of human freedoms and the pursuit of the common good.[31] Society itself is complex. Civil society is marked by ambiguities and clashes of interest and struggles between the weak and the strong that sometimes require governmental intervention. Yet the principle of subsidiarity would indicate that these matters should be solved at the lowest, most local level possible.[32] It also stresses the importance of "intermediary institutions" such as the family, the Church, social service agencies, and other social organizations in maintaining a just and peaceful society where the common good can be pursued.[33] In matters of urgency or overarching importance, state intervention can, under certain circumstances, be justified.[34]

The society-state distinction is illustrated in the history of the Catholic Church in Maryland (from whence I hail) and the United States. In the seventeenth century, amid the religious intolerance and strife in England, George Calvert envisioned the possibility of Catholics and Protestants living together peacefully in a colony in the New World.[35] Influenced by St. Thomas More, he believed that denying freedom of

---

[27] *Id. Cf.* Freedom, Truth, and Human Dignity 113–21 (David L. Schindler & Nicolas J. Healy Jr. trans., 2015), for further reflections on the distinction between society and the state.

[28] For a summary of principles of the Church's social teaching, see U.S. Conference of Catholic Bishops, Forming Consciences for Faithful Citizenship 20-25 (2015).

[29] For scale, see Brian Grim & Melissa Grim, *The Socio-Economic Contribution of Religion to American Society: An Empirical Analysis*, 12 Interdisc. J. Res. on Religion 3 (2016), http://faithcounts.com/Report/ (quantifying the economic impact of 344,000 religious congregations of all faiths at $418 billion annually, even before considering the economic impact of religious institutions and businesses).

[30] *See* Congregation For The Doctrine Of The Faith, Instruction On Christian Freedom And Liberation (Aug. 6, 1984).

[31] Compendium, *supra* note 25, at 418.

[32] *Id.* at 186.

[33] *Id.* at 187.

[34] *See infra* note 62 accompanying text.

[35] Matthew E. Bunson, *America's Catholic Colony*, Catholic Answers (Sept. 1, 2009), https://www.catholic.com/magazine/print-edition/americas-catholic-colony.

conscience undermined the common good.[36] Calvert, himself a part of the Catholic minority in England, managed to secure a land grant in a colony that would be called Maryland.[37] Maryland was not merely a haven for persecuted Catholics but rather was meant to be a place of religious toleration. It fell to George's son, Cecil, to carry out this adventuresome plan, which became a "business enterprise to which a noble cause was attached," according to historian Fr. Charles Connor.[38] So it was that two small ships, the *Ark* and the *Dove*, landed in 1634 at St. Clement Island off what is present-day St. Mary's County in Southern Maryland.[39] This noble experiment had its ups and downs. In 1649 the Maryland General Assembly passed the Toleration Act of 1649, also known as "An Act Concerning Religion," which ratified the founding vision of Maryland society.[40] Nonetheless, events in England – especially the enactment of the Penal Laws – led to a curtailment of this experiment in freedom but did not erase it from the memory of what became the Catholic minority in the colony of Maryland.[41] This early experience of religious tolerance would, in time, contribute to the US Constitution and Bill of Rights of the new republic.[42] An understated colonial Catholic society carved out for itself a way of existing at a time when the unjust penal laws were in force and thus helped preserve the ideals of freedom of conscience and religious toleration and influence the formation of a new form of government.

With the Constitution and the Bill of Rights, new doors were opened for Catholics and others. This, however, did not spell the end of religious intolerance in society. Catholics were still a minority religion and had to tread carefully. Even as their numbers grew and churches were built, Catholics resisted raising their profile and embracing all the organizational elements of the Roman Catholic Church in Europe.[43] Accordingly, the first archbishop of Baltimore, John Carroll (a cousin to the only Catholic signer of the Declaration of Independence), charted a cautious course in establishing the first Roman Catholic Diocese in the United States,

---

[36] *Two Acts of Toleration: 1649 and 1826*, http://msa.maryland.gov/msa/speccol/sc2200/sc2221/000025/html/intro.html.

[37] *George Calvert, First Lord Baltimore (c. 1580–1632)*, EXPLORING MARYLAND'S ROOTS: LIBRARY (2018), http://mdroots.thinkport.org/library/georgecalvert.asp.

[38] FR. CHARLES CONNOR, PIONEER PRIESTS & MAKESHIFT ALTARS: A HISTORY OF CATHOLICISM IN THE THIRTEEN COLONIES (2017).

[39] *The Story of the Ark & Dove . . .*, HISTORY OF ST. MARY'S CITY (2013), https://hsmcdigshistory.org/research/maritime-curation/ark-and-dove/.

[40] Kenneth L. Lasson, *Religious Freedom and the Church-State Relationship in Maryland*, 14 CATH. LAW. 4 (Winter 1968).

[41] For a fuller description of this history, see THOMAS W. SPALDING, THE PREMIER SEE 2–7 (1989).

[42] For the influence of colonial guarantees on the U.S. Constitution, see Interactive Constitution, NATIONAL CONSTITUTION CENTER, https://constitutioncenter.org/interactive-constitution#.

[43] Michael Davis Knowles et al., *Roman Catholicism*, ENCYCLOPEDIA BRITANNICA (July 19, 2017), https://www.britannica.com/topic/Roman-Catholicism.

namely, Baltimore.[44] As the first bishop in the United States, Carroll walked a fine line in a society that was sensitive to any form of interference from European monarchies and potentates. Lest he be thought subject to a foreign power (the pope), Carroll maintained that he was elected by his fellow clerics, an appointment Pope Pius VI merely confirmed.[45] Even so, Carroll faced, as would many of his successors, an anti-Catholic spirit embedded in American society. Carroll avoided building a gothic or baroque cathedral on the prominent Baltimore hill but instead built a neoclassical structure.[46] Designed by Benjamin Henry Latrobe, architect of the US Capitol, the Baltimore Cathedral harmonized with the architecture of the new republic.[47] Despite persistent expressions of anti-Catholicism, the Catholic Church in the United States grew steadily throughout the nineteenth century and by the early twentieth century had achieved a robust institutional form that continues to function to the present day.[48]

Among the most prominent archbishops of Baltimore was James Cardinal Gibbons, who served from 1877 until his death in 1921.[49] Gibbons skillfully led the hierarchy in his day in adapting the Church to American society while expanding its influence. In an 1887 speech, shortly after becoming a cardinal, Gibbons maintained that there was no conflict between one's being a loyal American and a loyal Catholic.[50] In the years that followed, Catholics, many of whom were European immigrants, assimilated into American society, so much so that, on the eve of the II Vatican Council (1962–65), some observers believed that anti-Catholic prejudice was virtually a thing of the past.[51] Unfortunately, that prejudice has proven to be a persistent strain and stain on our civil society, along with other forms of anti-religious prejudice and bigotry.[52]

---

[44] Thomas W. Spalding, *"A Revolution More Extraordinary": Bishop John Carroll and the Birth of American Catholicism*, 84 MD. HIST. MAG. 195, 200 (1989), http://msa.maryland.gov/megafile/msa/speccol/sc5800/sc5881/000001/000000/000336/pdf/msa_sc_5881_1_336.pdf.

[45] *Cf.* MICHAEL DAVID BREIDENBACH, CONCILIARISM AND AMERICAN RELIGIOUS LIBERTY, 1632–1835, at 185 (2013).

[46] *Id.*

[47] *Id.* at 167. *See also* JEFFREY A. COHEN & CHARLES E. BROWNELL, THE ARCHITECTURAL DRAWINGS OF BENJAMIN HENRY LATROBE 431 (1994). Latrobe's sketches for the Baltimore Cathedral are still displayed in the residence of the archbishop of Baltimore.

[48] JAMES HENNESSEY, AMERICAN CATHOLICS: A HISTORY OF THE ROMAN CATHOLIC COMMUNITY IN THE UNITED STATES 209 (1981).

[49] Timothy Walch, *James Cardinal Gibbons*, ENCYCLOPEDIA BRITANNICA (April 9, 2017), https://www.britannica.com/biography/James-Cardinal-Gibbons.

[50] For the text of this speech, see JOHN TRACY ELLIS, LIFE OF JAMES CARDINAL GIBBONS 308–09 (1952).

[51] Julie Byrne, *Roman Catholics and Immigration in Nineteenth-Century America*, DEP'T OF RELIGION, DUKE UNIV. (Nov. 2000), http://nationalhumanitiescenter.org/tserve/nineteen/nkeyinfo/nromcath.htm.

[52] Father Andrew Greeley called anti-Catholicism "the last acceptable prejudice." *See* Andrew M. Greeley, *Prejudiced Still*, AM. MAG.: JESUIT REV. (Oct. 20, 2003).

Thus, even in a legal framework that guarantees freedom of conscience, toleration, and religious freedom, the Church – like other groups in American society[53] – has faced a persistent anti-Catholicism on the part of the larger society. This same attitude takes on new forms as the Church's consistent teachings on the family, human sexuality, the value of unborn human life, and other issues become more and more countercultural. Anti-Catholicism is also fueled, no doubt, by scandals in the Church – especially the sexual abuse scandal[54] – and by the failure of many to live the faith they profess. In spite of such failures, the Church in the United States and elsewhere is right to seek and find in civil society "room" – societal "space" – for people of faith, for religious ministries and institutions, and for religious ideas and concepts.[55] Further, the Church seeks the right for members to conduct the entirety of their lives in accord with the teachings of their faith,[56] even as it asserts the right to be in the marketplace of ideas and to exert influence upon the formation of a just society. What the Church looks for in the wider society is not the right to dominate or rule but rather a spirit of toleration, even openness, not only to its teachings but also to its forms of worship and its faith-inspired ways of serving those in need. In addition to toleration and civility, the Church seeks respect for all kinds of "intermediary institutions" that stand between the power of the state and the individual conscience, including many types of faith-based institutions and other forms of free association.[57] These intermediary structures can and should contribute to the creation of conditions that aid and abet civil discourse among people of differing views. American Jesuit theologian Father John Courtney Murray would describe such societal toleration, openness, and respect of religion as a kind of unwritten pact, which he terms "articles of peace."[58]

---

[53] For accounts of prejudice against groups, see Brownstein, Chapter 2; Minter, Chapter 4; Leith Anderson, Chapter 12; Hoogstra et al., Chapter 25; Pizer, Chapter 29.

[54] Stefano Pitrelli & Sarah Pulliam Bailey, *Pope Francis Acknowledges Catholic Church's Bad Practices During the Sex Abuse Crisis*, WASH. POST (Sept. 21, 2017); Michael Lipka, *Most U.S. Catholics Call Addressing Clergy Sex Abuse a Top Priority*, PEW RESEARCH CTR. RELIGION & PUB. LIFE (DEC. 6, 2013), http://www.pewresearch.org/fact-tank/2013/12/06/most-u-s-catholics-call-addressing-clergy-sex-abuse-a-top-priority/.

[55] This is a widely shared desire. *See e.g., Vikas Shah, Religion, Science, and Society*, THOUGHT-ECON. (May 16, 2016), https://thoughteconomics.com/religion-science-and-society/ (interview with Rowan Williams, Archbishop of Canterbury, critiquing "the standard 'Western' narrative" that "religion at best is something private").

[56] *The Declaration on Religious Freedom, in* FREEDOM, TRUTH, AND HUMAN DIGNITY, THE SECOND VATICAN COUNCIL'S DECLARATION ON RELIGIOUS FREEDOM 17 (David L. Schindler & Nicolas J. Healy Jr. trans., 2015) ("The principle of religious freedom thus contributes in no small way to fostering a state of affairs in which men and women can without hindrance be invited to the Christian faith, embrace it of their own free will, and actively profess it in their whole way of life."). For another translation, see POPE PAUL VI, DECLARATION ON RELIGIOUS FREEDOM, *DIGNITATIS HUMANAE* (Dec. 7, 1965), http://www.vatican.va/archive/hist_councils/ii_vatican_council/documents/vat-ii_decl_19651207_dignitatis-humanae_en.html#.

[57] Richard M. Ebeling, *Free Markets, the Rule of Law, and Classical Liberalism*, FOUND. FOR ECON. EDUC. (May 1, 2004), https://fee.org/articles/free-markets-the-rule-of-law-and-classical-liberalism/.

[58] JOHN COURTNEY MURRAY, WE HOLD THESE TRUTHS 18 (1960).

Religious toleration is tested when religious tenets are countercultural. Indeed, the notion of toleration itself is incoherent when applied only to what is popular or commonly accepted. By contrast, Church teachings often *are* countercultural. Many Christians understand these teachings to be consonant with the dignity of the human person, created in God's image and called to love as God loves.[59] Not everyone agrees. But such disagreement ought not to lead to the silencing or belittling of religious voices. Further, it is not enough for society merely to tolerate the countercultural views of individuals. For religion is more than one's private spirituality; rather it has three dimensions: "historical, public, and communal."[60] Toleration should be extended to all three dimensions of the Church's mission. For example, our institutions of service should not be penalized or excluded from government programs for following church teachings or coerced by government mandates and policies to conform to the views of the prevailing culture.[61]

Coupled with toleration is civility. This is more than politeness. In the language of Pope Francis, we are called to foster "a culture of encounter."[62] This includes listening to one another, dialogue, a search for common ground, and respect for one another's identity and deeply held beliefs and convictions.[63] Civility is averse to putting pejorative labels on persons because of their convictions. Teachings such as the complementary relationship of man and woman in marriage should not be reduced to an "ism" or labeled as "bigotry."[64] Those who are convinced that marriage is between one man and one woman should not be equated with racial bigots.[65] Conversely, those who disagree with the Church's teaching on marriage should not be the objects of disparaging labels or epithets, either.[66]

More than politeness, civility should also extend to a respect for truth and a common desire to search for objective truth concerning the dignity of the human person and the common good of society. Dialogue is difficult without common ground rooted in objective truth about the dignity, rights, and responsibilities of the human person.

---

[59] *See, e.g., Sharing Catholic Social Teaching: Challenges and Directions*, U.S. CONF. OF CATH. BISHOPS, http://www.usccb.org/beliefs-and-teachings/what-we-believe/catholic-social-teaching/sharing-catholic-social-teaching-challenges-and-directions.cfm; *How Could Humans Have Evolved and Still Be Created in the "Image of God"?*, BIOLOGOS, https://biologos.org/common-questions/human-origins/image-of-god.

[60] FRANCIS CARDINAL GEORGE, A GODLY HUMANISM 131 (2015). For a discussion of religious organizations as devices to pursue shared religious aims, see Helfand, Chapter 11.

[61] For views on the role of funding, see Hollman, Chapter 23; Hoogstra et al., Chapter 25.

[62] Pope Francis has employed this phrase in many of his talks and writings. Among his earliest references to this phrase as pope was his 2013 Pentecost homily. *Pope Francis' Homily at Pentecost Mass*, ZENIT (May 19, 2013), https://zenit.org/articles/pope-francis-homily-at-pentecost-mass/.

[63] *Id.*

[64] For an insightful account of "civil rights simplisms" and their capacity to shrink possibilities for common ground, see Smith, Chapter 18.

[65] See Perry, Chapter 20, for critique of this standard analogy.

[66] See Minter, Chapter 4, and Pizer, Chapter 29, for hurtful things said of LGBT persons.

A lack of commonly shared truth undermines the human solidarity necessary for a healthy society. What is needed is an examination of an emerging fault line in our democracy: "a growing willingness to sacrifice objective truth for freedom."[67] A related fault line is reflected in the 2016 report of the US Civil Rights Commission, namely, a subordination of basic human freedoms to still-fluctuating and highly individualized views of what constitutes discrimination.[68] Leveling the charge of discrimination indiscriminately undermines respect for a healthy pluralism. Churches have the right not only to teach their members, but also to advocate broadly for laws and policies they believe are in accord with the common good. Not all schools and social services need be the same. Some can and should reflect their religious roots without fear of reprisal, just as religious persons and institutions must seek to build bridges wherever possible.

Even when met with toleration, civility, and openness, the Church recognizes that in every culture, including this one, it is never fully at home. The Letter to the Hebrews teaches: "We have here no lasting city."[69] The second-century author of the *Letter to Diognetus* put it this way:

> Christians are not distinguished from other men by country, language, or the customs which they observe. They do not inhabit cities of their own, use a particular way of speaking, nor lead a life marked out by any curiosity ... Instead they inhabit both barbarian and Greek cities – however things have fallen to each of them. And while following the customs of the natives in food, clothing, and the rest of ordinary life, they display to us their wonderful and admittedly striking way of life. They live in their own countries but they do so as those who are just passing through. As citizens they participate in everything with others yet they endure everything as if they were foreigners. Every foreign land is like a homeland to them and every land of their birth is like a land of strangers.[70]

In the same way, those who take their faith seriously and strive to make it the basis of their lives are not exempt from participating in the wider culture and contributing to the common good of society. Yet there is always a sense in which Christians and other committed religionists will have to discern when to confront the culture (and suffer the consequences) and when to try to transform the culture from within. Following in the footsteps of Archbishop John Carroll and James Cardinal Gibbons, we need to discern how and when to find common cause and common cultural expression with the wider society and how and when to resist the culture and the wider society. In the language of Pope Francis, Christians are called to be "missionary disciples" by bringing the faith to the peripheries of society, especially the poor

---

[67] *See* James Keating, *The Seminary and Western Culture: Relationships That Promote Recovery and Holiness* 14 NOVA ET VETERA 1099 (2016) (quoting Cardinal Francis George).

[68] *See* U.S. COMM'N ON CIVIL RIGHTS, PEACEFUL COEXISTENCE: RECONCILING NONDISCRIMINATION PRINCIPLES WITH CIVIL LIBERTIES (2016).

[69] *Hebrews* 13:14 (English Standard Version).

[70] *Letter to Diognetus, chapter 5*, CHRISTIAN HISTORY FOR EVERYTHING, https://www.christian-history.org/letter-to-diognetus.html.

and marginalized, and by taking part in ordinary daily life while bearing witness to that "wonderful and striking way of life" called Christianity.[71]

Faith-filled people hope that the wider culture will accord openness and civility to this "striking way of life." Sadly, that prospect currently seems elusive. Our culture is deeply divided, seems intent on excluding God and the Transcendent, and engages in identity politics to an alarming degree.[72] The conditions of the possibility for a fruitful dialogue and for the kind of peaceful coexistence first envisioned by Calvert seem to be lacking. Any fruitful dialogue between the Catholics, evangelicals, Mormons, and others within the LGBT community will require a good deal of difficult preparatory work and a shared willingness on the part of all to tone down rhetoric, to forego offensive labels, and to try, if nothing else, to find potentially productive areas of dialogue and cooperation. None of this is easy and all of it involves risk, yet it is worth the effort.

III GOVERNMENTAL PROTECTION OF GOD-GIVEN FREEDOMS

As noted earlier, society is logically and ontologically prior to the state. A just state is at the service of the wider society and provides the legal framework for the protection of God-given freedoms and rights while at the same time striving to maintain those conditions in which human dignity is fostered and the common good is pursued.

If the Church seeks from the wider society a spirit of toleration, openness, and respect for intermediary institutions, what does it seek from the state? This question is best answered in II Vatican Council's landmark "Declaration on Religious Freedom," issued December 7, 1965.[73] While not the first and only word of the Church regarding religious freedom, it is certainly the first document of an ecumenical council devoted solely to religious freedom. The architects of this document include the renowned American Jesuit theologian, Father John Courtney Murray, and then-Archbishop of Krakow, Karol Wojtyla, the future Pope St. John Paul II.[74] Its context is the aftermath of World War II, the rise of totalitarian states, and the freedom-aspiring states emerging from European colonialism.[75] Its teachings have continued applicability in our current context marked by religious persecution abroad and the erosion of religious freedom at home.

---

[71] POPE FRANCIS, *supra* note 9, at 119. Mike Aquilina, *The Role of the Christian Family in Evangelization – Salt of the Empire, See also* EARLY CHRISTIANS (Jan. 15, 2017), http://www.primeroscristianos.com/en/index.php/blogs/mike-aquilina/item/1745-salt-of-the-empire-the-role-of-the-christian-family-in-evangelization; George W. Rutler, *Christians "They Pass their Days on Earth, but They are Citizens of Heaven,"* FACEBOOK APOSTLES (May 18, 2015), https://facebookapostles.org/2015/05/18/christians-they-pass-their-days-on-earth-but-they-are-citizens-of-heaven-by-fr-george-w-rutler/.

[72] For a detailed treatment of identity politics today, see DeGirolami, Chapter 21.

[73] *The Declaration on Religious Freedom, supra* note 56.

[74] *Id.* at 162.

[75] Peri Pamir, *Nationalism, Ethnicity and Democracy: Contemporary Manifestations,* INT'L J. PEACE STUD. (1997), http://www.gmu.edu/programs/icar/ijps/vol2_2/pamir.htm.

According to the Declaration on Religious Freedom, the Church first seeks from government freedom from coercion.[76] Declaring that the human person has a right to religious freedom, the Declaration adds, "Such freedom consists in this, that all ... should be immune from coercion on the part of individuals, social groups, or any human power, so that no one is prevented from acting according to his conscience in private or in public, whether alone or with others, within due limits."[77]

This account of religious freedom reflects the American experience of limited government and the guarantees offered by the Constitution and the Bill of Rights.[78] The task of government is not to foster any specific religion but to protect all religious people and their institutions from undue constraints. The government should not enter into or try to settle religious questions and disputes;[79] Murray thought the government should declare itself "incompetent" in such matters, although the actual text of the Declaration does not go that far and was careful to circumscribe what the "due limits" of religious freedom might be.[80]

Among the due limits contemplated by the Declaration is that "just public order be observed."[81] In the Declaration, "what is meant by public order" is laid out with care:

> Society has the right to defend itself against possible abuses committed on the pretext of freedom of religion. It is the special duty of government to provide this protection. However, government is not to act in an arbitrary fashion or in an unfair spirit of partisanship. Its action is to be controlled by juridical norms which are in conformity with the objective moral order. These norms arise out of the need for the effective safeguard of the rights of all citizens and for the peaceful settlement of conflicts of rights, also out of the need for an adequate care of genuine public peace, which comes about when men live together in good order and in true justice, and finally out of the need for a proper guardianship of public morality.[82]

---

[76] *The Declaration on Religious Freedom, supra* note 56, at ¶ 2.

[77] *Id. See* Murray, *supra* note 58, at 48–78. *See also* U.N. *Universal Declaration of Human Rights*, 1948, for a similar view of religious liberty.

[78] For discussions of *Employment Division v. Smith*, 494 U.S. 872 (1990), and its impact on constitutional protection for religious freedom in the U.S., see Brownstein, Chapter 2; Laycock, Chapter 3; Helfand, Chapter 11; Eskridge, Chapter 22.

[79] For a discussion of the competence to decide religious questions in the United States, see Helfand, Chapter 11.

[80] David Schindler, *Freedom, Truth, and Human Dignity: An Interpretation of Dignitatis Humanae on the Right to Religious Freedom, in* FREEDOM, TRUTH, AND HUMAN DIGNITY, at 54–55 (noting the cautions by Wojtyla against accepting too readily limits on religious freedom for the sake of "public order" because public order claims could be expansive and arguing instead that limits on religious freedom for the sake of the common good must be grounded in the natural law).

[81] *The Declaration on Religious Freedom, supra* note 56, at ¶¶ 2, 3.

[82] *Id.* at ¶ 7.

Provision for common safety, wellbeing, and public morality follow from the fact that "[t]he right to religious freedom is exercised in human society: hence its exercise is subject to certain regulatory norms."[83]

Second, the Declaration on Religious Freedom teaches that respect for freedom of conscience is required of any just government that seeks to foster human dignity. Thus, the II Vatican Council taught that religious freedom is not merely a subjective disposition but rather is rooted in the very nature of the human person and is an essential and fundamental aspect of human dignity.[84] Elsewhere, in its Pastoral Constitution on the Church in the Modern World, the II Vatican Council describes conscience as the "most secret core" of the human person, a "sanctuary" where one "is alone with God, [w]hose voice echoes in his [or her] depths."[85] The conscience is oriented to truth and goodness, to the natural law written on the heart of each person, and to divinely revealed truths.[86] The conscience, then, is a law-perceiver rather than a lawgiver and must be coherently formed in the ways of truth, virtue, and goodness. Pope St. John Paul II taught that "the relationship between man's freedom and God's law is most deeply lived out in the 'heart' of the person, in his moral conscience."[87] Because conscience orients the human person toward truth as found in the natural law and in divine revelation, its judgments reached with rectitude must be obeyed by the person.[88] Consistent with that teaching, the Declaration on Religious Freedom describes freedom of conscience thus: "It is through the mediation of his conscience that man perceives and recognizes the precepts of divine law; he is bound in all his actions to follow his conscience faithfully, so he may come to God, his end. He is therefore not to be forced to act against his conscience."[89] In its description of the rights of conscience, the Declaration on Religious Freedom leads us to see that religious freedom is more than freedom from coercion.[90] Rather, religious freedom is oriented toward the unhampered search for truth: "by means of free inquiry, with the help of instruction and education, communication and dialogue, in which men and women share with one another the truth they have found or think they have found, so as to assist each other in seeking the truth."[91] Archbishop Wojtyla, among others, insisted that the Declaration on Religious Freedom be firmly based on the inseparable relationship between truth and freedom.[92]

---

[83] *Id.* at ¶7.

[84] *Id.* at 5.

[85] POPE PAUL VI, GAUDIUM ET SPES 16 (1965), http://www.vatican.va/archive/hist_councils/ii_vatican_council/documents/vat-ii_cons_19651207_gaudium-et-spes_en.html.

[86] *Id.*

[87] POPE JOHN PAUL II, VERITATIS SPLENDOR 54 (1993), http://w2.vatican.va/content/john-paul-ii/en/encyclicals/documents/hf_jp-ii_enc_06081993_veritatis-splendor.html.

[88] *Id.* at 58.

[89] *The Declaration on Religious Freedom, supra* note 56, at 6.

[90] *Id.* at 17.

[91] *Id.*

[92] Schindler, *supra* note 80, at 48–50, 98–101.

Third, while the government is not obliged to adopt as its own any given religion, the II Vatican Council teaches that government should recognize the value of religion for society, not to mention the immense contribution of religious persons and institutions to the good of society.[93] Indeed, the truths of natural law and the teachings of revelation shed much light on the right ordering of society toward compassion, justice, and peace. Far from countenancing discrimination against people of faith and their religious institutions, government should defend religious freedom as "an inviolable right" and "provide favorable conditions for fostering religious life."[94] Indeed, "government is to see to it that equality of citizens before the law, which is itself an element of the common good, is never violated, whether openly or covertly, for religious reasons. Nor is there to be discrimination among citizens."[95]

Fourth, government should respect not only the rights of religious individuals but also the rights of their religious institutions. This includes houses of worship but also social service agencies, hospitals, schools, and other institutions that serve the common good.[96] The Declaration on Religious Freedom explicitly connects the two, teaching that believers who open their hearts to God "in interior acts that are voluntary and free" have a right to "express those interior acts externally, participating with others in religious matters and professing [their] religion in a communal way."[97] The Declaration on Religious Freedom also teaches that the Church "claims for herself freedom as a society of men and women who enjoy the right to live in civil society according to the precepts of the Christian faith."[98] It further asserts that churches are entitled to "govern themselves according to their own norms" in fulfillment of their mission.[99] A corollary seems to follow. The dimensions of religious freedom are the same for individuals and groups. Both have the right to search for truth and for God.[100] Both have the right and duty to hold fast to the truth once it is known and "to order their whole lives in accord with [its] demands."[101] Both have the right to proclaim their faith within the Church and in public.[102] Religious freedom thus includes the rights of individuals to live their faith

[93] See *supra* note 29 for the scale of the good done for society.

[94] *The Declaration on Religious Freedom, supra* note 56, at ¶¶ 12–13.

[95] *Id.* at ¶ 6.

[96] For discussions of how central such protections are to institutions' missions, see Hollman, Chapter 23; Berg, Chapter 24; Hoogstra et al., Chapter 25.

[97] *The Declaration on Religious Freedom, supra* note 56, at ¶3; *See also* POPE BENEDICT XVI, *supra* note 6, at 25. ("The Church's deepest nature is expressed in her three-fold responsibility: of proclaiming the Word of God ... celebrating the sacraments ... and exercising the ministry of charity ... These duties presuppose each other and are inseparable.")

[98] *The Declaration on Religious Freedom, supra* note 56, at ¶20.

[99] *Id.* at ¶ 4.

[100] *Id.* (discussing needs of religious communities).

[101] *Id.* at ¶ 2.

[102] For a discussion of the importance of statutory protections for speech about marriage, family, and sexuality, see Adams, Chapter 32.

in the workplace and the rights of churches to remain true to the faith that inspired their various ministries, including those that serve people of differing faiths or no faith at all.

IV RESPONSIBILITIES OF PEOPLE OF FAITH AND THEIR INSTITUTIONS TOWARD SOCIETY AND THE STATE

Along with the demands of freedom there are correlative responsibilities for people of faith and their institutions toward society and the state. Among these are the following. First is to follow the example of Pope Francis who reminds us that each of us is made in the image and likeness of God and as such is deserving of treatment consistent with the human dignity we possess. This is at the heart of the 2006 statement of the US Conference of Catholic Bishops, "Ministry to Persons with a Homosexual Inclination," which states, "The commission of the Church to preach the Good News to all people in every land points to the fundamental dignity possessed by each person as created by God." The document continues,

> God has created every human person out of love and wishes to grant him or her eternal life in the communion of the Trinity. All people are created in the image and likeness of God and thus possess an innate human dignity that must be acknowledged and respected. In keeping with this conviction, the Church teaches that persons with a homosexual inclination must be accepted with respect, compassion, and sensitivity. We recognize that these persons have been, and often continue to be, objects of scorn, hatred, and even violence in some sectors of our society. Sometimes this hatred is manifested clearly; other times, it is masked and gives rise to more disguised forms of hatred. It is deplorable that homosexual persons have been and are the object of violent malice in speech or in action. Such treatment deserves condemnation from the Church's pastors wherever it occurs. Those who would minister in the name of the Church must in no way contribute to such injustice. They should prayerfully examine their own hearts in order to discern any thoughts or feelings that might stand in need of purification. Those who minister are also called to growth in holiness. In fact, the work of spreading the Good News involves an ever-increasing love for those to whom one is ministering by calling them to the truth of Jesus Christ.

The Holy Father has challenged the Church and her people to welcome and accompany those among us who feel marginalized or distant from the Church; we must embrace this challenge through our pastoral care and outreach to our sisters and brothers, including by using language responsibly without compromising religious convictions. People of faith should be loath to label even as they should loathe being labeled! Second, even as we wish religious freedom to be respected as a fundamental freedom, so too we should respect the fundamental freedoms and rights of others. For Catholics, human dignity and rights are known by reason and clarified by faith. Indeed, in the view of the Catholic Church the very idea of dignity and rights hinges on man's relationship to the Transcendent, to God. These fundamental rights include the right to life and to life's necessities – such as food, shelter, employment, and healthcare. To deny such rights is to engage in unjust discrimination. As stated earlier, there is broad recognition that not all will agree on what constitutes unjust discrimination.

Most, if not all, faith communities have resources and tools to help navigate through cultural complexity, whatever its sources. Perhaps the experience of engaging in robust ecumenical and interreligious dialogue can teach us how to go about improving the dialogue between faith and culture. Other resources and tools include the principles for moral cooperation, rules for discernment, the natural law tradition, and the respect of faith for reason. Most of all, it requires a willingness on the part of all to come together in search of common ground, rooted in objective truth.

The Church is immersed in the marketplace of ideas, the modern *"areopagus,"* and is even more immersed in serving the needs the poor, the vulnerable, the sick, and the newly arrived.[103] Society has the right to expect the Church to serve the common good and to build bridges wherever possible. The Church for her part has the right to be a distinctive voice that lives its distinctive vision in a distinctive way.

---

[103] REDEMPTORIS MISSIO, *supra* note 14, at 37.

14

Toward Collaboration

A *Perspective from* The Church of Jesus Christ of *Latter-day Saints*

Elder Von G. Keetch[1]

I MORAL AGENCY

A fundamental doctrine of The Church of Jesus Christ of Latter-day Saints is what we call "moral agency," the ability to choose right from wrong and to act for ourselves.[2] We believe the individual exercise of agency is essential to God's plan of salvation for each one of His children. We believe we must freely offer ourselves to God in thought, intent, word, and deed – that faith and goodness cannot be coerced or forced.

Freedom of conscience ensures that people can exercise their God-given agency in matters of faith. We uphold this freedom as a basic doctrinal principle of our faith and a fundamental human right. One of the Church's longstanding Articles of Faith, written in 1842, states, "We claim the privilege of worshiping Almighty God according to the dictates of our own conscience, and allow all men the same privilege, let them worship how, where, or what they may."[3]

Religious freedom in the Mormon view embraces not only the right to worship freely but also to speak and act based on one's religious beliefs.[4] Belief without

---

[1] Elder Von G. Keetch died unexpectedly on January 26, 2018 as this volume was being prepared. It is dedicated to his memory.

[2] *Agency*, THE CHURCH OF JESUS CHRIST OF LATTER-DAY SAINTS, https://perma.cc/3CZL-RPR9.

[3] *Articles of Faith* 11, THE CHURCH OF JESUS CHRIST OF LATTER-DAY SAINTS, https://perma.cc/96VV-NDRU.

[4] Elder Dallin H. Oaks, *Religious Freedom*, MORMON NEWSROOM (Oct. 13, 2009), https://perma.cc/3UR8-8E6R ("The free 'exercise' of religion obviously involves both the right to choose religious beliefs and affiliations and the right to 'exercise' or practice those beliefs."); Elder Jeffrey R. Holland, *Faith, Family, and Religious Freedom*, MORMON NEWSROOM (Feb. 26, 2015), https://perma.cc/ZAF3-5NNX ("To counter these trends every citizen should insist on his or her constitutional right to exercise one's belief and to voice one's conscience on issues not only in the privacy of the home or the sanctity of the pulpit but also in the public square and in the halls of justice. These are the rights of all citizens, including people, leaders, and organizations who have religious beliefs."); Elder D. Todd Christofferson, *Religious*

action means very little. Importantly, moral agency does not stop with the right of people to be religious. It includes the right *not* to be religious. It also includes the right of all people – including LGBT people – to live according to their core beliefs to the greatest extent reasonably possible.

This commitment to moral agency has been a core belief of the Church from its earliest days, both as a matter of doctrine and of practical experience with severe persecution. Joseph Smith, the first president of the Church, taught:

> We deem it a just principle ... that all men are created equal, and that all have the privilege of thinking for themselves upon all matters relative to conscience. Consequently then, we are not disposed, had we the power, to deprive anyone from exercising that free independence of mind which heaven has so graciously bestowed upon the human family as one of its choicest gifts.[5]

In sum, while there are of course limits to freedom of conscience and other personal freedoms, those limits should be narrow so as to allow as many people as possible the greatest degree of freedom so that each person can exercise his or her moral agency.

II RIGHT OF ASSOCIATION AND GATHERING VERSUS INVIDIOUS DISCRIMINATION

For Mormons, and for religious people in general, a vital aspect of freedom of religion is the right to freely associate with fellow believers. Jesus Christ taught, "For where two or three are gathered together in my name, there am I in the midst of them."[6] The need for religious people to gather with the faithful has always been a driving force behind the quest for religious liberty.

In their quest to found what they called "Zion" – meaning a community where all would be of one heart and one mind and there would be no poor[7] – Mormons sought to gather in New York, Ohio, Missouri, and Illinois – only to be driven out

---

Freedom – A Cherished Heritage to Defend, MORMON NEWSROOM (June 26, 2016), https://perma.cc/6RZM-DNFG ("The other First Amendment right protecting religion forbids the government from enacting laws 'prohibiting the free exercise' of religion. Notice the word 'exercise.' It protects the right to 'exercise' religion in our daily lives – not just to believe whatever we like or to worship privately in our homes and chapels, but to live openly and freely according to our faith as long as we respect the fundamental rights of others."); Elder Dale G. Renlund, *Our Good Shepherd*, ENSIGN 29, 32 (May 2017) ("Everyone, including people of religion, has the right to express his or her opinions in the public square.").

[5] THE CHURCH OF JESUS CHRIST OF LATTER-DAY SAINTS, TEACHINGS OF PRESIDENTS OF THE CHURCH: JOSEPH SMITH (2011), https://www.lds.org/manual/teachings-joseph-smith/chapter-29?lang=eng.

[6] *Matthew* 18:20 (King James Version).

[7] A. Don Sorenson, *Zion*, in ENCYCLOPEDIA OF MORMONISM 1624–26 (Stan L. Albrecht, et al. eds., 1992), http://contentdm.lib.byu.edu/cdm/compoundobject/collection/EoM/id/4391/show/4372.

each time by mob violence.[8] Eventually, we left the United States for Mexican territory, seeking refuge in what is now Utah.[9] There Mormons again sought to build a community of faith.

I mention all this because we need to be clear on something: we believe that the right of religious people to gather and associate with fellow believers who live the faith is absolutely essential to religious freedom. Without that, for most religious communities – and certainly for Mormons – there is no meaningful religious freedom. Faith communities must have wide autonomy to order their religious affairs, and not just with respect to core worshipping activities. That includes religious employment, religious schools, religious charities, and other activities that allow them to perpetuate their faith and carry out their religious missions.

To label the fundamental right of religious people to gather as "discrimination" is to do a serious injustice to people of faith and religious communities.[10] Discrimination is a powerful word. It carries with it a strong sense that the person or group is ignorant, intolerant, immoral, and bigoted and that their alleged "discriminatory" beliefs are destined for the ashbin of history. Such labels are counterproductive and drive wedges between people who otherwise might find common ground.

III THE CHALLENGE OF SHARED SPACE

Obviously, not all space can be religious space – just as not all space can be private intimate space. The Church understands that spaces such as the home, chapel, and internal church administration are different than the realm of government service or commerce.[11] Others share these spaces and therefore religious values cannot always prevail.

That is not to say that they can never prevail. But the Church recognizes that in commercial and other more public spheres religious freedom cannot be absolute. The commercial sphere, for example, has been highly regulated in many ways for well over a century – e.g., labor, safety, environmental, taxation, disability, and of course civil rights.[12] As we interact with each other in shared spaces, there must of necessity be more give and take; more willingness to compromise; more searching for ways to accommodate diverse needs in a pluralistic society.

---

[8] Ronald D. Dennis, *Gathering, in id.* at 536–37, http://contentdm.lib.byu.edu/cdm/compoun dobject/collection/EoM/id/4391/rec/1.

[9] Allan Kent Powell, *Utah Territory, in id.* at 1503–05, http://contentdm.lib.byu.edu/cdm/com poundobject/collection/EoM/id/4391/rec/1.

[10] U.S. Comm'n on Civil Rts., Peaceful Coexistence: Reconciling Nondiscrimination Principles With Civil Liberties (2016) (statement of Chairman Martin Castro), https://perma.cc/XLV6-63ET.

[11] Elder Lance B. Wickman, *The Crucible: The Atonement, Moral Agency, and the Law*, Mormon Newsroom (Feb. 17, 2017), https://perma.cc/JZ6R-4BAX.

[12] *Id.*

IV PLURALISM AND THE MORMON UNDERSTANDING
OF FAIRNESS FOR ALL

As religious worldviews clash with secular worldviews, tensions inevitably arise. Such tensions – between people with different faith traditions and between religious and secular traditions – have always been part of the American experience. As Americans, we know how to deal with these situations. We've been doing it – sometimes more successfully than others, but in the end always striving – from the outset. This is one of the core characteristics of America: that we can find workable solutions to accommodate people of extremely diverse backgrounds, beliefs, and needs.

Much of the solution to these tensions lies in the old American notion of "pluralism." We need an approach that reaffirms that fundamental disagreements can exist among intelligent, informed people of good will, including with respect to sexuality. We need an approach that to the greatest extent possible allows space for all people to live according to their fundamental beliefs and needs. We need an approach that seeks to resolve conflicts that may arise in our shared spaces by finding win-win solutions and avoiding demands for ideological purity. It means that neither freedom of conscience nor sexual rights will be absolute in all circumstances.

This is what the Church means by the notion of "Fairness for All, including people of faith." It is an approach that recognizes the diversity of human experience and needs. It is an approach that recognizes what we believe is the right of each person to exercise his or her moral agency in deciding how to live.

It is a goal that will not always be achieved. But it is a goal we must always earnestly strive for. If we view the contest between rights of conscience and sexual rights as a zero-sum game, then those with more power will always seek to annihilate the rights of those with less power. We are then left only with a question of who wields the bigger "hammer," recognizing full well that hammers change in size and force depending on the political cycle and the location.

Mormons believe there is a better way of moving forward – the time-tested way of pluralism and mutual understanding. Our efforts must be aimed at building respect-ful relationships and patterns of civility that enable us *both* to disagree vigorously about profoundly important matters *and* to affirm the broad right of all Americans to live according to their core beliefs. Certainly, this effort will not be easy. It never has been. But we believe it is very much worth pursuing.

15

Conscience Claims in Islamic Law

A Case Study

Intisar A. Rabb

In 1987, Ayatollah Ruhollah Khomeini, Iran's first Supreme Leader, issued a disarmingly simple *fatwā* on sex reassignment surgery:

> In the Name of God. Sex-reassignment surgery is not prohibited in Islamic law (sharī'a) if reliable medical doctors recommend it. God-willing, you will be safe and hopefully the people whom you mentioned might take care of your situation.[1]

With it, he addressed an important question posed by Maryam Mulk-Ara, a trans-gender woman born a man, who had long sought official sanction under Islamic law for sex-reassignment surgery (SRS). Surprisingly perhaps, subsequent Muslim religious and legal authorities in Iran now not only permit but partially subsidize SRS for members of Iran's trans community. Following Khomeini's *fatwā*, the government set up a *sex-change bureaucracy* – to borrow a term from Jeannie Suk and Jacob Gersen[2] – in order to simultaneously accommodate and regulate the newly permitted procedure for Iran's emerging trans community. The new structures turned Iran into a leading site for the surgeries and for medical tourism for SRS – second only to Thailand.[3]

Khomeini's *fatwā* has a long history that is anything but simple, and it bears implications for modern Islamic laws where a broad notion of *conscience claims* intersects with norms of equality and conventional morality. Those raising conscience claims in the United States, where religion is to be neither established nor curtailed,

---

[1] M. Alipour, *Islamic Sharī'a Law, Neotraditionalist Muslim Scholars, and Transgender Sex-Reassignment Surgery: A Case Study of Ayatollah Khomeini's and Sheikh al-Tantawi's Fatwas*, 18 INT'L J. TRANSGENDERISM 91, 96 (2017). Translations are by Alipour with slight modifications by the author. For versions of this *fatwā* in the Farsī original, see MUḤAMMAD MAHDĪ KARIMINIA, TAGHYĪR-I JINSIYAT AZ MANẒAR-I FIQH VA ḤUQŪQ 415–20 (2010).

[2] *See* Jacob Gersen & Jeannie Suk, *The Sex Bureaucracy*, 104 CAL. L. REV. 881 (2016) (describing a "sex bureaucracy" governing legal sexual conduct in the United States).

[3] Rochelle Terman, *Trans[ition] in Iran*, WORLD POL'Y INST. (2013), http://www.worldpolicy.org/transition-iran.

seek exemptions from general legal duties on the basis of religious belief. In contexts of countries with religious establishments like that of Iran, conscience claims become exemption requests *from* religious duties for some other, nonreligious reason.[4] In highlighting perspectives that shaped and emerged from this expanded notion of conscience claims, this chapter reviews the *fatwā*'s history and subsequent developments to assess a developing Islamic law of transsexuality and transgender rights.

This chapter has two aims. First, Sections I and II examine the *historical and doctrinal factors* behind the *fatwā*. What happens when demands for exemptions come from a minority group that Islamic legal doctrines historically have not accommodated? How and why did Islamic law decision-makers accommodate advances in medical technology and changes in cultural norms to legalize SRS? Hailed as unexpectedly progressive, the interpretive methods for doing so actually drew on *traditional* categories of gender in Islamic law that had been modified by similarly *traditional* European and American religious conceptions of the same.

Second, Section III considers rationales behind the conscience claims in this Islamic context, in order to explore a *comparative assessment* of approaches to resolving tensions between religion and equality norms. Iran's episode *almost* flips the US question about conscience claims, where a central concern is: whether and when the law should accommodate religious practice – or grant exemptions from general legal duties – particularly where laws imposing equality norms depart from an older "customary morality" that did not protect minority rights.[5] The answer may turn on many factors: a balancing of sincerity of belief against the state's interest in enforcing a law or in elevating norms of equality over liberty,[6] a law's overriding rationality and legitimacy,[7] arguments of complicity and third-party harms,[8] or other

---

[4] *Compare, e.g.*, Nejaime & Siegel, Chapter 6 (defining complicity-based conscience claims as "religious objections to being made complicit in the assertedly sinful") *with* DOUGLAS LAYCOCK, RELIGIOUS LIBERTY: THE FREE EXERCISE CLAUSE VOLUME 2 308 (2010) (equating "conscience claims" to conscientious objection on religious grounds and distinguishing them from religious autonomy or liberty claims).

[5] *See* NeJaime & Siegel, Chapter 6.

[6] *See* Sherbert v. Verner, 374 U.S. 398 (1963); Wisconsin v. Yoder, 506 U.S. 205 (1972).

[7] *See* Employment Division v. Smith, 494 U.S. 872 (1990) (holding that neutral laws of general applicability do not merit mandatory religious accommodation, so long as they bear a rational relationship to a legitimate government interest). In response to *Smith*, Congress passed RFRA in 1993 – allowing the federal government to "substantially burden a person's exercise of religion only if demonstrates that application of the burden to the person – (1) is in furtherance of a compelling governmental interest; and (2) is the least restrictive means of furthering that compelling governmental interest." 42 U.S.C. § 2000bb (2012). The Supreme Court then restricted RFRA to action by the federal government. City of Boerne v. Flores, 521 U.S. 507 (1997).

[8] Burwell v. Hobby Lobby, 134 S. Ct. 2751, 2760 (2014). For comment on the harms analysis, see, e.g., Doug Nejaime & Reva Siegel, *Conscience Wars: Complicity-Based Conscience Claims in Religion and Politics*, 124 YALE L.J. 2516, 2519–20, 2529–33 (2015); Amy Sepinwall, *Conscientious Objection, Complicity, and Accommodation*, in LAW, RELIGION AND HEALTH IN THE UNITED STATES 203–14 (Holly Lynch et al. eds., 2017).

metrics designed to determine acceptable departures from the law. While ritual law claims may be easy to accommodate – such as requests to pray or don certain dress that does not detract from work – US decision-makers addressing many conscience claims that are more social or transactional, like those of petitioners in *Masterpiece Cakeshop*,[9] must grapple with this entire range of questions.

In principle, Islamic law decision-makers must grapple with the same range of questions. But in Iran, they failed to do so. In such Islamic constitutional jurisdictions, where religion is the dominant basis for state law, the question becomes: whether and when the law should accommodate individual exemptions from (religion-based) laws of general applicability. There, gender, rather than equality, served as the starting point for both Iran's activist trans community and Iran's religious-legal officials. Consequently, there was no discussion of general principles that could determine acceptable departures from generally applicable religion-based duties, including whether medical advances or shifts in conventional morality could serve as valid means of updating certain religious norms. Nor was there discussion about weighing individual or third-party harm against a compelling state interest in enforcing religion-based laws. Still, that Islamic legal change came through a process of internal critique that accompanied shifts in medical technology, conventional morality, and notions of third-party harm has implications for assessing possible approaches to equality, nondiscrimination, and changing legal norms in broader Islamic contexts.

This chapter's comparative assessment of equality norms is thus short and rather anticlimactic for the Iranian context. The question in Iran *almost* flips the US question on its head because their "Islamic" assessment of a conscience claim did not actually touch on equality norms – by which I refer to common rights and obligations determined on the grounds of common human identity or citizenship rather than gender identity. By addressing narrow features of gender rather than equality, Iran's experience exemplifies a typical, though not essential, feature of Islamic legal interpretation. Bringing a wider scope to Islamic conscience claims might better inform Muslim-majoritarian contexts, such as Iran, as well as Muslim-minoritarian contexts in the United States and elsewhere.

I THE TRANSFORMATION OF MARYAM MULK-ARA

A *The First Petition: 1970s Pre-Revolutionary Iran*

It was not until almost a decade after Iran's 1979 Islamic Revolution that Maryam Mulk-Ara finally obtained the *fatwā* from Ayatollah Khomeini, giving her clear Islamic sanction to undergo SRS. Born in 1950 as Fereydoon, Mulk-Ara had for years identified more with the female gender than with her natal male biology.

---

[9] Masterpiece Cakeshop v. Colo. Civil Rights Comm'n, 138 S. Ct. 1719 (2018). For broader views, see McClain, Chapter 17; McConnell, Chapter 28.

Because Mulk-Ara's family opposed Mulk-Ara's "gender nonconformance," by age eighteen, Mulk-Ara decided to live alone.[10]

Mulk-Ara was fairly religious, fairly pragmatic, and fairly determined to find a solution. While reportedly avoiding relationships, Mulk-Ara dressed as a woman and persistently sought resolution to her dilemma from both secular and religious circles. While some elements of her story seem to have been embellished,[11] Mulk-Ara nevertheless seemed to have enjoyed broad access to influential power brokers.

In 1975, Mulk-Ara sought out an opinion from Ayatollah Khomeini, then exiled in Iraq. Khomeini advised Mulk-Ara to act as a woman where ritual law was concerned – in prayers, dress, and the like.[12] This first *fatwā* drew on an old opinion published in Khomeini's 1964 legal treatise about intersex people:

> It seems that sex-reassignment surgery for male-to-female and vice versa is not forbidden (*ḥarām*) [in Islam], and it is also not forbidden for a *khunthā* (intersex) undergoing it to be attached to one of the sexes [female or male]; and [if one asks:] is a woman/man obliged to undergo the sex reassignment surgery if the woman finds in herself [sensual] desires similar to men's desires or some evidence of masculinity in herself – or a man finds in himself [sensual] desires similar to the opposite sex or some evidence of femininity in himself? It seems that [in such a case] if a person really [physically] belongs to a [determined] sex, a sex reassignment surgery is not an obligatory [duty] (*wājib*), but the person is still eligible to change her/his sex to the opposite gender.[13]

But this opinion did not resolve Mulk-Ara's dilemma. "Not obligatory" and "eligible" were not the same as endorsement of her choice, and Khomeini's reference to intersex did not apply. Mulk-Ara still wondered: could she get a sex-change?[14]

B *The Second Petition: 1980s Post-Revolutionary Iran*

Dissatisfied with Khomeini's answer, the twenty-five-year-old Mulk-Ara nevertheless followed Khomeini's advice – continuing to dress as a woman, now with religious

---

[10] Observations here from Behzad Bloor, *Taghyīr-i jinsiyat dar Īrān*, BBC PERSIAN (2006); KARIMINIA, *supra* note 1, at 397–413, AFSANEH NAJMABADI, PROFESSING SELVES: TRANSEXU-ALITY AND SAME-SEX DESIRE IN CONTEMPORARY IRAN (2014) (interviewing Mulk-Ara and others); Alipour, *supra* note 1, at 91–103.

[11] For example, she reportedly met with the former Queen of Iran, Farah Pahlavi. *See, e.g.*, Alipour, *supra* note 1, at 94; NAJMABADI, *supra* note 10, at 158–62. But Mulk-Ara would have been thirteen years old on the reported date of the meeting, making it unlikely.

[12] Alipour, *supra* note 1, at 94; NAJMABADI, *supra* note10, at 158–62. These commentators report that she consulted Ayatollah Bihbahānī, but this is also unlikely as the jurist in Tehran by that name would have been Ayatollah Sayyid Muhammad Bihbahānī, who was long dead by then.

[13] *See* Khomeini, *Taḥrīr al-wasīla*, 2:626 (cited in Alipour 2017, at 96 (with modifications)); NAJMABADI, *supra* note 10, at 174–75 (also listing a second *fatwā* in Khomeini's treatise, at 2:73–55).

[14] Alipour, *supra* note 1, at 94; NAJMABADI, *supra* note 10, at 174–75.

sanction. The 1979 Revolution made that practice difficult. Zealous post-Revolutionary officials began enforcing "public gender codes," disrupting the more fluid and permissive idea of gender that had percolated prior to the Revolution.[15] Mulk-Ara's employers at the state radio and broadcasting network ridiculed her, instructed her to dress as a man, and required her to take hormones to accentuate male traits. She resigned or was fired.[16]

Mulk-Ara then sought a new solution. She went to the Speaker of Parliament, Ali Akbar Hashemi Rafsanjani, who referred her to two traditionally trained jurists with prominent government positions and, presumably, the ability to provide religious-legal guidance: the head of the judiciary, Abdolkarim Mousavi Ardebili, and Ahmad Jannati, a conservative leader of the Revolution who now heads Parliament's Assembly of Experts and its Guardian Council, which reviews laws for compliance with "principles of *sharī'a*."[17] As before, these jurists consulted Ayatollah Khomeini, who enjoyed virtually unassailable political and religious-legal authority as the Revolution's charismatic leader.[18] Khomeini gave the same answer as before.

Mulk-Ara determined that she must visit Khomeini himself. It took until 1987 to secure a meeting. Mulk-Ara arrived at Khomeini's residence, and the Supreme Leader listened intently to Mulk-Ara's life story and to testimony from doctors who had accompanied her. After deliberation, Khomeini issued the *fatwā* finally authorizing Mulk-Ara and similarly situated transsexual Muslims to undertake SRS.[19]

This meeting and the resulting *fatwā* were as high-profile as it gets. They transformed Mulk-Ara's personal experience into law. Then-President Ali Khamanei (who now serves as Supreme Leader, succeeding Khomeini) reportedly gifted Mulk-Ara a *chādor*, the full-body covering worn by some women in Iran. With it, Mulk-Ara finally had the support of the religious, governmental, and medical community to undergo male-to-female SRS.[20]

II AN EARLY ISLAMIC LAW OF TRANSSEXUALITY?

Neither of Khomeini's initial *fatwās* was fully acceptable to Mulk-Ara because those opinions seemed to be more about medieval Islamic rules for determining gender

[15] NAJMABADI, *supra* note 10, at 161.
[16] Alipour, *supra* note 1, at 94 (resigned); NAJMABADI, *supra* note 10, at 158–62 (fired).
[17] QĀNŪN-I ASĀSĪ-YI ĪRĀN [IRANIAN CONST.], art. 4 ("All civil, criminal, financial, economic, administrative, cultural, military, political, and other laws and regulations must be based on Islamic criteria."). The Iranian Constitution establishes Islamic law as state law in its constitutional rights and structure, as well as ordinary legislation. *See id.*, arts. 2, 12, and *passim*.
[18] Alipour, *supra* note 1, at 94; NAJMABADI, *supra* note 10, at 158–66, 174–75.
[19] Alipour, *supra* note 1, at 95; NAJMABADI, *supra* note 10, at 165–66. Further details reported in these and other accounts – such as beatings, the rescue by Khomeini's then ninety-year-old brother, the location of the home in Khomeini's former residence in Qom rather than in Tehran – are omitted because unlikely and in any case nonessential.
[20] Alipour, *supra* note 1, at 95.

than about her choice of gender. Historically, Islamic societies displayed cultural and legal norms that today strike most Muslims as contradictory and contrary to widespread understandings of Islamic law. First, medieval Muslim jurists elaborated an entire set of Islamic laws on intersexuality and asexuality beginning in Islam's founding period, from the seventh to ninth centuries. But they did not contemplate the modern question of whether one may choose a gender when one lacks at least some biological characteristics matching the chosen gender.[21] Second, these jurists tolerated expressions of male-male love. But they criminalized and severely penalized same-sex intimate relations.[22] Yet, all in all, there is no early Islamic law regulating *transgender/transsexuality* or *homosexuality*.

The early Islamic laws related to these questions, reviewed as follows, provide the legal backdrop necessary for understanding the new Islamic laws devised to address the concerns of Mulk-Ara and others in the trans community – who do not conceive of themselves as homosexual and who have religious and pragmatic reasons for transitioning.[23] The early laws also help situate the legal and cultural priors of the modern religious elite, who now dominate state law in Iran.

A *Different-Sex Affinity: Before Transsexuality*

In Islamic societies, there is a long history of socially constructed gender norms and nonconformists to those norms. As in other medieval societies, medieval Muslim jurists designated male and female as primary categories of gender and constructed rules of conduct on that basis. They then addressed instances where expressions of gender did not quite conform.[24]

Islamic legal treatises identify two main categories of biological gender nonconformance: eunuchs and people considered unsexed or asexual (*khaṣī*: castrated men, or *mamsūḥ*: those without apparent signs of genitalia), and intersex people (*khunthā*: those possessing elements of both male and female genitalia, also called hermaphrodites).[25] The first category occupied a sort of "in-between" space in Muslim societies. Legally and socially, they were gendered neither male nor female.

---

[21] *See, e.g.,* 9 MUWAFFAQ AL-DĪN IBN QUDĀMA, AL-MUGHNĪ 108–14 ('Abd Allāh b. 'Abd al-Muḥsin al-Turkī & 'Abd al-Fattāḥ Muḥammad al-ḥulw eds., 1986); *see also id.* at 2:233–34; 3:351; 6:600; 10:94–96, 236.

[22] *See, e.g.,* IBN QUDĀMA, *supra* note 21, at 12:348–51.

[23] *See, e.g.,* NAJMABADI, *supra* note 10, at 25 (reporting on a female-to-male transgender woman who preferred SRS to dressing and living as a man because he, his presumably female partner, and society would condemn the latter).

[24] *See, e.g.,* IBN QUDĀMA, *supra* note 21, at 10:94 ("A person must be either male or female, based on Qur'ānic verses [53:45, specifying that God created mates from males and females, and 4:1, specifying that men and women descended from Adam and Eve] ... So there is no third gender (*fa-laysa thamma khalq thālith*)").

[25] *See* KARIMINIA, *supra* note 1, at 57–63 (identifying categories), 97–130 (discussing the *khunthā*); *see also* IBN QUDĀMA, *supra* note 22, at 10:236 (listing categories), 9:109 (defining the *khunthā*).

They often served as guards or servants in royal courts, elite houses, and the Mosque in Medina – authorized to move relatively freely between spaces for men and women.[26]

The intersex category was more complex and Islamic laws more elaborate. On the notion that intersex persons *could* choose to align with one of the dominant gender categories – male or female – Islamic legal authorities generally directed that intersex people who had one organ more prominent and functional than the other must choose the gender that aligned with that organ. Persons for whom neither organ was prominent, the "ambiguous cases" (*khunthā mushkil*), could be treated as unsexed so long as they displayed no sexual preference for one gender.[27] Religiously and legally, all were accepted as God's creation. But socially, intersex persons were often isolated and maligned, as they simply did not conform to male-female categories. They bore the weight of choosing a gender and living by the associated norms of Islamic ritual law, family law, and other areas of law with rules that typically differ by gender.[28]

B *Same-Sex Relations: Before Homosexuality*

A third nonconforming category referred to social rather than biological markers of gender: the "effeminates" (*mukhannathūn*). Sources for the early history of Medina (located in modern western Saudi Arabia) point to a thriving culture of men who exhibited female gender markers. They adopted feminine dress, exhibited mannerisms coded as female, and were identifiable as a group of professional musicians who performed songs typically sung by women.[29]

---

[26] Alipour, *supra* note 1, at 92.

[27] See IBN QUDĀMA, *supra* note 21, at 9:109 (specifying that the determination for children relied upon the place of urination and that, upon reaching majority, still "ambiguous cases" could be determined by biological signs of puberty that specified belonging to the male or female gender category, or by the person simply claiming that "he" is a woman or a man, and that he or she could then marry the gender opposite the one he or she claimed), 9:114 (specifying that other categories of "ambiguous cases" could entail those from whom urine did not come from any particular place, or those without any genitalia at all, in which case the person could adopt one gender and conform to its rules for ritual law, marriage law, etc.).

[28] For colorful cases addressing *khunthā* designations, see IBRĀHĪM B. HĀSHIM AL-QUMMĪ (mid-3rd/9th c.), QAḌĀYĀ AMĪR AL-MU'MINĪN 'ALĪ B. ABĪ ṬĀLIB 73, 203 (*Fāris Ḥassūn Karīm* ed., 1382/[2003]) (reporting on early Iraqi cases in which 'Alī noted ways to distinguish the proper gender category for intersex people). Cf. KHALED EL-ROUAYHEB, BEFORE HOMOSEXUALITY IN THE ARAB-ISLAMIC WORLD, 1500–1800, at 65 (2005) (describing a case in which an Ottoman judge examined one 'Alī – thought to be a man – and ruled that he was actually an intersex person closer to being a woman, much to the litigant's delight).

[29] Everett K. Rowson, *The Effeminates of Early Medina*, 111 J. AM. ORIENTAL SOC'Y 671, at 672, 675, 679, 681 (1991). A later analog to the Medinan effeminates were the Moghul-Era and contemporary South Asian *hijras* – intersex or fully male-organed youth who grew up as male, later dressed and acted as female, and traditionally carried favor in the royal courts. *See* Alipour, *supra* note 1, at 92.

For these effeminates, Islamic laws governing gender were somewhat relaxed, despite the lack of any biological difference or "ambiguity," as with the unsexed and intersex. For example, in Islam's first century (seventh century CE), "effeminate" men were easily "admitted to women's quarters, on the assumption that they lacked sexual interest in women."[30] Some served as matchmakers and go-betweens, and many simply enjoyed women's company without desiring them romantically.[31] To be sure, there were occasions when some exhibited sexual interest in women by, say, commenting on a woman's appearance in a non-platonic way or conveying decidedly sensual descriptions of a woman to other men who lacked the access that the effeminate man enjoyed. Such men were then barred from women's quarters or banished from the city altogether.[32] On balance, effeminate men "enjoyed a position of exceptional visibility and prestige" when times were good and sexual tensions low; but they were never fully accepted and often decried when seen as attracted to women, engaging excessively in frivolous activities thought to detract from religion, or involved romantically with men.[33]

On this last point, a question remains about Islam's regulation of same-sex desire among effeminates or men who were otherwise gender-conforming. Consider Khaled El-Rouayheb's definitive work on this very theme. In it, he corrects an erroneous view of Muslims as historically opposed to same-sex love. He shows that many early Muslims lacked the modern notion of homosexuality, which emerged out of nineteenth-century Europe as encompassing identity and social standing, as well as gender and biology, expressions, and acts.[34] Thus for El-Rouayheb, the expansive nature of the modern notion of homosexuality can mislead attempts to understand gender norms in early Islamic law.[35] Rather than prohibiting or even effectively regulating most of those elements, Muslims tended to exhibit or allow widespread declarations of male-male love, often expressed as appreciation for pubescent boys alongside women.[36] To be sure, most jurists discouraged expressions of adult male love for male youth – some even prohibiting a man from looking at the faces of male youth if he did so with sexual desire. But jurists largely overlooked mere expressions of love.[37]

The major caveat: Islamic law did not tolerate at all sexual relations between men – even though proof and thus punishment were elusive. Any toleration of men's

---

[30] Rowson, *supra* note 27, at 675.

[31] *Id.* at 684.

[32] *Id.* at 677.

[33] *Id.* at 681.

[34] EL-ROUAYHEB, *supra* note 6, at 153–61.

[35] *Id.*

[36] While beautiful male youth featured in poetry were often fictive, El-Rouayheb argues that belletrists sometimes conveyed their own real amorous experiences and feelings. Further, the positive reception and popularity of their works, rather than disgust and derision, suggest a link to the values and assumptions of contemporary culture, just as the widespread acceptance of song lyrics expresses something about popular culture today. *Id.* at 75–77.

[37] *Id.* at 77, 111, 116.

odes to women and pubescent boys (who resembled women) reflected cultural mores of the societies at that time, and it was based on an understanding that men were not to act on their passions outside the confines of marriage. Marriage was understood to make licit intimate relations between a man and a woman, and jurists strictly prohibited pre- and extramarital sex as one of a small set of "fixed crimes and punishments" (*ḥudūd* laws) called *zinā* (fornication or adultery), which carried corporal or capital punishment.[38] Jurists further specified even harsher punishments for male-male intimate relations: all four Sunnī schools and the mainstream Shīʿī school laid out punishments ranging from flogging to capital punishment through stoning and other means.[39]

Punishments of pre- and extramarital sex were reportedly rare because allowable public expression of male passionate love for women and young men, together with a number of legal and procedural obstacles, made it difficult to prosecute disallowed private acts extending from that expression. Proof required a voluntary confession or witnesses to the act of penetration.[40] Any such evidence was highly unlikely, and even if available would typically trigger the "doubt canon" calling on judges to *avoid criminal punishment in cases of doubt*.[41] Nevertheless, criminalization and harsh sentencing rules for extramarital sex of any kind expressed moral condemnation of the act, even if Islamic societies tolerated expressions of the desire.

All told, the contradictory and competing treatments of gender in medieval Islamic law might be explained with reference to a fairly simple construction of two dominant gender categories – male and female – alongside in-depth discussion of intersex.[42] But that set of laws did not always track new gender categories, including transgender/transsexual categories. That was Mulk-Ara's problem with Khomeini's first two *fatwās*: drawing on early Islamic legal categories of gender, Khomeini did not initially address the concept of transsexual or transgender laws head-on.

III A MODERN ISLAMIC LAW OF TRANSSEXUALITY

A *The* Fatwā's *Making: Juristic Updating and Internal Critique*

Khomeini's third *fatwā*, reproduced at the outset of this chapter, squarely addressed Mulk-Ara's question on transsexuality with respect to shifts in law, medicine, and Iranian culture – the latter of which emerged through the trans community's increased activism. In law, the Revolution transformed secular Iran into an Islamic

---

[38] See *id.* at 111–51. On *ḥudūd* laws, see generally RUDOLPH PETERS, CRIME AND PUNISHMENT IN ISLAMIC LAW (2005); INTISAR A. RABB, DOUBT IN ISLAMIC LAW (2015).

[39] See EL-ROUAYHEB, *supra* note 6, at 111–51 (noting that all jurists punished active participants more harshly than passive participants). Jurists also characterized same-sex intimate relations either as a subset of *zinā* (fornication) or as an act called *liwāṭ* (for men) or *siḥāq* (for women), making the prohibition one against male-male intercourse, rather than homosexuality as a category. *Id.* at 125.

[40] EL-ROUAYHEB, *supra* note 6, at 123.

[41] *Id.* at 123–24. *See generally* RABB, *supra* note 36.

[42] *See supra* note 21 and accompanying text.

constitutional country where "the principles of *sharīʿa*," as defined by traditionally trained jurists, dominate. In medicine, technological advances made SRS safe and effective for the first time in the 1980s.[43] In cultural terms, as a member of the trans community at that time, Mulk-Ara led a persistent charge to secure the right to SRS and to be free to diverge from dominant gender norms. These three factors forced jurists to address novel questions related to emerging public transsexuality and transgender realities, using recognized rules of interpretation to expand Islamic law to accommodate both.

As noted, early Islamic legal sources do not clearly address modern notions of transsexuality and transgenderism. There was nothing in the Qurʾān or Sunna – the body of *ḥadīth reports* on the normative words and acts of the Prophet as well as, for the Shīʿī school of Islamic law that dominates in Iran, the normative words and acts of the series of twelve Imams who succeeded the Prophet. Finding no explicit texts, which would be dispositive, a Shīʿī jurist would consult the substantive rulings recorded as the result of earlier imāmic or juristic consensus (*ijmāʿ*) and practical reason (*ʿaql*). There, jurists would find permissions for intersex operations in certain circumstances and for particular reasons as had previously arisen in actual cases. But none of those doctrines addressed modern notions of transsexual or transgender norms to answer the question on elective SRS. And while a Sunnī jurist might analogize from the old laws to answer the new question, a Shīʿī jurist would not necessarily because doing so would appeal to the Sunnī method of analogical reasoning (*qiyās*), which Shīʿī jurisprudence officially rejects.[44]

To make a determination on SRS, Khomeini would have had to deploy the main interpretive tools designed to answer novel questions through interpretation (*ijtihād*): namely, a set of legal canons (*qawāʿid fiqhiyya*) and legal presumptions (*uṣūl ʿamaliyya*) used to fill gaps left by silences in the law.[45] Consistent with the usual practice of providing a direct answer to a targeted question only, Khomeini did not explain his *fatwā*. But some of his students later tried to explain its bases, with rationales on which the following analysis draws.

Khomeini considered at least two interpretive legal canons. First, he likely considered the *presumption of permissibility* (*aṣālat al-ibāḥa*) or *presumption of legality* (*aṣālat al-ḥiliyya*) and gave priority to a *presumption of exemption [from legal liability]* (*aṣālat al-barāʾa*) – among competing canons to the contrary – for all matters on which there is no clear statement in the foundational sources.[46] These

---

[43] Earlier reports of SRS were actually intersex transformations, in line with the early Islamic law of *khunthā*. *See* NAJMABADI, *supra* note 10, at 38–39, 169.

[44] On the Shīʿī legal texts and interpretive canons, see HOSSEIN MODARRESSI, INTRODUCTION TO LAW SHĪʿĪ LAW 3–4 (1984); MUḤAMMAD BĀQIR AL-ṢADR, LESSONS IN ISLAMIC JURISPRUDENCE (Roy Mottahedeh trans. 2003), 119–32.

[45] Alipour, *supra* note 1, at 98.

[46] *Id.* at 99 (noting the rule's basis in the famous verse in the Qurʾān, 17:15: that Muslims will not be punished without having received a message, and in a *ḥadīth* attributed to the Prophet that Muslims are not liable for what they do not know through clear evidence).

canons could easily justify both the designation of transsexual/transgender as a new gender category and the legality of SRS. Second, Khomeini's consultation with the medical and trans communities, which informed the broadly permissive ambit of his *fatwā*, may have also reflected the canon of necessity: *necessity makes licit otherwise prohibited acts (al-ḍarūrāt tubīḥ al-maḥḍūrāt)*. The state of the medical technology, medical advice, and transsexual/transgender status itself made SRS both necessary and permissible.[47] Third, the *fatwā* could also find support in the canon specifying a *presumption of the dominant actor [to dispose of that which is within his or her domain] (aṣālat al-taslīṭ)*, which entitles everyone to control what happens to his or her body and property. Limited to control in ways deemed "rational," this presumption fit easily with a norm of Shīʿī law under which changing the body is typically considered rational; note, for example, the religiously sanctioned, widespread Iranian industry in tattoos, piercings, and plastic surgery.[48]

In his post-Revolutionary rulings, Khomeini stressed another principle that gives *primacy to the role of time and place in* Islam's interpretive method, *ijtihād*:

> [I]jtihād is dynamic when considering two important factors of time and place. If a subject has a special [ruling] in *sharīʿa* [for] a particular time or place, the same subject, because of a different political and societal situation, might be changed in its [ruling]. It means that *ijtihād* can adapt to cultural conditions, which inevitably change over the passage of time and variation in place.[49]

These principles worked together with Khomeini's consultations of the trans and medical communities – psychologists and psychiatrists, physicians and surgeons – to produce the now-famous *fatwā*.[50]

B *The* Fatwā's *Limitations: Legal Authority, Bureaucracy, and Cultural Bias*

When Khomeini first addressed the question from exile, his position was limited. The science was insufficiently advanced to make a statement of wide application. This was true of the media and the trans community's organization, too. Moreover, as a senior jurist in exile, Khomeini's early *fatwās* may have been influential among the juristic and religious community who followed him at the time, but those opinions could not determine state law.

[47] *Id.* at 98. Some of Khomeini's students found difficulty in using the prior presumptions to justify SRS procedures because of discomfort with the idea of doctors seeing and touching patients' genitalia without necessity, and narrowed the ruling to "necessary" procedures.

[48] *Id.* at 98–99.

[49] *Id.* at 99 (noting that Khomeini came to this conclusion through his struggles with the Iranian regime before the Revolution and while leading the country afterward and that Khomeini used it to revisit old rulings in Islamic law that absolutely prohibited music, chess, and a woman's right to be elected to public office alongside questions of transsexual/transgender SRS – all reflecting a "new cultural situation regarding human life").

[50] *Id.*

By contrast, Khomeini's 1987 *fatwā* carried significant weight in Iran. Coming after the Revolution and his rapid rise to virtually absolute power, the *fatwā* translated his pro-SRS stance into Iranian law.[51] This is not to say that all jurists were forced to agree with him. The major Shī'ī jurists today agree on the permissibility of intersex surgeries (in line with medieval attitudes).[52] But they differ about the permissibility of SRS for those who have no biological gender ambiguity.[53]

Further, other jurists continued to study the question after the *fatwā*, sometimes reaching differing conclusions. For example, several jurists convened conferences of medical professionals and Islamic law experts in the 1980s and 1990s to consider the law in light of shifting facts surrounding SRS and other novel issues of gender and science. One jurist, Hujjatol Islam Muḥammad Mahdī Kariminia, wrote a dissertation on transsexuality and made it his mission to continue these conversations and to develop new rulings for marriage, divorce, inheritance, and the like.[54] Yet, Ayatollah Khomeini's charismatic leadership and religious authority meant that his *fatwā* on the matter carried dispositive weight, even after his death. It formed the basis for an entire state-sponsored system to provide support, oversight, and subsidies for SRS in Iran.[55]

Since, changes in media coverage and input from the trans community have helped shape both the law and social realities. Sensationalist tabloids before the 1980s published photos of "transgender" people as freaks and wonders, mislabeling intersex people; but by the 2000s, reputable papers published news about transsexuals and developments in the trans community. That coverage spread news about the trans community, raising awareness in rural communities about SRS's availability.[56]

Finally, the trans community itself sought change in religious and regulatory terms – through internal critique, using arguments recognized as authoritative in terms of Islamic law.[57] Both religiously observant members such as Mulk-Ara and her pragmatic counterparts knew that a *fatwā* from the top jurist would better entrench their rights than any legal instrument without it could. They also surmised

---

[51] NAJMABADI, *supra* note 10, at 174.

[52] *See, e.g.,* KARIMINIA, *supra* note 1, at 415–68 (collecting contemporary jurists' perspectives); Haider Hamoudi, *Sex and the Shari'a*, 39 FORDHAM INT'L L.J. 84 (2015) (citing *fatwā*s from Grand Ayatollah Sīstānī and Grand Ayatollah Abū al-Qāsim al-Khū'ī). *Cf.* Farrah Jabari, *Transexuality Under Surveillance in Iran: Clerical Control of Khomeini's Fatwas*, 10 J. MID. EAST. WOMEN'S STUDS. 31–32 (2014).

[53] *See, e.g.,* Hamoudi, *supra* note 50, at 85 (noting Khui's more skeptical stance, finding sex changes problematic).

[54] KARIMINIA, *supra* note 1, at 29–30. *See also* NAJMABADI, *supra* note 10, at 169, 177 (reporting Kariminia's observation that, whereas *fiqh* religious-legal reasoning seeks to solve problems, scientific reasoning seeks to find causes).

[55] *See* NAJMABADI, *supra* note 10, at 173–74 (distilling interviews).

[56] *Id.* at 35.

[57] *See generally* M. QASIM ZAMAN, MODERN ISLAMIC THOUGHT IN A RADICAL AGE: RELIGIOUS AUTHORITY AND INTERNAL CRITICISM (2012).

that regulation was better than legislation. Parliament conferred entitlements, not rights, they believed, and the legislative process was volatile, prolonged, and arduous. Moreover, it often produced unclear results. Thus instead of legislation, they pursued regulation backed by the weight of jurists as the more effective and authoritative vehicle for accommodation.[58] Mulk-Ara's story represents the importance of religious sanction for new areas of law such as SRS in an otherwise gender-conservative but religious-law recognizing society; indeed laws to meet her needs were folded into the Republic.[59]

Iran's new Islamic law of transsexuality, however, was no panacea for the trans community – in part because equality norms were not at the heart of legalizing SRS. Even after Khomeini's *fatwā* and the establishment of a legal SRS apparatus, trans people navigate onerous bureaucratic processes to obtain individual permissions and subsidies for SRS, are harassed by police for sexual deviancy, and must carry medical and state-conferred papers to avoid arrests. Social stigma persists and state agencies sometimes ignore the law. Case in point: Mulk-Ara worked for years to obtain official legal recognition of her status: from the Public Prosecutor, the Legal Medicine Organization, the Ministry of Health, and the Iranian security forces. She never got her state broadcasting job back; she received only a retirement deal. For seventeen years after the *fatwā*, she lived as a transgender person without getting SRS – until 2002, when she travelled to Thailand.[60] The Iranian scholar seeking to more fully elaborate newly expanded laws for transsexuals and transgender persons, Kariminia, believes that much work remains before courts, state officials, and society at large will accept the new developments.[61]

Significantly, the legal and social apparatus constructed for transsexuals and SRS encompasses only the trans community. Kariminia has emphatically insisted that new gender laws do not encompass homosexuals, who now generally operate on a don't-ask-don't-tell basis for fear of persecution if discovered in the act. Some commentators decry SRS permission as a sinister backdoor way of forcing gay people to change their biological gender to avoid homosexuality charges.[62] Gay communities wonder whether religious-legal or other avenues could open up rights discourse to their members – beyond the psychological-pathology discourse used

---

[58] NAJMABADI, *supra* note 10, at 213.

[59] *Id.* at 166.

[60] *Id.* at 166–67 (failing to specify why Mulk-Ara went to Thailand for SRS). For similar experiences of lengthy waiting times and discrimination, see, e.g., Nazila Fathi, *As Repression Eases, More Iranians Change Their Sex*, N.Y. TIMES (Aug. 2, 2004).

[61] *See* KARIMINIA, *supra* note 1, at 30; Najmabadi, *supra* note 10, at 185.

[62] *See, e.g.*, Sahar Bluck, *Transsexual in Iran: A Fatwa for Freedom?*, in LGBT TRANSNATIONAL IDENTITY AND THE MEDIA 59, 64–65 (C. Pullen ed., 2012); Zara Saeidzadeh, *The Legality of Sex Change Surgery and Construction of Transsexual Identity in Contemporary Iran* 7 (MA Thesis, Lund University, 2014).

now to exempt gay people from military service. But for Kariminia, the answer is an emphatic "no."[63]

This landscape is likely to remain so long as the discourse is framed in terms of identity as gender categories – used to assign Islam's traditional sets of rights and obligations for men and women – rather than equality, which would provoke contemplation of Islamic rights and obligations for all citizens, human beings, members of the community.[64] As Najmabadi put it:

> Given the religious sanction to sex change offered by Ayatollah Khomeini, the categorical bifurcation of non-heteronormative maleness played out quite differently in the Islamic Republic of Iran ... than it did in Europe and the United States. Being *transsexual*, rather than *gay* emerged as the more socially acceptable way of being a non-heteronormative male.[65]

In short, Iran's focus on gender in allowing SRS reified notions of gender at the expense of equality. SRS permissions had the effect of shoehorning the trans community into traditional gender modes rather than elevating both to incorporate equality norms.

IV CONCLUSION

Looking outside of Iran is instructive. In the Sunnī Muslim world, there have been three notable decisions on transsexuality and transgender matters.[66] Most prominently, the former head of al-Azhar, Sheikh Muḥammad Sayyid al-Ṭanṭāwī, like Khomeini, issued a *fatwā* permitting SRS. His ruling relied on arguments of advances in medicine and analogized it to earlier rulings for intersex people. That is, unlike Khomeini, Ṭanṭāwī derived his position by analogy from old laws for intersex procedures, which advised only gender-ambiguous people to choose a gender, such that the new *fatwā* seemed to advise against voluntary SRS without medical advice or necessity.[67] Nevertheless, by construing SRS as a medically advised procedure for transgender people who feel trapped in the wrong body, Egyptians eventually took his opinion as broadly permissive of SRS.[68]

---

[63] NAJMABADI, *supra* note 10, at 162.

[64] *Id.* at 162, 187.

[65] *Id.* at 162 (reflecting the sentiments of Kariminia, who focused on this new gender category).

[66] For more extensive surveys, see EQUAL RIGHTS TRUST, www.equalrightstrust.org. For Malaysian law, see Sima Barmania & Syed Mohamed Aljunid, *Transgender Women in Malaysia, in the Context of HIV and Islam: A Qualitative Study of Stakeholders' Perceptions*, 17 BMC INT'L HEALTH & HUMAN RTS. 1–10 (2017). On transsexuality elsewhere in the Muslim world, see, e.g., Unni Wikan, *Man Becomes Woman: Transsexualism in Oman as a Key to Gender Roles*, 12 MAN 304–19 (1977) (arguing that ostracized transsexual men helped define mainstream gender roles without new *fatwā*s or legal developments).

[67] See IBN QUDĀMA, *supra* note 21, 9:114, 10:94–96.

[68] For the *fatwā*'s text and case review, see Jakob Skovgaard-Petersen, *Sex Change in Cairo: Gender and Islamic Law*, 2 J. INT'L INST. 1–13 (1995); *see also* Alipour, *supra* note 1, at 95–97.

Courts in other Muslim-majority countries have ordered accommodations for trans persons on similarly narrow grounds. In 2009, the Supreme Court of Pakistan ordered government institutions to better provide for transgendered citizens. That court focused on dominant gender categories, characterizing trans persons as suffering gender disorders.[69] In 2014, a Malaysian appeals court struck down a 1992 law criminalizing transgender "cross-dressing."[70] After Malaysian states enacted a series of penal codes criminalizing men wearing women's attire in public,[71] one local state *muftī* – a jurist qualified to issue *fatwās* – submitted an affidavit to court calling the prohibitions a core "precept of Islam," despite a contrary historical record.[72] Declining to adjudicate that claim, the court noted that the *muftī* had failed to explicate Islam's precepts for appropriate dress for men who were *transgender* or who, in the court's terms, suffered from Gender Identity Disorder (GID).[73] Ultimately, the court over-turned the criminal convictions and law in question, finding that criminalizing transgender cross-dressing violated the Malaysian federal Constitution's fundamental rights to life, liberty, and dignity.[74] Significantly, the Malaysian court did not apply constitutional equality protections, concluding that to do so would *disadvantage* the

---

For the state-based discrimination and persecution of trans persons, see Jeffrey A. Redding, *Human Rights and Homo-Sectuals: The International Politics of Sexuality, Religion, and Law*, 4 Nw. J. Int'l Hum. Rts. 436, 439–40, 442–46 (2006).

[69] *See* Jeffrey A. Redding, *From "She-Males" to "Unix": Transgender Rights and the Productive Paradoxes of Pakistani Policing, in* Regimes of Legality: Ethnography of Criminal Cases In South Asia 258–89 (Daniela Berti & Devika Bordia eds., 2015). Exceptionally, Pakistani legislators followed the Supreme Court of Pakistan ruling with an equality-based bill to protect transgender persons. Transgender Persons (Protection of Rights) Act, art. 1(n) (2017). Introduced in August 2017, the bill has yet to become law.

[70] Khamis v. State (Negeri Sembilan) et al., Civil Appeal No. N-01-498-11/2012 (Malaysia Ct. App., Putrajaya, 2014).

[71] *Id.* at 4–5. *See also* Syariah Criminal Enactment of 1992 (Negeri Sembilan), Section 66 (enacted June 1993) ("Any male person who, in any public place wears a woman's attire or poses as a woman shall be guilty of an offence and shall be liable on conviction to a fine not exceeding one thousand *ringgit* or to imprisonment for a term not exceeding six months or both."). All thirteen Malaysian states prohibit men from dressing as women, and three states prohibit women from dressing as men. Human Rights Watch, *"I'm Scared to be a Woman": Human Rights Abuses Against Transgender People in Malaysia* (Sept. 24, 2014), features.hrw .org/features/HRW_reports_2014/Im_Scared_to_Be_a_Woman/.

[72] *Khamis v. State*, at *12 (citing the Muftī's Opinion). The *fatwā*-affidavit relies on the Malaysian discourse on transsexuality and transgender, which relies on conceptions of pathology – deeming biological males who express themselves as females to be the result of GID, which the Court in turn follows. *Id.* at *5–11.

[73] *Id.* at *12–13.

[74] *Id.* at *13 (citing Const. of Malaysia, art. 5(1)), *15 ("The existence of a law that punishes the gender expression of transsexuals, degrades and devalues persons with GID in our society ... [and] directly affects the appellants['] right to live with dignity, and is at odds with rights guaranteed by the federal constitution.").

transgender male petitioners, who would then be subject to enforcement of laws designed for non-transgender males.[75] Again, gender prevailed over equality.

With each conscience claim, decision-makers ignored or specifically excluded considerations of equality and its rationales, which might have provided an alternate basis for accommodation or exemption from religious laws. By focusing on Islamic exemptions from baseline *gender norms*, the permissions rested on necessity claims that allowed gender to be individually determined and regulated according to existing gender categories.

Consequently, existing approaches to conscience claims in Islamic law have been severely limited in application, making them unilluminating for comparative inquiry into cognate claims that arise in the United States. True, it is not that Islamic law lacks the tools to address norms of equality or conventional morality in addressing conscience claims. Rather, it is that these questions have rarely been considered in such terms in the Muslim world.

However, such norms *have* been considered in Muslim-minority contexts in at least one episode worth exploring. Consider *Cassius Clay [Muhammad Ali] vs. the United States*, in which Ali famously refused to submit for the Selective Service draft to fight in the Vietnam War, presenting himself as a conscientious objector to war on religious grounds. His Islamic interpretation was at odds with both the generally applicable legal duty and the cultural attitudes toward the war at the time. He narrowly won before the Supreme Court on technical grounds.[76] But the precedent

---

[75] *Id.* at *17–18 (citing CONST. OF MALAYSIA, art. 8(1)). In May 2016, a group of over fifty Muslim jurists in Pakistan issued a *fatwā* affirming the right of transgender men and women to marry under Islamic law, and urged the state to provide protection and ensure equal legal treatment. The *fatwā*, issued by Tanzeem Ittehad-i Ummat Pakistan, is generally understood to apply to the South Asian transgender community known as the *hijra* or *khawaja sara*. *See* Harry Cockburn, *Pakistani Muslim Clerics Say Transgender Marriages are Legal under Islamic Law*, THE INDEPENDENT (June 29, 2016). This *fatwā* too, was based on intersex laws: that trans people with visible signs of being male or of being female may marry members of the opposite sex. Significantly, it was couched in equality and equal protection terms, thus providing an exception to most treatments of the issue.

[76] Although Ali's objection initially seemed a selective rather than a general objection to war, as required for a draft exemption, Justice John Marshall Harlan determined that Ali was as a practical matter opposed to any war. A majority of Justices initially accepted the government's argument that Ali's objection was selective because "[t]here was ample evidence tending to show that [Ali] would not object to fighting with real weapons in a defensive war on behalf of Muslims... [and] his was not a general scruple against participation in war, but rather a refusal to fight in wars on the side of white persons." *See* Marty Lederman, *Muhammad Ali, Conscientious Objection, and the Supreme Court's Struggle to Understand "Jihad" and "Holy War": The Story of* Cassius Clay v. United States, SCOTUSBLOG (June 8, 2016). But with a law clerk's intervention, Justice Harlan learned that the Nation of Islam contemplated participation only in Armageddon-type battles, meaning "Ali was, as a practical matter, religiously opposed to fighting in any wars that might actually occur." *See id.* With Justice Thurgood Marshall recused, Harlan was initially assigned to write a 5–3 majority opinion affirming Ali's conviction. Harlan then changed his vote, leaving an undesirable 4–4 split that would have affirmed Ali's conviction. Despite Chief Justice Warren Burger's complaint that Justice Harlan had become an "apologist for the Black Muslims," Justices Blackmun, Brennan, Douglas, and Stewart all

matters,[77] both from his Islamic view and America's evolving view of equality and morality; the two eventually converged, long after the War and Ali's career ended. Unlike approaches to Islamic law in Muslim-majority societies, Ali's Islamic conscience claim emerged in a secular society, where claims to equality and liberty animated explicit discussions of war and draft duty. His experience is an example of a situation in which contemplation of a religious conscience claim – an *Islamic* conscience claim – eventually helped expand the scope of civil rights and produce shifts in the dominant cultural attitudes to an American war. This shift was accomplished by the Supreme Court granting an exemption (through reversal of the draft-dodging conviction). Although here, too, the Supreme Court did not grant the exemption explicitly on the basis of an equality norm, that principle animated the decision and the episode helped spur the judicial and public conversations in that direction soon after. One Washington, DC lawyer has seen a similar connection. He links the approach in *Clay v. United States* to the remand in *Zubik v. Burwell*: it is the Supreme Court's pragmatic approach to conscience claims that calls for crafting a palatable solution on principled grounds through more deliberation about the rationales on each side.[78]

seemed prepared to overturn the conviction. Yet, they disagreed on the grounds. They eventually settled on a compromise. In an unsigned opinion authored by Justice Potter Stewart, the Court reversed Ali's conviction without reaching the merits, sidestepping entirely "Justice Harlan's conclusion that Ali had a sincere religious objection to war 'in any form.'" *Id.* The opinion narrowly found that the appeals board might have impermissibly ruled against Ali because it assumed his beliefs were more racial than religious or a matter of convenience rather than sincerely held. *See* Clay v. United States, 403 U.S. 698, 704 (1971) ("[T]he Department was simply wrong as a matter of law in advising that the petitioner's beliefs were not religiously based and were not sincerely held.").

[77] *See* Jesse D.H. Snyder, *The Legacy of Muhammad Ali 45 Years After* Clay v. United States: *Why a Case on Selective Service Still Matters*, 16 Va. Sports & Ent. L. J. 34, 35, 37 (2016).

[78] *Id.* at 45–46.

16

Should an Amish Baker Sell a Cake
for a Same-Sex Wedding?

A *Letter on Toleration of LGBT Rights*
from Anabaptists to Evangelicals

Jason R. Moyer

Dirk Willems, escaping jail, runs away from a "thief catcher" on a cold day in the sixteenth-century Netherlands.[1] As an Anabaptist, a "rebaptizer," Willems is guilty of practicing an illicit form of Christianity.[2] Willems makes it across a body of water thinly covered with ice while his pursuer crashes through behind him. Although Willems enjoys the possibility of religious freedom with his oppressor flailing, drowning, and freezing, Willems risks that freedom, turning back instead to save the life of his pursuer. This *Martyrs Mirror* story ends with Willems burning on a pyre.

Today, conservative evangelicals understand religious freedom differently than do Anabaptists such as Willems.[3] He simply wanted to be left alone, tolerated, to practice his beliefs. By contrast, religious freedom for some conservative evangelicals means the opportunity to extend their values into the public sphere where they shape the law for others.[4] They seek to elect presidents or lawmakers with particular moral characters who follow a "Christian" voting plan or judges who interpret the

---

[1] See THIELEMAN J. VAN BRAGHT, THE BLOODY THEATER, OR, MARTYRS' MIRROR 741–42 (15th ed., 1987).

[2] Current Anabaptists include Mennonites, Brethren, Hutterites, and the Amish. For a contemporary perspective on Anabaptist theology, see GERALD J. MAST & J. DENNY WEAVER, DEFENSELESS CHRISTIANITY: ANABAPTISM FOR A NONVIOLENT CHURCH (2009).

[3] This chapter uses the term "conservative evangelicals" or "religious right" to describe what the Pew Research Center categorizes as the "evangelical Protestant tradition." Pew Research Ctr. Religion & Pub. Life Project, *America's Changing Religious Landscape*, https://perma.cc/J8C4-RWXT. Among the faith traditions included are the "southern Baptist Convention, the Assemblies of God, Churches of Christ, the Lutheran Church-Missouri Synod, the Presbyterian Church in America, other evangelical denominations, and many nondenominational congregations." *Id.* This chapter draws a distinction between "evangelicals" and evangelizing. Evangelizing in America can take many forms, one of which is the Anabaptist form of witness described in this chapter. *Id.*

[4] See Melling, Chapter 19, for critique of such broad religious freedom.

law similarly.[5] Additionally, they use litigation to secure a broad conception of religious freedom.[6] The Anabaptist witness demonstrated by the outstretched hand of Willems, pulling his enemy to safety provides a counterexample to the legal strategies used by Christians today to extend their agenda into US law. Willems wanted religious freedom, but not at the cost of the suffering of others.

This chapter asks what Willems' rescue of his pursuer can offer the contemporary debate about faith and sexuality. Section I uses the example of seventeenth-century Dutch Mennonites to argue that recent legislative efforts by conservative evangelicals overstep the Anabaptist tradition of religious toleration. Section II describes how the central Anabaptist theological concept yieldedness was tested in the US Supreme Court's landmark 1972 decision in *Wisconsin v. Yoder*.[7] Section III asks Christians to follow Willems by responding with self-sacrificial love when feeling threatened by an enemy.

Like all Christians, Anabaptists have varied opinions about sexuality from community to community. Anabaptists are united on one point: the stark moral difference between, on the one hand, what should take place within the body of believers and, on the other, how secular society functions.[8] We see Jesus' willing sacrifice and victorious resurrection as an instruction for defenseless living in the present. As the church embodies Jesus' life, our life together foreshadows a future where the wolf will lay down with the lamb and swords will be beaten into ploughshares.[9] In the time between Jesus' resurrection and God's return, we attempt to bear witness to God's peaceful reign by resisting coercive power in physical, social, and political relationships. Included in coercive power Anabaptists would reject is the use of lawsuits to achieve our ends.[10] By contrast, public advocacy for just laws in secular terms, or what we call "middle axioms," is appropriate.[11]

---

[5] For a discussion of identity politics, see DeGirolami, Chapter 21.

[6] For discussions of litigation by LGBT rights advocates and religious freedom advocates, see Helfand, Chapter 11; Leith Anderson, Chapter 12; Melling, Chapter 19; Ryan Anderson, Chapter 27; Pizer, Chapter 29. Some contend that the litigation secures the right to "reasonable disagreement" and is not "actual discrimination." *See* Ryan Anderson, Chapter 27.

[7] 406 U.S. 205 (1972).

[8] *See* JOHN HOWARD YODER, SCHLEITHEIM CONFESSION (1977).

[9] *Isaiah* 11:6 (King James Version) ("The wolf also shall dwell with the lamb, and the leopard shall lie down with the kid; and the calf and the young lion and the fatling together; and a little child shall lead them."); *Micah* 4:3 (King James Version) ("And he shall judge among many people, and rebuke strong nations afar off; and they shall beat their swords into plowshares, and their spears into pruning-hooks: nation shall not lift up a sword against nation, neither shall they learn war any more.").

[10] Anabaptists use the biblical call of *Matthew* 18:15–17 to describe how to resolve conflicts through reconciliation. This contrasts with the approach that other Christians might take to using lawsuits to extend their values into public life.

[11] Instead of violating the shared moral end of nonviolence through the use of coercive means such as litigation, Anabaptists use "middle axioms" that translate their arguments into the secular reasoning of the public sphere. *See, e.g.,* JOHN HOWARD YODER, THE CHRISTIAN

Before Christians attempt to protect their culture through coercive means from LGBT people by standing up for the religious legal right to not engage in commerce with LGBT persons by, for instance, not serving a wedding cake or refusing to make adoption placements with same-sex couples, then they should pause and consider the lesson that Willems teaches: he reached out his hand to save the person he felt most threatened by.

I THE BARE-BONES TOLERATION OF THE DUTCH MENNONITES

The statistical increase in the United States of "nones," those with no religious affiliation, combined with the overall decline in Christian religious affiliation, has bolstered the claim of many Christians that they are the threatened minority group.[12] As the argument goes, Christianity is on the decline and therefore so is society. The goal for these Christians is to (re)produce a type of civilization-shaping morality that will lead the world to its Godly future, or to follow the now famous Benedict option,[13] which essentially suggests that Christians head to the basement until the secular winds blow over and Christians can once again take their rightful place as the lead voice in whatever is left from the liberal-induced collapse of society. To some, the question of same-sex marriage is, for instance, merely a "fashionable ideology" that is threatening the breakup of society by compromising marriage's Godly function, which is "the great good of procreation."[14]

At one time, the legal efforts to push this traditional sexual mores into the law came from lawmakers, backed by constituencies who appealed to traditional majority values.[15] As a newly fashioned minority perspective, some Christians have adopted the tools of other minority groups, resorting to litigation rather than legislation. In this litigation, disparate faith groups present a united front.

Consider the litigation culminating in the Supreme Court's 2014 decision, *Burwell v. Hobby Lobby*.[16] The Supreme Court decided in favor of Hobby Lobby, which conscientiously objected to providing contraceptives to employees through

---

WITNESS TO THE STATE (2002); OXFORD CONFERENCE OF THE UNIVERSAL CHRISTIAN COUNCIL OF LIFE AND WORK ON CHURCH, COMMUNITY AND STATE (1937).

[12] *See* Pew Research Center, *supra* note 3 (reporting that the number of religiously unaffiliated adults or "nones" increased by roughly 19 million between 2007 and 2014, reaching roughly 56 million "nones" in 2014, surpassing both Catholics or mainline Protestants in number, although "nones" remain "second in size only to evangelical Protestants among major religious groups in the U.S.").

[13] ROD DREHER, THE BENEDICT OPTION: A STRATEGY FOR CHRISTIANS IN A POST-CHRISTIAN NATION (2017).

[14] *Manhattan Declaration: A Call of Christian Conscience*, FIRST THINGS, https://perma.cc/W8XE-YSF3.

[15] For a review of state constitutional bans on same-sex marriage and the degree of popular support at the time of passage, see Robin Fretwell Wilson, *Marriage of Necessity: Same-Sex Marriage and Religious Liberty Protections*, 64 CASE W. RES. L. REV. 1161, 1209 (2014).

[16] 134 S. Ct. 2751 (2014).

their healthcare coverage plan. Importantly, Hobby Lobby's appeal was brought under statutory protections enacted in 1993, the Religious Freedom Reformation Act, as well as constitutional Free Exercise precedence giving religious accommodations to three minority faith traditions: the Amish in *Wisconsin v. Yoder*, Seventh-Day Adventists in *Sherbert v. Verner*,[17] and Native American religion in *Employment Division v. Smith*.[18] Like these precedents, efforts to appeal to conservative evangelicals as a minority are bolstered by a social movement of "cross-denominational mobilization" that promotes the impression that Jerry Falwell's Moral Majority has become the moral minority.[19]

To think, however, that conservative Christians are becoming a minority is counterfactual. Pew Research Center data shows that 70 percent of Americans still self-identify as Christian; true, this represents a decline of 7.8 percent in the decade before 2014.[20] Although this may seem like a large drop-off, conservative evangelicals has not declined at all in that time.[21] Although the fear of the slippery slope to "European secularism" still holds sway in many Christian circles,[22] Pew's data shows that Christians as a group remain the majority in the United States – and conservative Christians with "moral majority" perspectives have not declined, they *increased* in the past ten years.

Despite continuing to occupy the majority position, conservative Christians today use strategies that more closely resemble a social movement to push their agenda, working from the ground up as a minority group to counter secularists who are perceived to have stripped America of its greatness. Litigation alerts flag victories and seek contributions.[23] They endlessly identify religious liberty threats that must immediately be addressed. With each new case, "Your Free Speech Hangs in the Balance of this Supreme Court Case."[24]

Part and parcel of this appeal to minority religious status, the religious right now marshals appeals to "complicity-based" rights of conscience.[25] When a conservative

---

[17] 374 U.S. 398 (1963).

[18] 494 U.S. 872 (1990). For views of *Smith*, see NeJaime & Siegel, Chapter 6; Helfand, Chapter 11.

[19] Douglas NeJaime & Reva B. Siegel, *Conscience Wars: Complicity-Based Conscience Claims in Religion and Politics*, 124 YALE L.J. 2202, 2544–52 (2015).

[20] Pew Research Center, *supra* note 3.

[21] *Id.* (showing that evangelical Protestants now total 62 million adults, an increase of 2 million since 2007, although with "margins of error," the actual increase "may have risen by as many as 5 million or remained essentially unchanged").

[22] For fears that the United States will follow Europe in certain respects, see Leith Anderson, Chapter 12.

[23] *See, e.g.,* the Alliance Defending Freedom, whose website opens with "FUND CRITICAL CASES
   Help defend religious freedom in these high-stakes legal battles across the nation." Alliance Defending Freedom, https://perma.cc/3KBZ-K6TC.

[24] *Id.*

[25] NeJaime & Siegel, *supra* note 19.

Christian baker refuses to serve a wedding cake for gay wedding, for instance, it is because the baker does not want to be "complicit" with what they see as a sin.[26] While complicity-conscience claims are not minority rights claims, they do appeal to victories in the minority religious protection tradition. For instance, Hobby Lobby appealed to *Wisconsin v. Yoder, Sherbert v. Verner, and Employment Division v. Smith*.[27] Because this approach continues the history of religious toleration, the framing tracks a minority asking for protection from the majority. This expansion of the minority-requests-toleration tradition demands a religious freedom that potentially sweeps in the liberty of others, such as their employees and customers. Because of this sweep, efforts to enlarge the zone of toleration to avoid complicity run up against third-party protections in the law.[28] The refusal to serve a gay couple, for instance, may both materially harm the gay couple by "deterring or obstructing access to goods and services" and demeaning them.[29]

Even with this shift to a minority perspective, one constant remains: the effort of Christians since Constantine to seek power by extending Christian beliefs into government and thereby position a single version of Christianity as the moral center of society. The latest complicity-based conscious claims fit this model as well by seeking to create a society where moral actions will be extended to employees and customers. This was also the case during the Reformation, with the early efforts at religious toleration.[30] Consider early efforts at religious toleration in the 1555 Peace of Augsburg that granted rulers in Lutheran Germany to choose the established religion of their territories, or before that the Swiss Confederation's efforts at peaceful religious coexistence between Reformed and Catholic cantons in the 1529 and 1531 *Landfrieden* treaties; in both instances, freedom of religion was limited to the governmental level.[31] One version of Christianity became the established religion of the government and was used to justify the mistreatment of religious minorities.[32] Anabaptists, on the contrary, do not seek to choose the government's

---

[26] Appellant's Reply Brief, Masterpiece Cakeshop, Inc. v. Craig, 2015 WL 13622552 (Colo. App.), at 6 ("He believes God granted him artistic and creative abilities and that he is religiously obligated to use those abilities in a manner that honors God.").

[27] 406 U.S. 205 (1972).

[28] The *Hobby Lobby* court found no third-party harms, as Laycock notes in Chapter 3. But see NeJaime & Siegel, *supra* note 19, describing possible overlooked harms to others from extending the government's accommodation for religious nonprofits to closely held for-profit corporations.

[29] NeJaime & Siegel, *supra* note 19, at 2566.

[30] *Toleration, in* OXFORD ENCYCLOPEDIA OF THE REFORMATION 1660–63 (H. J. Hillerbrand ed., 1996).

[31] Freedoms in the Peace of Augsburg may have been built upon the Swiss Confederation's 1529 and 1531 *Landfrieden* treaties that allowed different regions to establish either Reformed or Catholic religions. *See id.*

[32] For discussions of the no establishment norms and its connection to religious freedom, see Helfand, Chapter 11; Hollman, Chapter 23.

religion or to impose their own religion through laws. Instead, they seek freedom from a government to practice their religion.

Take, for instance, the case of seventeenth-century Swiss Anabaptists in the cantons of Zurich and Bern. They lived in territories whose governments not only protected borders and citizens from external (largely religious) threats, but also protected a specific assumption about Reformed Christian orthodoxy. The "hard-necked and unconvertable" Anabaptists, as a Reformed leader referred to them, refused on biblical grounds to take oaths, serve in the military, and hold weddings in the official state churches.[33] For their offenses, they were killed, stripped of property, and put in prison.

Mennonites in the Netherlands learned of this maltreatment and began sending funds and writing intercessory letters to Swiss government officials.[34] The Dutch Mennonites, although persecuted at one time, were successful business owners and well-regarded physicians in the seventeenth century. They had money and influence that they used to support their sisters and brothers many miles away. What united the Swiss and Dutch Anabaptists was their agreement in the Dordrecht Confession, which brought them together with Anabaptists across Europe into a cosmopolitan church.

Their letters appealed for the Swiss government to extend toleration to issues of religious conscience. In one 1643 tract, Dutch Mennonite Joost Hendricks argued against the "torture of conscience used by the Swiss" and in favor of "freedom of conscience."[35] Hendricks and the other intercessors focused on asking Swiss authorities to simply leave this dissenting religious movement alone to practice its beliefs. What makes this a notable request in seventeenth-century Europe is that, amidst governments with established churches, Hendricks did not attempt to argue against the Reformed theology that at worst backed the Anabaptist persecution and at best allowed it to happen. The Mennonite intercessors did not try to show how Reformed theology inaccurately understands the Bible or Jesus. Hendricks did not seek power or even legitimacy by making this appeal, but rather simple accommodation of a minority religious perspective to disagree.[36]

This early modern emphasis on freedom of religious conscience was not unique to Hendricks's letter but was included in many others as well. Neither was the emphasis on religious toleration particular to Dutch Mennonites. John Locke's 1689 *Letter on Toleration*, for example, which includes references to Anabaptists, made

---

[33] Jeremy Dupertuis Bangs, Letters on toleration: Dutch aid to persecuted Swiss and Palatine Mennonites 1615–1699 169–70 (2004).
[34] Gerald J. Mast, Separation and the Sword in Anabaptist Persuasion: Radical Confessional Rhetoric from Schleitheim to Dordrecht (2006).
[35] Bangs, *supra* note 33, at 90–91.
[36] For the importance of the right to be wrong, see Koppelman, Chapter 9.

these same points.[37] There is historical evidence of Locke interacting with Mennonites in the Netherlands during this time, as well as with William Penn, who eventually welcomed Anabaptists into Pennsylvania.[38] Given the importance of Locke to modern liberalism, it is clear that Dutch Mennonite intercessory letters are not the appeals of a strange religious tradition but are part of a broader intellectual current seeking healthier relationships between church and state.

Christians have not yet learned the many lessons from history about the problems that come when a territorial state adopts a particular religion. Toleration arguments have been extended by complicity conscience claims. Although a new strategy, it functions as Christendom has since its inception; it inappropriately attempts to extend a certain version of Christianity into government and society. This shifts toleration arguments from the Anabaptist appeal to "let me alone to practice my beliefs," to Christendom's claim to "let me make my beliefs society's beliefs." As Willems's flight from authorities and ultimate death for his faith underscores: the danger here is that people will again be hurt when a government extends legal protection to a privileged or governing religious assumption.

II ANABAPTIST YIELDEDNESS IN *WISCONSIN V. YODER*

The Anabaptist refusal to attempt to make their theology the state's theology is captured by the Amish term *Gelassenheit* or yieldedness. This term captures the "defenseless" posture that Anabaptists such as Willems take in relationship to violence:

> Rather than fight, sue, or prosecute when threatened or harmed by another, the Amish accept that a Christian should turn the other cheek as well as forgive and forget. Rather than join a protest or run for office when it appears that the civic order is becoming a mess, the Amish are convinced that their focus should be on living the Christian life within their own community.[39]

"Coercion" is the antagonist to yieldedness. For instance, in his 1944 book *War, Peace, and Nonresistance*, Guy Hershberger argues that even Gandhi's pacifist movement for Indian independence fell short of the high standard of Jesus' model of defenselessness. Gandhi's "primary purpose was to bring about the submission of the opposition through compulsion,"[40] albeit nonviolent pressure. Anabaptists do not follow the liberal pacifism that many conservatives detest, but instead assume a defenselessness made possible by confidence in the resurrection of Jesus. God has already established the world's reconciled future, the church simply needs to live

---

[37] JOHN LOCKE & RICHARD VERNON, LOCKE ON TOLERATION (Cambridge University Press, 2010); SUSAN L. TROLLINGER, SELLING THE AMISH: THE TOURISM OF NOSTALGIA 11 (2012).

[38] BANGS, *supra* note 33, at 11–68.

[39] TROLLINGER, *supra* note 37, at 11.

[40] GUY F. HERSHBERGER, WAR, PEACE, AND NONRESISTANCE 1 (1953).

into God's peaceful reign through reconciliatory relationships within the church community.[41] From there, the church turns in service toward the world. That is the "true evangelical faith" that will in God's time be universal.[42]

Given this perspective, it may seem odd that a case about the Amish children of Wallace Miller, Jonas Yoder, and Adin Yutzy in New Glarus, Wisconsin made it all the way to the Supreme Court.[43] Since the Amish do not sue others, they were not the party that pushed the case from court to court. The National Committee for Amish Religious Freedom (NCARF), a conservative religious freedom advocacy group, defended the families and funded their defense.[44] In the Amish community, children from the families stopped attending school after eighth grade, a violation of truancy laws in Wisconsin that required children to stay in school until the end of the school year in which a child turns sixteen.[45] The case ended with the court deciding in favor of Yoder because not to do so would violate the defendants' freedom to exercise their religion and pose an existential threat to the community's continuation.[46]

This was not the first run-in between this Amish community and the state of Wisconsin. Previous tensions arose over such issues as elementary school gym class. In defense of the Amish, two conservative state lawmakers, Frederick Kessler and Kenneth Merkel, "introduced legislation early in 1967 to exempt children from gym classes if they could demonstrate that participation 'conflicts with their religious practices.'"[47] In that case, showering and wearing gym clothes conflicted with the Amish beliefs in the importance of modesty.[48] The lawmakers unsuccessfully attempted to secure separate bathrooms for the Amish children. Just as with the legal question of LGBT bathroom usage today, the Amish children in New Glarus could have benefited from toleration of their specific needs, much as transgender individuals benefit from tolerant policies.[49]

---

[41] For an extended argument that the magnitude of good done by faith organizations can support a presumption in favor of exemptions, see Berg, Chapter 24.

[42] MENNO SIMONS, COMPLETE WRITINGS (1956).

[43] Yoder, *supra* note 7.

[44] SHAWN FRANCIS PETERS, THE *YODER* CASE: RELIGIOUS FREEDOM, EDUCATION, AND PARENTAL RIGHTS 5 (2003).

[45] Yoder, *supra* note 7.

[46] *Id.* at 219. The Court stressed how additional years of education would interfere with the Amish's community-preserving strategy. The Wisconsin law, it noted, "takes [youth] away from their community, physically and emotionally, during the crucial and formative adolescent period of life." State-supported high school could not, "in curriculum or social environment . . . impart the values promoted by Amish society." *Id.* at 211–12.

[47] PETERS, *supra* note 44, at 23.

[48] For a discussion of a recent attempt to rollback accommodations for religious modesty in New York's public pools, see Leith Anderson, Chapter 12.

[49] Conflicts that amplify the culture wars seem never-ending, but if reconciliation is possible, it will happen in part through finding common ground. The issues of bathrooms for Amish children and alternatives to civil weddings for the Swiss Anabaptists may be a good place to find

The Amish defendants only "warily permitted" a conservative religious advocacy group to create a defense on their behalf.[50] What stretched Amish yieldedness was NCARF's motivation to use the case to extend religious freedom over educational choice. The Amish families eventually won the case and by doing so left "an indelible mark on such areas as parents' rights, home schooling, and state regulation of religious schools."[51]

Although the arguments in *Yoder* were not made from the complicity-based claims used by conservative evangelicals today, this case stands as precedence in cases such as *Hobby Lobby* where conservative evangelicals attempt to take on the identity of the minority conscientious objector.[52] The sort of toleration that seventeenth-century Dutch Mennonites advocated for fits the demands of the Amish but is exceeded by the demands of both NCARF and the conservative Christians who use the case today. When the religious right on an unprecedented scale – far exceeding the impact of concessions made to a tiny Amish minority – uses minority religion cases to turn their moral values into law, it undermines the purpose of legal provisions designed for exceptional cases. The Amish simply wanted to be left alone to have their children finish schooling after eighth grade. In the case of *Yoder*, the Amish "didn't go to the law, the law came to them."[53]

The irony in *Yoder* is that it could be seen to have legally established the Amish religion by giving it a special religious place in society. Robert Bork argued, "In the name of the free exercise of religion, the Supreme Court, according to its own criteria, itself established a religion."[54] There is something fitting about the perception that the Amish are a moral center of American society. Tourists flock to Amish communities to see their hardworking "frontier" lifestyle; Thomas Jefferson recognized the Amish as the model of the "sturdy yeomen."[55]

However, establishing the Amish as a religion parts ways with a core Anabaptist tenet that the church has a more important mission in society than does the state. When the church either becomes the state through legal establishment *or* churches seek to extend their morality into law, it violates this core Anabaptist witness of defenselessness. Anabaptists seek nonconformity with the world because we believe

mutuality. For a discussion of the "bathroom issue" in efforts to secure state nondiscrimination protections for the LGBT community, see Wilson, Chapter 30.

[50] PETERS, *supra* note 44, at 5.

[51] *Id.* at 175.

[52] Although *Yoder* figures significantly in the religious right's efforts to carve out favorable treatment as the imposed-upon minority, in later cases, the justices chipped away at the interpretive framework they had used to shield the religious liberty of the New Glarus Amish. *Id.* at 175 (citing United States v. Lee, 455 U.S. 252 (1982), Goldman v. Weinberger, 475 U.S. 503 (1986), Bowen v. Roy, 476 U.S. 693 (1986), and Lyng v. Northwest Indian Cemetery Protective Association, 485 U.S. 439 (1988)).

[53] PETERS, *supra* note 44, at 55. Today there is an "Amish Steering Committee" that negotiates disagreements between their communities and the secular communities in which they live.

[54] *Id.* at 175.

[55] *Id.* at 152.

that the church's faithful witness is the location of God's righteousness. Governments exist to secure order in society, which God allows them to do with the use of the sinful tools of violence, but the church uses the tools of love and defenselessness as it looks for opportunities to turn around, make itself vulnerable, and help its enemy to safety.

III A CONCLUDING LETTER TO CHRISTIANS

The Anabaptist experience of being a minority religion should teach contemporary Christians how to respond when the world around them seems as if it is closing in. Each of us should position ourselves in the Willems story: are we the jailor or are we the victim escaping prison? Are we the minority or the majority? If, as the recent complicity-based appeals advanced by some suggest, one sees oneself as Willems, then one almost certainly will feel chased by an enemy across thin ice. Even if these appeals help one to secure religious freedom, a choice remains front and center: run for one's life or turn around and help the person that one sees as the enemy?

Our jailor may seem to be a different person depending on what sort of Christian we are. If one sits squarely within the mainline or evangelical left, the religious right may feel threatening. If one identifies as a member of the religious right, threats may seem to emanate from the secular culture, in the form of a gay couple seeking a wedding cake, adoption, or equal partner benefits.

Whatever one's starting point, by turning around and helping our pursuers, we may risk our own freedom, as Willems did, but the witness we perform by submitting ourselves to our enemy will allow us to show that we are followers of Jesus, the God of peace. It does not export anyone's morality – including a church's – to others, but simply lives that morality with the likeminded in community.

When a government provides a tolerant space for that, then it is doing the work that God has called it to do by keeping order in society, producing just laws for all, not just the religious.

So an Amish baker should bake a same-sex wedding cake. For Anabaptists yielding to others is a higher calling than is coercing others to conform to our moral standards even when they fall short of our standards. For evangelizing Christians, serving a same-sex wedding cake should be no more controversial than a pacifist Amish family serving whoopie pies to a motorcade of state officials protected by armed security.

The Amish view commerce with the outside world as an opportunity to share "their Christian witness through their visible different common life and daily practices."[56] If Amish bakers decide to only sell their cakes to those who fit their

---

[56] TROLLINGER, *supra* note 37, at xiv.

high moral standards, then they would need to stop selling to me and my Mennonite sisters and brothers who drive cars, use buttons, and carry cellphones. For a minority religious group, toleration does not involve becoming the moral center of a nation; it involves living in visibly different ways than society so that Christ's love shines through our church community to the world.

PART IV

Testing the Civil Rights Analogy

17

The Rhetoric of Bigotry and Conscience in Battles over "Religious Liberty v. LGBT Rights"

*Linda C. McClain**

I THE "BRUSH OF BIGOTRY"

Charges, denials, and countercharges of "bigotry" have a long history in debates over the evident conflict between LGBT rights and religious liberty.[1] In recent controversies, a frequent claim is that religious individuals who oppose changes in the legal definition of civil marriage and seek conscience-based exemptions from state non-discrimination laws that include "sexual orientation" as a protected category are being "branded" as bigots. Two prominent examples are the dissenting opinions in *Obergefell v. Hodges*,[2] in which the US Supreme Court held that same-sex couples "may exercise the fundamental right to marry in all States," and the arguments made in defense of merchants who object to providing wedding-related goods and services to same-sex couples, such as in *Masterpiece Cakeshop, Ltd. v. Colorado Civil Rights Commission*, which the Supreme Court will decide during its 2017–18 term. Critics of the application of nondiscrimination laws to such merchants even flip the (explicit or implicit) charge of bigotry to apply to the opponents of religious exemptions.

What does it mean to assert that a judicial opinion or a civil rights commission tars someone with the "brush of bigotry"?[3] Is a charge of bigotry inferred simply from

---

* Portions of this chapter draw from my forthcoming book, THE RHETORIC OF BIGOTRY AND CONSCIENCE: PAST AND PRESENT CONTROVERSIES OVER MARRIAGE AND CIVIL RIGHTS (forthcoming 2019), and are used with permission of the publisher.
[1] *See, e.g.,* William Raspberry, *Anita Bryant and Gay Rights: Bigotry or Prudence?,* WASH. POST (May 2, 1977).
[2] Obergefell v. Hodges, 135 S. Ct. 2584 (2015).
[3] U.S. v. Windsor, 133 S. Ct. 2675, 2696 (2013) (Roberts, C.J., dissenting) (critiquing Justice Kennedy's majority opinion for lacking evidence to attribute "sinister motive" for the Defense of Marriage Act and "tar the political branches with the brush of bigotry"); USCCB *Religious Liberty Chairman Responds to Statement of Chairman of U.S. Commission on Civil Rights* (Sept. 13, 2016), http://www.usccb.org/news/2016/16-117.cfm (quoting Archbishop Lori describing statements by Martin Castro, Chairman of the U.S. Commission on Civil Rights, as

asserting that society should learn from the past: that now-repudiated forms of discrimination – on the basis of race and sex – are relevant to protecting against discrimination on the basis of sexual orientation? Or from comparing past religious defenses of segregation and bans on interracial marriage with religious justifications for opposing marriage by same-sex couples? Are these analogies inapt because today's sincere religious believers have nothing in common with yesterday's segregationists? Indeed, does the label "bigot" better apply to public officials who show "intolerance" toward today's sincere believers by refusing them exemptions from nondiscrimination laws, driving them from the public square?[4]

These controversies reveal a number of puzzles. One puzzle is whether bigotry has to do with the motivation for a belief – is *sincerity* a defense to bigotry? The frequent contrast between the "sincere" opponent of same-sex marriage and the "racist bigot" of the past suggests the answer is yes. Common definitions of bigotry, however, suggest the answer may be no. If the core of bigotry concerns intolerance and prejudice toward another group's beliefs or a group itself, then a *sincere* white supremacist or anti-Semite or anti-Muslim could still be bigoted.[5]

Another puzzle concerns whether bigotry refers primarily to the content of a belief, that is, an *unreasonable* belief or an *irrational hatred or suspicion* of a group,[6] so that the *reasonableness* of a belief would counter a charge of bigotry. Or does "bigot" suggest a particular type of (bad) *character* of the person holding the view, with distinctive psychological or moral *traits* – holding views about a group inflexibly and obstinately, impervious to facts?[7] Or does the label "bigotry" signal an anachronistic and now-reviled view? On this definition, calling a position bigoted declares that it is (no longer) within the boundaries of civility and not an acceptable basis for supporting or opposing laws.

"reckless and painting those who support religious freedom with the broad brush of bigotry"). See also Lori, Chapter 13, for view that "[t]hose who are convinced that marriage is between one man and one woman should not be equated with racial bigots."; Ryan Anderson, Chapter 27.

4   Richard A. Epstein, *The Government's Civil Rights Bullies*, Defining Ideas (Sept. 26, 2016), http://www.hoover.org/research/governments-civil-rights-bullies. *See also* Stephen Smith, *Who's On Which Side of the Lunch Counter? Civil Rights, Religious Accommodation, and the Challenges of Diversity*, Pub. Discourse (Dec. 2, 2016) (arguing those who would deny religious exemptions are the true heirs of the segregationists).

5   *See Bigotry*, Free Dictionary, http://www.thefreedictory.com/bigotry (collecting several definitions mentioning "prejudice," "intolerance," and "obtuse or narrow-minded intolerance, especially of other races or religions").

6   *See id.* (quoting American Heritage Roget's Thesaurus defining "bigotry" as "irrational suspicion of a particular group, race, or religion").

7   *See, e.g.*, Gordon W. Allport, *The Bigot in Our Midst*, XL Commonweal 582, 583 (Oct. 6, 1944) (the "mental dynamics of bigotry" include the inability to take another's perspective or correct one's misinterpretations based on new information about a group); Stephen Eric Bronner, The Bigot: Why Prejudice Persists 7 (2014) ("[t]he bigot's prejudices rest on pre-reflective assumptions that become fixed, finished, and irreversible in the face of new knowledge").

As a window into these puzzles, this chapter assesses the rhetoric of "bigotry" and "conscience" in two contexts: (1) the US Commission on Civil Rights Report, *Peaceful Coexistence: Reconciling Nondiscrimination Principles with Civil Liberties,*[8] and (2) arguments made by the parties and *amici curiae* in *Masterpiece Cakeshop.* These contexts reveal a set of contrasting positions. First, defenders of religious liberty argue that to relate present-day objections based on conscience and sincerely held religious beliefs about marriage – and related arguments that those objections warrant exemptions from nondiscrimination laws – to past assertions of religious liberty in the context of objecting to complying with civil rights laws prohibiting race discrimination brands people – indeed, slanders them – as bigots. Today's sincere Christian (or Jew or Muslim) declining to create a wedding cake or otherwise affirm same-sex marriage is nothing like the racist (past or present) refusing to serve all black customers. And, some add, nothing like the homophobe refusing to serve any gay or lesbian customers. Instead, people of faith have championed civil rights and justice.

Those defending the extension of nondiscrimination laws to protect LGBT persons counter that history teaches lessons about past assertions of conscience and religious liberty, which were used to justify many forms of discrimination and exclusion. While courts themselves, for a time, accepted – and voiced – such religious justifications, courts have, for many decades, upheld nondiscrimination laws against such challenges. This past counsels caution about arguments that "free exercise" entails living out one's faith in the public square even when that includes denying customers goods and services. Further, the framing of "religious liberty v. LGBT rights" obscures the fact that religious traditions differ in their views and also evolve, sometimes spurred by legal change.[9]

Second, both contexts reveal competing views of the legitimate scope of modern public accommodations laws. Invoking Chief Justice William Rehnquist's opinion in *Boy Scouts of America v. Dale,* defenders of exemptions contend that the clash between religious liberty and LGBT rights stems from the (unwarranted) expansion of public accommodations laws beyond core (compelling) interests – *e.g.,* racial discrimination in hotels, restaurants, gas stations, and entertainment venues – to cover more places and more categories, such as sexual orientation and gender identity.[10] Title II of the Civil Rights Act of 1964, on this view, is the paradigm of a justified civil rights law.[11]

---

[8] U.S. COMM'N ON CIVIL RIGHTS, PEACEFUL COEXISTENCE: RECONCILING NONDISCRIMINA-TION PRINCIPLES WITH CIVIL LIBERTIES (2016).

[9] For calls for internal reexamination, see Gramick, Chapter 10; for discussions of persons straddling the LGBT and faith communities, see Minter, Chapter 4; Pizer, Chapter 29.

[10] Boy Scouts of America v. Dale, 530 U.S. 640, 664 (2000). For such a view, see Ryan Anderson, Chapter 27.

[11] 42 U.S.C. § 2000a (2012). For discussions of Title II's scope, see Laycock, Chapter 3; Wilson, Chapter 30.

Defenders of state public accommodations laws counter that the expansion of such laws reflects evolving understanding of the problems of prejudice and discrimination. While Title II is a landmark law, many states passed public accommodations laws long before Congress did, and expanded them in light of new insights and learning.[12] Apt here is Justice Stevens's statement, in his *Dale* dissent, that "every state law prohibiting discrimination is designed to replace prejudice with principle."[13]

Third, both sides agree on the importance of civility, tolerance, and pluralism, but disagree about what those commitments require. Supporters of people "of conscience" trying to "live out their faith" in the marketplace argue that robust protection of First Amendment freedoms everywhere – including the public square – is the only path to tolerance, civility, and peaceful coexistence. Defenders of full enforcement of modern civil rights law argue that civility and tolerance require that there be limits to acting on beliefs – however sincere and religiously motivated – in businesses open to the public; that is the "price of citizenship" that we pay in our "civic life."[14] In a religiously diverse nation, unless certain lines are drawn, every conscience would be "a law unto itself," raising "the prospect of constitutionally required religious exemptions from civil obligations of almost every conceivable kind."[15]

This chapter focuses primarily on the first set of contrasting arguments, since they most directly engage the rhetoric of bigotry and conscience.[16] It argues that the charge leveled by proponents of robust exemptions that people are being "branded as bigots" for their beliefs is often needless and provocative when directed at explanations about the constitutional limits of using religious and moral beliefs as a basis for (1) excluding others from a constitutional right or (2) denying them the protection of civil rights law. The mere step of drawing analogies between past and present forms of discrimination to point out how evolving understandings lead to recognition that such treatment lacks justification is not – in itself – a charge of bigotry. On the other hand, it is often needless and provocative for opponents of exemptions to indict religious belief as a "pretext" or "code word" for discrimination in order to justify limits to acting on such beliefs in the marketplace.[17] This chapter concludes

---

[12] For a chronology of state public accommodations laws extending to sexual orientation and gender identity, see Wilson, Chapter 30. For a listing of state anti-discrimination laws, see Appendix, Chapter 35.

[13] Dale, 530 U.S. at 664 (Stevens, J., dissenting).

[14] *See* Elane Photography, LLC v. Willock, 309 P.3d 53, 79–80 (N.M. 2013) *cert denied*, 134 S. Ct. 1787 (2014) (Bosson, J., concurring).

[15] Emp't Division v. Smith, 494 U.S. 872 (1990) (sustaining, against a Free Exercise challenge, denial of unemployment compensation when dismissal of employees for peyote ingestion was pursuant to a neutral, general applicable criminal law).

[16] For further elaboration, see LINDA C. MCCLAIN, THE RHETORIC OF BIGOTRY AND CONSCIENCE (forthcoming 2019).

[17] *See infra* III.A.1 for references.

with a brief comment on the oral argument in *Masterpiece Cakeshop*. During the argument, the parties and the justices debated the relevance of analogies to past civil rights battles and the Court's prior rulings upholding nondiscrimination laws. Also at issue was what the rhetoric of *Obergefell* implied about the requirements of civility and tolerance.

II THE US SUPREME COURT'S RHETORIC

The term "bigot" appears nowhere in the Supreme Court's four landmark opinions affirming the constitutional liberty and equality of gay men and lesbians: *Romer v. Evans, Lawrence v. Texas, United States v. Windsor*, and *Obergefell*.[18] In *Romer*, however, Justice Antonin Scalia's dissent charged Justice Anthony Kennedy's majority opinion as "verbally disparaging as bigotry" the "modest attempt by seemingly tolerant Coloradans to preserve traditional sexual mores" by passing a state constitutional amendment to bar "a politically powerful minority" (homosexuals) from "revis[ing] those mores through use of the laws."[19] What does it mean to brand someone as a bigot?

In *Windsor* and *Obergefell*, dissenters inferred a charge of bigotry from the majority's analogies between now-repudiated racial and sex-based inequality in the institution of marriage and exclusion of same-sex couples from marriage. Justice Samuel Alito pictured a future in which religious believers who "cling" to the traditional understanding of marriage could "whisper their thoughts [only] in their recesses of their homes," fearing that "if they repeat those views in public, they will risk being labeled [and treated] as bigots."[20]

The dissents also contrasted bigotry with conscience and sincerity. In *Obergefell*, Chief Justice John Roberts contended that the Court has "disparag[ed]" as "bigoted" the millions of Americans who, "as a matter of conscience, cannot accept same-sex marriage" or the Court's "better informed understanding" of marriage.[21] The passage in the *Obergefell* majority opinion that Roberts attacks warrants attention due to the

---

[18] Romer v. Evans, 517 U.S. 620 (1996) (holding that Colorado's Amendment 2, which prohibited any "protected status" based on "homosexual, lesbian, or bisexual orientation," violated the Equal Protection Clause of the Fourteenth Amendment of the U.S. Constitution); Lawrence v. Texas, 539 U.S. 558 (2003) (striking Texas law criminalizing consensual sodomy between two individuals "of the same sex" as violating constitutional "liberty" under the Due Process Clause of the of the 14th Amendment); United States v. Windsor, 570 U.S. 744 (2013) (striking portion of federal Defense of Marriage Act defining "marriage," for purposes of all federal laws pertaining to marriage, as only between one man and one woman and operating to deny federal recognition of same-sex marriages valid under state laws as violating the Due Process Clause of the Fifth Amendment); Obergefell, 135 S. Ct. 2584 (2015) (holding that same-sex couples have a fundamental right to marry as part of the "liberty" protected under the Due Process Clause of the Fourteenth Amendment).

[19] *Romer*, 517 U.S. at 636, 652 (Scalia, J., dissenting).

[20] *Obergefell*, 135 S. Ct. at 2642–43 (Alito, J., dissenting).

[21] *Id.* at 2626 (Roberts, C.J., dissenting).

central role it plays for both sides in post-*Obergefell* debates, including in *Masterpiece Cakeshop*. Justice Kennedy explained that constitutional rights – including the "right to marry" – arise not only from "history and tradition" but also from "a better informed understanding of how constitutional imperatives define a liberty that remains urgent in our own era."[22] Kennedy characterized opposition to same-sex marriage as based on "decent and honorable religious or philosophical premises," but explained: "when that sincere, personal opposition becomes enacted law and public policy, the necessary consequence is to put the imprimatur of the State itself on an exclusion that soon demeans or stigmatizes those whose own liberty is then denied."[23] Kennedy later stated that the First Amendment protects the ability of opponents of same-sex marriage to teach and advocate their beliefs, but the *state* may not "bar same-sex couples from marriage on the same terms as accorded to couples of the opposite sex."[24]

Critics of expansive nondiscrimination laws enlist Kennedy's opinion strategically to establish that believers seeking exemptions are not bigots; *Obergefell* promised that they would continue to be free to *express* their beliefs in the public square.[25] Defenders of state nondiscrimination laws, in turn, enlist *Obergefell*'s language to assert that such exemptions would put the state's "imprimatur" on religiously motivated discrimination.[26]

III BRANDING AS A BIGOT OR LEARNING FROM THE PAST?

Is it instructive to relate prior assertions of religious liberty and conscience in the context of opposition to laws barring discrimination on the basis of race to present-day assertions of religious liberty in the context of laws barring discrimination on the basis of sexual orientation and gender identity? Or does drawing such analogies brand people as bigots? The *Peaceful Coexistence* report (Report) released by the US Civil Rights Commission (Commission) and *Masterpiece Cakeshop* litigation illustrate competing answers.

A *The Civil Rights Commission's* Peaceful Coexistence *Report*

The Report's "Findings and Recommendations" nowhere use the rhetoric of bigotry in discussing the challenge of "reconciling nondiscrimination principles with civil liberties." Nonetheless, individual commissioners made oblique references to "bigotry." Parallels commissioners drew between religious justifications for racial segregation and the risks of religion – today – being used to justify "intolerance"

---

[22] *Id.* at 2602.
[23] *Id.*
[24] *Id.* at 2607.
[25] *See, e.g.,* Ryan Anderson, Chapter 27.
[26] *See, e.g.,* Melling, Chapter 19 (citing Kennedy's reference to the state's imprimatur).

and discrimination drew sharp criticism for "painting those who support religious freedom with the broad brush of bigotry."[27] Some critics, such as legal scholar Richard Epstein, asserted that the label "bigotry" better fits the "intolerant" commissioners.[28]

1 Analogies to the Past

The "Findings" link discrimination based on sexual orientation to other forms of discrimination, cautioning: "Religious exemptions to the protections of civil rights based upon classifications such as race, color, national origin, sex, disability status, sexual orientation, and gender identity, when they are permissible, significantly infringe upon these civil rights."[29] The Report recommends narrow tailoring of "religious exceptions to civil liberties and civil rights" because "[o]verly-broad religious exemptions unduly burden nondiscrimination laws and policies."[30]

Commission Chairman Martin R. Castro stated the following in connection with the Report's release:

> The phrases "religious liberty" and "religious freedom" will stand for nothing except hypocrisy so long as they remain code words for discrimination, intolerance, racism, sexism, homophobia, Islamophobia, Christian supremacy or any form of intolerance.[31]

Castro did not explicitly refer to "bigotry" in his statement. Still, "intolerance" and "discrimination" toward certain groups based on a group's belief or shared characteristic are, on many dictionary definitions, synonymous with bigotry.[32]

Castro insisted that the present "generation of Americans" must learn from past appeals to "religious liberty" used to justify slavery and racism:

> [T]oday, as in the past, religion is being used as both a weapon and a shield by those seeking to deny others equality. In our nation's past religion has been used to justify slavery and later, Jim Crow laws. We now see "religious liberty" arguments sneaking their way back into our political and constitutional discourses ... in an effort to undermine the rights of some Americans. This generation of Americans must stand up and speak out to ensure that religion never again be twisted to deny others the full promise of America.[33]

A rebuttal by several commissioners (including Castro) also shares this premise that, without vigilance, religion may be distorted to deny the equality of others. This

---

[27] USCCB Religious Liberty Chairman Responds, *supra* note 3.
[28] Epstein, *supra* note 4.
[29] Peaceful Coexistence, *supra* note 8, at 25 (Finding 3).
[30] *Id.* at 26 (Recommendation 1).
[31] Peaceful Coexistence, *supra* note 8, at 29 (statement of Chairman Martin R. Castro).
[32] *See Bigotry*, *supra* note 5 (listing synonyms).
[33] Peaceful Coexistence, *supra* note 8, at 29.

rebuttal also makes the implicit explicit: it *does* refer to bigotry and questions "sincerity."[34] The rebuttal decries a "new wave of laws" being proposed "to limit the freedoms of [LGBT] people" and to allow public and private actors to discriminate against them, including in commercial settings. The rebuttal refers to Mississippi's H.B. 1523 (the Protection of Conscience from Discrimination Act), North Carolina's H.B. 2, and various "bathroom bills" requiring transgender persons to use public facilities corresponding to their sex at birth.[35] This rebuttal asserts (in a section title): "These laws and proposals represent an orchestrated, nationwide effort by extremists to promote bigotry, *cloaked in the mantle of 'religious freedom.'*"[36]

Critics of the Report viewed the findings and recommendations and the commissioners' statements quoted earlier as tarring believers with the "brush" of bigotry. Commissioner Peter Kirsanow states that the "findings and recommendations lend credence to" Justice Alito's warnings, detailed earlier.[37] Kirsanow insisted that religious individuals "just want to be left alone" and not be forced by government – through nondiscrimination laws – to "associate" or to "speak."[38]

In her statement and rebuttal, Commissioner Gail Heriot quotes the prediction by legal scholar Mary Ann Glendon, in 2004 after Massachusetts began allowing same-sex couples to marry, of a "new era of intolerance and discrimination," in which "[e]very person and every religion that disagrees will be labeled as bigoted and openly discriminated against."[39]

Critical reactions to the Report focus particularly on Chairman Castro's statement.[40] In a letter to President Barack Obama, Senator Orin Hatch, Representative Paul Ryan, Archbishop William E. Lori, and sixteen other "American faith leaders" expressed "deep concern" about the Report. Citing Castro's statement, the letter demands that "no American citizen or institution be labeled by their government as bigoted because of their views and dismissed from the political life of our nation for holding those views."[41]

---

[34] *Id.* at 155, 160 (statement of Commissioners Achtenberg, Castro, Kladney, Narasaki, and Yaki Rebuttal).

[35] For critique of these laws, see Melling, Chapter 19; Pizer, Chapter 29; Wilson, Chapter 30.

[36] PEACEFUL COEXISTENCE, *supra* note 8, at 160 (statement of Commissioners Achtenberg, Castro, Kladney, and Yaki) (emphasis added).

[37] *Id.* at 42, 105 (statement of Commissioner Peter Kirsanow).

[38] *Id.* at 123.

[39] Mary Ann Glendon, *For Better for Worse*, WALL ST. J. (Feb. 25, 2004) (quoted in PEACEFUL COEXISTENCE, *supra* note 8, at 151 n. 52 (statement of Commissioner Gail Heriot and Rebuttal)).

[40] Nicholas Senz, *Obama Administration Says You're a Bigot if You Live Your Religion*, FEDERALIST (Sept. 19, 2016), http://thefederalist.com/2016/09/obama-administration-says-youre-bigot-live-religion.

[41] Letter from Most Reverend William E. Lori and Others to President Obama, Hon. Orrin G. Hatch, and Congressman Paul Ryan (Oct. 7, 2016).

2 Flipping the Charges of Bigotry and Intolerance

Some critics of the Report not only reject its implicit or explicit charge that opponents of nondiscrimination laws protecting LGBT people are bigots; they flip the charges of bigotry. Epstein insists that business owners who seek to live – and do business – according to their religious beliefs and are willing generally to serve gay and lesbian customers are not bigots. When they decline to violate their beliefs by helping to celebrate a same-sex marriage, their "conduct bears no relationship to a 'prejudiced or close-minded person, especially one who is intolerant or hostile towards different social groups.'"[42] By comparison:

> [T]he words "bigotry" and "phobia" clearly do apply to the five commissioners who happily denounce people like Stutzman [a florist who declined to arrange flowers for a gay customer's wedding] ... They show no tolerance, let alone respect, for people with whom they disagree ... They show deep prejudice and hostility to all people of faith.[43]

Simply to point out the appeal to religion in justifying prior forms of discrimination, as Castro does, is not to argue that religious beliefs equal bigotry. That said, there are better ways to express this point than Castro's rhetoric of pretext and weaponizing religion, as some of the arguments made in *Masterpiece Cakeshop* illustrate.

B *Masterpiece Cakeshop*

In *Masterpiece Cakeshop*, the Supreme Court will decide the appeal of the self-described "cake artist" Jack Phillips, who asks the Court to decide "whether applying Colorado's public accommodations law to compel artists to create expression that violates their sincerely held religious beliefs about marriage violates the Free Speech or Free Exercise Clauses of the First Amendment."[44] Phillips, the owner of Masterpiece Cakeshop, appeals a decision by the Colorado Court of Appeals that he violated the public accommodations provision of the Colorado Antidiscrimination Act (CADA) when, citing his religious beliefs, he declined to bake a cake for a celebration of Charlie Craig and David Mullins' wedding ceremony. The Colorado Court of Appeals affirmed a prior decision by the Colorado Civil Rights Commission, which upheld an administrative law judge's decision that Phillips violated CADA and that denying him an exemption did not violate his First Amendment rights.[45]

---

[42] Epstein, *supra* note 4 (using Wikipedia's definitions).
[43] *Id.*
[44] Brief for Petitioners, Masterpiece Cakeshop et al. v. Colorado Civil Rights Commission et al., No. 16–111, at I.
[45] Craig v. Masterpiece Cakeshop, 370 P.3d 272 (Col. Ct. App. 2015), *cert denied sub nom* Masterpiece Cakeshop v. Colorado Civil Rights Comm'n, 2016 WL 1645027 (Colo. 2016).

The rhetoric of bigotry and conscience has been deployed in this litigation by both sides to analogize between past and present civil rights battles. This section first examines arguments made by Phillips and his *amici*, then considers arguments made by respondents Colorado Civil Rights Commission (CCRC), Craig and Mullins, and their *amici*. On each side, only a minority of the *amicus* briefs explicitly use the rhetoric of bigotry – fourteen of those filed in support of Phillips; nine of those filed in support of respondents.[46] It is instructive to examine the usage of that term.

1 Arguments by Phillips and His Amici

Phillips and his *amici* contend that compelling him to "design" a "custom" wedding cake for a same-sex couple unconstitutionally forces him to "celebrate same-sex marriage," which he "in good conscience" cannot do, since he "seeks to live his life, pursue his profession, and craft his art consistently with his religious identity."[47] Phillips argues Colorado violated the First Amendment by compelling a private citizen "to utter what is not in his mind."[48] In support, Phillips invokes the famous compulsory flag salute case, *West Virginia v. Barnette*.[49]

These briefs also quote from Justice Kennedy's majority opinion in *Obergefell* and argue that a ruling against Phillips would fail to realize *Obergefell*'s "laudable effort to promote tolerance and mutual respect in a pluralistic national community."[50] Unless the Supreme Court reverses, the *amici* contend, it will send a message that Phillips is a bigot, a pariah, properly excluded from the public square – contrary to *Obergefell*'s "promise" to conscientious dissenters about their First Amendment rights. The path to peaceful coexistence lies in exemptions in case of such "decent and honorable" beliefs, so that people of faith are not driven from public life.[51] Their dignitary and other interests are harmed far more than those of a would-be customer denied service in the current gay-friendly marketplace.[52]

a SHOWING "HOSTILITY" TOWARD PHILLIPS'S RELIGION Phillips and several of his *amici* assert that the CCRC and the Colorado appellate court showed "hostility"

---

[46] This count reflects electronic searches of the briefs for "bigot," "bigoted," and "bigotry."
[47] Brief for Petitioners, *supra* note 44, at 14–17.
[48] *Id.* at 2.
[49] *Id.* at 3, 15 (citing W. Va. Bd. v. Barnette, 319 U.S. 624 (1943)). This chapter focuses more on Phillips's Free Exercise claim than his compelled expression/speech claim.
[50] Brief of Amici Curiae 34 Legal Scholars in Support of Petitioners, Masterpiece Cakeshop et al. v. Colorado Civil Rights Commission et al., No. 16–111, at 14–17, at 27. All the amicus briefs from this litigation are available at: http://www.scotusblog.com/case-files/cases/masterpiece-cakeshop-ltd-v-colorado-civil-rights-commn/.
[51] For similar views, see Ryan Anderson, Chapter 27.
[52] For other weighing of burdens, see Laycock, Chapter 3.

toward his religion. They cite this remark made by a commissioner in proceedings before the CCRC:

> Freedom of religion and religion have been used to justify all kinds of discrimination throughout history, whether it be slavery, whether it be the [H]olocaust, … we can list hundreds of situations where freedom of religion has been used to justify discrimination. And to me it is one of the most despicable pieces of rhetoric that people … use their religion to hurt others.[53]

Amicus Liberty Counsel argues this remark illustrates that CCRC has "fully embraced [the idea] that religious beliefs must take a back seat to eliminating what it views as discrimination based on sexual orientation, because religious freedom is just an excuse to justify hurting other people."[54] Phillips argues that the CCRC's "disdain" for his "religious views" is also evident from its permitting three other bakers to decline to create cakes with "offensive" messages expressing disapproval of same-sex marriage.[55] *Amicus* William Jack, who requested those three cakes, contends that the CCRC "expressed hostility towards [his] traditional religious views" as being "odious."[56]

It bears noting that, in affirming the CCRC's ruling against Phillips, the Colorado Court of Appeals neither denied the "sincerity" of Phillips's religious beliefs about marriage nor called him a "bigot." The court did, however, draw on precedents rejecting religious defenses to public accommodations laws to explain that the freedom to act on religious beliefs has limits. It cited *Newman v. Piggie Park Enterprises*, a 1966 case in which the federal district court in South Carolina refused "to lend credence or support to [the restaurant owner's] position that he has a constitutional right to refuse to serve members of the Negro race in his business establishment upon the ground that to do so would violate his sacred religious beliefs."[57] Quoting *Piggie Park*, the Colorado court explained that, while free exercise includes a "'right to espouse beliefs of [one's] own choosing,'" it does not include "the absolute right to exercise and practice such beliefs in utter disregard of the clear constitutional rights of other citizens."[58] So, too, the court reasoned, if Masterpiece Cakeshop wishes to operate as a "public accommodation" and "conduct business" in Colorado, CADA "prohibits it from picking and choosing customers based on their sexual orientation."[59]

---

53 Brief for Petitioners, *supra* note 44, at 43.
54 Brief of Amicus Curiae Liberty Counsel in Support of Petitioner Seeking Reversal, at 40.
55 Brief for Petitioners, *supra* note 44, at 40–43.
56 Brief of Amici Curiae William Jack and the National Center for Law and Policy in Support of Petitioners, at 2, 16.
57 *Masterpiece Cakeshop*, 370 P.3d at 280.
58 *Id.* at 291 (quoting Newman v. Piggie Park Enterprises, 256 F. Supp. at 941, 945 (D.S. C. 1966), aff'd, 377 F.2d 433 (4th Cir. 1967), aff'd, 390 U.S. 400 (1968) (per curiam)).
59 *Id.* at 292.

In concluding that CADA, a neutral law of general applicability, was constitutional, the court related the US Supreme Court's recognition of states' "compelling" interest in eliminating discrimination on the basis of race and sex in places of
public accommodation to Colorado's interest in eliminating discrimination in such
places on the basis of sexual orientation. It concluded that CADA "creates a
hospitable environment for all consumers," which "prevents the economic and
social balkanization prevalent when businesses decide to serve only their own
'kind.'"[60]

b MERCHANTS OF "GOOD CONSCIENCE" ARE NOT BIGOTS Phillips and his *amici*
contrast the religious believer with "decent and honorable" beliefs about marriage
with the racist and the homophobe. Phillips, "a conscientious man of faith," "gladly
serves people from all walks of life, including individuals of all races, faiths, and
sexual orientations," but simply "declines all requests ... to create custom artistic
expression that conflicts with his faith."[61] This conscience-driven refusal to express a
message, in this instance "celebrating same-sex marriage," one *amicus* argues, is not
the "invidious discrimination" like that at the core of laws banning discrimination in
public accommodations; in those instances, "a merchant objects to serving some
people just because and on the ground that they are black, or female ... or gay."[62]

A number of *amici* enlist the rhetoric of bigotry in urging the Supreme Court to
reverse. In arguing that Phillips has been "branded" a bigot, some remind the Court
of the prediction in Justice Alito's *Obergefell* dissent: "Colorado has unquestionably
labeled and treated Petitioner as a bigot."[63] The *amicus curiae* brief filed by Sherif
Girgis and Robert George suggests that denying Phillips's claim will "tell him – and
all traditional Muslims, Orthodox Jews, and Christians – that acting on beliefs
central to his identity is wrong, benighted, even bigoted"; *Obergefell* "expressly"
rejects sending such a message.[64] Asserting that Craig and Mullins "suffered no
material harm" from Phillips' refusal, another *amicus curiae* brief emphasizes the
harms suffered by Phillips: "the State has effectively branded him a bigot and
rendered him something of an outcast, seriously harming his reputation in the
community."[65]

c REJECTING ANALOGIES TO PAST CIVIL RIGHTS STRUGGLES *Amici* for Phillips
argue that past civil rights struggles are not relevant to Phillips's refusal of service

---

[60] *Id.* at 293–94.
[61] Brief for Petitioners, *supra* note 44, at 8–9, 52.
[62] Brief of Amici Curiae 34 Legal Scholars, *supra* note 50, at 13.
[63] Brief of North Carolina Family Values Coalition and the Family Research Council as Amici
Curiae in Support of Petitioners, at 22.
[64] Brief of *Amicus Curiae* Sherif Girgis Supporting Petitioners, at 17. Robert George appears as
counsel of record.
[65] Brief of the Ethics & Religious Liberty Commission of the Southern Baptist Convention et al.
in Support of Petitioners, at 30.

to Craig and Mullins: "Public-accommodations concerns of past eras are not present here."[66] One reason is that "the artist plainly did not act out of invidious discrimination" but instead out of concern not to "violate [his] conscience."[67] Another is the distinction between genuine public accommodations, "like restaurants and hotels," and "customized pieces of art," like wedding cakes.[68] A third is that Craig and Mullins "had immediate access to other artists,"[69] unlike racial minorities discriminated against under the Jim Crow practices that Title II sought to end. Some *amici* treat Title II as the paradigm of a narrowly tailored public accommodations law, contrasting CADA as an inappropriate expansion of nondiscrimination law that, instead of remedying discrimination, now is a "source" of it.[70] Such expansion has led, as Chief Justice Rehnquist predicted in *Dale*, to clashes with First Amendment rights.

Other *amici* concede the general legitimacy of including "sexual orientation" protections in nondiscrimination law, but argue that goods and services related to same-sex weddings are a special case. One brief asserts that Phillips simply refuses to "use his artistic gifts to provide a particular service" because he believes it "contrary to God's law and biblical teachings."[71] Notably, the *amicus* brief filed by Utah Republican State Senators argues that, "in Republican-controlled 'red' states, the lack of protections for LGBT [sic] in places of public accommodations leave them exposed to potential abuses most Americans would find deplorable."[72] But red states such as Utah, they argue, have not extended their public accommodations law to include "sexual orientation" out of concern that such laws might not adequately protect the First Amendment rights of "conscientious objectors" such as Phillips.[73]

d DOWNPLAYING THE ROLE OF RELIGION IN PAST DEFENSES OF RACISM AND DISCRIMINATION Some *amici* reject any comparison between Phillips's "decent and honorable" beliefs about marriage and religious justifications for segregation and antimiscegenation laws. For example, in his brief, Ryan T. Anderson of the Heritage Foundation (who is also writing for this volume) contrasts opposition to interracial marriage, rooted in "racist bigotry," with support for marriage as a

---

[66] Brief for the States of Texas, Alabama, et al. as Amici Curiae in Support of Petitioners, at 3.
[67] *Id.* at 3.
[68] *Id.*
[69] *Id.*
[70] Brief of Liberty Counsel, *supra* note 54, at 18.
[71] Brief of *Amici Curiae* 34 Legal Scholars, *supra* note 50, at 26.
[72] Brief of *Amici Curiae* Utah Republican State Senators in Support of Petitioners and Reversal, at 3. The brief notes that Utah passed "compromise" legislation "add[ing] sexual orientation to the state's housing and employment discrimination laws," in employment and housing, but could not reach agreement on a similar expansion of its public accommodations law. *Id.* at 24–25. For an account of Utah's law and why it did not address public accommodations, see Adams, Chapter 32.
[73] Brief of *Amici Curiae* Utah Republican State Senators, *supra* note 72, at 4–11.

"conjugal union of husband and wife," rooted in "decent and honorable premises."[74]

To rule for Phillips would send "no message about the supposed inferiority of people who identify as gay," but instead a message "that citizens who support the historic understanding of marriage are not bigots and that the state may not drive them out of business and civic life."[75]

Anderson downplays the pervasiveness and sincerity of religious rationales marshaled in the past for racial segregation and against interracial marriage: the "wicked system of white supremacy" was rooted in "bigotry," "animus," and convictions about racial hierarchy. For Anderson, political leaders' appeal to theology to justify racial "subordination" showed how religion "was perverted to justify racism and slavery."[76] Missing is recognition that white segregationists vehemently denied charges of bigotry and insisted they were waging a war of morality and conscience, with God on their side.[77] The "theology of segregation" sounded in pulpits and pages of the Congressional Record.[78] Further, even some who came to oppose legal segregation believed that there were "decent and honorable" grounds for opposing interracial marriage. In 1963, when asked whether racial integration would lead to "inter-marriage," President Harry Truman, who issued an executive order initiating the desegregation of the military and created the President's Commission on Civil Rights, answered: "I hope not. I don't believe in it. The Lord created it that way. You read your Bible and you'll find out."[79]

e THE DEMANDS OF TOLERANCE Some *amici* assert that Colorado has been *intolerant* toward Phillips and his sincere religious beliefs. Thus, Epstein repeats the charges of intolerance he sounded against Commissioners on the US Civil Rights Commission, decrying "state coercion" against "the few vulnerable family firms" – such as Masterpiece – that raise conscience-based objections"; the brief asserts that Phillips "and others like him have repeatedly been victimized by such actions."[80]

---

[74] *Amicus Curiae* Brief of Ryan T. Anderson, Ph.D. and African-American and Civil Rights Leaders in Support of Petitioners, at 3–4. *See also* Ryan Anderson, Chapter 27 (urging that governments can "address minorities" precise needs without punishing reasonable citizens for acting on decent and honorable beliefs).

[75] *Amicus Curiae* Brief of Ryan T. Anderson, *supra* note 74, at 3–4. *See also* Ryan Anderson, Chapter 27, for similar claim that protecting Phillips's "freedom here sends no message about the supposed inferiority of those identifying as gay; it sends no message about sexual orientation at all. It says that citizens who support the historic understanding of sex and marriage are not bigots".

[76] *Amicus Curiae* Brief of Ryan T. Anderson, *supra* note 74, at 15–16.

[77] For examples, *see* McClain, *supra* note 16.

[78] *See, e.g.,* Reverend G.T. Gillespie, *A Southern Christian Looks at the Race Problem*, S. Presbyterian J. (June 5, 1857), reprinted at 103 Cong. Rec. A6511 (Aug. 9, 1957) (85th Cong., 1st Sess.).

[79] James E. Fleming & Linda C. McClain, Ordered Liberty 173 (2013) (citation omitted).

[80] Brief of *Amici Curiae* Law and Economics Scholars in Support of Petitioners, at 22–23.

Another brief asserts that "secular ideologies increasingly employ the strong arm of the state to advance their causes, promoting tolerance and respect for some while ruthlessly suppressing others," forgetting that "tolerance is a two-way street."[81] This argument that Colorado was intolerant toward Phillips prefigures Justice Kennedy's chiding of Colorado at oral argument that "tolerance is most meaningful when it's mutual;" Colorado, Kennedy asserted, "has been neither tolerant nor respectful of Mr. Phillips' religious beliefs."[82]

2 Arguments by Respondents and Their Amici

Of the forty-six *amicus* briefs filed on behalf of respondents CCRC and Craig and Mullins, only nine explicitly use the terms "bigot," bigoted," or "bigotry," and just six do so in their argument.[83] None explicitly labels Phillips a bigot. Do they, nonetheless, imply that he is one? This section examines some of those briefs, using one as a doorway into examining an argument that some commentators view as labeling religious persons as bigots: "we have heard this before and should learn the lessons of history." Many *amici* argue that the long history of asserting a variety of First Amendment justifications for racial and sex discrimination – and of courts eventually rejecting such justifications – affords reasons for courts to reject present-day religious and other justifications for sexual orientation discrimination in the context of marriage, or, more broadly, for LGBT discrimination. The same "principles" that underlie landmark federal public accommodations laws apply to the expansion of state laws to include sexual orientation (and, some *amici* add, gender identity). They warn that recognizing exemptions based on conscience or religious beliefs threatens to reverse hard-won progress in protecting civil rights and may put the state's "imprimatur" on discrimination.

a DO AMICI BRAND PHILLIPS AS A BIGOT? The *amicus* brief filed by the Lambda Legal Defense and Education Fund *et al.* refers to bigotry not in marketplace discrimination but in violence against LGBT persons:

Because anti-LGBT discrimination is pervasive and results in fears that hostility may lurk behind any counter or storefront, this community has created "safe spaces," in which to relax and let down their guard ... Tragically, as the violent Pulse nightclub massacre in Florida last year shows, even in such safe spaces

---

[81] Brief of North Carolina Values Association, *supra* note 63, at 3–4.
[82] Transcript of Oral Argument, Masterpiece Cakeshop v. Colorado Civil Rights Comm'n, No. 16–111, at 62.
[83] Three amicus briefs refer to "bigotry" only in the statements of interests of amici as organizations dedicated to fighting bigotry.

members of the LGBT community may be targets of life-shattering, even life-ending bigotry.[84]

Putting the stamp of governmental approval on discrimination has "dangerous repercussions," including more discrimination and an increased risk of anti-LGBT violence. The brief mirrors the *Peaceful Coexistence* report in defending Colorado's nondiscrimination law's choice of "a path of peaceful coexistence and equal access in public life."[85] The brief does not question the sincerity of Phillips' religious belief, but explains the "dangerous ripple effects" of recognizing religious or creative expression exemptions to nondiscrimination laws. Enlisting *Obergefell*, the brief cautions: "When even 'sincere, personal opposition' to treating LGBT people equally 'becomes enacted law and public policy, the necessary consequence is to put the imprimatur of the State itself on exclusion that soon demeans or stigmatizes those whose own liberty is then denied.'"[86]

A second brief does not explicitly call Phillips a bigot, but observes that *Loving* and *Bob Jones University* illustrate that "much prejudice against people of different races in the United States was justified on religious grounds, and racists often still base their bigotry on their religious faith."[87] The brief warns that precedents such as *Bob Jones* might be at risk if the Court allows "religious preferences and beliefs" to be sufficient to exempt Phillips from CADA. The brief counters Phillips's theory that Craig and Mullins suffered minimal harm, being denied service at a *particular* business: "The true harm comes from being the victim of bigotry, and not necessarily that from the inconvenience of seeking alternative providers."[88]

A third brief states: "CADA forbids discrimination on the basis of sexual orientation – whether motivated by pure bigotry, secular morality, or religious belief."[89] The brief presents Phillips's free exercise claim as a "sympathetic case," posing a dilemma of "conscience." Nonetheless, invoking *Smith*, it warns that there is no principled limit to the conscience exemption Phillips seeks, anticipating numerous clashes between "commands of conscience" and laws "that protect fundamental rights, equal protection, health and safety, free markets, or other social goods."[90]

A fourth brief that mentions "bigotry," filed by the Central Conference of Rabbis, rejects the oppositional framing of "religious liberty versus LGBT rights," pointing to "broad religious support for LGBT nondiscrimination."[91] The explicit reference to

[84] Brief of *Amici Curiae* Lambda Legal Defense and Education Fund, Inc. et al. in Support of Respondents, at 37–38.
[85] *Id.* at 3.
[86] *Id.* at 39–40 (quoting *Obergefell*, 135 S. Ct. at 2602).
[87] Brief of *Amici Curiae* the Center for Inquiry et al. in Support of Respondents, at 25.
[88] *Id.* at 26–27.
[89] Brief of Church-State Scholars as *Amici Curiae* in Support of Respondents, at 4.
[90] *Id.* at 12 (quoting *Smith*, 494 U.S. at 890). For other discussion of *Smith*, see Brownstein, Chapter 2; Laycock, Chapter 3; Krotoszynski, Chapter 7.
[91] Brief for *Amici Curiae* the Central Conference of Rabbis in Support of Respondents, at 18–19.

bigotry occurs when the brief recounts some religious leaders' opposition to Mississippi's HB 1523: "Rabbi Jeffrey Simons perceived [HB 1523] as being 'not about religion … [but] about bigotry.'"[92]

Another brief critiques the claim by Phillips and his supporters that people of faith are being branded as bigots when public accommodations laws are applied to them: "Opponents contend that they are the victims of secularism – positioned as bigots and pariahs – then leverage that narrative to assert that they are not bigots at all because they are not discriminating based on sexual orientation. Instead, they are making a choice to reject *conduct* – marriage."[93] The brief positions this attempt to distinguish between identity (status) and conduct (marriage) in a longer history of opposing "civil rights gains for the LGBT community." Notably, this brief does not rely on analogies to racial discrimination, but charts the shifting rationales offered to oppose civil rights for LGBT people, interlacing the Court's own trajectory from *Bowers v. Hardwick* to *Obergefell* and its rejection of the status-conduct distinction.[94]

b LEARNING FROM THE PAST The *amicus* brief filed by Massachusetts, along with eighteen other states and the District of Columbia, illustrates a theme in many briefs filed in support of upholding Colorado's law: "history has taught us to be wary" of the assertion of Free Exercise claims to justify "refus[ing] equal service to certain members of the public based on its owner's personal beliefs."[95] Public accommodations laws are "a centerpiece of state efforts to combat the economic, personal, and social harms caused by invidious discrimination," including that experienced by LGBTQ people.[96]

The argument that "we have heard this kind of claim before"[97] draws direct analogies between the role of religious beliefs to justify racial and sexual orientation discrimination. In *Piggie Park*, the brief observes, the Supreme Court characterized as "patently frivolous" the business owner's assertion of a constitutional right not to violate his "sacred religious beliefs" about segregation as the reason for his "refusal to serve members of the Negro race."[98] It then asserts: "Businesses today have no more of a right to justify their discrimination against LGBTQ individuals on religious grounds."

Motive for discrimination, the brief insists, does not matter. Thus, to Phillips' question "whether the States' compelling interest in combatting discrimination

---

[92] *Id.* at 20 (citation omitted).

[93] Brief of *Amici Curiae* Legal Scholars in Support of Equality in Support of Respondents, at 10.

[94] *Id.* at 14–19.

[95] Brief of Massachusetts et al. as *Amici Curiae* in Support of Respondents, at 2.

[96] *Id.* at 2, 4–10. For an argument that LGBT discrimination is separable from the invidious discrimination that provoked Title II, see Ryan Anderson, Chapter 27.

[97] Brief of Massachusetts et al., *supra* note 95, at 2.

[98] *Id.* at 26 (citing *Piggie Park*, 390 U.S. at 402 n.5). For distinctions between religious arguments made to support racial discrimination and those made in the wedding context, see Perry, Chapter 20.

extends to discrimination motivated by 'sincerely held religious beliefs,'" the brief insists "the answer is a resounding 'yes.'"[99]

The Massachusetts brief's single reference to "bigotry" appears in the context of citing the recent violence in Charlottesville and the sizable minority of the public who disapprove of interracial marriage:

> It remains a sad fact of American society that bigoted beliefs are disturbingly prevalent. Under Petitioners' theory, an anti-Semitic baker could refuse to sell a wedding cake to a Jewish couple because he does not wish 'to create expression that he considers objectionable.' ... And a racist architect could refuse to design a family home for an interracial couple on the same grounds.[100]

While the First Amendment "tolerates all manner of odious speech in the public square," the brief adds, it does not insulate businesses from liability for such refusals.[101]

Without referring to bigotry, the NAACP Legal Defense and Educational Fund also sounds the theme of learning from history, relating the denial of service to three would-be customers in 2012 – Mr. Mullins, Mr. Craig, and Mr. Craig's mother (Deborah Munn) – to the denial of service at a barbeque to three African-American customers in 1964 – leading to *Piggie Park*.[102] The brief observes that, at the time of the Court's decision, the restaurant owner's "religious beliefs were relatively mainstream." He was not viewed as "fringe or disingenuous," making the Court's ruling all the more significant.[103]

This brief highlights the appeal to religious beliefs to justify now-repudiated forms of discrimination, emphasizing that such beliefs were not isolated, marginal positions, but sincerely and widely held and articulated. "[T]he overarching lesson of *Piggie Park*, *Bob Jones*, and *Loving* is that this Court has repeatedly and unambiguously rejected religious-based justifications for differential treatment ... for good reasons: the government has a compelling interest in combating discrimination in its various forms."[104] *Amicus* American Bar Association adds that such "historic decisions" as *Piggie Park* and *Bob Jones* contributed to the eventual emergence of a "settled social consensus" despite the many "passionate" and "sincere" moral and religious objections to Title II: "business owners who offer their goods and service to the public cannot claim constitutional sanctuary from public accommodations laws."[105]

---

[99] Brief of Massachusetts et al., *supra* note 95, at 21.
[100] *Id.* at 32.
[101] *Id.*
[102] Brief of Amicus Curiae NAACP Legal Defense & Educational Fund, Inc. in Support of Respondents, at 2–3.
[103] *Id.* at 14 (citing media coverage of Mr. Bessinger).
[104] *Id.* at 15.
[105] Brief of the American Bar Association as *Amici Curiae* In Support of Respondents, at 5, 21.

At the *Masterpiece Cakeshop* oral argument, the liberal justices brought up *Piggie Park*, along with other civil rights era cases, in questioning petitioners' First Amendment claims.[106] They expressed concern that an exemption could undermine the entire structure of nondiscrimination laws.[107] On the other hand, after observing that "the racial analogy obviously is very compelling," Chief Justice Roberts pointed out that *Obergefell* "went out of its way to talk about the decent and honorable people who may have opposing views."[108] Phillips, on this reading of *Obergefell*, is morally distinct from a racist. Whether this distinction is enough to justify exempting him from Colorado's laws remains to be seen.

IV CONCLUSION

Charges of "branding as a bigot" often stem from analogies between past and present forms of exclusion and injustice. These charges are often needless and provocative. The mere step of drawing analogies between past and present forms of discrimination to point out how, over time, new insights and evolving understandings lead to recognition that such treatment lacks justification is not a charge of bigotry. Nor should a charge of bigotry be inferred simply from explanations about the constitutional limits of using religious and moral beliefs as a basis for (1) excluding others from a constitutional right (such as the fundamental right to marry) or (2) denying them the protection of civil rights laws. On the other hand, it is needlessly provocative to indict religious beliefs as a "pretext" or "code word" for discrimination in order to explain that there must be limits to acting on such beliefs – however sincere – in the marketplace. The better path, modeled by Justice Bosson's concurring opinion in *Elane Photography*, is to speak in terms of the requirements of civility and tolerance, or the "price of citizenship" in a pluralistic society.[109] Bosson attempted to address the business owners "with utmost respect," while explaining that their freedom to live out their religious beliefs "wherever they lead" in their personal lives must have some limits in "our civic life," including public accommodations. He focuses on the strength of the state's interest in the terms of that civic life to show the force of analogy: "the [state] legislature has made it clear that to discriminate in business on the basis of sexual orientation is just as intolerable as discrimination directed toward race, color, national origin, or religion."[110]

What will the Supreme Court say about whether this "price of citizenship" is too high? It is always difficult to read tea leaves predicting the outcome in closely watched cases, but the oral argument suggested that concern for "tolerance and mutual respect" may prove key to Justice Kennedy, widely believed to be the crucial

[106] Oral Argument, *supra* note 82, at 20–21 (Justice Sotomayor).
[107] *Id.* at 43–44 (Justice Souter).
[108] *Id.* at 73.
[109] *See Elane Photography*, 309 P.3d at 79–80 (Bosson, J., concurring).
[110] *Id.*

fifth vote for the majority. Kennedy appeared troubled *both* by Phillips's efforts to draw lines to carve out an exception from state nondiscrimination laws for "compelled expression" *and* by a lack of tolerance and respect shown by the Commission toward Phillips's religion. Kennedy focused on whether the comment of one of the commissioners, discussed earlier, expressed "hostility" toward Phillips' religion. Kennedy chided counsel for the CCRC for its treatment of Phillips, admonishing that "tolerance is essential in a free society" and should be "mutual."[111] Kennedy also seemed sympathetic to the argument that public accommodations laws like CADA could exempt merchants like Phillips, so long as a gay couple could readily find the same good or service elsewhere. Even so, he expressed concern that a ruling for Phillips could allow a "boycott" of "gay marriage" and be "an affront to the gay community."[112] Perhaps the Court may avoid ruling on the merits, given the many quagmires about finding any line that would not undermine nondiscrimination law – not to mention its own precedents (including *Obergefell*). It might, for example, remand to afford the Commission (minus the "hostile" Commissioner) or the Colorado legislature a chance to craft some kind of exemption that would not be an "affront" to would-be customers such as Craig and Mullins, but also show (in Kennedy's words) more tolerance and respect toward Phillips. If nothing else, the *Masterpiece* litigation shows the many constitutional and political commitments at stake and the importance from learning from the past as states attempt to protect against discrimination, based on evolving insights and understandings. The path forward from *Obergefell* to a more tolerant and respectful society is being charted by the Court, federal and state lawmakers, civil rights advocates, and scholars in volumes such as this.

---

[111] Oral Argument, *supra* note 82, at 62.
[112] *Id.* at 27.

18

Against "Civil Rights" Simplism

How Not to Accommodate Competing Legal Commitments

Steven D. Smith

Contrary to earlier assurances, the legalization of same-sex marriage and the advancement of LGBT rights have in recent years generated numerous conflicts between nondiscrimination laws and the conscientious reservations of some merchants or professionals – reservations that resonate with longstanding commitments to freedom of religion and freedom of expression.[1] These conflicts are often in the news: most everyone has heard of the wedding photographer case, the florist case, and the baker cases.[2] So, how should society attempt to resolve these conflicts between legal commitments sounding variously in equality, freedom of religion, and freedom of expression?

How such conflicts are resolved is a crucially important but formidably difficult question, to which there is not a simple answer. In fact, that is this chapter's essential claim: there is no simple way to resolve the conflicts between nondiscrimination laws and the commitments to the freedoms of religion and expression. This may seem like a disappointingly paltry contribution to the very important discussion undertaken in this volume. But the claim is more significant than it seems for one key reason: so many of those who weigh in on the issue – judges, lawyers, advocates generally – seem to believe that there *is* a simple way to resolve the conflicts.[3] More specifically, many or even most advocates attempt or purport to resolve the conflicts by one or both of two simple expedients: they ascribe unsavory or reprehensible motives to their opponents, or they draw simplistic analogies to other controversies that go under the generic label of "civil rights."[4]

---

[1] For examples of such assurances, see Steven Smith, *What* Masterpiece Cakeshop *Is Really About*, Pub. Discourse (Oct. 24, 2017), https://perma.cc/M6ZZ-N7GE .

[2] For other instances, see McClain, Chapter 17; Wilson, Chapter 30.

[3] *See, e.g.*, Melling, Chapter 19.

[4] *See* Kirsten Powers, *Jim Crow Laws for Gays and Lesbians?*, USA Today (Feb. 18, 2014), https://perma.cc/4YTU-YWHQ.

Such "civil rights" simplism fails to generate just or stable resolutions to the controversies. More generally, and more troublingly, such simplisms do great damage to the fabric of our society and our civil discourse. In the unlikely event that scholars, judges, lawyers, and citizens generally could be persuaded to forbear from such rhetorically powerful but simplistic approaches, it is at least possible that society might make progress toward achieving more just and enduring resolutions of the conflicts that divide us.

Section I of this chapter discusses reasons why particular kinds of simplistic arguments have come to be common and almost mandatory in contemporary discourse. Section II considers and criticizes one virtually ubiquitous and simplistic form of argumentation – the ascription of *animus* or hatred to one's opponents. Section III considers and criticizes a different but also familiar form of argumentation – the lumping together of discrete issues with different histories and different sociological features under the general heading of "civil rights." The Conclusion suggests that a more constructive and healthy public discourse will need to become at once more prudential and more visionary than these familiar simplisms attempt to be.

I THE PARADOXICALLY IMPOVERISHED CONDITION OF CONTEMPORARY PUBLIC DISCOURSE

The almost irresistible appeal of the simplistic approaches is best appreciated against the backdrop of the impoverished condition of our public discourse. Other things being equal, of course, simplicity is generally deemed a virtue in a position or theory, as the maxim known as Ockham's razor instructs us.[5] Further, the limitations of a sound-bite political culture will in many contexts make rhetorical simplicity virtually mandatory. But even beyond these generic and perennial advantages, "civil rights" simplisms flourish like weeds in the barren field of contemporary public discourse for a number of reasons.

The dismal condition of current discourse is a phenomenon on which critics of various philosophical and political inclinations have commented. Philosopher Ronald Dworkin, for example, contended that "[w]e have not managed to construct even the beginnings of a decent public argument about … matters [of human rights, religious freedom, taxes, and other public issues]."[6] He thought that "our politics are now so debased that they threaten our standing as a genuine democracy."[7] Actually, Dworkin issued this indictment just over a decade ago, but does anyone suppose that he would have offered a more positive assessment if he had lived to witness the 2016 primary and general elections?

---

[5] *Occam's Razor*, ENCYCLOPEDIA BRITANNICA, https://perma.cc/E3HF-FC3C (preferring, of two competing theories, the simpler explanation).

[6] RONALD DWORKIN, IS DEMOCRACY POSSIBLE HERE? 127 (2006).

[7] *Id*. at 130.

In one sense this situation is puzzling because it might seem that education and communication are more advanced and universally available today than they have been in other places and historical periods, and that virtually all the moral and political thought of the past two or three millennia is now available to most Americans with the click of a mouse. So, one might think that public deliberations ought to be richer and more sophisticated today than they have ever been. But, paradoxically, the very abundance of political and moral perspectives and theories can work to make public discourse more pathetically threadbare.

That is because public discourse needs to proceed on premises that are shared – to proceed within an area of "overlapping consensus," to borrow philosopher John Rawls's familiar formulation.[8] Or so it may seem.[9] This apparent imperative may derive either from normative political philosophy (like Rawls's) or from mundane political prudence: it is easier to reason with people if you start with premises that they accept. But as normative perspectives and positions multiply and are increasingly all over the map, the area of "overlapping consensus" is likely to shrink, almost to the vanishing point. Thus, by contrast to the kinds of searching discussions that can flourish among people who share substantive premises and a fundamental normative framework (libertarians, economists, Kantians, natural law theorists), advocates who enter into the public arena may find themselves with few shared views from which to reason.

And yet there are still a few ideas or propositions that are generally if not universally shared among Americans. Consider three. One such proposition is that the satisfaction of desires or preferences is, *prima facie*, a good thing. Indeed, that idea helps to explain the influence of economics, and the near ubiquity of instrumentalist reasoning (even in constitutional law[10]) and of rational choice theory and similar modes of thought in academic contexts. And yet it seems that many of the deepest human concerns and commitments – concerns and commitments that we tend to designate with terms like "rights," "justice," "human dignity," and "conscience" – resist being instrumentalized or are instrumentalized only at the cost of serious distortion.

For these sorts of concerns, society typically wants to engage in a more "moral" or "normative" deliberation. At least two additional shared propositions can serve to advance that sort of deliberation. (1) It is bad or wrong to act out of mere hatred or (as the courts like to say) "*animus.*" Gratuitous deprivations or indignities are to be

---

[8] JOHN RAWLS, A THEORY OF JUSTICE 340 (1971) (arguing that overlapping consensus on justice can occur even when there are "considerable differences in citizens' conceptions of justice provided that these conceptions lead to similar political judgments").

[9] STEVEN D. SMITH, THE DISENCHANTMENT OF SECULAR DISCOURSE (2010) (questioning whether the idea that discourse proceeds from shared premises accurately describes society's actual practices and experiences). Even so, the idea of shared premises operates to impose constraints on what is deemed acceptable.

[10] For an insightful discussion of this phenomenon, see ROBERT F. NAGEL, CONSTITUTIONAL CULTURES 106–12 (1989).

deplored: utilitarians, Kantians, and natural lawyers can agree on that point. (2) Racial segregation was shameful and wicked and, conversely, the campaign to overcome racial segregation – a campaign commonly referred to as "the Civil Rights movement" – was a righteous development of which Americans should be proud.[11]

It is hardly surprising, and perhaps inevitable, that in a sea of turbulent disagreement and unmoored rhetoric, advocates of all kinds would attempt to anchor their normative arguments and agendas to these two secure islands of consensus. This chapter does not challenge either of these points of consensus by arguing, perversely, that hatred is to be encouraged[12] or by denying the justice of the campaign against racial segregation. And yet these reference points, however venerable, provide severely limited normative resources for deliberating about complex public issues such as those posed by the conflicts between commitments to equality and to religious and expressive freedoms. A discourse largely confined to such resources is too simple for the task; it quickly becomes strained and distorted, with unfortunate consequences.

II ASCRIBING *ANIMUS*

If one of the few secure premises available in public discourse is that it is wrong to act from hatred or *animus*, then advocates have an incentive to advance their causes by portraying their opponents as hateful in general or toward particular classes of people. And so it is not surprising that this sort of demonizing rhetoric has become virtually ubiquitous in American politics and culture today: advocates routinely denounce their opponents as bigots or "haters," or as racist, misogynist, homophobic, xenophobic, or antireligious.

Such accusations are pervasive on blogs and social media and bumper stickers. But they make their appearance in more official and respectable settings as well. The Supreme Court's decision in *United States v. Windsor*[13] centrally depended on the accusation that in adopting the Defense of Marriage Act, Congress had acted from "animus" or "the bare desire to harm a politically unpopular group."[14] (Prudently, in *Obergefell v. Hodges*,[15] the Court backed away from this rhetorical strategy of denigration in favor of a more respectful treatment.[16]) In his opinion in the recent

---

[11] ELIZABETH MENSCH & ALAN FREEMAN, POLITICS OF VIRTUE (1993).

[12] *Cf.* Josh Hafner, *"Turn on the Hate"? Steve Bannon's Cynicism Spreads Online*, USA TODAY (Nov. 16, 2016), https://perma.cc/WL6S-JP44 (discussing reported advice of presidential advisor Stephen Bannon: "Let the grassroots turn on the hate, because that's the ONLY thing that will make them do their duty.").

[13] 133 S. Ct. 2675 (2013).

[14] Steven D. Smith, *The Jurisprudence of Denigration*, 48 U. C. DAVIS L. REV. 675 (2014) (tracing and criticizing the majority's claims of animus).

[15] 135 S. Ct. 2584 (2015).

[16] *See, e.g., id.* at 2602 ("Many who deem same-sex marriage to be wrong reach that conclusion based on decent and honorable religious or philosophical premises, and neither they nor their beliefs are disparaged here.").

report of the US Commission on Civil Rights entitled (without any apparent sense of irony) *Peaceful Coexistence*,[17] Chairman Martin Castro indicated that the phrases "religious liberty" and "religious freedom" are hypocritical "code words for discrimination, intolerance, racism, sexism, homophobia, Islamophobia, [and] Christian supremacy."[18] Though stridently presented, Castro's view was hardly idiosyncratic; he joined three other commissioners in a statement that described proposed protections for religious freedom as hypocritical manifestations of "intolerance and animus."[19]

To be sure, hatred and bigotry are real phenomena; they are, arguably, part of the human make-up. And yet arguments that centrally turn on ascriptions of *animus* to large classes of people are likely at best to vastly oversimplify a complex set of beliefs, perspectives, and motivations. At worst, they are flatly implausible. Consider, for example, the much-discussed *Arlene's Flowers* case.[20] The defendant in the case, Baronelle Stutzman, is a Christian florist whose beliefs include the ideas that (a) she should love other people as herself and (b) marriage is a divine institution limited to unions between a man and a woman. In accordance with these beliefs, Stutzman sold thousands of dollars' worth of arranged flowers to Robert Ingersoll, over a nine-year period, without reservation, with full knowledge that Ingersoll is gay and that many of the arrangements were intended for his same-sex partner, Curt Freed, and for occasions such as Valentine's Day or birthdays.[21] Stutzman considered Ingersoll a good friend. But when Ingersoll asked her to do the floral arrangements for his wedding to Freed, she politely declined, recommending three other florists who would be good for the job; she gave Ingersoll a hug and wished him well. She has indicated that she would be willing to sell Ingersoll the "raw materials," or the flowers themselves, that could be used for a wedding; her objection was to using her artistic gifts to do the actual arranging, thereby personally helping to celebrate a union that she believes is contrary to God's law.

That of course led to a set of lawsuits for discrimination.[22] For her part, Stutzman claimed that it is a violation of her religious freedom for the state to force her to violate her beliefs. In Chairman Castro's understanding, this claim is evidently to be interpreted as hypocritical and as disguised "homophobia." But all of the facts of the case render such an interpretation not merely uncharitable, but utterly implausible.

---

[17] U. S. Comm'n on Civil Rights, Peaceful Coexistence: Reconciling Nondiscrimination Principles with Civil Liberties (Sept. 2016).

[18] *Id.* at 25 (Statement of Chairman Martin R. Castro).

[19] *Id.* at 30, 40 (Statement of Commissioners Achtenberg, Castro, Kladney, and Yaki) [hereinafter *Commissioners' Statement*]. *See also id.* at 32 (describing "[t]hreats to civil liberties, cloaked as 'religious freedom' protection bills"); *id.* at 33 (describing such measures as "thinly-veiled attempts to turn back the clock" and describing the proposed federal First Amendment Defense Act as "hypocrisy").

[20] State v. Arlene's Flowers, Inc., 389 P.3d 543 (Wash. 2017) *vacated*, 138 S. Ct. 2671 (2018).

[21] *See* Warren Richey, *A Florist Caught Between Faith and Financial Ruin*, Christian Sci. Monitor (July 12, 2016), https://perma.cc/935E-GL3U.

[22] For details on the suits, see McClain, Chapter 17; Wilson, Chapter 30.

The problem with such arguments, however, is not simply that they are likely to be false. Their more destructive consequences lie in the damage such rhetoric does to the character of the relevant actors and, more generally, to the fabric of civil society.

Think about the qualities of character expressed and cultivated when rhetoric is based on ascriptions of hatred. The targets of such accusations – namely, those who are dismissed by distant outsiders as hypocritical and hateful even though they themselves know otherwise – are of course likely to feel resentful, abused, and alienated. Justified or not, these perceptions do not contribute to a healthy, positively engaged civic character.

Even more importantly, perhaps, consider the significance of such ascriptions to the ascribers themselves. If the practice were not so depressingly familiar, it would seem quite extraordinary for someone confidently to attribute hypocrisy and hateful motives to thousands or millions of people whom he has never met and who at least purport to be acting on more honorable considerations. Who, other than perhaps God, could possibly claim the ability to penetrate past other people's outward professions and see into their hearts and minds in the way such attributions purport to do? Such attributions are thus hubristic on a grand scale; they are also deeply uncharitable (since what the ascribers discern or think they discern in their fellow citizens is essentially irrational and malicious).

More generally, such ascriptions reflect a sort of Manichean or "light versus darkness" view of humanity that from a less fervent perspective appears quite fantastic. Given the ubiquity today of the rhetoric of ascribed hatred, it appears that millions of Americans essentially perceive humanity as divided into two main classes: people (like themselves) who are reasonable and good-hearted and tolerant, and people (like their opponents) who in important matters act not from legitimate reasons, but rather from hatred or irrational bigotry. The appeal of this Manichean outlook is understandable. Beyond offering a sure and simple way of relating to a vexingly complex social world, the outlook provides cheap moral reassurance: to be included the congregation of the blessed, it is evidently enough for a person to feel and express indignation or contempt toward the large and menacing crowd of the "haters." This phenomenon – the self-righteousness, the insufferable smugness – is readily discernible in much public discourse today. Was virtue ever achieved at so little cost or effort?

Though powerfully attractive, the Manichean perspective so grossly oversimplifies a vastly more complex human reality (in which hatred may be one element, but only one, and one likely to be distributed *across* our various political divides, not merely on one side of them) that it descends into mere delusion. On such delusions and comfortable self-delusions, not only mutual deliberation and mutual respect but even self-knowledge become all but impossible. It seems unlikely that the American project, or any political project, can prosper or perhaps even endure on such a foundation of rampant and mutually accusatory delusion.

III "CIVIL RIGHTS" AS AN INSTRUMENT OF EQUIVOCATION

Another secure reference point in contemporary normative discourse is the acknowledged justice of the Civil Rights movement to end racial segregation. Unsurprisingly, therefore, arguments about competing commitments to nondiscrimination and to religious or expressive freedom frequently make straightforward analogies to, and attempt to draw decisive conclusions from, that campaign and its supposed lessons.[23]

One familiar form of this strategy replies to a florist's or baker's or photographer's claim to be excused from helping to celebrate a same-sex marriage by declaring that if the claim were accepted, a similar exemption would have to be granted to people (if there are any) who assert religious objections to helping with an interracial marriage.[24] But any exceptions to laws forbidding racial discrimination would be anathema; or so even the proponents of religious accommodation are likely to agree.[25] And so it follows – QED – that exemptions must be denied in the same-sex marriage cases as well.

Arguments from analogy are common enough, of course, in life and especially in law: the common law method centrally depends on arguments from analogy as lawyers and judges draw on precedents in reaching conclusions in current cases. But common law argumentation has typically been complex and nuanced, drawing on similarities between the present and earlier cases, but also scrutinizing the various differences. In his classic study, Professor Karl Llewellyn identified sixty-four different techniques by which common law courts have invoked and extended, but also distinguished and limited, precedents.[26]

Applied to conflicts among commitments to equality, religious freedom, and expressive freedom, this common law method would no doubt identify similarities between the campaign against racial segregation and the current controversies involving same-sex marriage, but it would also call attention to important differences. Such differences are real and potentially significant. More generally, the various agendas that are commonly lumped together under the heading of "civil rights" exhibit some common features but also fundamental differences.

Some of these differences are historical: the sometimes tragic or sordid history of relations among races is quite a different narrative from the history of relations

---

[23] *See, e.g., Commissioners' Statement, supra* note 14, at 31–32.

[24] This is perhaps the most common objection I have encountered in my occasional efforts to defend religious objections in the recent cases involving same-sex marriage. The argument was evidently centrally featured in the oral argument in the Washington Supreme Court in the Arlene's Flowers case. *See* Gene Johnson, *Case of Florist Who Denied Service for Gay Wedding is Heard,* ASSOCIATED PRESS (Nov. 15, 2016), https://perma.cc/36CP-UASK.

[25] Counsel for Baronelle Stutzman took this position in the oral argument in *Arlene's Flowers. See id.* For an argument distinguishing refusals based on religious views of interracial marriage from refusals based on same-sex marriage, see Perry, Chapter 20.

[26] KARL LLEWELLYN, THE COMMON LAW TRADITION 48 (1960).

between sexes or between people with different sexual orientations. In the latter histories, there are inequities and abuses, to be sure, but nothing quite equivalent to chattel slavery and the Civil War. And other races or ethnic groups – Native Americans, Asians, and Hispanics – may have experienced entirely different histories.

Because of these different histories and for other reasons, the various agendas placed under the heading of "civil rights" also implicate significantly different sociological realities. With respect to race, for example, blacks in America have typically been a mostly identifiable numerical minority that has during some periods been segregated so that interracial interactions have in some contexts been minimized: in some regions of the country, white Americans may have had little or no contact at all with black Americans.[27] Women, by contrast, though mostly identifiable, have not been a minority; and though sometimes segregated by gender *roles*, they have not been *physically* separated in the way racial minorities have been. Virtually every American male will have lived with and had close personal interactions with a mother, perhaps a sister or daughter, and often a wife. As a class, gays and lesbians will have still other distinctive characteristics. Like blacks and unlike women, they have been a numerical minority;[28] like women and unlike blacks, they have not on the whole been kept separated from the rest of society; unlike both blacks and women, they have had considerable though hardly complete control over whether they are identifiable as belonging to a distinctive class.

Given these potentially important historical and sociological differences, a strategy for dealing with perceived intolerance with respect to one kind of characteristic may or may not be an appropriate strategy for dealing with intolerance or subordination based on a different characteristic.[29] Constitutional doctrine as it has evolved has clearly, if clumsily, reflected an awareness of this point. Consider the unilluminating, and almost comical, "tiers of scrutiny" in which racial classifications are subjected to "strict scrutiny," while gender classifications are treated with "intermediate scrutiny"; courts seem altogether uncertain about what sort of "tier" or "level" or "scrutiny" to use in dealing with sexual orientation.[30] But the doctrine at least reflects an awareness that the different issues call for different analyses and responses. Public bathrooms segregated by race are wholly unacceptable. By contrast, bathrooms segregated by sex have, at least until recent complications arose, been considered unproblematic.[31]

---

[27] For patterns across time, see Trevon Logan & John Parman, *The National Rise in Residential Segregation*, NBER Working Paper No. 20934 (Feb. 2015), http://www.nber.org/papers/w20934.

[28] For statistics, see Minter, Chapter 4; Warbelow, Chapter 31.

[29] For a similar observation from a LGBT advocate, see Jonathan Rauch, *Gay Rights, Religious Liberty, and Nondiscrimination: Can a Train Wreck Be Avoided?*, 2017 U. Ill. L. Rev. 1195.

[30] *See* Michael Stokes Paulsen, *Everything You Need to Know About Constitutional Law*, Pub. Discourse (May 19, 2015), https://perma.cc/Q962-3UT3.

[31] See Wilson, Chapter 30, for evidence that the "bathroom" question has operated to block state sexual orientation and gender identity nondiscrimination laws since the narrative first arose.

The differences in these relationships and their attendant problems may be obscured by classifying the variety of issues – racial segregation, gender or sex relations, and issues of sexual orientation and gender identity – all under the heading of "civil rights." The classification thus implies that the issues are essentially similar, or are simply different manifestations of some basic common phenomenon – hatred, perhaps, or "discrimination," or irrational prejudice. Insofar as they mask fundamental differences and imply an illusory equivalence among the issues, however, these terms, "civil rights" and "discrimination,"[32] merely serve to promote equivocations that dampen deliberation.

If these various issues and challenges are fundamentally different in character, so also the actual or hypothetical religious objections to interracial marriage and same-sex marriage are quite different in character. In a heavily biblically oriented cultural context, to be sure, people will be motivated to present and defend their opinions in biblical vocabulary (in much the same way that in an English-speaking country people will typically present their views *in English*). Thus, in a context in which the Bible is a common source and in which slavery and later racial segregation are part of the dominant culture – as they were in the antebellum and Jim Crow South – it is hardly surprising that some people would offer religious or biblical accounts of these practices. And yet, the fact remains that religious arguments against inter-racial marriage have extremely weak grounding both in the Bible and in the Christian tradition: the religious argument is mostly a perverse artefact of one lamentable part of the American experience. Moreover, even those who con-demned interracial marriage typically did not deny that such unions were in fact marriages.[33]

The religious objection to same-sex marriage, by contrast, is quite different.[34] Though the issue continues to provoke much debate, the objection at least can claim to be consistent with long-standing Christian traditions and supported by the authoritative pronouncements of major religious authorities, including the magisterium of the Roman Catholic Church.[35]

On these questions, to be sure, different religious believers, including different professing Christians, will reach different conclusions.[36] But that fact underscores the crucial point – namely, that it is simply facile to discredit or dismiss the religious

Importantly, Title IX bans discrimination on the basis of sex in higher education, but allows for separate, comparable changing and restroom facilities for each gender. *See* Title IX, 20 U.S.C. §§ 1681–88 (2012); 44 C.F.R. § 106.33 (2017).

[32] *See* Richard W. Garnett, *Religious Accommodations and – and Among – Civil Rights: Separation, Toleration, and Accommodation*, 88 S. Cal. L. Rev. 493 (2015).

[33] *See* David R. Upham, *Interracial Marriage and the Original Understanding of the Privileges or Immunities Clause*, 42 Hastings Const. L. Q. 213 (2015).

[34] *See* Lori, Chapter 13; Ryan Anderson, Chapter 27.

[35] *Catechism of the Catholic Church*, Art. 6, 2331–36 (1994); Greenawalt, Chapter 8.

[36] *See* Gramick, Chapter 10; Leith Anderson, Chapter 12; Lori, Chapter 13; Hoogstra et al., Chapter 25; Ryan Anderson, Chapter 27.

objection to same-sex marriage asserted by someone like Baronelle Stutzman by observing that religious arguments were also made for slavery or for antimiscegenation laws. The tactic is comparable to saying that society can disregard the scientific evidence for evolution or climate change since arguments purporting to be based on "science" have also been given for phlogiston or the flat earth or six-day creationism or all sorts of absurd or frivolous propositions. In religion, as in science, the undeniable occurrence of bad arguments is no warrant for dismissing *all* arguments as bad.

Courts may to be sure believe that they are incompetent or constitutionally forbidden to assess the merits of different religious claims, and hence to distinguish between strong religious arguments and weak ones.[37] But if such a prohibition precludes a court from saying that the (contested but substantial) religious objection to same-sex marriage is fundamentally different from the (frivolous) religious objection to interracial marriage, the prohibition should equally preclude the court from treating the objections as practically equivalent in strength. And so it should be no answer to a religious objection to same-sex marriage that a *different* religious objection to a *different* practice would likely not be honored with an exemption. To do that is in effect to seize on the fact of bad or bad faith religious arguments to dismiss and disparage, in broad-brush terms, a source and style of normative thought that has undoubtedly been a central part of the American political tradition and that for many Americans is still a central and essential element of their existence. Such disparagement is ill calculated to support the American project as a stable and inclusive element.

IV CONCLUSION

This chapter argues that two very common and simplifying approaches to resolving conflicts among competing legal commitments ought to be eschewed as unlikely to produce just and stable results and as damaging to our civil society and public discourse. But the question inevitably arises: if we should not resolve conflicts in these familiar and simplistic ways, how then *should* we go about resolving such conflicts?

This chapter does not try to answer that question; on the contrary, the chapter suggests that no simple answer is available. Of course, readers or listeners often have little patience for this sort of reticence. If you cannot say anything constructive, they may think, you should not say anything at all. And it is just possible that from this mostly negative or critical presentation, and by a sort of process of elimination, some more positive suggestions may tentatively emerge.

Although terms like *"animus,"* "civil rights," "discrimination" (and for that matter "public" as in "public-private" or "public accommodation") may figure in

---

[37] *See, e.g.,* Rayburn v. Gen. Conference of Seventh-Day Adventists, 772 F.2d 1164, 1166, 1168 (4th Cir. 1985); *see generally* Michael A. Helfand, *Litigating Religion,* 93 B.U. L. Rev. 493 (2013).

deliberations, and in formulations of competing positions,[38] it would be a mistake to suppose that any of those concepts can somehow deliver the correct answer. Rather, if we aspire to be more mature and responsible in our deliberations, we will probably need to be both more earthily prudential and more loftily visionary than the "civil rights" simplisms attempt to be. *Prudential*, in that we will need to closely consider the various conflicts and diversities that come into play in their own right and on their own merits – to deal with the "facts on the ground" – without supposing that we can deduce adequate answers from simplistic analogies to earlier conflicts and achievements. And *visionary*, in that we will need to think about what the diverse and inclusive community to which we aspire would look like and then try to devise strategies to achieve that sort of community.

It is not the intention of this chapter to commit yet another simplism by suggesting that terms like "diversity" or "inclusiveness" can in themselves yield definite and satisfactory resolutions. The terms "diversity" and "inclusiveness" typically carry positive resonances, but the truth is that we do not and should not want to include every kind of diversity in our communities. Ku Klux Klanners and neo-Nazis, for example, reflect diverse elements that we might be very happy to do without.

So, what kind of diversity do we want? By now, hopefully, there is a general consensus if not a universal agreement that we – in a guarded sense of "we" – want a community that is racially inclusive. And perhaps most of us have come to value a community in which gays and lesbians can participate in public life, including the marketplace, without having to deny or hide that dimension of their personalities.

But do we want a community in which devout Christians like Baronelle Stutzman can participate in public life and in the marketplace without concealing or suppressing their convictions? And if so, what strategies might promote that sort of inclusiveness? Or conversely, are traditional Christians like Stutzman comparable to the Ku Klux Klanners? Would we prefer a community in which the Baronelle Stutzmans of the world remain out of sight – by staying at home or in church, or at least by checking their religious commitments at the door before entering the public arena? These are the sorts of questions that ultimately confront us.

To be sure, it is not clear that we collectively possess either the will or the capacity to arrive at satisfactory answers to such questions. It is surely more exhilarating just to try to crush the opposition if we think we have the power to do so.[39] One must be cautious about too quickly or naively embracing compromises that some people have (in complete good faith) proposed but that may have little staying power.[40]

---

[38] *See, e.g.*, Krotoszynski, Chapter 7; Melling, Chapter 19; Wilson, Chapter 30. For dissection of charges of bigotry in debates over competing rights, see McClain, Chapter 17.

[39] *See, e.g.*, Mark Tushnet, *Abandoning Defensive Crouch Constitutionalism*, BALKINIZATION (May 6, 2016), https://perma.cc/UR9E-PUVF.

[40] *See* Steven D. Smith, *Die and Let Live? The Asymmetry of Accommodation*, 88 S. CAL. L. REV. 703 (2015).

Still, if the American project is to proceed in any sort of just and inclusive fashion, then it will be necessary at some point to devise nonideal but broadly acceptable resolutions of the conflicts among competing legal and cultural commitments. And we will surely not achieve such resolutions by ascribing reprehensible motives to those who disagree with us or by invoking simplistic analogies to the Civil Rights movement. We will need to work harder and do better than that. More specifically, we will need to articulate and defend our visions of what community in America should look like. If we manage to do that, the various analogies to different aspects of the so-called Civil Rights movement will fall into place naturally enough.

19

Heterosexuals Only

Signs of the Times?

Louise Melling

The United States is in a moment of change and, with it, conflict.[1] Advances for equality for LGBT people and for women are facing resistance, including resistance rooted in religious beliefs. In myriad contexts, the question arises whether and when those objecting to laws prohibiting discrimination should be exempted from compliance with them. State legislatures, for example, debate and pass measures that provide heightened protection for religious freedom that can strengthen claims for exemptions.[2] They pass laws that permit adoption agencies, counselors, and county clerks to claim an exemption to nondiscrimination laws.[3] Institutions go to court seeking permission to refuse to comply with nondiscrimination laws that provide no religious exemption. Businesses wanting to refuse to serve LGBT people,[4] employers objecting to complying with the federal rule requiring insurance coverage for contraception,[5] health-care institutions resisting providing services and information

---

[1] This chapter draws in significant part from an article, *Religious Refusals to Public Accommodations Laws: Four Reasons to Say No*, published in 38 Harv. J.L. & Gender 177 (2015).

[2] E.g., Ind. Code §§ 34-13-9-1 to -3 (2015) (Religious Freedom Restoration Act).

[3] E.g., Mich. Comp. Laws §§ 722.124e–722.124f (2017) (permitting adoption agencies to reject parents for religious reasons); Tenn. Code Ann. § 63-22-302 (2016) (allowing counselors and therapists to deny services that conflict with their religious beliefs); N.C. Gen. Stat. § 51-5.5 (2015) (allowing magistrates to recuse themselves from performing duties related to marriage ceremonies to which they religiously object).

[4] E.g., Craig v. Masterpiece Cakeshop, Inc., 370 P.3d 272, 276 (Colo. App. 2015), *cert. denied sub nom.* Masterpiece Cakeshop, Inc. v. Colo. Civil Rights Comm'n, No. 15SC738, 2016 WL 1645027 (Colo. Apr. 25, 2016), *and rev'd.* Masterpiece Cakeshop, Ltd. v. Colo. Civil Rights Comm'n, 138 S. Ct. 1719 (2018); State v. Arlene's Flowers, Inc., 389 P.3d 543 (Wash. 2017), *cert. granted, judgment vacated, remanded,* 138 S. Ct. 2671 (2018); Elane Photography, L.L.C. v. Willock, 309 P.3d 53 (N.M. 2013), *cert. denied,* 134 S. Ct. 1787 (2014); Gifford v. McCarthy, 137 A.D.3d 30 (N.Y. 3d Dept. 2016).

[5] E.g., Burwell v. Hobby Lobby Stores, Inc., 134 S. Ct. 2751 (2014); Zubik v. Burwell, 136 S. Ct. 1557 (2016).

to LGBT people or to women,[6] religiously affiliated schools refusing to hire or retain single women who are pregnant[7] or gay staff who get married,[8] and pharmacies refusing to serve women who seek to fill prescriptions for contraception,[9] are all turning to the courts for a license to discriminate. The Trump administration's efforts to grant such licenses are sparking litigation or threats of litigation.[10] And, in its 2017–18 term, the US Supreme Court will decide whether the Free Exercise Clause provides a constitutional right to discriminate.[11]

This chapter articulates the harms that flow from such exemptions, whether required as a matter of Supreme Court jurisprudence or permitted in legislation. Section I focuses on the harms to the individual that arise when places of public accommodation – businesses that open their doors to the public – assert a right to refuse services to LGBT people, often in the context of wedding services.[12] In this context, more than in any other context, the cost of exemptions is too often discounted in public discourse.[13] Religious exemptions in this context constitute

---

[6] E.g., N. Coast Women's Care Med. Grp., Inc. v. San Diego Cty. Superior Court, 189 P.3d 959 (Cal. 2008); *see also* Franciscan All., Inc. v. Burwell, 227 F. Supp. 3d 660 (N.D. Tex. 2016) (enjoining provision in Patient Protection and Affordable Care Act barring discrimination based on gender identity and termination of pregnancy).

[7] E.g., Richardson v. Northwest Christian University, 242 F. Supp. 3d 1132 (D. Or. 2017); Dias v. Archdiocese of Cincinnati, No. 1:11–CV–00251, 2013 WL 360355 (S.D. Ohio Jan. 30, 2013); Hamilton v. Southland Christian Sch., Inc., 680 F.3d 1316 (11th Cir. 2012); *see also* Herx v. Diocese of Fort Wayne–S. Bend, Inc., 48 F. Supp. 3d 1168 (N.D. Ind. 2014).

[8] E.g., Complaint, Billard v. Charlotte Catholic High Sch., No. 3:17–CV–00011 (W.D.N.C. Jan. 11, 2017) (stayed pending resolution of *Masterpiece Cakeshop*); Complaint, Zmuda v. Corp. of the Catholic Archbishop of Seattle, No. 14-2-07007-1 (Wash. Super. Ct. Mar. 6, 2014) (case settled).

[9] E.g., Stormans, Inc. v. Wiesman, 794 F.3d 1064 (9th Cir. 2015), *cert. denied*, 136 S. Ct. 2433 (2016); Morr-Fitz, Inc. v. Quinn, 976 N.E.2d 1160 (Ill. App. Ct. 2012).

[10] E.g., Pennsylvania v. Trump, No. CV 17-4540, 2017 WL 6398465 (E.D. Pa. Dec. 15, 2017), *appeal docketed*, 18–1253 (3d Cir. Feb. 15, 2018). The Pennsylvania case is one of eight filed to challenge interim final rules that greatly expanded exemptions for those entities objecting the Affordable Care Act rule requiring insurance coverage for contraception on religious or moral grounds. *See* Religious Exemptions and Accommodations for Coverage of Certain Preventive Services Under the Affordable Care Act, 82 Fed. Reg. 47,792–01 (Oct. 13, 2017); Moral Exemptions and Accommodations for Coverage of Certain Preventive Services Under the Affordable Care Act, 82 Fed. Reg. 47,838–01 (Oct. 13, 2017).

[11] Craig v. Masterpiece Cakeshop, Inc., 370 P.3d 272 (Colo. App. 2015), *cert. denied sub nom.* Masterpiece Cakeshop, Inc. v. Colo. Civil Rights Comm'n, No. 15SC738, 2016 WL 1645027 (Colo. Apr. 25, 2016), *and rev'd.* Masterpiece Cakeshop, Ltd. v. Colo. Civil Rights Comm'n, 138 S. Ct. 1719 (2018).

[12] This chapter thus focuses on the refusals of *institutions* – stores, inns, reception halls, and other businesses – to provide services because of religious beliefs. Different questions arise where the issue concerns an exemption for an institution that primarily hires or serves only people of its own faith, or for an individual.

[13] The voices of those seeking an exemption also need to be heard as part of any robust discourse. For an exposition of the competing claims, see Laycock, Chapter 3. Sound policy decisions require hearing the consequences of any policy choice. It is the first step toward appreciating and accepting responsibility for the positions we advocate or enact.

state-sanctioned discrimination with the concomitant humiliation and stigma for those refused service. And they betray the promise of equality reflected in the underlying nondiscrimination mandate, be it one set forth by a court or a legislature. Section II addresses the way in which exemptions do not ease conflict but rather serve to contest, and undermine, the underlying rule of nondiscrimination. Indeed, as Section II shows, exemptions serve the normative function of continuing to cast LGBT people generally, and same-sex couples in particular, as immoral, thus undermining the project of full legal equality. Finally, Section III briefly concludes that sanctioning exemptions in this context, where the law has not done so in other contexts, calls into question our commitment to nondiscrimination for LGBT people.

I EXEMPTIONS DISCRIMINATE, SHAME, AND STIGMATIZE

By definition, religious exemptions to nondiscrimination laws give institutions the right to discriminate: with exemptions, the state sanctions the refusal, rooted in faith, to comply with laws prohibiting discrimination. In the context now the subject of debate, that means that inns, bakeries, floral shops, dress shops, tuxedo rentals, photography studios, and reception halls, among others, could, with the state's blessing, refuse to serve a couple because they are of the same sex.[14] In other words, a business could put an actual or metaphorical sign, "Heterosexuals Only," in the window of the bridal shop, over the wedding cake case, or on the website page describing rental space for weddings. The attendant harms are multiple.

There is the immediate and obvious harm of being told, "We don't want your kind here." There is harm no matter how kindly the words are spoken, no matter how heartfelt and deep the objection is. It is the harm of being rejected because of who you are, because you are a member of a class long disfavored and long subject to discrimination. It is the kind of rejection that silences, shames, and kills.[15]

---

[14] Courts have recognized that refusal to serve couples in this context constitutes discrimination. *See, e.g.*, Craig v. Masterpiece Cakeshop, Inc., 370 P.3d 272, 281 ("But for their sexual orientation, Craig and Mullins would not have sought to enter into a same-sex marriage, and but for their intent to do so, Masterpiece would not have denied them its services.").

[15] *See* Rose Saxe, *It's Always Been About Discrimination for LGBT People*, ACLU Speak Freely (Dec. 21, 2017), https://perma.cc/3NFW-WWGB (detailing and contextualizing harm of refusal). Another ACLU colleague recently recounted a story of his shame upon being subject to housing discrimination. When he first moved to New York, an apartment complex told him it had nothing available, although it had just told his work colleague there were lots of listings. Unlike his then–coworker, my colleague is black. Although the facts were as strong as they can be to make a claim of discrimination, my colleague didn't file a complaint: "I was too ashamed."

During the enactment of the Civil Rights Act of 1964 (1964 Act), the Senate Commerce Committee spoke to these harms in the context of public accommodations:

The primary purpose ... is to solve this problem, the deprivation of personal dignity that surely accompanies denials of equal access to public establishments. Discrimination is not simply dollars and cents, hamburgers and movies; it is the humiliation, frustration, and embarrassment that a person must surely feel when he is told that he is unacceptable as a member of the public.[16]

Roy Wilkins of the National Association for the Advancement of Colored People spoke similarly about the 1964 Act:

The truth is that the affronts and denials that this section, if enacted, would correct are intensely human and personal. Very often they harm the physical body, but always they strike at the root of the human spirit, at the very core of human dignity.[17]

And, in the context that is the focus of this chapter, the mother of a gay man denied a cake for his wedding said, "It was never about the cake. It was about my son being treated like a lesser person."[18]

The Supreme Court has also articulated the dignitary harm of discrimination. When striking down gender-based preemptory challenges in jury selection, the Court stated that such discrimination can be an "assertion of ... inferiority" that "denigrates the dignity of the excluded" and "reinvokes a history of exclusion."[19] This harm extends to individuals denied benefits and recognition by virtue of sexual orientation and gender identity. In *United States v. Windsor*, for example, the Court emphasized how the Defense of Marriage Act effectuated not just a denial of the economic benefits tied to marriage, but also a "differentiation [that] demeans the couple."[20]

These statements, however, do not capture the entirety of the harm. Nondiscrimination laws function to accord recognition and to embrace and

---

[16] Heart of Atlanta Motel, Inc. v. United States, 379 U.S. 241, 291–92 (1964) (Goldberg, J., concurring) (quoting S. Rep. No. 88–872, at 16 (1964)).

[17] S. Rep. No. 88–872 (1964), *reprinted in* 1964 U.S.C.C.A.N. 2355, 2369.

[18] Deborah Munn, *It Was Never About the Cake*, Huffington Post (Feb. 2, 2016), https://perma.cc/PG2T-CCAA. It is no answer to suggest that there is no problem in affording businesses exemptions because no reasonable couple or person would want the services or goods of an unwilling provider. Consider what the progress for equality for women or people of color would look like if this had been the approach.

[19] J.E.B. v. Ala. *ex rel.* T.B., 511 U.S. 127, 142 (1994).

[20] United States v. Windsor, 133 S. Ct. 2675, 2694 (2013); *see also, e.g.*, Stewart v. Heineman, 296 Neb. 262, 287–88 (Neb. 2017) (discussing stigma and humiliation of LGBT people being excluded from foster care programs); Marvin Lim & Louise Melling, *Inconvenience or Indignity? Religious Exemptions to Public Accommodations Laws*, 22 J.L. & Pol'y 705, 711–18 (2014) (collecting cases discussing dignitary harm of discrimination).

open doors to those who were traditionally excluded. They hold a promise that the power of the law will be used to end a second-class status. Exemptions to these laws undermine the traditionally stigmatized group's belief that the community will ever give them a fair shake. That is true even if exemptions are claimed only in small pockets of society. An example illustrates this point. Assume the law protects against LGBT discrimination in public accommodations, with an exemption for establishments with a religious objection. What happens when you are turned away at an inn consistent with the law's exemption? How do you feel as you approach the next reception desk? And the next one? Or the next time you go on vacation? How long do the humiliation and anxiety linger, even if only one inn turns you away?[21] The promise of equality is not real or robust if it means you can be turned away. It takes but one metaphorical – or actual – "Heterosexuals Only" sign to make an LGBT person question whether the society is in fact embracing her and her kind.[22]

What is more, this continued discrimination is state-sanctioned. The state, if it enacts a public accommodations law with an exemption, has given the businesses a permission slip. As Justice Anthony Kennedy remarked with respect to marriage equality:

> When that sincere, personal opposition [to same-sex marriage based on decent and honorable religious or philosophical premises] becomes enacted law and public policy, the necessary consequence is to put the imprimatur of the State itself on an exclusion that soon demands or stigmatizes those whose own liberty is then denied.[23]

Admittedly business owners with religious objections to nondiscrimination laws too speak of the stigma and harm they endure in this debate – of being called a bigot and of being pushed out of the marketplace because of their beliefs.[24] The cost to these business owners cannot be denied. But there is no cost-free option. Either businesses retain a right to deny LGBT people service, or we commit to ending the legacy of

---

[21] *See* Debbie Munn, *A Mom's Valentine's Day Message to Her Son, and LGBT Kids Everywhere*, DAILY BEAST (Feb. 14, 2018) (detailing how being turned away changed her son and his husband when they seek services), https://perma.cc/9YCG-3KBF; *see also* Saxe, *supra* note 15 ("[O]nce we are refused, every time we approach the door of a store, we wonder how we will be treated and are more likely to hide who we are.").

[22] A referral to a business willing to provide the service does not mitigate the harm. To say otherwise is to suggest the issue is really the cake, the hamburger, or the hotel room. A referral simply amends the metaphorical sign to read: "Wedding cakes for heterosexuals only. Gays served down the street." The same costs attend.

[23] Obergefell v. Hodges, 135 S. Ct. 2584, 2602 (2015); *see also* Allen v. Wright, 468 U.S. 737, 755 (1984) ("[S]tigmatizing injury ... is one of the most serious consequences of discriminatory government action.").

[24] *E.g.*, Sherif Girgis, *Nervous Victors, Illiberal Measures: A Response to Doug NeJaime and Reva Siegel*, 125 YALE L.J.F. 399, 404–05 (2016).

discrimination against LGBT people. If we care about LGBT equality, the price of exemptions with its attendant harms is too great.

II EXEMPTIONS UNDERMINE AND ERODE
NONDISCRIMINATION LAWS

Proponents of exemptions often argue that they will quiet the storm, ease resistance, and in fact advance LGBT rights. The argument has intuitive appeal. It is about accommodating difference, embracing pluralism, respecting religious beliefs, and, in the context this chapter addresses, managing change. Change is hard. Everyone resists some change, and often with deep conviction, so an effort to respect both sides – by acknowledging how hard change is and how hard no change is – makes sense. At their core, the calls for exemptions also often rest on a claim that they are part of a necessary compromise for progress or that more gradual change will be longer lasting. History, however, complicates this narrative.

Consider the lessons from efforts to advance women's equality by protecting their right to control fertility. The decades that followed *Roe v. Wade*[25] have brought waves of laws permitting institutions and individuals to refuse to provide abortions.[26] For example, forty-three states currently permit healthcare institutions to refuse to provide abortion services, and forty-five states permit individual healthcare providers to similarly refuse.[27] The exemptions continue to expand, going beyond the performance of abortions to a right to refuse conduct that might be seen as facilitating abortion. For example, since 2004, federal, state, and local government agencies and programs have risked losing federal dollars if they "subject[] any institutional or individual health-care entity to discrimination on the basis that the health-care entity does not provide, pay for, provide coverage of, or refer for abortions."[28] Requirements that health care providers give patients information and referral assistance as a condition of refusing to provide certain medical care[29] or that they attend to women

---

[25] 410 U.S. 113 (1973).

[26] Douglas NeJaime and Reva Siegel trace this expansion of refusal measures to what they refer to as complicity-based conscience claims. Douglas NeJaime & Reva B. Siegel, *Conscience Wars: Complicity-Based Claims in Religion and Politics*, 124 YALE L.J. 2516 (2015).

[27] GUTTMACHER INST., STATE POLICIES IN BRIEF: REFUSING TO PROVIDE HEALTH SERVICES (2018), https://perma.cc/47WR-GFJQ. Twenty-seven of the states that permit hospitals to refuse to provide abortions had passed their laws by the end of 1974. NeJaime & Siegel, *supra* note 26, at 2583 n.89.

[28] This rule, known colloquially as the Weldon Amendment, is an appropriations rider. *See* Consolidated Appropriations Act, 2010, Pub. L. No. 111–117, § 508(d)(1), 123 Stat. 3034, 3280 (2009).

[29] E.g., Pregnancy Care Ctr. of Rockford v. Rauner, No. 2016–MR–741 (Ill. Cir. Ct. Dec. 20, 2016) (challenge to amendment requiring providers that decline to participate in medical procedures to provide information and referral assistance).

before and after an abortion are contested.[30] Even rules requiring insurance coverage of birth control – rules adopted to further women's equality – are disputed.[31]

Exemptions in this context have thus not functioned to quiet the storm. They have not served to carve out a narrow space to which those who resist can retreat. Rather, the push has been for ever-expanding exemptions to rules governing all manner of interactions in the public sphere.[32]

A similar pattern is emerging in the LGBT arena. Provisions in marriage laws stating explicitly that clergy and houses of worship cannot be required to perform or recognize marriages to which they object have not lessened the call for exemptions. Rather, there is an increasing call for measures to ensure that anyone objecting on religious grounds to marriages of same-sex couples need not in any way facilitate or acknowledge the marriage. This means businesses demand a right to refuse to provide services[33] and employers to refuse to provide partner benefits.[34] There are measures to permit government officials to refuse to register a marriage[35] and even a state law, with a parallel measure proposed in Congress,[36] to prohibit any institution or individual from being penalized for acting consistently with a belief that marriage is between a man and woman or that sex is proper only in the context of such a marriage.[37] This is not surprising as some who advocate for exemptions for those who oppose marriage for same-sex couples look to the religious refusals laws governing abortion as a model.[38]

---

[30] Danquah v. Univ. of Med. & Dentistry of N.J., No. 2:11-cv-06377-JLL-MAH (D.N.J. Nov. 22, 2011) (challenge by nurses to any requirement they provide services to women before and after abortions, including having patient change into a gown, checking patient's temperature, and reviewing discharge instructions).

[31] *E.g.*, Zubik v. Burwell, 136 S. Ct. 1557 (2016); Burwell v. Hobby Lobby Stores, Inc., 134 S. Ct. 2751 (2014).

[32] As a matter of law as well, following the Supreme Court's decision in *Hobby Lobby*, any exemption in a nondiscrimination law will almost surely fan, not calm, conflict. In *Hobby Lobby*, the Court looked to the accommodation for nonprofit religiously affiliated organizations as a predicate for holding that closely held for-profit corporations could not be required to provide insurance for contraception. 134 S. Ct. at 2781–83. More specifically, when assessing whether the rule was narrowly tailored, the Court reasoned that if the government could accommodate nonprofit corporations with religious objections to the rule, it presumably could accommodate for-profit companies with religious objections too. *Id.* Looking forward then, any exemption included in a statute may well give rise to litigation arguing that it must be extended under federal RFRA, which governs federal laws, or an available state RFRA. For a listing of state laws, see Appendix, Chapter 35.

[33] *See supra* note 4 and accompanying text.

[34] *See* Pidgeon v. Turner, 538 S.W.3d 73 (Tex.), *cert. denied*, 138 S. Ct 505 (2017).

[35] *E.g.*, N.C. Gen. Stat. § 51–5.5 (2015).

[36] First Amendment Defense Act, S. 2525, 115 Cong. (2018).

[37] *E.g.*, Miss. Code Ann. §§ 11–62–1 to -3 (2016).

[38] *E.g.*, Ryan Anderson & Sherif Girgis, *Against the New Puritanism*, in John Corvino, Ryan T. Anderson & Sherif Girgis, Debating Religious Liberty and Discrimination 112–13 (2017) ("The law should treat those who believe that marriage unites man and woman . . . as it has treated prolife hospitals, doctors, and others in the wake of *Roe v. Wade*.").

The call for ever-expanding exemptions has consequences. The exemptions punch a hole in the tapestry of nondiscrimination laws. Like the underlying non-discrimination laws, they set a norm – in this context, one that casts doubt on the morality of the underlying status and conduct.

Again, the story of the laws governing abortion provides a cautionary tale. As the recitation provided earlier illustrates, for more than two decades, federal and state laws have sanctioned hospitals and health-care institutions to refuse to provide abortion because of religious objections.[39] These laws send a message that it is appropriate in the eyes of the state to keep abortion, and those who seek it, at arm's distance. This norm has led nurses to claim a right even to refuse women care before and after their abortions – a right not to take blood pressure or to ensure a woman has a ride home.[40] In other words, the legal norm that has been established fosters a cultural norm of shunning – of treating those who get abortions – the vast majority of whom are women[41] – as untouchable.[42] It fosters the notion that abortion, and the women who seek it and medical staff who provide it, are immoral. It is no wonder, given that norm, that the right of women to control their fertility continues to be so hotly contested.

Religious exemptions in the context of LGBT rights pose the same risks. Every such exemption, and even the debate over the measure, legitimates opposition to LGBT equality and functions to question the very morality of the underlying right.[43] Every exemption in the marriage context stands for the norm that it is acceptable to act in the public sphere on the premise that marriage for same-sex couples is immoral and the power of the state is there to support that stance. That is not the path to LGBT equality.

III EXEMPTIONS QUESTION OUR COMMITMENT TO LGBT EQUALITY

The current conflict over the propriety of exemptions rooted in religion to laws barring discrimination is not a new one. Rather, it is a conflict that is in many ways

---

[39] *See supra* notes 25–32 and accompanying text.

[40] Brief for Defendants in Opposition to Plaintiffs' Application for Preliminary Injunctive Relief at 10–16, Danquah v. Univ. of Med. & Dentistry of N.J., No. 2:11–CV–06377–JLL–MAH (D.N.J. Nov. 22, 2011).

[41] Men who are transgender and nonbinary people assigned female at birth also seek abortions. To date, restrictions on abortions, however, have targeted non-transgender women.

[42] The norm is all the more powerful because it is bolstered by doctrines that say the state can use its power to discourage abortion and thus discourage the exercise of a constitutional right. *See* Planned Parenthood of Se. Pa. v. Casey, 505 U.S. 833, 878 (1992). The state may also bar government funds from supporting abortion in any way – and thus may ban abortion in public hospitals and federal insurance programs, Webster v. Reproductive Health Servs., 492 U.S. 490 (1989); Harris v. McRae, 448 U.S. 297 (1980), and bar abortion information and referrals in publicly funded programs, Rust v. Sullivan, 500 U.S. 173 (1991).

[43] Proponents of exemptions do not contest this point. Sherif Girgis, for example, states, "[i]n a diverse society, religious liberty always creates moral stigma." *See supra* note 38, at 406. The claim in this chapter is not that this debate is illegitimate but rather that it has consequences.

predictable. Such claims for exemptions come at critical moments of advances in civil rights when there is a call for a change in the social rules addressing discrimination.[44]

Indeed, this very debate has played out in the context of race and, to some degree, gender.[45] Many, including those whose beliefs at that time dictated separation of the races, resisted racial equality and integration.[46] Even the courts invoked these religious doctrines in upholding convictions for violations of antimiscegenation laws,[47] penalties for African Americans who refused to sit in the "colored car,"[48] and fines imposed on Berea College for integrating.[49]

Resistance in the name of religion continued even after arguments in favor of racial segregation lost currency and the legal norms changed. The House version of the 1964 Act as originally passed included an accommodation that wholly exempted religiously affiliated employers from its terms banning discrimination in employment.[50] The 1964 Act ultimately passed without the exemption.[51] A barbeque franchise resisted compliance with the 1964 Act, refusing to serve African Americans on the ground that the 1964 Act "contravene[d] the will of God."[52] The court rejected the defense, stating that while the franchise

---

[44] James Esseks, Director of the ACLU's LGBT & HIV Project, refers to this strategy of calling for exemptions as "Plan B," with "Plan A" taking the form of advocating against the change in legal norms. *See* Rod Dreher, *Does Faith = Hate*, Am. Conservative (Oct. 9, 2013), http://perma .cc/XBA4-DTSF ("[T]he most important goal at this stage is not to stop gay marriage entirely but to secure as much liberty as possible for dissenting religious and social conservatives while there is still time."). *See also, e.g.*, Brief of the General Conference of Seventh-Day Adventists and the Becket Fund for Religious Liberty as Amici Curiae in Support of Neither Party, Obergefell v. Hodges, 135 S. Ct. 2584 (No. 14–556), 2015 WL 1022705, at 12 ("[I]t is not surprising that a scholarly consensus has emerged that giving legal recognition to same-sex marriage may result in widespread and foreseeable church–State conflict.").

[45] *See* Brief Amici Curiae of Julian Bond, et al. in Support of the Government at 10–19, Sebelius v. Hobby Lobby Stores, Inc., 134 S. Ct. 2751 (2014) (No. 13–354), 2014 WL 491245 (recounting ways in which religion was invoked to support slavery, segregation, and discrimination against women – as well as to support social change – and then to demand exemptions from laws prohibiting discrimination).

[46] *Id.*

[47] *See, e.g.*, Green v. State, 58 Ala. 190, 195 (1877) (upholding conviction for interracial marriage, reasoning God "has made the two races distinct").

[48] *See, e.g.*, W. Chester & Philadelphia R. R. Co. v. Miles, 55 Pa. 209, 213 (1867) (reversing judgment in favor of an African-American woman who refused to sit in "colored" section of train car, relying in part on the fact that "the Creator" made two distinct races, which "God has made ... dissimilar," and "the order of Divine Providence" dictates that the races should not mix).

[49] *See* Berea Coll. v. Commonwealth, 94 S.W. 623, 626 (Ky. 1906), *aff'd*, 211 U.S. 45, 58 (1908).

[50] *See* Equal Emp't Opportunity Comm'n v. Pac. Press Publ'g Ass'n, 676 F.2d 1272, 1276–77 (9th Cir. 1982) (recounting legislative history of 1964 Act).

[51] *Id.*

[52] Newman v. Piggie Park Enters., Inc., 377 F.2d 433, 438 (4th Cir. 1967) (Winter, J., concurring), *aff'd and modified on other grounds*, 390 U.S. 400 (1968).

owner "has a constitutional right to espouse the religious beliefs of his own choosing ... he does not have the absolute right to exercise and practice such beliefs in utter disregard of the clear constitutional rights of other citizens."[53] Most famously, Bob Jones University and its companion plaintiff, Goldsboro Christian Schools, invoked religion to resist integration in education.[54] In the Supreme Court, the schools argued that the loss of their tax-exempt status because of their discriminatory policies violated their Free Exercise rights.[55] The Supreme Court rejected the claim, reasoning that "the interests asserted by petitioners cannot be accommodated with [the] compelling governmental interest" in "eradicating racial discrimination in education – discrimination that prevailed, with official approval, for the first 165 years of this Nation's constitutional history."[56] Thus, although the nation's efforts to achieve integration met with resistance based on religious beliefs, neither the courts nor Congress countenanced religious exemptions to laws barring discrimination based on race.

What are we then saying about our commitment to LGBT equality if we embrace exemptions here? Why would we reason differently? Any number of rationales are offered to justify exemptions in the LGBT context where they have been rejected previously: the move for LGBT equality is still new and reflects a big change, race has a unique place in American history, and laws affecting racial discrimination are subject to the highest level of scrutiny. But each of these arguments ultimately comes down to a basic proposition: that the state interest in ending discrimination based on sexual orientation and gender identity is different and lesser. But what does that mean about how we think about equality? If we tolerate pockets of discrimination against LGBT people and enshrine that notion in our laws, the law will construct a second-class version of equality.[57] We should reject requests to discriminate that are rooted in religion today, just as we rejected them fifty years ago.[58]

---

[53] Newman v. Piggie Park Enters., Inc., 256 F. Supp. 941, 945 (D.S.C. 1966).
[54] Bob Jones Univ. v. United States, 461 U.S. 574, 580–82 (1983).
[55] *Id.* at 603.
[56] *Id.* at 604.
[57] The second-class status cannot be justified by the different levels of scrutiny afforded race, gender, and sexual orientation under the federal Constitution. Those tiers reflect a difference in judicial scrutiny given the rationales the state offers to justify differential treatment, not the value we put on the goal of ending discrimination. Stated otherwise, we would not say that a state's interest in ending discrimination against women is not compelling because sex discrimination is subject to intermediate scrutiny. *See* Roberts v. U.S. Jaycees, 468 U.S. 609, 624 (1984) (goal of eliminating gender discrimination in public accommodations serves a compelling state interest).
[58] *See supra* notes 45–56.

IV CONCLUSION

Our country is at a critical juncture in the effort to end discrimination based on sexual orientation and gender identity in the law and culture. The question is, will our laws accommodate those who object on religious grounds? If we care about the promise of equality and making that equality robust, this chapter argues, the answer must be no. It is not a vision without cost, but neither is the alternative. The price of sanctioning, with the force of law, the message that we do not serve your kind here is too great, no matter the motivation.

20

Conscience v. Access and the Morality of Human Rights, with Particular Reference to Same-Sex Marriage

Michael J. Perry

Little remains to be said about "conscience v. access"[1] that has not already been said – and often well said. Or so it seems to me. (Not that a consensus has been achieved. Far from it.) But "little" is not "nothing." The aim of this chapter: to bring the morality of human rights to bear and to do so with particular reference to conscience-based opposition to same-sex marriage. The chapter proceeds in three sections. Section I presents the relevant parts of the morality of human rights: the human right to moral freedom and the human right to moral equality. Sections II and III pursue the implications of those two rights for, respectively, interracial marriage (Section II) and same-sex marriage (Section III).

I THE MORALITY OF HUMAN RIGHTS: HEREIN OF MORAL FREEDOM AND MORAL EQUALITY

A Global Political Morality: Human Rights, Democracy, and Constitutionalism presents and defends the morality of human rights, which is mainly, though not solely, a political morality – indeed, the first truly global political morality in history.[2] Here, "political morality" means:

"(a) a set of norms about how government – whether a particular government or group of governments, a particular kind of government, or every government – should act towards the human beings over whom it exercises power; in particular, a set of norms specifying what government should not do to the human beings over

---

[1] The phrase "conscience v. access" occurred to me as I was reading a paper by Robin Fretwell Wilson, *Unpacking the Relationship Between Conscience and Access, in* LAW, RELIGION, AND HEALTH IN THE UNITED STATES (Holly Fernandez Lynch, I. Glenn Cohen & Elizabeth Sepper eds., 2017), https://ssrn.com/abstract=2912515.

[2] *See* MICHAEL J. PERRY, A GLOBAL POLITICAL MORALITY: HUMAN RIGHTS, DEMOCRACY, AND CONSTITUTIONALISM (2017).

whom it exercises power, or what government should do for them, or both; and (b) the rationales that warrant, or are thought to warrant, the norms."[3]

The conscience v. access controversy implicates two human rights that are core parts of the morality of human rights: the human right to moral freedom and the human right to moral equality.[4]

A Moral Freedom

The human right to moral freedom, discussed at length in A *Global Political Morality*,[5] is the right to the freedom to live one's life in accord with one's moral convictions and commitments, including, of course, one's religiously based moral convictions and commitments.[6] Some human rights – such as the right not to "be subjected to torture or to cruel, inhuman or degrading treatment or punishment"[7] – are unconditional, in the sense that the rights forbid (or require) government to do something, *period*. Some other human rights, by contrast, are conditional, in the sense that the rights forbid (or require) government to do something *unless certain conditions are satisfied*. The human right to moral freedom is – and as a practical matter must be – conditional: it forbids government to ban or otherwise impede certain choices, thereby abridging one's freedom to live in accord with one's moral convictions and commitments, *unless* each of three conditions is satisfied:

- *The legitimacy condition:* the government action at issue (law, policy, etc.) must serve a legitimate government objective.[8] The specific government action at issue might not be the law (policy, etc.) itself but that the law does not exempt the protected conduct.
- *The least burdensome alternative condition:* the government action – which, again, might be that the law does not exempt a specific action – must

---

[3] *Id.* at 7.

[4] *Id.* at 55–64.

[5] *See id.* at 63–87.

[6] A GLOBAL POLITICAL MORALITY argues that the "right of privacy" entrenched in the constitutional law of the United States is best understood as the American version of the human right to moral freedom. *See* PERRY, *supra* note 2, at 142–45.

[7] Both Article 5 of the Universal Declaration of Human Rights and Article 7 of the International Covenant on Civil and Political Rights state: "No one shall be subjected to torture or to cruel, inhuman or degrading treatment or punishment." *See* Universal Declaration of Human Rights, G.A. Res. 217(III)A, ¶ 5, U.N. Doc. A/RES/217(III) (Dec. 10, 1948). *See also* International Covenant on Civil and Political Rights, G.A. Res. 2200 (XXI), ¶ 7, U.N. Doc. A/Res/2200 (XXI) (Dec. 16, 1966).

[8] The United Nations' Siracusa Principles state: "Whenever a limitation is required in the terms of the Covenant to be 'necessary,' this term implies that the limitation: (a) is based on one of the grounds justifying limitations recognized by the relevant article of the Covenant, ... [and] (c) pursues a legitimate aim." *See* U.N. Comm'n on Human Rights, *The Siracusa Principles on the Limitation and Derogation Provisions in the International Covenant on Civil and Political Rights*, ¶ 10, U.N. Doc E/CN.4/1985/4 (Sept. 28, 1984).

be necessary to serve the legitimate objective, in the sense that the action serves the objective significantly better than would any less burdensome government action.[9]

- *The proportionality condition:* the legitimate objective served by the government action must be sufficiently weighty to warrant the burden imposed by the government action.[10]

According to the human right to moral freedom, government must accommodate a conscience-based claim for exemption from an otherwise applicable law or policy, such as a policy of military conscription, unless each of the three foregoing conditions is satisfied.[11]

All of the human rights comprised by the morality of human rights are rights against government.[12] That is the sense in which the morality of human rights is a *political* morality. Some of the rights comprised by the morality of human rights are rights not only against government but also against some or all other human beings. That is the sense in which the morality of human rights, although *mainly* a political morality, is not *solely* a political morality.

Given its content, the right to moral freedom is a right only against government; under the right, government is the sole duty-bearer.[13] As the next section explains, by contrast, the right to moral equality, given its content, is a right against all human beings; under the right, all human beings are the duty-bearers.[14]

B Moral Equality

The human right to moral equality, discussed more fully in A *Global Political Morality*,[15] is the right of every human being to be treated as the moral equal of

---

[9] *Id.* at ¶ 11 ("In applying a limitation, a state shall use no more restrictive means than are required for the achievement of the purpose of the limitation.").

[10] *Id.* at ¶ 10 ("Whenever a limitation is required in the terms of the Covenant to be 'necessary,' this term implies that the limitation: ... (b) responds to a pressing public or social need, ... and (d) is proportionate to that aim.").

  Obviously, the right to moral freedom would provide no meaningful protection for practices covered by the right if the consistency of a ban or other policy with the right was to be determined without regard to whether the policy's benefit was proportionate to the policy's cost.

[11] *See, e.g.,* U.N. Human Rights Comm., *Mr. Yeo-Bum Yoon and Mr. Myung-Jin Choi v. Republic of Korea,* U.N. Doc. CCPR/C/88/D/1321–1322/2004 (2006) (ruling that the human right to moral freedom – specifically, Article 18 of the International Covenant for Civil and Political Rights – requires parties to the International Covenant to provide for conscientious objection to military service). For relevant discussion, see JOCELYN MACLURE & CHARLES TAYLOR, SECULARISM AND FREEDOM OF CONSCIENCE 89–91 (2011).

[12] *See* James Nickel, *Human Rights, in* THE STANFORD ENCYCLOPEDIA OF PHILOSOPHY (Edward N. Zalta eds., Spring 2017), https://perma.cc/65YB-FANS.

[13] *See* Leif Wenar, *Rights, in* THE STANFORD ENCYCLOPEDIA OF PHILOSOPHY (Edward N. Zalta eds., Fall 2015), https://perma.cc/6WBS-F3EQ.

[14] *Id.*

[15] *See* PERRY, *supra* note 2, at 55–62.

every other human being, in this sense: as equally entitled with every other human being to be treated – as no less worthy than any other human being of being treated – "in a spirit of brotherhood," just as Article 1 of the Universal Declaration of Human Rights states that "all human beings" should be treated.[16] The most common bases for treating some human beings as morally inferior, as less worthy than some other human beings, if worthy at all, of being treated "in a spirit of brotherhood" – the most common bases, that is, for demeaning and even dehumanizing some human beings[17] – have been, as listed both in Article 2 of the Universal Declaration and in Article 26 of the International Covenant on Civil and Political Rights, "race, colour, sex, language, religion, political or other opinion, national or social origin, property, birth or other status."[18] Because, as Article 1 of the Universal Declaration states, "all human beings ... should act towards one another in a spirit of brotherhood," all bear the duty of moral equality, not just government.[19]

II MORAL FREEDOM, MORAL EQUALITY, AND INTERRACIAL MARRIAGE

Imagine the following scenario: because a florist is morally opposed to interracial marriage, she refuses to sell to an interracial couple an arrangement of flowers for the couple's upcoming wedding. The florist believes that interracial marriage is contrary to God's will.[20] A court determines that the florist's refusal violates the state's nondiscrimination law, imposes a fine on her, and orders her not to refuse such requests in the future. In contesting the fine and order, the florist argues that under the state's constitutional law, which protects the right to moral freedom, government must exempt her refusal from the state's nondiscrimination law.

She is mistaken. The state need not exempt her refusal. Why not? Again, the human right to moral equality, given its content, is a right against all persons, even if,

---

[16] The Universal Declaration states, in Article 1, that "[a]ll human beings are born free and equal in dignity and rights ... and should act towards one another in a spirit of brotherhood." Universal Declaration of Human Rights, G.A. Res. 217(III)A, ¶ 5, U.N. Doc. A/RES/217(III) (Dec. 10, 1948). As a right against government, the human right to moral equality forms the core of the right to equal protection entrenched in the constitutional law of the United States. See PERRY, *supra* note 2, at 57–62.

[17] See DAVID LIVINGSTONE SMITH, LESS THAN HUMAN: WHY WE DEMEAN, ENSLAVE AND EXTERMINATE OTHERS 20 (2011); Richard Rorty, *Human Rights, Rationality, and Sentimentality, in* ON HUMAN RIGHTS (OXFORD AMNESTY LECTURES) 111, 112–14, (Stephen Shute & Susan Hurley eds., 1994); David Livingstone Smith, *The Essence of Evil*, AEON (Oct. 24, 2014), https://perma.cc/PFK8-BUB5.

[18] International Covenant on Civil and Political Rights, G.A. Res. 2200 (XXI), ¶ 2, U.N. Doc. A/Res/2200 (XXI) (Dec. 16, 1966).

[19] Universal Declaration of Human Rights, G.A. Res. 217(III)A, ¶ 1, U.N. Doc. A/RES/217(III) (Dec. 10, 1948).

[20] For more on this view historically, see William N. Eskridge Jr., *Noah's Curse: How Religion Often Conflates, Status, Belief, and Conduct to Resist Antidiscrimination Norms*, 45 GEORGIA L. REV. 657 (2011).

for understandable reasons, the right is not enforced against all persons in all contexts. (For example, the right is not enforced in the context of one's decisions about whom to admit to one's circle of friends.) If it were to exempt the florist's refusal, government, as this chapter explains in the next paragraph, would be accommodating an act that violates the human right to moral equality. This government need not accommodate an act that violates the right to moral equality; indeed, this government should not accommodate such act, given its commitment to the human right to moral equality. Government's justification for refusing to exempt the florist's refusal is obviously sufficiently weighty: there is no less burdensome way for the government to serve the compelling objective of not accommodating a violation of a human right to which it is and should be committed.[21]

Why would the government be accommodating an act that violates the human right to moral equality if it were to exempt the florist's refusal? How does the florist's refusal violate – in what way does it violate – the human right to more equality?

American history demonstrates that in the United States, the view on which the florist's refusal is based – "interracial marriage is immoral" – is an aspect of an ideology, white supremacy, that is directly contrary to the very foundation of the human right to moral equality.[22] Even if the florist in our imagined scenario, like many before her, explains that her moral opposition to interracial marriage is solely on the basis of her (inherited) belief that interracial marriage is contrary to God's will, the fact remains that in the United States, the phenomenon of moral opposition to interracial marriage makes no discernible sense except as an aspect of the ideology of white supremacy.[23] That moral opposition to interracial marriage and the ideology of white supremacy are *logically* independent of one another – that one can affirm the former but not the latter without being illogical – is beside the point. As a "real world" matter, moral opposition to interracial marriage is finally explicable, even in its "God's will" version, only as an aspect of the ideology of white supremacy.[24] Something philosopher John Corvino has observed is relevant here: "[T]he very point of antimiscegenation laws is to signify and maintain the false and pernicious belief that nonwhites are morally inferior to whites."[25]

Thus, the florist's refusal violates the human right to moral equality. Given government's commitment to that human right, government need not – indeed,

---

[21] *See* PERRY, *supra* note 2, at 154. See Wilson, Chapter 30, for an approach that requires businesses to serve all customers, but permits the owner to satisfy the business's duty with employees and subcontractors.

[22] SHERYLL CASHIN, LOVING: INTERRACIAL INTIMACY IN AMERICA AND THE THREAT TO WHITE SUPREMACY 42–66 (2017).

[23] *Id.*

[24] *See* Ian Millhiser, *When "Religious Liberty" Was Used to Justify Racism Instead of Homophobia*, THINKPROGRESS (Feb. 27, 2014), https://perma.cc/6UXQ-KDS6. A prominent example of the phenomenon Millhiser discusses is in Mississippi Governor Theodore G. Bilbo's book, TAKE YOUR CHOICE: SEPARATION OR MONGRELIZATION (1946).

[25] John Corvino, *Homosexuality and the PIB Argument*, 115 ETHICS 3, 501, 509 (2005).

should not – exempt the florist's refusal to facilitate an interracial marriage from the state nondiscrimination law.[26]

III MORAL FREEDOM, MORAL EQUALITY, AND SAME-SEX MARRIAGE

Now, imagine another scenario.[27] Because a florist is morally opposed to same-sex marriage, a florist refuses to sell to a same-sex couple an arrangement of flowers for the couple's upcoming wedding. (The florist is not morally opposed to selling flowers to – and has long sold flowers to – persons who happen to be, and whom she knows to be, gay, lesbian, transgender, etc.) The florist believes that a same-sex "marriage" – in her judgment, a faux marriage – is contrary to God's will. A court determines that the florist's refusal violates the state nondiscrimination law, imposes a fine on her, and orders her not to refuse such requests in the future. In contesting the fine and order, she argues that under the state's constitutional law, which protects the right to moral freedom, government must exempt her refusal from the state nondiscrimination law. Is she, like the florist in the previous scenario, mistaken?

As a "real world" matter, moral opposition to same-sex marriage – in contrast to moral opposition to interracial marriage – is readily explicable other than as an aspect of an ideology or sensibility according to which some human beings are morally inferior to others. More specifically, and as this section explains, moral opposition to same-sex marriage is readily explicable other than as an aspect of homophobic bigotry.

The view that gays and lesbians are morally inferior is sadly familiar. Judge Richard Posner, writing about the "irrational fear and loathing of" gays and lesbians, has observed that they, like the Jews with whom they "were frequently bracketed in medieval persecutions[,] . . . are despised more for what they are than for what they do."[28] The Connecticut Supreme Court echoed that observation in its decision

---

[26] *But cf.* JOHN D. INAZU, CONFIDENT PLURALISM: SURVIVING AND THRIVING THROUGH DEEP DIFFERENCE 74–79 (2016) (discussing Bob Jones University v. United States, 461 U.S. 574 (1983)).

[27] This scenario is based on the facts in State of Washington v. Arlene's Flowers, Inc., 389 P.3d 543 (Wash. 2017). For the details of other refusals by wedding vendors, see McClain, Chapter 17; Smith, Chapter 18; Wilson, Chapter 30.

[28] RICHARD POSNER, SEX AND REASON 346 (1992). As history teaches, an "irrational fear and loathing" of any group often has tragic consequences. The irrational fear and loathing of gays and lesbians is no exception. There is, for example, the horrible phenomenon of "gay bashing." "The coordinator of one hospital's victim assistance program reported that 'attacks against gay men were the most heinous and brutal I encountered.' A physician reported that injuries suffered by the victims of homophobic violence he had treated were so 'vicious' as to make clear that 'the intent is to kill and maim.'" ANDREW KOPPELMAN, ANTIDISCRIMINATION LAW AND SOCIAL EQUALITY 165 (1996). As "[a] federal task force on youth suicide noted[,] because 'gay youth face a hostile and condemning environment, verbal and physical abuse, and rejection and isolation from family and peers,' young gays are two to three times more likely

recognizing same-sex marriage, noting that gays and lesbians are often "'ridiculed, ostracized, despised, demonized and condemned' merely for being who they are."[29] Professor Andrew Koppelman, who is also writing for this volume, has rehearsed some especially grim examples, including "the judge's famous speech at Oscar Wilde's and others' sentencing for sodomy, one of the most prominent legal texts in the history of homosexuality, [which] 'treats the prisoners as objects of disgust, vile contaminants who are not really people, and who therefore need not be addressed as if they were people.'"[30] Koppelman continues

> From this it is not very far to Heinrich Himmler's speech to his SS generals, in which he explained that the medieval German practice of drowning gay men in bogs "was no punishment, merely the extermination of an abnormal life. It had to be removed just as we [now] pull up stinging nettles, toss them on a heap, and burn them."[31]

So society should not discount the possibility that for some persons, their moral opposition to same-sex marriage is premised on or informed by a view – homophobic bigotry – that is contrary to the human right to moral equality.[32]

But that something is true for some persons who are morally opposed to same-sex marriage[33] does not entail that it is true for all or even most persons who are morally opposed to same-sex marriage. The belief that same-sex sexual conduct is immoral does not assert, imply, or presuppose that those who engage in the conduct are morally inferior human beings, any more than the claim that theft is immoral asserts, implies, or presupposes that those who steal are morally inferior human beings. (By contrast, "the very point of antimiscegenation laws" was to implement "the false and pernicious belief that nonwhites are morally inferior to whites."[34]) This is not to deny that some "of the antigay animus that exists in the U.S. is just like racism, in the virulence of the rage it bespeaks and the hatred it directs towards those who are its objects."[35] But "[n]ot all antigay views ... deny the personhood and equal citizenship of gay people."[36] As legal scholar Robert Nagel has emphasized,

---

than other young people to attempt and to commit suicide." *Id.* at 149. See also Minter, Chapter 4, for the scale of the public health crisis experience by LGBT youth.

[29] Kerrigan v. Comm'r of Public Health, 957 A.2d 407, 445–46 (Conn. 2008).

[30] Andrew Koppelman, *Are the Boy Scouts Being as Bad as Racists? Judging the Scouts' Antigay Policy*, 18 Pub. Aff. Q. 363, 372 (2004).

[31] *Id.*

[32] *See* Shannon Gilreath & Arley Ward, *Same-Sex Marriage, Religious Accommodation, and the Race Analogy*, 41 Vermont L. Rev. 237, 244–45 (2016); *see also* Michael Jensen, *I Oppose Same-Sex Marriage (and No, I'm Not a Bigot)*, ABC News (May 27, 2015), https://perma.cc/4UZ5-WUAN.

[33] *See id.*

[34] *See* Corvino, *supra* note 25, at 509.

[35] Andrew Koppelman, *You Can't Hurry Love: Why Antidiscrimination Protections for Gay People Should Have Religious Exemptions*, 72 Brook. L. Rev. 125, 145 (2006).

[36] *Id.*

"[t]here is the obvious but important possibility that one can 'hate' an individual's behavior without hating the individual."[37]

Consider, as a prominent example of "hating the sin but not the sinner," the teaching of the magisterium – of the pope and the bishops – of the Roman Catholic Church, who are leading opponents of "legislative and judicial attempts, both at state and federal levels, to grant same-sex unions the equivalent status and rights of marriage – by naming them marriage, civil unions or by other means."[38] According to the magisterium's teaching, it is immoral not just for same-sex couples but for anyone and everyone – even a man and a woman who are married to one another – to engage in (*i.e.*, pursuant to a knowing, uncoerced choice to engage in) any sexual conduct that is "inherently nonprocreative."[39] Same-sex sexual conduct – like contracepted male-female sexual intercourse, masturbation, and both oral and anal sex – is inherently nonprocreative. Because "[w]hat are called 'homosexual unions' . . . are inherently nonprocreative," declared the Administrative Committee of the US Conference of Catholic Bishops, they "cannot be given the status of marriage."[40] As Joseph Cardinal Ratzinger who later became Pope Benedict XVI stated in 2003, speaking for the Congregation for the Doctrine of the Faith: because homosexual acts "close the sexual act to the gift of life . . . homosexual acts go against the natural moral law."[41] Nonetheless, the pope and bishops also insist that all human beings, gays and lesbians no less than others, are equally beloved children of God.[42] "[Our teaching] about the dignity of homosexual persons is clear. They

---

[37] *See* Robert F. Nagel, *Playing Defense in Colorado*, 6 WM & MARY BILL RTS. J. 167, 201 (1997).

[38] *U.S. Catholic Bishops' Administrative Committee Calls for Protection of Marriage*, U.S. CONFERENCE OF CATHOLIC BISHOPS (Sept. 10, 2003), https://perma.cc/RDA6-5WG8.

[39] *See* LESLIE WOODCOCK TENTLER, CATHOLICS AND CONTRACEPTION: AN AMERICAN HISTORY (2004).

[40] *U.S. Catholic Bishops' Administrative Committee Calls for Protection of Marriage, supra* note 38. *See also* Congregation for the Doctrine of the Faith, *Considerations Regarding Proposals to Give Legal Recognition to Unions Between Homosexual Persons* (June 3, 2003), https://perma.cc/7XR4-EEAB.

[41] *Id. See* David Hollenbach, *Religious Freedom and Law: John Courtney Murray Today*, 1 J. MORAL THEOLOGY 69, 75 (2012):

> The United States Catholic Bishops have adopted particularly pointed public advocacy positions on . . . resistance to gay marriage and public acceptance of the legitimacy of same sex relationships. The Bishops' 2007 statement *Forming Consciences for Faithful Citizenship* was a formal instruction by the U.S. hierarchy covering the full range of the public dimensions of the Church's moral concerns. In this document, . . . echoing the affirmation by the Catechism of the Catholic Church that homosexual acts "are contrary to the natural law" and that "under no circumstances can they be approved," the bishops oppose[d] "same-sex unions or other distortions of marriage."

[42] *U.S. Catholic Bishops' Administrative Committee Calls for Protection of Marriage, supra* note 38. *See also* HELEN M. ALVARÉ, PUTTING CHILDREN'S INTERESTS FIRST IN U.S. FAMILY LAW AND POLICY: WITH POWER COMES RESPONSIBILITY (2018). *Cf.* Eskridge, *supra* note 20, at 704.

must be accepted with respect, compassion, and sensitivity. Our respect for them means that we condemn all forms of unjust discrimination, harassment or abuse."[43]

The magisterium's teaching that "inherently nonprocreative" sexual conduct is immoral – no less than an interpretation of a religious scripture according to which same-sex "marriage" is contrary to God's will – is a constitutionally inadequate basis for excluding same-sex couples from civil marriage.[44] But this does not mean that in the United States today, moral opposition to same-sex marriage is generally, much less invariably, an aspect of homophobic bigotry. Recall, in that regard, the late Justice Antonin Scalia's dissenting opinion (joined by Justice Clarence Thomas) in *United States v. Windsor*, in which Justice Scalia strenuously objected to what he perceived to be the majority's unwarranted accusation that all who are morally opposed to same-sex marriage have "hateful hearts"; that they are "unhinged members of a wild-eyed lynch mob ... an enemy of human decency ... In the majority's telling," lamented Justice Scalia, "this story is all black-and-white: Hate

---

The Vatican's 1975 Declaration *Persona Humana* announced that "homosexual acts" are "disordered," but also acknowledged the modern distinction between sexual orientation and sexual acts. The next year, the National Conference of Catholic Bishops responded with a more gay-tolerant document, "To Live in Christ Jesus," which said this: "Homosexuals, like everyone else, should not suffer from prejudice against their basic human rights. They have a right to respect, friendship and justice. They should have an active role in the Christian community." Different dioceses adopted slightly different readings of these documents. For example, the Church in the state of Washington interpreted the pronouncements to support the conclusion that *"prejudice against homosexuals is a greater infringement of the norm of Christian morality than is homosexual orientation or activity."*

[R]eflecting a strong turn in public opinion toward toleration for gay people, the American Catholic Church was subtly readjusting its doctrinal stance toward homosexuality. According to the Vatican, men and women with homosexual tendencies "must be accepted with respect, compassion, and sensitivity. Every sign of unjust discrimination in their regard should be avoided." After fighting the nondiscrimination law in Massachusetts through the 1980s, Catholic dioceses acquiesced in similar laws adopted by Catholic Connecticut in 1991 and Catholic Rhode Island in 1995. Archbishop John Francis Whealon of Hartford, Connecticut said this in 1991: "The Church clearly teaches that homosexual men and women should not suffer prejudice based on their sexual orientation. Such discrimination is contrary to the Gospel of Jesus Christ and is always morally wrong." Many Connecticut legislators took the Archbishop's statement as tacit approval of the nondiscrimination measure (adorned with religious liberty-protective exemptions). The Roman Catholic shift in emphasis – not necessarily a shift in precise doctrine – was representative of organized religion in America, as public opinion shifted strongly toward toleration of gay Americans and same-sex couples.

Id. For a discussion of Pope Francis's engagement with LGBT members of the Catholic Church, see Gramick, Chapter 10.

[43] *U.S. Catholic Bishops' Administrative Committee Calls for Protection of Marriage, supra* note 38.

[44] *See* PERRY, *supra* note 2, at 137–52. For a nuanced account that charges of animus and other "civil rights simplisms" cannot chart the correct answer to conflicts between faith and sexuality, see Smith, Chapter 18.

your neighbor or come along with us."[45] Similarly, in his dissenting opinion in *Obergefell v. Hodges*, Chief Justice John Roberts, joined by Justices Scalia and Thomas, wrote:

> Perhaps the most discouraging aspect of today's decision is the extent to which the majority feels compelled to sully those on the other side of the debate. The majority offers a cursory assurance that it does not intend to disparage people who, as a matter of conscience, cannot accept same-sex marriage. That disclaimer is hard to square with the very next sentence, in which the majority explains that "the necessary consequence" of laws codifying the traditional definition of marriage is to "demea[n] or stigmatiz[e]" same-sex couples. The majority reiterates such characterizations over and over. By the majority's account, Americans who did nothing more than follow the understanding of marriage that has existed for our entire history – in particular, the tens of millions of people who voted to reaffirm their States' enduring definition of marriage – have acted to "lock ... out," "disparage," "disrespect and subordinate," and inflict "[d]ignitary wounds" upon their gay and lesbian neighbors. These apparent assaults on the character of fairminded people will have an effect, in society and in court ... It is one thing for the majority to conclude that the Constitution protects a right to same-sex marriage; it is something else to portray everyone who does not share the majority's "better informed understanding" as bigoted.[46]

Let us assume that the florist in our imagined scenario is not a homophobic bigot but that she nonetheless agrees with – or, if she is a Catholic, that she at least defers to – the magisterium's teaching concerning "inherently nonprocreative" sexual conduct, a teaching as Lori and Gramick note elsewhere in this volume that long antedates the relatively recent emergence of the moral, political, and constitutional controversies over same-sex marriage. In that case, her refusal to sell to the same-sex couple a flower arrangement for their upcoming wedding is not fairly regarded as an act that violates the human right to moral equality.

However, this conclusion does not necessitate that the florist's conscience-based request for an exemption from the state nondiscrimination law be granted. Whether it should be granted depends on the answers to further questions[47] – including, not least, these two: Would granting such requests have the effect of making it difficult for same-sex couples to gain access to the wedding-related services they seek? Because of the continued virulence of homophobic bigotry in some parts of American society, are the florist's and similar refusals commonly experienced by

---

[45] United States v. Windsor, 133 S. Ct. 2675, 2697, 2707, 2708, 2710, 2711 (2013) (Scalia, J., dissenting).

[46] Obergefell v. Hodges, 135 S. Ct. 2584, 2626 (2015) (Roberts, J., dissenting).

[47] *See* KENT GREENAWALT, EXEMPTIONS: NECESSARY, JUSTIFIED, OR MISGUIDED? 84 (2016); Kent Greenawalt, *Individual Conscience and How It Should Be Treated*, 31 J. L. & RELIGION 306 (2016).

same-sex couples (and others) as demeaning, dehumanizing, hurtful rejections,[48] even when, as in our imagined scenario, a particular refusal is not based on homophobic bigotry and so does not violate the human right to moral equality?

IV CONCLUSION

The intuition of many persons may be that the conscience-based claim for an exemption pressed by the florist who is morally opposed to same-sex marriage presents a more complex and difficult issue than the conscience-based claim for an exemption pressed by the florist morally opposed to interracial marriage. What this chapter serves to provide is a rational vindication of that intuition; it serves to explain why as *a matter of principle* – specifically, *as a matter of the human right to moral equality* – the two conscience-based claims merit different responses,[49] even if it is not unreasonable for lawmakers, in legislating, or for judges, in adjudicating, to reach the conclusion that, all things considered, the former claim too should be rejected.[50]

---

[48] Gilreath and Ward certainly experience such refusals as demeaning, dehumanizing, hurtful rejections. *See* Shannon Gilreath & Arley Ward, *supra* note 32.

[49] Consider, in that regard, *Trinity Western University v. The Law Society of Upper Canada* (2006), 131 O.R. 3d 113 (Can. Ont. C.A.), in which the British Columbia Court of Appeal ruled in favor of accrediting Trinity Western University's new law school notwithstanding the university's requirement that students wanting to attend TWU sign a covenant that opposes same-sex marriage. It is safe to assume, I think, that had the university required students wanting to attend TWU sign a covenant that opposed interracial marriage, the court would not have ruled in TWU's favor.

[50] If it is not unreasonable to conclude that the former claim too should be rejected, it does not follow that it is unreasonable to conclude that the former claim should be *granted*. Why assume that there is no room for a reasonable difference of judgments about the matter? For an argument that in *State of Washington v. Arlene's Flowers, Inc.*, 389 P.3d 543 (Wash. 2017), the Washington Supreme Court should have done what it eventually declined to do – grant the florist's conscience-based claim for an exemption – see the Brief for the Legal Scholars in Support of Equality and Religious and Expressive Freedom as Amici Curiae in Support of Appellants, 2016 WL 6126873 (Wash.) (Appellate Brief). Consider the range of views articulated in the U.S. Commission on Civil Rights report, U.S. Comm'n on Civil Rights, Peaceful Coexistence: Reconciling Nondiscrimination Principles with Civil Liberties (2016).

21

On the Uses of Anti-Christian Identity Politics

Marc O. DeGirolami

To ask about the relationship of Christianity and American law and politics is to probe a fraught and discomfiting subject. There are reasonable and measured responses that acknowledge the centrality of Christianity as a historical and cultural matter and its continuing, though diminished and diminishing, relevance and influence. Why, then, does the relationship between Christianity and American law continue to excite such fervid reactions?

American law is the product of a centuries-long Western legal tradition that has been deeply informed by Christian understandings of the nature of law and individual rights – as well as the proper allocation and limits of government power that include the separation of powers and the division of authority between national and state governments.[1] Magna Carta, for example, which was drafted in significant part by Archbishop of Canterbury Stephen Langton, is in many ways the ancestor of foundational American rights including the right to due process of law and other bedrock limits on government power. What is known and broadly praised today as the distinctively American conception of "separation of church and state" is essentially a piece of Christian political theology.[2]

True, the more temporally proximate historical source of American law and politics is the seventeenth- and eighteenth-century Enlightenment, and one of the primary projects of thinkers of this period was to separate ecclesiastical from civil authority. Yet many of the most influential figures on, and of, the American founding (John Locke, George Washington, John Adams, James Madison, Patrick Henry, and even Thomas Jefferson, to name only a few) assumed and directed their arguments toward a distinctively Christian commonwealth and advanced

---

[1] *See generally* HAROLD J. BERMAN, LAW AND REVOLUTION: THE FORMATION OF THE WESTERN LEGAL TRADITION (1983).

[2] Marc O. DeGirolami, *The Two Separations, in* THE CAMBRIDGE COMPANION TO THE FIRST AMENDMENT AND RELIGIOUS LIBERTY (Michael Breidenbach & Owen Anderson eds., forthcoming 2019).

distinctively Christian theological arguments in support of their views.[3] Statesmen of the stature of Jefferson and Justice Joseph Story debated whether, and in what sense, Christianity was "part of the common law" of England and the United States.[4] As late as the turn of the twentieth century, the Supreme Court, in deciphering the meaning of a federal statute, declared with confidence that "this is a Christian nation."[5] It relied on what were at that time common cultural and legal assumptions, as well as a "mass of organic utterances" drawn from colonial charters, state constitutions, and common law decisions, among others.[6] And Christianity has also been the major religion of the United States as a matter of political culture: its holidays, its solemnizing rituals, its civic and moral structures and strictures (such as those concerning marriage, for example), and its public language and symbols ("In God We Trust"; "One Nation Under God"; "God Bless America") continue to provide perhaps the most widely shared set of common, American cultural assumptions, though, to be sure, ones whose salience is weakening.[7]

At the same time, the Constitution does not rest on the authority of any church or religious institution; indeed, the Establishment Clause of the First Amendment expressly states that the federal government is not to make laws respecting religious establishments, and this proscription has been extended by the Supreme Court to apply against the states.[8] The Religious Test Clause precludes Congress or the president from imposing a formal test-oath on putative federal office holders.[9] There is to be no Church of the United States that is aligned with and controlled by the political and legal authority, and no religious orthodoxy can delimit membership in the political class. The United States is not to be a theocracy. In this important sense, law and politics in the United States are secularized – disentangled and set apart from religious authority.[10]

The archetypal case of religion for these purposes is Christianity, since Christianity is the dominant religion of the American historical experience, and the Anglican Church is the church-state model that the American founders had immediately before them. With the coming of religious pluralism in the United States, the rise of nonbelievers as well as the so-called Nones and the respective legal challenges these groups pose,[11] and the fragmentation and diminution of the mainline Protestant

---

[3] *Id.*

[4] *See* THE SACRED RIGHTS OF CONSCIENCE (Daniel L. Dreisbach & Mark David Hall eds., 2010).

[5] Holy Trinity Church v. United States, 143 U.S 457, 471 (1892).

[6] *Id.*

[7] *See generally* Robert N. Bellah, *Civil Religion in America*, 96 J. AM. ACAD. ARTS & SCI. 1 (1967).

[8] *See* Everson v. Bd. of Ed. of Ewing Twp., 330 U.S. 1 (1947).

[9] *See generally* Paul Horwitz, *Religious Tests in the Mirror: The Constitutional Law and Constitutional Etiquette of Religion in Judicial Nominations*, 15 WM. & MARY BILL RTS. J. 75 (2006).

[10] For additional discussion of the Establishment Clause, see Hollman, Chapter 23.

[11] *See generally* Daniel Cox & Robert P. Jones, *America's Changing Religious Identity*, PUB. RELIGION RESEARCH INST. (2017), https://perma.cc/AK6V-X6YT (reporting that nearly one out

Christianity that was so widely shared for most of the country's history,[12] Christianity plays a much less important cultural role than it once did. These trends are likely to strengthen, and Christianity's influence to weaken, in coming decades.

This description of the American relationship to Christianity may be contestable in its details, but whatever objections may be lodged against it somehow fail to get at the heart of the dispute. That is because the real fight is not about historical or descriptive accuracy but the nature of American identity and to what extent the historical past should inform that identity – not about the kind of country America has been but about the kind America is and should aspire to be.

This chapter cannot hope to trace the complete and ongoing history of that disagreement. Nor is it necessary to do so, since criticisms of Christian nationalists as well as the "Christian Right" are well rehearsed and abundant.[13] This chapter instead focuses on one manifestation of a more recent and parallel phenomenon – anti-Christian American nationalism. It briefly discusses a distinctive variety of anti-Christian identity politics inspired by one particular legal source: an obscure provision of a document often called the Treaty of Tripoli of 1796 (Treaty of Tripoli), which states that "the government of the United States is not, in any sense, founded on the Christian religion."[14] The uses to which the phrase has been put are more important than its confused historical meaning. In evaluating anti-Christian identity politics in some of these uses, this chapter considers the recent claim by Professor Mark Lilla that contemporary Americans – and American liberals in particular – ought to abandon "the politics of identity" in favor of a politics of shared citizenship.[15]

Lilla is right that identity politics – the formation of political allegiances in conformity with, and for the promotion of, particular notions of the modern self – as practiced today have corroded the commonalities that remain among Americans. Identity politics also render compromise on various culture-war issues more difficult:

---

of four Americans identify as spiritual but religiously unaffiliated and are on average younger than self-identified Christians); Mark L. Movsesian, *Defining Religion in American Law: Psychic Sophie and the Rise of the Nones* (European University Institute, Working Paper, 2014). For discussion of the significance of the rise of Nones, see Leith Anderson, Chapter 12.

[12] *See generally* JOSEPH BOTTUM, AN ANXIOUS AGE: THE POST-PROTESTANT ETHIC AND THE SPIRIT OF AMERICA (2014).

[13] *See* DeGirolami, *supra* note 2.

[14] Treaty of Peace and Friendship Between the United States of America and the Bey and Subjects of Tripoli of Barbary, Article XI (1796), https://perma.cc/BT6P-89W6. The full text of Article XI reads:

As the government of the United States of America is not in any sense founded on the Christian Religion,-as it has in itself no character of enmity against the laws, religion or tranquility of Musselmen,-and as the said States never have entered into any war or act of hostility against any Mehomitan nation, it is declared by the parties that no pretext arising from religious opinions shall ever produce an interruption of the harmony existing between the two countries.

[15] MARK LILLA, THE ONCE AND FUTURE LIBERAL: AFTER IDENTITY POLITICS 14–15 (2017).

any policy or legal victory for the opposition, however small, takes on greater symbolic importance and must therefore be resisted all the more fiercely. Yet the pathologies of identity politics are only symptoms of a more potent sickness in American political and cultural life. Americans, as citizens, share less and less. They disagree in deepening ways about the nature of the political and moral good, about justice, and about what sort of people Americans are and aspire to be. In short, identity politics are not the cause of, but a response to, political and cultural fragmentation. And anti-Christian identity politics, like Christian identity politics, represent one strain of that response – one ostensible common meeting point for a nation whose people are increasingly disaffected with and alienated from one another.

I ARTICLE XI AND ANTI-CHRISTIAN IDENTITY POLITICS

Christian identity politics are nothing new. Scholars have long debated the question whether the American founders were more influenced by Christian (principally Calvinist) or secular Enlightenment understandings.[16] Some emphasize the founding generation's straightforward relation of revealed religion, reason, and natural rights, as well as religious sources and baselines while others, likely a majority, minimize these and focus on secular sources. The debate is the sort that will never be won because there is sufficient historical evidence, amenable to all manner of supple interpretive acrobatics, to warrant many different conclusions.

It is difficult enough to disentangle and measure the relative strength of religious influences on a single political or judicial figure – on George Washington or John Adams, for example, or Joseph Story or Antonin Scalia. It seems an utterly hopeless undertaking to say with any confidence about an entire country with as variegated a history as that of the United States that "we are a Christian nation." Indeed, when commentators are bold enough to claim that the United States has been a Christian nation from its founding, they are perhaps best understood as arguing about America's present and future rather than its past.[17] Often what these commentators advocate as a historical and cultural recovery is in fact a rather untested and novel legal and political program.

---

[16] The contests among historians and political writers are summarized effectively from the secularist perspective in Steven K. Green, *Understanding the "Christian Nation" Myth*, 2010 CARDOZO L. REV. DE NOVO 245 (2010).

[17] For one example, see former Alaska governor Sarah Palin's statement in 2009: "I think we should ... go back to what our founders and our founding documents meant. They're quite clear that we should create law based on the God of the Bible and the 10 Commandments." *Interview by Bill O'Reilly with Sarah Palin, Former Governor of Alaska*, FoxNews (May 6, 2009), https://perma.cc/39FJ-68BH.

Yet just as there are Christian-nation advocates, so, too, are there partisans of an anti-Christian nation view – those who view something fundamentally and constitutively American in the rejection of Christianity or features of it. In the recent report of the US Commission on Civil Rights entitled *Peaceful Coexistence: Reconciling Nondiscrimination Principles with Religious Liberty*, for example, Commission Chairman Martin Castro headlined his statement with an epigraph: "The government of the United States is not, in any sense, founded on the Christian religion."[18] The line is attributed to John Adams, and there is no other direct reference to it. The rest of Chairman's Castro's short statement tends to refer to "religion" in general. And the Commission's report generally does not refer to Christianity in specific, but to conflicts between "religion" or "religious freedom" and newly emerging rights of sexual liberty and equality.

But the chairman saw fit to single out Christianity as well as the evils of "Christian supremacy."[19] By doing so, he provided an overarching, symbolic theme to the Commission's findings and recommendations. The Commission's most critical comments were leveled at those cases and laws in which particular Christian scruples and beliefs were accommodated when they conflicted with nondiscrimination norms.[20] Its highest praise was bestowed on those cases in which particular Christian scruples and beliefs either were not accommodated or were expressly subordinated in the conflict with nondiscrimination norms.[21] "[T]hroughout history," the Commission's findings and recommendations explain, "religious doctrines accepted at one time later become viewed as discriminatory, with religions changing accordingly."[22] "Religious liberty," the chairman stated, "was never intended to give one religion dominion" and "[t]his generation of Americans must stand up and speak out" against any such pretensions.[23] For Chairman Castro and the Commission, the government's responsibility is to stimulate what they see as salutary changes. And, as the cases cited by the Commission make clear, no religion is in need of more vigorous monitoring for its "supremacist" tendencies than Christianity.

The message is in fact quite clear. Christianity – or at least certain prominent kinds of Christianity – must and will change, by compulsion if necessary. Americans simply are not the sort of people who will tolerate, let alone accommodate, Christian

---

[18] *See* U.S. COMM'N ON CIVIL RIGHTS, PEACEFUL COEXISTENCE: RECONCILING NONDISCRIMINATION PRINCIPLES WITH RELIGIOUS LIBERTY 29 (statement of Chairman Martin R. Castro), https://perma.cc/W8HN-PPCR.

[19] *See id.; see also id.* at 115, 122 (statement and rebuttal of Commissioner Gail Heriot (quoting Commissioner Castro)).

[20] *Id.* (citing Hosanna-Tabor Evangelical Lutheran Church and Sch. v. E.E.O.C., 565 U.S. 171 (2012); Burwell v. Hobby Lobby Stores, Inc., 134 S. Ct. 2751 (2014); Religious Freedom Restoration Act, 42 U.S.C. § 2000bb-4 (1993)).

[21] *Id.* (citing Christian Legal Soc. Chapter of the Univ. of California, Hastings Coll. of the Law v. Martinez, 561 U.S. 661 (2010); Obergefell v. Hodges, 135 S. Ct. 2584 (2015)).

[22] *See* PEACEFUL COEXISTENCE, *supra* note 18, at 26, Finding 7.

[23] *Id.* at 29 (statement of Chairman Castro).

views – about morality, justice, and the political good – should those views conflict in any way with nondiscrimination norms, and particularly those essential norms concerning sexuality and equality. Americans ought to be hostile to Christianity under such circumstances. Christianity is in this sense inimical to the American project – un-American. Indeed, one can hear in the chairman's and in the Commission's rhetoric distinctive echoes of what John Courtney Murray once remarked as the "nativist inspiration," "visible in the constant use of the adjectives 'American' and 'un-American' as the ultimate categories of value."[24] The epigraph gives the chairman's statement a distinctively and powerfully anti-Christian flavor: to be truly American, to understand America's history as well as its future, is precisely to reject Christianity of this sort.

Before considering these claims further, a brief word is necessary about the mysterious historical genesis of the epigraph. Its source was not Adams, as Commissioner Gail Heriot also notes in her rebuttal;[25] indeed, its authorship is something of an enigma. The phrase is located in Article XI of the Treaty of Tripoli, which was negotiated in 1797 by the United States and the nominally Ottoman city-states of Algiers, Tripoli, Morocco, and Tunis for protection against the depredations of pirates in the surrounding waters.[26] These pirates routinely, and with the tacit blessing of the so-called Barbary States, targeted, captured, and enslaved Christians. The United States had at one time been protected by the English navy, and thereafter by the French in the aftermath of the American Revolutionary War, but after suffering substantial losses at sea, the United States now needed to form a new treaty with these powers.

Certainly more important than the language of the treaty was the sum to be paid to the Barbary States, which had declared themselves at war with all Christian states that did not pay tribute. The amount was staggering; indeed, the enormity of the gift might lead one to suspect that there was a sizable temptation to say just about anything in order to avoid having to pay any more money. As the treaty itself puts it rather emphatically after it lists all of the ransom: "And no further demand of tributes, presents or payments shall ever be made."[27]

There is serious doubt about whether Article XI was part of the original treaty at all. The Treaty of Tripoli was originally drafted in Arabic and was subsequently translated into English before being submitted to President Adams and the US Senate. A Dutch scholar of the Arabic language writing in the 1930s, Christiaan Snouk Hurgronje, who examined the original document, concluded that Article XI

---

[24] John Courtney Murray, *Paul Blanshard and the New Nativism*, THE MONTH 191, 215–16 (1951).
[25] *See* PEACEFUL COEXISTENCE, *supra* note 18, at 115, 124, n.12 (statement and rebuttal of Commissioner Gail Heriot).
[26] *Supra* note 14.
[27] *Supra* note 14, at Article X.

had no equivalent in the original Arabic.[28] Somebody seems to have added Article XI after the treaty was drafted and signed by the Barbary states, but before it was ratified by the president and the Senate; the strong suspicion is that one of the American emissaries to Algiers, Joel Barlow, slipped it in.[29] Barlow had been raised in conservative Connecticut, but after an extended stay in France and a warm flirtation with Girondist leaders beginning in 1788, he had rather ostentatiously abandoned Christian orthodoxy for Enlightenment Rationalism. He was made a French citizen in the early 1790s.

Yet however Article XI made its way into the translated Treaty of Tripoli, it was ratified unanimously by the Senate and signed by the president. What is perhaps most remarkable is that not a word of protest was raised against it in 1797. Federalists and Republicans approved it without any objection, and indeed, seemingly without any debate at all. Adams signed it into law without comment – the same John Adams who would write only a decade later in a letter to Benjamin Rush, "The Bible contains … the most perfect morality … that was ever conceived upon earth. It is the most republican book in the world, and therefore I will still revere it … [W]ithout national morality a republican government cannot be maintained."[30]

There are ways to explain this silence, though they are speculative. Part of the answer might depend upon the meaning of the phrase "not, in any sense, founded on the Christian religion." One possible interpretation is that no single ecclesiastical denomination is established in the United States. Such establishments were the norm in several states at the time (including in Adams's native Massachusetts and, of course, in England), but it would have been uncontroversial to say that there was no similar national establishment in the United States. Indeed, that interpretation would have comported with the Establishment Clause. The rest of the Treaty of Tripoli discusses the fairly banal details of the agreement – what is to be done with the subjects and goods of ships seized by the parties, the compensation paid to the Barbary States, passports that must be produced for inspection, the forbidding of pillage should a ship of the other party wash up on shore, and the like.

Article XI might therefore have been intended as an assurance to the Bey and the Barbary States that the United States would not renege on the terms of the agreement on the ground of national Christian hostility to Islam. That is, Article XI establishes the terms of the relationship between nations with very different religious traditions, as the remainder of the text of the Article makes plain.

---

[28] See TREATIES AND OTHER INTERNATIONAL ACTS OF THE UNITED STATES OF AMERICA 2:371 (Hunter Miller ed., 1931–48).

[29] See MORTON BORDEN, JEWS, TURKS, AND INFIDELS 77 (1984).

[30] See Letter from John Adams to Benjamin Rush (Feb. 2, 1807). See also JOHN ADAMS, A DEFENSE OF THE CONSTITUTIONS OF GOVERNMENT IN THE UNITED STATES OF AMERICA, Preface (1788) ("[I]t can no longer be called in question" that "authority in magistrates and obedience of citizens can be grounded on reason, morality, and the Christian religion.").

Of course, other interpretations are possible. Perhaps the language does mean to disavow Christianity more broadly as a basis for American government, as the language "in any sense" might suggest. In that case, however, one wonders why such an affirmation should be made in the middle of a geopolitical treaty otherwise having little to do with these issues.

At any rate, this intriguingly opaque history contrasts starkly with the straightforward uses to which Article XI has been put since its drafting, and especially in the twentieth century. In 1955, for example, the American Association for the Advancement of Atheism declared with great conviction that George Washington was Article XI's author.[31] It has been subsequently trotted out with dutiful ceremony for the proposition that through it, "the founding fathers" thereby made a decisive and indelible statement – one which "transcends its authorship" – about "the role of religion in our government."[32]

This is likewise the sort of meaning ascribed to Article XI by Chairman Castro and the Commission. It is a reading that concerns not its historical meaning, but its embodiment of who and what we are as Americans. Article XI, on this view, expresses something timeless and constitutive about America that regards its historical, political, and cultural association with Christianity (conservative Christianity, especially) as an embarrassment, anathema, or un-American. In this sense, Article XI has taken on independent significance quite distinct from its own history as an emblem of anti-Christian American identity.

II ABANDONING IDENTITY POLITICS?

Setting aside the absence of any real connection between the historical evidence and this sort of symbolic use of Article XI, its use in a report such as the Commission's is cause for other concern as well. At the present American legal and cultural moment, compromises between those with traditional Christian views and those who advocate for new and expanding sexual egalitarian rights are extraordinarily complex and difficult to achieve.[33] As the work of one of the volume editors, Professor Robin Wilson, and other similarly minded moderate scholars has shown, compromise requires the careful delineation and apportioning of legal rights and obligations in which victories for the other side are not seen as battles lost or territory ceded in a zero sum game.[34] Compromise becomes impossible when "each side is

---

[31] *See* Sherman D. Wakefield, *The Treaty With Tripoli of 1796–97*, Progressive World 27–30 (1955).

[32] *See generally The Great Debate of Our Season*, Mother Jones (2005).

[33] For hurdles facing state lawmakers today, see Wilson, Chapter 30.

[34] *See* Robin Fretwell Wilson, *Bargaining for Religious Accommodations: Same-Sex Marriage and LGBT Rights After Hobby Lobby, in* The Rise of Corporate Religious Liberty 264–68 (2016). For the views of lawmakers, see Adams, Chapter 32; Leavitt, Chapter 33.

intolerant of the other; each side wants a total win"; and each side views any defeat, however minor, as empowering the enemy.[35]

Anti-Christian American identity politics, like their pro-Christian counterpart, render compromise extremely unlikely. They are a singularly effective means of entrenching and exacerbating political polarization, as those with traditional Christian views on matters of sexuality and morality are no longer simply fellow citizens with different opinions, but fundamentally wicked and anti-American. Once Christians who hold positions that do not conform to contemporary orthodoxies become the symbols of what must be vanquished, it is no longer possible even to speak together with them, let alone to negotiate over legal arrangements.

It may be in part for this reason that Mark Lilla, in his recent book *The Once and Future Liberal*, argues that identity politics should be abandoned. The perennial romantic impulse to merge the political and the personal – to achieve a politics "where the answers to the questions *Who am I?* and *What are we?* are exactly the same" – has been a particularly powerful political force in the United States since the mid-twentieth century.[36] Lilla explains:

> What all these groups wanted from politics was more than social justice and an end to war. They also wanted there to be no space between what they felt inside and what they did out in the world. They wanted to feel at one with political movements that mirrored how they understood and defined themselves as individuals. And they wanted their self-definition to be recognized.[37]

The shifts described by Lilla have affected the law as well, and perhaps in no area more profoundly than constitutional law. The Supreme Court's view of the fundamental purposes of the First Amendment, for example, steadily changed during the twentieth century from justifications that emphasized truth seeking and common democratic deliberative processes to those that made authenticity and self-actualization paramount.[38] Likewise, the Court's contemporary conception of individual liberty more broadly in its "substantive due process" jurisprudence has assumed a distinctively self-definitional and solipsistic cast. Legal rights are now not about what people do, but about who they are.[39]

Lilla writes as a liberal and for a liberal-progressive audience. Though he praises the advances in social justice that he argues have resulted from an embrace of

---

[35] Douglas Laycock, *Religious Liberty and the Culture Wars*, 2014 ILL. L. REV. 839, 879. For views on how the election of President Donald Trump has affected this dynamic, see Laycock, Chapter 3.

[36] LILLA, *supra* note 15, at 72.

[37] *Id.* at 76.

[38] *See* Marc O. DeGirolami, *Virtue, Freedom, and the First Amendment*, 91 NOTRE DAME L. REV. 1465 (2016).

[39] *See* Planned Parenthood v. Casey, 505 U.S. 833, 851 (1992) (plurality op.) ("At the heart of liberty is the right to define one's own concept of existence, of meaning, of the universe, and of the mystery of human life.").

identitarian concerns, he bemoans the shift in focus of American liberal politics from commonality to difference: "[W]hat replaced a broad political vision was a pseudo-political and distinctly American rhetoric of the feeling self and its struggle for recognition."[40] The favored political locution is no longer "Speaking as an American," but instead "Speaking as an X," in which identity as X gives the speaker a uniquely privileged position to offer an opinion on a given subject, and where "the winner of the argument will be whoever invoked the morally superior identity."[41] This leaves Americans of different backgrounds and beliefs with no points to debate together, no commonalities, and indeed, nothing to say to one another at all, as "what replaces argument ... is taboo."[42]

Liberals, Lilla argues, must develop a vision for the American future that "convinces people, from very different walks of life, in every part of the country, that they share a common destiny and need to stand together."[43] Identity politics – including, though he does not specifically invoke them, the sort of anti-Christian identity politics represented by the symbolic uses of Article XI – are pernicious obstructions for a society that, in the end, must elevate "democratic persuasion over aimless self-expression" and "citizenship over group identity or personal identity."[44] Identity politics not only make the hard work of the compromisers impossible, but they also stunt the possibility of constructing any future political foundation of common American solidarity.

III ANTI-CHRISTIAN AMERICAN IDENTITY POLITICS AS A SYMPTOM OF CULTURAL DISSOLUTION

Lilla persuasively makes the case for the corrosiveness of identity politics – for their effectiveness in further fraying the political and cultural bonds shared by Americans. But his recommendations seem utterly implausible. Political vision and invocations of "citizenship" based on a shared sense of national destiny cannot simply be manufactured or purchased or wished into existence in the absence of agreement about what makes for a good life, what constitutes a just society, and what is truly constitutive of American nationhood. Political vision of this kind depends upon the capacity to create and embrace a common and unifying tradition, even if in part a mythologized one, that speaks to these matters. There is a reason that identity politics thrive and flourish: at present we have no such unifying tradition.

The champions of anti-Christian identity politics hope to provide an ersatz replacement to fill this considerable hole in modern American public life: if we Americans cannot tell you who we are, at least we can tell you with great certitude

---

[40] LILLA, *supra* note 15, at 78.
[41] *Id.* at 90.
[42] *Id.* at 91.
[43] *Id.* at 102.
[44] *Id.* at 104.

who we are not: we are not Christian. In this view, America's cultural and civic essence lies in the repudiation of orthodox Christian views, and the concomitant disavowal of whatever is Christian in our collective past, concerning fundamental questions of human anthropology, politics, justice, and ethics.

Christians who hold these views today are propounders of "hate," an ascription that is itself a powerful marker of American civic decay – of a "debased and divisive" political and cultural discourse.[45] The more, and the more deeply, Americans disagree with one another about moral and political questions – and the more these matters become not so much subjects of American civic disagreement as discrete, irreconcilable, and fixed standpoints among distinctive identitarian groups that happen to live alongside one another in America – the less there remains to say to one another as Americans.

One thing does remain, however: the *ad hominem* ascription to one's adversaries of hatred, ill will, malevolent motivation, or, as the Supreme Court recently put it, "the bare desire to harm."[46] That "taboo," as Lilla put it, endures after the end of the argument. Resort to this particular discursive device is damaging, not least because it makes appeals to a shared political vision impossible.[47] Indeed, it is hard to imagine anything more perfectly calculated to destroy any lingering American commonalities.

IV CONCLUSION

The political theorist Jacob Levy has recently written that identity politics have become the preferred mode in which groups of Americans "fight[] for political justice by drawing on the commitment that arises from targeted injustice."[48] Groups with specific political grievances can react to and mobilize effectively against real injustices in the law more effectively than if, for example, they were compelled to appeal to an imagined set of shared American premises.

But Levy's praise for this function of identity politics misses something important about the civic conditions that inspire and foster them. Identity politics are at least as much symptomatic of deep disagreements about justice as they are direct arguments about justice. They are a reflection of, and a response to, the steady dissolution of the sorts of civic connections and cohesions on matters of justice and morality that once provided a foundation (a thin foundation, perhaps, but still a sturdy one) for Americans to debate and argue together about their political present and future. Perhaps it is at least some small evidence of the possibility – if not of civic

---

[45] *See* Steven D. Smith, *The Jurisprudence of Denigration*, 48 U.C. Davis L. Rev. 675 (2014).

[46] United States v. Windsor, 133 S. Ct. 2675 (2013).

[47] *Id.*

[48] Jacob T. Levy, *The Defense of Liberty Can't Do Without Identity Politics*, Niskanen Ctr. (Dec. 13, 2016), https://perma.cc/8S45-XFQ7.

reconstruction, then at least of the continuing vitality of the maxim, *audi alteram partem* – that a volume like this one is possible.

And yet, in their increasingly salient anti-Christian form, identity politics perform a related but slightly different function. In this context, "the government of the United States is not, in any sense, founded on the Christian religion" represents a rallying cry for national unity around a common enemy – Christian orthodoxy – in what is otherwise a growing wasteland of civic estrangement. As Chairman Castro put it, it is the duty of Americans, *qua* Americans, to unite together against the prepossessions and hegemonic tendencies of Christianity. In these terms, anti-Christian identity politics might well be enlisted as the sort of basis for civic solidarity for which liberals such as Lilla have been searching. To be united against something is not the same as to be united for something, but it is nevertheless a kind of commonality that may well become stronger as the influence of Christianity in America diminishes.[49] Whether anti-Christian identity politics can serve this function – the liberal-progressive reconstitution of American civic life for a bitterly and seemingly irremediably fragmented nation – remains to be seen.

[49] *See* Cox & Jones, *supra* note 11.

PART V

Strings Attached?

Government Support of Religion and Religious Institutions

22

Marriage Equality, Traditionalist Churches, and Tax Exemptions

William N. Eskridge, Jr.

On June 26, 2015, the US Supreme Court ruled in *Obergefell v. Hodges* that the Fourteenth Amendment to the US Constitution requires all states to issue marriage licenses to same-sex couples.[1] One concern, voiced at oral argument in *Obergefell*, is that constitutionally required marriage equality might support a state requirement that all churches, synagogues, and mosques celebrate such marriages or face revocation of their tax exemption as charitable institutions by a state or the federal government. There has not been any significant effort, either inside or outside the federal government, to penalize religious institutions in the years after *Obergefell*,[2] but there is no doubt that such a fear exists among religious groups and institutions that support only traditional marriage as a matter of faith.[3]

While it is beyond the capacity of an academic to calm such fears, this chapter will demonstrate that federal statutory and constitutional law would prevent churches from being penalized in this manner federally. Indeed, the chapter will

---

[1] Obergefell v. Hodges, 135 S. Ct. 2584 (2015).

[2] It is worth noting that among the states that voluntarily embraced same-sex marriage by ballot or legislative measures all – with the exception of just Delaware – protected the tax-exempt status of religious organizations. See CONN. GEN. STAT. § 46b-150d (2013); D.C. CODE § 46–406(e) (2013); MD. CODE, FAM. LAW §§ 2–201, 2–202 (2013) (lacking amendments present in 2012 Md. Laws § 3); 2012 Md. Laws § 3; MINN. STAT. ANN. § 363A.26 (2013); N.H. REV. STAT. ANN. § 457:37(III) (2013); N.Y. DOM. REL. LAW § 10-b(1) (2013); R.I. GEN. LAWS ANN. § 15–3–6.1 (2013); VT. STAT. ANN. tit. 18, § 5144(b) (2013); WASH. REV. CODE ANN. § 26.04.010(5) (2013); S. 1, 27th Leg., 2nd Special Sess. 2 (Haw. 2013); S. 10 § 209(a-10), 98th Gen. Assemb., Reg. Sess. (Ill. 2013); *see also* ME. REV. STAT. tit. 19-A, § 655 (2013) (codifying ballot initiative to enact same-sex marriage). *See generally* Robin Fretwell Wilson, *When Governments Insulate Dissenters from Social Change: What* Hobby Lobby *and Abortion Conscience Clauses Teach About Specific Exemptions*, 48 U. C. DAVIS L. REV. 703, 788 (2014).

[3] *See* Michael J. DeBoer, *Compelling Reasons to Retain Tax Exemptions for Religious Institutions (Part 1)*, ETHICS & RELIGIOUS LIBERTY COMMISSION SOUTHERN BAPTIST CONVENTION (June 7, 2016), https://perma.cc/52X5-WMX; *see e.g.* Margaret F. Brinig, *Belonging and Trust: Divorce and Social Capital*, 25 BYU J. PUB. L. 271 (2011).

argue that it is not in the public interest or in the interests of the LGBT rights movement to penalize churches that cleave to traditional marriage and reject marriage equality. The literature on social capital helps to understand this broader point. Theorists are concerned that the United States is hemorrhaging social capital needed for democratic flourishing, and the marriage issue has the potential to exacerbate that loss.[4] The last thing a progressive social movement ought to do is attack core religious institutions. The welfare of the country, the LGBT community, and the Constitution require a hands-off approach for the foreseeable future – and especially an assurance that federal and state tax exemptions for charitable institutions not be imperiled by a church's adherence to traditional marriage.

I SHORT HISTORY OF CHALLENGES POSED BY MARRIAGE EQUALITY TO RELIGIOUS INSTITUTIONS

Marriage equality for committed lesbian and gay couples was not a salient national issue until the Hawaii Supreme Court ruled in May 1993 that Hawaii's statutory bar to same-sex marriages constituted sex discrimination subject to strict scrutiny.[5] The decision set off a national debate: Should other states recognize Hawaii same-sex marriages if they occurred? Within Hawaii, there was a fierce political clash, first within the legislature between 1994 and 1997 and then in a popular referendum on the issue, in 1998.[6]

In Hawaii, The Church of Jesus Christ of the Latter-day Saints (LDS Church), the second largest denomination in the state,[7] worried that if the courts were to eliminate the state's bar to same-sex marriages, the state would try to force Mormons (members of the LDS Church) to celebrate those marriages. To protect its interest in religious liberty, the LDS Church sought to intervene in the pending same-sex marriage lawsuit. Rejecting intervention, the Hawaii Supreme Court ruled that state statutory law clearly barred government retaliation against any church along these lines.[8] Moreover, the court said, any state requirement that churches celebrate marriages contrary to their faith would violate the Free Exercise Clause of the First Amendment to the US Constitution.[9]

---

[4] *See* Brinig, *supra* note 3, at 283.
[5] Baehr v. Lewin, 852 P.2d 44 (Haw. 1993), *reaffirmed but modified on reconsideration*, 852 P.2d 74 (Haw. 1993).
[6] *See generally* David Orgon Coolidge, *The Hawai'i Marriage Amendment: Its Origins, Meaning and Fate*, 22 U. HAW. L. REV. 19, 36–38 (2000).
[7] Matthew Brown, *Hawaii's Largest Faiths Oppose Same-Sex Marriage Bill*, DESERET NEWS (Oct. 15, 2013), https://perma.cc/WZ4K-22L4 .
[8] Baehr v. Miike, 910 P.2d 112, 114–15 (Haw. 1996) (affirming the trial judge's refusal to allow LDS Church intervention). *See generally* GREG PRINCE, MORMONS AND GAYS (forthcoming 2018).
[9] *Baehr*, 910 P.2d at 115.

The US Supreme Court agrees with the Hawaii Supreme Court on this precise question. Indeed, Justice Antonin Scalia raised it at oral argument in *Obergefell*.[10] He asked counsel for the lesbian and gay couples, Mary Bonauto, whether constitutional marriage rights for those couples would impose a duty upon traditionalist faiths to celebrate those marriages. Speaking for the many LGBT rights groups on brief in the case, Bonauto answered that the Free Exercise Clause would protect those faith traditions. Justices Ruth Bader Ginsburg and Sonia Sotomayor immediately agreed with Bonauto's point. No justice objected to this view.

In *Hosanna-Tabor Evangelical Lutheran Church and School v. EEOC*,[11] a unanimous Supreme Court held that the Free Exercise Clause, as well as the Establishment Clause, bar the federal government from applying nondiscrimination laws to church personnel decisions regarding its ministers and other faith officials. Chief Justice John Roberts' opinion for the Court relied on the established First Amendment rule that the state cannot regulate any "internal church decision that affects the faith and mission of the church itself."[12] Indeed, a concurring opinion by Justice Samuel Alito was even more specific. "The First Amendment," he added, "protects the freedom of religious groups to engage in certain key religious activities, *including the conducting of* worship services and other *religious ceremonies and rituals*, as well as the critical process of communicating the faith."[13]

The Court's decision in *Obergefell* itself, then, was icing on a cake already well frosted. While rejecting faith-based arguments supporting the limitation of civil marriage to one man, one woman, Justice Anthony Kennedy's opinion for the Court went out of its way to agree with Bonauto's, Ginsburg's, and Sotomayor's understanding of the Religion Clauses: "The First Amendment ensures that religious organizations and persons are given proper protection as they seek to teach the principles that are so fulfilling and so central to their lives and faiths, and to their own deep aspirations to continue the family structure they have long revered."[14]

Another issue raised at the *Obergefell* oral argument is considered by many to represent a more serious threat to churches performing only traditional marriages. Churches are exempt from federal income tax, and donations to such institutions are tax deductible, because they are "charitable institutions" under the Internal Revenue Code (IRC). The IRC defines "charitable institution" to include those

---

[10] These statements about the *Obergefell* oral argument are drawn from the official transcript, which is consistent with my recollection sitting in the Supreme Court that day. *See generally* Transcript of Oral Argument 38, Obergefell v. Hodges, 135 S. Ct. 2584 (2015) [hereinafter *Obergefell* Transcript].

[11] Hosanna-Tabor Evangelical Lutheran Church v. E.E.O.C., 565 U.S. 171 (2012).

[12] *Id.* at 190.

[13] *Id.* at 199 (Alito, J., concurring) (emphasis added). For extended treatment of *Hosanna-Tabor*, see Helfand, Chapter 11; Hollman, Chapter 23.

[14] *Obergefell*, 135 S. Ct. at 2607 (dictum).

"organized and operated exclusively for religious, charitable, scientific, testing for public safety, literary, or educational purposes."[15] Justice Alito asked then-Solicitor General Donald Verrilli whether marriage equality would have any consequences for the tax breaks for churches refusing to perform same-sex marriages. At the end of a stellar argument, Verrilli stumbled in answering this question:

> You know, I – I don't think I can answer that question without knowing more specifics, but it's certainly going to be an issue. I – I don't deny that. I don't deny that, Justice Alito. It is – it is going to be an issue.[16]

Neither the solicitor general nor his many briefing assistants apparently had thought of that issue. But it was of great concern to Justice Alito and many other informed religious observers. Why?

Essential background to the Alito-Verrilli exchange was the Supreme Court's controversial opinion in *Bob Jones University v. United States*.[17] In response to concerns that the tax code was subsidizing private segregated academies and colleges, such as Bob Jones University, the Internal Revenue Service (IRS) issued Revenue Ruling 71–477 that curtailed the potential federal income tax advantages to such institutions.

> Both the courts and the [IRS] have long recognized that the statutory requirement of being "organized and operated exclusively for religious, charitable, ... or educational purposes" was intended to express the basic common law concept [of "charity"].... All charitable trusts, educational or otherwise, are subject to the requirement that the purpose of the trust may not be illegal or contrary to public policy.[18]

Based on the "national policy to discourage racial discrimination in education," the IRS ruled that "a private school not having a racially nondiscriminatory policy as to students is not 'charitable' within the common law concepts reflected in [IRC] sections 170 and 501(c)(3)."

By the time the University's case reached the Supreme Court, Bob Jones University admitted students of color but still refused to allow interracial dating or marriages.[19] All nine justices treated this policy as one that discriminated because of race, and eight justices ruled that the statutory exemption for charitable educational institutions was inapplicable to those violating the fundamental public policy against

---

[15] IRC § 501(c)(3), 26 U.S.C. § 501(c)(3) (2012); *see* IRC § 170(c), 26 U.S.C. § 170(c) (2012) (including a similar definition for taxpayer deductions for charitable contributions).

[16] *Obergefell* Transcript, *supra* note 10, at 38.

[17] Bob Jones Univ. v. United States, 461 U.S. 574 (1983).

[18] Revenue Ruling 71–447, 1971–2 Cum. Bull. 230 (quotations in text), upheld in *Bob Jones*.

[19] *Bob Jones University Drops Mixed-Dating Ban*, L.A. TIMES (Mar. 4, 2000), https://perma.cc/7CWF-4E7Z.

race discrimination.[20] More surprisingly, all nine justices rejected Bob Jones's free exercise claim.[21] Bob Jones University's reading of the Bible committed it to exclusion of persons engaged in sexual relationships with someone of another race; such relationships were, according to millions of southern fundamentalists, contrary to the Word of the Lord.[22] Hence, the university claimed that denying it a tax benefit solely because it was following the Will of God was a violation of the Free Exercise Clause.[23] Not a single justice found the claim meritorious.[24]

The IRS's revenue ruling, and the threat of rigorous enforcement by the Carter administration, alarmed many in the southern fundamentalist community and mobilized many evangelical Christians to support Governor Ronald Reagan for president.[25] Reagan won the presidency with such support. As president, he backed Bob Jones University's quest to remain tax exempt on appeal – but the Supreme Court disagreed. And the Supreme Court's decision in *Bob Jones* doubled the alarm within evangelical and fundamentalist communities.[26] Ever since marriage equality became a prominent issue in national politics, persons of faith have worried that their churches might lose the same tax exemption that Bob Jones University did.[27] That concern surfaced in the Alito-Verrilli exchange, and again in the dissenting opinion written by the chief justice in *Obergefell*. He warned that the "tax exemptions of some religious institutions would be in question if they opposed same-sex marriage. . . . Unfortunately, people of faith can take no comfort in the treatment they receive from the majority today."[28]

II *BOB JONES*: NO THREAT TO CHURCHES HEWING TO TRADITIONAL MARRIAGE

How should the solicitor general have answered Justice Alito's question? Mindful of the solicitor general's caution about how much he or she should commit the federal

---

[20] *Bob Jones University*, 461 U.S. at 592. *See infra* Section II.A for underpinnings of that public policy.

[21] *Id.* at 585.

[22] William N. Eskridge, Jr., *Noah's Curse: How Religion Often Conflates Status, Belief, and Conduct to Resist Antidiscrimination Norms*, 45 GA. L. REV. 657 (2011) (describing traditional religious beliefs that scripture bars racial integration and different-race marriages). For a contrast between religiously based opposition to interracial marriage and to same-sex marriage today, see Perry, Chapter 20.

[23] *See Bob Jones University*, 461 U.S. at 602–03.

[24] *Id.* at 585.

[25] *See* Juan Williams, *Reagan, The South and Civil Rights*, NPR (June 10, 2004), https://perma.cc/X7Z3-E5E3.

[26] *See* Amanda Marcotte, *It Wasn't Abortion That Formed the Religious Right. It Was Support for Segregation*, SLATE (May 29, 2014), https://perma.cc/VED2-JPAU (describing the response to the *Bob Jones* decision).

[27] *See* Laurie Goodstein & Adam Liptak, *Schools Fear Gay Marriage Ruling Could End Tax Exemptions*, N.Y. TIMES (June 24, 2015), https://perma.cc/SX4M-4HAD.

[28] *Obergefell*, 135 S. Ct. at 2626 (Roberts, C.J., dissenting).

government to any future policy, the answer to Justice Alito's question is this: don't worry. For the foreseeable future, *Bob Jones* poses no threat to the tax exemptions accorded churches, synagogues, mosques, and other places of worship, as well as core religious institutions. Was the chief justice simply wrong to call these tax exemptions into question? Yes. I say this as a student of statutory interpretation, a scholar of constitutional law, and a longtime supporter of marriage equality for LGBT people.

A *Agency Practice and the Internal Revenue Code*

Consider first the limitations of *Bob Jones*, both on its face and as applied by the IRS. Its holding was that the national policy against race discrimination is so powerful and pervasive that it overwhelmed the important public policy encouraging private charity, religion, and education.[29] As the opinion for the Court emphasized, not only were the Reconstruction Amendments centrally concerned with race discrimination, but Congress and the president had adopted a series of statutes and executive orders targeting race discrimination.[30] Indeed, Bob Jones University was acting illegally when it excluded potential students because of race.[31]

Neither the Supreme Court nor any appellate court has expanded *Bob Jones* to penalize private educational institutions that discriminate on any ground other than race. The IRS has followed an exceedingly narrow approach to the public policy exception to section 501(c)(3), revoking or denying exemptions only when a charitable institution has, like Bob Jones University itself, engaged in open race discrimination or blatantly illegal activity.[32] Thus, charitable institutions that discriminate on the basis of sex, gender, disability, and other quasi-suspect or possibly suspect traits have not seen their tax-exempt status come under scrutiny. Within a month of *Obergefell*, the Commissioner of Internal Revenue announced that "[t]he IRS does not view *Obergefell* as having changed the law applicable to section 501(c)(3) determinations or examinations. Therefore, the IRS will not ... change existing standards in reviewing applications for

---

[29] *Bob Jones University*, 461 U.S. at 592. For more on the societal good done by houses of worship and faith-based charities, see Lori, Chapter 13; Berg, Chapter 24.

[30] *Bob Jones University*, 461 U.S., at 594–95.

[31] 42 U.S.C. § 1981 (2012); Olatunde Johnson, *The Story of* Bob Jones University v. United States *(1983): Race, Religion, and Congress's Extraordinary Acquiescence*, in WILLIAM N. ESKRIDGE, JR. ET AL., EDS., STATUTORY INTERPRETATION STORIES 126, 151 (2011).

[32] Nicholas A. Mirkay, *Globalism, Public Policy, and Tax-Exempt Status: Are U.S. Charities Adrift at Sea?*, 91 N.C. L. REV. 851, 871 (2013) (stating that the IRS will deny tax-exempt status for charitable institutions that engage in "racial discrimination, civil disobedience, or certain illegal activity"). For the perspective of a former IRS policy official, see Marcus Owens, Bob Jones, Obergefell, *and the IRS*, AHLA CONNECTIONS (2016).

exemption under section 501(c)(3) or in examining the qualification of section 501(c)(3) organizations."[33]

Moreover, if the IRS were to apply the *Bob Jones* exception more broadly, the last place the agency would start would be with churches, for reasons of tax law and administration. Sex discrimination is an established quasi-suspect classification, yet the IRS has been completely acquiescent when applying section 501(c)(3) to churches that openly discriminate on the basis of sex – from the Roman Catholic Church and other denominations that will not ordain women as priests or other officials, to the Southern Baptist Convention, the LDS Church, and other denominations demanding that women who marry men assume primarily domestic roles.[34] Even if *Obergefell* had elevated sexual orientation to be a quasi-suspect classification for constitutional purposes, which it did not do, it is hard to imagine that the IRS would go after the many churches declining to perform same-sex marriages when the IRS is unwilling to deny those same denominations tax exemptions because of their established sex discrimination.

This practical point will likely be dispositive. In 2018, a large majority of America's churches and mosques (and many synagogues) did not perform or recognize same-sex marriages.[35] Any effort by the IRS to deprive all of these churches, mosques, and synagogues their tax exemption would be tantamount to repealing section 501(c)(3) for religious institutions. Not only would such a move be politically inconceivable, but would probably be overridden by the Supreme Court, which takes a dim view of big policy moves by an agency that are not clearly supported by the statutory plan.[36]

Indeed, Congress's structuring of the IRC requires the IRS to afford special treatment to churches.[37] For example, most charitable organizations must apply to the IRS for tax-exempt status – but not churches, for they are entitled to their tax exemption automatically by virtue of being churches.[38] Most tax-exempt organizations must make annual filings of detailed financial reports – but not churches, which are largely exempt from such filings.[39] Finally, churches even enjoy special

---

[33] Mark Lehman & David Dorn, *Obtaining Tax Exempt Status for Religious Institutions*, 7 COLUM. J. TAX LAW – TAX MATTERS 7–8 (2016)(quoting and analyzing IRS Commissioner's statement in response to *Obergefell*).

[34] *See generally* William N. Eskridge, Jr., *Latter-day Constitutionalism: Sexuality, Gender, and Mormons*, in THE CONTESTED PLACE OF RELIGION IN FAMILY LAW (Robin Fretwell Wilson ed. 2018). For a discussion of such decisions as distinctions rather than a brand of discrimination, see Ryan Anderson, Chapter 27.

[35] *See* David Masci & Michael Lipka, *Where Christian Churches, Other Religions Stand on Gay Marriage*, PEW RES. CTR. (Dec. 21, 2015), https://perma.cc/8M39-3ZKC.

[36] *E.g.*, Gonzales v. Oregon, 546 U.S. 243 (2006) (outlining the "major questions exception" to judicial deference to agency interpretations).

[37] Samuel D. Brunson & David J. Herzig, *A Diachronic Approach to Bob Jones: Religious Tax Exemptions After* Obergefell, 92 IND. L.J. 1175, 1203–04 (2017).

[38] *Churches, Integrated Auxiliaries, and Conventions or Associations of Churches*, IRS, https://perma.cc/UB99-EDCQ.

[39] *Id.*

procedural protections that discourage IRS audits. "The IRS appears to have largely internalized the legislative and judicial deference given churches."[40] Not only has the agency avoided application of *Bob Jones* to religiously affiliated organizations in general, but "[e]ven in the area of racial discrimination, where it has the strongest explicit mandate and has, in fact, revoked exemptions, it has not revoked the exemption of a single discriminatory church."[41]

B *Religious Freedom Restoration Act of 1993*

There has been a significant change in the law since *Bob Jones*, namely, the enactment of the Religious Freedom Restoration Act of 1993 (RFRA).[42] Consistent with its earlier decision in *Bob Jones*, the Supreme Court in *Employment Division v. Smith* ruled that general, nondiscriminatory state laws or rules do not violate the Free Exercise Clause unless they are inspired by religion-based animus.[43] Congress sought to override *Smith* with RFRA. This law prohibits the government from taking any action that "substantially burden[s] a person's exercise of religion," unless the government proves that the burden "is in furtherance of a compelling governmental interest" and "is the least restrictive means of furthering that compelling governmental interest."[44] Although the Supreme Court has struck down the application of RFRA to state discrimination, because it was beyond Congress's Fourteenth Amendment authority, the Court has treated RFRA as binding on the federal government.[45] And states have enacted parallel protections.[46]

Would *Bob Jones* be decided the same way under RFRA? Certainly, a good argument can be made for the same result. Denying a religious university's tax exemption because of its racially discriminatory admissions policy "substantially burden[s] a person's exercise of religion," now that the Supreme Court has definitively ruled that "person" includes corporate bodies and even for-profit companies.[47] But it makes sense to say that denying the tax exemption "is the least restrictive means of furthering [a] compelling governmental interest" in eradicating racial discrimination throughout society. So, *Bob Jones* is defensible under RFRA, but would the same result follow when the government interest is eradicating sexual

---

[40] *Id.* at 1204.
[41] *Id.*
[42] Religious Freedom Restoration Act of 1993 (RFRA), 107 Stat. 1488, codified at 42 U.S.C. § 2000bb (2012).
[43] Employment Div., Dep't of Human Res. v. Smith, 494 U.S. 872 (1990).
[44] RFRA, *supra* note 42.
[45] *Compare* City of Boerne v. Flores, 521 U.S. 507, 532–36 (1997) (striking down RFRA as it applies to state and local governments) *with* Hobby Lobby v. Burwell, 134 S. Ct. 2751 (2014) (applying RFRA to regulate federal administrative rules substantially affecting religious free exercise).
[46] See Appendix, Chapter 35, for state laws.
[47] Hobby Lobby, 134 S. Ct. at 2768.

orientation discrimination, rather than race discrimination? Existing Supreme Court case law says no. The famous Boy Scouts case held that a state policy against sexual orientation discrimination was not sufficiently compelling to justify an infringement on the Boy Scouts' right of expressive association.[48]

A broad reading of *Obergefell* would call that holding into question. Although the Court's opinion rested primarily on the fundamental due process right to marry, the opinion also relied on equal protection analysis. Indeed, the Court's reasoning emphasized the irrationality of sexual orientation as a basis for government exclusions and the historical mistreatment of this minority group.[49] Such reasoning supplies much of the analysis that would justify strict or quasi-strict scrutiny under the Court's sex and disability discrimination precedents. Those precedents suggest that heightened scrutiny should apply to classifications that (1) disadvantage a minority that has been treated unfairly by the state and has traditionally been politically powerless, (2) are not generally correlated with the needs of rational public policy, and, most controversially, (3) are immutable traits.[50] Indeed, an excellent argument can be made that most anti-LGBT discrimination, like the marriage exclusion, is also discrimination because of sex.[51] Finally, the Supreme Court's earlier decision invalidating the Defense of Marriage Act rested upon the equal protection component of the Fifth Amendment and clearly applied something tougher than rational basis review.[52]

It remains to be seen whether the Supreme Court will recognize sexual orientation as a new suspect or quasi-suspect classification. Since 1988, the justices have not expanded the short list of quasi-suspect or suspect classifications.[53] Indeed, the Court may not do so until Congress passes the kinds of sexual orientation super-statutes similar to the race discrimination laws that formed the backbone of *Bob Jones* or the sex discrimination laws that were cited as a reason for heightened scrutiny of sex-based classifications.[54] Such super-statutes remain controversial within our political system, but they are also key to the RFRA analysis. Has *Congress* – not just the Court or the President – announced that ending sexual orientation discrimination is a

---

[48] Boy Scouts of Am. v. Dale, 530 U.S. 640 (2000).

[49] *Obergefell*, 135 S. Ct. at 2596–97 (describing history of unjust discrimination against gay men and lesbians); *id.* at 2604 (rejecting laws that seek to disparage or subordinate gay men and lesbians); *id.* at 2606 (citing the stories of the lesbian and gay plaintiffs in the cases before the Court as examples of families worthy of equal respect from the state).

[50] Cleburne v. Cleburne Living Center, 473 U.S. 432 (1995).

[51] Andrew Koppelman, *Why Discrimination Against Lesbians and Gay Men Is Sex Discrimination*, 69 N.Y.U. L. Rev. 197, 208 (1994).

[52] United States v. Windsor, 133 S. Ct. 2675 (2013); *see id.* at 2708 (Scalia, J., dissenting) (arguing that the Court's equal protection analysis of DOMA was equally applicable to state exclusions of homosexual marriages).

[53] The last expansion of (quasi-)suspect classifications occurred with *Clark v. Jeter*, 486 U.S. 456 (1988) (nonmarital births). It is notable that the Court has struck down many sexual orientation classifications since 1996, yet has never addressed the level of scrutiny issue.

[54] Frontiero v. Richardson, 411 U.S. 677 (1974) (plurality opinion).

compelling public interest that would justify abridgments of religious free exercise under authority delegated by Congress to the IRS? Notice how this analysis tracks the IRS's current practice, which denies tax exemptions only to charitable institutions that openly discriminate because of race (in violation of powerful statutory, executive, and judicial rules) or that defy criminal and other serious laws adopted by Congress.

A number of commentators have urged the IRS to deny tax exemptions to charitable institutions that discriminate on the basis of a classification the Court treats with strict scrutiny (*i.e.*, race and ethnicity).[55] In my view, the approach should be one that hews more carefully to congressional action, but under either approach one must wait and see what becomes of *Obergefell* and the Court's other LGBT rights cases. The country is moving toward treatment of sexual orientation, and gender identity, as irrelevant to public policy[56] – but the Supreme Court may or may not follow the country's lead, and constitutional norms may lag behind or pioneer public norms, depending upon the personnel and the philosophies represented on the Court in the next generation. As norms evolve, sooner or later, charitable institutions that openly discriminate on the basis of sexual orientation will find their tax exemptions in peril – but this analysis does not quite apply to churches, which enjoy the additional protections of the Free Exercise Clause.

C Free Exercise Clause

In the short and medium term – several decades into the future – the IRS for practical, statutory, and political reasons will not penalize churches, synagogues, mosques, and other institutions of worship that authorize only traditional marriages. If it did so, RFRA would stand in its way. And so would the Constitution. I believe it would violate the Religion Clauses if the IRS said that Mormon, Catholic, and Baptist churches must lose their federal charitable institutions exemption because they will not celebrate same-sex marriages.

Although the Supreme Court in *Employment Division v. Smith* ruled that laws of general application will not violate the Free Exercise Clause unless they carry a discriminatory intent, the Court subsequently in *Hosanna-Tabor* ruled that Title VII – a statute of general application that protects against religion-based job discrimination – could not constitutionally be applied to a church's decision about whom it can employ as a proper minister.[57] Recall that the chief justice's opinion for the Court reasoned that the Religion Clauses protect any "internal church decision that affects the faith and mission of the church itself."[58] As argued earlier in this chapter,

---

[55] Brunson & Herzig, *supra* note 37 at 1208–13 (discussing such a proposal).
[56] *See* Anna Brown, *5 Key Findings About LGBT Americans*, Pew Res. Ctr. (June 13, 2017), https://perma.cc/YK7K-HYVB.
[57] *Hosanna-Tabor*, 565 U.S. at 196.
[58] *Id.* at 190.

this reasoning assures churches that the state cannot require them to celebrate the marriages of lesbian and gay couples.

Does this reasoning also assure churches that states cannot take away a tax benefit based upon this kind of discrimination? Religion Clause doctrine suggests the same answer. In *Sherbert v. Verner*, the Supreme Court ruled that the state could not refuse to provide unemployment compensation benefits to a worker who was discharged because he would not work on the day his faith tradition considered the Sabbath: "Government may neither compel affirmation of a repugnant belief, nor penalize or discriminate against individuals or groups because they hold religious views abhorrent to the authorities."[59] Indeed, although *Employment Division v. Smith* curtailed the breadth of the Free Exercise Clause, the Court was careful to recognize the ongoing validity of *Sherbert*.[60] Read together, *Hosanna-Tabor* and *Sherbert* suggest that the Free Exercise Clause prohibits a judicial or agency interpretation of section 501(c)(3) that would extend the *Bob Jones* public policy exception to churches refusing to celebrate lesbian or gay marriages. As a principle of statutory interpretation, the Supreme Court has admonished judges to interpret ambiguous laws to avoid constitutional problems exactly like this one,[61] so even if the denial of tax exemption were not flatly unconstitutional, it should be avoided.

For this reason, synagogues refusing to celebrate marriages between Jews and gentiles have never found their section 501(c)(3) exemption even questioned. Nor have churches refusing to allow women to officiate at religious wedding ceremonies. Nor have houses of worship that will not celebrate different-race marriages. For example, in July 2017, Chastity Bumgardner and Henry Lawrence were all set to get married at the Pleasant Valley Community Church in Piketon, Ohio – until the church's pastor discovered that Lawrence is a black man and refused to allow his church to be used for such a service.[62] The church continues to enjoy its tax exemption, and that ought not be surprising. If read literally, *Hosanna-Tabor* would protect a church against Title VII liability even if the church refused to elevate people of color to ministerial positions.

Admittedly, one can read *Hosanna-Tabor* more narrowly, as the case only involved a claim of sex discrimination. If one read *Obergefell* broadly – supporting the notion of sexual orientation as a suspect classification – and *Hosanna-Tabor* narrowly, one could argue that the Constitution permits the IRS to revoke tax exemptions for churches that refuse to celebrate either different-race or same-sex marriages. As to the latter possibility, much as I support marriage equality and think

---

[59] Sherbert v. Verner, 374 U.S. 398, 402 (1963).
[60] *Smith*, 494 U.S. at 884.
[61] Northwest Austin Municipal Utility Dist. No. 1 v. Holder, 557 U.S. 193 (2009) (Roberts, C.J.).
[62] For the news account, see *Interracial Couple Spurned*, ABC News (July 10, 2017), https://perma.cc/TLJ3-W6C7. For the current tax-exempt status of this church, see *Nonprofit & 501c Organizations Piketon, OH*, TaxExempt World (Sept. 20, 2017), https://perma.cc/9FDC-JLWZ.

it would benefit from more denominational support, I do not think this would be good for the country, or even for LGBT people.

III DEMOCRATIC PLURALISM, SOCIAL CAPITAL THEORY, AND RELIGIOUS FREE EXERCISE

Consider a broader public law perspective on the tax-exemption issue. Our democracy is a pluralistic one, and its legitimacy rests upon both foundations, as well as dignified treatment of all its citizens. On the one hand, major public policy initiatives are more legitimate if adopted by elected representatives who can be held accountable by voters. On the other hand, policies that accommodate the most urgent needs of as many relevant social groups as possible are more legitimate than policies taking away rights from one salient social group and handing them over to another. *Obergefell* is vulnerable to both kinds of legitimacy critiques: the Court trumped the views expressed by more than 60 percent of the voters in all four states, and the decision was read by traditional family values groups as harming them for the benefit of LGBT persons.[63] To be sure, the Court tried to soften both critiques, the first by pointing to the extensive state-by-state deliberation that occurred before the Court acted[64] – and that led to marriage licenses in thirty-six or thirty-seven states and the District of Columbia – and the second by emphasizing the privacy, free exercise, and parental rights retained by traditionalists.[65] As to the latter point, *Obergefell* can be read to support the analysis developed earlier in this chapter.

Courts need to avoid raising the stakes of politics by one-sided treatment of issues that intensely but evenly divide the polity.[66] Justice Kennedy's bow to religious liberty in *Obergefell* should be read in this spirit: the federal government should not use marriage equality as a reason to penalize churches that disagree.[67] This section of the chapter pushes further, to argue that theories of social capital support a go-slow approach that accommodates marriage equality skeptics.

Professor Robert Putnam defines social capital as "features of social life – networks, norms, and trust – that enable participants to act together more effectively to pursue shared objectives."[68] In *Bowling Alone*, Putnam distinguishes between thick ties of intimacy engendered by *bonding groups* and thin ties of generalized trust

---

[63] *See* John Stonestreet, *Christian Leaders Respond to* Obergefell v. Hodges: A *Symposium*, BREAK POINT (June 26, 2015), https://perma.cc/3X38-PPV5.

[64] *Obergefell*, 135 S. Ct. at 2605.

[65] *Id.* at 2625–26.

[66] William N. Eskridge Jr., *Pluralism and Distrust: How Courts Can Support Democracy by Lowering the Stakes of Politics*, 114 YALE L.J. 1279 (2005).

[67] *Obergefell*, 135 S. Ct. at 2591.

[68] Robert D. Putnam, *The Strange Disappearance of Civic America*, THE AMERICAN PROSPECT no. 24 (Winter 1996). *See also* Jenny Onyx & Paul Bullen, *Measuring Social Capital in Five Communities*, 36 J. APPLIED BEHAV. SCI. 23 (2000).

facilitated by *bridging groups.*[69] He maintains that both thin and thick ties, both bridging and bonding groups, are necessary for the formation of strong social capital – and that social capital is positively correlated with social cohesion, a well-functioning democracy, and social and economic flourishing.[70] An important factor in this conclusion is the ability of social capital to build trust, a social glue that has been increasingly diluted in recent American history. Under this theory, any attempts to impose top-down discipline on our society's most significant bonding institutions – of which churches are one – would undermine the chance for peaceful bridging or for thin ties to develop in communities, thereby eroding the trust that Putnam identifies as being instrumental to social capital. Conversely, allowing churches to maintain the freedom to hew to their traditions would promote bottom-up discussions within faith traditions, bonding, and would leave room for interfaith dialogue, bridging.

Other theorists offer similar lessons, from rational choice perspectives. For example, Professor Francis Fukuyama argues that economic flourishing rests upon the trust and openness to cooperation entailed in social capital, for this makes it easier to form associations and drives down the transactions cost of economic activity.[71] Furthermore, his theory is skeptical of extreme claims from both sides of cultural debates.[72] Absolutist theories of equality, including a broad reading of *Bob Jones*, undermine trust in the new minority and do not necessarily promote social solidarity. But absolutist libertarian theories, such as those rejecting *Bob Jones*, ignore the ways that the state shapes and affects social norms.

IV CONCLUSION

It is not in the best interests of the LGBT rights movement to insist upon disciplining churches for not following the Supreme Court's lead. In my view, lesbian and gay marriages are good for gay people, good for the children they are raising, good for the faith traditions celebrating those marriages, and good for America. I am confident that the next generation of Americans will agree with me – which means that many faith traditions left to their own devices will move toward toleration or acceptance of marriage equality.[73] And I think some faith traditions will not move toward a tolerant stance, but I do not see them swallowing gay marriage under pressure from the state; the history of Christianity and other religions suggests that

---

[69] Robert D. Putnam, Bowling Alone: The Collapse and Revival of American Community 136, 234 (2000).

[70] *Id.* at 234; *accord*, Mark S. Granovetter, *The Strength of Weak Ties*, 78 Am. J. Soc. 1360 (1973).

[71] Francis Fukuyama, *Social Capital and the Global Economy: A Redrawn Map of the World*, 74 Foreign Aff. 89, 89–103 (1995). *See also* Daron Acemoglu & James Robinson, Why Nations Fail: The Origins of Power, Prosperity, and Poverty (2012).

[72] *See* Fukuyama, *supra* note 71.

[73] Eskridge, *supra* note, 34. For demographic differences in views, see Brownstein, Chapter 2.

resistance or martyrdom is just as likely as acquiescence or acceptance of state-approved norms.

The best approach for the state to take is grounded in what Professor Robert George calls "pluralist perfectionism," where the government instructs and nudges, but citizens and their groups have a wide range of choice.[74] The more private and bonding a social activity is (the more like decisions about family), the more the state should emphasize pluralism, but the more public and bridging an activity is (the more like government action itself), the more the state should emphasize perfectionist norms, though perhaps limited to norms where there is social consensus.

[74] Robert P. George, *Making Men Moral: Civil Liberties and Public Morality* (1993); Sherif Girgis, *Nervous Victors, Illiberal Measures*, 125 YALE L.J.F. 399 (2016).

23

Why Money Matters

LGBT Rights and Religious Freedom

Holly Hollman

Political and theological debates over LGBT rights have been particularly contentious. Perhaps that is to be expected when addressing matters as personal as sexuality, identity, and religious beliefs, in a scorching political climate.[1] In public debates about specific LGBT legal protections, such as those involving public accommodations or employment laws, differing sides often oversimplify the conflict in ways that make compromise – or even meaningful dialogue – impossible. At times, these sides have distorted the meaning of religious freedom beyond recognition from a historical and legal perspective, undermining the public's understanding of and support for religious freedom.

Casting conflicts between LGBT nondiscrimination rights and claims for exemptions based on religious objections in absolute terms is especially harmful. Efforts to secure LGBT nondiscrimination protections face religious and other objections that are presented as demands for religious liberty. At the same time, religiously based objections and claims for exemptions from LGBT nondiscrimination protections are often dismissed as bigotry masquerading as "religious liberty" unworthy of any legal consideration.[2] As others have observed, this framing of the debate has prevented legislation that would protect both LGBT rights *and* religious freedom.[3] While cultural changes and differences in religious opinions about LGBT rights have created challenges for some religious institutions, common ground in religious teachings and religious liberty principles can bridge significant divisions.

The legal tradition in the United States of protecting religious liberty seldom operates in absolute terms. Instead, religious liberty is protected in a variety of ways

---

[1] Christopher Ingraham, *However Divided You Think Our Politics Are, This Chart Shows That It's Actually Way Worse*, WASH. POST (July 22, 2016), https://perma.cc/X6SW-N7JZ.
[2] For a discussion of such claims as a "civil rights simplism," see Smith, Chapter 18.
[3] *See* Adams, Chapter 32.

in the law depending on the context.[4] Whether a claim of religious liberty justifies specific legal protection, particularly an exemption from an otherwise applicable law, depends on a number of factors. Other contributors to this book describe the variety of religiously grounded conflicts related to increased LGBT protections and how shifting legal standards for free exercise cases affect the prospects for resolution.[5] To illustrate the fallacy of absolute claims, this chapter focuses on another contextual issue: government funding and religious institutions.[6]

Protecting the religious autonomy of religious institutions, in particular of churches and other houses of worship, is directly related to constitutional constraints on government support of religion. The connection is an undeniable theme that runs throughout religious liberty law and shapes expectations about that freedom. While the scope of restrictions on government funding of religious institutions is contested and the precise contours of the church autonomy doctrine are not clearly defined, the interplay between these two concerns is significant. It is reflected in the US Supreme Court's decisions and in how the nation negotiates the scope and extent of religious liberty protections. In public debates about LGBT nondiscrimination rights and religious liberty, however, the implication of government funding is often overlooked, which leads to a harsher landscape for negotiating differences.

As debates about same-sex marriage and LGBT rights continue in the wake of *Obergefell*,[7] greater attention to the context of particular conflicts is necessary to preserve the religious liberty Americans enjoy. By paying attention to historical and practical considerations about the role of government funds in our religious liberty tradition, we can better understand and negotiate the balance of interests between

---

[4] By its design, the First Amendment to the United States Constitution encompasses two distinct guarantees that together protect religious freedom, although religious freedom is not always protected in the same way. "Congress shall make no law respecting an establishment of religion, or prohibiting the free exercise thereof." U.S. Const. amend. I. The Religion Clauses – No Establishment and Free Exercise – are the twin pillars that support the architecture of our first freedom, embodying distinct views, both of which are essential to understanding various claims and ensuring religious liberty. For example, the Constitution protects an individual's right to worship (free exercise) and protects against government-sponsored religion (no establishment).

[5] *See* Brownstein, Chapter 2; Laycock, Chapter 3; NeJaime & Siegel, Chapter 6; Helfand, Chapter 11; Smith, Chapter 18; Eskridge, Chapter 22; Berg, Chapter 24; Pizer, Chapter 29.

[6] While religiously based claims for exemptions to nondiscrimination laws are also made by individuals and commercial businesses, this chapter focuses on religious organizations and how expectations for the scope of nondiscrimination and religious-based exemptions vary for them in different contexts. For a discussion of claims pressed by individuals and commercial businesses, see McClain, Chapter 17; Smith, Chapter 18; McConnell, Chapter 28; Wilson, Chapter 30.

[7] *See* Obergefell v. Hodges, 135 S. Ct. 2584, 2607 (2015) ("The First Amendment ensures that religious organizations and persons are given proper protection as they seek to teach the principles that are so fulfilling and so central to their lives and faiths, and to their own deep aspirations to continue the family structure they have long revered.").

religious autonomy and nondiscrimination in different contexts.[8] By rejecting the false frame of absolute rights, society may be able to move forward in a way that is less divisive and more consistent with the religious liberty tradition that has served America so well. History, law, and practical experience teach us that money matters to the resolution of many religious liberty conflicts. Recognizing the interplay between claims for government funding and claims for religious exemptions is one aspect of embracing a shared understanding of religious liberty and moving beyond the current stalemate.

I CONSTITUTIONAL HISTORY TEACHES US THAT MONEY MATTERS

The relationship between government financial support and autonomy of religious entities goes back to the beginning of this country. Many early state constitutions included protections for religious liberty that banned government funding of religion and religious institutions.[9] They were written in response to legal arrangements in Europe and in the American colonies where tax support and government control of churches had been common. Likewise, the US Constitution and the First Amendment represented a break from the colonial experience of the Founders, providing a new vision of religious liberty that separated the institutions of religion and government at the federal level.

From a historical and textual perspective, the First Amendment protects religious liberty in a way that tells us money matters. The Free Exercise Clause protects against interference in religious exercise and provides no expectation of government support for religious beliefs and practices. The Establishment Clause provides a structural limitation on government advancement of religion that prohibits direct government funding of religious activities and religious ideas. While there is disagreement among academics, advocates, and jurists over which legal standards should apply in many specific religious liberty cases, there is no doubt that the First Amendment was adopted because of concerns related to tax support of religion.[10]

---

[8] This chapter explores the issue of government funding and religion as an important factor in negotiating the boundaries of religious liberty. It recognizes, however, that deep conflicts between LGBT equality and religious opposition to same-sex marriage persist apart from any discussion of government funding.

[9] *See* Brief of Baptist Joint Committee for Religious Liberty and General Synod of the United Church of Christ as Amici Curiae Supporting Respondent, Trinity Lutheran Church of Columbia v. Comer, 137 S. Ct. 2012 (2017).

[10] *See* Ira C. Lupu & Robert Tuttle, Secular Government Religious People 5 (2014) ("Through various kinds of religious establishments, governments declared and enforced orthodox beliefs, imposed taxes to support ministers and churches, and compelled attendance at worship."). *See also* Michael W. McConnell, *Establishment and Disestablishment at the Founding, Part 1: Establishment of Religion*, 44 Wm. & Mary L. Rev. 2105, 2131 (2003) (finding six categories of establishment: "(1) control over doctrine, governance, and personnel of the church; (2) compulsory church attendance; (3) financial support; (4) prohibitions on worship

Avoiding government sponsorship and control of religion – and specifically avoiding tax support of religious activities – is at the heart of what "no establishment" means. It is also one of the reasons houses of worship have held a special place in religious liberty law – one that requires special safeguards to avoid government-funded religion, as well as one that receives favorable treatment under the law to reduce government interference and to protect religious autonomy.[11]

The process of disestablishment in the colonies – separating the institutions of religion and government and specifically ensuring that churches were supported by voluntary offerings instead of coerced taxation – marked a significant improvement for religious liberty. The benefits were twofold. Religious dissenters and other citizens were no longer forced to support the established churches – allowing churches to flourish or fail on their own – and the government was no longer deemed to have authority in matters of religion. The efforts of Baptists and other religious dissenters who opposed taxation to support state establishments are well documented.[12] In our current political context, however, the relationship between the prohibition on funding religion and freedom for religion is often forgotten.[13] Our country's embrace of religious liberty is deeply rooted and reflected in the separation of the institutions of religion and government. It recognizes that religion must be funded by voluntary offerings, not compulsory taxation, and that in matters of religious doctrine, practice, and polity, religion follows its own understandings, not those imposed by the state.

---

in dissenting churches; (5) use of church institutions for public functions; and (6) restriction of political participation to members of the established church.").

[11] For a collection of state "no establishment" constitutional provisions, see Amici Curiae, *supra* note 9. For a selection of state religious exemptions to nondiscrimination statutes, see Brief of the General Conference of Seventh-Day Adventists and the Becket Fund for Religious Liberty as Amici Curiae Supporting Neither Party, Obergefell v. Hodges, 135 S. Ct. 2584 (2015). Religious liberty protections are found in more than 2,000 federal and state laws. *See* James E. Ryan, *Smith and the Religious Freedom Restoration Act: An Iconoclastic Assessment*, 78 VA. L. REV. 1407, 1445 (1992).

[12] *BGAV Bibliography: Early Baptists and Their Allies on the Meaning of Religious Liberty*, BAPTIST JOINT COMM. FOR RELIGIOUS LIBERTY, https://perma.cc/32ZW-PE6X (compilation of primary and secondary sources); Melissa Rogers, *Traditions of Church-State Separation: Some Ways They Have Protected Religion and Advanced Religious Freedom and How They Are Threatened Today*, 18 J. L. & POLITICS 277, 277–94 (2002).

[13] *See* LUPU & TUTTLE, *supra* note 10, at 74–112 (reviewing the history and evolution of law regarding the funding of religious institutions). *See also* Trinity Lutheran Church of Columbia, Inc., 137 S. Ct. 2012, 2035 (2017) (Sotomayor, J., dissenting) ("The course of this history shows that those who lived under the laws and practices that formed religious establishments made a considered decision that civil government should not fund ministers and their houses of worship. To us, their debates may seem abstract and this history remote. That is only because we live in a society that has long benefited from decisions made in response to these now centuries-old arguments, a society that those not so fortunate fought hard to build.").

II LAWS AND POLICIES RECOGNIZE THAT MONEY MATTERS

Church-state law developed in ways that demonstrate and reinforce the importance of the twofold benefits of disestablishment: keeping government out of essential religious matters and avoiding tax support for religion. In religious liberty law and practice, these two concerns remain intertwined and should inform current conflicts. Failure to acknowledge that money matters in our religious liberty tradition feeds the damaging all-or-nothing narratives. It emboldens those who would deny all religious exemptions *and* those who advocate for the broadest religious exemptions to LGBT nondiscrimination laws. This failure ignores the highly contextual nature of religious liberty law and breeds mistrust, making it more difficult to live with our deepest differences. Two strains in religious liberty law – one that supports religious autonomy and one that prevents government-sponsorship of religion – are instructive.

Consider first the church autonomy doctrine, a well-established aspect of church-state law that provides a basis for keeping government out of religious affairs. Grounded in both principles of free exercise and no establishment, church autonomy provides the strongest constitutional basis for religious exemptions from civil laws. Legal recognition of this doctrine arose out of cases mostly involving intra-church property conflicts. In some disputes over church property or personnel, the real question is who controls the church, which may involve questions of church polity reflecting theology. The Supreme Court has held that civil courts are unqualified to decide cases that would require them to determine inherently religious questions, and that absent evidence of fraud or collusion, courts should defer to the church's own understandings.[14] In general, church autonomy recognizes a zone of freedom in essential religious matters that limits government regulation of churches in ecclesiastical matters, which span from questions of doctrine to governance, polity, and administration. This nonintervention principle rightly assumes that churches and other closely related entities, while by no means beyond the reach of the law, are special and given special constitutional treatment.[15] Dedicated to religious purposes, they are not funded by the government and have broad autonomy to control their property and other resources in accord with their religious principles.

Another aspect of church-state law recognizes the longstanding role of religiously affiliated organizations, such as hospitals and charities, in providing government-funded social services. Carefully structured financial arrangements between religiously affiliated organizations and government social services programs have long

---

[14] For a general discussion of church autonomy, see Douglas Laycock, *Towards a General Theory of the Religion Clauses: The Case of Church Labor Relations and the Right to Church Autonomy*, 81 COLUM. L. REV. 1373, 1402–14 (1981).

[15] For a discussion of the autonomy accorded churches and affiliated organizations, see Helfand, Chapter 11.

been accepted as constitutional.[16] Such arrangements recognize the importance of regulatory safeguards to achieve public purposes, including avoiding the unconstitutional government funding of religion. Participation of religious institutions in such government-funded programs requires competing for grants on an equal basis with nonreligious providers and generally abiding by the same government regulations.[17] This approach assumes that government-funded services are provided to meet government purposes without regard to religion and that any explicitly religious activities of participating religious entities are fully separated in time or place from services funded by direct government aid.[18]

While church autonomy emphasizes the uniqueness and independence of religious institutions and supports exemptions for religion, financial partnerships between government and religious institutions emphasize secular goals of government and demand accountability to achieve public purposes. Claims of church autonomy, rooted in the separation of religion and government, are necessarily diminished when religious institutions take government money. Likewise, expectations of nondiscrimination and government accountability increase where a religious institution is providing government-funded services.

Financial partnerships between religious institutions and the government gained greater public attention in the late 1990s with the introduction of a policy known as "charitable choice," and in 2001 when President George W. Bush launched his "faith-based initiative."[19] These efforts, broadly intended to expand the role of religious institutions in partnering with the government, resulted in policy changes that continued (with some changes) through the Obama administration. They also highlighted tensions between the claims of religious institutions for autonomy and

---

[16] Bradfield v. Roberts, 175 U.S. 291 (1899) (upholding government payments to a religiously affiliated hospital); Bowen v. Kendrick, 487 U.S. 589 (1988) (upholding participation of religious groups in providing government-funded social services but remanding for a determination of whether groups were pervasively sectarian or whether "grant funds are being used in such a way as to have a primary effect of advancing religion").

[17] *But see* Exec. Order No. 13279, 67 Fed. Reg. 77141 (Dec. 12, 2002) (stating faith-based organizations that provide federally funded social services may retain religious characteristics in the organization's name, organizational structure, and facilities, so long as the federal government money is not paying for inherently religious activities). While the majority of this executive order could be viewed as restating current assumptions about religious affiliates, one highly controversial aspect permitted religious organizations to use religious criteria in hiring and employment decisions even within the government-funded program. *Id.* at § 204(c). *See also Hiring Law for Groups Following a Higher Law: Faith-Based Hiring and the Obama Administration*, Pew Res. Ctr. (Jan. 30, 2009), https://perma.cc/WE84-Q6AY (interview with Ira "Chip" Lupu, F. Elwood and Eleanor Davis Professor of Law, the George Washington University Law School).

[18] Exec. Order No. 13559, Sec. 1. 75 Fed. Reg. 71319 (Nov. 17, 2010) (amending Exec. Order No. 13279, 67 Fed. Reg. 77141 (2002)).

[19] For a brief overview of the program and its strengths and weaknesses, *see* Holly Hollman, *Protecting Religious Liberty and Preventing Discrimination in Government-Funded Partnerships*, Report From the Capital (Feb. 2017), https://perma.cc/33RT-RD8Y.

for government funding. Whether designed to increase the autonomy of providers or to strengthen the constitutional foundation of financial partnerships, federal executive policy sparked closer examination of the complexities of protecting religious freedom in the context of government funding. The result has been regulations based on bipartisan recommendations that clarify how such partnerships should operate in compliance with church-state law and public expectations to protect beneficiaries and providers. Significant controversy and political debate, however, continue to surround questions of religious hiring and nondiscrimination in government-funded programs.[20]

Apart from the debate about religious hiring in government-funded programs, laws prohibiting discrimination in employment demonstrate that religious liberty is protected differently in different contexts. "Religion" is typically treated as a protected category in nondiscrimination law, alongside race, sex, national origin, and other characteristics. Such laws protect religious liberty by valuing religion and diversity and preventing one's religion from being a disqualification for employment. Employment laws also protect religious liberty in a different way that promotes the free exercise and autonomy interests of religious entities. Employment laws that prohibit discrimination based on protected categories (including religion) typically exempt religious organizations (as defined by statute and applicable case law) from the prohibition on religious discrimination.[21] As a result, a religious organization may choose to hire only persons who share the same religious tradition (coreligionists) or only those who agree to a certain statement of faith. An entity that does not meet the statutory definition of a religious organization, however, could be held liable for making unfavorable employment decisions based on an applicant's or employee's religion.[22]

The Supreme Court has upheld the religious exemption for religious organizations found in Title VII of the 1964 Civil Rights Act,[23] which is the primary federal law that prohibits discrimination in employment. The Court found it to be a permissible accommodation of religion, even for positions that do not perform religious duties.[24] More recently, the Supreme Court upheld the ministerial

---

[20] *See, e.g.,* Robin Fretwell Wilson, *Squaring Faith and Sexuality in Religious Institutions: The Unique Challenge of Sports,* 34 L. & INEQ. 385 (2016); Carl Esbeck, *Federal Contractors, Title VII, and LGBT Employment Discrimination: Can Religious Organizations Continue To Staff on a Religious Basis?,* 2015 OXFORD J.L. & REL. 368 (2015).

[21] *See generally Religious Discrimination,* U.S. EQUAL EMP'T OPPORTUNITY COMM'N, https://perma.cc/H7MM-X2YQ.

[22] For cases, see Wilson, *supra* note 20, at Appendix.

[23] 42 U.S.C. § 2000e (2012).

[24] *See* Corp. of Presiding Bishop of The Church of Jesus Christ of Latter-day Saints v. Amos, 483 U.S. 327, 335 (1987) ("[I]t is a permissible legislative purpose to alleviate significant governmental interference with the ability of religious organizations to define and carry out their religious missions."). *But see* Estate of Thornton v. Caldor, Inc., 472 U.S. 703, 710 (1985) (striking a Connecticut statute that provided Sabbath observers with an absolute and unqualified right not to work on their chosen Sabbath as violating the Establishment Clause: "The

exception, an application of the church autonomy doctrine, which precludes the application of *any* nondiscrimination laws to the employment of clergy, recognizing the importance of churches defining their message by deciding who will speak for them.[25] The ministerial exception, like Title VII and similar state employment laws, illustrate a central point: religious liberty of religious institutions is protected, but not in absolute terms. Religious liberty and nondiscrimination are both important government interests, and they are protected differently in the context of different types of entities and job positions.[26]

By contrast, nondiscrimination in government-funded social service programs serves an essential government interest where less deference to religious autonomy is due. Participating religious providers recognize that when using government resources, they must provide services without regard to religion – they cannot discriminate against government beneficiaries based on religion.[27] A privately funded program conducted by a religious organization, of course, may integrate religious activity or limit services to persons within a community that fit its religious mission. Claims of religious autonomy and for exemptions from nondiscrimination laws can be difficult to defend in a government-funded program.

Some religious institutions argue that hiring according to religion is necessary to maintain the special character of the organization and perform its work, even in a government-funded program.[28] Yet religious organizations that enter financial partnerships with the government do so to provide secular services and are prohibited from using such funds for religious activities. While such organizations are often presumed not to discriminate with government funds, some claim an absolute right to religious freedom that ignores the important way that religious identity and belief is protected as a protected category alongside race, sex, and national origin. Denying someone a government-funded job based on religion, like denying someone a job with a secular employer on that basis, runs counter to principles of religious liberty.

First Amendment ... gives no one the right to insist that in pursuit of their own interests others must conform their conduct to his own religious necessities." (quoting Otten v. Baltimore & Ohio R. Co., 205 F.2d 58, 61 (2d Cir. 1953))).

[25] *See* Hosanna-Tabor Evangelical Lutheran Church & Sch. v. EEOC, 565 U.S. 171, 184, 191 (2012) ("The Establishment Clause prevents the Government from appointing ministers, and the Free Exercise Clause prevents it from interfering with the freedom of religious groups to select their own ... the ministerial exception is not limited to the head of a religious congregation."); Amos, 483 U.S. at 329 ("Section 702 of the Civil Rights Act of 1964 ... exempts religious organizations from Title VII's prohibition against discrimination in employment on the basis of religion.").

[26] While Title VII's religious exemption for religious hiring applies broadly to organizations that meet the statute's definition of religious organization, the exemption applies only to decisions made *based on religion*, as opposed to other legally protected categories. See Wilson, *supra* note 20, for cases. The ministerial exception reaches a broader range of claims but applies only to "ministers," a narrow category of employees most closely associated with church autonomy.

[27] *See* Exec. Order No. 13559, *supra* note 18. But see Exec. Order No. 13831, 83 Fed. Reg. 20715 (May 3, 2018), which seems to eliminate this important beneficiary protection.

[28] See Esbeck, *supra* note 20, for cases.

Applying religious criteria to the use of public funds undercuts the separation of church and state that protects religious liberty. It harms the government's interest in providing benefits and services on a nondiscriminatory basis.

Of course, nondiscrimination in employment law is a key battleground in debates about LGBT rights and religious liberty even outside of faith-based partnerships with government, as this volume shows. As a matter of religious autonomy, religious institutions want to be free to hire according to religion, including with regard to teachings and tenets about sexuality. While many cities and states ensure LGBT nondiscrimination in employment, LGBT status is not explicitly protected by Title VII. Conflict over religious hiring in government-funded programs is a substantial part of the background against which broader conflicts between advocates for LGBT nondiscrimination and religious entities that oppose such protections have deepened. Failure to acknowledge how money affects competing claims in the arena of government-funded services makes it more difficult to negotiate LGBT protections and to preserve the autonomy of religious institutions in other contexts.

III PRACTICAL EXPERIENCE SHOWS US THAT MONEY MATTERS

As others in this volume discuss, religious teachings about sexuality and understandings about whether civil laws should protect rights based on LGBT status differ widely between religious groups, as well as within religious communities. Some religious traditions advocate for legal protections for LGBT individuals and support marriage equality for same-sex couples, some oppose all recognition of sexual orientation and gender identity as protected bases for nondiscrimination, and others fall somewhere in between. Diverse religious opinions in a rapidly changing cultural and legal landscape create challenges for religious institutions but do not have to create a religious liberty crisis. Common ground in religious teachings about care for others can help bridge sharp differences in many cases.[29] Separation of church and state principles, including those that recognize the relationship between government funding and religious liberty, may also prove helpful. The hard work of understanding another person's perspective and the need to respect another's desire to live consistently with his or her deepest values are necessary first steps toward building public consensus to protect religious liberty and LGBT people in a variety of contexts.

In the meantime, religious institutions at the center of our religious liberty tradition – churches and their essential ministries – will continue to advance their beliefs and practices, maintaining and advancing specific religious precepts through worship, instruction, and evangelism without relying on government funds. Reflecting the diversity of those communities, many faithful individuals will work to

---

[29] For a powerful call to protect our LGBT neighbors from within the Catholic tradition, see Gramick, Chapter 10.

advocate for public policies consistent with their religious beliefs. Where such entities operate independent from government, there is less political pressure to apply nondiscrimination laws at odds with the entity's religious teachings. To the extent that such entities seek and accept government resources, however, it is not surprising to see expectations of accountability and equality, including LGBT nondiscrimination, come to the fore.

As our constitutional history and legal traditions teach, the issue that connects government funding and nondiscrimination norms is control. In some circumstances, such as in hiring for religious organizations (and hiring ministers in particular), houses of worship and other religious entities claim religious liberty rights that may outweigh the state's interest in nondiscrimination or are beyond the state's competence to decide.[30] Deferring to religious understandings and avoiding interference with religion in a context that is primarily religious protects religious freedom. Keeping the institutions of government and religion separate in this way recognizes that institutions of religion and government have distinct roles and responsibilities that are best maintained through independence from one another. They typically also have distinct sources of funding. The government has no authority in and should not exercise control over religious doctrine. And to maintain their identity, churches and other houses of worship in particular should be shielded from government control. The independence of religious institutions also supports deference to religious autonomy when weighed against competing government interests. In many other contexts, including most commercial or government employment, religious liberty will be better protected by enforcing nondiscrimination laws that prohibit religious discrimination against employees or customers. In religiously affiliated nonprofits, which sit at the boundary of these spheres especially when receiving government funding, the lines may not be quite so clear and are worth negotiating further.[31]

Failure to appreciate that government funding undercuts claims for autonomy will likely harm our tradition of religious liberty. In *Trinity Lutheran Church of Columbia, Inc. v. Comer*,[32] the so-called playground case, the Supreme Court addressed the relationship between government funding and churches. While the case marks the first time the Court has upheld a direct government grant to a church, the Court did not reject the basic premise of the Establishment Clause, which forbids government advancement of religion. Instead, it found a narrow free exercise right to participate in a particular kind of government-funded program. The

---

[30] For a discussion of the state's competence to decide questions of religion, see Helfand, Chapter 11.

[31] In the context of religious colleges and universities, this point is further complicated by a variety of funding mechanisms, including student aid. *See, e.g.* Ibby Caputo & Jon Marcus, *The Controversial Reason Some Religious Colleges Forgo Federal Funding*, THE ATLANTIC (July 7, 2016), https://perma.cc/NAF6-E4AR.

[32] 137 S. Ct. 2012 (2017).

Court's decision does not support government funding of religious exercise and teaching or the funding of churches in general. It leaves for another day many questions about the status of laws that prohibit government funding of religious institutions.

For the majority, the government program at issue was simply a public safety program that did not involve religion. With a carefully worded footnote, Chief Justice John Roberts limited the departure from the "no-aid to churches" rule, stating: "This case involves express discrimination based on religious identity with respect to playground resurfacing. We do not address religious uses of funding or other forms of discrimination."[33] Even so, within the first pages of the majority opinion, the Court emphasized that the church preschool admits students of any religion, reinforcing the important connection between government funding and nondiscrimination. While Trinity Lutheran Church certainly has the right to use its own resources for preschool education that incorporates daily religious activities and to maintain its property solely for private use, receipt of government funds even for a safety program brings pressure to serve the public without discrimination based on religion or other category.[34]

Indeed, religious liberty would be hard to understand if the Court found that the state must allow churches to participate in a funding program that then left the church free to use government resources for religious purposes. The Court's decision in *Trinity Lutheran Church* affirms that religious institutions have the right to receive generally available government benefits for health and safety, such as sidewalks and police and fire protection. But they do not have the right to exercise control over how those benefits and resources are used. Who would think that a church could insist that the police officers who arrive to investigate a robbery at the church must be members of the church's religion? Or that the government employee assigned to help children cross an intersection near a religious school could not be a member of the LGBT community? At the same time, most people expect that those who work for a church can be required to uphold church teachings. That foundational understanding supports religious autonomy and control over private religious resources and state control over public secular resources.

---

[33] *Id.*, at 2024.

[34] Likewise, the voucher program upheld in Zelman v. Simmons-Harris, 536 U.S. 639, 645 (2002), prohibited discrimination by all participating schools based upon race, religion, or ethnicity. The majority held that the program, which included religious schools, did not violate the Establishment Clause because the taxpayer funding only reached the school as a matter of "true private choice." In Christian Legal Society v. Martinez, 561 U.S. 661 (2011), the Court rejected a challenge to the University of California at Hastings's all-comers policy for student organizations. Instead, it upheld the school's nondiscrimination policy as a reasonable, viewpoint-neutral condition on access to the student-organization forum. "The First Amendment shields CLS against state prohibition of the organization's expressive activity, however exclusionary that activity may be. But CLS enjoys no constitutional right to state subvention of its selectivity." *Id.* at 669.

While some advocates of LGBT nondiscrimination and some advocates of religious liberty pursue their agendas as if the other side's claims threaten their existence, our religious liberty tradition demonstrates there is room for both, though not on absolute terms. Respect for autonomy and the absence of government funding of houses of worship allow religious communities to maintain teachings that may be at odds with nondiscrimination laws and other public expectations that are essential in secular settings. Public demands for LGBT equality, like other cultural changes, may pressure and influence religious institutions to be more inclusive,[35] but significant changes within religious organizations will rest on doctrinal commitments and beliefs of faith communities.

IV CONCLUSION

To sustain religious liberty as the crown jewel of America's democracy, the public must understand and respect the historical and legal tradition, as well as its practical utility. A polarized political culture has taken a toll on our shared understanding of what religious freedom entails. In public debates about LGBT nondiscrimination, the term "religious liberty" is often used with little attention to our country's history and founding legal principles. Religious liberty can be a unifying value for individuals with very different religious and political beliefs if one remembers that religious liberty is not protected the same way in every context. Recognizing the importance of context when weighing competing interests is crucial.

Religious institutions – houses of worship in particular – hold a special place in the law, separate from other arenas where competing government interests are stronger. That special place is best guarded when such institutions maintain their independence from government by avoiding government funding. Demands for religious liberty in current debates about LGBT nondiscrimination rights should not be addressed in a vacuum. If the goal is to uphold religious liberty for all while protecting the LGBT community against discrimination, we should talk frankly about how the nation has delicately balanced similar competing claims in the past and avoided absolute claims.

---

[35] For a discussion of responses by some religious universities to secular norms, see Hoogstra et al., Chapter 25.

24

Freedom to Serve

Religious Organizational Freedom, LGBT Rights, and the Common Good

Thomas C. Berg

The conflicts rage on between nondiscrimination claims by LGBT persons and religious-freedom defenses by traditionalist organizations. The bulk of the conflicts will likely involve nonprofit religious schools or social services that claim that having to hire openly gay employees, facilitate same-sex adoptions, or take other actions would conflict with their religious identity.

I have advocated for protecting both same-sex couples and religious objectors,[1] and I remain interested in arguments that can cut across our polarized cultural-political lines. This chapter explores one argument for the freedom of religious organizations – an argument aimed at people in the middle, who may support same-sex marriage but are open to protecting objectors.[2]

Recently, religious organizations seeking protection from government restrictions have emphasized that they seek "freedom to serve" others. The US Catholic bishops have made that phrase central to their campaign for religious liberty in disputes over same-sex marriage, the Obama administration's contraception mandate, and other issues. "If religious liberty is not respected," the bishops argue, "all people ... are deprived of the essential contribution to the common good, be it in education, health care, feeding the hungry, civil rights, and social services that the Church and other people of faith make every day."[3] This "common good" argument for religious freedom, also articulated by Archbishop William Lori in Chapter 13, stands distinct

---

[1] *See, e.g.*, Thomas C. Berg & Douglas Laycock, *Protecting Same-Sex Marriage and Religious Liberty, in* Religion and Equality: Law in Conflict 167, 171 (W. Cole Durham & Donlu Thayer eds., 2016).

[2] For survey evidence that there are such Americans, see Laycock, Chapter 3.

[3] *Religious Liberty*, U.S. Conference of Catholic Bishops, https://perma.cc/SS29-9M9T. Conservative evangelical Protestants have sounded similar themes. Stephen V. Monsma & Stanley W. Carlson-Thies, Free to Serve: Protecting the Religious Freedom of Faith-Based Organizations (2015).

from other arguments, such as preserving the autonomy of individual believers or limiting the power of government.

The common-good argument is worth examining in detail. It will likely figure in future litigation and legislative debates over nondiscrimination and religious freedom. Resting claims for religious freedom on contributions to the social good raises complications: above all, it may seem to make freedom a matter of policy rather than rights. But this chapter argues that the common-good argument, when properly defined, is a legitimate, indeed important strain in America's tradition of religious-freedom rights, as Section I explains.

In a roughly analogous way, Section II argues, same-sex-marriage rights found support in considerations of the common good as well as individual autonomy. Same-sex partners' care for each other and for their children figured importantly in *Obergefell v. Hodges*[4] and in legislative and public support for marriage equality. Recognizing this parallel, and others, between marriage rights and religious-freedom rights might encourage us to give weight to both rights.[5] Section III then catalogs the contributions of religion and religious organizations. Sections IV and V, respectively, respond to objections that may be raised and suggest principles for the proper scope of religious freedom.

I HOW DO RELIGION'S SOCIETAL CONTRIBUTIONS RELATE TO RELIGIOUS FREEDOM?

Discussing religious organizations and the "common good" requires acknowledging at the outset that religiously motivated conduct can have negative effects, some serious, on others. For example, discrimination against LGBT persons can materially reduce their access to jobs or important services; in some cases, it can cause jolting surprise or public embarrassment.[6]

But conservative religion is often dismissed as a mere cover for irrationality and bigotry, and that is a canard. A balanced, accurate picture requires consideration of the ways in which free religious practice in America contributes to social good. Before presenting the evidence of those contributions, however, it is important to consider whether and how religion's societal contributions are relevant to religious freedom as (A) a consideration of social policy and (B) a right.

---

[4] 135 S. Ct. 2584 (2015).

[5] *See, e.g.,* Thomas C. Berg, *What Same-Sex-Marriage and Religious-Liberty Claims Have in Common,* 5 Nw. J. L. & Soc. Pol'y 206 (2010).

[6] For deeply personal accounts of such harms, see Minter, Chapter 4; Melling, Chapter 19; Pizer, Chapter 29.

A *Social Policy*

Certainly, any positive social contributions by religious organizations provide a policy argument for protecting them from governmental interference that might hamper their work. Adopting sound policy toward a given activity requires balancing its positive and negative aspects. And religious freedom – at least in the form of exemptions from generally applicable laws – is often a matter of legislative discretion.[7] The US Supreme Court has said that legislatures may adopt religious exemptions, although in cases of truly generally applicable laws the Free Exercise Clause does not require it.[8]

B *Religious-Freedom Rights*

But do religion's societal contributions support religious freedom not simply as a policy but as a right? Grounding religious freedom on these contributions might suggest that it should protect only those religions that those in power agree with or view as beneficial. But that would clash with the fundamental constitutional principles that government must not discriminate among religions[9] and that a religion need not be "acceptable … or comprehensible to others in order to merit First Amendment protection."[10]

Two qualifications about linking religious freedom to contributions to the common good are crucial. First, any particular organization's ability to invoke religious freedom should not depend at the threshold on whether the organization contributes, or is perceived as contributing, to the common good. Rather, religion's contributions are a reason to have a general principle protecting religious freedom. That principle then protects free exercise for religions of all kinds (subject to appropriate limits). Second, common-good arguments are not the only argument for religious freedom. They operate alongside other arguments based on preserving personal autonomy or placing structural limits on government.

Subject to those qualifications, religion's contributions are relevant in multiple ways, even to religious freedom as a right.

1 Motivation

Consider a practical fact: people will be inclined to protect a freedom only if they believe that, on the whole, it plays some positive role in society. Only if they think free expression is valuable overall will they protect it for obnoxious political

---

[7] For a discussion of legislative considerations, see Adams, Chapter 32; Leavitt, Chapter 33.

[8] Employment Division v. Smith, 494 U.S. 872, 890 (1990).

[9] Larson v. Valente, 456 U.S. 228, 244–45 (1982).

[10] Thomas v. Review Board, 450 U.S. 707, 714 (1981).

harangues or hateful Westboro Church picketers.[11] So, too, for freedom of religion. Countering jaundiced views of religion – showing its contributions – can move people to consider religious freedom arguments rather than dismiss them out of hand.[12]

2 Justifications

Religion's social contributions provide not just motivations, but also normative justifications, for protecting religious freedom. First, as Alan Brownstein has observed, one major purpose for civil rights and liberties is to prevent those in power from "focus[ing] on one characteristic of a person – their race, religion, national ancestry or sexual orientation – and act[ing] as if that one attribute determines the value of the person."[13] Gays and lesbians "are a lot more than their sexual orientation and conduct" – and likewise, "traditional religions are a lot more than one allegedly discriminatory belief might suggest."[14] As Douglas Laycock and I have argued, LGBT persons and religious conservatives "are each viewed as evil by a substantial portion of the population"; thus, "each is subject to substantial risks of intolerant and unjustifiably burdensome regulation."[15] Understanding the contributions of religion, including traditional religion, helps establish that certain restrictions on it are intolerant or excessive.

Second, and relatedly, America's religious freedom tradition rests in part on the premise that religious organization provide a vital means for individuals to develop and exercise "civic virtue" – a regard for others' interests that government cannot mandate, and that is necessary to preserve order and harmony in a free society.

Nearly all the framers thought that popular government required morality in the citizenry. Most of them thought religion an important contributor to morality; many thought it crucial. George Washington emphasized that morality and religion were "indispensable" to political prosperity, "the firmest props of the duties of men and citizens" – and that "reason and experience both forbid us to expect that national morality can prevail in exclusion of religious principle."[16] John Adams said, "We have no government armed with power capable of contending with human passions

---

[11] Snyder v. Phelps, 562 U.S. 443 (2011) (holding that the church's picketing of a funeral was protected by the Free Speech Clause).

[12] See Lori, Chapter 13, for discussion of study quantifying religious congregations' economic impact at $418 billion annually.

[13] Alan Brownstein, *Gays, Jews, and Other Strangers in a Strange Land: The Case for Reciprocal Accommodation of Religious Liberty and the Right of Same-Sex Couples to Marry*, 45 U.S.F. L. Rev. 389, 405–06 n.47 (2010).

[14] *Id.*

[15] Berg & Laycock, *supra* note 1, at 171.

[16] George Washington, *Farewell Address* (Sept. 19, 1796), https://perma.cc/E37K-GZFC.

unbridled with morality and religion."[17] These "civic republican" framers – particularly concerned with the virtues that would enable people to govern themselves – emphasized "the basic place and utility of all peaceable religions in a well-governed society."[18] In the Northwest Ordinance of 1787, Congress resolved that "religion, morality, and knowledge, being necessary to good government and the happiness of mankind, schools and the means of education shall be forever encouraged."[19]

More recently, Timothy Hall has argued that religious organizations help generate virtue by providing a concrete context "in which individuals become sharers of a common life, and thus have occasion to acquire an other-regarding disposition."[20] Mary Ann Glendon similarly situates the First Amendment in a "structural" account of the Bill Rights, under which the rights provide "'positive protection' for certain structures of civil society" – including religious organizations – that "promote self-government" and act as "seedbeds of civic virtue."[21] These modern writers reiterate the themes of Alexis de Tocqueville, who observed that "[i]n no country in the world has the principle of association been more successfully used ... than in America."[22] A mass democratic society, Tocqueville said, had to rely on smaller groups because "[f]eelings and opinions are recruited, the heart is enlarged, and the human mind is developed by no other means than the reciprocal influence of men upon each other."[23]

According to the main strain of the American tradition, however, religion can only promote civic virtue if it is largely voluntary. Sponsorship of a favored religion, James Madison and others warned, would corrupt it and undermine its capacity to nurture and mobilize civic virtue. As Hall puts it, government had to be satisfied "with the strategy of indirection": "preserv[ing] a zone of autonomy in which religious groups can create those dispositions to virtue which the republic needs but whose creation it cannot command."[24] Thus a civic republican like John Adams could say, "We should begin by setting conscience free ... When all men of all religions ... enjoy equal liberty, property ... and an equal chance for honors and power[,]we may expect that improvements will be made in the human character and the state of society."[25]

---

[17] *John Adams to Massachusetts Militia* (Oct. 11, 1798), https://perma.cc/996W-UWK7 ("Our Constitution was made only for a moral and religious People. It is wholly inadequate to the government of any other.").

[18] JOHN J. WITTE, JR. & JOEL A. NICHOLS, RELIGION AND THE AMERICAN CONSTITUTIONAL EXPERIMENT 37 (4th ed., 2016).

[19] *Northwest Ordinance* art. 3 (July 13, 1787), https://perma.cc/DG97-QE2U.

[20] Timothy L. Hall, *Religion and Civic Virtue: A Justification of Free Exercise*, 67 TULANE L. REV. 87, 88 (1992).

[21] Mary Ann Glendon, *Structural Free Exercise*, 90 MICH. L. REV. 477, 543 (1991).

[22] ALEXIS DE TOCQUEVILLE, 1 DEMOCRACY IN AMERICA 191 (Henry Reeve trans., 1899).

[23] *Id.* at 117.

[24] Hall, *supra* note 20, at 120–21, 124–25.

[25] *Letter to Dr. Price, Apr. 8, 1785, in* 8 THE WORKS OF JOHN ADAMS (Charles F. Adams ed., 1853), https://perma.cc/F7RL-ZS57.

But how can a common-good or civic-virtue rationale support protecting religious practice when it conflicts with generally applicable laws, such as prohibitions on invidious discrimination? After all, such a law shows that a democratic majority has determined that the practice conflicts with civic norms.

For an answer, return to George Washington, this time to his 1789 letter to a Quaker assembly.[26] Washington had a rocky history with Quakers, whose refusal to serve in the Revolutionary army was widely viewed as treasonous.[27] His 1789 letter chided them gently for their refusal but proceeded to defend their rights:

> Your principles and conduct are well known to me; and it is doing the people called Quakers no more than justice to say, that (except their declining to share with others the burden of the common defense) there is no denomination among us, who are more exemplary and useful citizens.
>
> I assure you very explicitly, that in my opinion the conscientious scruples of all men should be treated with great delicacy and tenderness; and it is my wish and desire, that the laws may always be as extensively accommodated to them, as a due regard to the protection and essential interests of the nation may justify and permit.

The letter's two paragraphs are connected. Washington, who valued religion largely for its support of civic morality, still supported "extensively accommodat[ing]" religious conscience when it violated a mandate such as contributing to the common defense. He supported accommodation because, among other reasons, Quakers overall were "exemplary and useful citizens" – largely as a result of the same belief system that led them to refuse military service.

In short, an act may deserve protection, even though society deems it non-virtuous, because it stems from an overall pattern of living with evident virtues. This perspective combines the goods of pluralism and civic virtue. Protection of dissenting conscience can promote the common good by keeping the dissenter not merely free, but free to serve others. Organizations advance societal goals from a variety of perspectives, in a variety of ways: many of them make "uncommon contributions to the common good."[28] Forcing an organization to change or minimize a feature of its distinctive identity risks undercutting the organization's distinctive contributions inspired by that identity. These reasons justify a presumption – not an absolute right, but a presumption – that organizations should be free to maintain their identity as they provide services to others.

---

[26] *George Washington to the Society of Quakers* (Oct. 13, 1789), https://perma.cc/2R3R-KARL.

[27] *See, e.g.,* Vincent Philip Munoz, *George Washington on Religious Liberty*, 65 Rev. Pol. 11 (Winter 2003).

[28] Stanley Carlson-Thies, *Faith-Based Organizations Can Strengthen the Religious Freedom They Need*, Institutional Religious Freedom Alliance, https://perma.cc/2Q59-XAW6.

II SAME-SEX MARRIAGE RIGHTS AND THE COMMON GOOD

Recognizing the virtues or contributions of "uncommon" groups is particularly appropriate for the clash between LGBT nondiscrimination and religious liberty. The right to same-sex civil marriage itself has relied significantly on claims of civic virtue. Marriage equality prevailed in the courts and public opinion for many reasons, but among them was that same-sex couples wanted to marry to pursue similar virtues as straight couples: love, commitment, and family.

Begin with *Obergefell*, where the Supreme Court held that same-sex couples fit within the traditional right to marry for several reasons – some sounding in individual autonomy, but others sounding in responsibility and commitment. That commitment benefits the partners: it "offers the hope of companionship and understanding and assurance that while both still live there will be someone to care for the other."[29] But it also benefits others. "The right to marry ... safeguards children and families"; because "many same-sex couples provide loving and nurturing homes to their children, ... [e]xcluding [them] from marriage thus conflicts with a central premise of the right."[30] Marriage "is a keystone of our social order," the Court added – citing Tocqueville and thereby implying that marriage is a keystone, a vital form of association, because it serves social goals that government itself cannot directly achieve.[31]

Similar arguments appear in the literature advocating marriage equality as a matter of not just "civil rights" but "civil responsibility"[32] – in William Eskridge's words, not just "sexual liberty" but "civilized commitment."[33] Jonathan Rauch cataloged how equality would benefit both gay people and the rest of society, serving marriage's three "essential social functions": "providing a healthy environment for children, ... helping the young (especially men) settle down and make a home, and providing as many people as possible with caregivers."[34] Earlier, Andrew Sullivan pioneered the argument that gay marriage, "[l]ike straight marriage, ... would foster social cohesion, emotional security, and economic prudence" and "also help nurture children."[35] Rauch defended (gay) marriage as vital intermediate association:

---

[29] 135 S. Ct. at 2600.
[30] *Id.* at 2590, 2600 (citing evidence on same-sex households with children, from Brief for Gary J. Gates as Amicus Curiae, at 4–6, 2015 WL 1021451).
[31] 135 S. Ct. at 2601.
[32] Jonathan Rauch, Gay Marriage: Why It's Good for Gays, Good for Straights, and Good for America 67 (2008).
[33] William N. Eskridge, Jr., The Case for Same-Sex Marriage: From Sexual Liberty to Civilized Commitment (1996).
[34] Rauch, *supra* note 32, at 76.
[35] Andrew Sullivan, *Here Comes the Groom*, New Republic (Aug. 28, 1989), https://perma.cc/9Z3C-57KT. *See also* Eskridge, *supra* note 33, at 13 (arguing that denying same-sex marriage was "antifamily and antichildren").

"no institution or government program can begin to match the love of a devoted partner."[36]

These "common good" arguments might sound like matters of policy rather than constitutional right.[37] But *Obergefell* emphasized them in its constitutional reasoning, to show how same-sex unions serve the purposes of the right to marriage. Social virtues can likewise help ground religious freedom as a right.

Of course, "civil responsibility" arguments for marriage equality have triggered strong criticisms from some LGBT advocates. Critics assert that marriage is patriarchal and constricting,[38] and that *Obergefell*, in its "glorification of marriage, … effectively work[s] the very humiliation of [nonmarital relationships] that the majority condemns in restrictive marriage laws."[39] Again, however, the point here is simply that *Obergefell* emphasized marriage's social virtues and used them to ground same-sex marriage as a right, not just social policy.

Moreover, this grounding in social virtues was probably crucial to marriage equality's success in public opinion. After initial legislative defeats, advocates learned from opinion research that they "'had to convince people that gay couples were trying to join this institution'" rather than fundamentally change it.[40] They responded with the "Why Marriage Matters" campaign, whose "message was 'love, commitment, family'" – "invit[ing] straight people to empathize with gay people" and "shift[ing] focus from minority rights to points of commonality."[41] This approach successfully targeted the "movable middle."[42]

Claims to marriage and to religious freedom can both rest in part on the recognition that people with practices that are unfamiliar or objectionable to others can still contribute to the common good. That approach may seem quixotic in today's culture wars, when each side increasingly sees its opponents "as selfish, as threats to the nation, even as unsuitable marriage material."[43] The 2016 election has deepened such polarization; the overwhelming Trump vote among white evangelicals may cement the left's conviction that those voters cannot possibly contribute to

[36] Rauch, *supra* note 32, at 78.

[37] Eskridge, *supra* note 33, chs. 5, 6.

[38] See *id.* at 60–62, 75–85 (discussing and responding to such arguments).

[39] Susan Frelich Appleton, Obergefell's *Liberties: All in the Family*, 77 Ohio St. L.J. 919, 956 (2016).

[40] Molly Ball, *How Gay Marriage Became a Constitutional Right*, The Atlantic (July 1, 2015), https://perma.cc/VV82-DCKY (quoting Lanae Erickson Hatalsky of the policy group Third Way).

[41] Nathaniel Frank, *How Gay Marriage Finally Won at the Polls*, Slate (Nov. 7, 2012), https://perma.cc/W3KX-56FW.

[42] Nathaniel Frank, Awakening: How Gays and Lesbians Brought Marriage Equality to America 278 (2017).

[43] Emily Badger & Niraj Chokshi, *How We Became Bitter Political Enemies*, N.Y. Times (June 15, 2017), https://perma.cc/8MK7-UDWP.

the common good.[44] Yet the inconvenient fact remains that religious organizations – conservative ones as much as any – contribute substantially to serving others.[45]

III RELIGIOUS VOLUNTARISM AND THE COMMON GOOD: EVIDENCE

A substantial body of evidence indicates that religious organizations still play the important role the founders envisioned in serving others and the common good, as this section enumerates.

A *Benefits to Religious Individuals*

First, religious identity provides benefits to the individual adherents, benefits that may be lost if the individuals have to suppress or compromise it. Multiple studies, summarized by leading researcher Ram Cnaan, indicate that religious identity increases morale, reduces fear of death, reduces suicides, and has other positive effects.[46] Religious involvement correlates with physical health, although it's unclear whether that reflects causation or mere correlation. Studies also show "a strong correlation between religious participation and avoidance of crime and substance abuse."[47] "The preponderance of the evidence ... suggests that religion is modestly helpful in the areas of prosocial behavior, personal and social adjustment, life satisfaction and well-being, and physical symptomatology."[48]

Cnaan's findings indicate that these benefits come not from individual faith but overwhelmingly from participation in a religiously based "social support network."[49] Similarly, Robert Putnam and David Campbell find that although religious persons score high on indicators of "good neighborliness" – volunteering or donating to causes, attending civic or club meetings – the effects arise almost entirely from participation in religious social networks, such as

---

[44] For the personal account of hostility after the 2016 election from the president of the National Association of Evangelicals, see Leith Anderson, Chapter 12.

[45] *See* Lori, *supra* note 12.

[46] RAM A. CNAAN, THE NEWER DEAL: SOCIAL WORK AND RELIGION IN PARTNERSHIP 139 (1999).

[47] *Id.* at 150.

[48] *Id.* at 156. Other work shows that, across dozens of studies, "greater religiousness ... facilitate[s] marital functioning," although the effects are "small." *See* Robin Fretwell Wilson, *Divorcing Marriage and the State Post-Obergefell*, *in* THE CONTESTED PLACE OF RELIGION IN FAMILY LAW (Robin Fretwell Wilson ed., 2018) (reviewing studies showing that religious married couples, on balance, are "happier than nonreligious married couples, less likely to divorce, more collaborative, and more faithful, and less likely to report domestic violence, even after controlling for other demographic factors").

[49] Cnaan, *supra* note 46, at 139.

"having close friends at church," and "taking part in small groups at church."[50] These findings segue to the central topic of this chapter: the contributions of religious organizations.

B *Social Contributions of Religiously Based Service Organizations*

A significant body of evidence documents religious organizations' service to others in areas such as education, prisoner rehabilitation and reentry, crime prevention, antipoverty efforts, and disaster relief. As Stephen Monsma concluded: "[I]f violations of religious-freedom rights would cause a significant number of faith-based organizations to go out of business, to withdraw from certain areas of service, or to reduce their size, ... a crisis of the first magnitude would exist in the nation's social safety net."[51] To assess religious organizations' contributions, Monsma posed three questions:

(1) How many faith-based organizations are actively providing services to how many persons, and what proportion of services in that are[a]? ...
(2) Are these faith-based organizations filling a niche that governmental or nonprofit secular agencies would have a difficult time filling? ...
(3) Are faith-based organizations largely religious in name only, ... or is their religious character something that is alive and meaningful to them in shaping their identity, their motivation for what they are doing, and how they go about doing it?[52]

The third factor, centrality of religious identity, estimates the likelihood that religious organizations would cease or curtail their work if forced by regulations to violate their religious identity. The two preceding factors – the magnitude and distinctiveness of faith-based services – estimate the losses that would follow if religious organizations took that step. It is worth unpacking each.

1 Magnitude

In the same vein as Monsma, Cnaan concludes from a study of Philadelphia service providers:

> Religious organizations represent a major part of the American welfare system. Tens of thousands of people in the Philadelphia area are being helped by all kinds of programs, from soup kitchens to housing services, from job training to educational

---

[50] Robert D. Putnam & David E. Campbell, American Grace: How Religion Unites and Divides Us 444, 472 (2010).

[51] Stephen V. Monsma, Pluralism and Freedom: Faith-Based Organizations in a Democratic Society 16 (2011).

[52] *Id.* at 19. For a view of what should qualify as religious organization as religious, see Hill, Chapter 26.

enhancement classes. One can only imagine what would happen to the collective quality of life if these religious organizations would cease to exist.[53]

Consider also evidence of magnitude in various fields of social service:

- Catholic Charities USA provides more Americans with social services than any entity except the federal government:[54] 8.3 million different persons in 2016.[55] The evangelical Salvation Army provides 55 million meals yearly and nightly shelter for 10 million people.[56]
- Catholic hospitals and health-care facilities form the nation's largest private nonprofit health-care system, caring for one in six hospital patients and typically providing a disproportionate share of public-health and specialty services.[57]
- According to a recent study of homeless shelters in eleven cities nationwide, "[f]aith-based organizations provide nearly 60% of the Emergency Shelter Beds, what many consider the 'safety net of all safety nets' for the homeless population."[58]
- Among America's private overseas-relief agencies, 33 percent were faith-based in 2005, "deliver[ing] almost half of the nongovernmental international assistance." World Vision, the large evangelical agency that has faced legal controversies over its faith-based hiring policies, has "'more staff members [40,000] than CARE, Save the Children, and the worldwide operations of [USAID] – combined.'"[59]
- If faith-based adoption agencies were to disappear, according to the CEO of the National Council for Adoption, "the whole [adoption] system would collapse on itself."[60]

---

[53] Cnaan, *supra* note 46, at 275–76.

[54] *See* Laury Oaks, *Catholic Church*, in 1 Poverty in the United States: An Encyclopedia of History, Politics, and Policy 131, 131 (Gwendolyn Mink & Alice O'Connor eds., 2004).

[55] *Catholic Charities USA*, Letter to United States House of Representatives (Jan. 17, 2018), https://perma.cc/S9TQ-4WXK.

[56] *The Salvation Army, 2017 Annual Survey* 5, https://perma.cc/T5BU-X6UA. Brief *Amicus Curiae* of U.S. Conference of Catholic Bishops et al., at 14, *in* Zubik v. Burwell, 136 S. Ct. 1557 (2016), https://perma.cc/KQF8-M96B [hereinafter "USCCB Brief"]. *See id.* at 6–26 (summarizing magnitude and distinctiveness of religious organizations' services).

[57] U.S. Conference of Catholic Bishops, *Catholic Health Care, Social Services and Humanitarian Aid*, https://perma.cc/8TYJ-KQSJ (reporting 2014 figures showing 645 Catholic hospitals serve 87,972,910 patients annually); *Obama Risks $100 Billion if Catholic Hospitals Close*, Fiscal Times (Mar. 1, 2012), https://perma.cc/79MR-S5FS.

[58] Byron Johnson & William H. Wubbenhorst, Assessing the Faith-Based Response to Homelessness in America: Findings from Eleven Cities 20 (2017), https://perma.cc/Y7YN-HRDB.

[59] Monsma, *supra* note 51, at 21 (quoting Nicholas D. Kristof, *Learning from the Sins of Sodom*, N.Y. Times (Feb. 28, 2010), at Wk11).

[60] *Id.* at 30; *id.* at 31 (quoting interview with Chuck Johnson).

2 Distinctiveness

If religious organizations facing legal conflicts cease or curtail their services, will other organizations replace them? It is doubtful, given not only the magnitude of the services but their distinctiveness. "Faith-based organizations often fill a niche that either government or large, secular social service agencies would have a hard time filling."[61] A few examples:

- Nonprofit church-owned hospitals "save more lives, release patients from the hospital sooner, and have better overall patient satisfaction ratings."[62]
- In the area of education, according to Anthony Bryk, "accumulated evidence [from two decades of studies] indicates that average [student] achievement is somewhat higher in Catholic high schools than in public high schools, and ... that Catholic high schools may be especially helpful for disadvantaged students." Bryk's own fieldwork confirmed that "the largest [advantage of Catholic schools was] for the most disadvantaged students."[63]
- Faith-based adoption agencies are "especially effective in placing special needs children who usually are hard to place."[64] For example, distinctively high percentages of adoptions by Catholic Charities and Bethany Christian Services in 2009 involved, respectively, special-needs and older children.[65]

Scholarship suggests various reasons for the religious providers' advantages. First, "they have faith-rooted beliefs into which they can tap to motivate and encourage" beneficiaries and others.[66] For example, faith-based prisoner reentry programs can "'affect returning prisoners in ways that other programs do not'" because they "'can help create the conditions for personal transformation, provide inspiration, and motivate individuals to achieve individual goals.'"[67] Bryk attributes the "Catholic

---

[61] *Id.* at 42.

[62] David Foster et al., *Hospital Performance Differences by Ownership* 1 (June 2013), https://perma .cc/GP7R-JF9E (determining ownership from the American Hospital Association 2011 Hospital Survey Database).

[63] ANTHONY S. BRYK ET AL., CATHOLIC SCHOOLS AND THE COMMON GOOD 58, 246–48 (1993). Other measured advantages of Catholic schools come from the social capital they provide to their neighborhoods. *See* MARGARET F. BRINIG & NICOLE STELLE GARNETT, LOST CLASS-ROOM, LOST COMMUNITY: CATHOLIC SCHOOLS' IMPORTANCE IN URBAN AMERICA (University of Chicago Press 2014) (finding that when Catholic schools close, social capital in neighborhood declines and social/physical disorder increases).

[64] MONSMA, *supra* note 51, at 31.

[65] *Id.* (citing MARY L. GAUTIER & ANNA CAMPBELL BUCK, CATHOLIC CHARITIES USA: 2009 ANNUAL SURVEY, at 36 (2010)); USCCB Brief, *supra* note 56.

[66] MONSMA, *supra* note 51, at 39 (quoting report of the Michigan Prisoner ReEntry Initiative, ISSUES OF FAITH, JUSTICE, AND FORGIVENESS: WORKING WITH FAITH-BASED ORGANIZATIONS TO FOSTER DIVERSITY OF MISSION 2 (Sept. 2008)).

[67] *Id.* at 39.

school effect" – greater achievement for the least advantaged – to several factors, among them "an inspirational ideology" motivating both students and teachers.[68]

A second source of distinctiveness lies in faith-based organizations' capacity to mobilize grassroots networks of volunteers, donations, and other resources. For example, Catholics, blacks, and white evangelicals (Hispanic and Anglo) – three groups very likely to dissent from progressive laws on sexual issues[69] – are also, according to sociologist John DiIulio,

> the three religious communities that figure most prominently in serving members and nonmembers alike. Each [group] showers volunteer hours and money on nonmembers who tend to be unlike members in terms of race, socioeconomic status, or religion.[70]

Similarly, Robert Putnam and David Campbell document how religious identity is more effective than nonreligious identity in mobilizing people to volunteer and donate. That holds not just for "religious" causes, as the authors define them (uniquely religious activities such as worship or proselytizing), but also for "secular" causes (service to the needy even when done in a religious setting).[71] "[R]egular churchgoers are more than twice as likely to volunteer to help the needy, compared to demographically matched Americans who rarely, if ever, attend church."[72] In the area of prisoner rehabilitation, "[t]he vast majority of the many thousands of correctional volunteers tend to come from religious congregations."[73] In short, "[t]here is no other source that is more volunteer-rich than America's houses of worship": they "not only mobilize labor for the church itself, but are also feeder systems for many other nonprofit and voluntary organizations."[74]

The benefits accrue not only to service recipients but to volunteers themselves. Cnaan summarizes one study concluding that "religious organizations are key teachers of [concrete] political and civic skills," such as "letter-writing, participating in decision-making meetings, ... and giving presentations or speeches in public forums"; many survey respondents said they learned these skills in "their church work."[75] Another study concluded that because congregation-based social services give their members so many "opportunities for volunteer work and political

---

[68] Bryk, *supra* note 63, at 303–04.

[69] For demographic views on issues such as same-sex marriage and abortion, see Brownstein, Chapter 2; Greenawalt, Chapter 8; Leith Anderson, Chapter 12.

[70] JOHN J. DiIULIO, JR., GODLY REPUBLIC: A CENTRIST BLUEPRINT FOR AMERICA'S FAITH-BASED FUTURE 158 (2007).

[71] PUTNAM & CAMPBELL, *supra* note 50, at 445.

[72] *Id.* at 446.

[73] BYRON R. JOHNSON, MORE GOD, LESS CRIME: WHY FAITH MATTERS AND HOW IT COULD MATTER MORE 197 (2012).

[74] *Id.* (citing, as to "volunteer-rich," MARC A. MUSICK & JOHN WILSON, VOLUNTEERS: A SOCIAL PROFILE 308–10 (2007)).

[75] Cnaan, *supra* note 46, at 189.

participation," "religion is the predominant institution working against the class bias in American civic engagement."[76]

In short, substantial evidence shows that voluntary religious organizations today still play the role of nurturing civic virtue that many founders expected. Religious organizations are not alone; secular agencies fill this role, too, and should enjoy associational rights.[77] But religious organizations have shown a distinctive power to mobilize energy to serve others, often by addressing their personal and spiritual challenges. It is very risky to impose regulation on religious organizations that, by burdening their religious identity, might lead them to cut their services.[78] In Washington's words, we should be "reluctan[t]" to "indulge the supposition" that government or other secular agencies will make up the losses.[79]

3 Importance of Religious Identity

Finally, do religiously affiliated organizations regard their religious identity as important – so important that they will stop providing services rather than violate or change their tenets? Often they do. World Vision's general counsel explains that agency's need to be able to hire persons committed to its tenets: "'We are not just another humanitarian organization, but a branch of the body of Christ ... The key to our effectiveness is our faith, not our size. If we would lose our birthright, if we ever would not be able to determine our team, we'd lose our vision.'"[80]

Religious-liberty conflicts have prompted organizations to exit. Catholic Charities branches in Massachusetts, Illinois, and the District of Columbia stopped performing adoptions because of rules requiring them to place children with same-sex couples.[81] The states lost the benefit of the organizations' experience and contacts, especially concerning hard-to-place children with special needs. "In this all-or-nothing gambit," Robin Fretwell Wilson writes, "Catholic Charities lost, prospective adoptive parents lost, and so did many children in Massachusetts."[82] Likewise, several nonprofit challengers to the contraception mandate warned that they would

---

[76] *Id.* at 154.
[77] See Helfand, Chapter 11, for a discussion of associational rights.
[78] See Laycock, Chapter 3, for critique of laws that require conscientious objectors to choose between following their faith or shuttering their operations and, in the case of individuals, abandoning their occupations.
[79] Washington, Farewell Address, *supra* note 16.
[80] MONSMA, *supra* note 51, at 25 (quoting World Vision Vice President and Chief Legal Officer Steven T. McFarland).
[81] Laurie Goodstein, *Illinois Bishops Drop Program Over Bias Rule*, N.Y. TIMES (Dec. 29, 2011), at A16; Patricia Wen, *Catholic Charities Stuns State, Ends Adoptions*, BOS. GLOBE (Mar. 11, 2006), at A1.
[82] Robin Fretwell Wilson, *A Matter of Conviction: Moral Clashes Over Same-Sex Adoption*, 22 B.Y.U. J. PUB. L. 475, 493 (2008).

cease providing services rather than pay for medicines they believed to be sinful.[83] The government that triggers such conflicts engages in "a high-stakes game of chicken"[84] – one that it is sensible to avoid, given the contributions that religious organizations make, unless regulation is truly necessary.

IV ANSWERS TO OBJECTIONS

Having set forth the "common good" argument for religious freedom, I now consider two significant objections to it.

A *What Good Comes from Organizations Whose Practices Negatively Affect Others?*

Studies may show the value of religious organizations in general, but current religious-freedom controversies involve specific acts that violate laws protecting interests of others: nondiscrimination laws, the contraception mandate, and so forth. Some judges and scholars now advocate denying protection, or even forbidding it as unconstitutional, whenever an activity causes more than a *de minimis* "harm to third parties."[85] These critics say, in effect, that religious acts harming others have no civic value. Does protection here exceed, by definition, the bounds of the civic-virtue rationale?

Surely not. First, as noted earlier in this chapter, if civic virtue generally favors a presumptive right of religious organizational freedom, then that presumptive right should extend to all religious organizations. Effects on others surely relate to the scope of religious freedom: the government interests that limit the right. But they should not eliminate protection altogether.

Second, the empirical dynamics of faith-based services give reason to protect even activities that affect others' legal rights. Many of the contributions of religious organizations to others involve Catholic and evangelical entities. Recall that they are among the groups that "figure most prominently in serving members and nonmembers alike."[86] These groups have also had the most prominent recent

---

[83] *See, e.g.*, Robin Fretwell Wilson, *Calculus of Accommodation: Contraception, Abortion, Same-Sex Marriage, and Other Clashes Between Religion and the State*, 53 B.C. L. REV. 1417, 1448–49 (2012)(quoting, e.g., statements of Belmont Abbey College's president and Francis Cardinal George of Chicago).

[84] *Id.*

[85] *See, e.g.*, Nelson Tebbe et al., *How Much May Religious Accommodations Burden Others?*, http://papers.ssrn.com/sol3/papers.cfm?abstract_id=2811815 (forthcoming in ELIZABETH SEPPER ET AL., LAW, RELIGION, AND HEALTH IN THE UNITED STATES (2017)). *Cf.* Frederick Mark Gedicks & Rebecca G. Van Tassell, *RFRA Exemptions from the Contraception Mandate: An Unconstitutional Accommodation of Religion*, 49 HARV. C.R.-C.L. L. REV. 343, 349–50 (2014) (arguing that an accommodation that shifts any "material costs" onto other individuals violates the Establishment Clause).

[86] *See supra* note 51 and accompanying text.

conflicts with generally applicable regulations such as nondiscrimination laws and the contraception mandate.[87]

The effectiveness of these groups may be no accident. They are what I have called "partly acculturated": they reach out to the broader culture, providing services and employment to nonmembers, but simultaneously they maintain certain faith-based standards of conduct that depart from societal norms.[88] They differ both from insular, fully "unacculturated" groups (say, small sects) and from fully "acculturated" groups that regularly look to general societal norms (say, mainline Protestants).

There are reasons to hypothesize that "partly acculturated" groups have advantages in providing services. Social scientists studying religion have documented and analyzed how "strict" churches tend to inspire greater commitment from their members than do lenient groups.[89] Economist Laurence Iannoccone argues that by making strict behavioral demands, organizations "mitigate[e] free-rider problems that otherwise lead to low levels of member commitment and participation."[90] Reviewing surveys of participation in different religious groups, Iannaccone concludes that a group's "distinctiveness, costliness, or strictness" does more to explain high rates of participation than does any other factor.[91]

Anthropologist William Irons describes costly or unpopular religious practices as "signals of commitment" by the community's members.[92] Cooperation within a group requires trust, which is threatened by free riding but bolstered by "signals of commitment [that are] hard to fake." Because people are less likely to fake costly or unpopular practices, "we should expect that more costly religions are more effective at creating intragroup cooperation."

But the commitment and discipline of an organization's members will provide limited social benefits if the organization directs its activities wholly inwardly. Moreover, a group that is too strict or insular may "scare off many potential members" and remain tiny.[93] Therefore, groups that combine strict features with openness to nonmembers may be especially vigorous in providing social services. That Catholics and evangelicals combine these elements may explain their prominence in providing services. They offer examples of a strong religious identity that invigorates operations and attracts donors, clients, and volunteers.

---

[87] See Leith Anderson, Chapter 12, and Hoogstra et al., Chapter 25, for specific instances.

[88] Thomas C. Berg, *Partly Acculturated Religious Activity: A Case for Accommodating Religious Nonprofits*, 91 NOTRE DAME L. REV. 1341, 1343–48 (2016).

[89] The literature begins with DEAN KELLEY, WHY CONSERVATIVE CHURCHES ARE GROWING: AN ESSAY IN RELIGIOUS SOCIOLOGY (1972).

[90] Laurence Iannaccone, *Why Strict Churches Are Strong*, 99 AM. J. SOC. 1180, 1183 (1994).

[91] *Id.* at 1200.

[92] William Irons, *Religion As a Hard-to-Fake Sign of Commitment*, in EVOLUTION AND THE CAPACITY FOR COMMITMENT 292, 298–99 (Randolph Nesse ed., 2001), https://perma.cc/FX3L-MC5K.

[93] Iannaccone, *supra* note 90, at 1202.

A partly acculturated organization's norms will sometimes conflict with laws defining the rights of others. Opponents claim that the organization is harming third parties; the organization claims freedom to follow its tenets and identity. If partly acculturated activity offers distinctive contributions to society, we should not refuse protection simply because the activity affects nonmembers in a way that contravenes a law. We should try to protect religious freedom, not just for insular organizations but also for those participating in the broader society. Protection cannot be absolute, and harms to third parties are relevant; but they are not conclusive. As Section V discusses, legislators can fashion approaches to avoid subordinating one set of interests to the other.[94]

Although there is evidence that partly acculturated groups such as evangelicals and Catholics are particularly vigorous in serving others, that proposition remains largely a hypothesis. In future research, it would be helpful to examine whether groups with a strong sense of religious distinctiveness have an advantage in providing services.

B *Does Religious Organizations' Importance Call for Strict Regulation?*

Religious organizations' very prominence might argue against accommodating them. Perhaps they cannot be protected from regulation, because they affect too many other people when they contravene general laws.

Sensible protection is usually possible, however, because although religious providers are important, ample alternatives also exist. What matters is not only the religious sector's size but also its distinctive contribution. Some beneficiaries and employees want, or willingly accept, a religious setting; religious providers can reach them while other providers reach other population segments. Families can choose to send their children to traditional Catholic schools; evangelical students with traditional views can attend evangelical colleges; LGBT students can find more suitable options at public or liberal-oriented private schools.

Consider, for example, the 2016 controversy over a California bill ramping up regulation of religious colleges that have rules disfavoring same-sex or transgender conduct. Introduced in response to alleged instances where Christian colleges expelled students for same-sex behavior or assigned transgender students to housing based on their biological sex at birth, the bill would have eliminated exemptions from nondiscrimination laws for any college whose students received Cal Grants, the state counterpart to federal Pell grants for low-income students.[95]

---

[94] See Laycock, Chapter 3, for the judgment that laws can be fashioned to protect LGBT persons from discrimination while "protecting the consciences of religious conservatives in all but the hardest cases"; Adams, Chapter 32, for an instance involving tax-paid clerk issuing marriage licenses in Utah; Leavitt, Chapter 33, for a critique of administrative overreach resulting in winners and losers.

[95] Tyler Wood, *Chapter 888: Exemptions to Anti-Discrimination Laws in Higher Education: What You Don't Know Could Hurt You*, 48 U. Pac. L. Rev. 575 (2017).

The bill provoked furious charges that it would "not only violate religious liberty ... [but also] discriminate against [Hispanic] communities," since Hispanics are disproportionately served by the affected evangelical and Catholic colleges.[96] In an op-ed, Los Angeles's Catholic archbishop and a black Pentecostal bishop wrote that there was insufficient reason to inflict such harms, since "no one is compelled to attend a private religious college."[97] "Those who do make a deliberate decision because they are seeking an academic environment and community where they can live, learn and serve with others who share their beliefs, values and aspirations."

Facing these arguments about religious colleges' contribution to the common good, the bill's sponsor pared the bill back to a requirement that colleges give notice of their policies against same-sex or transgender conduct.[98] The California debate thus came to focus on two factors: notice of a religious college's policy and the availability of alternative providers. These factors point the way toward the appropriate scope of protection for religious organizations.

V THE COMMON GOOD AND THE SCOPE OF PROTECTION

Begin with notice. It is important that clients and employees of religious organizations are made reasonably aware of religious standards that might affect them and might conflict with applicable law. Without some form of notice, they may find themselves subject to unexpected standards of conduct that they cannot easily escape. The California bill, therefore, legitimately retained the provision designed to ensure that LGBT students knew colleges' policies before deciding whether to attend. Fortunately, when an organization holds itself out as religious – a congregation or a meaningfully religious nonprofit – it usually thereby gives such notice. There is often a "reasonable expectation that employees who work for churches and religious-affiliated non-profits understand that their employers are focused on advancing a religious mission."[99]

Religious organizations that do not have explicit religious elements in their programs should make it reasonably apparent to employees – through a handbook, contract, or other means – that religious norms may apply. A general statement to that effect should suffice. The employer should not be required to state each

---

[96] Press Release, *National Hispanic Leaders Oppose California Bill SB 1146*, RELIGION NEWS SERV. (July 19, 2016), https://perma.cc/F8ZR-77TX.

[97] Archbishop Jose Gomez & Bishop Charles Blake, *California Bill SB 1146 Threatens Minorities and the Poor*, FOX NEWS OPINION (Aug. 10, 2016), https://perma.cc/97R7-3FUZ.

[98] *See* Patrick McGreevy, *State Senator Drops Proposal That Had Angered Religious Universities in California*, L.A. TIMES (Sept. 1, 2016), https://perma.cc/6WF8-E35Z. For the importance of notice, see Pizer, Chapter 29.

[99] Micah Schwartzman et al., *Hobby Lobby and the Establishment Clause, Part III: Reconciling Amos and Cutter*, BALKINIZATION (Dec. 9, 2013), https://perma.cc/U8EG-K5NH. See Helfand, Chapter 11, for such a view.

particular tenet in detail; such a rule would constantly trip up organizations trying in good faith to maintain their identity.

The second concept is that of alternatives, which make it possible to avoid, or exit from, religious rules. When alternatives exist, the government should not force a religious social service organization to violate its religious identity merely to ensure clients' unfettered choice of providers. But religious organizations may be denied exemption when they occupy "chokepoints," where they can substantially limit others' access to services or employment.

Typically, however, objecting religious organizations are a small part of a much larger range of providers, secular and religious, most of which have no objection. In the California dispute, students had multiple college options beyond the objecting Catholic and evangelical institutions: there was insufficient reason to harm these institutions' students by disqualifying them from state grants. Likewise, in the cases involving Catholic adoption agencies and nondiscrimination requirements, there were generally numerous agencies happy to place children with same-sex couples.[100] Accommodation could have preserved religious agencies' ability to deliver effective services consistent with their beliefs, without depriving anyone of meaningful access.

VI CONCLUSION

As the success of same-sex marriage movement shows, the case for a right can become stronger, in courts and in public opinion, when it connects to social virtues as well as to personal autonomy. Religious organizations today continue to play roles that have historically provided one rationale for religious freedom: they develop civic-mindedness, mobilize resources to serve others, and pursue the common good from the "bottom up." This rationale can help ground sensible, responsible standards of protection for religious organizations in cases of conflict with nondiscrimination laws and other modern regulations.

---

[100] *See, e.g.*, Dale Carpenter, *Let Catholics Discriminate* (Mar. 31, 2006), https://perma.cc/N7D5-LFHR (noting that in Massachusetts, "[g]ay couples could still adopt through dozens of other private agencies or through the state child-welfare services department itself").

PART VI

Educational Institutions in the Age of Same-Sex Marriage

25

Two Paths

Finding a Way Forward at Covenantal Universities

Shirley V. Hoogstra, Shapri D. LoMaglio, and Brad Crofford

A significant cause of social unrest in America today is how two threads of the American fabric interweave: deeply held religious beliefs and equal treatment of persons under the law, most centrally here the LGBT community. Americans are grappling with whether these two foundational concepts can peaceably coexist.[1] One set of institutions that has been at the forefront of this question is faith-based institutions of higher education, whose views on human sexuality are increasingly in the minority amidst a broader cultural shift.[2]

Covenantal universities – that is, universities that express faith in every aspect of the institution[3] – contribute significantly to American higher education and society. These institutions must be allowed not only to claim their religious heritage as a historical marker, but also to be guided by faith commitments as they educate and shape young adults in their faith. Just as society leaves room for secular commitments in the pursuit of knowledge and preparation of the next generation to lead full, impactful lives, it must leave room for religious ones, as well. Allowing covenantal universities to arm students with the skills "to think deeply, to act justly, and to live wholeheartedly as Christ's agents of renewal in the world"[4] benefits not only students, but also broader society.

This chapter first explores the spiritual concerns of university students. Then, it introduces covenantal universities as a part of the United States' higher education landscape that is uniquely suited to meet such needs. Third, it examines the holistic

---

[1] *See, e.g.*, Kelsey Dallas, *How to Help Millennials Care More About Religious Freedom*, DESERT NEWS (Aug. 20, 2017), https://perma.cc/VN72-FX5L (noting that students at Christian colleges and universities may be more sympathetic to religious rights but still have concerns about harming the LGBT community).

[2] *U.S. Public Becoming Less Religious*, PEW RES. CTR.: RELIGION & PUB. LIFE (Nov. 3, 2015), https://perma.cc/JJ3Y-XSJK.

[3] Michael W. Lee, *What Is a Christian School?*, PERSPECTIVE (Jan. 11, 2006), https://www.cherokeechristian.org/wp-content/uploads/2013/10/BadMyth-fivearguments.pdf.

[4] *See Who We Are*, CALVIN COLLEGE, https://perma.cc/J5SG-TF4D.

rationale behind such institutions' faith-based policies and practices. Fourth, it describes how such policies may run afoul of secular society's shifting values and explores how such conflicts can be reconciled. Finally, it outlines two possible paths forward: a continued conflict as each position seeks dominance, or a mutual understanding where each group acknowledges the importance of the other's rights.

I THE SPIRITUALITY OF COLLEGE STUDENTS

Social science has confirmed what we have observed in our own interactions with college students over the years – students are spiritual beings. Scholars at the University of California at Los Angeles (UCLA) conducted a seven-year study of college students' spirituality.[5] They note, "The 'big questions' that preoccupy students are essentially spiritual questions: Who am I? What are my most deeply felt values? Do I have a mission or purpose in my life? Why am I in college? What kind of person do I want to become? What sort of world do I want to help create?"[6]

The implications of such important questions extend beyond the student to impact society. University leaders discussing the UCLA study's findings write:

> technical knowledge alone will not be adequate for dealing with some of society's most pressing problems: violence, poverty, crime, divorce, substance abuse, and the religious, national, and ethnic conflicts that continue to plague our country and our world. At root, these are problems of the "heart," problems that call for greater self-awareness, self-understanding, equanimity, empathy, and concern for others.[7]

Students seek answers to such questions through their college experiences. The aforementioned study finds that: "More than eight in ten report that 'to find my purpose in life' is at least a 'somewhat' important reason for attending college ... and two-thirds of new freshmen say that it is either 'very important' or 'essential' that college 'helps you develop your personal values' and 'enhances your self-understanding.'"[8] The desire for spiritual development as part of education is further reflected in the approximately $27 billion spent on faith-based primary and secondary education[9] and $43 billion spent on faith-based higher education annually in the United States.[10]

It is understandable that students pursue higher education with the objective of spiritual development; after all, though students can certainly grow spiritually

---

[5] *Attending to Students' Inner Lives: A Call to Higher Education*, HIGHER EDUC. RES. INST. 4, https://perma.cc/9SDD-JL2A.

[6] ALEXANDER W. ASTIN, HELEN S. ASTIN & JENNIFER A. LINDHOLM, CULTIVATING THE SPIRIT: HOW COLLEGE CAN ENHANCE STUDENTS' INNER LIVES 1 (2011).

[7] *Attending to Students' Inner Lives, supra* note 5, at 4.

[8] ASTIN, et al., *supra* note 8, at 3.

[9] Brian J. Grim & Melissa E. Grim, *The Socio-Economic Contribution of Religion to American Society: An Empirical Analysis*, 12 INTERDISC. J. RES. ON RELIGION 1, 6 (2016).

[10] *Id.*

elsewhere, "an institution of higher education is one of the places where the question of what living is for can be pursued in an organized way … not just a place for the transmission of knowledge, but a forum for the exploration of life's mystery and meaning."[11]

Yet, as later interviews in UCLA's longitudinal study revealed, students' educational experiences all-too-often did not help them explore these questions: "in the follow up survey only 19% of college juniors report that their faculty frequently encourage them to explore questions of meaning and purpose, and 58% report that their faculty never encourage them to explore religious/spiritual matters."[12] (And this is despite the fact that "81 percent of teaching faculty consider themselves to be 'spiritual,' and 64 percent, 'religious'"![13])

New York Times columnist David Brooks offers one potential explanation for this disjunction, noting that "[m]ost universities have gotten out of the business of spiritual and character development, and they've adopted a research ideal."[14] This ideal "teaches students how to do things but less why they should do them and less how to think about what is their highest and best life. To ask about the meaning of life is to appear unprofessional."[15]

Spiritual development is neither easy nor inevitable, but instead requires structures, expectations, and relationships that enable students to flourish. Despite often providing otherwise good educations, not all institutions of higher education have been up to the task. Faith-based colleges and universities provide a unique environment for students' spiritual growth.

II THE ROLE OF COVENANTAL UNIVERSITIES

The spirituality of American students is reflected in the religious diversity of the American higher education landscape. The faith-based sector of higher education represents roughly a third of the private market in the United States. Of the 3,099 private, degree-granting institutions, 1,014 are religiously affiliated.[16] These institutions reflect their religious character in different ways: some in their founding documents, some through their board of trustees, and some by making available religious worship and instruction consistent with their religious tradition and

---

[11] Anthony T. Kronman, Education's End: Why Our Colleges & Universities Have Given Up on the Meaning of Life (2007).

[12] *Attending to Students' Inner Lives*, supra note 5, at 5.

[13] Astin, et al., *supra* note 6, at 8.

[14] David Brooks, *The Cultural Value of Christian Higher Education*, CCCU (July 10, 2017), https://perma.cc/RGX5-E8LF.

[15] *Id.*

[16] Daniel Frost, *Sexually Conservative Religious Universities and Tax Exemption*, J. Church & State (July 7, 2016), https://perma.cc/8K6U-MGTG (estimating that there are 1,014 religious institutions).

theological perspective.[17] Others ensure that their religious character permeates all aspects of their institution, including their hiring, curriculum, and student life programming.[18] Institutions associated with the Council for Christian Colleges and Universities (CCCU) fall into this last category.

The American academy has been diverse from its founding,[19] and religious colleges have always been an essential component of that diversity. Indeed, two of the first three colleges in the United States, Harvard and Yale, were founded to train clergy.[20] Institutional diversity has made the American higher education system the best in the world.[21] The diverse array of options allows every student to find a college or university that best fits them and affords them the greatest chance for educational success and for leading rich, fulfilling lives. Beyond being spiritual (as described in the previous section), young Americans are also religious: despite a decline from earlier generations, 27 percent of Millennials in the United States attend church weekly, and 38 percent say that religious belief is important or very important to them.[22] It is no surprise that young adults would pursue higher educational experiences that reflect the fullness of the lives they expect to lead after college.

Not all religiously affiliated institutions make students' moral and spiritual development a central thrust of their work as educators, but many do. As Figure 25.1 shows, institutions span a spectrum of religiosity. Some are seminaries, which teach students theology and the skills needed to assume sacred responsibilities. Others are covenantal, where religious beliefs and values permeate all dimensions of the institution, from students' development to faculty scholarship, and where the community's members share a commitment to those values. Others may have ongoing religious affiliations that influence aspects of the institutions (such as governance or the availability of religious instruction or community), be only nominally religious, or be explicitly secular. Institutions may fluctuate between these categories over time. For example, a seminary might add programs of broader instruction that transform it into a covenantal institution, or an institution that was originally

---

[17] Michael W. Lee, *What Is a Christian School?*, PERSPECTIVE (Jan. 11, 2006), https://www .cherokeechristian.org/wp-content/uploads/2013/10/BadMyth-fivearguments.pdf.

[18] *See* KAYE COOK & CYNTHIA NEAL KIMBALL, IS A CHRISTIAN COLLEGE EDUCATION "WORTH IT"? WORLDVIEW DEVELOPMENT AMONG CHRISTIAN COLLEGE STUDENTS AS A MODEL FOR THE LARGER ACADEMY (2011), https://perma.cc/Q2BV-QJU7.

[19] Even among the earliest institutions in the United States, there was a variety of institutional types: religious, women's, public, and private colleges. *See e.g. College History*, MORAVIAN COLL., https://perma.cc/VG4H-LD9L; *History*, UNIV. OF DELAWARE, http://www.udel.edu/ about/history.

[20] *See Harvard in the 17th and 18th Centuries: Religion*, HARV. UNIV. ARCHIVES, https://perma.cc/ GRU5-WFB2; *Traditions & History*, YALE, https://www.yale.edu/about-yale/traditions-history.

[21] *See* Abigail Hess, *The 12 Best Universities in the World*, CNBC (Oct. 24, 2017), https://perma.cc/ Q2BV-QJU7 (indicating that ten of the top twelve universities in the world are located in the United States).

[22] *U.S. Public Becoming Less Religious*, PEW RES. CTR.: RELIGION & PUB. LIFE (Nov. 3, 2015), https://perma.cc/PPN5-2LHZ.

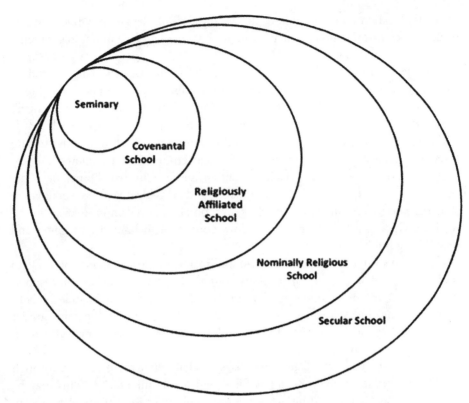

FIGURE 25.1 Degrees of religious infusion[23]

covenantal might abandon religious commitments to the point of being only nominally religious.

At covenantal universities, students' spiritual development is pursued alongside gaining an excellent grounding in the academic discipline of their choice. As one example, students at Malone University complete twenty Spiritual Formation Opportunity credits each semester, which the university sees as "a vital portion of the holistic growth of each student."[24] Students decide which events to attend, and "[o]ptions include everything from large worship gatherings to small Bible studies, with diverse leaders and topics, as well as opportunities scheduled throughout the day and week, all in an effort to effectively minister to today's college student."[25] Beyond the experiential component, there is often an academic component, with many covenantal universities requiring Bible or theology courses as part of the

[23] Reproduced from Robin Fretwell Wilson, *Squaring Faith and Sexuality: Religious Institutions and the Unique Challenges of Sports*, 34 L. & INEQ. 385 (2016).
[24] *Spiritual Formation Opportunities*, MALONE UNIV., https://perma.cc/2BJR-DJ9A.
[25] *Id.*

general education core curriculum. For example, Biola University undergraduate students take thirty credit hours of biblical studies – enough for a minor in the field – regardless of their major.[26]

The 143 institutions affiliated with the CCCU in the United States, including Malone University and Biola University, comprise about 15 percent of all religiously affiliated institutions in the United States, represent just under 5 percent of all private degree-granting institutions, and educate about 450,000 students each year.[27] They have graduated more than three million alumni.[28] CCCU members share three basic educational commitments: (1) Biblical Truth – the integration of biblical truth into every aspect of the academic enterprise; (2) Christian Formation – the moral and spiritual formation of their students; and (3) Gospel Witness – graduating students who make a difference for the common good as redemptive voices in the world.[29] These private religious institutions contribute to human flourishing and exist for the public good.

CCCU institutions' commitment to biblical truth leads them not only to include biblical studies as part of the required core curriculum or offer opportunities for spiritual experiences, but also to ask the faculty to include in both their teaching and scholarship how the lens of faith informs the topic under discussion. Beyond instruction, faculty and staff serve as professional as well as spiritual mentors to students, whether formally or informally. As Trevecca Nazarene University president Dan Boone asks: "What better place to work through doubts and questions than a campus filled with godly mentors?"[30] This may be why seniors at CCCU institutions are more likely than their peers at public or other private, non-profit universities to rate their interactions with faculty, student services staff, administrative staff, and academic advisors as "very good" or "excellent."[31]

III THE LOGIC OF FAITH-BASED POLICIES AND PRACTICES

This commitment to the students' moral and spiritual formation leads CCCU institutions to create policies and practices that they believe will help strengthen the spiritual lives of students. The importance of practices in forming students cannot be overstated. In *Desiring the Kingdom*, philosopher James K. A. Smith calls

---

[26] *Bible Courses*, Biola Univ., https://perma.cc/2P8D-4XRC.
[27] CCCU analysis of Integrated Postsecondary Education System (IPEDS) data for 2014–15, https://perma.cc/D6GB-G3DH.
[28] *About*, CCCU, https://perma.cc/32NK-3HSG.
[29] *Membership*, CCCU, https://perma.cc/NGS4-H5YR.
[30] Dan Boone, A Charitable Discourse 173 (2010).
[31] *CCCU Analysis of 2016–2017 Data*, Nat'l Surv. of Student Engagement, https://perma.cc/NYV8-DD9M.

into question the assumption that our worldviews shape our actions, compellingly arguing that instead our actions and practices shape our worldviews.[32] Smith writes:

[E]ducation is not primarily a heady project concerned with providing *information*; rather, education is most fundamentally a matter of *formation*, a task of shaping and creating a certain kind of people. What makes them a distinctive kind of people is what they love or desire – what they envision as "the good life" or the ideal picture of human flourishing. An education, then, is a constellation of practices, rituals, and routines that inculcates a particular vision of the good life by inscribing or infusing that vision into the heart (the gut) by means of material, embodied practices.[33]

This has important implications for education, as it reflects that education does not solely occur in classrooms or as a transfer of knowledge between professor and student. Rather, the formation that is education happens throughout all parts of the university experience, whether in a class, chapel, stadium, or elsewhere. As Boone writes, "Our dorm life is an extension of the academic classroom because there we learn respect for property, problem solving, relational integrity, sharing, and all the other values that help us live peacefully in a community."[34]

Faith-based policies at covenantal universities encompass a wide variety of issues and circumstances, such as standards for behavior, living arrangements, and service to the community. They frequently include routine attendance at chapel (*i.e.*, weekly or daily religious services formally organized by the institution) and a "community covenant" that sets expectations for healthy living in a variety of areas, such as demonstrating self-restraint in alcohol consumption or avoiding pornography, while also encouraging students to exercise humility and pursue kindness and relational harmony with others. Additionally, most CCCU institutions have single-sex dormitories with a policy that limits hours when guests of the opposite sex can visit, enabling residents to feel at home on their dormitory floor and encouraging each floor to develop a sense of community. While the exact nature of such policies may vary by school or residence type, they are also intended to uphold the biblical belief that sexual conduct is best expressed in the context of marriage between a man and a woman. Such policies are not limited to students; CCCU institutions also have institutional policies for employees to follow biblical teaching as that institution understands it. There is an internal consistency to this: if a covenantal institution is to be a place where faith-based commitments are upheld and expressed by the community, then all members of the community must make this commitment to one another.

---

[32] James K.A. Smith, Desiring the Kingdom: Worship, Worldview, and Cultural Formation (2009).

[33] *Id.*

[34] Boone, *supra* note 30, at 172.

Not all such policies are inward-oriented or proscriptive as covenantal universities are also committed to graduating students who make a difference for the common good. This is reflected in the institutions encouraging, or sometimes even requiring, service to the community. Because of this service orientation, students at CCCU institutions are both more likely to volunteer and perform more hours of community service than the average college student.[35] The personal responsibility and communal dedication underlying the practices above create graduates who keep their financial commitments,[36] speak truth to power, and stand up for the marginalized and downtrodden.

These policies stem from a deep-rooted understanding of the proper relationship between God, ourselves, and our neighbors – and their breadth and interconnectedness ought not be minimized. These policies and practices create a tapestry that reflects the institution's biblical mission. Like pulling a thread, changes that might from the outside appear minor or inconsequential may nevertheless undermine the internal consistency of the community's faith commitments and thereby mar the whole. Thus, when changes occur, they should originate within the campus community to ensure consistency.

IV THEOLOGICAL COMMITMENTS AND SECULAR SOCIETY

Faith-based policies have sometimes drawn charges of both discrimination[37] and hypocrisy by some in secular society.[38] How then should one reconcile the sincere beliefs of covenantal universities with the expectation in secular society for equal treatment, especially in regards to LGBT persons? Answering this question, as well as the charges of discrimination and hypocrisy, requires both clarification and confession.

---

[35] *Building the Common Good: The National Impact of Council for Christian Colleges & Universities (CCCU) Institutions* (2017) (showing that CCCU students have a participation rate of 35.2% in community service, and those who volunteer do so for an average of thirty-eight hours), https://perma.cc/X8PP-9773; *College Students*, CORP. FOR NAT'L & CMTY. SERV., https://www.nationalservice.gov/vcla/demographic/college-students (showing that 25.7% of college students volunteer, and those who do volunteer do so for an average of thirty-four hours).

[36] CCCU analysis of 2014 data from College Scorecard, https://perma.cc/PRB2-KH6E (showing that the 3-year, 5-year, and 7-year student loan repayment rates for graduates of CCCU institutions are higher than the national average and higher than the rates for graduates of private nonprofit, public, and for-profit universities).

[37] PEACEFUL COEXISTENCE: RECONCILING NONDISCRIMINATION PRINCIPLES WITH CIVIL LIBERTIES, U.S. COMM'N ON CIVIL RIGHTS (2016) [*hereinafter* PEACEFUL COEXISTENCE]. *See also* Tom Gjelten, *In Religious Freedom Debate, 2 American Values Clash*, NPR (Feb. 28, 2017), https://perma.cc/MTS4-PVQ4.

[38] PEACEFUL COEXISTENCE, *supra* note 37, at 122 ("The phrases 'religious liberty' and 'religious freedom' will stand for nothing except hypocrisy so long as they remain code words for discrimination, intolerance, racism, sexism, homophobia, Islamophobia, Christian supremacy or any form of intolerance.").

The belief that sexual intimacy is given as a gift to a woman and man in marriage is based in the biblical narrative. For covenantal universities, the interpretation of the Bible is at the core of the integration of faith into the life and work of the community. The Christian life is one of knowing the love and grace of God, and as a result living a life empowered by the life and words of Jesus. Part of being a follower of Jesus is to eschew sinful behavior, including what have been described as the seven deadly sins (pride, greed, lust, anger, gluttony, envy, and sloth). Yet, only Christ could live the perfect life, which is why Christians believe that Jesus, who gave his own life out of love, is worthy of emulation. The Christian life thus includes caring for the sick, the hungry, the imprisoned, the naked, and the lonely, and exhibiting love, joy, peace, patience, kindness, goodness, faithfulness, gentleness, and self-control.[39] Policies and practices at covenantal universities are made with these beliefs and goals in mind.

However, policies are implemented by people. Whether at faith-based universities[40] or other universities,[41] LGBT students do not always experience a community of love, respect, patience, and kindness. The research shows that LGBT students face social exclusion or other negative experiences related to their sexual orientation or gender identity. A study of sexual minorities on Christian college campuses found a less than ideal outcome given the high standards for community life:

> [t]he students we studied don't seem to find much of an articulated vision in their Christian communities for realistically holding their life experience at the intersection of sex and religion/spirituality. What they saw modeled reportedly felt rather simplistic and not grounded in real life … [m]ost perceived that they were left to figure this out as best they can.[42]

In this sense, Christian colleges – and, indeed, American higher education more broadly – are not yet doing as well as students need or would like. Covenantal universities want what is spiritually best for students, and they desire to care for students who are reconciling their orientation with their faith commitments, yet the experience of working through a minority orientation or identity is hard for many students. Despite these difficulties, students seek to hold and develop both their faith and their sexual identity at covenantal universities. The aforementioned study found that the students were "typically highly religious/spiritual and want to develop in a setting where they can consider both sexual and religious/spiritual development,"

---

[39] *Galatians* 5:22–23.

[40] *See* MARK A. YARHOUSE, JANET B. DEAN, STEPHEN P. STRATTON & MICHAEL LASTORIA, LISTENING TO SEXUAL MINORITIES: A STUDY OF FAITH AND SEXUAL IDENTITY ON CHRISTIAN COLLEGE CAMPUSES (2018); CHRISTOPHER YUAN, GIVING A VOICE TO THE VOICELESS (2016).

[41] *See* Patricia A. Tetreault, Ryan Fette, Peter C. Meidlinger & Debra Hope, *Perceptions of Campus Climate by Sexual Minorities*, 60 J. HOMOSEXUALITY 947 (2013); YARHOUSE et al., *supra* note 40.

[42] YARHOUSE et al., *supra* note 40.

even when they may disagree on campus policies.[43] Covenantal universities can help students grow in these areas.

All universities, including covenantal universities, find themselves embedded in a larger cultural context that is shaping the communities they serve. Recent studies confirm that the American public's views on sexual orientation and gender *are* quickly shifting. A Pew Research Center report from 2016 finds:

> One-in-five U.S. adults say their views on homosexuality have changed over the past few years, and most say they have become more accepting. Among the most common reasons given for changing viewpoints are having a friend or family member who is gay or lesbian and coming to the belief that people are free to live their lives however they choose.[44]

Christians are responding to this significant shift. Authors such as psychologist Mark Yarhouse, ethicist Andrew Walker, theologian Wesley Hill, and others are creating resources for understanding sexual orientation and gender identity and offering Christ-like responses.[45]

There are also legal dimensions to the question of how to reconcile sincerely held religious beliefs and the experience of LGBT persons in broader society. Engaging issues and searching for a path forward is what higher education has always done. Specifically, the CCCU's legislative staff has been charged with examining if there is a way to not only codify rights for religious persons and organizations originating from the First Amendment, but also explore if there is a theological and civic rationale for new civil rights for LGBT persons as part of the same effort.[46] These tangible steps build credibility for the faith community and underline our commitment to living into a "confident pluralism" where civil society respects and allows differing points of view to coexist. Others have joined CCCU in this effort.[47]

A Gospel response at its best allows people to deeply understand and have compassion for the complexities of the human experience even while holding to different theological beliefs. Indeed, differing beliefs need not result in the other's dignity being dismissed. John Inazu in his book, *Confident Pluralism*, argues that, in a confidently pluralistic society, "[w]e can embrace pluralism precisely because we

---

[43] *Id.*

[44] *Where the Public Stands on Religious Liberty vs. Nondiscrimination*, Pew Res. Ctr. (Sept. 28, 2016), https://perma.cc/SV4N-JWU6.

[45] Mark A. Yarhouse, Understanding Gender Dysphoria: Navigating Transgender Issues in a Changing Culture (2015); Andrew T. Walker & R. Albert Mohler, God and the Transgender Debate (2017); Wesley Hill, *A Necessary Pairing: The Theology of Marriage and of Compassion*, CCCU (2017), https://perma.cc/Q7RD-6X7C.

[46] Shapri D. LoMaglio, *Fairness for All*, CCCU (2017), https://perma.cc/WA32-XBEH.

[47] *See* Leith Anderson, Chapter 12.

are confident in our own beliefs, and in the groups and institutions that sustain them."[48] This is not easy – it requires practice. In *Awaiting the King*, James K. A. Smith posits that a pluralistic society needs individuals with "specific dispositions of tolerance, humility, and patience," virtues that religious communities are uniquely able to instill through their practices.[49] Christian faith has always called believers to "love our neighbor"[50] and to pray for peace and prosperity of the city and country in which we live.[51]

A model of this respect for diverse values and approaches is David Coleman, president and chief executive officer of the College Board, defending Wheaton College's contribution to the academy despite others' criticisms of its religious beliefs. He writes:

> There are policies at Wheaton with which I disagree, but disagreement must not tempt us to banish difference but instead should spur us to look harder. We have institutions in the Catholic, Protestant, Evangelical, and Jewish traditions that all live their identities in diverse ways and bring valuable resources to bear on students' academic, personal, and civic development. If students want to further both their intellectual and spiritual development at an accredited religious institution, if they feel they will learn best in that kind of setting, if they want to be part of a community that has a faith tradition (often not their own), they should have that option, with federal aid. It's a wonderful thing and a source of strength that we have religious diversity among our institutions of higher education.[52]

Coleman's fair-minded, even-handed approach is a model worth emulating. He acknowledges the contribution of faith-based institutions, without denying his disagreements. Similarly, support for the equal treatment of LGBT persons in the public square, such as in public accommodations or housing, need not come at the expense of denying institutional faith commitments that animate the institution's missions and guide institutional policies. Indeed, the faith commitments described in Section III of this chapter describe how covenantal universities organize them-selves, not necessarily how society ought to operate. As Gordon-Cromwell Theological Seminary president Dennis Hollinger writes, "Christians today should not be seeking a privileged establishment of their faith – the Christendom model – but rather the freedom to express their faith in the contexts that are most pertinent to their faith – their churches and various institutions."[53]

---

[48] John D. Inazu, Confident Pluralism: Surviving and Thriving Through Deep Difference 7 (2016).

[49] James K.A. Smith, Awaiting the King: Reforming Public Theology 146 (2017).

[50] *See Matthew* 22:35–40 (King James Version).

[51] *See Jeremiah* 29:7 (King James Version).

[52] David Coleman, *No, Wheaton College's Accreditation Should Not Be Revoked*, Nat'l Rev.
(July 30, 2014), https://perma.cc/Z72A-V5VT.

[53] Dennis Hollinger, *Religious Freedom, Civil Rights, and Sexuality*, CCCU (June 9, 2017),
https://perma.cc/3WZD-ELAD.

The humility, openness to discussion and study, and comity described earlier in this chapter are important steps for moving forward. Of course, though Americans disagree with one another's beliefs, neither secular values nor religious values have a monopoly on the pursuit of truth – both require an element of faith. Neither a supreme being's presence nor an afterlife can be definitively proven or disproven; so, too, with the origins of the universe or the inherent dignity of the human person. We understand that there are aspects to our religion – or, indeed, any religion – that strike outsiders as odd or outlandish, and the ability to express such disagreements is part of a plural society. However, just as society leaves room for secular commitments in the pursuit of knowledge and preparation of the next generation to lead full, impactful lives, it should also leave room for religious ones.

V PRESERVING PLURALISM IN HIGHER EDUCATION

Even while recognizing that covenantal universities ought to be permitted to operate in the United States, some nonetheless argue they should be treated differently by the government because of their religious commitments. For instance, some advocate that their eligibility for government funding should be limited because "[t]he ... government should not be funding discrimination."[54] However, it is critical that generally available government funding not be restricted because of an institution's religious mission and policies. To limit funding in this way risks unintended consequences in student choice and would, in effect, unfairly privilege the values and belief of secular institutions of higher education[55] over those of faith-based institutions.

Proposed legislation in California from 2016 demonstrates the impossible choice confronting covenantal colleges and their students if government funding is restricted. An early version of SB 1146 would have narrowed California's religious

---

[54] *See e.g.*, Susan M. Shaw, *Federal Funding Is Not a Form of Religious Liberty*, Huffington Post (Dec. 17, 2015), https://perma.cc/78MZ-7GWX.

[55] As noted in Section III, the practices at institutions of higher education shape students, regardless of whether the university or college is religious or secular. Smith writes:

> An education, then, is a constellation of practices, rituals, and routines that inculcates a particular vision of the good life by inscribing or infusing that vision into the heart (the gut) by means of material, embodied practices. And this will be true even of the most instrumentalist, pragmatic programs of education (such as those that now tend to dominate public schools and universities bent on churning out "skilled workers") that see their task primarily as providing *in*formation, because this is a vision of the good life that understands human flourishing in terms of production and consumption. Behind the veneer of a "value-free" education concerned with providing skills, knowledge, and information is an education vision that remains formative. There is no neutral, nonformative education; in short, there is no such thing as a "secular" education.

> James K.A. Smith, Desiring the Kingdom: Worship, Worldview, and Cultural Formation 26 (2009) (emphasis in original).

exemptions for faith-based institutions of higher education, which would have affected policies ranging from admissions and housing to curriculum and employ-ment.[56] As written, this legislation would have required institutions to either comply with new requirements or cause their students to lose eligibility for Cal Grants – need-based grants worth about $9,000 per year.[57] After a major advocacy push from faith-based institutions (including CCCU institutions), other faith-based organiza-tions, and the Association of Independent California Colleges and Universities, the final legislation required institutions with exemptions from Title IX to "disclose to current and prospective students, faculty members, and employees the basis for claiming or having the exemption and the scope of the allowable activities provided by the exemption."[58]

Were SB 1146 to have passed in its earlier form and covenantal universities to have maintained their faith-based policies, it would have prevented the students with the greatest financial need from attending the institution of their choice. Meanwhile, those students from high-income families who were not eligible for Cal Grants would have been unaffected; they could still attend the university of their choice. This dynamic would be similar if such restrictions were placed on federal Pell Grants, student loans, federal work study, or other financial aid. In this way, the negative impacts of policies restricting government funding to faith-based institu-tions are unfairly concentrated. This is particularly unfortunate given that low-income and first-generation college students at private colleges and universities – including faith-based institutions – are far more likely to graduate than their peers at public universities.[59] Ultimately, because of persistent and authentic efforts made by the public officials in Sacramento and Christian college leadership, relationships were built that resulted in discussion and consultation about future legislation instead of assumptions and surmising about the intentions of the other. This is a model worth emulating.

In short, a diversity of institutions within the American higher education system honors student choice. Students committed to their faith should be able to utilize federal and state support for education at whatever institution they believe will best help them achieve academic and life success. The ability of students to choose institutions that serve their educational and spiritual goals should be within the

---

[56] *Preserve Faith-Based Higher Education*, Biola Univ., https://perma.cc/B3QN-TB6U.

[57] *Id.*; *What is a Cal Grant?*, Cal. Student Aid Commission, https://perma.cc/6KPB-GNCH.

[58] *Preserve Faith-Based Higher Education*, *supra* note 56.

[59] *Expanding Access and Opportunity: How Small and Mid-Sized Independent Colleges Serve First-Generation and Low-Income Students*, Council for Indep. Coll. 27 (Mar. 2015), https://perma.cc/23PW-TFJ3 (showing that the four-year graduation rate for first-generation students at private, nonprofit nondoctoral and doctoral universities are 42% and 43% versus 18% and 26% at public, nondoctoral and doctoral universities, respectively; showing that four-year graduation rates for low-income students at private, nonprofit non-doctoral and doctoral universities are 36% and 48% versus 13% and 22% at public, nondoctoral and doctoral universities, respectively).

reach of all students, not just those who are wealthy, but also those who are middle or lower income who qualify for federal or state aid.[60]

VI CONCLUSION

To move forward, we should look back. The First Amendment of the US Constitution acknowledges that Americans will not only have religious thoughts that they hold in their minds, but that religious belief will manifest itself in religious exercise.[61] Furthermore, the framers recognized that people with likeminded beliefs, religious or not, would gather together around and form organizations that reflected the shared convictions and values of the community,[62] and they believed people should be free to do so without government interference.[63] The right of assembly, all too often overlooked in favor of the "the enfeebled right of expressive association," remains vital for our nation's well-being.[64] Finally, they recognized that preventing the imposition of a state religion required the government to treat religious persons and their institutions equal to their secular counterparts.[65]

While quick to point to these rights, the US religious community has not always modeled well the constitutional principle that the Constitution was designed to protect minority rights.[66] It has not always heeded Supreme Court justice Hugo Black's wisdom: "I do not believe that it can be too often repeated that the freedoms of speech, press, petition and assembly guaranteed by the First Amendment must be

---

[60] *Federal and State Funding of Higher Education: A Changing Landscape*, PEW CHARITABLE TR. (June 11, 2015), https://perma.cc/B99W-HZCS; Thomas G. Mortenson, *State Funding: A Race to the Bottom*, AM. COUNCIL ON EDUC., https://perma.cc/K4J3-AFKW.

[61] Although the US Supreme Court's decision in *Employment Division v. Smith* allowed neutral rules of general applicability to burden religious beliefs, the Court noted that Americans can reflect special solicitude toward religious belief and practice through specific protections in the law:

> Just as a society that believes in the negative protection accorded to the press by the First Amendment is likely to enact laws that affirmatively foster the dissemination of the printed word, so also a society that believes in the negative protection accorded to religious belief can be expected to be solicitous of that value in its legislation as well.

Emp't Div., Dep't of Human Res. of Or. v. Smith, 494 U.S. 872, 890 (1990). Other rights may also be implicated, such as associational rights. *See* JOHN INAZU, *LIBERTY'S REFUGE: THE FORGOTTEN FREEDOM OF ASSEMBLY* (2012).

[62] Roberts v. United States Jaycees, 468 U.S. 609 (1984).

[63] *See* U.S. CONST. amend. I.

[64] INAZU, *supra* note 61, at 4.

[65] *See* U.S. CONST. amend. I.; Trinity Lutheran Church of Columbia, Inc. v. Comer, 137 S. Ct. 2012 (2017).

[66] *See* Andrew R. Lewis, *Abortion Taught Conservative Christians to Argue for Minority Rights – As They're Doing Today in Masterpiece Cakeshop*, WASH. POST (Dec. 5, 2017), https://perma.cc/RQ7J-VGYV.

accorded to the ideas we hate, or sooner or later they will be denied to the ideas we cherish."[67]

We are at a moment in our nation's history during which both the religious community and the LGBT community have to decide between conflict or comity, "between two constitutional visions: a radical sameness that destroys dissenting traditions or the destabilizing difference of a meaningful pluralism."[68] They could continue decades-long legal battles, ones that could cut deep into the cartilage of important religious and associational rights and could undermine the ability of other groups of peoples with conflicting values to live together in the future. They could choose public relations campaigns that vilify and demean, misrepresent and mistreat.

Conversely, they could choose another path forward, one that reflects that the Constitution is capacious enough to protect minority rights, one that does not sacrifice one group's rights at the expense of another, one that protects diversity and pluralism rather than quashing it. We should model that there is strength in diversity by preserving societal pluralism into the future. We should acknowledge that even when our group is not in the minority – and perhaps *especially* when we are not the minority[69] – the rights of minority populations must be protected. This is a moment that will be remembered by the future. May we choose the best path forward, together.

---

[67] Communist Party v. Subversive Activities Control Board, 367 U.S. I, 137 (1961) (Black, J., dissenting).

[68] INAZU, *supra* note 61, at 184.

[69] *See* Paul A. Djupe, Andrew R. Lewis & Ted G. Jelen, *Rights, Reflection, and Reciprocity: Implications of the Same-Sex Marriage Debate for Tolerance and the Political Process*, 93 POL. & RELIGION 630 (2016) (showing that when individuals consider how their own rights could be at stake, they are more likely to tolerate rights for groups they dislike).

26

God and Man and Religious Exemptions in the Modern University

B. Jessie Hill

What does it mean to say that a college or university is "religious" in the eyes of the law? In the United States, there are certain benefits that go along with having the identity of a "religious" institution of higher learning. These benefits may include the ability to claim exemptions from various generally applicable laws under the Religious Freedom Restoration Act (RFRA);[1] immunity for hiring decisions under the ministerial exception;[2] immunity from labor regulation;[3] and specific statutory exemptions under the federal laws that prohibit discrimination in hiring and in education, Title VII of the Civil Rights Act of 1964 (Title VII) and Title IX of the Education Amendments of 1972 (Title IX).[4] It is therefore important to consider carefully which institutions should qualify for these exemptions.

The topic of religious exemptions – their appropriateness in general, their proper scope, and the conditions under which they may be claimed by an individual or institution – has been widely discussed in the scholarly literature.[5] But the topic of exemptions specifically for religious universities has not been covered as broadly.[6]

The issue of religious exemptions for universities is unique, and interesting, for two reasons. First, universities occupy a sort of middle ground between

---

[1]   42 U.S.C. §§ 2000bb–2000bb-4 (2012).

[2]   Hosanna-Tabor Evangelical Lutheran Church & Sch. v. E.E.O.C., 565 U.S. 171, 188 (2012); Petruska v. Gannon Univ., 462 F.3d 294, 306 (C.A.3 2006).

[3]   N.L.R.B. v. Catholic Bishop of Chicago, 440 U.S. 490, 507 (1979).

[4]   42 U.S.C. §§ 2000e to 2000e-17; 20 U.S.C. §§ 1681–1688 (2012). Of course, religious universities are also entitled to the benefits generally available to all nonprofit universities, including secular universities, such as tax exemption. Because such benefits are not unique to religious institutions, they are not considered here. For a discussion of tax exemption, see Eskridge, Chapter 22.

[5]   See, e.g., KENT GREENAWALT, EXEMPTIONS: NECESSARY, JUSTIFIED, MISGUIDED? (2016); NELSON TEBBE, RELIGIOUS FREEDOM IN AN EGALITARIAN AGE (2017).

[6]   There are a few recent, prominent exceptions. See, e.g., Robin Fretwell Wilson, *Squaring Faith and Sexuality: Religious Institutions and the Unique Challenge of Sports*, 34 LAW & INEQ. 385 (2016); Kif Augustine-Adams, *Religious Exemptions to Title IX*, 65 KAN. L. REV. 327 (2016).

unquestionably religious institutions, such as houses of worship, and more clearly secular institutions, such as bakeries, floral shops, and Hobby Lobby.[7] On the one hand, many universities have longstanding religious affiliations; they may be controlled by religious groups and have explicitly religious missions of which they give notice. These institutions benefit from the protections of both academic freedom and religious freedom.[8] On the other hand, many of the more venerable universities in the United States began as pervasively religious institutions with a primary mission of training ministers but have moved away from that mission and that religious identity over time; now, many a university's religious affiliation is more a historical artifact than a true indicator of institutional identity.[9] What is more, these institutions also participate in an educational marketplace, competing with non-religious counterparts for the best students, faculty, and staff; this competition often results in the schools' employing and serving those who do not share their religious values. Indeed, some such institutions are particularly prestigious, and as a result they wield considerable market power.

Second, the mission of a university is different from that of other institutions. Universities exist to produce and promote knowledge, embodying an ethic of openness and critical inquiry. Moreover, they play an important role in not only the intellectual, but also the social, emotional, and perhaps even spiritual development of their students, who generally enter the institution at a critical and formative time in their lives.[10] It is therefore important to consider what impact a particular set of rules about religious exemptions may have on that mission, as well as on the students whose development is entrusted to religious schools.

The issue of religious exemptions for colleges and universities now sits in the midst of considerable uncertainty over the scope of certain nondiscrimination laws. For example, under the Obama administration, the US Department of Education, the US Department of Justice, and the US Equal Employment Opportunity Commission (EEOC) took the position that the term "sex," for purposes of federal civil rights protections, included not only biological sex but also sexual orientation and gender identity.[11] Recent litigation has also led to an expansion of the definition of

---

[7] Religiously affiliated hospitals might be another such "middle ground" type of institution.

[8] Some religiously affiliated institutions may not extend academic freedom protections to their faculty. For views, see, e.g., Michael McConnell, *Academic Freedom in Religious Colleges and Universities*, 53 L. & CONTEMP. PROBLEMS 303 (1990); Matthew Finkin, *On Institutional Academic Freedom*, 61 TEX. L. REV. 817 (1983); Douglas Laycock, *Academic Freedom, Religious Commitment, and Religious Integrity*, 78 MARQUETTE L. REV. 297 (Winter 1995).

[9] *See, e.g.*, Hoogstra et al., Chapter 25; John W. Coakley, *Rutgers College and the Reformed Dutch Church*, 17 RUTGERS J. L. & RELIGION 379, 379 (2016) (*citing* David B. Potts, *American Colleges in the Nineteenth Century: From Localism to Denominationalism*, HIST. OF EDUC. Q. 373–75 (1971)).

[10] See Hoogstra et al., Chapter 25, for discussion of spiritual development.

[11] *See, e.g.*, DOE-DOJ Joint Dear Colleague Letter on Transgender Students (May 13, 2016), https://perma.cc/BP2L-79Z5.

"sex" under Title VII and Title IX.[12] These developments have raised the stakes for some religious colleges and universities that may now find themselves on the wrong side of nondiscrimination laws if they limit married student housing to opposite-sex married couples, for example, or if they wish to terminate an employee who has married someone of the same sex.[13] Although the Trump administration has pulled back on the Obama administration's broader interpretation of Title IX,[14] the federal courts may continue to read the statute as encompassing sexual orientation and gender identity discrimination.

The scope of nondiscrimination laws as applied to religious institutions was further put into question by the US Supreme Court's 2014 decision in *Burwell v. Hobby Lobby*.[15] The specific holding in that case was that the plaintiffs – closely held corporations with large numbers of employees whose owners incorporated religious statements into their companies' missions – were persons who exercise religion within the meaning of RFRA.[16] The Court reached this conclusion only as a matter of statutory interpretation. Still, after *Hobby Lobby*, some commentators wonder just how broad the class of institutions that may be considered to exercise religion might be, including in other religious exemption contexts.[17] Thus, at the same time that the scope of federal civil rights protections have expanded, the scope of religious exemptions has expanded as well, creating more points of potential conflict between religious institutions and the state over the applicability of these protections.

Given this widening conflict, the imperative of finding common ground becomes particularly pressing. The goal of this chapter is therefore to suggest some principles for analyzing the exemption claims of religious universities on which, hopefully, individuals on all sides can agree. This chapter begins by providing some brief background, in Section I, on the various exemptions that may be relevant to religious universities. As Section I explains, these many exemptions have distinct but overlapping coverage. Importantly, Section I also highlights the various interests that must be taken into account when considering the propriety of exemptions in the university context. Section II then identifies some principles for determining when a university should be able to claim a religious exemption by suggesting factors that agencies and courts might use in order to balance the competing interests identified in Section I.

---

[12] *See, e.g.*, Zarda v. Altitude Express, Inc., 883 F.3d 100 (2d Cir. 2018); Hively v. Ivy Tech Cmty. Coll. of Indiana, 853 F.3d 339, 341 (7th Cir. 2017); Schroeder ex rel. Schroeder v. Maumee Bd. of Educ., 296 F. Supp. 2d 869, 880 (N.D. Ohio 2003).

[13] *See, e.g.*, Augustine-Adams, *supra* note 6, at 338.

[14] DOE-DOJ Joint Dear Colleague Letter (February 22, 2017) (rescinding Dear Colleague Letter of May 13, 2016); Brief for the United States as *Amicus Curiae*, Zarda v. Altitude Express, Inc., 883 F.3d 100 (2d Cir. 2018), 2017 WL 3277292 (arguing that discrimination based on sexual orientation is not discrimination based on sex under Title VII).

[15] 134 S. Ct. 2751 (2014).

[16] *Id.* at 2765–66, 2768–75.

[17] *See, e.g.*, Zoë Robinson, *What Is a "Religious Institution"?*, 55 B.C. L. REV. 181 (2014).

I EXEMPTIONS AND THEIR BENEFICIARIES

Some of the most significant exemptions that a religious university may claim from generally applicable laws include exemption from those Title IX requirements that are inconsistent with its tenets; the exemption from Title VII for discrimination in employment on the basis of religion; the constitutionally grounded exemption from labor regulation by the National Labor Relations Board; the ministerial exception, which immunizes religious universities from legal scrutiny of hiring and firing decisions with respect to "ministerial" employees; the specific regulatory exemption from the contraception mandate under the Patient Protection and Affordable Care Act (ACA); and the general exemption under RFRA that any "person" may claim to avoid complying with legal mandates that substantially burden that person's exercise of religion.

This chapter does not question the premise that exemptions from generally applicable legal requirements may sometimes be appropriate for religious colleges and universities. Instead, the issue explored here is whether a *particular* religious college or university should be entitled to claim an exemption based on religious belief or affiliation. As discussed later in the chapter, courts and agencies have often been called upon to decide which characteristics of a college or university render it sufficiently religious to qualify for a particular exemption. Each statutory or regulatory carve-out has yielded its own test or family of tests that courts and regulatory bodies are expected to apply in determining the applicability of the rule. Despite the specificity and context-sensitivity of these tests, however, the tests rely on many of the same factors in determining religiosity. In addition, they largely aim to protect the same constellation of interests on the part of the university, its students, and the public. The primary goal of these exemptions is to protect the institutional autonomy of religious associations and avoid excessive governmental entanglement with religion, while nonetheless advancing the generally applicable law's goals of equity and inclusion and avoiding unnecessary third-party harms.

A *The Exemptions and Their Limits*

In some instances, agencies have been left to put meat on the skeleton of a generically worded statutory exemption for religious institutions. For example, Title IX's provision for religious institutions permits universities to be exempt from the statute's sex discrimination prohibitions when a given requirement "would not be consistent with the religious tenets of such organization" if the school "is controlled by a religious organization."[18] Notably, institutions seeking a waiver under Title IX are required to request exempt status explicitly.[19]

---

[18] 20 U.S.C. § 1681(a)(3) (2012).

[19] 34 C.F.R. 106.12(b) (2017) ("An educational institution which wishes to claim the exemption ... shall do so by submitting in writing to the Assistant Secretary a statement ... identifying the provisions of this part which conflict with a specific tenet of the religious

The Department of Education applies an informal test to determine whether a school possesses the degree of religiosity necessary to claim the exemption. For a university to qualify, it must be a divinity school or other program designed to train students for a religious vocation; or it must require faculty, students, or employees to belong to or accept a particular religion; or – as a sort of catch-all category:

> Its charter and catalog, or other official publication, contains explicit statement that it is controlled by a religious organization or an organ thereof or is committed to the doctrines of a particular religion, and the members of its governing body are appointed by the controlling religious organization or an organ thereof, and it receives a significant amount of financial support from the controlling religious organization or an organ thereof.[20]

As one commentator notes, the Title IX exemption has never been litigated, so there is no authoritative judicial construction of the statutory language.[21]

The scope of the religious exemption to the ACA's contraceptive insurance coverage mandate was also initially a matter of administrative determination, although it later became the subject of extensive litigation as well. In its original form, this exemption was quite narrow and would have excluded any entity that did not primarily serve and employ coreligionists.[22] Considerable back-and-forth negotiation and litigation ensued regarding the scope of the exemption, which was initially extended to a narrow group of religious entities such as churches and their integrated social services operations (but not to religious colleges and universities) and subsequently broadened to include virtually any employer with a conscientious objection.[23]

---

organization."). The Department of Education's Office for Civil Rights currently makes an archive of this information available, *Religious Exemptions Index*, U.S. DEP'T OF EDUC., OFFICE FOR CIVIL RIGHTS, https://perma.cc/AH8X-TG43. It appears that requests for exemption have increased in recent years. *See* HUMAN RIGHTS CAMPAIGN, HIDDEN DISCRIMINATION: TITLE IX RELIGIOUS EXEMPTIONS PUTTING LGBT STUDENTS AT RISK 11 (2015).

[20] *Exemptions from Title IX*, U.S. DEP'T OF EDUC., OFFICE FOR CIVIL RIGHTS, https://perma.cc/G4SR-GS6X (emphasis added). Kif Augustine-Adams has carefully examined the evolution of the federal government's approach to religious exemptions and explains that this policy was never codified but is still the test used for this determination. Augustine-Adams, *supra* note 6, at 330.

[21] Augustine-Adams, *supra* note 6, at 327.

[22] Group Health Plans and Health Insurance Issuers Relating to Coverage of Preventive Services Under the ACA, 76 Fed. Reg. at 46,626.

[23] Some of this process is described in Univ. of Notre Dame v. Sebelius, 743 F.3d 547, 548–51 (7th Cir. 2014), *cert. granted, judgment vacated sub nom.* Univ. of Notre Dame v. Burwell, 135 S. Ct. 1528 (2015). *See also* Zubik v. Burwell, 136 S. Ct. 1557 (2016); Religious Exemptions and Accommodations for Coverage of Certain Preventive Services Under the Affordable Care Act, 82 Fed. Reg. 47792 (modifying the prior rule by greatly broadening eligibility for exemption); Moral Exemptions and Accommodations for Coverage of Certain Preventive Services Under the Affordable Care Act, 82 Fed. Reg. 47,838, 47,841 (interim final rule Oct. 6, 2017) (same). For critique of the Trump administration's broadened exemptions, see NeJaime & Siegel, Chapter 6.

Similarly, and relatedly, much ink has been spilled over the question of who can qualify for exemptions under RFRA, a broadly worded statute that protects the religious exercise of any "person[]" from being "substantially burden[ed]" by acts of the federal government.[24] In *Hobby Lobby*, the Supreme Court decided that a closely held corporation employing approximately 13,000 people could be a "person" that exercises religion under the statute.[25] At the same time, several colleges and universities have challenged the federal government's contraceptive coverage requirement as a substantial burden on their religious exercise under RFRA.[26] It appears that the religious schools' right to invoke RFRA, as a person exercising religion, went unchallenged.

Courts have also filled the gap with a variety of tests to elucidate Title VII's exemption from its general prohibition on religious discrimination in employment.[27] One scholar has summarized these tests as "(1) the secularization test, (2) the sufficiently religious test, (3) the primarily religious test, and (4) the *LeBoon* test."[28] Together, these tests consider factors such as actual control; financial support; clarity of mission; requirements imposed on faculty with respect to religious conduct or belief; engaging in religious activities as part of school activities; self-presentation (*i.e.*, how the institution holds itself out); and the university community's membership – whether it is primarily composed of coreligionists or is more diverse.[29]

Finally, courts have on occasion extended exemptions to religious institutions due to constitutional constraints on generally applicable legislation that contained no explicit exemption. The ability of religiously affiliated colleges and universities to claim the ministerial exception – an immunity from suit over employment decisions pertaining to high-level ministerial employees – appears to be largely uncontroversial.[30] Where the issue has squarely arisen, courts have applied factors like those applied in the Title VII and Title IX contexts to determine whether an educational institution can invoke the exception. Thus, in *Kirby v. Lexington Theological*

---

[24] 42 U.S.C. § 2000bb-1(a) (2012). Some states have statutory analogs to RFRA that constrain state government. See Appendix, Chapter 35, for state RFRAs. For analysis and critique of RFRAs in this volume, see Laycock, Chapter 3; NeJaime & Siegel, Chapter 6; Smith, Chapter 18.

[25] *Hobby Lobby*, 134 S. Ct. at 2769.

[26] *See, e.g., Univ. of Notre Dame*, 743 F.3d at 554; Wheaton Coll. v. Burwell, 50 F. Supp. 3d 939, 947 (N.D. Ill. 2014), *aff'd*, 791 F.3d 792 (7th Cir. 2015).

[27] 42 U.S.C. § 2000e-1(a) exempts from its prohibitions a "religious corporation, association, educational institution, or society with respect to the employment of individuals of a particular religion to perform work connected with the carrying on by such corporation, association, educational institution, or society of its activities."

[28] Roger W. Dyer, Jr., *Qualifying for the Title VII Religious Organization Exemption: Federal Circuits Split over Proper Test*, 76 MO. L. REV. 545, 546–47, 554–60 (2010).

[29] *Cf.* Wilson, *supra* note 6, at 485–87.

[30] Petruska v. Gannon Univ., 462 F.3d 294 (3d Cir. 2006); Kant v. Lexington Theological Seminary, 426 S.W.3d 587, 593–96 (Ky. 2014). For more on the scope of the ministerial exception, see Helfand, Chapter 11; Melling, Chapter 19.

Seminary, the Kentucky Supreme Court held that a theological seminary was a religious institution that could claim the protection of the ministerial exception, stating, somewhat vaguely, that the exception could be invoked "whenever [an] entity's mission is marked by clear or obvious religious characteristics."[31] The court then pointed to the fact that the school was financially supported by the Christian Church (Disciples of Christ), in return for which it was charged with training ministers and advancing the church's mission. The court also considered it significant that religious study was required for all students and that the seminary's "bylaws and governing structure" indicated a close relationship with the church.[32] The court was not dissuaded by the fact that the school employed non-members of the faith.[33] Similarly, the California Court of Appeal found that the exception applied to Chapman University. Although vaguely referring to those institutions protected by the ministerial exception as "church-related institutions," the court took pains to note the relationship between Chapman University and the Christian Church (Disciples of Christ) in its overall mission, structure, and inclusion of religious teachings in its curriculum.[34]

Similarly, religious universities are entitled to exemption from labor regulation under the National Labor Relations Act (NLRA), because such regulation might otherwise raise constitutional concerns.[35] After years of case-by-case decision-making by the National Labor Relations Board about whether a particular religious school was religious enough to obtain this exemption, the US Court of Appeals for the DC Circuit decided in *University of Great Falls v. NLRB* that the exemption should be granted to any nonprofit school affiliated with or controlled by a religious entity that "holds itself out to students, faculty and community" as religious.[36]

In sum, a wide array of tests has been applied to determine which higher education institutions are sufficiently religious to claim exemptions from various civil rights laws. Though the language of those tests differs widely, they tend to focus on many of the same formal and substantive attributes. Those factors – not all of which are considered for each type of exemption – are as follows:

(1) the existence of a *formal religious affiliation* and visible structural markers of that affiliation, including a financial relationship and a relationship of formal hierarchy or control;

---

[31] Kirby v. Lexington Theological Seminary, 426 S.W.3d 597, 609 (Ky. 2014) (quoting Hollins v. Methodist Healthcare, Inc., 474 F.3d 223 (6th Cir. 2007)).

[32] *Id.* at 610–11.

[33] *Id.* at 610.

[34] Schmoll v. Chapman Univ., 70 Cal. App. 4th 1434, 1437, 1439 (1999).

[35] *Catholic Bishop*, 440 U.S. at 507.

[36] Univ. of Great Falls v. N.L.R.B., 278 F.3d 1335, 1343 (D.C. Cir. 2002) (quoting Universidad Central de Bayamon v. N.L.R.B., 793 F.2d 383, 400 (1st Cir. 1985)). The NLRB itself has not acquiesced in the DC Circuit's interpretation of what the Constitution requires, however. Saint Xavier Univ. & Serv. Employees Int'l Union, Local 1, 365 NLRB No. 54 (Apr. 6, 2017) (upholding NLRB jurisdiction over nonreligious employees of a religious school).

(2) the *pervasiveness of the religious mission*, both in the university's formal documents and in the substance of its instruction and relationship with employees and other community members;

(3) the school's willingness to *educate and employ those who do not share its mission*;

(4) the *visibility of the school's religious commitment*, as suggested by the likelihood that employees, faculty, students, and even prospective students will be aware of it; and

(5) *nonprofit status*.

B *The Balance of Interests*

Arguably, the different kinds of exemptions described previously in this chapter serve distinct purposes and interests. For example, the ministerial exception, mandated by both the Free Exercise Clause and the Establishment Clause, ensures that religious organizations are free to choose those who will lead them on their way and speak on their behalf; its origins lie in the prohibition on the state choosing ministers for the church.[37] RFRA, by contrast, is tied more closely to the rationales behind individual free exercise rights, and its statutory language echoes that jurisprudence.[38] RFRA is largely aimed at immunizing individuals or associations from negative consequences arising from specific exercises of religion that might otherwise violate the law. Put differently, one might say that RFRA aims to avoid spiritual harm to religious individuals and entities. And the exemptions under Title IX and Title VII are geared toward protecting religious organizations both from excessive government intrusion in their internal affairs and from being forced to trade their religious convictions for the right to exist and participate in the educational marketplace alongside secular schools.

Yet, viewed from a slightly greater distance, it is apparent that these exemptions aim to balance roughly the same set of interests. At the highest level of generality, all of these exemptions are concerned with protecting institutional autonomy. Institutional autonomy, in turn, is supported by various rationales that are relevant here. First, religious associations are seen as inherently valuable because they bolster individual free exercise – and may even be considered essential to it.[39] To go a step further, some have pointed out that religious associations are, essentially, greater than the sum of their parts; group worship is a unique form of worship, which must be given room to exist and which cannot be reduced to individual religious practices.[40] And relatedly, Professor Lawrence Sager has argued that religious institutions are protected from

---

[37] Hosanna-Tabor Evangelical Lutheran Church & Sch. v. E.E.O.C., 565 U.S. 171, 181–87 (2012).

[38] 42 U.S.C. § 2000bb(a); 42 U.S.C. § 2000bb-1 (2012).

[39] *See, e.g.,* Christopher C. Lund, *Free Exercise Reconceived: The Logic and Limits of Hosanna-Tabor,* 108 Nw. U. L. Rev. 1183, 1197 (2014).

[40] *See, e.g.,* Helfand, Chapter 11; Richard W. Garnett, *Do Churches Matter? Towards an Institutional Understanding of the Religion Clauses,* 53 Vill. L. Rev. 273, 293–94 (2008) (describing

government intervention because they are comprised of intimate, enduring relationships formed around common values that in some cases support free expression but
perhaps more importantly "nurture the development and well-being of their
members" while creating a structure for individuals to "find [their] own way."[41]

Second, religious institutions play a unique and valuable role in society. They
serve as counterpoints to the state, offering competing norms and values, and as
such, they play an important role in supporting a pluralistic and robust civil
society.[42] They cannot play this role if the state is able to impose its own secular
values and views on the institution's members, or even if it can put an excessively
heavy thumb on the scale of the organization's deliberations. Third, religious institutional autonomy is desirable because the state is uniquely incompetent to decide
religious questions, which are often involved when religious tenets are claimed to
come into conflict with legal requirements.[43] Arguably, all of the religious autonomy goals animating the exemptions available to religious universities are encompassed within these three rationales.

At the same time, the exemptions are often crafted with the goal of balancing
religious autonomy interests against other interests – here, primarily, the interests in
equality and inclusion of those affected by the institutions. Another way of thinking
about this interest is as an interest in avoiding third-party harms – that is, harms to
individuals who are not religious "insiders."[44] For example, although students,
faculty, and staff at a religiously affiliated college are usually aware of the nature
of the institution's religious commitment, they may have varying degrees of awareness of the requirements by which they are actually bound and therefore may or may
not have meaningfully consented to them.[45] Moreover, religious schools compete
with one another and with nonreligious schools for students, faculty, and staff.
Students compete for admission to the best schools, which in turn wield enormous
power in the marketplace. The religious affiliation of the institution may not be in
the foreground for many students, and it may not be emphasized by the college or

---

churches as "institutions that are not reducible to the rights and interests of their members and
employees").

[41] Lawrence Sager, *Why Churches (and, Possibly, the Tarpon Bay Women's Blue Water Fishing
Club) Can Discriminate, in* THE RISE OF CORPORATE RELIGIOUS LIBERTY 77, 86 (Micah
Schwartzman, Chad Flanders & Zoë Robinson eds. 2016) (citing Seana V. Shiffrin, *What Is
Really Wrong with Compelled Association?*, 99 Nw. U. L. REV. 839 (2005)).

[42] *See, e.g.*, Richard W. Garnett, *Religion and Group Rights: Are Churches (Just) Like the Boy
Scouts?*, 22 ST. JOHN'S J. LEGAL COMMENT. 515 (2007). For the scale of good works done by
houses of worship, see Berg, Chapter 24.

[43] *See, e.g.*, Ira C. Lupu & Robert W. Tuttle, *The Mystery of Unanimity in* Hosanna-Tabor
Evangelical Lutheran Church & School v. EEOC, 20 LEWIS & CLARK L. REV. 1265 (2017).

[44] For an extended discussion of third-party harms, see NeJaime & Siegel, Chapter 6; Melling,
Chapter 19; for a discussion of whether members have impliedly consented, see Helfand,
Chapter 11.

[45] For examples, see *infra* notes 51–53.

university in its marketing materials.[46] Thus, there is a risk that students, faculty, or staff may find themselves accepting the terms of membership in a religious community without fully understanding the implications of that membership.

In addition to these concerns about institutional autonomy and third-party harms – which may apply to all sorts of religious institutions – there are special concerns pertaining to institutions of higher education. These concerns pull in opposing directions. On the one hand, private, religious universities may be sites for the creation and reinforcement of norms and attitudes that stand in opposition to certain mainstream liberal values. A school that is dominated by an explicitly religious worldview, for example, may embrace values, an approach to pedagogy, and a code of conduct that are atypical for a modern university. As John Garvey, president of the Catholic University of America, explained in his inauguration address: "We deliver one message about materialism, sex, self-sacrifice, and alcohol; our children see another in school and the media. Our lesson gains credibility if the children see a community of people they know and admire living it."[47] This important function performed by religious schools supports both the school's interest in religious freedom (and academic freedom) and the public interest in supporting a diversity of educational options – diversity among rather than within institutions.

On the other hand, college is a time and place in which young people may learn to question, perhaps for the first time, some of their longest-held beliefs about the world, if not their very identities. Universities are so greatly valued in society in part because of their vital role in creating, challenging, and re-creating knowledge. "The job of colleges and universities is to articulate, examine, and judge whether any particular idea (regardless of its affinity to religion) is worthy of being called knowledge."[48] Critical thinking and questioning are essential to performing this task. Thus, the notion of a university as a place for the perpetuation of particular, well-defined values is arguably in tension with the public mission of that institution – if not with the very idea of it. Moreover, it has undoubtedly not escaped the notice of university administrators – even, or perhaps especially, those at religiously affiliated schools – that college is a time when many students realize their sexual identity. This creates a particular difficulty for students attending religious schools, since religious norms and the claimed exemptions often center on sexual ethics.

Finally, it is worth noting that American institutions of higher learning are somewhat unique in their heavy dependence on government funding.[49] In addition

---

[46] For a discussion of the ways in which "covenantal" colleges and universities foreground their mission, see Hoogstra et al., Chapter 25.

[47] John Garvey, Inaugural Address at the Catholic University of America, *Intellect and Virtue: The Idea of a Catholic University* (Jan. 25, 2011), https://perma.cc/J8WT-EFXM.

[48] Douglas Jacobsen & Rhonda Hustedt Jacobsen, No Longer Invisible: Religion in University Education 93 (2012).

[49] Pew Charitable Ctr., Federal and State Funding of Higher Education: A Changing Landscape 9, 11–12 (2015), https://perma.cc/7PZ3-WLAG.

to (usually) benefitting from nonprofit status, universities receive large dollar amounts in federally funded student financial aid and – for research universities – federal research funding. This fact alone suggests two more conflicting interests at work: the interest of taxpayers in not supporting discriminatory conduct or policies, and the interest of schools in maintaining independence despite their need for government subvention.[50]

II WHICH UNIVERSITIES SHOULD QUALIFY?

An approach that seeks common ground on the question of exemptions for religious colleges and universities would attempt, to the greatest extent possible, to accommodate all of the various interests just identified. Of course, to do that is a highly complex task, and it is not the goal of this brief chapter to specify a detailed rule for determining whether a college or university is entitled to claim an exemption from any or all generally applicable civil rights laws. Instead, this section presents some overarching principles, arguing that there are values worth protecting on both sides of the exemption issue, and that the goal should be to work toward reconciling them.

One approach to religious exemptions for institutions of higher education might be to require a certain "degree" of religiosity before an institution can qualify. Religious colleges and universities, of course, vary widely in terms of the extent to which their religious mission permeates the educational and social environment. On one end of the spectrum might be a school such as Liberty University, which has described its mission in a letter to the US Department of Education as "glorify[ing] God by 'equipping men and women in higher education in fidelity to the Christian faith expressed through the Holy Scriptures, the orthodox religious and moral foundations of that education being a central and perpetual purpose and mission.'"[51] In that letter, Liberty claimed a right to discipline female students who have abortions, because the university's policy allows for such discipline.[52] On the other end of the spectrum would perhaps be a school such as Georgetown, whose religious affiliation may not even be apparent at first glance.[53]

One might argue, then, that only schools possessing the qualities of a close, intimate, voluntary association merit special protection from the intrusion of state law. The rationales for protecting institutional autonomy generally assume that the institution being protected is such an association – one that is central to the

---

[50] For views on how government support complicates the analysis of whether to exempt religious actors, see Melling, Chapter 19; Eskridge, Chapter 22; Hollman, Chapter 23; Berg, Chapter 24.

[51] Letter to Dep't of Educ. (Jan. 16, 2014), https://perma.cc/BMM3-9UVV (quoting Liberty University's articles of incorporation).

[52] *Id.*

[53] Georgetown's website front barely mentions its Catholic affiliation, for example. Its front-page text refers as often to Georgetown's commitment to "social justice" as it does to its Jesuit tradition. GEORGETOWN UNIV., https://perma.cc/V5FF-X5AF.

identities of the individuals who belong to it. The visibility and pervasiveness of a university's religious commitment, as well as the religious homogeneity of its students, faculty, and staff would be obvious factors for making this determination.

However, several problems arise from this approach. One obvious problem is that of line-drawing: How are courts and agencies to decide how religious is religious enough? Consider, for example, what to do with Grand Canyon University, a for-profit Christian college. One reporter noted that Grand Canyon University described itself as a Christian university and required students to do coursework in religion or philosophy but did not require a statement of faith from its professors or staff.[54] In addition, this approach may unfairly penalize more pluralistic, ecumenical schools. As one court observed, "If the [u]niversity is ecumenical and open-minded, that does not make it any less religious, nor [government] interference any less a potential infringement of religious liberty."[55] Yet at the same time, such "open" institutions are also less likely to need or seek exemptions from civil rights laws in the first place.[56] And a narrow exemption from a specific requirement, or even a limited ministerial exception claim with respect to a high-level employee, might be easier to claim than a broad immunity from a significant civil-rights provision that would affect a large number of students, faculty, and staff.

Moreover, to the extent the relevant question is whether a university constitutes a close association, some well-known religious universities may not qualify for exemptions. As noted earlier in this chapter, the more liberal religious institutions may not qualify as the sort of close, homogeneous associations contemplated here. As explained in Section I.B., however, granting exemptions from civil rights laws to universities raises particular concerns because of the unique nature of universities. They usually command considerable power in a national education marketplace. They also arguably owe to their students a space in which to develop and possibly change their identities. And they often benefit from massive quantities of taxpayer funding. A high bar for exemptions to civil rights laws is arguably a small price to pay, given the benefits such institutions enjoy and the significant responsibilities they shoulder.

---

[54] *See* Elizabeth Redden, *For-Profit, For God*, INSIDE HIGHER ED (Aug. 3, 2009), https://perma .cc/PP4P-Q8S8 (discussing the potential for conflict between for-profit status and Christian affiliation).

[55] Univ. of Great Falls v. N.L.R.B., 278 F.3d 1335, 1346 (D.C. Cir. 2002).

[56] For example, both Notre Dame University and Liberty University brought suit to seek total exemption from the contraceptives mandate. Georgetown, by contrast, has not litigated the issue but chose to accept the Obama administration's proffered accommodation; it thus denies coverage for students but informs them that they can get cost-free contraception through a third party. *FAQS Student Health Insurance 2017–2018 Plan Year*, GEORGETOWN UNIV. STUDENT HEALTH SERVS., https://perma.cc/788U-BJA8. Liberty University has also requested exemptions from Title IX, whereas Notre Dame has not. *Religious Exemptions Index, supra* note 19. Moreover, perhaps staking out a middle-ground position – or perhaps generating concerns about its sincere need for exemption – Notre Dame has changed its stance with respect to covering some contraceptives. *See* Emma Green, *Notre Dame Switches Its Position on Birth-Control Coverage – Again*, THE ATLANTIC (Feb. 7, 2018), https://perma.cc/7EKD-WHP6.

Ultimately, attention to the pervasiveness of an institution's religious mission is likely to minimize the danger of excessively burdening religious outsiders. If an institution is pervasively religious, it is less likely to employ and matriculate individuals who do not share its beliefs; it is therefore less likely that its community members will be burdened by the exemption. The opposite can be said of more open and ecumenical institutions, which are less likely to seek exemptions in the first place, given their more liberal orientation.

A second way to mediate between the interests of religious entities and the interests of third parties is to require strong forms of notice, so that nonadherents will be as informed as possible of the details of their commitment when they choose to work or study at a religious institution. In particular, schools should be required to give advance notice of both their religious commitments *and* the implications of those commitments for a particular legal requirement in order to claim an exemption from that requirement. Currently, in the Title IX context, a college or university must seek a waiver from the Department of Education when claiming an exemption. This process requires the school to identify the conflict between a specific requirement of Title IX and the institution's religious tenets. In general, this is not a procedure that is required under Title VII, RFRA, or the ministerial exception. Requiring Title IX-style notice could go a long way toward alleviating the burdens placed on unwitting or nonconsenting members of the community who do not necessarily share the institution's religious orientation, without greatly burdening the schools. However, such a requirement would only be effective in giving notice to potential community members if it is treated as a prerequisite to making an exemption claim.[57]

To be sure, the requirement of notice will not alleviate all conflicts between religious institutions and their individual members. In particular, because many people's sexual identity is still developing during their college years, some students may not discover until after they have joined the university community that their sexual identity puts them in conflict with their school's rules and commitments. In some such cases, it may be possible for the student to reconcile his or her sexual identity with the commands of his or her faith – perhaps with the assistance of the university's faculty and staff. In other cases, the conflict will remain irreconcilable, and it may be inevitable that courts will be called upon to intervene and engage in sensitive line-drawing.

Finally, courts and agencies should be allowed to consider an institution's sincerity of belief. For example, they might consider whether the institution is consistent with respect to its own rules and its own tenets. They should be able to consider whether the institution seeking one exemption has sought exemptions to

---

[57] This is not the case in the Title IX context. *See Exemptions from Title IX*, U.S. Dep't of Educ., Office for Civil Rights, https://perma.cc/K3UY-HTJZ ("Religious institutions that have neither sought nor received prior written assurance from OCR may still invoke their exemption after OCR receives a Title IX complaint.").

other general laws, in order to protect other core religious tenets, or has instead attempted to pick and choose which exemptions it wishes to seek. When universities attempt to invoke religious exemptions – particularly in the context of litigation – the stakes are generally quite high. The incentive to claim religious status is similarly great, especially in the face of highly fact-intensive discrimination claims, which often require a jury to make determinations of individuals' private motives.[58] The broader and more deferential the exemption, the greater the temptation to claim it. Thus, courts and agencies should not shy away from making sincerity determinations when the question arises.

One objection to this approach is that it may raise Establishment Clause concerns; it appears to come dangerously close to asking government actors (whether courts or agencies) to decide ecclesiastical or doctrinal questions, such as whether a particular religion's tenets conflict with a nondiscrimination law, or whether an institution "qualifies" for its claimed denominational status. Under the ministerial exception, for example, a court is not permitted even to consider the reason for a ministerial employee's firing – not even to determine whether it is pretextual.[59] Yet, in the Title IX context, this is precisely what is required. And schools seeking those exemptions – which are routinely granted – have no difficulty articulating their religious values and mission, nor the conflict with their tenets created by the law's nondiscrimination provisions. Articulating one's values is, arguably, simply the price of the exemption. Additionally, to say that courts and agencies should require some such specific showing on the part of the university is not to rule out a somewhat deferential consideration of that showing.

III CONCLUSION

In his 1951 classic, *God and Man at Yale*, William F. Buckley, Jr. famously excoriated his *alma mater* for imposing a relentlessly secularist worldview upon its students. For this the book is well remembered. Perhaps less famously, he also urged Yale's alumni to strike back, using their money and power to force Yale to reimpose the traditional Protestant values of its founding. In one sense, then, the title of this chapter is ironic, in that it hopes to avoid a back-and-forth struggle in the name of imposing particular religious or secular values by suggesting principles for finding common ground on the issue of religious exemptions for colleges and universities. At the same time, however, Buckley's argument also reveals just how profoundly important the American university is – not just to those within it, but also to those outside it. It is for precisely this reason that it is a site of cultural conflict, as well as a particularly urgent site for mediating that conflict.

---

[58] B. Jessie Hill, *Kingdom Without End? The Inevitable Expansion of Religious Sovereignty Claims*, 20 LEWIS & CLARK L. REV. 1177, 1198 (2017).

[59] *Hosanna-Tabor*, 565 U.S. at 194.

PART VII

The Challenges of Public Accommodations

27

Challenges to True Fairness for All

How SOGI Laws Are Unlike Civil Liberties and Other Nondiscrimination Laws and How to Craft Better Policy and Get Nondiscrimination Laws Right

Ryan T. Anderson

Public debates about sensitive issues of culture, identity, and sexuality often get tangled up in terms and concepts. In particular, we confuse "rights" and "needs" in ways that in turn confuse our understanding of the appropriate role of government in these arenas. Untangling this knot is a first step toward fruitful debate of these sensitive issues.

There are certain rights that everyone possesses irrespective of their identity. Among these are the right to life, liberty (including religious liberty), and the pursuit of happiness. Government exists to protect, not violate, these rights. At the same time, there are certain needs that everyone has, regardless of their identity. Government, in some cases, has an obligation to help people meet those needs, and in other cases, it has an obligation to allow people to meet them on their own, by prohibiting others from preventing any person from meeting his own needs. So, for instance, government directly meets the needs of the poor through certain welfare programs, and it also prevents private entities from blocking people from meeting their own needs through certain nondiscrimination statutes.

Some argue that people are blocking LGBT citizens' ability to meet their needs, necessitating a governmental response. If a governmental response is necessary, any response helping citizens must not unduly impede decent interactions or civil liberties such as freedoms of speech, association, and religion. As Americans continue to disagree about sex and marriage, Americans must find ways to help every citizen meet his or her needs without weaponizing the redefinitions of marriage, sex, and gender in ways that prevent others from exercising their rights and meeting their needs. SOGIs should not become tools of intolerance.

If a nondiscrimination policy is needed to, in a specific context, protect citizens from mistreatment that hampers their full participation in civil society, such policies ought to be shields, not swords.

But SOGI policies *are* being used as swords to "punish the wicked," as the biggest financial backer of SOGIs, Tim Gill, has put it.[1] Lawmakers, public-interest firms, civil rights commissioners, and judges seem to agree with Gill that SOGIs should be wielded in this fashion. For many, it is not sufficient that same-sex couples can marry in the state's eyes; their relationships must count as marriages in the eyes of their fellow citizens, who must be forced to facilitate such unions. Likewise, not only must citizens be free to adopt transgender identities, others must be forced to accept them.

In brief, policies intended to allow LGBT people to meet their needs are being used illiberally to impose a new sexual orthodoxy on the nation. But as the US Supreme Court in its same-sex marriage decision, *Obergefell v. Hodges*, acknowledged, doing so is unjustified: the conviction that male and female are created for each other "has been held – and continues to be held – in good faith by reasonable and sincere people here and throughout the world."[2] Indeed, the Supreme Court added, many "reach that conclusion based on decent and honorable religious or philosophical premises, and neither they nor their beliefs are disparaged here."[3] Any fair policy will take heed of this point; it will address minorities' precise needs without punishing reasonable citizens for acting on decent and honorable beliefs.

Policy makers should not assume that the best solution is to add "four words and a comma"[4] – that is, to insert "sexual orientation, gender identity" into existing laws crafted to respond to racism and sexism, as nearly all SOGI laws do.[5] To avoid punishing good actions and interactions, lawmakers must carefully specify what constitutes "discrimination" on the basis of "sexual orientation" and "gender identity." Lawmakers should carefully consider which entities to regulate to keep burdens to a minimum.[6] And they should accommodate freedoms of speech, association, and religious liberty. On each of these dimensions, our law has treated racial discrimination differently from sex-based discrimination. This chapter highlights and analogizes these differences. It shows what constitutes discrimination and how to distinguish invidious discrimination from fair distinctions and reasonable disagreements.

After considering analogies to race and sex, this chapter considers analogies to religion, addressing two common charges against skeptics of SOGI laws: that it is inconsistent to support religious liberty but not SOGI nondiscrimination policies and that it is inconsistent to support bans on religious discrimination but not SOGI

---

[1] Andy Kroll, *Meet the Megadonor Behind the LGBTQ Rights Movement*, ROLLING STONE (June 23, 2017), https://perma.cc/7783-K5YU (specifying $500 million investment).

[2] Obergefell v. Hodges, 135 S. Ct. 2584, 2594 (2015). For similar views about tradition and history of belief about traditional marriage, see Greenawalt, Chapter 8; Perry, Chapter 20.

[3] Obergefell, 135 S. Ct. at 2594.

[4] Eric Berman, *Senate Democrats to Propose "Four Words and a Comma" Anti-Discrimination Bill*, WIBC (Oct. 6, 2015), https://perma.cc/6NN7-8MAE.

[5] *See* Appendix, Chapter 35.

[6] *See* Laycock, Chapter 3; Adams, Chapter 32.

discrimination. As to the first objection, constraints on the government for the sake of all citizens can be appropriate in a way that coercion of some citizens for the sake of others may not. As to the second, religion nondiscrimination laws have not been used to impose a religious orthodoxy on the nation, but SOGI nondiscrimination laws are being used to impose a sexual orthodoxy, despite reasonable differences on questions such as the nature of marriage.

Anti-gay and anti-transgender bigotry exists and should be condemned. But support for marriage as the union of husband and wife is not anti-gay.[7] The conviction that sex is a biological reality is not anti-transgender.[8] Just as Americans have combatted sexism without treating pro-life medicine as sexist, any public policy necessary to help people who identify as LGBT meet their needs should be crafted to respect the consciences of reasonable people who act on good-faith beliefs about marriage and gender identity. Not every disagreement is discrimination. And our laws should not suppose otherwise.

I ANALOGIES TO RACE AND SEX

This section first explores the meaning of discrimination itself and then parses invidious discrimination from other lawful distinctions premised on convictions that are respectful and should be respected.

A *Definitions of Key Terms*

Taken in its broad sense of making distinctions, discrimination is inevitable.[9] In the moralized, pejorative sense, discrimination involves mistreatment based on irrelevant factors. For clarity, this chapter uses "distinguish" as a neutral term and "discriminate" to refer to wrongful distinctions – those based on irrelevant factors. One distinguishes *or* discriminates based on X when one takes X as a reason for treating someone differently.[10] Of course, there might be some traits on which one both distinguishes and discriminates, and disentangling the two can take work. A school distinguishes based on sex when it creates male and female bathrooms; it

---

[7] *See* RYAN T. ANDERSON, TRUTH OVERRULED: THE FUTURE OF MARRIAGE AND RELIGIOUS FREEDOM (2015).

[8] *See* RYAN T. ANDERSON, WHEN HARRY BECAME SALLY: RESPONDING TO THE TRANSGENDER MOMENT (2018).

[9] Very different actions are often lumped together under the heading of "discrimination," as Professor Kent Greenawalt notes: (a) unjust categorizations, (b) arbitrary categorizations that are not themselves unjust, and (c) appropriate categorizations, such as when colleges offer admission to the students who performed most strongly on college aptitude tests. *See* Kent Greenawalt, *Probabilities, Perceptions, Consequences, and "Discrimination": One Puzzle About Controversial "Stop and Frisk,"* 12 OHIO ST. J. CRIM. L. 181, 189 (2014).

[10] *See* JOHN CORVINO, RYAN T. ANDERSON & SHERIF GIRGIS, DEBATING RELIGIOUS LIBERTY AND DISCRIMINATION 163–68 (2017).

discriminates based on sex when it allows men to study economics while forcing women to stick to home economics.[11] However, doctors neither distinguish nor discriminate based on sex when they decline to perform abortions, as the sex of the pregnant person plays no role in doctors' reasoning.

SOGI laws fail to specify appropriately what constitutes discrimination based on sexual orientation and gender identity.[12] This allows for over-enforcement. To illustrate this point, it is useful to consider several different cases of putative "discrimination" based on race and sex. Public policy is nuanced enough to capture important differences between race and sex; it should do the same with regard to SOGI.

B *Invidious Discrimination Is Rightly Unlawful*

Invidious discrimination is rooted in unfair, socially debilitating ideas about individuals' abilities or proper social status. Racially segregated water fountains are a clear example of race-based discrimination: their creators took race into account where it was utterly irrelevant in order to treat blacks as socially inferior.[13] That is what made the practice invidious race-based discrimination. Given that such discrimination was entrenched, widespread, and state-sponsored, Congress rightly stepped in.[14]

Likewise, throughout much of American history, girls and women were not afforded educational opportunities equal to those available to boys and men.[15] This form of discrimination took sex into consideration where it was irrelevant. It treated girls and women differently precisely because of their sex, depriving them of educational opportunities for which they were qualified. That unjustified treatment is what made it invidious discrimination. Addressing its entrenchment justified Congress's passage of Title IX of the Education Amendments of 1972 (Title IX).[16]

C *Appropriate, Lawful Distinctions Should Not Be Classified as Discrimination*

Yet, Title IX's implementing regulations made clear that sex-specific housing, bathrooms, and locker rooms were not forms of unlawful discrimination.[17] Such policies take sex into consideration, but not invidiously. They treat both sexes

---

[11] *See* 45 C.F.R. §§ 618.405, 618.410 (2017) (implementing Title IX).

[12] See Adams, Chapter 32, for delineations in the context of housing and hiring nondiscrimination laws.

[13] See Perry, Chapter 20, for a discussion of the need for a federal ban on racial discrimination.

[14] Title II of the Civil Rights Act, 42 USCA § 2000a (b) (2012) (banning discrimination on the basis of race, color, religion, or national origin in "public accommodations"). For more on the scope of public accommodations under this law, see Laycock, Chapter 3; Wilson, Chapter 30.

[15] See Hill, Chapter 26, for the genesis of Title IX.

[16] 20 U.S.C. §§ 1681–1688 (2012).

[17] *See* 44 C.F.R. § 106.33 (2017) ("A recipient may provide separate toilet, locker room, and shower facilities on the basis of sex, but such facilities provided for students of one sex shall be comparable to such facilities provided for students of the other sex.").

equally because they take sex into consideration – they distinguish on the basis of sex – only where it is relevant. Specifically, biological sex-specific rules respect bodily sexual differences where those raise legitimate privacy interests.

It would serve equality only in the most artificial (and unimportant) sense to force men and women to undress in front of each other. Indeed, Justice Ruth Bader Ginsburg, writing for the Supreme Court in *United States v. Virginia*, which held that the Virginia Military Institute had to become coeducational, took it for granted that the Court's decision "would undoubtedly require alterations necessary to afford members of each sex privacy from the other sex in living arrangements."[18] Likewise, when critics decades earlier had argued that the Equal Rights Amendment would have required unisex intimate facilities, Ginsburg, who was then a Columbia Law School professor, dismissed this claim "emphatically not so. Separate places to disrobe, sleep, perform personal bodily functions are permitted, in some situations required, by regard for individual privacy. Individual privacy, a right of constitutional dimension, is appropriately harmonized with the equality principle."[19]

While privacy requires separate facilities for males and females, it cannot justify race-specific facilities, which is why the latter discriminate invidiously. Hence, our civil rights laws abolished separate facilities for blacks and whites, but not for males and females. Note that policymakers did not treat sex-specific intimate facilities as discriminatory in the first place, and thus they did not require exemptions for a subset of regulated actors.[20] As the regulations themselves reflected, protected statuses for race and sex do not carry precisely the same legal implications. The scope of bans on discrimination on the basis of each characteristic requires tailoring, considering the status's relevance and what scope is required to restore a group's equal opportunity. Unfortunately, SOGI laws have not been carefully tailored in either drafting or application.

D *Some Actions Neither Distinguish Nor Discriminate*

If sex-specific intimate facilities legitimately distinguish between sexes, pro-life medical practices make nothing hinge on sex at all. That only women can get pregnant has no bearing on the judgment of a doctor or nurse who refuses to kill the unborn, a judgment based on respect for prenatal life. It would be a misapplication of sex nondiscrimination law to say that a Catholic hospital refusing to perform abortions is discriminating based on sex at all. Even those who support abortion access need not support coercing pro-life doctors or hospitals to perform them, since

---

[18] 518 U.S. 515, 550 n. 19 (1996).

[19] Eugene Volokh, *Prominent Feminist: Bans on Sex Discrimination "Emphatically" Do Not "Require Unisex Bathrooms,"* WASH. POST (May 9, 2016), https://perma.cc/6NXV-NCSX; Ruth Bader Ginsburg, *The Fear of the Equal Rights Amendment*, WASH. POST (Apr. 7, 1975), https://www.washingtonpost.com/news/volokh-conspiracy/wp-content/uploads/sites/14/2016/05/ginsburg.jpg.

[20] See *supra* note 14.

any disparate impact created by pro-life practices does not prevent women from obtaining abortions elsewhere.[21]

Thus, three distinct strains of "discrimination" emerge:

- Invidious discrimination, in which an irrelevant factor is (wrongfully and harmfully) taken into consideration – racially segregated water fountains are an example;
- Distinctions that should *not* count as unlawful discrimination, in which a distinguishing factor is taken into consideration precisely because it is relevant, and no one is wronged or harmed[22] – sex-specific intimate facilities would be one example; and
- Policies that do not involve distinctions based on a given trait at all (even if they have disparate impact on a group with that trait), which our law can tolerate without hampering the affected group's participation in civil society – pro-life medicine would be an example.

To avoid unduly burdening sensible and often crucial practices, a prerequisite for any policy addressing the needs of LGBT people must be that it is warranted on the basis of invidious discrimination.

E *Distinguishing SOGI Discrimination from Sexual Disagreement*

What SOGI advocates suggest constitutes invidious discrimination can be further divided in two categories: actual discrimination and reasonable disagreement. Consider a florist who refused to serve all LGBT customers simply because of their LGBT identity. The florist would be discriminating on the basis of sexual orientation or gender identity because he takes these characteristics into consideration precisely to then treat his customers differently.[23] Such discrimination would be invidious because there is no connection between the decision to sell flowers and a customer's gender identity or same-sex sexual desire.

---

[21] On how access and conscience may both be protected, see Greenawalt, Chapter 8; Perry, Chapter 20.

Sometimes the disparate impact created by private actors on a group is extensive enough to hamper that group's full participation in society, in which case the law may regulate private actors even though the private actors neither discriminate against the group nor draw distinctions based on a defining trait. Consider disabled Americans. The Americans with Disabilities Act legitimately regulated businesses that might otherwise neither distinguish nor discriminate based on ability – simply because businesses' *tendency to overlook* the needs of people with disabilities was widespread enough to deprive such people of full participation in civil society. 42 U.S.C. § 12181 (2012).

[22] A range of views on third-party harm courses across this volume. *See* Laycock, Chapter 3; NeJaime & Siegel, Chapter 6; Melling, Chapter 19; Berg, Chapter 24; Hill, Chapter 26; and McConnell, Chapter 28.

[23] *See, e.g., Tennessee Hardware Store Puts Up No Gays Allowed Sign*, USA Today (July 2015).

Jack Phillips, by contrast, did not discriminate – or even distinguish – based on sexual orientation when he refused to design and bake a same-sex wedding cake. He did not take his customer's sexual orientation into consideration at all.[24] He declined to use his artistic abilities to create a custom cake to celebrate a same-sex wedding because he objected to same-sex marriage, based on the common Christian belief that such partnerships are not marital (along with many other relationships – sexual and not, dyadic and larger, same- and opposite-sex).[25] Nowhere need Phillips's reasoning have even referred to the partners' sexual orientation, much less any ideas or attitudes about gay people as a class (good or bad, explicit or not).

Both Justice Samuel Alito and Justice Anthony Kennedy seemed to grasp the importance of this point during oral arguments in *Masterpiece Cakeshop*. When Phillips declined to create a same-sex wedding cake, Colorado wouldn't even recognize – let alone issue – same-sex marriage licenses. Justice Alito observed that Phillips' customer couldn't get the state of Colorado to recognize his relationship as a marriage, "[a]nd yet when he goes to this bake shop, and he says I want a wedding cake, and the baker says, no, I won't do it, in part because same-sex marriage was not allowed in Colorado at the time, he's created a grave wrong . . . How does that all that fit together?"

Indeed. Colorado should have never declared Phillips guilty of discrimination in the first place. And – in what might prove to be the most important comment made during oral argument – Justice Kennedy appeared to reject the ACLU's argument that opposition to same-sex marriage *just is* discrimination against people who identify as gay. Kennedy explained Phillips's beliefs: "Look, suppose he says, 'I have nothing against gay people,' he says. 'But I just don't think they should have a marriage because that's contrary to my beliefs. It's not their identity; it's what they're doing.'" In response to the ACLU's claim that this is sexual-orientation discrimination, Kennedy responded "[y]our identity thing is just too facile."

It wasn't his customer's identity that motived Phillips at all.[26] It is even clearer that Phillips's reason for refusing to bake the wedding cake did not rest on the invidious purpose of avoiding contact with others on equal terms, as was the case with Jim Crow laws.[27] As Phillips said to the same-sex couple, "I'll make you birthday cakes, shower cakes, sell you cookies and brownies, I just don't make cakes for same-sex weddings."[28] He sought only to avoid complicity in what he considered one

---

[24] See Ryan T. Anderson, *Disagreement Is Not Always Discrimination: On Masterpiece Cakeshop and the Analogy to Interracial Marriage*, 16 GEO. J. L. & PUB. POL'Y 123 (2018), https://papers.ssrn.com/sol3/papers.cfm?abstract_id=3136750.

[25] See 3 JOHN FINNIS, HUMAN RIGHTS AND COMMON GOOD: COLLECTED ESSAYS 315–88 (2011); JOHN WITTE JR., FROM SACRAMENT TO CONTRACT: MARRIAGE, RELIGION, AND LAW IN THE WESTERN TRADITION (2d ed. 2012); SCOTT YENOR, FAMILY POLITICS: THE IDEA OF MARRIAGE IN MODERN POLITICAL THOUGHT (2011).

[26] For more on this see Anderson, *supra* note 24.

[27] See generally NIKKI L. M. BROWN & BARRY M. STENTIFORD, THE JIM CROW ENCYCLOPEDIA (2008).

[28] Affidavit of Jack Phillips, at 168, ¶79, https://perma.cc/PX5V-XZE3.

distortion of marriage among others – as shown by his refusal to create divorce cakes as well.

By and large, such refusals simply reflect what the Supreme Court has recognized as a disagreement about marriage among people of good faith motivated by honorable premises.[29] Applying nondiscrimination policy here amounts to an enforcement of sexual orthodoxy on reasonably disputed questions. It punishes people for acting on reasonable views of marriage.

This is seen most clearly in the case of Catholic Charities adoption agencies. They decline to place children with same-sex couples not because of a couple's sexual orientation, but because of the conviction that children deserve both a mother and a father. These agencies believe that men and women are not interchangeable, that mothers and fathers are not replaceable. Catholic Charities does not think that people who identify as LGBT cannot love or care for children; instead they believe that the two best dads in the world cannot make up for a missing mom, and the two best moms in the world cannot make up for a missing dad. This policy does not take sexual orientation into consideration at all.[30] It simply reflects a reasonable disagreement about the importance of both mothering and fathering.[31]

Opposition to interracial marriage, however, was invidious discrimination based on race.[32] Antimiscegenationists opposed interracial marriage precisely because one of the spouses was black, and therefore supposedly incompetent, impure, or threatening to whites.[33] This opposition rested on the idea that blacks were inferior and thus should not interact with whites on an equal plane, least of all in marriage. Thus, a baker refusing to bake for an interracial wedding discriminates invidiously on the basis of race. He takes that factor – race – into consideration and does so where it is irrelevant. His behavior thus perpetuates damaging myths about blacks that impede their full participation in society. This is only confirmed by the fact that antimiscegenation laws (and beliefs) are outliers in history, having arisen only in cultures that had race-based castes.[34] For all these reasons, when the Supreme Court struck down bans on interracial marriage, it did not and could not say that opposition to miscegenation "has been held – and continues to be held – in good faith by reasonable and sincere people here and throughout the world," as *Obergefell* did.

Meanwhile, support for marriage as the conjugal union of husband and wife has been a human universal until just recently, whatever a culture thought about sexual

[29] *See* Obergefell v. Hodges, 135 S. Ct. 2584, 2602, (2015); *see also* Dep't of Fair Emp't and Hous. v. Cathy's Creations, Inc., BCV-17–102855 (Cal. Super. 2016) (affirming a baker's right to refuse to bake a wedding cake for a lesbian couple).

[30] *See* Corvino, Anderson & Girgis , *supra* note 10; Ryan T. Anderson, Truth Overruled: The Future of Marriage and Religious Freedom (2015).

[31] *See* Greenawalt, Chapter 8.

[32] *See* Loving v. Virginia, 388 U.S. 1 (1967).

[33] For an extended discussion of differences between objections to same-sex marriage and interracial marriage, see Perry, Chapter 20.

[34] *See, e.g.*, *What Is Caste Discrimination*, https://perma.cc/68VN-J88G.

orientation or same-sex relations. This view of marriage is based on the capacity that a man and a woman possess to unite in a conjugal act, create new life, and unite that new life with both a mother and a father. Whether ultimately sound or not, this view is reasonable and disparages no one. If *Obergefell* was about respecting the freedom of people who identify as gay to live as they wish, the law should respect the same freedom of Americans who believe in the conjugal understanding of marriage. No doubt many people oppose the conjugal view of marriage. But, to quote the *Obergefell* Court, when that "personal opposition becomes enacted law and public policy, the necessary consequence is to put the imprimatur of the State itself on an exclusion that soon demeans or stigmatizes those whose own liberty is then denied." Nondiscrimination law should be a shield to protect, not a sword to demean, stigmatize, and deny liberty to traditional Muslims, Jews, Christians, and other believers.[35]

Charges of discrimination based on gender identity often suffer from similar problems. *The Washington Post* recently reported that a woman sued a Catholic hospital for its refusal to perform a sex-reassignment procedure on her that entailed removing her healthy uterus.[36] Comments in the *Post's* story conflate actual discrimination with reasonable disagreement, a common phenomenon:

> "What the rule says is if you provide a particular service to anybody, you can't refuse to provide it to anyone," said Sarah Warbelow, the legal director for the Human Rights Campaign. That means a transgender person who shows up at an emergency room with something as basic as a twisted ankle cannot be denied care, as sometimes happens, Warbelow said. That also means if a doctor provides breast reconstruction surgery or hormone therapy, those services cannot be denied to transgender patients seeking them for gender dysphoria, she said.[37]

Twisting an ankle differs crucially from sex reassignment surgery. A hospital that refused to treat the twisted ankles of transgender people simply because of their gender identity would be discriminating invidiously, but a hospital that declined to remove the healthy uterus of a woman identifying as a man would not be engaging in gender-identity discrimination. In the first case, the hospital takes a patient's transgender identity into consideration and then treats the patient worse precisely on that ground, where gender identity is utterly irrelevant. But in the second case, the gender identity of the patient does not even enter the decision. Just as pro-life physicians do not kill unborn babies, regardless of the pregnant person's sex, some

---

[35] For views of same-sex marriage by faith tradition, see Leith Anderson, Chapter 12.
[36] Sandhya Somashekhar, *Catholic Groups Sue Over Obama Administration Transgender Requirement*, WASH. POST (Dec. 29, 2016), https://perma.cc/JM85-QLBB.
[37] *Id.* See Greenawalt, Chapter 8, for federal conscience protections, which extend to objections to sterilize another person.

doctors refuse to remove healthy uteruses from anyone, regardless of their gender identity.[38] Their decision simply reflects reasonable disagreement over the best medicine for gender dysphoria and the nature of medicine altogether (whether, for example, a healthy organ should ever be removed from a healthy body).[39] We should not use nondiscrimination policies to enforce orthodoxy on reasonably disputed issues of medical care. That would make nondiscrimination laws swords, not shields.

Just as reasonable medical treatments for gender dysphoria do not discriminate based on gender identity, neither do reasonable policies on sex-specific facilities. The bathroom, locker room, and housing policies at stake in this debate make reasonable – and explicitly lawful under federal law – distinctions based on "sex": anatomy, physiology, and biology. These policies do not take gender identity into account, much less do so invidiously. It is not because some people wear suits and ties and others wear dresses that there are separate bathrooms and locker rooms for men and women. The existence of sex-specific intimate facilities is explained not by our internal sense or social expressions of gender, but by our external manifestations of biology and the need for bodily privacy.[40]

By contrast, it would be invidious discrimination based on gender identity to say that students who identified with their biological sex could use one water fountain, while others had to use another. This would involve taking transgender status into account where it is irrelevant.

Thus, lawmakers should not use SOGI laws to coerce actions rooted in the conjugal view of marriage, medical practices rooted in reasonable views about medicine and bodily integrity, or policies about intimate facilities that reflect reasonable views of privacy. These reasonable actions should not be banned under SOGI laws, just as bans on sex-based discrimination do not force pro-lifers to perform abortions. Rather than simply granting exemptions from SOGI laws to allow some regulated actors to follow such policies, lawmakers should not ban those policies in the first place.

II SOGI LAWS, RELIGIOUS LIBERTY, AND RELIGIOUS NONDISCRIMINATION POLICIES

This section responds to two common charges of inconsistency in this position: that it is inconsistent to support (A) religious liberty but not SOGI laws, and (B) bans on discrimination based on religion but not based on SOGI. Both arguments miss telling differences between these policies. Neither position is inconsistent.

---

[38] This is particularly true for Catholic hospitals that decline to perform any sterilization procedures. *See* United States Conference of Catholic Bishops, *Ethical and Religious Directives for Catholic Health Care Services, Fifth Edition,* (2009), https://perma.cc/J84M-52WR.

[39] *See* ANDERSON, *supra* note 8.

[40] *See id.*

Under nondiscrimination laws, the government coerces some citizens on behalf of others. By contrast, civil liberties limit the government's ability to coerce others in order to protect the personal freedom of all. Thus, nondiscrimination laws force some to live by the majority's values while religious liberty laws protect the interest of all to live by their own beliefs. And while nondiscrimination policies can be justified in certain circumstances, there is no human right to them, as there is to religious liberty.

There are subtler but no less important contrasts between bans on SOGI non-discrimination and bans on religious nondiscrimination. Religious nondiscrimination policies directly protect one component of the common good. SOGI laws as currently crafted and applied do not. Bans on religious discrimination shield people from being penalized by others for participating in the fundamental human good of religion, which is itself a constitutive part of the common good.[41] But no such fundamental human good is at stake with current SOGI nondiscrimination policies as enforced. Policy crafted to help LGBT people meet their needs, in the ways described previously and later in this chapter, *could* function as shields to enable citizens to flourish and not as swords, and thus could be related to the common good. But SOGI laws as currently drafted and enforced are being used to compel people to embrace a new sexual orthodoxy that tears down social barriers to the pursuit of sexual autonomy. But such autonomy is not itself an intrinsic human good or part of the common good. In fact, to the extent that SOGI laws promote sexual autonomy as the new orthodoxy, they undermine crucial components of the common good: marriage and the personal and social norms and virtues that protect and promote it.

This last point returns to the fact that SOGI nondiscrimination laws are used as swords to punish reasonable people for acting on honorable beliefs – as religion (and other) nondiscrimination laws are not. That is, bans on religion-based discrimination are not used to force religious organizations to violate their sincere beliefs. Nor are they used to force secular organizations or anyone else to violate theirs. Religious nondiscrimination laws have not been used, for example, to force Planned Parenthood to hire pro-life Catholics. No one filled a legal complaint claiming it was unlawful religion-based discrimination when Mozilla Firefox forced out CEO Brendan Eich because he had donated to California's marriage initiative – even though his donations were rooted in his religious identity and its constitutive beliefs. Likewise, when A&E suspended Phil Robertson from *Duck Dynasty* because he expressed support for biblical views of sexuality, Americans who objected to this decision did not allege that it violated religion nondiscrimination policies. Religious nondiscrimination laws simply do not seek to impose religious orthodoxy on the country.

---

[41] *See* Corvino, Anderson & Girgis, *supra* note 10.

SOGI nondiscrimination policies *are* used to impose sexual orthodoxy. They are used to force Catholic schools to employ people who undermine their sexual values and evangelical bakers to lend their artistic talents to messages about marriage with which they disagree.[42] SOGI laws are intended to "punish" people of good will who simply seek the freedom to lead their lives in accordance with their beliefs about human sexuality. Religious nondiscrimination laws are not used to punish those the majority considers wrong on religion – just the opposite, these protections are equally available to all religions, including minority faiths.

This difference flows partly from differences in how SOGI and religious nondiscrimination laws are interpreted. SOGI laws are read to protect not only LGBT identities but also forms of associated conduct. But the laws themselves rarely address which conduct counts, leaving human rights commissioners and judges free to decide that it is gender identity discrimination for Planet Fitness to base locker room access on biology, not identity, and that it is sexual orientation discrimination for Catholic Charities to seek out a mom and a dad for every child. [43]

But the law is much more nuanced about when it does or does not protect conduct (in addition to status) under other nondiscrimination laws. Religious nondiscrimination laws apply to status and certain religiously inspired conduct, but not to such an extent as to impose a religious orthodoxy – *i.e.*, to force other actors to undermine their own missions. Planned Parenthood cannot refuse to hire a pro-choice Jew because he wears a yarmulke, but it can refuse to hire a pro-life Jew, even when his pro-life convictions flow from his Jewish status and identity. This leaves Planned Parenthood free to make reasonable distinctions based on its mission, even when living by that mission has a disparate impact on people with a certain religious identity and conduct.

Similarly, even if same-sex relationships flow from gay and lesbian identities, supporters of conjugal marriage should not be coerced under SOGI nondiscrimination laws to relent on convictions around marriage. Likewise, even if cross-dressing flows from transgender identity, a policy against biological males entering a women's locker-room should not be viewed as discrimination based on gender identity.[44] Indeed, as noted, sex nondiscrimination laws already allow for such reasonable policies. As for race nondiscrimination laws, they apply almost exclusively to status – what, after all, is the conduct that flows from race? And so, while race

---

[42] See Hill, Chapter 26, for discussion of Title VII protections for religious hiring; for discussion of *Masterpiece Cakeshop*, see McClain, Chapter 17; Smith, Chapter 18; and McConnell, Chapter 28.

[43] Amanda Prestigiacomo, *Michigan Court Tells Woman She'll Have To Accept Men in Her Gym Locker Room*, DailyWire (June 6, 2017), https://perma.cc/Q4EN-EHHP. See also Adams, Chapter 32, for discussion of facilities regulation in Utah's hiring and housing SOGI nondiscrimination law; Greenawalt, Chapter 8; and Berg, Chapter 24, for discussion of adoption placement.

[44] For cases interpreting sex discrimination to encompass gender identity or sexual orientation, see Hill, Chapter 26.

nondiscrimination laws impose an orthodoxy on the nation – colorblindness – that result is justified because no conduct flows from race and there is no reasonable, decent, and honorable alternative view.[45]

Thus, SOGI nondiscrimination policies are fundamentally unlike civil rights laws that protect against discrimination on the basis of race, sex, and even religion. The latter do not burden other fundamental values, but reflect nuanced understandings of what constitutes unlawful discrimination, and are not used as a sword to enforce orthodoxy against people with reasonable, decent, and honorable disagreements, but as a shield to protect people from unjust discrimination that prevents their full participation in society and their ability to flourish.

III NEED FOR POLICY SHAPES THE PROTECTIONS AND DEFINITIONS

When crafting any necessary policy to allow people who identify as LGBT to meet their needs without undermining the common good, lawmakers must (1) precisely identify the need to be met, (2) tailor the scope of any remedy, (3) carefully determine which circumstances count as invidious discrimination and which do not, and (4) avoid gratuitous burdens on conduct flowing from reasonable disagreement or on the rights of conscience, religion, and speech. Of course, what counts as a gratuitous burden will depend on the needs being addressed.[46]

When Congress enacted the Civil Rights Act of 1964 (1964 Act), blacks were treated as second-class citizens. Individuals, businesses, and associations across the country, without justification, excluded blacks in ways that caused grave material and social harms, market forces did not act as a corrective, and all this occurred with the tacit and often explicit backing of government. A resort to the law was necessary.[47] And because race is almost always irrelevant, and discrimination on its basis was so firmly entrenched, the Act appropriately allowed only very limited exemptions once a business was defined as a covered public accommodation.[48]

---

[45] For similar sentiment about race discrimination, see Perry, Chapter 20.

[46] While SOGI laws, as currently drafted and applied, are not justified, that does not exclude the idea of more tailored policies that would address the mistreatment of LGBT people and at the same time would leave all Americans – not just the lucky few who are sufficiently well-connected to be exempted from SOGI laws – free to act on their good-faith convictions. The fundamental starting point of any such policy discussion, however, would be an examination of the need to ban SOGI discrimination at all. To date, very little attention has been given to what exactly the policy need is. *See* Ryan T. Anderson, *How to Think About Sexual Orientation and Gender Identity (SOGI) Policies and Religious Freedom*, HERITAGE FOUND. (Feb. 13, 2017), https://perma.cc/VLU3-L7WY.

[47] Title II of the Civil Rights Act, 42 U.S.C. § 2000a(1)-(6) (2012). Portions of this paragraph are adapted from CORVINO, ANDERSON & GIRGIS, DEBATING RELIGIOUS LIBERTY AND DISCRIMINATION, *supra* note 10.

[48] See Laycock, Chapter 3, for discussion of the limited number of establishments reached under the 1964 Act; Wilson, Chapter 30, for the purpose behind this limited reach.

Contrast sex-based discrimination. The scope of federal nondiscrimination law was narrower in the first place and allowed broader exemptions because of differences in the nature and history of racism and sexism. For example, federal law, even today, does not ban sex discrimination in public accommodations. And the ban on sex discrimination in education expressly allows for sex-specific intimate facilities for any actors, and it offers broad exemptions for religious liberty claimants.[49] In other words, the scope of regulation, definition of discrimination, and extent of religious liberty exemptions differed materially between race and sex discrimination bans because these two characteristics are different and give rise to different policy needs.

Likewise, sexual orientation and gender identity are different from both sex and race (and from each other). There is no analogue of Jim Crow laws for LGBT people. There are no denials of the right to vote, no lynchings, no signs over water fountains saying "Gay" and "Straight." Of course, bigotry against LGBT individuals exists and our communities must fight it. But it would be too crude – and too burdensome on important interests in religion, speech, and the like – to adopt for SOGI nondiscrimination laws the breadth of coverage meant to respond to Jim Crow laws and then tack on some exemptions.

That becomes clear when one considers the cases to which SOGI laws are controversially applied. These involve an astonishingly small number of business owners who cannot in good conscience support same-sex wedding celebrations. Most, like Jack Phillips, treat gay people with respect while simply declining to help celebrate or facilitate same-sex weddings.[50] Professor Andrew Koppelman, a long-time LGBT advocate, acknowledges as much:

> Hardly any of these cases have occurred: a handful in a country of 300 million people. In all of them, the people who objected to the law were asked directly to facilitate same-sex relationships, by providing wedding, adoption, or artificial insemination services, counseling, or rental of bedrooms. There have been no claims of a right to simply refuse to deal with gay people.[51]

Not only is there no movement to deny LGBT people access to markets, goods, or services, there is a reason why there have been "no claims of a right to simply refuse to deal with gay people": no faith teaches it.[52] In this vein, as one of this volume's

---

[49] 20 U.S.C. §§ 1681–1688 (2012).

[50] See Smith, Chapter 18, for the importance of this fact; McConnell, Chapter 28, for record citations.

[51] Andrew Koppelman, *A Zombie in the Supreme Court: The Elane Photography Cert Denial*, 7 ALA. C.R. & C.L. L. REV. 77, 77–95 (2016).

[52] David Bernstein & Doug Laycock, *Guest Post from Prof. Doug Laycock: What Arizona SB1062 Actually Said*, WASH. POST (Feb. 27, 2014), https://perma.cc/3LLL-FWDA (quoting longtime same-sex marriage supporter Douglas Laycock: "I know of no American religious group that teaches discrimination against gays as such, and few judges would be persuaded of the sincerity of such a claim. The religious liberty issue with respect to gays and lesbians is about directly facilitating the marriage, as with wedding services and marital counseling.").

editors, Robin Fretwell Wilson, noted a decade ago, "The religious and moral convictions that motivate objectors to refuse to facilitate same-sex marriage simply cannot be marshaled to justify racial discrimination."[53]

In sum, the refusals of wedding vendors such as Phillips have nothing like the sweep or shape of racist or sexist practices. They do not span every domain; they do not even cover just the professional sphere – they focus only on marriage and sex. They are about refusing to communicate certain messages about marriage, not avoiding contact with certain people.[54] Thus, Barronelle Stutzman, who declined to create floral arrangements to celebrate the same-sex wedding of a client whom she had served for nearly ten years, clearly did not think gay people vicious, incompetent, or unproductive. She did not think they mattered less or deserved shunning. She employed gay people and served them faithfully as clients, gladly creating anything else they requested.[55] As Professor Koppelman writes, "These people are not homophobic bigots who want to hurt gay people."[56]

The few cases of refusals that have garnered media attention – cases involving cake designers, a florist, and a photographer – hardly diminish a single person or couple's range of opportunities for room, board, or entertainment. If businesses started to refuse service specifically to gay individuals, it is hard to imagine a sector of commerce or a region of the United States where media coverage would not provide a remedy swift and decisive enough to restore access in days or shutter the business. The LGBT community's political influence is profound and still growing. When corporate giants such as the NBA, the NCAA, Apple, Salesforce, Delta, and Coca-Cola threaten to boycott states over laws merely giving believers their day in court,[57] it is hard to see the case for legally sanctioning the one baker in the state who cannot make same-sex wedding cakes.

Finally, progressives such as Professor Koppelman have noted that cultural acceptance weakens the case for legal regulation: "With respect to the religious condemnation of homosexuality, this marginalization is already taking place. But that does not mean that the conservatives need to be punished or driven out of the marketplace. There remains room for the kind of cold respect that toleration among exclusivist religions entails."[58] Elsewhere Koppelman expands: "The reshaping of

---

[53] Robin Fretwell Wilson, *Matters of Conscience: Lessons for Same-Sex Marriage from the Healthcare Context*, in SAME-SEX MARRIAGE AND RELIGIOUS LIBERTY: EMERGING CONFLICTS 101 (Douglas Laycock et al., eds. 2008).

[54] See Smith, Chapter 18, for claims by a Washington photographer, Barronelle Stutzman; McConnell, Chapter 28, for recitation of Phillips' claims.

[55] *See* Smith, Chapter 18; Barronelle Stutzman, *Why a Friend Is Suing Me: The Arlene's Flowers Story*, SEATTLE TIMES (Nov. 9, 2015), https://perma.cc/4BG5-2WAA.

[56] Andrew Koppelman, *Gay Rights, Religious Accommodations, and the Purposes of Antidiscrimination Law*, 88 S. CAL. L. REV. 619, 625 (2015).

[57] *See* John Schuppe, *Corporate Boycotts Become Key Weapon in Gay Rights Fight*, NBC NEWS (Mar. 16, 2016), https://perma.cc/5X6P-67K9. For defense of RFRAs, see Laycock, Chapter 3; for state RFRAs, see Appendix, Chapter 35.

[58] Koppelman, *supra* note 56, at 626.

culture to marginalize anti-gay discrimination is inevitable. To say it again: The gay rights movement has won. It will not be stopped by a few exemptions. It should be magnanimous in victory."[59]

IV CONCLUSION

In 1993, in *Bray v. Alexandria Women's Health Clinic*, the Supreme Court resolutely rejected the argument that pro-lifers are inherently discriminatory: "[w]hatever one thinks of abortion, it cannot be denied that there are common and respectable reasons for opposing it, other than hatred of, or condescension toward (or indeed any view at all concerning), women."[60]

The same is true when it comes to marriage as the union of husband and wife: there are common and respectable reasons for supporting it that have nothing to do with hatred or condescension. But this is not true when it comes to opposition to interracial marriage – and this is where the analogies to racism break down. When the Supreme Court struck down bans on interracial marriage, it did not say that opposition to interracial marriage was based on "decent and honorable premises" and held "in good faith by reasonable and sincere people here and throughout the world." It did not say it, because it could not say it.

As a result, following *Obergefell*, our policy toward supporters of the conjugal view of marriage should mirror our policy toward pro-lifers after *Roe* – not our policy toward racists after *Loving*. After *Roe*, Americans did not use sex nondiscrimination law as a sword to punish pro-lifers. Just the opposite: they enacted legislation at the local, state, and federal levels to protect the rights of pro-life Americans not to be punished by government for living out their beliefs. The Church and Weldon Amendments have protected the conscience rights of pro-life medical personnel to refuse to perform or assist with abortions, and the Hyde Amendment and Mexico City policy prevent the use of federal taxpayer money to support abortion.[61]

Likewise, governments must avoid penalizing people for acting on their view that marriage is the union of husband and wife, that sexual relations are properly reserved for such a union, or that maleness and femaleness are objective biological realities. Protections for such citizens need not undermine the valid purposes of laws meant to allow LGBT people to meet their needs – such as eliminating the public effects of anti-gay bigotry – because support for conjugal marriage is not anti-gay. Protecting freedom here sends no message about the supposed inferiority of those identifying as gay; it sends no message about sexual orientation at all. It says that citizens who support the historic understanding of sex and marriage are not bigots. It ensures their

---

[59] *Id.* at 628.
[60] *See* Bray v. Alexandria Women's Health Clinic, 506 U.S. 263, 267–68 (1993).
[61] *See* Greenawalt, Chapter 8. For more on the Mexico City Policy, see *The Mexico City Policy: An Explainer*, KAISER FAMILY FOUND., https://perma.cc/P2BN-9ZRR.

equal social status and opportunities. It protects their businesses, livelihoods, and professional vocations, and (perhaps eventually) professional licenses in fields such as medicine and law.[62] And it benefits the rest of society by allowing traditional people of faith in good conscience to continue offering social services and education.

In short, pro-life conscience protections do not undermine *Roe v. Wade* or women's equality. Like pro-life conscience protections, conscience protections for conjugal marriage supporters do nothing to undermine *Obergefell* or LGBT equality. Both protect human dignity and human rights for dissenters from prevailing social norms. Both promote the common good.

---

[62] For specific protections against professional discipline in the Utah Compromise, see Adams, Chapter 32.

28

Dressmakers, Bakers, and the Equality of Rights

Michael W. McConnell

Around the time briefs were being written in the *Masterpiece Cakeshop*[1] case and Washingtonians were preparing for the 2016 inauguration festivities, the *Washington Post* ran a story in its Arts and Entertainment section entitled, "Should Designers Dress Melania and Ivanka? The Question Is More Complex than It Seems."[2] According to the article, President-elect Trump had run a campaign that inspired "waves of racism and violence" and "[w]hether to associate with him ha[d] become a moral question." One designer, Sophie Theallet, publicly declared she would not design a dress for the first lady, explaining that "as an independent fashion brand, we consider our voice an expression of our artistic and philosophical ideas." The article stated that a designer like Theallet

> sees fashion as a way of expressing her views about beauty and the way women are perceived in society. Fashion is her tool for communicating her world vision. In the same way that a poet's words or a musician's lyrics are a deeply personal reflection of the person who wrote them, a fashion designer's work can be equally as intimate.

The article went on to explain the difference between selling "wares" off the rack "at retail" and "making one-of-a kind garments for individuals." According to the article, that difference explains "why declining to dress a celebrity is not the equivalent of refusing service."

Toward the end of the article, the writer expresses her own view. Noting that other designers "would happily, and without reservation, create a splendid wardrobe for the incoming first lady," the writer concludes: "for those designers for whom fashion serves as their voice in the world, they should not feel obligated to say something in which they do not believe."

---

[1] 137 S. Ct. 2290 (2017) (granting cert.).
[2] All quotations here are from Robin Givhan, *Should Designers Dress Melania and Ivanka? The Question Is More Complex Than It Seems*, WASH. POST (Jan. 12, 2016), https://perma.cc/2SRE-GB6Y.

There do not seem to have been any angry letters to the editor. No one insisted that a dressmaker who enters commerce has an obligation to serve all comers and forfeits any right to withhold services on moral or ideological grounds. No one wrote that designing a dress is not a form of expression. Presumably, while some Americans might agree with Sophie Theallat's decision not to lend her skills to the Trump inauguration and others might disagree, no one would question the expressive nature of the activity or disagree with the *Washington Post* writer's conclusion that "those designers whose work serves as their voice in the world should not feel obligated to say something in which they do not believe." In fact, it is a common feature of American life for people to refuse to do business with those with whom they have moral or ideological disagreements. Several Rockettes refused to dance at the Trump inaugural.[3] Pro-life women can refuse to be treated by doctors who perform abortions.[4] PayPal refused to build a production facility in a state that enacted a law it disapproved of about transgender bathrooms.[5] Political consultants (some of them) work only for politicians they favor.[6] Actors can decline roles in productions that communicate a racist message – even if their own roles have no such message.[7] Sports leagues have refused to compete in a state that passed a Religious Freedom Restoration Act.[8] I know a public relations agency that would not do work for the local Catholic diocese because of the Catholic positions on same-sex marriage and abortion. And the US Supreme Court has already – unanimously – held that an economic boycott based on race, namely a boycott of white-owned businesses, is a constitutionally protected form of protest.[9] The dressmakers profiled in the *Washington Post* are just the latest example.

I HOW DOES THIS COMPARE TO *MASTERPIECE CAKESHOP?*

This brings us back to *Masterpiece Cakeshop*. The legal issue in that hotly contested case is whether a Colorado baker named Jack Phillips can be punished for refusing

---

[3] Katie Rogers & Gia Kourlas, *A Trump Inauguration Casualty: The Silent, Smiling Rockettes*, N.Y. TIMES (Jan. 18, 2017), https://perma.cc/3CRU-BUC8?type=image.

[4] Wendy Wright, *Should Patients Be Limited to Only Pro-Abortion Health Providers?*, CONCERNED WOMEN FOR AM. (July 7, 2011), https://perma.cc/9KUD-HRT5; Matthew S. Bowman & Christopher P. Schandevel, *The Harmony Between Professional Conscience Rights and Patients' Right of Access*, 6 PHOENIX L. REV. 31 (2012).

[5] Jon Schwartz & Elizabeth Weise, *PayPal Withdraws Planned N.C. Expansion Due to Anti-gay Law*, USA TODAY (Apr. 6, 2016) https://perma.cc/JZC2-6N3L.

[6] For examples of consultants who work for candidates with specific viewpoints, see STRATEGIC CAMPAIGN GROUP, https://perma.cc/ZL2J-P4PG (Republican candidates) and FELDMAN STRATEGIES, https://perma.cc/3BVR-AH27 (Democratic candidates).

[7] *See, e.g.*, Rebecca Strasburg, *Backstage Experts Answer: When Is It OK to Turn Down a Role*, BACKSTAGE (Apr. 22, 2015), https://perma.cc/6KK8-8H4Y.

[8] Dennis O'Donnell, *NCAA Final Four Boycott over Indiana Religious Freedom Law Would Be Wrong*, CBS SF BAY AREA NEWS (Mar. 31, 2015), https://perma.cc/YJ9M-D84M.

[9] NAACP v. Claiborne Hardware, Inc., 458 U.S. 886 (1982).

to create a custom cake for an event of which he morally disapproves.[10] In all but one respect, his circumstances are identical to those of Sophie Theallet, the dress designer. Like Theallet, Phillips regards his creative work as his "voice in the world" and as reflecting his view of beauty and of marriage.[11] Like Theallet, Phillips has moral qualms about the event and does not wish to "associate" with it.[12] Like an inaugural gown, a wedding cake is an expression of its designer's "values" and "point of view" – even if the dress contains no words and no symbols specifically referring to Trump.[13] It is the event at which the dress (or cake) would be used that supplies the expressive context – not necessarily anything particular to the dress (or cake). Like dress designers, Phillips distinguishes between selling off-the-shelf items to a customer on a retail basis and "making one-of-a-kind garments [or cakes] for individuals."[14] And just as there are many designers "who would happily, and without reservation, create a splendid wardrobe for the first lady," the record in the Colorado case shows that there were dozens of bakers in close proximity to Masterpiece Cakeshop who would happily create a cake for their occasion.[15] This means there is no practical burden on Melania or on the couple from the denial of service – only the insult that comes from knowing that another human being disapproves, which is precisely what the dressmaker and the baker wish to communicate, and the government has no right to prevent.

As the dressmaker news story illustrates, there is no genuine doubt that artisans express themselves in their creations and in their decisions not to associate with events that are inconsistent with their beliefs and values. If *Masterpiece Cakeshop* had arisen in any other cultural context, civil libertarians would easily recognize the expressive character of the decision to create (or refuse to create) dresses and cakes

[10] Masterpiece Cakeshop v. Colorado Civil Rights Commission, No. 16-111, Order Granting Certiorari (June 26, 2017), https://perma.cc/GB2E-Q7WF ("The question presented is: Whether applying Colorado's public accommodations law to compel Phillips to create expression that violates his sincerely held religious beliefs about marriage violates the Free Speech or Free Exercise Clauses of the First Amendment.").

[11] Appellant's Reply Brief, Masterpiece Cakeshop, Inc. v. Craig, 2015 WL 13622552 (Colo. App.), at 6 ("He believes God granted him artistic and creative abilities and that he is religiously obligated to use those abilities in a manner that honors God. (*Id.* at 475, ¶ 62.)").

[12] *Id.* ("Nor will Phillips create wedding cakes honoring same-sex marriages, regardless who orders them, because Phillips believes that God ordained marriage as the sacred union between one man and one woman, (*id.* at 476, ¶ 67.), and that marriage exemplifies the relationship between Christ and His followers. (*Id.* at 469, ¶ 61–63.)").

[13] *Id.* ("That Phillips' artistic creations may not include words is irrelevant to the question of whether they are expression protected by the First Amendment, for 'the Constitution looks beyond written or spoken words as mediums of expression.' *Hurley*, 515. U.S. at 569.").

[14] Brief of Petitioner, Masterpiece Cakeshop, Ltd. v. Colorado Civil Rights Commission, 2017 WL 3913762 (U.S.), 9 (U.S. 2017) ("These limitations on Phillips's custom work have no bearing on his premade baked items, which he sells to everyone, no questions asked.").

[15] Appellant's Reply Brief, *supra* note 11, at 22 ("There are some 300 other bakeries in the Denver area that are available to fulfill such requests. The State has no vital interest in compelling Phillips personally to provide such a non-essential service, especially when scores of other bakeries are ready and willing to do so.").

for ceremonial events. The only difference between the baker and the dress designer is that the dress designer disapproves of the Trump inauguration while the baker disapproves of same-sex weddings. Unfortunately, for some people, that makes all the difference.

Once we recognize that the creation of symbolic objects such as inaugural gowns and wedding cakes can be expressive, it ceases to be surprising that the First Amendment extends its protection – even to what one justice during oral argument derisively dismissed as mere "food."[16] The Supreme Court has long recognized that nonverbal conduct, such as the burning of a draft card to protest the war,[17] sleeping in a park to protest treatment of the homeless,[18] or wearing an army uniform in an antiwar film[19] is entitled to a measure of constitutional protection. To be sure, the government can regulate the material impacts even of expressive conduct, but it cannot use its power to regulate conduct as a backdoor way of punishing its communicative content. And it cannot force people engaged in an expressive activity to create or convey messages they disagree with.

It has been argued, nonetheless, that the *Masterpiece Cakeshop* case is not really about freedom of expression. The Colorado law, according to an *amicus* brief written by a distinguished lawyer and academic, "does not regulate the creation of messages," but only the selection of customers.[20] The challengers to the Colorado law "have a First Amendment right to pick their message, but not to choose their customers based on sexual orientation."[21] That is a plain misstatement of the facts. The record shows that the Colorado baker, Phillips, happily produces goods for customers without regard to their sexual orientation.[22] He does not discriminate among types of customer; instead, he (like the dressmaker) refuses to create cakes that celebrate ideas of which he disapproves. He is the mirror image of a gay photographer who refuses to provide his services to an evangelical rally *against* same-sex marriage. The photographer is not discriminating on the basis of religion; he is not anti-evangelical; he is opposed to the message of the rally. By the same

---

[16] Transcript of oral arguments, Masterpiece Cakeshop, Ltd. v. Colorado Civil Rights Commission, 2017 WL 6025739 (U.S.), 14 (U.S. Oral. Arg. 2017) ("Justice Sotomayor: So that begs the question, when have we ever given protection to a food? The primary purpose of a food of any kind is to be eaten.").

[17] U.S. v. O'Brien, 391 U.S. 367 (1968).

[18] Clark v. Cmty. for Creative Non-violence, 468 U.S. 288.

[19] Schacht v. U.S., 398 U.S. 58 (1970).

[20] Brief of Floyd Abrams, et al., Masterpiece Cakeshop v. Colorado Civil Rights Commission, No. 16–111 at 2 (Oct. 30, 2017), https://perma.cc/W7UZ-GA94 ("Colorado does not regulate the creation of messages . . . [T]he Colorado law does not seek to regulate messages but to prohibit discrimination against customers.").

[21] *Id.*

[22] Brief of Petitioner, Masterpiece Cakeshop, Ltd. v. Colorado Civil Rights Commission, 2017 WL 3913762 (U.S.), 8–9 (U.S. 2017).

token, Jack Phillips does not discriminate against customers on the basis of their sexual orientation. He refuses to bake cakes that celebrate a same-sex wedding, which he regards as contrary to God's will.

The State of Colorado is regulating the services of bakers on the basis of their ideological viewpoint. Three pro-same-sex-marriage bakers were approached and asked to bake cakes to be served at anti-same-sex events, and all three refused.[23] When the disappointed customers complained to the Colorado authorities, invoking the theory that businesses have an obligation to serve all comers, the state responded that these bakers were not discriminating against particular customers but simply refusing to assist events they found "offensive."[24] Exactly the same is true of Phillips. The inconsistent treatment of the cases makes clear that the state is simply playing favorites: punishing speech with which it disagrees, protecting speech with which it agrees. That violates fundamental principles of the First Amendment.

II LESSONS FROM THE NOT-SO-DISTANT PAST

The closest analogy in the Supreme Court's cases is the unanimous decision in *Hurley v. Irish-American Gay, Lesbian, and Bisexual Group of Boston.*[25] In that case, a veterans group organized a parade on St. Patrick's Day, allowing a wide and seemingly miscellaneous collection of groups to march.[26] The case arose because the organizer refused to allow a group to march carrying a banner announcing themselves as the "Irish American Gay, Lesbian, and Bisexual Group of Boston."[27] The parade organizers did not discriminate against gay or lesbian parade marchers as such – indeed they made no inquiry into the sexual orientation of anyone marching in the parade – but they objected to the message conveyed by the banner, and refused to include it as part of their parade.[28] Because the parade organizers allowed a wide variety of groups to march, the Massachusetts courts defined the parade as a "public accommodation," much as the Colorado courts have defined Masterpiece Cakeshop as a public accommodation – meaning that it was forbidden to

---

[23] *See* discussion of Jack v. Azucar Bakery, Jack v. Gateaux, Ltd., and Jack v. Le Bakery Sensual, Inc. in Brief of Amici Curiae William Jack and the National Center for Law and Policy in Support of Petitioners, Masterpiece Cakeshop, Ltd. v. Colorado Civil Rights Commission, 2017 WL 4004521 (U.S.) (U.S. 2017).

[24] Craig v. Masterpiece Cakeshop, Inc., 370 P.3d 272, 282 n.8 (Colo. Ct. App. 2015).

[25] 515 U.S. 557 (1995).

[26] Hurley, 515 U.S. at 560.

[27] Irish-American Gay, Lesbian and Bisexual Group of Boston v. Boston, 636 N.E.2d 1293, 1295 (Mass. 1994).

[28] "Petitioners disclaim any intent to exclude homosexuals as such, and no individual member of GLIB claims to have been excluded from parading as a member of any group that the Council has approved to march. Instead, the disagreement goes to the admission of GLIB as its own parade unit carrying its own banner." Hurley, 515 U.S. at 572.

discriminate on various identity grounds, including sexual orientation.[29] The Massachusetts courts held that exclusion of the group violated the public accommodations law.[30] Describing the parade as lacking the element of expression for purposes of the First Amendment, the Massachusetts court held that forcing the inclusion of the group carrying the banner would not violate the First Amendment.[31] The court issued an order forcing the parade organizers to include the gay and lesbian group to march in the future.

The Supreme Court reversed. It began by noting that public accommodation laws are "well within the State's power" and "do not, as a general matter, violate the First or Fourteenth Amendment."[32] A public accommodations law "does not, on its face, target speech or discriminate on the basis of its content, the focal point of the prohibition being rather on the act of discriminating against individuals in the provision of publicly available goods, privileges, and services on the proscribed grounds."[33] Nonetheless, the Court held that "[i]n the case before us, ... the Massachusetts law has been applied in a peculiar way" namely, that its enforcement action was not based on exclusion of any individuals on the basis of their sexual orientation, but instead on the decision of the organizers not to allow the group to march under its banner.[34] The state's order "essentially requir[ed] petitioners to alter the expressive content of their parade" by including a message they did not approve.[35] "[O]nce the expressive character of both the parade and the marching GLIB [Irish-American Gay, Lesbian and Bisexual Group of Boston] contingent is understood," the Court explained, "it becomes apparent that the state court's application of the statute had the effect of declaring the sponsors' speech itself to be the public accommodation," in violation of "fundamental rule of protection under the First Amendment, that a speaker has the autonomy to choose the content of his own message."[36] Nor does it matter that the dispute arose in the context of the commercial marketplace. The right to "autonomy to control one's own speech," the Court stated, is "enjoyed by business corporations generally and by ordinary people."[37]

The same logic should apply in *Masterpiece Cakeshop*. As in *Hurley*, the state's public accommodation law on its face is unobjectionable, but as in *Hurley*, the "peculiar" application of the law tramples on First Amendment rights. When the baker refuses customers not on the basis of their own protected characteristics, but because he does not wish to embrace their message, the law ceases to be an

---

[29] *See* Mass. G.L. c. 272, §§ 92A & 98 and Colo. Rev. Stat. Ann. §§ 24-34-301(7), 24-34-601(1).
[30] Irish-American Gay, Lesbian and Bisexual Group of Boston, 636 N.E.2d 1293.
[31] *Id.* at 1300.
[32] *Hurley*, 515 U.S. at 573.
[33] *Id.*
[34] *Id.*
[35] *Id.* at 572.
[36] *Id.*
[37] *Id.* at 574.

anti-discrimination statute in the ordinary sense and becomes a regulation of speech. Even if Phillips's own "specific expressive purpose" were difficult to discern (and it is not), he has the same right that the parade organizers in *Hurley* had "not to propound a particular point of view."

Some may say that this prioritizes one right over another – the right of freedom of speech, or perhaps the freedom of religion – over the right not to suffer invidious discrimination. However, this is a misunderstanding. Instead, a decision in favor of the baker would put these rights on an equal plane. The rights of freedom of speech and religion do not entail the right to compel others to support, participate in, or endorse the exercise of the right. Dissenters have the right to express their views, but no right to complain if other people disapprove. It does not violate their dignity for other individuals to abhor their message, and they have no claim of "discrimination" if other individuals refuse to cooperate in or carry their messages. No one doubts that an artist or artisan can refuse to assist a political party or ideological movement he or she opposes. No one doubts the right to refuse to perform in or assist in a worship service. We prohibit religious discrimination,[38] but a Jewish printer does not have to print church programs declaring Jesus to be the messiah. We prohibit racial discrimination, but a singer cannot be compelled to perform the national anthem at an NAACP convention if she objects to that organization's policies. There is no need to draw lines between architects, speech writers, public relations firms, photographers, musicians, bakers, or florists: no one engaged in an expressive activity can be compelled to use their talents in support of a cause they disapprove of. This has always been true in America. To say that same-sex weddings are on an equal plane is not to treat the right of same-sex marriage as second class in any way. It simply treats this new right with the same respect, and the same limits, that the older rights of speech and religion have long been treated.

III CONCLUSION

The *Washington Post* was right. Dress designers have no obligation to create an inaugural gown for Ivanka or Melania Trump. "[A]s for those designers for whom fashion serves as their voice in the world, they should not feel obligated to say something in which they do not believe."[39] The Trump inauguration stands for ideas that many Americans do not share, and an inaugural gown – even without specific words or markings – is part of the symbolism of that event. A wedding is no less symbolic. Nor is the cake. The fashioning of expressive symbols cannot be compelled.

[38] Title VII of the Civil Rights Act of 1964, 42 U.S.C. § 2000e (2012).
[39] Givhan, *supra* note 2.

29

It's Not About the Cake

Against "Altaring" the Public Marketplace

Jennifer C. Pizer

Let's be honest. The national conversation is not really about wedding cakes and who pees where. It is about whether LGBT people are equal in this country and whether we are entitled to be treated like everyone else in public life.

Two 2017 cases challenged the US Supreme Court to decide whether religious objections to who LGBT persons are can justify discrimination by commercial businesses, licensed medical and social service providers, and even government employees. In one, the Supreme Court agreed to decide whether Jack Phillips was entitled to refuse to sell a wedding cake to Charlie Craig and David Mullins.[1] In the second, the Court declined to decide whether a Mississippi law that permits religion-based discrimination against same-sex couples and transgender people in numerous contexts violates the Establishment Clause or the Equal Protection Clause.[2]

These cases paralleled more than 100 bills in 30 states that year proposing to expand religious rights to discriminate or to target transgender people,[3] who already are among the most marginalized and vulnerable members of our society.[4] Prior years had witnessed similar legislative floods.[5] For Attorney General Jeff Sessions,

---

[1] Masterpiece Cakeshop, Ltd. v. Colo. Civil Rights Comm'n, No. 16–111, 137 S. Ct. 2290 (2017).

[2] Protecting Freedom of Conscience from Government Discrimination Act, MISS. CODE ANN. § 11–62-1 (2016), https://perma.cc/X29J-YQPX; Barber v. Bryant, 827 F.3d 671 (5th Cir. 2017), *cert. denied*, 2018 U.S. LEXIS 113 (U.S. Jan. 8, 2018) (No. 17–547).

[3] *See* Julie Moreau, *129 Anti-LGBTQ State Bills Were Introduced in 2017, New Report Says*, NBC NEWS (Jan. 12, 2018), https://perma.cc/7TWU-LVEP; Sarah Warbelow & Breanna Diaz, *2017 State Equality Index*, HUMAN RIGHTS CAMPAIGN FOUND. 6 (2017), https://perma.cc/3HAX-Z296 (identifying bills).

[4] *See generally* Sandy E. James et al., *The Report of the 2015 U.S. Transgender Survey*, NAT'L CTR. FOR TRANSGENDER EQUALITY (2016), https://perma.cc/L5VB-GZG3 [hereinafter *U.S. Transgender Survey*].

[5] *See* Sarah Warbelow & Breanna Diaz, *LGBTQ–Related Bills Considered in 2016*, HUMAN RIGHTS CAMPAIGN FOUND. (2016), https://perma.cc/YYQ4-ZKMZ [hereinafter *LGBTQ–Related Bills Considered in 2016*].

this outpouring was to be expected: "[M]any Americans ... are concerned about what this changing cultural climate means for the future of religious liberty."[6]

This chapter offers reassurance – and a caution. First, inclusion and equal treatment of LGBT people and their families is not a threat to religious liberty as that important right has been understood for generations. Just as there is no war on Christmas,[7] Christian beliefs and freedom of worship are not under attack. But, debilitating discrimination against LGBT people does pervade America, diminishing countless lives that deserve equal freedom, dignity, and opportunity. Much of this discrimination, though certainly not all, is done in the name of religion. Permission to discriminate in a business, public services agency, or government function has not been – and must not become – an element of protection for religious exercise. The First Amendment, the Supreme Court instructs, "embraces two concepts – freedom to believe and freedom to act. The first is absolute but, in the nature of things, the second cannot be. Conduct remains subject to regulation for the protection of society."[8]

Thus, for example, Americans have officially rejected racial segregation regardless of religious motivation.[9] Likewise, Help Wanted ads are no longer segregated by sex and, despite the religious objections of some, women can be primary wage earners, practice law, and drive school buses.[10] More recently, courts have applied this lesson to protect unmarried heterosexual couples' access to rental housing.[11]

The core principle in these cases has allowed our society to function with more cohesion than many other societies: everyone must be treated equally in public life

---

[6] Jeff Sessions, *Here's The Speech Jeff Sessions Delivered to Christian First Amendment Lawyers*, THE FEDERALIST (July 13, 2017), https://perma.cc/WSX3-72L7 [hereinafter *Prepared Remarks to ADF*].

[7] *Compare War on Christmas*, FOX NEWS INSIDER, https://perma.cc/YH3J-6762, *and* JOHN GIBSON, THE WAR ON CHRISTMAS: HOW THE LIBERAL PLOT TO BAN THE SACRED CHRISTIAN HOLIDAY IS WORSE THAN YOU THOUGHT (Sentinel Trade Publisher 2006), *with* Dan Cassino, *How Fox News Created the War on Christmas*, HARV. BUS. REV. (Dec. 9, 2016), https://perma.cc/X5Q9-H5XC, *and* Liam Stack, *How the "War on Christmas" Controversy Was Created*, N.Y. TIMES (Dec. 19, 2016), https://perma.cc/L5UD-6FWV.

[8] Cantwell v. Connecticut, 310 U.S. 296, 303–04 (1940).

[9] In *Newman v. Piggie Park Enters., Inc.*, 390 U.S. 400 (1968), the Supreme Court described free exercise defenses to nondiscrimination law as "patently frivolous." *Id.* at 403 n.5. *See also* Bob Jones Univ. v. United States, 461 U.S. 574, 580, 583 n.6 (1983) (rejecting Christian religious objection to interracial mixing); Loving v. Virginia, 388 U.S. 1, 3 (1967) (rejecting religious defense of antimiscegenation law).

[10] *See* EEOC v. Fremont Christian Sch., 781 F.2d 1362, 1369–70 (9th Cir. 1986) (rejecting religion-based restriction of spousal benefits to male employees' wives); *contra* Bradwell v. Illinois, 83 U.S. 130, 141 (1873) (Bradley, J., concurring) (justifying the denial of a law license because women are "to fulfil the noble and benign offices of wife and mother. This is the law of the Creator."). *See also* Bollenbach v. Bd. of Educ., 659 F. Supp. 1450, 1473 (S.D.N.Y. 1987) (finding women entitled to jobs driving buses despite Hasidic male students' religious objection).

[11] *See, e.g.*, Smith v. Fair Emp't and Hous. Comm'n, 913 P.2d 909, 928–29 (Cal. 1996); Swanner v. Anchorage Equal Rights Comm'n, 874 P.2d 274, 279–80 (Alaska 1994).

notwithstanding particular sects' religious objections to who others are and to how they live. The civil rights framework premised on that principle has served America well through generations of equality movements. To weaken it now because of objections to LGBT people likely would corrode the structure needed to protect everyone, including those who may be tomorrow's discrimination targets as demographics shift.

I LGBT PEOPLE REMAIN SIGNIFICANTLY UNPROTECTED

Full civic equality for LGBT people will not harm anyone else. There is enough equality to go around. But, persuading the American public to let go of entrenched myths and prejudices remains challenging. The struggle for the freedom to marry itself took more than forty years.[12] Sharing individual stories and showing that LGBT people pose no threats to others mattered immensely. States defending heterosexuals-only marriage laws eventually stopped contending that LGBT people are too unstable, too promiscuous, and too threatening to children to be allowed to marry.[13] Later, opposition boiled down to contorted claims that heterosexual couples would stop marrying and their children would suffer if same-sex couples could marry[14] – suppositions neither correct nor relevant, as the Supreme Court determined.[15]

Although baseless and illogical, arguments that LGBT people pose some sort of threat to children and to society's core institutions are all-too-familiar. "Queer" people are not a new phenomenon.[16] Over the generations, LGBT Americans have been defamed as sexual predators of children, deviant, and mentally ill.[17] Loving

---

[12] *See, e.g.*, Baker v. Nelson, 191 N.W.2d 185, 186 (Minn. 1971).

[13] *See* Baehr v. Miike, 1996 WL 694235, at 8 (Haw. 1st Cir. 1996).

[14] *See, e.g.*, DeBoer v. Snyder, 772 F.3d 388, 404–06 (6th Cir. 2014).

[15] Obergefell v. Hodges, 135 S. Ct. 2584, 2590 (2015).

[16] HIDDEN FROM HISTORY: RECLAIMING THE GAY AND LESBIAN PAST (Martin Duberman et al., eds., 1989); JONATHAN NED KATZ, GAY AMERICAN HISTORY: LESBIANS & GAY MEN IN THE U.S.A.: A DOCUMENTARY HISTORY (1992).

[17] Anita Bryant's "Save Our Children" campaign succeeded in driving repeal in 1974 of Dade County, Florida's Nondiscrimination Ordinance. LILLIAN FADERMAN, THE GAY REVOLUTION: THE STORY OF THE STRUGGLE 330–33 (2016). Such political attacks continued and, nearly forty years later, a "child predator" campaign tanked Houston's Equal Rights Ordinance by impugning transgender women. *See* Alexa Ura, *Bathroom Fears Flush Houston Discrimination Ordinance*, TEXAS TRIB. (Nov. 3, 2015), https://perma.cc/M28X-RF3D. *See also* VITO RUSSO, THE CELLULOID CLOSET (1987) (examining demonizing images of homosexuality in Hollywood films). The American Psychiatric Association only removed homosexuality from its DIAGNOSTIC AND STATISTICAL MANUAL OF MENTAL DISORDERS (DSM) in 1973. *See* Douglas Kimmel & Linda Garnets, *What a Light It Shed: The Life of Evelyn Hooker, in* PSYCHOLOGICAL PERSPECTIVES ON LESBIAN, GAY, AND BISEXUAL EXPERIENCES 40–44 (Linda Garnets & Douglas Kimmel eds., 2d ed., 2003) [hereinafter PSYCHOLOGICAL PERSPECTIVES]. Before the DSM's change, "treatment" included castration, lobotomy, electroshock therapy, and aversion therapy, more commonly now called "conversion therapy" or "reparative therapy." *Id.* at 41. "Conversion therapy" continues today despite no evidence of success and considerable evidence of

relationships have been deemed abominations and criminalized, and our children taken.[18] Service to our country has been deemed unworthy and dangerous.[19] Until recently, being said to be LGBT was seen to so tarnish one's reputation that damages for defamation were presumed.[20] More tangibly, LGBT Americans have been subject to hate crimes at staggering rates.[21]

Some contend the tide has turned and LGBT people now are accepted, making those who still object to same-sex relationships or gender transition the true victims of discrimination.[22] This is counterfactual. Anti-LGBT hostility and discrimination remain pervasive in this country.[23] Lambda Legal's Help Desks received more than 6,000 requests for assistance annually in 2016 and 2017.[24] Spanning coast to coast, callers asked for help with harassment and refusals of service in every imaginable

---

harm. *See* Douglas Haldeman, *The Practice and Ethics of Sexual Orientation Conversion Therapy*, *in* PSYCHOLOGICAL PERSPECTIVES 681–98 (Linda Garnets & Douglas Kimmel eds., 2d ed., 2003); King v. Gov. of New Jersey, 767 F.3d 216, 238 (3d Cir. 2014) (upholding state law banning such treatment of minors by licensed mental health professionals); Pickup v. Brown, 740 F.3d 1208, 1232 (9th Cir. 2014) (same).

[18] *See, e.g.*, Bowers v. Hardwick, 478 U.S. 186, 196–97 (1986) (Burger, C.J., concurring) (upholding criminalization of same-sex adult intimacy in one's home, citing "millennia of moral teaching"), *rev'd by* Lawrence v. Texas, 539 U.S. 558, 578 (2003); Bottoms v. Bottoms, 457 S.E.2d 102, 108 (Va. 1995) (transferring custody from lesbian mother to maternal grandmother based on disapproval of mother's lesbian relationship, citing state's criminal sodomy law).

[19] Thomasson v. Perry, 80 F.3d 915, 923 (4th Cir. 1996) (en banc), *cert. denied*, 519 U.S. 948 (1996) (upholding military discharge of member who self-identified as gay); High Tech Gays v. Defense Indus. Sec. Clearance Office, 895 F.2d 563, 574 (9th Cir. 1990) (upholding Defense Department policy of heightened security standards for lesbian and gay job applicants); Cook v. Gates, 528 F.3d 42, 42 (1st Cir. 2008) (upholding military's subsequent "Don't Ask, Don't Tell" policy, which permitted LGB people to serve as long as their sexual orientation was kept secret). The Don't Ask, Don't Tell Repeal Act of 2010 finally allowed LGB persons to openly serve in the military. Pub. L. No. 111–321, 124 Stat. 3515 (2010), however, President Trump has restricted service by transgender people. *See* Karnoski v. Trump, 2017 WL 6311305 (Dec. 11, 2017).

[20] *See* Yonaty v. Mincolla, 97 A.D.3d 141, 146 (N.Y. App. Div. 2012) (reviewing history).

[21] *See, e.g.*, U.S. Bureau of Justice Statistics, *Hate Crime Victimization, 2004–2015* (Apr. 2015), https://perma.cc/99CB-MP5A (showing 22% of hate crimes reported from 2011–15 were based on sexual orientation).

[22] *See, e.g.*, Ryan Anderson & Robert George, *Liberty and SOGI Laws: An Impossible and Unsustainable "Compromise,"* WITHERSPOON INST. (Jan. 11, 2016), https://perma.cc/3FT3-B4DA [hereinafter *Liberty and SOGI Laws*].

[23] *See, e.g.*, Harvard T.H. Chan School of Public Health, *Discrimination in America: Experiences and Views of LGBTQ Americans* (Nov. 2017), https://perma.cc/8UF3-RA8E (finding that, *inter alia*, a majority of LGBTQ Americans have experienced slurs and that they or an LGBTQ friend or family member have experienced threats, harassment or violence because of their sexuality or gender identity) [hereinafter *Discrimination in America*]; Christy Mallory & Brad Sears, *Evidence of Discrimination in Public Accommodations Based on Sexual Orientation and Gender Identity: An Analysis of Complaints Filed with State Enforcement Agencies, 2008–2014*, WILLIAMS INST. (Feb. 2016), https://perma.cc/HW4V-GT3Q (finding LGBT people file public accommodations discrimination complaints based on sexual orientation and gender identity proportionately as often as people of color and women file complaints based on race and sex); *U.S. Transgender Survey*, *supra* note 4.

[24] *See Legal Help Desk*, LAMBDA LEGAL, https://perma.cc/KF4Y-YLU5.

context from retail sales and restaurants, to child care services, to public transportation.

Advocates for business owners' ability to refuse same-sex couples say exemptions would pose little risk to LGBT people because few businesses would turn away those customers.[25] Lambda Legal submitted a brief to the Supreme Court presenting a representative set of firsthand accounts of just such refusals, which ranged literally from cradle to grave:[26]

- Before pregnancy: The treatment of Lupita Benitez, my client, a lesbian, whose San Diego doctors refused her a routine infertility procedure, donor insemination, after a year of preparation, due to their Christian fundamentalist beliefs.[27]
- At birth: The religion-based rejection of a Nashville lesbian couple by a local midwife, later by every other midwife in town, and by the childbirth trainer who barred the couple from group classes saying other couples would object to them.[28]
- At death: Jack Zawadski, an eighty-two-year-old man in Picayune, Mississippi had prearranged funeral services for his husband – his partner of fifty-two years, whose health was failing. The funeral home staff refused to care for his husband's body, saying, "This goes against everything I believe in. I'm a Christian."[29]

Couples experience problems traveling. A Hawaii B&B refused Diane Cervelli and Taeko Bufford a room because the owner "felt uncomfortable having lesbians in her house" – she considered homosexuality "detestable" and believes it "defiles our land," citing her religious beliefs.[30]

Many service denials came out of the blue, frustrating ordinary tasks. A Missouri CPA refused to file a married gay couple's tax return, proclaiming "[w]e are a Christian organization."[31] In an Illinois post office, a clerk refused to change a transgender man's name on a post office box, laughing at him and reciting Catholic beliefs.[32]

---

[25] Brief for Petitioners at 54–55, Masterpiece Cakeshop Ltd. v. Colo. Civil Rights Comm'n, No. 16–111, 137 S. Ct. 2290 (Aug. 31, 2017), 2017 WL 3913762.

[26] Brief of Amici Curiae Lambda Legal Defense and Education Fund, Inc. et al., Masterpiece Cakeshop, Ltd. v. Colo. Civil Rights Comm'n No. 16–111 (Oct. 30, 2017), 2017 WL 5127317, https://perma.cc/DDP2-NTTQ [hereinafter *Lambda Brief*].

[27] N. Coast Women's Care Med. Grp., Inc. v. San Diego Cty. Superior Court, 189 P.3d 959, 962 (Cal. 2008), https://perma.cc/B8YA-8K5K.

[28] *Lambda Brief, supra* note 26, at 17–18.

[29] *See* Zawadski v. Brewer Funeral Servs., No. 55CI1:17-CV-00019-CM (Miss. Pearl River Cty. Cir. Ct. June 14, 2017), https://perma.cc/B763-SQWA.

[30] Cervelli v. Aloha Bed & Breakfast, 2018 WL 1027804 (Feb. 23, 2018), https://perma.cc/DHA3-C8AU.

[31] *Lambda Brief, supra* note 26, at 31–32.

[32] *Id.* at 31.

Some refusals are frightening: denials of emergency roadside service, harassment by service technicians in one's home, and being ejected by taxi drivers at night in dangerous areas.[33] Violence occurs, too. Hate crimes against LGBT people remain wildly disproportionate, with murders of transgender people a particularly devastating manifestation of queer- and trans-phobia.[34]

That the possibility of refusal lurks behind every store counter is not just a matter of inconvenience – having to go to another bakery or restaurant. It inflicts emotional pain, disruption, and added financial costs; LGBT people live with stress and fear of what next, causing health to suffer and altering life plans.[35] Whatever the motivation, discrimination can have long-term deleterious effects.[36] However, religious voices often make things worse.[37]

Sadly, being refused service because of who one is leaves lasting damage.[38] Laws prohibiting discrimination in public accommodations, the Supreme Court

---

[33] *Id.* at 9; Aimee Green, *Lesbian Couple Sues Broadway Cab, Driver for $38,000 after Left beside Interstate 84*, THE OREGONIAN (July 28, 2014), https://perma.cc/MRV5-NAZZ.

[34] *See, e.g.*, Los Angeles County Human Relations Commission, *2016 Hate Crime Report*, https://perma.cc/8GVX-AR3L (reporting that LGBT people are the group most frequently targeted for hate crime, that the 118 crimes based on sexual orientation in 2016 comprised "nearly one-quarter of all hate crimes," and that 81% of anti-LGBT crimes were violent); Mark Lee, *A Time To Act: Fatal Violence Against Transgender People in America 2017*, HUMAN RIGHTS CAMPAIGN FOUND., https://perma.cc/R2A6-JDBR ("Over the past five years, more than 100 transgender people have been killed in the United States.").

[35] *See, e.g.*, Sejal Singh & Laura Durso, *Widespread Discrimination Continues to Shape LGBT People's Lives in Both Subtle and Significant Ways*, CTR. FOR AM. PROGRESS (May 2, 2017), https://perma.cc/MY7Z-A7ZA; Mark Hatzenbuehler, *Structural Stigma: Research Evidence and Implications for Psychological Science*, 71 AM. PSYCHOLOGIST 742, 742–51 (2016), http://dx.doi.org/10.1037/amp0000068; Edward Alessia et al., *Prejudice Events and Traumatic Stress among Heterosexuals and Lesbians, Gay Men, and Bisexuals*, 22 J. AGGRESSION, MALTREATMENT & TRAUMA 510, 510–26 (July 2013), http://www.tandfonline.com/doi/full/10.1080/10926771.2013.785455#.UfAdNxaTLiM.

[36] Ilan Meyer & David Frost, *Minority Stress and the Health of Sexual Minorities*, 252–66, *in* HANDBOOK OF PSYCHOLOGY & SEXUAL ORIENTATION (Charlotte Patterson & Anthony D'Augelli eds., 2012), https://perma.cc/BZG6-YVCH; Vickie Mays & Susan Cochran, *Mental Health Correlates of Perceived Discrimination Among Lesbian, Gay, and Bisexual Adults in the United States*, 19 AM. J. PUB. HEALTH. 1869, 1870 (2001).

[37] Ilan Meyer et al., *The Role of Help-Seeking in Preventing Suicide Attempts among Lesbians, Gay Men, and Bisexuals*, WILLIAMS INST. (June 2014), https://perma.cc/659H-GZQU (finding LGBT people who sought help from religious or spiritual sources more likely to commit suicide than those who sought treatment from a health-care provider or no treatment at all); Maurice Gattiss et al., *Discrimination and Depressive Symptoms Among Sexual Minority Youth: Is Gay-Affirming Religious Affiliation a Protective Factor?*, ARCH. SEX. BEHAV. 1589, 1589 (2014).

[38] Some may contend the refusals are based not on customers' identity, but on their (presumed) conduct. However, as the Supreme Court teaches, "Our decisions have declined to distinguish between status and conduct in this context." Christian Legal Society v. Martinez, 561 U.S. 661, 689 (2010) (referencing Lambda Legal's amicus brief). Just as a tax on yarmulkes is a tax on Jews, *id.*, objecting to a gay person living as a gay person – loving, marrying, and building a family with a same-sex partner – is objecting to who that person is.

observed, "eliminate [the] evil" of businesses serving only those "as they see fit," which demeans both the individual and society as a whole.[39]

Obviously, not all discrimination is the same. The treatment of African Americans in this country – past and still – is uniquely horrifying and morally bankrupt.[40] But the legal principle is the same: public accommodations laws "serve interests of the highest order."[41] That principled affirmation of common humanity and equal value is no less true and important today than it has been throughout American history.

II TARGETING LGBT PEOPLE

As same-sex couples gained the freedom to marry in more states, Kentucky and Kansas greenlighted religion-based discrimination.[42] Over the governor's veto, Kentucky in 2013 boosted its state Religious Freedom Restoration Act (RFRA), which had been patterned on the federal RFRA, to require the government to prove "by clear and convincing evidence that it has a compelling governmental interest" before the government can limit conduct motivated by religious belief.[43] Kansas followed suit with hardly any public objection.[44]

In 2014, a national furor erupted when the Arizona legislature approved a revision of its RFRA that would allow private citizens to mount a RFRA defense when sued under civil rights laws.[45] Although Arizona's civil rights statutes did not list sexual orientation or gender identity among the characteristics on which discrimination was forbidden, and the existing municipal ordinances imposed only limited penalties, those who championed SB 1062 were forthright and adamant: the expanded religious rights were "needed" to permit businesses to turn away same-sex couples.[46] US Senators John McCain and Jeff Flake, both Republicans,

---

[39] Heart of Atlanta Motel v. United States, 379 U.S. 241, 250, 259 (1964).

[40] *See generally* MICHELLE ALEXANDER, THE NEW JIM CROW (2010); DERRICK BELL, AND WE ARE NOT SAVED: THE ELUSIVE QUEST FOR RACIAL JUSTICE (1987); JAMES BALDWIN, THE FIRE NEXT TIME (1963).

[41] Roberts v. United States Jaycees, 468 U.S. 609, 624 (1984).

[42] German Lopez, *Kentucky's Religious Freedom Law Gives Students the Green Light to Discriminate Against LGBT Peers*, VOX (Mar. 21, 2017), https://perma.cc/Q6VR-HYJN.

[43] House Bill No. 279 (Ky. 2013) (codified as KAN. REV. STAT. ANN § 446.350 (2013)).

[44] 2013 Kan. Sess. Laws 147 (codified as KAN. STAT. ANN. § 60–5302 (2013)).

[45] 2014 Arizona Senate Bill 1062. *See* Jennifer Pizer, *Shields Not into Swords: Stopping the Misuse of Religious Freedom for Discrimination, in* LOVE UNITES US: WINNING THE FREEDOM TO MARRY IN AMERICA 323, 329–30 (Kevin Cathcart & Leslie Gabel-Brett eds., 2016) [hereinafter *Shields Not Into Swords*].

[46] *See, e.g.*, Howard Fischer, *SB 1062 Author Makes a Final Appeal to the Governor for Bill Passage*, KNAU ARIZ. PUBLIC RADIO (Feb. 28, 2014), https://perma.cc/37CP-4S87.

joined major business leaders trying to protect the state's reputation.[47] They pleaded with then-Governor Jan Brewer to block the measure, which she eventually did.[48]

In 2015, as marriage equality cases sped to the Supreme Court, Indiana took center stage. In a private ceremony, then-Governor Mike Pence, surrounded by self-identified fundamentalist clergy, signed SB 101, an expanded RFRA.[49] When the photo went public, Pence could not offer an explanation that was not anti-gay.[50] As in Arizona, business leaders joined advocates' censure of Pence and the new law, stressing that LGBT Hoosiers had only insufficient, municipal-level protections from discrimination, which the RFRA threatened to override.[51] Although the national denunciation successfully drove an amendment exempting civil rights protections from the RFRA, the legislature balked at passing state-level equality guarantees for LGBT people, and has done so consistently since then.[52]

While Indiana drew the most sustained rebuke, legislators in more than two dozen states launched more than 100 anti-LGBT bills in 2015.[53] After the Supreme Court's *Obergefell v. Hodges* decision in June of that year, the 2016 bill count nearly doubled.[54]

Mississippi House Bill 1523[55] gave the broadest authorization to discriminate against LGBT people in the name of religious freedom in a state with among the fewest SOGI protections in the country.[56] The bill was modeled on the federal First Amendment Defense Act (FADA) bill, which would prevent the government from "impos[ing] a penalty" under federal law on individuals and institutions if they act on a religious belief that "marriage is or should be recognized as the union of one man and one woman, or that sexual activity is properly reserved to such a marriage" – in other words, that same-sex couples should not marry or have sex.[57] Mississippi's bill, called the "Protecting Freedom of Conscience from Government Discrimination Act," added a third ground for religious refusal – a belief that gender is binary and determined by external observation or genetics at birth, and that gender

---

[47] *See Shields Not Into Swords, supra* note 45, at 325 n.3, 329; Howard Fischer, *Pressure Grows for Veto of Arizona's SB 1062*, CAPITOL MEDIA SERVS. (Feb. 23, 2014), https://perma.cc/K57V-BT88.

[48] Catherine Shoichet & Halimah Abdullah, *Arizona Gov. Jan Brewer Vetoes Controversial Anti-Gay Bill, SB 1062*, CNN (Feb. 26, 2014), https://perma.cc/L5R8-55UE.

[49] Tom Cook, *Gov. Mike Pence Signs "Religious Freedom" Bill in Private*, INDYSTAR (Apr. 2, 2015), https://perma.cc/T9PC-Y9M3.

[50] *See Shields Not Into Swords, supra* note 45, at 323–24.

[51] *Id.* at 325–329.

[52] *See Indiana's Equality Profile*, MOVEMENT ADVANCEMENT PROJECT, https://perma.cc/7GAL-Q6YA.

[53] Sarah Warbelow & Xavier Persad, *2015 State Equality Index, LGBT-Related Bills Considered in 2015*, HUMAN RIGHTS CAMPAIGN FOUND. (2016), https://perma.cc/C9TG-KBDC.

[54] *LGBTQ–Related Bills Considered in 2016, supra* note 5.

[55] House Bill No.1523 (Miss. 2016) (codified as MISS. CODE ANN. § 11–62-1 (2016)).

[56] *See generally Mississippi's Equality Profile*, MOVEMENT ADVANCEMENT PROJECT, https://perma.cc/E7H6-TPQL.

[57] H.R. 2802, 114th Cong. (1st Sess. 2015); S. 1598, 114th Cong. (1st Sess. 2015).

transition can never be a medically appropriate treatment for gender dysphoria.[58] As in the federal FADA bill, HB 1523 defined "impos[ing] a penalty" to include ineligibility for public employment or taxpayer-funded contracts or grants to serve the public when nondiscrimination would be required.

This meant LGBT people and sexually active, unmarried, non-LGBT people all could be refused service by individuals, private businesses, medical and social services agencies, licensed health professionals, schools, foster and adoptive parents, religiously affiliated organizations, and even some government actors.[59] Governor Bryant signed the bill into law in April 2017.[60]

The impact was immediate. Brandiilyne Mangum-Dear, a pastor, and her wife, Susan Mangum, who had founded Mississippi's first and only LGBT-affirming church, Metropolitan Community Church, received threatening calls on the church phone.[61] A truck emblazoned with a swastika parked outside the church, causing members to fear entering even after the church posted security guards at the doors.

Brandiilyne and Susan joined others and challenged HB 1523.[62] The federal district court in Mississippi enjoined the statute, finding that its special exemptions for specified religious views violate the Establishment Clause, and the overt targeting of same-sex couples and transgender people violates the Equal Protection Clause.[63] On appeal, the Fifth US Circuit Court of Appeals reversed and remanded on a technical ground, saying plaintiffs lacked legal standing to sue because the law had not taken effect, rejecting our clients' claim of injury based on government religious endorsement.[64] The Supreme Court declined to review the decision.[65]

HB 1523 is the most sweeping "religious exemptions" bill to gain state legislative approval. It signals a notable shift in focus, from broad RFRAs designed to create rights to special religion-based treatment in any context to FADAs focusing explicitly on marriage and sometimes gender identity, and to other bills targeting transgender people. Bills to create focused exemptions, such as in medical services and education, also appeared, underlining the anti-LGBT *animus*.

With many bills, public funding is at stake. Consider professionally licensed social and medical services – the government partners closely with and subsidizes these professionals through Medicare, Medicaid, and other programs. When a publicly funded health professional places religious standards above professional standards, it should sound alarms.

---

[58] *See supra* note 5.

[59] *Id.*

[60] Miss. Code Ann. § 11–62-3 (2016).

[61] Susan Sommer, *In Bad Faith*, Lambda Legal Impact (Summer 2017), https://perma.cc/DFY7-85KP.

[62] Barber v. Bryant, 193 F.Supp.3d 677 (S.D. Miss. 2016).

[63] *Id.* at 716.

[64] Barber v. Bryant, 860 F.3d 345, 357 (5th Cir. 2017).

[65] *See* Barber v. Bryant, *supra* note 62.

As of December 2017, seven states – North Dakota, Virginia, Michigan, Mississippi, Alabama, South Dakota, and Texas – have enacted laws to allow child welfare agencies to refuse to make placements based on religious objections and to impose anti-LGBT religious beliefs on children in state care.[66] Such beliefs often include that a same-sex orientation is sinful or sick but "curable" through so-called conversion therapy, which has been recognized as ineffective and often damaging.[67] Many glibly say that LGBT potential parents and those of other faiths can go elsewhere to adopt but let's be honest: rejection of qualified parents means more children languishing in the system and others, especially LGBT children, placed in hostile environments.[68] Although only 5 percent of these anti-LGBT bills passed in 2017, the hostile rhetoric that follows bill introduction takes a toll on LGBT people, the states considering them, and all people of good will.[69]

Let's be honest about another fact: these bills concern places of *public* accommodation – commercial and professional services offered to the general *public*, regulated to protect the *public*, and usually funded *publicly*. They are meant to allow targeted rejection of LGBT people whenever we make ourselves known – to make us hide our relationships and conform, at least outwardly, to common gender expectations.[70] These bills are not about protecting churches from hostile interlopers; the First Amendment already does that. They are not about protecting clergy's right to refuse to solemnize any marriage contrary to doctrine. That, too, already is secure.[71] Instead, these bills aim to undercut now-longstanding norms of the public marketplace and create special rights to discriminate, whether nondiscrimination protections exist yet or not. Yet, Attorney General Sessions, Vice President Pence, and others, including some respected scholars, contend these exemptions for religiously motivated conduct are appropriate because "[r]eligious rights [are] natural rights, not subject to government infringement" – meaning government lacks power

---

[66] ALA. CODE 1975 § 26–10D-2 (2017); S.D. CODIFIED LAWS § 26–6-38 (2017); TEX. HUM. RES. CODE ANN. § 45.004 (2017); MISS. CODE ANN. § 11–62-5 (2016); MICH. COMP. LAWS. § 722.124e (2015); VA CODE ANN. § 63.2–1709.3 (2012); N.D. CODIFIED CODE § 50–12-03 (2003).

[67] King v. Gov. of New Jersey, 767 F.3d 216, 238 (3d Cir. 2014); Pickup v. Brown, 740 F.3d 1208, 1232 (9th Cir. 2014).

[68] Charlene Aaron, *Texas Adoption Law Seen as Major Victory for Religious Freedom*, CBN NEWS (Oct. 25, 2017), https://perma.cc/4MRT-4NAJ (quoting bill sponsor); Family Equality Council, https://perma.cc/YFB9-5BUY.

[69] Gregory Herek, *Anti-Equality Marriage Amendments and Sexual Stigma*, 61 SOC. ISSUES 413, 413 (2011); GLENDA RUSSELL, VOTED OUT: THE PSYCHOLOGICAL CONSEQUENCES OF ANTIGAY POLITICS (2000).

[70] These include expectations about both gender expression and gender of one's romantic partner. See discussions in Glenn v. Brumby, 663 F.3d 1312 (11th Cir. 2011) (holding gender identity discrimination is a form of sex discrimination) and Hively v. Ivy Tech Cmty. Coll., 853 F.3d 339 (7th Cir. 2017) (en banc) (same for sexual orientation discrimination).

[71] The existing constitutional protection has been reconfirmed without controversy in numerous state marriage equality laws (*e.g.*, 2013 Hawaii Laws 2nd Sp. Sess. Act 1 (S.B. 1), codified at HRS § 572-D), and in Utah's SOGI nondiscrimination law.

to regulate.[72] As a blanket statement, that obviously cannot be true. Regardless of religious command, human sacrifice is not permitted, men may not beat their wives and children, marry more than one person at a time, or keep slaves; stoning one's neighbor is forbidden, no matter if he (or she) seduced another's wife.[73] "An eye for an eye" remains a metaphor. The important protections for religious freedom set out in federal and state law cannot extend beyond the point where others will be hurt.[74]

President Donald Trump announced his executive order on religious liberty as protecting conservative religious groups from faith-based persecution. In his words, "the federal government has used the power of the state as a weapon against the faith community, bullying and even punishing Americans of faith."[75] No American, Trump proclaimed, "should be forced to choose between the dictates of the federal government and the tenets of their faith." Ever?

It is counterfactual for Christians to claim to be a persecuted minority. Nearly 70 percent of Americans identify as some form of Christian.[76] By contrast, the LGBT population amounts to less than 5 percent.[77] So who holds social dominance and who, generally speaking, is vulnerable?

III IMPACTS ON THIRD PARTIES

The bakers, florists, and others who refuse to treat gay customers like other customers explain their religious objection as a need to not be "complicit" in what the business owners consider these customers' sinful or sham marriages or other wrongful conduct.[78] Doctors who routinely provide insemination services to heterosexual

---

[72] *Prepared Remarks to ADF, supra* note 6; Will Drabold, *Here's What Mike Pence Said on LGBT Issues Over the Years*, TIME (July 15, 2016), https://perma.cc/43YZ-ZZVJ; Robert George et al., *The Argument Against Gay Marriage: And Why It Doesn't Fail*, WITHERSPOON INST. (Dec. 17, 2010), https://perma.cc/4KTQ-8ZN6.

[73] *Leviticus* 20:10.

[74] *See, e.g.*, United States v. Lee, 455 U.S. 252, 263 n.3 (1982). *Accord* Trinity Lutheran Church of Columbia v. Comer, 137 S. Ct. 2012, 2029 n.3 (2017). See also discussion in Jennifer Pizer, *Navigating the Minefield: Hobby Lobby and Religious Accommodation in the Age of Civil Rights*, 9 HARV. L. & POL'Y. REV. 1, 18 (2015).

[75] Presidential Executive Order, *Promoting Free Speech and Religious Liberty* (May 4, 2017), https://perma.cc/YQR8-GFSQ; White House, *President Trump Hosts Faith Leaders at the White House* (May 4, 2017), https://perma.cc/4ZMG-QUCG. *See also* Attorney General Memorandum, Prohibition on Improper Guidance Documents (Nov. 16, 2017), https://perma.cc/US55-WCTB.

[76] Pew Research Ctr., *America's Changing Religious Landscape* (May 12, 2015), https://perma.cc/5M8C-W46C.

[77] Gary Gates, *LGBT Demographics: Comparisons Among Population-Based Surveys*, WILLIAMS INST. (Sept. 2014), https://perma.cc/KXR4-BXA6 (showing estimates across national surveys of 2.2%–4.0%); Andrew Flores et al., *How Many Adults Identify as Transgender in the United States*, WILLIAMS INST. (June 2016), https://perma.cc/LX3K-BSHM (calculating 0.6% of U.S. adults identify as transgender).

[78] Brief of 67 Catholic Theologians and Ethicists as Amici Curiae in Support of Hobby Lobby Stores, Inc., Hobby Lobby Stores, Inc. v. Burwell, 134 S. Ct. 2751, 2014 WL 316716 (2014), at * 6.

patients withheld that medical care from Lupita Benitez, claiming complicity.[79] The owners of Hobby Lobby Stores, who do not line-item-veto other coverage from the company health plan, said they would be complicit in their 13,000 employees' individual reproductive decisions if the plan covered birth control.[80] Before *Hobby Lobby* arrived in the Supreme Court, then-Judge Neil Gorsuch described complicity this way in a concurring appellate opinion approving the owners' religious objection to their employees' use of birth control:

> All of us face the problem of complicity. All of us must answer for ourselves whether and to what degree we are willing to be involved in the wrongdoing of others. For some, religion provides an essential source of guidance both about what constitutes wrongful conduct and the degree to which those who assist others in committing wrongful conduct themselves bear moral culpability.[81]

Strikingly, Gorsuch made no mention of the impact on employees and their families if company owners' religious beliefs are allowed to override neutral, generally applicable, laws that benefit workers. Justice Alito's decision for the Supreme Court took pains to quantify the impact on employees as "precisely zero" – something that cannot be said if, as under Sessions' new guidance, all objecting employers are treated like churches.[82] Providing the decisive fifth vote in *Hobby Lobby*, Justice Kennedy emphasized that workers' interests – including protections against discrimination – are compelling and must not be sacrificed to accommodate others' religious interests.[83]

With all religion claims, society should ask: Will accommodation of one person's objection to standard norms have adverse impacts on others? Being held to laws that protect everyone equally is not persecution. Preventing one person from discriminating against others is not discrimination against that person. These are merely essential qualities of peaceful coexistence in a pluralistic society.[84] This is what equality means.

Religious freedom certainly does guarantee the right to *believe* that engaging in commercial transactions constitutes an endorsement of customers' beliefs, traditions, family structure, or gender expression. But, it must not include the right to

---

[79] North Coast Women's Care Medical Group, 189 P.3d 959, 962 (Cal. 2008).

[80] Burwell v. Hobby Lobby Stores, Inc., 134 S. Ct. 2751, 2765 (2014).

[81] Hobby Lobby Stores, Inc. v. Sebelius, 723 F.3d 1114, 1152 (10th Cir. 2013).

[82] *Id.* at 2760; HHS Press Office, *Trump Administration Issues Rules Protecting the Conscience Rights of All Americans* (Oct. 6, 2017), https://perma.cc/V5Y2-TY44; Rachel Zoll et al., *Sessions' Order to Accommodate Religious Objections Undercuts LGBT Protections*, Chicago Trib. (Oct. 6, 2017), https://perma.cc/YW8H-YPQM.

[83] *Hobby Lobby*, 723 F.3d at 2787 (Kennedy, J., concurring).

[84] *See generally* U.S. Comm'n on Civil Rights, Peaceful Coexistence: Reconciling Non-discrimination Principles with Civil Liberties (Sept. 7, 2016), https://perma.cc/XLV6-63ET.

act to the detriment of third parties. Courts appropriately have recognized that society cannot function if each person is "a law unto himself."[85]

Because America is not a theocracy, no amount of religious sincerity justifies civil law and public institutions that demean and discriminate against same-sex couples or impede needed medical care for transgender people. Those who condone differential discrimination against LGBT people are mistaken about what the law must require.[86]

Consider the demands of the US Conference of Catholic Bishops (USCCB) and others for exemption from the nondiscrimination provisions of the Patient Protection and Affordable Care Act (ACA) and federal contracts and grants.[87] Requiring large hospital systems and health plans to operate according to nondiscrimination rules, and other professional norms, is not religious intolerance. At one time, charity hospitals were operated by churches with donations from within the faith.[88] Today institutions solicit business from the general public, are paid by secular insurance plans and taxpayer-funded programs such as Medicare, and employ people of many faiths. They should be expected to serve the public at large per professional standards of care and without discrimination against patients or personnel.

Arguments of endorsement are equally flawed. Obeying a law does not mean agreeing with that law – whether a civil rights law, tax provision, or traffic and land use rules.

The baker and other objecting parties nonetheless contend that creating custom goods is an expression of endorsement, which, as a matter of free speech law, they should not be compelled to make. A key element of First Amendment protection for expression is that those who see the end product must understand the idea the would-be artist intends to convey.[89] No one believes bakers convey their personal approval of every marriage for which they create and sell a cake.

---

[85] Employment Div., Ore. Dept. of Human Res. v. Smith, 494 U.S. 872, 879 (1990) (quoting Reynolds v. United States, 98 U.S. 145, 167 (1879)); United States v. Carroll, 567 F.2d 955, 957 (10th Cir. 1977).

[86] *See, e.g.*, Ryan Anderson, *Liberty and SOGI Laws, supra* note 22; *Prepared Remarks to ADF, supra* note 6.

[87] *See, e.g.*, USCCB, *Nondiscrimination in Health Programs and Activities*, RIN 0945-AA02 (Nov. 6, 2015), https://perma.cc/NS8P-6TJD (claiming religious right to forbid gender transition-related care and deny spousal benefits for employees' same-sex spouses); *Letter to Obama from Faith Leaders*, WASH. POST (July 1, 2014), https://perma.cc/H9F4-5GZW.

[88] *See, e.g.*, Dolores Liptak & Grace Bennett, SEEDS OF HOPE: THE HISTORY OF THE SISTERS OF PROVIDENCE, HOLYOKE, MASSACHUSETTS (1999) (describing late nineteenth- and early twentieth-century history of women religious providing medical, social services, and other charity care).

[89] *See* Spence v. Washington, 418 US 405, 409–11 (1974) (holding both subjective and objective considerations bear on whether conduct constitutes protected expression); Rumsfeld v. Forum for Academic & Institutional Rights, Inc., 547 U.S. 47, 63–64 (2006) (explaining actor can dispel potential inference from required conduct with explicit speech); State v. Arlene's Flowers, Inc., 389 P.3d 543, 557–59 (Wash. 2017) *vacated,* 138 S. Ct. 2671 (2018) (distinguishing flower arranging from inherently expressive conduct from which observer understands message).

But here again, let's be honest. Expression aside, some people, for religious or other personal reasons, want to avoid treating LGBT people the same as others in their commercial transactions. So it matters that, from *United States v. Lee* to *Hobby Lobby*, the Supreme Court has repeatedly affirmed a core principle: each person's exercise of religion must end when it starts to harm another.[90]

Persons of faith have a role to play in this – they can work to avoid conflict between their religious commitments and others' interests.[91] The medical student who has strong religious views about whether gay couples should have children can consider internal medicine or ophthalmology rather than infertility care.

Thus, the baker can decide on religious grounds against making and selling Halloween cakes. He can bake beautiful Yule logs only for friends who share his faith. But whatever he chooses to make and offer for sale *to the general public* he must sell to everyone in compliance with laws that protect everyone, including civil rights laws.[92]

Society must stand firm on this principle for everyone's benefit. Today, this dispute extends beyond cakes and flowers, to funeral services and haircuts.[93] Indeed for years, it has been about housing, employment, lodging, and medical care. Equal treatment in the mall, the market, and motels is not too much to ask.[94]

IV THE EXISTING CIVIL RIGHTS FRAMEWORK SHOULD NOT BE ALTERED TO ALLOW DISCRIMINATION

Existing nondiscrimination frameworks have been essential for achieving inclusion, safety, and equal treatment of historically disenfranchised groups. The religious exemptions in those laws have worked reasonably well for the most part. As LGBT people now step forward – challenging falsehoods and insisting upon equal citizenship in both law and fact – it is simply another chapter of this familiar American story.

---

[90] United States v. Lee, 455 U.S. 252, 260–61 (1982) ("When followers of a particular sect enter into commercial activity as a matter of choice, the limits they accept on their own conduct as a matter of conscience and faith are not to be superimposed on statutory schemes which are binding on others in that activity.").

[91] E.g., Wisconsin v. Yoder, 406 U.S. 205, 220 (1972); Smith v. Fair Emp't and Hous. Comm'n, 913 P.2d 909, 919 (Cal. 1996).

[92] See further discussion in Douglas NeJaime & Reva B. Siegel, *Conscience Wars: Complicity-Based Conscience Claims in Religion and Politics*, 124 Yale L.J. 2516 (2015).

[93] E.g. Zawadski v. Brewer Funeral Servs. No. 55CI1:17-CV-00019-CM (Miss. Pearl River Cty. Circ. Ct. June 14, 2017), https://perma.cc/B763-SQWA; *Oliver v. The Barbershop*, LAMBDA LEGAL, https://perma.cc/R2TX-HMB5.

[94] *See generally* Douglas NeJaime, *Marriage Inequality: Same-Sex Relationships, Religious Exemptions, and the Production of Sexual Orientation Discrimination*, 100 CAL. L. REV. 1169 (2012).

A collaborative search for common ground can take place even as social change continues. Hearts and minds generally shift toward acceptance of diversity, including sexual orientation and gender diversity, when people get to know each other.

This happens within families, as well as in congregations, social groups, schools, workplaces, and legislative bodies. Acceptance accelerates when people of good will engage. From the LGBT perspective, engagement should begin with an honest recognition of persistent anti-LGBT biases that impact so many in our communities – the hate crimes, harassment, discrimination, disproportionate poverty, health disparities, and other challenges.[95] To be sure, there has been significant progress. But so much more is needed.

LGBT individuals, same-sex couples, and their families all need both full legal equality and further evolution in public attitudes.[96] Toward that goal, determined advocates of good will on both sides achieved a breakthrough in Utah in 2015 by adding sexual orientation and gender identity nondiscrimination protections to the state's existing employment and housing civil rights laws.[97] That success – often now referred to as "the Utah compromise" – came after years of intensive negotiations between Equality Utah and lawyers representing the LDS Church, with essential commitment from legislative leaders as well as national experts on various sides providing suggestions.[98]

Since then, Utah's breakthrough has had some appeal to legislators in other states who have felt stuck politically between the LGBT community's calls for equal legal protections and opposing voices insisting upon religious exemptions. But, consistently with this chapter's consistent cautions: the Utah's compromise was a milestone, not a model. Without question, Utah's enactment of any civil rights protections for LGBT people would have been notable given the LDS Church's dominant influence in the state and its intense, longstanding opposition to LGBT rights, most visibly including its substantial financial and rhetorical support for the 2008 Proposition 8 initiative that stripped same-sex couples of the freedom to marry in California.[99]

---

[95] *See generally* authorities cited *supra* notes 21, 23, and 34. *See also* M.V. Lee Badgett et al., *New Patterns of Poverty in the Lesbian, Gay, and Bisexual Community*, WILLIAMS INST. (June 2013), https://perma.cc/7PHC-D8G4; David Lick et al., *Minority Stress and Physical Health Among Sexual Minorities*, WILLIAMS INST. (Oct. 2013), https://perma.cc/NRB2-MQTN; Jennifer Pizer et al., *Evidence of Persistent and Pervasive Workplace Discrimination Against LGBT People*, 45 LOY. L.A. L. REV. 715 (2012) (compiling research results).

[96] *See, e.g.*, Pavan v. Smith, 137 S. Ct. 2075, 2077 (2017) (reversing decision that denied marital presumption to married same-sex parents seeking birth certificate for child identifying both parents); *Discrimination in America, supra* note 23.

[97] S.B. 296 Gen. Sess. (Utah 2015) (codified as 2015 UTAH CODE ANN. § 57–21-2.7).

[98] Dennis Romboy, *Utah Legislature Passes Two "Historic" Anti-Bias, Religious Rights Bills*, DESERET NEWS (Mar. 11, 2015), https://perma.cc/3XZJ-GUE5.

[99] *See California Proposition 8, the "Eliminates Right of Same-Sex Couples to Marry" Initiative*, BALLOTPEDIA (2008), https://perma.cc/M6KF-V8T5 (showing Church's heavy involvement in financing Proposition 8); Fred Karger, *Should the Mormon Church Pay Taxes?*, HUFFINGTON POST (Dec. 16, 2017), https://perma.cc/V73W-HYUK.

From that place, Church leadership travelled a distance to support employment and housing nondiscrimination protections for queer people (while maintaining firm opposition to marriage equality). Meanwhile, local LGBT community advocates had to persist through years of false starts, frustration, and religiously inspired condemnation.[100] The breakthrough deserves credit for honoring key principles. Critically, the new law added sexual orientation and gender identity into the existing nondiscrimination framework, treating all covered personal characteristics the same and with the same religious exemptions. In other words, the law uses the same standards for all forms of prohibited discrimination and did not lessen any existing protections when protections for LGBT people were added.

Despite those important fairness measures, Utah's law is not the model for other states for at least two reasons. First, Utah's religious exemptions are uniquely capacious because religiously affiliated institutions control a huge part of the market in the state and, as Senator J. Stuart Adams acknowledges in this volume, Utah's underlying law always omitted them. Second, the new nondiscrimination law did not reach public accommodations – but this is an area of persistent, harmful discrimination, for which no federal litigation approach currently is available.[101]

The educational and organizing work needed to build support for comprehensive, effective nondiscrimination laws is being done as urgently as possible. Public discussion about law *and* values is at the heart of social change, and of that work. The goal is to change how people treat each other first. In time, what people understand about each other often changes, too. Academically, there are hard, interesting questions, as this volume shows. But from a practical, real-human-beings perspective, focusing on common ground and potential for mutual concern and respect makes us a better, stronger society. And then the legal drafting becomes far easier.

V CONCLUSION

My maternal grandmother was Irish, Catholic, and devout. Her husband, my grandfather, identified as a Yankee Protestant, with ardently anti-Vatican views. Trapped in their determined disagreement, my mother was often miserable. She converted to Judaism before marrying my father; they raised us in those traditions Her parents were aghast; her mother feared for her soul.

---

[100] Troy Williams & Clifford Rosky, *Laws Should Protect Practice of Faith, Reject LGBT Discrimination*, Deseret News (Feb. 22, 2015), https://perma.cc/PHS6-GBZ2; Clifford Rosky, *Religious Liberties and Gay Rights*, Deseret News (Mar. 1, 2012), https://perma.cc/Q79W-7ZZB.

[101] *Compare, e.g.*, Hively v. Ivy Tech Cmty. Coll., 853 F.3d 339, 339 (7th Cir. 2017) (en banc) (holding Title VII's sex discrimination ban covers sexual orientation discrimination) *and* Whitaker v. Kenosha Unified School District, 858 F.3d 1034 (7th Cir. 2017) (Title IX and gender identity) *with* 42 U.S.C. § 2000a (2012). Title II of the Civil Rights Act of 1964 does not bar sex discrimination in public accommodations).

My grandmother was fixed in her views of many things – her faith and her love of opera and the sea. When I came out as a lesbian in college, she was surprised and curious. Over time, she came to welcome my gay friends to her Thanksgiving table. She wanted to know them. She cared about deeper truths. "The priests are men. They try their best, but they're not right about everything," she said.

Like my grandmother, my mother-in-law also had deeply rooted beliefs. For her, the path to accepting her daughter's relationship with me took more than twenty years. But she, too, was motivated by love to try. My wife and I married a week before our twenty-fourth anniversary. The weekend of our wedding, my mother-in-law formally welcomed me into the family. Two months later, at eighty-nine, she died.

Love and equality are deeper truths. They guide us to reconciliation if we are willing to see what matters most. When we open our eyes to our common humanity, segregation of some and treatment of them as lesser seems strange, unsettling, and ugly.

Let us open our eyes to the tasks ahead. For many of us queer people, this will not be easy. Too many of us grew up in stultifying denial of our true selves, with ostracism hovering if we made a revealing move. For some, inner gashes from years of Sunday sermons damning us have not healed. It takes patience and a leap of faith to listen with an open heart to those who sincerely believe we sin because we love. In return for that earnest listening, we need bakeries, barber shops, and bowling alleys to be open equally to all. None should be an altar for sacrificing anyone's civil rights. It is a fair and beneficial bargain all around.

30

Bathrooms and Bakers

How Sharing the Public Square Is the Key to a Truce in the Culture Wars

Robin Fretwell Wilson

Too often, conflicts over LGBT rights and religious freedom follow a familiar pattern: partisans on both sides press uncompromising positions, knowing they leave no room for the other side. Sometimes, legislators – in cooperation with stakeholders or independently – fashion approaches that make room for all sides, as shown in the chapters by Senator J. Stuart Adams (Chapter 32) and Governor Michael Leavitt (Chapter 33). When they do not, however, laws written with different, older conflicts in mind govern conflicts *or* legislatures enact one-sided measures largely responsive only to one constituency – in both cases, a kind of "purity" model elevates one community's interests over others'. When legislators do not consciously make room for all, parties resort to litigation, which, by its nature, yields only one winner.

Americans overwhelmingly believe that LGBT people should not be treated differently just for being gay or trans. 71 percent favor protections for LGBT people "against discrimination in jobs, public accommodations, and housing."[1] Three in four say it should be illegal for an employer "to fire someone for being gay or lesbian."[2] Four of five believe it is already illegal to refuse to serve someone because of their sexual orientation or gender identity (together, SOGI).[3] A slim majority, 53 percent, oppose laws that require trans persons to use bathrooms corresponding to their sex at birth, while 39 percent favor them.[4]

But when asked whether bakers and other wedding vendors should be able to decline to assist weddings when guided by faith, Americans are split. As Douglas

---

[1] Robert P. Jones, Daniel Cox, Betsy Cooper & Rachel Lienesch, *Beyond Same-Sex Marriage: Attitudes on LGBT Nondiscrimination Laws and Religious Exemptions from 2015 American Values Atlas*, PRRI (Feb. 18, 2016), https://perma.cc/S235-23PS.

[2] Emily Swanson, *Americans Think It Should Be Illegal to Fire Someone for Being Gay, Don't Realize It's Not Already*, HUFFINGTON POST (June 19, 2014), https://perma.cc/7SUB-BM2Q.

[3] *Id.*

[4] Daniel Cox & Robert P. Jones, *Majority of Americans Oppose Transgender Bathroom Restrictions*, PRRI (Mar. 10, 2017), https://perma.cc/A3QJ-5BML.

Laycock notes in Chapter 3, "48% support[] religious exemptions in the wedding cases and 49% oppose[] exemptions." Presumably Americans share the intuition expressed the day after *Obergefell v. Hodges*[5] by former Solicitor General Ted Olson, an instrumental figure in realizing marriage equality across the United States: "[B]eing asked to participate in a wedding, to perform a wedding, to sing in a wedding, to ... be a wedding planner" is different than "walk[ing] into a bakery on the street and want[ing] to buy a pie or a doughnut ... People have the right to refuse personal services with respect to things like that on a religious basis."[6]

This chapter shows that despite considerable support for LGBT rights *and* for protections for those who ask not to assist with marriages for faith-based reasons, a purity model reigns across most of the United States: access by LGBT persons to public places follows a red/blue fault line. Notably, twenty-two states and the District of Columbia protect LGBT persons from discrimination in employment, housing, or public accommodations through state laws; two of these protect against discrimination based only on sexual orientation.[7] These laws were passed before marriage equality came on the scene; until Utah enacted its protections as to housing and hiring, no Republican-led legislature had enacted a SOGI. None of the public accommodations laws leave room for wedding vendors like Masterpiece Cakeshop's owner Jack Phillips, whose case the US Supreme Court decided this term.[8] By contrast, twenty-nine states extend no protection in state law from discrimination in public accommodations to the LGBT community, muting the need for step-offs from performing religiously infused wedding services. These states are overwhelmingly Republican, with Republicans dominating both legislative chambers and, with rare exception, are led by Republican governors.[9] Significant numbers of residents in these states self-identify as religious.[10]

There are hopeful signs that sorely needed protections against discrimination in public accommodations can be extended to the full LGBT community. All across the nation, LGBT advocates and people of faith are sitting down to discuss more nuanced laws that protect both communities in the areas most core to them. Sometimes legislators participate in – and mediate – these conversations. In other cases, stakeholders are meeting on their own.

---

[5] 135 S. Ct. 2584 (2015).

[6] Jennifer Rubin, *Where Do We Go From Here on Gay Rights?*, WASH. POST (June 29, 2015), https://perma.cc/3NSP-NA6H.

[7] *See* Appendix, Chapter 35.

[8] Masterpiece Cakeshop, Ltd., v. Colo. Civil Rights Comm'n, No. 16-111, slip op. (U.S. June 4, 2018). For views on Phillips's case and the reasons he advances for being permitted to decline to make cakes for same-sex weddings, see McClain, Chapter 17; Melling, Chapter 19; Ryan Anderson, Chapter 27; McConnell, Chapter 28; and Pizer, Chapter 29.

[9] *See infra* Fig. 1; *State Partisan Composition*, NAT'L CONFERENCE OF STATE LEGIS. (Jan. 30, 2018), https://perma.cc/8PX4-Z5SL. Nebraska's legislature is unicameral and nonpartisan; Nebraska has a Republican governor. Louisiana's Senate (25–14) and House (61–41) are majority-Republican; the governor is a Democrat.

[10] *See* Robin Fretwell Wilson, *Marriage of Necessity: Same-Sex Marriage and Religious Liberty Protections*, 64 CASE W. RES. L. REV. 1161, 1221 (2014).

But two hurdles to enacting legislation banning LGBT discrimination in public places loom large: bathrooms and bakers.

First deployed in 2008, the bathroom narrative is simple and strikingly effective: giving trans people equal access to facilities, opponents contend, threatens the safety of others.[11] This claim is not anchored in evidence about risks from trans people.[12] Still, as Section I shows, there has been no new statewide public accommodations law banning SOGI discrimination since the bathroom narrative took hold. This means the safety claim must be met head-on for new nondiscrimination laws to be tenable.

Importantly, federal regulators cannot push through the impasse blocking protections for LGBT persons – assuming the Trump Administration wanted to – because, as Jennifer C. Pizer notes in Chapter 29, Title II of the Civil Rights Act of 1964 does not bar discrimination on the basis of "sex." That bare fact precludes the extension to SOGI discrimination, as the Obama administration did in hiring, education, and other realms.[13]

Section II documents the growing importance of objections from a tiny handful of wedding vendors across the nation. Refusals by bakers, photographers, florists, and others to facilitating same-sex weddings for religious reasons have placed them at odds with, and in violation of, SOGI nondiscrimination laws written long before marriage equality became the law of the land. To date, no public accommodations law has allowed exceptions *once* a group has been defined as needing protection *and* a business has been defined as a "public accommodation." In other words, the business is all-in or all-out. This means that in places that ban SOGI discrimination, businesses that would gladly serve LGBT patrons for everything but religiously infused services like weddings, as Phillips and others say they would,[14] face legal sanction, protracted litigation, and even closure – just as if they had said "No Gays Allowed."[15]

Section III argues that the key to a truce in the culture war between faith and sexuality rests on rejecting a binary model that treats all services alike – all-in or all-out, no matter how religiously infused. As the lack of new state laws since 2008 illustrates, both sides still marshal enough influence to be in "blocking positions," freezing the status quo. Because SOGI laws have not historically made fine distinctions, the fight over new public accommodations laws has become an existential one for people of faith: oppose SOGIs in order to keep religious business owners afloat or

---

[11] *See infra* Section I.
[12] *See* Robin Fretwell Wilson, *The Nonsense About Bathrooms: How Purported Concerns Over Safety Block LGBT Nondiscrimination Laws and Obscure Real Religious Liberty Concerns*, 20 LEWIS & CLARK L. REV. 1373 (2017).
[13] *See* Laycock, Chapter 3; Melling, Chapter 19; Hill, Chapter 26; Pizer, Chapter 29; and *Introduction* for descriptions and status of regulations and cases.
[14] *See* McClain, Chapter 17, and McConnell, Chapter 28, for accounts; *infra* Section II.
[15] *Tennessee Hardware Store Puts Up "No Gays Allowed" Sign*, USA TODAY (July 1, 2015), https://perma.cc/M23K-4D84.

risk closure.[16] LGBT people see the fight for new SOGI laws as existential, too: to avoid the humiliation and pain of being turned away.[17] This section sketches a new vision: regulate the business, not individual workers, so that every couple who walks in is served with dignity but no specific individual must perform any given service.

Section IV concludes that our familiar purity-model approaches do not adequately account for the interests of all in an evenhanded way. In three-fifths of America, LGBT people can be told "we don't serve people like you." In two-fifths, people of faith can be told "get over your faith or get out of business." Across all of America, the public square belongs only to one side.

Unless America finds news ways to share the public square, it will remain a checkerboard of injustice to someone. For a people that cares deeply about justice for all, that result is a shame, whether one lives in Alabama or New York.

I LGBT PEOPLE IN RED AMERICA

As noted, most people see denials of service based on characteristics irrelevant to the service as wrong – demeaning to the person refused, to the LGBT community, and to all of us. Yet, the United States is a checkerboard of public accommodation nondiscrimination laws, as Figure 30.1 shows.

Twenty-nine states provide no statewide protection to LGBT persons against being refused service in public spaces such as restaurants and hotels. Three states, Arkansas, Tennessee, and North Carolina, affirmatively bar the enactment of local nondiscrimination laws protecting LGBT people, measures being litigated or scheduled to sunset.[18] A minority, twenty-one states and the District of Columbia, protect members of the LGBT community from being denied service by public establishments – two on the basis of sexual orientation only.[19]

---

[16] *Preserve Freedom, Reject Coercion*, COLSON CTR. FOR CHRISTIAN WORLDVIEW, https://perma .cc/HFP2-CP4L ("We therefore believe that proposed SOGI laws, including those narrowly crafted, threaten fundamental freedoms, and any ostensible protections for religious liberty appended to such laws are inherently inadequate and unstable.").

[17] For more on dignitary harms and law's expressive value, see NeJaime & Siegel, Chapter 6; Melling, Chapter 19; and Pizer, Chapter 29. For law's expressive effect, see Cass R. Sunstein, *On the Expressive Function of Law*, 144 U. PA. L. REV. 2021, 2025-26 (1996) (noting a law's statement about a subject "may be designed to affect social norms and in that way ultimately to affect both judgments and behavior... [A]n appropriately framed law may influence social norms and push them in the right direction").

[18] *See* Ark. Act No. 137 (2015); Protect Fayetteville v. City of Fayetteville, 510 SW 3d 258 (Ark. 2017) (holding Fayetteville SOGI ordinance conflicted with state law); Tennessee Pub. Ch. 278 (2011); Howe v. Haslam, 2014 WL 5698877 (Tenn. Ct. App. 2014); 2016 N.C. Sess. Laws 3, *repealed by* 2017 N.C. H.B. 142 (preempting local laws until December 1, 2020).

[19] *See* Appendix, Chapter 35. New York interprets its Human Rights Laws to cover transgender people. 9 N.Y. Code of Rules and Regs. §466.13.

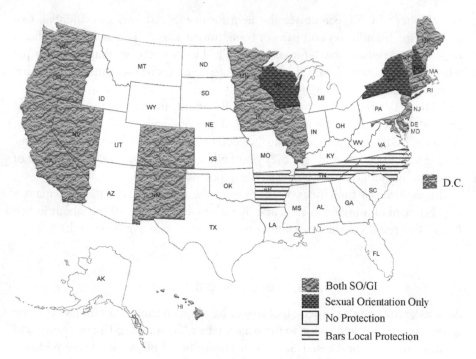

FIGURE 30.1 Public accommodations nondiscrimination laws (as of July 1, 2018)

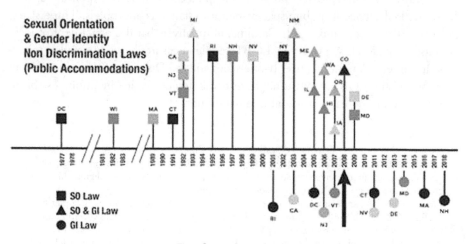

FIGURE 30.2 Timeline of nondiscrimination laws

As Figure 30.2 documents, although state SOGI laws date back to 1977, for the half-decade preceding and including 2008, states protected the full LGBT community in the nondiscrimination laws they enacted. That abruptly stopped in 2008.

After 2008, states have enacted LGBT protections in stages or added gender identity discrimination.[20] But the United States has seen no wholly new nondiscrimination law for all LGBT people in public accommodations since 2008, when the bathroom narrative emerged.

By recasting basic protections against SOGI discrimination as "allowing men to enter women's restrooms and locker rooms – defying common sense and common decency," opponents have stopped new laws, such as the Houston HERO Ordinance.[21] Opponents have also swept aside local ordinances protecting LGBT persons' full enjoyment of facilities. In North Carolina, for example, state legislators preempted Charlotte's SOGI, directing instead that all public accommodations require patrons to use the bathroom of their birth. The law provoked boycotts, travel bans, and numerous lawsuits before being mostly repealed.[22] Yet, despite the punishing backlash North Carolina experienced, the 2017 legislative year saw a raft of "bathroom-of-one's-birth laws" proposed across the country.[23] In 2018, campaigns for statewide office and initiatives to repeal local ordinances are being waged around bathroom access.[24]

Lawmakers who seek to enact protections for the full LGBT community in other realms, such as housing, must now contend with the "bathroom bill" label, too – even though sharing a bathroom with another member of the public is, patently, not an issue when renting an apartment for one's own use.[25] The move by regulators in Massachusetts, Iowa, and elsewhere to extend SOGI protections to houses of worship and other places previously considered off-limits only inflames matters further.[26] While those efforts have stalled or been disavowed,[27] careful line-drawing between the secular and sectarian can lower the stakes when writing nondiscrimination laws.[28]

---

[20] Maryland and Delaware enacted protections after 2008, while Connecticut, Massachusetts, and Nevada broadened pre-2008 bans on sexual orientation discrimination to include trans people. *See* Wilson, *Marriage of Necessity, supra* note 10, at 1383. New Hampshire recently joined those states by extending its ban to gender identity discrimination. *See* Appendix, Chapter 35.

[21] Houston, Tex., Ordinance 2014–530 (May 14, 2014).

[22] *See* Wilson, *Marriage of Necessity, supra* note 10.

[23] For citations and critique, see Melling, Chapter 19; Pizer, Chapter 29.

[24] *See, e.g., Stop Wagner*, https://perma.cc/QRR2-CFHS; *Protect Our Privacy*, ALASKA FAMILY COUNCIL, https://perma.cc/GF7E-7NS9.

[25] *Sign the Petition: Stop Governor Wolf's Bathroom Bills*, PAFAMILY.ORG, https://perma.cc/A8K5-GC5E ("Some things just shouldn't be shared. Tell Gov. Wolf: No Bathroom Bill.").

[26] *Sexual Orientation and Gender Identity: A Public Accommodations Provider's Guide to Iowa Law*, IOWA CIV. RTS. COMM'N, https://perma.cc/5D5U-FTEA; *Gender Identity Guidance*, MASS. COMM'N AGAINST DISCRIMINATION (Sept. 1, 2016) at 4–5, https://web.archive.org/web/20160915014340/http://www.mass.gov/mcad/docs/gender-identity-guidance.pdf.

[27] *See Gender Identity Guidance*, MASS. COMM'N AGAINST DISCRIMINATION (revised Dec. 5, 2016), https://perma.cc/3NDP-ZHR8; Chris Johnson, *Anti-LGBT Group Withdraws Lawsuit Against Mass. Trans Law*, WASH. BLADE (Dec. 12, 2016), https://perma.cc/N7L9-D2N4.

[28] *See* Adams, Chapter 32.

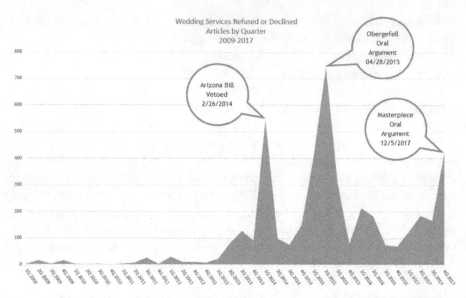

FIGURE 30.3 Reporting on wedding vendors declining to do service

On "bathroom" access, balancing two sets of interests is not hard: without fanfare and without trouble, Utah imposed a duty in its 2015 hiring and housing LGBT nondiscrimination law on all employers to accommodate trans workers' decisions to use the bathroom of their choice; employers retained discretion to adopt reasonable facility and grooming rules.[29] In the near- and mid-terms, however, the impulse to regulate *every* place people gather may defeat attempts to enact protections against discrimination in clearly warranted places: restaurants, bars, hotels, and other sectarian places.[30]

II RELIGIOUS WEDDING VENDORS IN BLUE AMERICA

Enacting new public accommodation laws faces a second, seemingly insurmountable hurdle: What to do about the baker, photographer, florist, or other wedding vendor conflicted over facilitating same-sex weddings? Here, the fires of resistance have been stoked by numerous stories of small wedding vendors who declined to facilitate same-sex marriages for religious reasons, as Figure 30.3 shows.[31]

---

[29] *Id.*

[30] *Accord* Melling, Chapter 19 ("Different questions arise where the issue concerns an exemption for an institution that primarily hires or serves only people of its own faith, or for an individual.").

[31] A search of LexisNexis's "News" database on March 2, 2018 for media accounts in U.S. jurisdictions yielded 4,443 discrete articles dating back to 2009. The specific search read "(gay or transgender or lgbt** or "sexual orientation") and wedding and (refus! or declin! w/5 serv!)." The oldest story described efforts to convince the Connecticut legislature to protect

Lawsuits followed these refusals, including two discussed at length in this volume, *Masterpiece Cakeshop, Ltd. v. Colorado Civil Rights Commission* and *State v. Arlene's Flowers, Inc.*[32]

In the court of public opinion, small business owners conflicted over same-sex marriage have been treated like religious martyrs by some and pariahs by others.[33]

In courts of law, religious business owners have lost every case – until 2018.[34] In *Cathy's Creations*, for the first time, a state court held that the First Amendment right of a religious baker to be free from compelled speech outweighed the government's interest in preventing dignitary harm to a lesbian couple through its public accommodations law.[35] The Court candidly acknowledged:

> No matter how the court should rule, one side or the other may be visited with some degree of hurt, insult, and indignity. The court finds that any harm here is equal to either complainants or [Cathy's Creations' owner], one way or the other. If anything, the harm to [the owner] is the greater harm, because it carries significant economic consequences.

While the Supreme Court largely declined to address the free speech issues posed in *Masterpiece Cakeshop*, instead deciding the case based on antireligious sentiment that corrupted the adjudication, the outcomes under the literal terms of state nondiscrimination laws in Phillips's and *every other case* until *Cathy's Creations* were prefigured. All ran afoul of SOGI laws written years before marriage equality *without* this specific conflict in mind, as Figure 30.4 shows.

In *Masterpiece Cakeshop*, for instance, Phillips's refusal occurred in 2012, two years before same-sex marriages first became legal in Colorado in 2014.[36] Colorado's

---

wedding-service providers in its same-sex marriage law. Daniela Altimari, *Catholics Press Their Case*, HARTFORD COURANT (Mar. 7, 2009), A1.

[32] Masterpiece Cakeshop, No. 16-111, slip op. State v. Arlene's Flowers, Inc., 389 P. 3d 543 (Wash. 2017) vacated and remanded, Order List, 585 U.S. __ (June 25, 2018), https://perma .cc/3X9Z-ADQQ. For other cases decided under laws predating marriage equality, see Elane Photography, LLC v. Willock, 309 P.3d 53 (N.M. 2013) *cert denied*, 134 S. Ct. 1787 (2014) (photographer); In the Matter of Klein, Case Nos. 44–14 & 45–14 (Or. Bureau of Labor & Industries 2015), https://perma.cc/QV27-Z5YB (religious bakers' denial of wedding cake for same-sex wedding); Complaint, Odgaard v. Iowa Civ. Rights Comm'n (Case No. CVCV046451 (Iowa Dist. Ct. Oct. 7, 2013), https://perma.cc/WM6G-V6AW (Mennonite art gallery owners' refusal to rent venue for same-sex wedding ceremony).

[33] *Compare* Curtis M. Wong, *Sweet Cakes By Melissa Receives Donations After Judge Rules They Owe $135,000 To Lesbian Couple*, HUFFINGTON POST (Feb. 2, 2016), https://perma.cc/ZG2D-NVEF, *with* Tom Coyne, *Memories Pizza Reopens After Gay Wedding Comments Flap*, WASH. TIMES (Apr. 9, 2015), https://perma.cc/UT9A-K3CW.

[34] Zack Ford, *12 Things Conservatives Have Predicted Would Happen Now That Marriage Equality Is Law*, THINKPROGRESS (June 29, 2015), https://perma.cc/L48R-L7WL.

[35] Dep't of Fair Emp't and Hous. v. Cathy's Creations, Inc., BCV-17–102855 (Cal. Super. Ct. of Kern) (Feb. 5, 2018) (finding no violation of state SOGI by religious baker refusing to bake custom wedding cake for lesbian couple, where couple was referred to a different baker who baked the cake).

[36] Masterpiece Cakeshop, 370 P.3d 272; *Same-Sex Marriage Officially Legal in Colorado*, KTTV NEWS (Oct. 8, 2014), https://perma.cc/7TGC-H923.

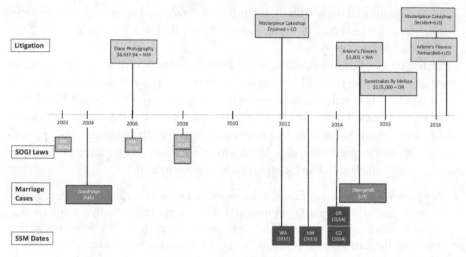

FIGURE 30.4 Enactment of SOGI laws in relation to same-sex marriage recognition

underlying law prohibiting discrimination in public accommodations was enacted in 2008, six years before marriage equality was recognized in Colorado and at a time when, as Figure 30.3 showed, the media paid little attention to same-sex wedding services, then largely a hypothetical possibility.[37] Obviously, when legislators cannot fully anticipate a need, as then, they cannot write specific rules to reconcile all the interests implicated; that is, they cannot tailor nondiscrimination laws written to address the central harm – persons being turned away from places like restaurants and hotels – while also avoiding the spillover to religiously infused services like weddings.

For many of these owners, their choice was "not about refusing service [to anyone] on the basis of sexual orientation or dislike for another person who is preciously created in God's image."[38] Betty Odgaard, owner of Görtz Haus Gallery,

---

[37] 2008 Colo. Sess. Laws 341 (May 29, 2008) (effective on passage). The earliest high-profile case pitting the rights of wedding vendors against the rights of same-sex couples also preceded marriage equality, Elane Photography, 309 P.3d 53 (N.M. 2013) *cert denied*, 134 S. Ct. 1787 (2014). There, a New Mexico wedding photographer declined to take pictures for a same-sex commitment ceremony in 2006. *Id.* The SOGI law under which the photography business was fined was enacted in 2004 – before any U.S. jurisdiction had conducted same-sex marriages and almost a decade before marriage equality became a reality in New Mexico, in 2013. N.M. STAT. § 28–1–7 (2004) (approved on March 10, 2004, effective July 1, 2014); Goodridge v. Dep't of Pub. Health, 440 Mass. 309, 798 N.E.2d 941 (2003) (legalizing same-sex marriage); Goodridge v. Dep't of Public Health, 2004 WL 5064000 (May 17, 2004) (trial court order upon remand; first marriages on this date); Griego v. Oliver, 316 P.3d 865 (N.M. 2013).
[38] Barronelle Stutzman, *Why a Friend Is Suing Me: The Arlene's Flowers Story*, SEATTLE TIMES (Nov. 9, 2015), https://perma.cc/4BG5-2WAA.

closed the gallery to all marriages rather than do same-sex marriages. The business later folded.[39] She felt conflicted about participating in the sanctification of same-sex marriages. "I would never discriminate in any area[,] that's not who I am. I just couldn't celebrate their wedding because of my faith."[40] Odgaard is not alone; marriage remains a religious occasion for half of all Americans, as Adams notes (Chapter 32).

So, too, with Barronelle Stutzman, who felt being asked to make flowers for her long-time client Rob Ingersoll and his husband Curt forced her to "choose between my affection for Rob and my commitment to Christ. As deeply fond as I am of Rob, my relationship with Jesus is everything to me. Without Christ, I can do nothing."[41] Stutzman's objection had less to do with Rob and Curt and more to do with Jesus. Odgaard's and Stutzman's marriage-focused objections may be parsed from objections to the couple themselves.[42]

Contrast wedding-focused objections to ones premised on homosexuality. Aaron Klein of Sweet Cakes by Melissa, which was ordered to pay $135,000 in fines and damages for refusing to bake a custom cake for a same-sex couple, quoted a Bible verse to one of the brides' mothers that labels same-sex relations "an abomination."[43] Unlike marriage-related objections, the basis for this objection *and* the protected ground, sexual orientation, are one and the same – they cannot be parsed: the objection is to serving the person at the counter precisely *because of* who they are.[44] Preexisting SOGIs make no distinction between refusals directed at a people and refusals tied to one's deeply held faith convictions about marriage.

Some, however, lump all these motivations together. True, "it was not the legality of marriage equality that was responsible for [businesses' repercussions]; it was laws

[39] The Odgaards sold the gallery building to a local church, saying, "If it can't be a gallery anymore, [a church] is the next best thing. We're pretty tickled." Kevin Hardy, *After Gay Marriage Controversy, Görtz Haus Now a Church*, DES MOINES REG. (Oct. 27, 2015), https://perma.cc/K3HT-VLFB.

[40] Curtis M. Wong, *Iowa's Görtz Haus Learns That Refusing to Host Gay Weddings Is Bad for Business*, HUFFINGTON POST (Feb. 2, 2016), https://perma.cc/GN5G-KTH9.

[41] *Supra* note 38.

[42] Both businesses employ LGBT workers and otherwise serve LGBT people. *See* McClain, Chapter 17; Smith, Chapter 18; Appellant's Brief, Washington v. Arlene's Flowers, Inc., No. 91615-2 (Wash. 2015) at 9–10, 13 (noting Stutzman "has employed and served those who identify as gay, lesbian and bisexual, and their sexual orientation did not affect how she viewed them as employees, customers and friends"). *See also* Elane Photography, 309 P.3d 53 (N.M. 2013) *cert denied*, 134 S. Ct. 1787 (2014), Petition for a Writ of Certiorari, No 13-585 (2013), at 7, https://perma.cc/25YJ-6UHP ("[T]he Huguenins gladly serve gays and lesbians.").

[43] In the Matter of Klein, Case Nos. 44-14 & 45-14, 5–6 (Or. Bureau of Labor & Industries 2015), https://perma.cc/QV27-Z5YB (finding one bride's mother told the same-sex couple that the baker told her "her children were an abomination unto God").

[44] *See* Frank Bruni, *Bigotry, the Bible and the Lessons of Indiana*, N.Y. TIMES (Apr. 3, 2015), https://perma.cc/XJ25-8QSH (arguing people "should know better than to tell gay people that they're an offense. And that's precisely what the florists and bakers who want to turn them away are saying to them").

guaranteeing equal access to goods and services."[45] But these laws preceded marriage equality itself.

Treating refusals premised on marriage as if a business told a customer to "get the hell out of my shop" not only disserves persons of faith like Odgaard and Stutzman who are struggling to balance the demands of faith with the demands of the law – it disserves the LGBT community. That conflation *is* the roadblock to progress.

The key to progress for both sides is to meld their respective interests. Just as one baker forced out of business by laws that penalize adherence to widely held religious beliefs about marriage is one too many,[46] one LGBT person excluded for just being gay or trans should be one too many, as well.

As the next section illustrates, the false assumption that regulation of public accommodations has always followed a purity model, and therefore the public square has never been shared, is frustrating honest attempts at combining protections for sexual minorities with protections for people of faith.

III NONDISCRIMINATION LAWS AND THE PURITY MODEL MYTH

The key to a truce in the culture war between faith and sexuality rests on rejecting a binary model that treats all services by businesses on Main Street identically. As noted earlier, public accommodations laws today do not make fine distinctions *once* a class is defined as "protected" *and* a business on Main Street is regulated. But that all-in structure masks an important fact: our federal public accommodations laws and those of twenty-two states and DC reach a subset of all businesses open to the public or none at all.[47] In fact, outside the states that have SOGIs now, laws sweeping widely and laws sweeping narrowly are almost evenly split, as this section shows.

Whatever the sweep of public accommodations nondiscrimination laws, it is possible to keep religious wedding vendors in business while *not* turning gay couples away, just as it is possible to authorize businesses to share restrooms in a way that preserves the dignity and privacy of all patrons.

Lawmakers should not conflate duties placed on regulated businesses, however broadly defined, to serve all people with a duty on any *individual, even the owner,* to provide a religiously infused service. These are legally distinct. As Olson intimated shortly after *Obergefell*, they are morally distinct, too. The primary thrust of public accommodations laws is that no one who comes into a shop is told to get out, no one is sent down the street. That overarching goal can be accomplished by regulating the

---

[45] Ford, *supra* note 34. *See also* Robin Fretwell Wilson, *The Calculus of Accommodation: Contraception, Abortion, Same-Sex Marriage, and Other Clashes Between Religion and the State,* 53 B.C. L. Rev. 1417 (2012) (noting nondiscrimination laws spill over to contexts not imagined).

[46] *See* Ryan Anderson, Chapter 27.

[47] *See* Appendix, Chapter 35; Section III.A.2.

business, not every person in it. Pushing this distinction expressly into law would go a long way towards ensuring that sorely needed protections for the LGBT community do not come at the expense of shop owners' livelihoods.

A *Scope of Nondiscrimination Laws Reveal a Deeply Pluralistic America*

This subsection first diagrams the narrow scope of Title II and then places state laws on a continuum from targeted coverage to the broader, all-in coverage of some state laws.

1 Title II's Targeted Scope

Title II reaches a short list of places – inns and transient lodging, places that sell food for consumption on site, gas stations, entertainment venues, and establishments that contain these kinds of places for their patrons – and proscribes discrimination on a narrow set of bases: "race, color, religion, or national origin."[48] These places track the "common law notion that innkeepers and common carriers had an obligation to accept all 'travellers [sic].'"[49] "Private clubs or establishment[s]" fall outside Title II's coverage,[50] erecting a private/public distinction.[51] To trigger Title II, an establishment must affect commerce or be supported by state action.[52] This scope makes obvious a fact often overlooked: federal public accommodations law has never required all businesses to serve all comers.[53]

Contrast this narrow scope with the far more capacious scope of the Americans with Disabilities Act (ADA), which expressly encompasses retail establishments, all "service establishment[s]," "social service center establishments," including adoption agencies, and places of "public gathering."[54] While "religious organizations or

---

[48] 42 U.S.C. § 2000a (b) (2012).

[49] Phyllis Coleman, *eHarmony and Homosexuals: A Match Not Made in Heaven*, 30 QUINNIPIAC L. REV. 727, 741–42, n. 85–88 (2012).

[50] 42 U.S.C. § 2000a (e) (2012) (expressly exempting "a private club or other establishment not in fact open to the public, except to the extent that the facilities of such establishment are made available to the customers or patrons" within Title II's scope).

[51] For importance of this boundary, see Krotoszynski, Chapter 7. The boundary between public and private has been probed in a dizzying array of circumstances. *See* David S. Cohen, *The Stubborn Persistence of Sex Segregation*, 20 COLUM. J. GENDER & L. 51, 115 n. 287 (2011) ("As a representative sample, country clubs, private membership organizations, mosques, health clubs and gyms, golf courses, local Franco-American fraternal clubs, and fishing and hunting clubs have had to litigate whether they were permitted to segregate based on sex under state anti-discrimination laws.").

[52] 42 U.S.C. § 2000a (2012).

[53] *See* NeJaime & Siegel, Chapter 6; McConnell, Chapter 28.

[54] Americans with Disabilities Act, 42 U.S.C. § 12181(7) (2012). Even cast broadly, ADA duties have been anchored to "physical place" so that an employer benefit plan fell outside its coverage. *See* Kolling v. Blue Cross & Blue Shield of Michigan, 318 F.3d 715 (6th Cir. 2003).

entities controlled by religious organizations" are expressly exempted,[55] it is difficult to imagine much that is not covered.

The narrowness of Title II's scope versus the ADA's is shown in cases interpreting Title II to exempt service establishments like hair salons. Take, for example, *Halton v. Great Clips, Inc.*[56] There, former employees and customers brought suit in federal court against a Great Clips franchise, alleging it refused to provide relaxers and "fades" – services predominantly sought by African Americans – while offering "permanents" to white customers. Plaintiffs charged violations of Title II and Ohio's public accommodations nondiscrimination law.

In granting summary judgment for the defendant business and owner on the Title II claim, the district court noted that, as a "threshold matter," Title II "clearly does not include retail stores and food markets because there has been little if any discrimination in the operation of these establishments."[57] For this proposition, it cited *Newman v. Piggie Park Enterprises*.

While courts "have found health spas, golf clubs, and beach clubs" to be covered by Title II as places of entertainment, the court would have been "hard-pressed to find that the hair services offered by [Great] Clips could be deemed 'entertainment.'"[58]

As a service establishment, Great Clips was simply not contemplated by Title II's definition. "[I]f Congress wanted to include ... a service establishment, it could have amended Title II" to encompass such businesses.[59] Given the ADA's breadth and Title II's circumscribed scope, "inaction by Congress could not be mere oversight or an expectation that courts would broadly interpret the statute to include basically any type of establishment."[60] That Great Clips was located in a shopping plaza did not suffice to bring it within Title II. That "reading of the statute would bring every establishment in any mall or any shopping center within the statute's purview," a result Congress did not intend.[61]

Ironically, *Great Clips* relied upon *Newman v. Piggie Park Enterprises*, a case invoked across this volume. Pizer says of *Piggie Park* that "Americans have officially rejected racial segregation regardless of religious motivation;"[62] Louise Melling says restaurant franchise owners may "espouse the religious beliefs of his own choosing,"

---

[55] 42 U.S.C. § 12187 (2012).
[56] 94 F. Supp. 2d 856 (N.D. Ohio 2000).
[57] *Id.* at 862 (citing Newman v. Piggie Park Enterprises, 377 F.2d 433 (4th Cir. 1967), *aff'd*, 390 U.S. 400 (1968)).
[58] 94 F. Supp. 2d at 862.
[59] *Id.*
[60] *Id.*
[61] *Id.* at 863 (noting Title II would encompass businesses that have "a covered establishment" on premises, like a sit-down restaurant). Plaintiffs' claims went forward under Ohio law which regulates any "place for the sale of merchandise." 94 F. Supp. 2d at 870; Ohio Rev. Code § 4112.01(9).
[62] *See* Pizer, Chapter 29.

but do "not have the absolute right to exercise and practice such beliefs in utter disregard of the clear constitutional rights of other citizens."[63] Linda McClain notes the Colorado court in *Masterpiece Cakeshop* cited *Piggie Park* for the same proposition,[64] as does the majority in *Masterpiece Cakeshop*.[65] But for all the emphasis placed on *Piggie Park*, the United States Court of Appeals for the Fourth Circuit observed:

> The sense of [Title II's] plan of coverage is apparent. Retail stores, food markets, and the like were excluded from the Act for the policy reason that there was little, if any, discrimination in the operation of them. Negroes have long been welcomed as customers in such stores.[66]

Congress never found a need for regulating retail establishments – or any businesses outside the narrow band covered by Title II. In other words, Congress never reached the butcher, the baker, or the candlestick maker.

2 The Variable Scope Under State Nondiscrimination Laws

State laws take a range of approaches, from the ADA's broad coverage to Title II's narrow one.[67] California's Unruh Civil Rights law typifies the former. It reaches "the full and equal accommodations, advantages, facilities, privileges, or services in all business establishments of every kind whatsoever."[68] Other states hew closely to federal law in specifying enumerated *places*. Ohio is representative: it covers "any inn, restaurant, eating house, barbershop, public conveyance by air, land, or water, theater, store, other place for the sale of merchandise, or any other place of public accommodation or amusement of which the accommodations, advantages, facilities, or privileges are available to the public."[69]

---

[63] *See* Melling, Chapter 19 (quoting *Piggie Park*, 390 U.S. 400 at 945).

[64] *See* McClain, Chapter 17 (citing *Masterpiece Cakeshop*, 370 P.3d at 291 (quoting *Piggie Park*, 390 U.S. 400 at 945)).

[65] Masterpiece Cakeshop, No. 16-111, slip op. at 9.

[66] 372 F.2d at 476 (citing remarks of Senator Humphrey).

[67] *Compare* Coleman, *supra* note 49, at 741–42 ("Even though the federal statute continues to define public accommodations narrowly, state laws now typically include just about all businesses.").

[68] Cal. Civil Code §51.

[69] Ohio Rev. Code 4112.01(A)(9). In interpreting a similar list in a gambling probation statute, Ohio's Attorney General read "other place of public accommodation" to refer to places like those preceding it in the statute, like "hotel[s], restaurant[s], tavern[s], store[s], arena[s], hall[s]." Ohio Attorney General Op. 75–005 (Jan. 30, 1975), http://www.ohioattorneygeneral.gov/getattachment/1318d384-9d4d-40bf-bf82-a2ee85c6b37e/1975-005.aspx. Whether a particular place is "public" depends on its use. *Id.*

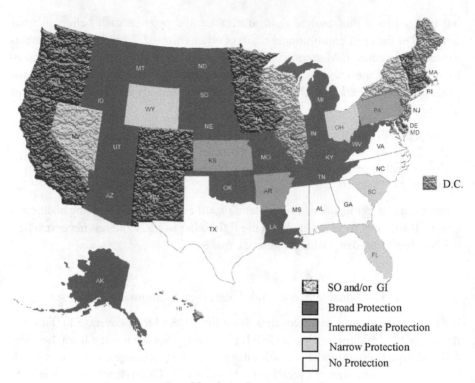

FIGURE 30.5 Breadth of nondiscrimination laws

Not all states cast the net as widely as possible, as Figure 30.5 shows. Indeed, America is a checkerboard on scope of nondiscrimination laws, just as it is with whether LGBT persons are protected from discrimination.[70]

Twenty-eight states follow the California all-in model, including some that have extended SOGI nondiscrimination protection to the LGBT community, such as Washington, and some that have not, such as Arizona.[71] Eight states hew to the

[70] Based on the text of scope provisions only, laws characterized here as broad cover all conceivable businesses. Laws with intermediate coverage anchorage coverage to a physical location and enumerated type of business but reach services, too. Narrow laws do not include a reference to services and hinge on enumerated places.

[71] *See* Appendix, Chapter 35, Col. 3 (listing Alaska, Arizona, California, Colorado, Connecticut, Delaware, Hawaii, Idaho, Indiana, Iowa, Kentucky, Louisiana, Massachusetts, Michigan, Minnesota, Missouri, Montana, Nebraska, New Mexico, North Dakota, Oklahoma, Oregon, South Dakota, Tennessee, Utah, Vermont, Washington, and West Virginia).

States often mirror federal law in not reaching private entities. *See, e.g.*, Wis. Stat. 106.52 (2015) ("'Public place of accommodation or amusement' does not include a place where a bona fide private, nonprofit organization or institution provides accommodations . . . to the following individuals only: a. Members of the organization or institution. b. Guests named by members . . . c. Guests named by the organization").

Even when a state's public accommodations law covers a longer list of businesses, scope questions arise. This is because "[h]istorically, public accommodations provided essential

federal government's specified-list of regulated places approach.[72] Six states, all in the Bible belt, have no public accommodations law protecting anyone from discrimination in public places.[73] Eight states and DC follow a middle course, focusing on places but explicitly including within the category of public accommodations businesses that provide "services."[74] Thus, state laws can be arrayed on a continuum between Title II's narrow and California's "all-in" approaches.

Despite the rhetoric that all businesses must serve all comers, that has not been the rule across America.[75] Query whether states that have not enacted SOGI nondiscrimination protections will be willing to include LGBT persons within the state's protections absent a new model for accommodating religious persons in such laws.

B *Regulating the Bakery, Not the Baker*

Underpinning the purity model is the notion that no departure can be tolerated from the way in which racial nondiscrimination has been addressed in this country. Enacted at a time of great racial division, the Civil Rights Act of 1964 (1964 Act) ameliorated many of the effects of discrimination based on race,[76] which has blighted our nation.

---

products or services but later cases include other, non-required businesses." Coleman, *supra* note 49. For instance, dating services have been found to be covered even when not statutorily enumerated. *See, e.g.*, Lahmann v. Grand Aerie of Fraternal Order of Eagles, 43 P.3d 1130, 1135–36 (Or. Ct. App. 2002).

[72] *See* Appendix, Chapter 35, Col. 3 (listing Florida, Nevada, New York, Rhode Island, Ohio, South Carolina, Wisconsin, and Wyoming).

[73] These states are Alabama, Georgia, Mississippi, North Carolina, Texas, and Virginia.

[74] *See* Appendix, Chapter 35, Col. 3 (listing Arkansas, District of Columbia, Illinois, Kansas, Maine, Maryland, New Hampshire, New Jersey, and Pennsylvania).

[75] Title II's narrow scope alleviates the pressure under a no-exceptions-once-regulated-approach because it reaches some but not all storefronts on Main Street. For example, small dental offices would not be regulated as public accommodations under federal law or the law of some states. *See* Robin Fretwell Wilson, *When Governments Insulate Dissenters From Social Change: What Hobby Lobby and Abortion Conscience Clauses Teach About Specific Exemptions*, 48 U.C. DAVIS L. REV. 703, 758–59 n.271 (2014). Thus, not all businesses a person might encounter walking down Main Street are regulated public accommodations, avoiding the question legally of whether professionals should be regulated exactly as businesses selling goods.

Because of scope limitations, some wedding vendors remain outside state SOGI laws. *See* Amy Lynn Photography Studio v. City of Madison, Case No. 17CV0555 at 3 (Wis. Cir. Ct. 2017), http://www.adfmedia.org/files/AmyLynnPhotographyJudgmentWisconsin.pdf (quoting WIS. STAT. § 106.52(1)(e)1 (2015))(finding no violation by Wisconsin photographer operating online business from her home because statute encompassed only businesses with a "physical storefront").

[76] Since the 1964 Act's passage, Americans have become increasingly intolerant of racial intolerance. Consider approval of marriages between "blacks and whites," where public support has leapt from about 10% in 1964 to 87% in 2013. *See* Frank Newport, *In U.S., 87% Approve of*

Change resulted in part because the 1964 Act permits no exceptions for smaller businesses.[77] As the president of the AFL-CIO said in testimony submitted to Congress:

> A Negro seeking service at a small lunch counter can be just as hungry as the one who stops at Howard Johnson's. The public accommodations bill is too important to be compromised by limiting either the size or type of establishment covered or the means of enforcing the right to equal service. We need a public accommodations bill with teeth in it.[78]

Congress did not regulate every "type of establishment," but it understood the "public-spirited proprietor will benefit from an enforceable public accommodations measure" applied uniformly to whatever establishments are covered; without blanket treatment for regulated businesses, the "public establishment [that] wants to do the right thing, but [is] concerned lest their competitors gain an advantage by continuing old discriminatory practices," may be disadvantaged in the marketplace and dissuaded from positive change.[79]

While the 1964 Act left aside small homeowners who rent rooms in their home, known as the Mrs. Murphy exception, the rationale for leaving them aside – "the right to privacy in one's residence" – "[had] no applicability to a small commercial hotel, a small restaurant, a bowling alley, or a barbershop."[80] Being turned away from a storefront on Main Street "carr[ied] different social meanings" than being refused by a private homeowner. "While a tired black family might bitterly resent [the homeowner's] decision, they would understand themselves as victims of her personal choice – and this is categorically different from the institutionalized humiliation imposed by a hotel clerk who rejects them.'"[81]

Congress expressly rejected a small lunch counter exception mirroring the small employer exception in Title VII of the 1964 Act.[82] An "explicit cutoff – in either dollar volume or number of employees – should [not] be written into this bill to

---

Black-White Marriage, vs. 4% in 1958, GALLUP (July 25, 2013), http://www.gallup.com/poll/163697/approve-marriage-blackswhites.aspx.

[77] Brian K. Landsberg, *Public Accommodations and the Civil Rights Act of 1964: A Surprising Success?*, 36 HAMLINE J. PUB. L. & POL'Y 1 (2014).

[78] *Civil Rights – Public Accommodations: Hearings Before the S. Comm. on Commerce S. 1732, a Bill to Eliminate Discrimination in Public Accommodations Affecting Interstate Commerce*, 88th Cong. 1259 (1963) (statement of Walter P. Reuther, President, International Union, United Automobile Workers).

[79] *Id.; see also Civil Rights – Public Accommodations, supra* note 78, at 257. (Statement of Senator Javits) ("I do not believe Congress should itself discriminate against the larger businesses in favor of the smaller ones, in order to permit the latter the capability of racial discrimination.").

[80] *Id., supra* note 77, at 1260 (statement of Mr. Reuther). *See generally* Robin Fretwell Wilson, *Bargaining for Civil Rights: Lessons from Mrs. Murphy for Same-Sex Marriage and LGBT Rights*, 95 B.U. L. REV. 951, 975 (2015) (noting that the Mrs. Murphy exceptions were premised on privacy, associational rights, civil rights, and political expediency, as well as "the difficulty and cost of enforcement and the collateral costs of federalizing interpersonal relationships").

[81] BRUCE ACKERMAN, WE THE PEOPLE: THE CIVIL RIGHTS REVOLUTION 142 (2014).

[82] 42 U.S.C. § 2000e(b) (2012) (exempting employers with fewer than 15 employees).

exempt outright smaller businesses."[83] Including such exemptions would "negate the moral and human base for this legislation."[84] And making some exceptions would undercut the assurance given that all Americans would be treated alike regardless of race.[85] Within a regulated category, such as hotels, "virtually universal coverage facilitated compliance by removing the fear that, if a public accommodation desegregated, its customers could flee to one that remained segregated."[86]

On the Senate floor, Vermont Senator Winston Prouty explained that "[t]he evil [Congress] seek[s] to remove is the degradation of a man in his use of the common privileges because his skin is not the proper color. The affront is to his dignity."[87] "Discrimination," the Senate report to the 1964 Act explained, "is not simply dollars and cents, hamburgers and movies; it is the humiliation, frustration, and embarrassment that a person must surely feel when he is told that he is unacceptable as a member of the public."[88]

The 1964 Act sought to erase institutionalized humiliation, the primary evil of discrimination.[89] When a group can be freely denied access to businesses open to others, it signals to that group that it is inferior and not valued as members of the polity.[90]

The lesson of the 1964 Act is this: no one should be turned away from a business on Main Street open to everyone else. Treating customers with dignity requires that regulated businesses serve all customers. The stricture can be honored *without* running religious people out of the public square – by regulating the business, not individual workers, so that every couple who walks in is served with dignity but no specific individual must perform any given service.

New SOGI laws should make clear that, as to weddings, religious owners can fulfill duties imposed on their businesses without personally performing a given service. Larger business can hire a new employee to perform the service if existing employees, as a matter of faith, cannot. Small business owners of businesses where there is a high probability that the owner or a family member would be asked to do the service personally would retain the discretion to hire a new employee to assist the business to fulfill its new duty or to put in place arrangements with contractual partners to assist as needed.

---

[83] "[A] Negro should not be forced to decide whether the particular hotel or motel he is approaching is one large enough to treat him like any other fellow American. *"Civil Rights – Public Accommodations," supra* note 78 (Statement of Senator Javits).

[84] *Id.*

[85] *Id.*

[86] Landsberg, *supra* note 77, at 9–10 (quoting ACKERMAN, *supra* note 81, at 142).

[87] 110 CONG. REC. 8258 (1964).

[88] Heart of Atlanta Motel, Inc. v. United States, 379 U.S. 241, 291–92 (1964) (quoting S.Rep. No.872, 88th Cong., 2d Sess., 16).

[89] ACKERMAN, *supra* note 81.

[90] Holning Lau, *Transcending the Individualist Paradigm in Sexual Orientation Antidiscrimination Law*, 94 CALIF. L. REV. 1271 (2006); Nan. D. Hunter, *Accommodating the Public Sphere: Beyond the Market Model*, 85 MINN. L. REV. 1591 (2001) (describing the significance of citizenship).

For the smallest businesses, hiring new workers may be too costly, placing a premium on the need for legislators to leave the discretion afforded by contract law to subcontract with others to fulfill the obligation. If a business cannot afford to hire a new employee, a new duty on the business to serve all customers in all services can effectively force an owner to *personally* provide a particular service *unless* flexibility to cover the service through a subcontractor is baked in. Such a duty will, of course, apply whether a business is incorporated or conducted as a sole proprietorship.

The ability to use independent contractors to fulfill contracts for goods and routine services already exists in the background law of most states. The business remains on the hook contractually for the service, is liable for breach, and must ensure performance – just as businesses do when acting through employees.[91]

Now, if one sees SOGI laws as devices to run religious people out of the public square or to expunge certain views from society – a feature, not a bug[92] – this idea will be wholly unacceptable. But if the goal is to avoid the humiliation and dignitary losses LGBT persons experience all too frequently across the United States today,[93] then parsing between the business and owners accomplishes this.

IV CONCLUSION

Without a new model for sharing the public space, we risk perpetuating a culture war between faith and sexuality, a war no one can win.

No one should be turned away from a business open to all on Main Street. But neither should persons of faith effectively be barred from operating small businesses that focus on, or only sometimes cater to, weddings. To borrow a quip, bakeries cannot be choosers. But individual business owners should be allowed to decide how the cake is baked.

As Andrew Sullivan said once, neither side will "conquer intolerance with intolerance."[94] Finding flexible approaches that keep both parties in the public square is not only right and decent, it offers the best hope for "changing minds and hearts."

---

[91] Jared G. Kramer, *When Should Contracts Be Assignable? An Economic Analysis* 7 (Harvard Law Sch. John M. Olin Center for Law, Economics, & Business, Discussion Paper No. 484 (Aug. 2004) ("As a matter of contract default rules, contract rights can generally be assigned, and contract obligations can generally be delegated to others.").

[92] *Compare* Bruni, *supra* note 44 (quoting a prominent gay philanthropist as saying "church leaders must be made 'to take homosexuality off the sin list'").

[93] See NeJaime & Siegel, Chapter 6; Melling, Chapter 19; and Pizer, Chapter 29, for poignant accounts.

[94] Andrew Sullivan, *The Morning After In Arizona*, THE DISH (Feb. 27, 2014), http://dish.andrew sullivan.com/2014/02/27/the-morning-after-in-arizona/.

PART VIII

Reflections from Advocates, Legislators, and Policymakers

31

Sound Nondiscrimination Models and the Need to Protect LGBTQ People in Federal Law

Sarah Warbelow

Lesbian, gay, bisexual, transgender, and queer (LGBTQ) people are a part of the rich tapestry that makes up America. Located in every corner of this country,[1] unbound by class, race, or religion, LGBTQ people may quite literally be your brother, aunt, child, neighbor, postal carrier, or doctor. Being LGBTQ is normal[2] and ought to be unremarkable; certainly a person's sexual orientation or gender identity is irrelevant to their ability to excel in the workplace, be a great tenant, thoughtfully choose a gift at the mall, or contribute in any other way to that complex fabric that forms life in the United States. Yet, a history of invidious discrimination, including criminalization,[3] has left its ugly mark on the current lives of LGBTQ people.

The patchwork of laws prohibiting discrimination on the basis of sexual orientation and gender identity[4] mirror a political class conflicted about whether to embrace their neighbors.[5] In contrast, fair-minded Americans from across the political spectrum support the adoption of national nondiscrimination laws that explicitly include LGBTQ people.[6] However, one of the challenges for advocates is

---

[1] Williams Inst., *Just the Facts: LGBT Data Overview* 2015, UCLA SCH. OF LAW, https://perma.cc/F3PH-29JL.

[2] Jack Drescher, *Out of DSM: Depathologizing Homosexuality*, 5 BEHAV. SCI. 565, 572 (2015). The American Psychiatric Association delisted sexual orientation from the DIAGNOSTIC AND STATISTICAL MANUAL OF MENTAL DISORDERS in 1973, with similar moves to reflect the fact that "a transgender identity is not a disorder." *See also, The Psychology of Transgender*, AM. PSYCH. ASS'N (Nov. 19, 2015), https://perma.cc/DK76-3NX6.

[3] *See, e.g.*, Lawrence v. Texas, 539 U.S. 558 (2003); People v. Archibald, 296 N.Y.S.2d 834 (App. Term 1968), *aff'd*, 27 N.Y.2d 504, 260 N.E.2d 871 (1970).

[4] Sarah Warbelow & Breanna Diaz, 2017 *State Equality Index*, HUMAN RIGHTS CAMPAIGN FOUND. (2017).

[5] Daniel Cox & Joanna Piacenza, *Nearly One-Quarter of Americans Oppose Same-Sex Marriage While Supporting Nondiscrimination Laws*, PUB. RELIGION RES. INST. (2015).

[6] *Id.*

that people believe protections are such common sense that they must already exist.[7] Unfortunately, LGBTQ people are subject to a grab bag of protections including incomplete and inconsistently interpreted federal laws in addition to widely varying state level laws.[8] Recently at the federal level, critical nondiscrimination protections have been undermined or dismantled through rollbacks of administrative regulations combined with lax or no enforcement. State legislatures have similarly engaged in attacks against the LGBTQ community, with more than 500 anti-LGBTQ pieces of proposed legislation introduced over the last three years. Caught in the middle are LGBTQ people who are simply trying to live their lives and fulfill their dreams without being subjected to discriminatory treatment at every turn.

Uniform federal nondiscrimination laws are desperately needed to ensure that when Americans engage in the public square, prejudices do not determine destiny. Making the assumption that an individual's core identity – whether race, religion, sexual orientation, gender identity, or any other protected characteristic – is predictive of their capacity to contribute is unacceptable. Ensuring equal treatment under the law is fundamental to the American ethos, and nondiscrimination laws for LGBTQ people fulfill that promise.

I FEDERAL CIVIL RIGHTS LEGISLATION AND RELIGIOUS EXEMPTIONS

A *Religious Opposition to Civil Rights and Racial Equality*

While odious to most people today, opposition to civil rights legislation prohibiting race discrimination partially rested on religious grounds. Individuals, religious organizations, and even government actors argued that segregation was supported by the Bible, arguments used to support antimiscegenation laws and state-sanctioned defiance of *Brown v. Board of Education.*[9] Our nation's most prominent leaders including congressmen, judges, and governors cited these claims.[10] Twice-elected Governor of Mississippi and US Senator Theodore Bilbo stated, "there is every reason to believe

---

[7] Peter Moore, *Poll Results: Discrimination*, YouGov (June 18, 2014), https://perma.cc/72QH-3EA7.

[8] For state nondiscrimination laws, see Appendix, Chapter 35.

[9] Linda C. McClain, *The Civil Rights Act of 1964 and "Legislating Morality": On Conscience, Prejudice, and Whether "Stateways" Can Change "Folksways,"* 95 B.U. L. Rev. 891, 917 (2015) (citing Fay Botham, Almighty God Created the Races: Christianity, Interracial Marriage, and American Law, 131–57 (2009) (explaining the role of "Southern White Protestant theology of race" in creating antimiscegenation laws)).

[10] *See, e.g.,* Loving v. Virginia, 388 U.S. 1 (1967) (quoting trial judge's statement regarding interracial married couple Mildred and Richard Loving: "Almighty God created the races white, black, yellow, malay and red, and he placed them on separate continents. And, but for the interference with his arrangement, there would be no cause for such marriage. The fact that he separated the races shows that he did not intend for the races to mix.").

that miscegenation and amalgamation are sins of a man in direct defiance to the will of God."[11] Even pastors made these claims. Pastor James Burks characterized integration in a sermon shortly after *Brown* as "another stepping stone toward the gross immorality and lawlessness that will be characteristic of the last days."[12]

The debate around the Civil Rights Act of 1964 (1964 Act) ultimately asked the question of whether Congress could "legislate morality" in response to atrocities depicted across the South during the civil rights movement.[13] Opponents of the bill proposed a blanket exemption for religious organizations, arguing that, as social institutions, these groups were part of a larger freedom of association, guaranteed by the "natural law" that also promoted segregation.[14] Such exemptions were defended on the basis that, "although the federal government was legislating morality, it would not attempt to become involved in social relationships."[15] Although this proposal failed, Title VII of the Civil Rights Act of 1964 (Title VII) provides an exemption for religious employers.[16]

Even after passage of the 1964 Act, business owners resisted complying with the law, arguing they should be allowed to continue to discriminate based on religious belief regarding segregation. In the 1968 US Supreme Court case *Newman v. Piggie Park Enterprises*, the owner of a South Carolina barbecue restaurant argued that his religious belief caused him to oppose any racial integration, including in his restaurants.[17] The Supreme Court rejected the assertion that a business owner's religious beliefs allowed him to refuse to comply with public accommodation law, holding that the owner "has a constitutional right to espouse the religious beliefs of his own choosing, however, he does not have the absolute right to exercise and practice such beliefs in utter disregard of the clear constitutional rights of other citizens."[18]

The experiences of people of color and LGBTQ people, where the communities do not overlap, have very different historical roots and frequently different modern manifestations of discrimination. Still, the federal laws that have been adopted to address discrimination on the basis of race, religion, national origin, and sex provide important insights into how sexual orientation and gender identity can fit into an existing framework.

---

[11] THEODORE G. BILBO, TAKE YOUR CHOICE: SEPARATION OR MONGRELIZATION 91 (1946).

[12] Jane Dailey, *Sex, Segregation, and the Sacred After Brown*, 91 J. AM. HIST. 1 (Apr. 23, 2006).

[13] McClain, *supra* note 9, at 891–95.

[14] *Id.* at 913 (referencing Civil Rights Commission: Hearings on S. 1117 and S. 1219 Before the Subcomm. On Constitutional Rights of the Comm. on the Judiciary, 88th Cong. 41–43 (1963) (statement of Sen. Sam J. Ervin, North Carolina)).

[15] *Id.* at 912 (referencing Civil Rights: Hearings on H.R. 7152 as Amended by Subcomm. No. 5 Before the H. Comm. on the Judiciary, 88th Cong. 2700 (1963) (statement of Robert F. Kennedy, Att'y Gen. of the United States)).

[16] *See* Hill, Chapter 26.

[17] Newman v. Piggie Park Enters., Inc., 390 U.S. 400 (1968).

[18] *Id.*

B Religious Exemptions in Current Civil Rights Laws

Currently, religious organizations benefit from a broad set of religious exemptions to federal nondiscrimination law. These expansive exemptions amply protect religious employers and organizations from government intrusion in employment and housing.

The Supreme Court has noted that the US Constitution gives "special solicitude to the rights of religious organizations."[19] Despite the important role of these exemptions, the Supreme Court has also recognized that the government has a unique, compelling interest in protecting against employment discrimination. In *Burwell v. Hobby Lobby*, the Supreme Court held that the Religious Freedom Restoration Act (RFRA) exempted some employers with religious objections from complying with the contraceptive coverage mandate implemented under the Patient Protection and Affordable Care Act. Writing for the majority, Justice Samuel Alito rejected "the possibility that discrimination in hiring ... might be cloaked as a religious practice to escape legal sanction."[20] He wrote: "[O]ur decision today provides no such shield. The Government has a compelling interest in providing equal opportunity to participate in the workforce[.]"[21]

C Title VII and the Ministerial Exception

Title VII currently provides an exemption from the ban on employment discrimination based on religion. Sections 702(a) and 703(e) exclude from coverage any "religious corporation, association, or society," as well as "a school, college, university or other educational institution or institution of learning if (i) the organization is, in whole or in part, owned, supported, controlled, or managed by a religious corporation, association, or society or (ii) the curriculum of the organization is directed toward the propagation of a religion."

Decades of case law interpreting Title VII have made clear that this includes a broad range of organizations. Federal courts have found many types of religious entities, well beyond houses of worship alone, to be eligible, including:

- a retirement home operated by Presbyterian Ministries,[22]
- a newspaper published by the First Church of Christ, Scientist,[23]
- Christian elementary schools and universities,[24] and

---

[19] Hosanna-Tabor Evangelical Lutheran Church and School v. EEOC, 565 U.S. 171, 200 (2012).

[20] 134 S. Ct. 2751 (2014).

[21] *Id.*

[22] EEOC v. Presbyterian Ministries, 788 F. Supp. 1154 (W.D. Wash. 1992).

[23] Feldstein v. Christian Science Monitor, 555 F. Supp. 974 (D. Mass. 1983).

[24] *See, e.g.,* Ganzy v. Allen Christian School, 995 F. Supp. 340 (E.D.N.Y. 1998); Killinger v. Samford University, 113 F.3d 196 (11th Cir. 1997); Little v. Wuerl, 929 F.2d 944 (3d Cir. 1991).

- a nonprofit medical center operated by the Seventh-Day Adventist Church.[25]

In addition to Title VII's religious exemption, the Supreme Court has identified a "ministerial exception" under the First Amendment that religious organizations are entitled to use in their employment practices. As articulated in *Hosanna-Tabor Evangelical Lutheran Church & School v. EEOC*, a case regarding a discrimination claim brought by a teacher at a religious school, the "ministerial exception" applies to employees serving in roles beyond the traditional ministerial role.[26] Federal courts have found a variety of religious organization employees to be exempt from non-discrimination laws including:

- a cemetery employee who organized religious services,[27]
- a theology professor,[28] and
- a music director.[29]

However, employees serving in "purely custodian or janitorial" roles have not been considered ministerial.[30] Similarly, an organist who had no control over order of service and no contact with parishioners fell outside of the scope of the exception.[31]

Neither Title VII nor the "ministerial exception," however, permits any secular employer to discriminate based on individual prejudices, morals, or religious-based beliefs. This is true of all civil rights laws, including those that protect Christians, Jews, and other religious individuals from discrimination. A secular employer, organization, or company that markets its goods and services to the general public cannot circumvent civil rights laws for a religious purpose. No civil rights statute restricts the ability of a person to hold contrary beliefs, based on religion or otherwise. The purpose of civil rights laws historically has been to ensure fundamental fairness so that individuals are able to live and work in environments free of discrimination.

D Fair Housing Act

Religious entities are exempt from the 1968 Fair Housing Act with regard to the sale, rental, or occupancy of a dwelling owned by the organization for noncommercial purposes.[32] In addition, the law exempts single family homes sold or rented by the owner as well as rooms or units for rent where there are no more than four units and

---

[25] Young v. Shawnee Mission Med. Ctr., 1988 U.S. Dist. LEXIS 12248 (D. Kan. 1988).
[26] Hosanna-Tabor, 565 U.S. 171.
[27] Fisher v. Archdiocese of Cincinnati, 6 N.E.3d 1254 (Ohio Ct. App. 2014).
[28] *See, e.g.*, Klouda v. Sw. Baptist Theological Seminary, 543 F. Supp. 2d 594 (N.D. Tex. 2008).
[29] Starkman v. Evans, 198 F.3d 173 (5th Cir. 1999).
[30] E.E.O.C. v. Roman Catholic Diocese, 213 F.3d 795 (4th Cir. 2000).
[31] Archdiocese of Washington v. Moersen, 925 A.2d 659 (Md. 2007).
[32] 42 U.S.C. § 3607 (2012).

the owner lives on the premises.[33] While the latter provision is not explicitly or only a religious exemption, it effectively allows people of faith to take into consideration the religious beliefs of individuals with whom they will be sharing close living quarters.

E *Exemptions in Practice*

The majority of the statutory religious exemptions in federal civil rights law have existed since the 1960s. Well-established norms have arisen and the majority of businesses and institutions understand their obligations under law.[34] These norms include the idea that religious organizations – including hospitals, schools, nursing homes, and shelters – ought to be able to ensure that people holding roles that are fundamental to an organization's ability to pursue its religious mission share the religious viewpoints of the organization. However, those norms also establish that organizations are not at liberty to discriminate with impunity; while a Jewish organization may have the ability to ensure that a Jewish person fills non-ministerial roles, the organization would be prohibited from discriminating against an applicant for that role on the basis of race or national origin.[35] Suggesting that there is consensus on where and how to draw these lines is disingenuous, however the principles that underlie the law are fairly well accepted. Religious organizations must have the freedom to establish and express their religious beliefs, but their right to do so is limited, as every constitutional right is ultimately limited, by their active participation in a diverse civil society that has struggled with discrimination throughout its history.

II A BRIEF HISTORY OF DISCRIMINATION AGAINST LGBTQ PEOPLE

Despite recent advances in civil rights, including nationwide marriage equality, LGBTQ people have historically suffered from federally sanctioned discrimination, family rejection, and social isolation. Same-sex attraction was not only pathologized but criminalized throughout the twentieth century. As late as 1973, same-sex attraction was considered a curable mental illness by mainstream mental health organizations.[36] Courts across the country began to use antisodomy laws to specifically target same-sex behavior in the early 1970s. These laws categorized same-sex sexuality as "sexual misconduct" and "deviate sexual intercourse."[37] Individuals arrested for violating antisodomy laws not only faced imprisonment and fines but also often had their names

---

[33] 42 U.S.C. § 3603 (2012).

[34] *Breaking News: EEOC/OFCCP Proposed Merger Resulting in Unexpected Allies*, NAT'L L. REV. (May 23, 2017), https://perma.cc/389Z-49HP.

[35] *Questions and Answers: Religious Discrimination in the Workplace*, EQUAL EMP. OPPORTUNITY COMM'N (Jan. 31, 2011), https://perma.cc/22UP-KFTR.

[36] Drescher, *supra* note 2.

[37] Nancy J. Knauer, *LGBT Elder Law: Towards Equity in Aging*, 32 HARV. J. L. & GENDER 302 (2008).

published in local papers. When the Supreme Court overturned Texas's sodomy statute in 2003, thirteen additional states had active laws criminalizing same-sex sexual activity.[38]

In addition to being targeted by sodomy laws, transgender people and gender nonconforming lesbian, gay, and bisexual (LGB) people were also subject to municipal and state laws prohibiting cross-dressing and "disguise." These laws were widespread, found in every corner of the country.[39] Criminalization resulted in severe social ostracism, job loss, eviction, and social isolation for generations of LGBTQ men and women.[40]

Service members suspected of being LGBTQ were dismissed from the military with dishonorable discharges – making basic tasks such as finding employment, renting an apartment, or qualifying for a loan difficult and embarrassing, if not impossible.[41] The federal government also purged suspected LGBTQ civil servants in the 1950s. LGBTQ civil servants were determined to be a security risk and "bad for morale." As one Senate report stated, "[o]ne homosexual can pollute an entire office."[42] The threat of unchecked discrimination in federal employment persisted until President Bill Clinton signed an executive order in 1993 banning discrimination on the basis of sexual orientation and President Barack Obama signed an order protecting transgender federal workers in 2014.[43]

State-sanctioned discrimination was not merely an artifact of laws adopted pre-1900 or even pre-2000. Recent discrimination can be found in the more than thirty states that adopted constitutional amendments barring same-sex couples from marrying – the last adopted by North Carolina in 2012 – making them and their families strangers to the state-granted rights, benefits, and obligations of this civil institution.[44] Echoes of this harsh discrimination still permeate the hearts and minds of the generations that survived it.

A *Real People, Real Discrimination*

Despite recent advancements towards LGBTQ equality, our community continues to face systemic discrimination in schools, housing, health care, and on the job.

---

[38] Lawrence v. Texas, 539 U.S. 558, 562 (2003).

[39] WILLIAM N. ESKRIDGE, JR. & NAN D. HUNTER, SEXUALITY, GENDER, AND THE LAW 54 (3d ed. 2011).

[40] Knauer, *supra* note 37.

[41] Dave Philipps, *Ousted as Gay, Aging Veterans Are Battling Again for Honorable Discharges*, N.Y. TIMES (Sept. 6, 2015), https://perma.cc/M33Y-5UQT.

[42] ESKRIDGE & HUNTER, *supra* note 39.

[43] *Facts About Discrimination in Federal Government Employment Based on Marital Status, Political Affiliation, Status as a Parent, Sexual Orientation, and Gender Identity*, EEOC, https://perma.cc/K5KZ-3DUW; *Fact Sheet: Taking Action to Support LGBT Workplace Equality Is Good for Business*, WHITE HOUSE OFFICE OF PRESS SEC'Y (July 21, 2014), https://perma.cc/3C59-KDCN.

[44] *State Laws and Constitutional Amendments Targeting Same-Sex Relationships*, LAMBDA LEGAL (June 3, 2013), https://perma.cc/6JX6-PVGE .

During the Obama administration, the federal government directly addressed this discrimination, implementing concrete nondiscrimination provisions and interpreting existing statutes to directly improve the lives of LGBTQ people across the nation. However, recent actions by the Trump administration have threatened these protections, including a departure from standard legal interpretation of statutes such as Title VII and Title IX of the Education Amendments of 1972 (Title IX) that aim to effectively exclude LGBTQ people and families from their protections.

Even in the absence of routine federal data collection and consistently enforced federal nondiscrimination laws, discrimination against LGBTQ people is well documented. According to the Pew Research Center, 21 percent of LGBTQ adults have experienced employment discrimination, with 5 percent having experienced discrimination within the year prior to the survey.[45] Where sexual orientation and gender identity are covered by state employment nondiscrimination laws, the rates of complaints filed by LGBTQ people are comparable to the rates of complaints filed by people of color and women.[46] An investigation conducted by the US Department of Housing and Urban Development found that "same-sex couples experience discrimination in the online rental housing marketing relative to heterosexual couples," with adverse treatment of same-sex couples present in all US metropolitan areas.[47]

Fear of discrimination causes many LGBTQ people to avoid seeking health care; when they do seek care, LGBTQ people are not treated consistently with the respect that all patients deserve. In a recent study, 56 percent of LGB people and 70 percent of transgender and gender nonconforming people reported experiencing discrimination by health-care providers – including refusal of care, harsh language, and physical roughness – because of their sexual orientation or gender identity.[48] A startling 27 percent of transgender respondents and 8 percent of LGB respondents reported that they had been denied necessary health care because of their gender identity or sexual orientation.[49] Delay and avoidance of care due to fear of discrimination compounds the significant health disparities experienced by LGBTQ people as a group.[50] For example, 28 percent of transgender people reported that they postponed or avoided seeking treatment when sick or injured for fear of facing discrimination.[51]

---

[45] Anna Brown, *As Congress Considers Action Again, 21% of LGBT Adults Say They Faced Workplace Discrimination*, PEW RES. CTR. (Nov. 4, 2013), https://perma.cc/V7TZ-ARNT.

[46] Christy Mallory & Brad Sears, *Evidence of Employment Discrimination Based on Sexual Orientation and Gender Identity*, WILLIAMS INST. (Oct. 2015), https://perma.cc/566J-EDYF.

[47] *See* Samantha Friedman et al., *An Estimate of Housing Discrimination Against Same-Sex Couples*, U.S. DEP'T OF HOUS. & URBAN DEV., OFFICE OF POL'Y DEV. & RES. (June 2013) https://perma.cc/7Q3K-VTN2.

[48] *When Health Care Isn't Caring* 5, LAMBDA LEGAL (2010), https://perma.cc/XK9B-W9LM.

[49] *Id.*

[50] *See, About LGBT Health*, https://perma.cc/VNN6-Y6VM.

[51] Jaime M. Grant et al., *Injustice at Every Turn: A Report of the National Transgender Discrimination Survey* 6, NAT'L CTR. FOR TRANSGENDER EQUAL. & NAT'L GAY & LESBIAN TASK FORCE (2011).

B *Impact of Discrimination on LGBTQ People*

Beyond the immediate effects of a lost job or denial of services, discrimination against LGBTQ people results in psychological and social harm. Consistent, pervasive messages that being LGBTQ is immoral, deviant, or unworthy of legal protections takes a toll even when the individual rejects the validity of the message. While attitudes towards LGBTQ people have changed significantly, more than a quarter of Americans still believe that homosexuality should be discouraged rather than accepted[52] and nearly the same percentage believe that same-sex relationships should be illegal.[53]

Ballot measures amending state constitutions to deny same-sex couples access to marriage provided researchers with the ability to examine effects of negative messaging on the well-being of LGB people. During these campaigns, states residents were subjected to intense messaging demonizing same-sex relationships.[54] Unsurprisingly, LGB people who lived in states while the campaign was happening experienced significantly more psychological distress than LGB people living in states without campaigns.[55] Not surprisingly, LGBTQ people who have experienced discrimination have markedly higher levels of stress than their non-LGBTQ peers.[56] Prolonged stress can lead to ulcers, diabetes, heart attacks, and strokes.[57]

The effects of discrimination on LGBTQ youth are particularly alarming.[58] LGBTQ students are twice as likely as their non-LGBTQ peers to be verbally harassed or physically attacked.[59] Nearly all LGBT youth report hearing negative messages about being LGBTQ, particularly at school, on the internet, and from their peers.[60] More than half also report hearing negative messages from religious leaders and elected leaders.[61] Research shows that there is an increased risk of suicidal thoughts or suicide attempts by victims of bullying.[62] Bullied students also experience high levels of anxiety, depression, and loneliness[63] and have lower academic achievement.[64]

---

[52] Hannah Fingerhut, *Support Steady for Same-sex Marriage and Acceptance of Homosexuality*, PEW RES. CTR. (May 12, 2016), https://perma.cc/X58P-TFKY.

[53] *Gay and Lesbian Rights*, GALLUP (Mar. 7, 2018), https://perma.cc/TBF9-CBQV.

[54] Sharon Scales Rostosky et al., *Marriage Amendments and Psychological Distress in Lesbian, Gay, and Bisexual (LGB) Adults*, 56 J. COUNSELING PSYCHOL. 56 (2009).

[55] *Id.*

[56] *Stress in America: The Impact of Discrimination*, AM. PSYCH. ASS'N (Mar. 10, 2016), at 8.

[57] *Stress Effects on the Body*, AM. PSYCH. ASS'N, https://perma.cc/Z8HH-RCP6.

[58] *See* Minter, Chapter 4.

[59] *See Growing Up LGBT in America*, Human Rights Campaign (2012), at 16.

[60] *Id.* at 18.

[61] *Id.*

[62] *See* Anat Brunstein Klomek et al., *Suicidal Adolescents' Experiences with Bullying Perpetration and Victimization During High School as Risk Factors for Later Depression and Suicidality*, 53 J. ADOLESCENT HEALTH S37 (2012).

[63] Ken Rigby, *Consequences of Bullying in Schools*, 48 CAN. J. PSYCH. 583 (2003).

[64] Gwen M. Glew et al., *Bullying, Psychosocial Adjustment, and Academic Performance in Elementary School*, 159 ARCHIVES PEDIATRIC ADOLESCENT MED. 1026 (2005).

Nondiscrimination laws are not a panacea for the victimization experienced by LGBTQ people, but they begin to lay the groundwork for broader social change. They also send a critically important message of belonging and acceptance. Unfortunately, Congressional inaction and state-sanctioned discrimination coupled with efforts to roll back the rights of LGTBQ people will likely lead to continued discrimination and negative health outcomes for LGBTQ people.

III LGBTQ PEOPLE IN THE ERA OF TRUMP

On the campaign trail, President Trump claimed that he would be the better friend to LGBTQ people than his opponent,[65] and many pundits speculated that, as a New Yorker accustomed to interacting with LGBTQ people, Trump would not make rolling back rights for LGBTQ people a part of his administrative goals.[66] His choice of Mike Pence as a running mate was an early signal that even if Trump was indifferent to LGBTQ equality, his administration would be influenced by individuals with records of opposition to civil rights for LGBTQ people.[67] In the first year of office alone, the Trump administration took significant steps to undermine rights for LGBTQ people.

A *Transgender Students*

In 2016, the Departments of Justice and Education issued comprehensive guidance to ensure that transgender students were being treated fairly and with dignity in public, federally funded schools, including having equal access to sex-segregated facilities, such as restrooms and locker rooms consistent with their gender identity.[68] This guidance was based upon both a statutory interpretation of Title IX as well as a growing body of case law finding that US civil rights laws prohibiting discrimination on the basis of sex also encompass gender identity.[69] Eleven states and state officials, led by Texas Attorney General Ken Paxton, filed suit challenging the guidance weeks after it was issued.[70] After a Texas federal judge issued a nationwide hold on

---

[65] Jeremy Diamond, *Donald Trump to LGBT Community: I'm a "Real Friend,"* CNN (June 13, 2016), https://perma.cc/QN32-L96U.

[66] Maggie Haberman, *Donald Trump's More Accepting Views on Gay Issues Set Him Apart in* G.O.P., N.Y. TIMES (Apr. 22, 2016), https://perma.cc/6T3Z-PH4W.

[67] *See* Amanda Holpuch, *Before He Was Trump's Running Mate, Mike Pence Led the Anti-LGBT Backlash*, THE GUARDIAN (Oct. 4, 2016), https://perma.cc/YM73-SSCR.

[68] *Dear Colleague Letter on Transgender Students*, U.S. DEP'T OF EDUC. & U.S. DEP'T OF JUSTICE (May 13, 2016), https://perma.cc/9A7R-27P9.

[69] *See e.g.*, Schwenk v. Hartford, 204 F.3d 1187, 1200 (9th Cir. 2000); Rosa v. Park W. Bank & Trust Co., 214 F.3d 213, 215–16 (1st Cir. 2000); Smith v. City of Salem, 378 F.3d 566 (6th Cir. 2004 Glenn v. Brumby, 663 F.3d 1312 (11th Cir. 2011)).

[70] Complaint, Texas v. United States, 201 F. Supp. 3d 810 (N.D. Tex. 2016) (Civil Action No. 7:16-cv-00054-O).

the guidance's enforcement, the Obama administration responded by requesting that the court limit the hold to the states filing suit.[71]

Two days after Jeff Sessions was confirmed as attorney general in February 2017, the Department of Justice (DOJ) moved to end the Obama administration's challenge to a nationwide injunction against enforcement of the guidance, allowing the nationwide hold to continue.[72] That decision was swiftly followed by a formal rescission of the guidance by Sessions and Secretary of Education Betsy DeVos.[73] The White House statements on the issue made clear that the president supported the rescission.[74] Despite a May 2017 ruling by the US Court of Appeals for the Seventh Circuit that Title IX protects transgender students from discrimination, including with respect to accessing restrooms consistent with the students' gender identity,[75] the Department of Education's Office for Civil Rights refuses to investigate claims filed by transgender students on that basis.[76]

B Transgender Service-Members

Transgender people had been barred from military service as a result of outdated medical policies adopted by the Department of Defense (DoD). Unlike the statutory ban known as "Don't Ask, Don't Tell" which required Congressional action to overturn,[77] the ban on transgender military service was just policy and required only action by the DoD to update it. In July 2015, the Pentagon announced a working group to study how to modify existing regulations to allow open military service by transgender people.[78] Approximately one year later, Defense Secretary Ash Carter announced that the military had adopted a new policy, effective immediately, that protected currently serving transgender people from discharge solely based on their gender identity.[79] New transgender recruits were to be permitted to join by the summer of 2017.[80]

---

[71] Defendant's Motion to Clarify. *Id.*

[72] Kevin Bohn, *Justice Department No Longer Fighting Injunction on Transgender School Guidance*, CNN (Feb. 11, 2017), https://perma.cc/JW5D-85MT.

[73] Jeremy W. Peters, *Trump Rescinds Rules on Bathrooms for Transgender Students*, N.Y. Times (Feb. 22, 2017), https://perma.cc/C37W-K8DJ.

[74] *Id.*

[75] Whitaker v. Kenosha Unified Sch. Dist. No. 1 Bd. of Educ., 858 F.3d 1034 (7th Cir. 2017). *See also* Dodds v. Dept. of Education, 845 F.3d.217 (6th Cir. 2016).

[76] Moriah Balingit, *Education Department No Longer Investigating Transgender Bathroom Complaints*, Wash. Post (Feb. 12, 2018), https://perma.cc/TWM4-NQRA.

[77] Don't Ask, Don't Tell Repeal Act of 2010 (codified at 10 U.S.C. § 654 (2012)).

[78] Press Release, *Statement by Secretary of Defense Ash Carter on DOD Transgender Policy*, U.S. Dep't of Def. (July 13, 2015), https://perma.cc/TBM2-UZGT.

[79] Terri Moon Cronk, *Transgender Service Members Can Now Serve Openly, Carter Announces*, DoD News (June 30, 2016), https://perma.cc/9SWU-E8W9.

[80] *Id.*

According to the Williams Institute, there are approximately 15,500 actively serving transgender members of the US military, making DoD the largest employer of transgender people in America.[81] In addition to the United States, eighteen other nations, including the United Kingdom, Australia, Canada, and Israel, allow transgender people to serve openly in their militaries.[82]

On July 26, 2017, President Trump posted a series of early morning tweets announcing, "The United States Government will not accept or allow transgender individuals to serve in any capacity in the U.S. Military."[83] In response, fifty-six retired generals and admirals released a joint statement warning Trump's transgender military ban would degrade military readiness.[84] A formal memorandum directing the military to continue the ban on enlistment by those they learn are transgender was issued by Trump in August[85] even though the US armed forces are currently facing recruitment challenges, including for high-demand positions such as linguists, health-care providers, social workers, and aviators.[86]

C *Executive Order on Religious Liberties*

During the second week of Trump's presidency, the draft of an executive order that could provide an unprecedented license to discriminate leaked to advocates and reporters across Washington, DC.[87] Under the draft executive order, every federal agency could be required to rescind every nondiscrimination regulation and program instruction protecting LGBTQ people in housing and homelessness programs, health-care nondiscrimination regulations, child welfare regulations, and beyond.[88] The leaked document provided a bleak and unfiltered glimpse at the Trump roadmap for undermining civil rights protections in the name of religion.

On May 4, 2017, the White House published an executive order instructing the attorney general to provide guidance to all agencies on "interpreting religious liberty

---

[81] Gary J. Gates & Jody L. Herman, *Transgender Military Service in the United States*, Williams Inst. (2014), https://perma.cc/8NY8-82M2.

[82] Paul LeBlanc, *The Countries That Allow Transgender Troops to Serve in Their Armed Forces*, CNN (July 27, 2017), https://perma.cc/2DK9-JADN.

[83] Jeremy Diamond, *Trump to Reinstate US Military Ban on Transgender People*, CNN (July 26, 2017), https://perma.cc/7Y69-9JL7 (images of original tweets imbedded).

[84] General John R. Allen, USMC (retired) et al., *Fifty-Six Retired Generals and Admirals Warn That President Trump's Anti-Transgender Tweets, If Implemented, Would Degrade Military Readiness*, Palm Ctr. (Aug. 1, 2017), https://perma.cc/T4CR-8AAX.

[85] *Presidential Memorandum for the Secretary of Defense and the Secretary of Homeland Security*, Office of the President (Aug. 25, 2017), https://perma.cc/T4CR-8AAX.

[86] John Grady, *Panel: Pentagon Facing Future Recruiting Challenge Due to Lack of Candidates*, U.S. Naval Inst. News (Oct. 12, 2017), https://perma.cc/U93X-AYCP; Leo Shane III, *Congress Could Give Fitness Waivers to More Troops As It Targets High-Demand Skills*, Mil. Times (Mar. 1, 2017), https://perma.cc/HDX7-6RB4.

[87] Sarah Posner, *Leaked Draft of Trump's Religious Freedom Order Reveals Sweeping Plans to Legalize Discrimination*, The Nation (Feb. 1, 2017), https://perma.cc/CH3Z-MRZL.

[88] *Id.*

protections in Federal law."[89] This sweeping approach threatened an unprecedented expansion of religious exemptions affecting employment, services, and programs. Revisiting federal law, regulations, and policies will almost certainly have significant implications for LGBTQ people. In essence, the executive order sidesteps the question of how and where the administration will permit discrimination against LGBTQ people – delegating the details to Attorney General Jeff Sessions.

Attorney General Sessions will almost certainly seek to apply an expansive interpretation of RFRA to areas of the law that were not implicated in *Hobby Lobby*, as well as potentially treating closely held for-profit corporations as religious organizations throughout federal law.

D DOJ Refusal to Protect LGBTQ People Under Existing Federal Laws

A growing body of federal case law holds that discrimination on the basis of sexual orientation[90] and gender identity[91] are forms of sex discrimination. The Equal Employment Opportunity Commission, the independent agency tasked with enforcing federal employment nondiscrimination laws, has determined that Title VII covers employment discrimination against LGBTQ people[92] and accepts complaints accordingly.[93] During the Obama administration, Attorney General Eric Holder issued a memo instructing DOJ staff to treat gender identity discrimination as a form of sex discrimination and clarified that the DOJ Civil Rights Division was authorized to bring claims on behalf of transgender people.[94]

Under Attorney General Sessions, the DOJ filed an *amicus* brief in *Zarda v. Altitude Express*, a case about a gay man terminated from his job for mentioning his sexual orientation, arguing that Title VII could not be used to remedy sexual orientation discrimination.[95] DOJ was not a party to the case and was under no obligation to offer its views to the US Court of Appeals for the Second Circuit. The

---

[89] Exec. Order No. 13798, 82 Fed. Reg. 21675 (May 4, 2017).

[90] *See, e.g.*, Hively v. Ivy Tech Cmty. Coll., 853 F.3d 339 (7th Cir. 2017) (en banc); Winstead v. Lafayette Cty. Bd. of Cty. Comm'rs, 197 F. Supp. 3d 1334 (N.D. Fla. 2016); Isaacs v. Felder, 143 F. Supp. 3d 1190, 1193 (M.D. Ala. 2015); Videckis v. Pepperdine Univ., 100 F. Supp. 3d 927, 937 (C.D. Cal. 2015); Smith v. Avanti, 249 F. Supp. 3d 1194 (D. Colo. 2017).

[91] *See supra* note 68.

[92] *See* Baldwin v. Foxx, E.E.O.C. Appeal No. 0120133080, 2015 WL 4397641 (July 16, 2015); Macy v. Dep't of Justice, EEOC Appeal No. 0120120821, 2012 WL 1435995 (Apr. 20, 2012).

[93] *What You Should Know About EEOC and the Enforcement Protections for LGBT Workers*, EEOC, https://perma.cc/W7RD-SLQL. *See also* EEOC v. Scott Med. Health Ctr., 2016 WL 6569233 (W.D. Pa. Nov. 4, 2016); EEOC v. Pallet Co., d/b/a IFCO Systems NA (D. Md., Civ. No. 1:16-cv-00595-CCB) (filed Mar. 1, 2016, settled June 28, 2016).

[94] *Memorandum on the Treatment of Transgender Employment Discrimination Claims Under Title VII of the Civil Rights Act of 1964*, OFFICE OF THE ATT'Y GEN., U.S. DEP'T OF JUSTICE (Dec. 15, 2014), https://perma.cc/AY73-PXPB.

[95] Brief for the United States as Amicus Curiae Supporting Defendants-Appellees, Zarda v. Altitude Express, Inc., No. 15–3775, 883 F.3d 100 (2d Cir. 2018).

decision to weigh in was a gratuitous effort to advance the narrative that LGB people are not protected by landmark civil rights laws.

A few months later, at the direction of Sessions, DOJ rescinded the Holder memo. Sessions replaced Holder's instructions to DOJ to actively protect transgender people with a memo saying that nondiscrimination protections under Title VII do not apply to transgender people.[96] DOJ instructed all US attorneys to adopt this position in pending and future matters.[97] The new policy directly conflicts with years of interpretation from both the US Supreme Court[98] and federal circuit courts.[99] Sessions openly directed DOJ to ignore their responsibilities in protecting the civil rights of all Americans.

E Data Collection

LGBTQ inclusion within federal surveys and data collection instruments is key to ensuring that LGBTQ people are being adequately served by federal programs and receiving the services and support they are entitled to under federal law. LGBTQ people have been included in numerous federal surveys for almost a decade. However, the Trump administration has engaged in a targeted effort to erase LGBTQ people from these data collection efforts and, thus, from program discussions altogether.

For example, in 2012, the Administration for Community Living (ACL) recognized that older adults experiencing isolation because of their sexual orientation or gender identity may be recognized as a population with a "greatest social need" for purposes of Older Americans Act (OAA) programs.[100] Given previous recognition as a "greatest social need population" by the Department of Health and Human Services, having a sexual orientation question – and the inclusion of a gender identity question – within the OAA survey promotes the development of data-driven public policy that does the most good and furthers the OAA's purposes. Comprehensive, uniform data collection is an essential tool to ensure that LGBTQ seniors have equal access to the federal programs and services to which they are entitled.

---

[96] *Memorandum on the Revised Treatment of Transgender Employment Discrimination Claims Under Title VII of the Civil Rights Act of 1964*, OFFICE OF THE ATT'Y GEN., U.S. DEP'T OF JUSTICE (Oct. 4, 2017), https://perma.cc/MUP2-BK6A.

[97] *Id.*

[98] The memo contends that "Title VII's prohibition on sex discrimination encompasses discrimination between men and women." This conflicts with two Supreme Court cases, *Oncale v. Sundowner Offshore Servs.*, 523 U.S. 75 (1998) (holding that sexual harassment of a male by another male is prohibited by Title VII), and *Price Waterhouse v. Hopkins*, 490 U.S. 228 (1989) (holding that sex stereotyping is a form of sex discrimination prohibited by Title VII).

[99] *See supra* note 68.

[100] *LGBT Populations and "Greatest Social Need,"* NAT'L RES. CTR. ON LGBT AGING (2012), https://perma.cc/EB4Y-LY4N.

On March 13, 2017, ACL published a Federal Register notice with a link to the 2017 draft survey stating that there were "no changes" to the survey. However, there was a single, significant change. ACL had removed the question pertaining to sexual orientation – the only alteration to the survey from 2016 to 2017. A correction was issued in the Federal Register eleven days later, after swift public outcry.[101] However, the public comment period was not lengthened to account for the notice error. Undoubtedly due to the explosive public response – almost 5,000 Human Rights Campaign members and supporters alone spoke out against the change – ACL published a new draft in June including LGB older adults, but still excluding transgender seniors.[102]

The Trump administration has also capitalized on nonsubstantive, clerical errors to rescind agency actions that would serve the LGBTQ community. For example, in March 2017, the Department of Housing and Urban Development (HUD) published a notice withdrawing critical data collection and notice requirements for two of the Department's flagship LGBTQ programs. The withdrawn notice provided data collection and implementation guidelines for evaluating the LGBTQ Youth Homelessness Prevention Initiative operated in coordination with the True Colors Fund. As described by HUD, this "first-of-its-kind" initiative was designed to "identify successful strategies for ensuring that no young person is left without a home because of their sexual orientation or gender identity."[103] This project began with two pilot communities in 2014 in hopes of developing a model for preventing LGBTQ youth homelessness that could be replicated by other communities. The rescission of this important survey element will undoubtedly make replicating this impressive project nationwide challenging.

IV UNDER SIEGE IN STATE LEGISLATURES

Despite broad-based support for LGBTQ equality and the Supreme Court's definitive decision in *Obergefell v. Hodges* leading to marriage equality nationwide, some state lawmakers have continued to advance an anti-LGBTQ agenda. Over the past three years, more than 500 anti-LGBTQ bills were filed in state legislatures around the country.[104] Fortunately, with the support of fair-minded people at the grassroots level, hard work by advocates, and public outcry from the business community, approximately 94 percent of those bills were defeated.[105] In 2017, legislators in 30

---

[101] Robin Knauer Maril, *Trump's Administrative Abuse and the LGBTQ Community* 5, HUMAN RIGHTS CAMPAIGN FOUND. (2017).

[102] *Id.*

[103] HUD Exchange, *LGBTQ Youth Homelessness Prevention Initiative Overview* (June 2015), https://perma.cc/8KZ9-EJAU.

[104] Warbelow, *supra* note 4.

[105] *Id.*

states filed 129 bills designed to restrict the rights of LGBTQ individuals and their families; only 12 were enacted – a passage rate of less than 10 percent.[106]

The onslaught of anti-LGBTQ legislation in the states began in 2015, with many state legislatures hurrying to try to limit *Obergefell*'s scope. The most successful and highest profile legislation of 2015 was related to religious refusals.[107] In contrast, 2016 saw a pivot to anti-transgender legislation, such as a school bathroom exemption which would have prohibited transgender students in South Dakota from accessing restrooms consistent with their gender identity, vetoed by the state's Republican governor,[108] followed by North Carolina's HB 2, the first state law mandating anti-transgender discrimination by government entities.[109] While the trend of targeting transgender people, particularly transgender children, continued into 2017 – Texas's failed SB 6, and special session revision SB 3, are particularly high-profile examples – the anti-LGBTQ legislation that was most successful in 2017 tended to be narrower, single-issue religious exemption bills that permit discrimination in public education and the provision of taxpayer-funded child welfare services.[110]

The bills permitting discrimination in taxpayer-funded child welfare services highlight an ongoing concern over attempts to inoculate certain government contractors and grantees from nondiscrimination requirements if those government contractors would like to selectively withhold their services from parents or children to whom the provider has a religious or moral objection. In practice, that could include same-sex couples, LGBTQ individuals, couples or individuals of faiths different from that of the agency, single parents, or married couples where one prospective parent had previously been divorced.[111] These laws can result in children being left in legal limbo rather than being placed with a qualified family prepared to provide the child with a much-needed temporary or forever home.

Mississippi's HB 1523, which was passed in 2016 but suspended by a federal court before being allowed to take effect in June 2017, is the most egregious example of an active anti-LGBTQ law in the country.[112] The law allows taxpayer-funded, faith-based organizations to justify discrimination against LGBTQ people, single mothers, and unwed couples without fear of losing a contract or grant to provide critical social safety net services the state has engaged with them to provide all Mississippians. In a moment of crisis where a taxpayer-funded faith-based

---

[106] *Preview 2018: Pro-Equality and Anti-LGBTQ State and Local Legislation*, HUMAN RIGHTS CAMPAIGN FOUND. (2018).

[107] *See, e.g.*, Brian Eason, *Official: RFRA Cost Indy Up to 12 Conventions and $60M*, INDYSTAR. COM (Jan. 26, 2016), https://perma.cc/N3B9-UZZG.

[108] H.B. 1008, 2016 Leg. Assemb., 91st Sess. (S.D. 2016).

[109] H.B. 2, 2016 Gen. Assemb., 2d Extra Sess. (N.C. 2016).

[110] HUMAN RIGHTS CAMPAIGN FOUND., *supra* note 106.

[111] Cathryn Oakley, *Disregarding the Best Interest of the Child: Licenses to Discriminate in Child Welfare Services*, HUMAN RIGHTS CAMPAIGN FOUND. (2017).

[112] H.B. 1523, 2016 Leg. Assemb., Reg. Sess. (MS 2016).

organization was providing emergency shelter on behalf of the government, the organization could, for example, refuse to acknowledge the marriage of a same-sex couple who was seeking emergency shelter for their family, or could refuse to give a transgender person access to facilities consistent with their gender identity. Religious organizations are entitled to their religious viewpoints, and, generally speaking, the state cannot and should not be regulating their ability to practice or express their faith. However, when engaged in taxpayer-funded activity, state contractors and grantees should not be given a license to discriminate against members of the public they have been paid to serve. It is the government's responsibility to serve everyone, and any entity acting on behalf of the state who is unwilling to serve the public on a nondiscriminatory basis should not be receiving taxpayer funds.

V CONCLUSION

The purpose of nondiscrimination laws is quite simple: ensure that all of the people who make up the diverse fabric of American society are able to engage in that society on their merits, and are not held back by irrelevant factors such as their race, religion, sex, national origin, or any other characteristic that does not impact their ability to contribute to our shared society. Sexual orientation and gender identity are such characteristics. LGBTQ people should not be denied the opportunity to work, live, or have equal access to public places or services simply because of who they are or whom they love. Neither should people of faith – which is why nondiscrimination laws have long protected people of all faiths from discrimination on the basis of religion.

The same laws can, and do, easily ensure the rights of both people of faith and LGBTQ people in the same way that laws can and do provide equal protections to people on the basis of both race and religion. No one deserves to have their ability to go about their daily lives hampered because of discriminatory behavior – and when Americans agree that discrimination on the basis of these irrelevant characteristics is wrong, it becomes clear that proposals with major exemptions or loopholes are unacceptable.

Discrimination on the basis of sexual orientation and gender identity is wrong. That means that to the extent that jurisdictions have forbidden discrimination on the basis of other protected classes, it must forbid sexual orientation and gender identity discrimination on the same terms. Conversely, laws extending nondiscrimination protections to LGBTQ people must do so without eroding the existing civil rights laws that have previously been extended to other characteristics. All should be treated the same, as no one group's rights are more or less valuable or ought to be bargained away. Exemptions to nondiscrimination laws that single out any part of the LGBTQ community for treatment different from others should not be accepted; that includes exemptions that deny transgender people equal access to all public places, spaces, and services, including sex-segregated spaces or sex-specific dress codes. It also includes exemptions that suggest or insist that religious organizations operating in the public sphere – including those operating as government contractors – may have a special, protected right to discriminate against LGBTQ people. Religious organizations operating in their private sphere have every right to determine what they believe and how to express that belief, but when they cross into the public square, they are and always have been expected to engage with the rules of civil society. If they are, or traditionally have been, forbidden from discrimination when they are operating in the public square – as government contractors, places of public accommodation, or employers – it is both appropriate and necessary that they be expected to refrain from discriminating on the basis of sexual orientation and gender identity. While there are undoubtedly those who resist the idea that LGBTQ people deserve equal treatment under the law, the purpose of nondiscrimination laws is to remind us all that treating people equally – and not allowing artificial, discriminatory barriers to dictate anyone's fate – enhances the society that we all share.

32

Cultivating Common Ground

Lessons from Utah for Living with Our Differences

Senator J. Stuart Adams

Across the United States, there is a palpable sense of uncertainty about whether tensions between gay rights and religious liberty will ever subside. After *Obergefell v. Hodges*,[1] a majority of the country finds itself with a new civil right handed down by court decision, with little to no statutory law to answer the predictable questions that have arisen. Must those who adhere to a traditional view of marriage facilitate marriages even when doing so violates their deeply held religious beliefs? Does the answer depend on whether the person or entity is a church, a private citizen, or a government employee? Can a church lose its tax exemption for declining to facilitate or celebrate a marriage it cannot recognize as a matter of its faith? Does it matter if the entity contracts with the government to provide services to children and families or if a person or business provides commercial goods for weddings, as in *Masterpiece Cakeshop, Ltd. v. Colorado Civil Rights Commission*,[2] a case presently decided by the US Supreme Court? These and other downstream concerns after *Obergefell* echo with an age-old question: When do the rights of one person stop and those of another begin?

Same-sex marriage decisions rippled across America even before *Obergefell*, with Utah at the leading edge.[3] Like a majority of states, Utah found itself grappling with a state same-sex marriage ban that had been struck and no playbook for how to proceed – not even a statewide nondiscrimination law.

The swirling uncertainty clouded matters not just for faith communities and individual believers, but for gay couples, too. Consider this: Who would preside over marriage for gay couples wanting to marry? At the time that same-sex marriage was recognized in Utah, Utah law imposed no duty for anyone to marry heterosexual

---

[1] 135 S. Ct. 2584 (2015).
[2] No. 16–111, 2017 WL 4232758 (U.S. Aug. 31, 2017).
[3] Kitchen v. Herbert, 961 F. Supp. 2d 1181 (D. Utah 2013), *aff'd*, 755 F.3d 1193 (10th Cir. 2014).

couples, let alone gay couples.[4] Like Americans across the country who see marriage as a religious event,[5] many in Utah expressed concern about being asked to legally bring into existence a relationship that they could not assist with as a matter of faith. This should surprise no one since Utah is the second most religious state in America.[6] But Utah had no ready answers.

Even in parts of the country that had preexisting statewide laws banning sexual (SOGI) discrimination, as just under half the states did then and do today, those laws all predated same-sex marriage.[7] Laws written without same-sex marriage in mind cannot, by their very terms, assure traditional religious believers that they need not fear legal repercussions for speaking in favor of traditional marriage or for supporting those in traditional marriages through religious counseling and marriage retreats or in sundry other ways.

At times of great social change, people naturally look to legislators to forge common ground where others only see legal battlefields. When legislators do not act, courts are left to decide competing rights without the advantages of the legislative process, which affords opportunities such as hearings for multiple stakeholders to weigh in. Without the opportunity to forge common ground, communities that have a tremendous amount at stake pursue answers in court, which often results in winner-takes-all outcomes.

The easiest thing for the Utah State Legislature to have done would have been to provide assurance to the religious community only. But we charted a new path: We gave much-needed protections to *two* communities often pitted against one another – people of faith and the full LGBT community. This resulted in a stable law that has brought peace, security, and respect to all Utahns.

Plowing the field for common ground is hard work. It requires sensitivity to the diverse needs of a state's many citizens, respect for the state's body of preexisting law, and sometimes new thinking about how to maximize freedom for all our citizens, without offending equality, liberty, religious freedom, and other values we hold dear.

This chapter charts the evolution of Utah's marriage and nondiscrimination law from a constitutional amendment barring same-sex marriage to attempts to enact nondiscrimination protections to a two-bill package. That package protected the full LGBT community from discrimination in housing and hiring while cementing more protections around marriage than any other state in America.[8] As the majority

---

4   *See infra*, note 86.
5   Marriage Update, Rasmussen Reports (June 25, 2015), https://perma.cc/U7L6-WL8B (finding that 50% of Americans "consider marriage a religious institution").
6   Mark Kellner, *Utah Is Second Most-Religious State, Mississippi Ranks First and Vermont Last*, DESERET NEWS (Feb. 5, 2014), https://perma.cc/3Y7J-J5R3.
7   *See* Wilson, Chapter 30.
8   Robin Fretwell Wilson, *Bargaining for Religious Accommodations: Same-Sex Marriage and LGBT Rights After Hobby Lobby, in* THE RISE OF CORPORATE RELIGIOUS LIBERTY 265–68 (Micah Schwartzman, Chad Flanders & Zoë Robinson eds., 2016).

whip in the Utah Senate, I carried the bill that answered many of the then-unanswered questions. This chapter offers lessons for the challenges facing the United States as it struggles with the scripts we have inherited for navigating religious freedom and LGBT rights – scripts that affirm the value of only one community. Utah wrote a new script about peaceful coexistence and living with our differences, even when they go to things as deep as attraction or the God we worship.

In a tolerant, inclusive, peaceful America, we can write new scripts that ensure that all of us can live according to those things most dear to us, without fear of repercussions.

·I UTAH'S EVOLVING SCRIPT ON MARRIAGE

The saga over same-sex marriage unfolded in Utah much as it did in most of the country. In 2015, Utah received same-sex marriage by judicial decision with no positive law surrounding it.

At the time, only twenty-one states and the District of Columbia banned discrimination based on sexual orientation or gender identity in housing, hiring, and public accommodations.[9] As explained later in this chapter, Utah's landmark legislation provided protections against discrimination for the full LGBT community in housing and hiring.[10] Some states had statutory protections around marriage because those states had enacted laws recognizing same-sex marriage.[11] Otherwise, the country was a blank slate.

The case law of some states subjects religious burdens to heightened scrutiny,[12] other states police infringements on religious belief or practice with state Religious Freedom Restoration Acts.[13] Some do both.[14]

---

[9] *See* Appendix, THE CONTESTED PLACE OF RELIGION IN FAMILY LAW 541–43 (Robin Fretwell Wilson ed., 2018). The states banning discrimination based on sexual orientation or gender identity in housing, hiring, and public accommodations are California, Colorado, Connecticut, Delaware, Hawaii, Illinois, Iowa, Maine, Maryland, Massachusetts, Minnesota, Nevada, New Hampshire, New Jersey, New Mexico, New York, Oregon, Rhode Island, Vermont, Washington, and Wisconsin, as well as the District of Columbia. *See* Appendix, Chapter 35, at Col. 2.

[10] *See infra* Section IV.

[11] Robin Fretwell Wilson, *When Governments Insulate Dissenters from Social Change: What Hobby Lobby and Abortion Conscience Clauses Teach About Specific Exemptions*, 48 U.C. DAVIS L. REV. 703 (2014).

[12] These states include Alaska, Arkansas, Hawaii, Indiana, Kansas, Maine, Massachusetts, Michigan, Minnesota, Mississippi, Montana, New York, North Carolina, Ohio, Pennsylvania, Tennessee, Virginia, Washington, and Wisconsin. *See* Appendix, Chapter 35, at Col. 1.

[13] These states include Alabama, Arizona, Arkansas, Connecticut, Florida, Idaho, Illinois, Indiana, Kansas, Kentucky, Louisiana, Mississippi, Missouri, New Mexico, Oklahoma, Pennsylvania, Rhode Island, South Carolina, Tennessee, Texas, and Virginia. *See* Appendix, Chapter 35, at Col. 1.

[14] These states include Arkansas, Indiana, Kansas, Mississippi, Pennsylvania, Tennessee, and Virginia. *See* Appendix, Chapter 35, at Col. 1.

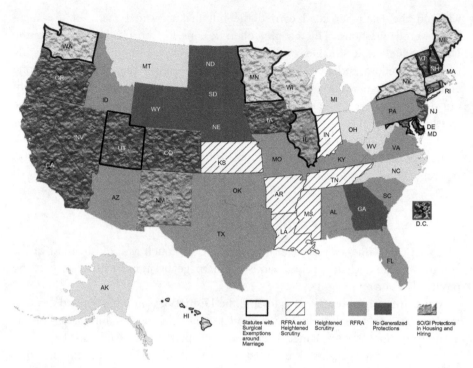

FIGURE 32.1 Patterns of religious liberty protections and SOGI nondiscrimination laws

Utah had neither a RFRA nor heightened scrutiny of religious burdens in its constitution and still does not.[15] In 2015, it did not protect the LGBT community from discrimination of any kind.

As Figure 32.1 details, six states today follow this pattern of not giving special protection to religion or the LGBT community.[16] But most speak to religious protections *or* LGBT rights. Some states give special protection to religious believers through constitutional guarantees *and* state RFRAs.[17] Some give heightened protection only in their state constitutions,[18] others only through a RFRA.[19] Eleven states and the District of Columbia give protections to the LGBT community but make no

---

[15] *See* THE CONTESTED PLACE, *supra* note 9, at 541–43.

[16] These states are Georgia, Nebraska, North Dakota, South Dakota, West Virginia, and Wyoming. *See* Appendix, Chapter 35, at Cols. 1 & 2.

[17] These states are Arkansas, Indiana, Kansas, Mississippi, Pennsylvania, Tennessee, and Virginia. *See* Appendix, Chapter 35, at Cols. 1 & 2.

[18] These states are Alaska, Hawaii, Maine, Massachusetts, Michigan, Minnesota, Montana, New York, North Carolina, Ohio, Washington, and Wisconsin. *See* Appendix, Chapter 35, at Col. 1.

[19] These states are Alabama, Arizona, Connecticut, Florida, Idaho, Illinois, Kentucky, Louisiana, Missouri, New Mexico, Oklahoma, Rhode Island, South Carolina, and Texas. *See* Appendix, Chapter 35, at Col. 1.

general concessions for religious practice.[20] A number give special statutory protections for religious practice and protect LGBT persons from discrimination.[21] Roughly half of the states that banned discrimination against LGBT persons made specific rules for marriage.[22]

RFRAs allow faith communities to do good work and protect religious minorities from government overreach – both important to Utahns. But we concluded quickly that a RFRA was not adequate to provide answers to what should happen around marriage, for three reasons. First, a RFRA had not been successfully invoked at that point against a nondiscrimination statute despite twenty-three years of history.[23] Unlike RFRA, legislative protections for specific religious practices around marriage give courts greater clarity about how the legislature intends for specific disputes to be resolved and are more likely to be enforced.[24]

Second, RFRA requires parties to litigate in order to get clarity about what is permitted and what is not. That litigation is taxing financially and emotionally. Worse, it is wholly unnecessary if it is within the power of the legislature to decide, *ex ante*, where one party's rights end and another's begins. As will be apparent later in this chapter, legislators have the ability to craft new solutions that avoid having to pick winners and losers – in other words, to cultivate ways to avoid having one person's interests come at the expense of another. But only legislatures have the institutional competence to write those new scripts. RFRA leaves courts largely to pick winners and losers under older, less nimble scripts.

Third, Utah faced this question shortly after Arizona's attempt to revise its existing RFRA sparked boycotts and damaged the state's image.[25] Religious stakeholders during the debate expressed a desire for RFRA "to stave off gay rights,"[26] something RFRA is largely incapable of doing.[27] But that misunderstanding tarnished RFRAs. After Arizona, enacting RFRAs has become politically costly, if not impossible.[28]

---

[20] These states are California, Colorado, Delaware, Iowa, Maryland, Nevada, New Hampshire, New Jersey, Oregon, Utah, Vermont, and the District of Columbia. *See* Appendix, Chapter 35, at Cols. 1 & 2.

[21] These states are Connecticut, Illinois, New Mexico, and Rhode Island. *See* Appendix, Chapter 35, at Cols. 2 & 5.

[22] *See supra* note 9 (listing Connecticut, Delaware, Hawaii, Illinois, Maine, Maryland, Minnesota, New Hampshire, New York, Rhode Island, Vermont, Washington, and the District of Columbia).

[23] See Laycock, Chapter 3, for evaluation of success of RFRAs claims asserted against nondiscrimination statutes.

[24] *See generally* Wilson, *supra* note 11.

[25] Libby Hill, *Some Call It Religious Freedom, Others Call It Anti-Gay. Here's a Look at the Battle in Some States*, L.A. TIMES (Apr. 5, 2016), https://perma.cc/74YZ-GNKX.

[26] Juliet Eilperin, *After Veto in Arizona, Conservatives Vow to Fight for Religious Liberties*, WASH. POST (Feb. 27, 2014), https://perma.cc/MX42-YMAD.

[27] *See supra* note 26.

[28] *See* Emma Margolin, *Did Indiana and Arkansas Kill "Religious Freedom" for Everyone Else?*, MSNBC (Apr. 3, 2015), https://perma.cc/FS63-CTSV.

During the same session in which Utah enacted landmark legislation described later in this chapter, a RFRA-type bill was introduced but died in the Utah Senate.[29]

A *Utah's Marriage Law and LGBT Ordinances before Same-Sex Marriage*

In November 2004, Utah passed a Constitutional amendment by an "overwhelming" margin recognizing marriage only between a man and a woman, one of eleven states that passed similar amendments that year[30] after Massachusetts first recognized same-sex marriage by court decision.[31] At the time, I stood with my colleagues in the House of Representatives, where I served, as we passed that amendment. I felt it went to the core of values I and other Utahns consider most dear: family, sexuality, and religious beliefs. We believed we had bulletproofed traditional marriage.

Not long after, in 2008, a small contingent of mostly Democrat legislators began introducing nondiscrimination legislation in the House to protect LGBT persons from discrimination in housing and hiring, with little traction.[32] During that same period, Utah municipalities began enacting nondiscrimination ordinances, led first by Salt Lake City in 2010.[33] By 2015, eleven cities and towns and three counties had passed LGBT employment and housing nondiscrimination protections.[34] However, none protected against discrimination based on gender identity. This patchwork of local rules created inconsistencies across Utah for employers operating in more than one jurisdiction. Because they were written before same-sex marriage in Utah, the ordinances could not have included specific protections around traditional marriage, even though the municipalities included categorical exemptions for religious employers.[35]

After Salt Lake City enacted its nondiscrimination ordinance in 2010, another nondiscrimination bill was introduced in the House.[36] It was followed in 2011 and 2012 by Senate bills that died without a hearing or were tabled.[37] In 2013, Senator Stephen Urquhart introduced SB 262, which was sent to the Senate floor but was never debated.[38]

---

[29] H.B. 322, Gen. Sess. (Utah 2015).
[30] Utah Const. art. I, § 29; James Dao, *Same-Sex Marriage Issues Key to Some G.O.P. Races*, N.Y. Times (Nov. 4, 2014), https://perma.cc/QC7E-76KP.
[31] *Goodridge v. Department of Public Health*, 798 N.E.2d 941 (Mass. 2003).
[32] *See* S.B. 148, Gen. Sess. (Utah 2011); H.B. 305, Gen. Sess. (Utah 2010); H.B. 267, Gen. Sess. (Utah 2009).
[33] *See* Salt Lake City Ordinance No. 63 (2009), https://perma.cc/9TMM-NNWE.
[34] *See* Equality Utah, *Housing and Workplace Discrimination in Utah* 15 (Jan. 2011), https://perma.cc/DTK3-YVFF; Human Rights Campaign, *Cities and Counties with Non-Discrimination Ordinances That Include Gender Identity*, https://perma.cc/X57G-KTX8.
[35] *Id.*
[36] H.B. 305, Gen. Sess. (Utah 2010).
[37] S.B. 148, Gen. Sess. (Utah 2011); S.B. 51, Gen. Sess. (Utah 2012).
[38] S.B. 262, Gen. Sess. (Utah 2013).

Then, on December 20, 2013, Judge Robert Shelby handed down *Kitchen*.[39] *Kitchen* gave no guidance about how to implement such a fundamental shift in state policy, nor did it provide protections for those who adhere to a traditional view of marriage or have strongly held religious beliefs.

There was significant tension on both sides. Some Utahns wanted to secede from the union.[40] Others felt that *Kitchen* was a harbinger of even more successes. In 2014, Senator Urquhart introduced SB 100.[41] Frustrated by the lack of progress, LGBT supporters taped "blue notes" to legislators to the Senate chamber doors, Martin Luther-style, demanding that SB 100 be heard in committee.[42] They blocked entrances to committee rooms and the governor's office; thirteen people were arrested.[43]

The state immediately appealed *Kitchen* to the US Court of Appeals for the Tenth Circuit.[44] Judge Shelby declined to stay his decision, but the US Supreme Court ordered a stay.[45] As the substantive appeal percolated at the Tenth Circuit, our legislative leadership, despite great social pressure, held all relevant legislation; we needed clarity from the Tenth Circuit.

On June 25, 2014, the Tenth Circuit affirmed Judge Shelby's ruling.[46] On November 4, 2014, the US Supreme Court denied *certiorari*.[47] The stay was lifted and couples began marrying.[48]

For communities that feel on the outside looking in, courts can be important agents of change, as *Kitchen* shows. Yet, the recognition of new civil rights by courts almost always creates as many new questions as are answered. However, legislatures are where all citizens can be heard, whether their interests are directly implicated or they simply care deeply about the state, its citizens, and their welfare. With a raft of unanswered questions, Utah's Legislature had to step in and fill the gap.

---

[39] Kitchen v. Herbert, 755 F.3d 1193 (10th Cir. 2014).

[40] *How Utah's Compromise Could Serve as a Model for Other States*, NPR (June 1, 2016), https://perma.cc/358X-ML94.

[41] S.B. 100, Gen. Sess. (Utah 2014).

[42] Bob Henline, *"Operation Blue Note" Underway at Utah State Capitol*, SALT LAKE MAG. (Feb. 3, 2014), https://perma.cc/EV5L-G3R8.

[43] Dennis Romboy & Lisa R. Roche, *Protesters Arrested After Blocking Senate Committee Room*, KSL (Feb. 10, 2014), https://perma.cc/3EG2-XAPE.

[44] Lee Davidson, *Utah Legislators May Rewrite State Law on Gay Marriage*, SALT LAKE TRIB. (Oct. 6, 2014), https://perma.cc/2DSM-JXAL.

[45] Brooke Adams & Lindsay Whitehurst, *Supreme Court Halts Utah Gay Marriages Pending Appeal*, SALT LAKE TRIB. (Jan. 7, 2014), http://archive.sltrib.com/story.php?ref=/sltrib/news/57357406-78/court-utah-state-stay.html.csp.

[46] Kitchen, 755 F.3d 1193.

[47] 135 S. Ct. 265 (2014).

[48] Dennis Romboy, *Same-Sex Marriage Now Legal in Utah*, DESERET NEWS (Oct. 6, 2014), https://perma.cc/8NFF-V4SS.

Many legislators were frustrated by *Kitchen*. Most gave a rumored LGBT non-discrimination bill little hope of passage. Several proposals for religious liberty legislation were expected, too, including the RFRA mentioned earlier. With both types of bills moving down the tracks, the rights of Utahns were on a collision course.

B *An Unprecedented Request for an Alternative to Intolerance*

Then, something unprecedented happened. On the second of our forty-five day session,[49] The Church of Jesus Christ of Latter-day Saints, sometimes called The LDS Church or Mormon Church (the Church), held a press conference.[50] The Church requested the Utah Legislature find a way to combine protections for religious liberty and for LGBT persons from discrimination in employment and housing.[51]

Elder Jeffrey R. Holland, a member of the Church's governing Quorum of the Twelve Apostles, finished the press conference with a call for "an alternative to the rhetoric and intolerance that for too long has come to characterize national debate."[52]

The Church urged the legislature to follow one overarching principle: "fairness for all" – that is, an "approach that balances religious freedom protections with reasonable safeguards for LGBT people – specifically in areas of housing, employment and public transportation, which are not available in many parts of the country."[53] This desire to protect both communities has its genesis in one of the Church's fundamental beliefs: "We claim the privilege of worshiping Almighty God according to the dictates of our own conscience, and allow all men the same privilege, let them worship how, where, or what they may."[54] To say the Church's announcement generated a tectonic shift in the dialogue would be an understatement.

The legislature put this principle into law, creating a space for everyone to act according to individual conscience – whether a member of the LGBT community, a person of faith, or both. Bringing all the stakeholders to the table – and keeping them there – was a formidable challenge, especially when advocates for different communities sometimes prioritized different needs.

Judicial rulings, particularly around heated social conflicts, create winners and losers – one side's perspective emerges victorious. The legislative process has the

---

[49] *See* Michelle L. Price, *Utah Legislature Enters Final Days of Session*, Daily Herald (Mar. 11, 2013), https://perma.cc/39J7-DMXN.

[50] The Church of Jesus Christ of Latter-day Saints, *Transcript of News Conference on Religious Freedom and Nondiscrimination* (Jan. 27, 2015), https://perma.cc/EPR3-B6L6.

[51] *Id.*

[52] *Id.*

[53] *Id.* (statement of Elder Dallin H. Oaks).

[54] The Church of Jesus Christ of Latter-day Saints, *Articles of Faith* (1842), https://perma.cc/95XY-RVLW.

advantage of negotiation and compromise; it tempers absolutes while allowing both sides to share in the gains and losses.

Our session's time limitation proved advantageous. It placed everyone under immense pressure, focusing stakeholders on finding an acceptable balance. A few weeks into the session, the coeditor of this volume, Professor Robin Fretwell Wilson, visited Utah to speak at a conference. Given her expertise,[55] I asked Professor Wilson to help with drafting the bill. She volunteered her time and expertise until the legislative session ended. Without her involvement, that of Professor Cliff Rosky of the University of Utah's College of Law, an influential voice within Equality Utah,[56] representatives of The Church of Jesus Christ of Latter-day Saints and other faith traditions, and our own legislative counsel, our efforts would not have been successful. Remarkably, with days left in the session, we had cultivated common ground.

II CONTOURS OF COMMON GROUND

Together, SB 296 and 297 were dubbed by the press as the Utah Compromise. In drafting the two bills, we were guided by a number of principles.

A *Involve Everyone and Listen Earnestly*

We did what legislators should do: get stakeholders across the spectrum to find constructive solutions. We sat down with members of Utah's LGBT community, social conservatives, and business leaders. Many were familiar to us as seasoned advocates at the statehouse, others we had never met, especially from the LGBT community. We listened to stories they shared of feeling like outcasts and second-class citizens. Putting a human face to legislative needs changed the tenor of the discussion. Similarly, those who expressed concerns for religious liberty, as I did, felt listened to and respected, as well. That process was not only best done legislatively, it could only be done legislatively.

B *Meet Each Side's Core Needs*

The Utah Compromise gives the LGBT community more protections than it had in New York at the time.[57] SB 296, the Employment and Housing Antidiscrimination Amendments, modified Utah's Antidiscrimination Act and the Utah Fair

---

[55] SAME-SEX MARRIAGE AND RELIGIOUS LIBERTY: EMERGING CONFLICTS (Douglas Laycock, Anthony R. Picarello & Robin Fretwell Wilson eds., 2008).

[56] *See e.g.*, Clifford J. Rosky, Perry v. Schwarzenegger *and the Future of Same-Sex Marriage Law*, 53 ARIZ. L. REV. 913 (2011).

[57] *See* Office of N.Y. State Office of the Attorney Gen. Eric T. Schneiderman, *The Sexual Orientation Non-Discrimination Act (SONDA)*, https://perma.cc/5QG2-5H37.

Housing Act to protect the full LGBT community from discrimination.[58] The inclusion of not only sexual orientation, but also gender identity, as illicit grounds for hiring or housing decisions puts Utah on a short list of states with these protections.[59] Incidentally, the law did not reach public accommodations because no municipal law had reached so far, and we did not have the benefit of the thinking of our municipal counterparts on questions such as those raised by *Masterpiece*.

Protection of the transgender population was not easy in a deeply conservative and religious state.[60] But inclusion of the full LGBT community was a must-have for Equality Utah and others. And it proved positive, resolving issues much of the country still struggles with.[61]

As noted next, SB 296 also maintained Utah's existing carve-out of religious entities in employment, but expanded it to include religious primary and secondary schools, as well as the Boy Scouts.[62] SB 296 carried forward and extended somewhat similar carve-outs in the housing context, too.[63]

We were cognizant of the need not to roll back at-will employment or hobble employers unduly. Under SB 296, employers have a duty to meet the gender-based needs of all employees. Employers control the workplace environment through reasonable dress and grooming standards and reasonable policies that preserve "sex-specific facilities," like restrooms.[64] This permits them to respect the privacy of transgendered employees and their coworkers by means as simple as locked stalls or an individual restroom.

C Leave in Place Existing Law as Much as Possible

Creating a whole new set of rights and obligations *only as to* sexual orientation and gender identity might have created unintended consequences. We feared we would inadvertently fail to replicate something from existing law in a new, separate chapter. And having a single, all-inclusive nondiscrimination law proved important to the LGBT community, too.[65]

We began with the existing scaffolding of Utah's law, which protected Utahns from discrimination in housing and hiring of the basis of race, sex, color, national

---

[58] S.B. 296, Gen. Sess. (Utah 2015); Utah Code § 34A–5–106 (2015).
[59] *See supra* Section I.
[60] *See* Philip Bump, *America's Reddest and Bluest Places*, Wash. Post (Dec. 4, 2014), https://perma.cc/LS9H-XDZ4.
[61] *See* Minter, Chapter 4; Pizer, Chapter 29.
[62] Utah Code §§ 34A–5–102(i), 57-21-2(1), 57–21–3(b) (2015).
[63] § 57–21–3 (4)(a)(i) (2015).
[64] § 34A-5-109.
[65] Zack Ford, *Utah Bill Would Ban LGBT Discrimination, With Some Big Exceptions*, Think Progress (Mar. 6, 2015), https://perma.cc/RB7G-BVA2.

origin, religion, age, and disability and categorically set aside religious organizations.[66] In practice, this meant that churches were not regulated as employers, nor
were their wholly owned subsidiaries.

SB 296 also maintained the fifteen-employee threshold for discrimination
claims,[67] ensuring that Utah's small family-run businesses could nimbly manage
their workplaces according to their values without government interference. Some
fault Utah for not increasing the number of employees a business could have and
remain outside the nondiscrimination structure.[68] Raising the limit in preexisting
Utah law, however, would have meant either rolling back existing nondiscrimination protections for people of color and other protected classes or creating a two-tier
structure in which LGBT discrimination receives less protection. Both results
offended principles of just and fair treatment, in our view. And both were unnecessary given the capaciousness of Utah's existing treatment for employers, one of the
most generous in the nation.

Preexisting protections for religious liberty were not disturbed either. SB 296 and
297 instructed courts not to interpret provisions "to infringe upon the freedom of
expressive association or the free exercise of religion" protected by the United States
and Utah constitutions.[69]

D *Give Clarity About the Duties Owed*

Definitions do a lot of the important work in statutes. One tricky definition was
"gender identity," where we believed a medically objective definition would provide
the needed clarity for employers and employees about when duties and protections
were triggered. Borrowing the documentation requirement from Connecticut and
other states with a longer history of protecting transgender individuals,[70] we agreed
on the following definition:

> "Gender identity" has the meaning provided in the [American Psychiatric Associ-
> ation's] Diagnostic and Statistical Manual (DSM-5). A person's gender identity can
> be shown by providing evidence, including, but not limited to, medical history,
> care or treatment of the gender identity, consistent and uniform assertion of the
> gender identity, or other evidence that the gender identity is sincerely held, part of a
> person's core identity, and not being asserted for an improper purpose.[71]

---

[66] Utah Code §§ 34A-5-102(1)(i)(ii)(A)-(C), 34A-5-104 (2015).

[67] § 34A-5-102(a)(i)(D).

[68] Andrew T. Walker & Russell Moore, *Is Utah's LGBT-Religious Liberty Bill Good Policy?*,
Ethics & Religious Liberty Comm'n of the S. Baptist Convention (Mar. 6, 2015), https://
perma.cc/38BR-CQRG (describing the fifteen-employee limit as an "arbitrary threshold").

[69] Utah Code §§ 34A-5-111, 63G-20-103(1) (2016).

[70] Conn. Gen. Stat. § 46a-51 (2016). *See also* Del. Code tit. 19, § 710 (2014).

[71] § 34A-5-102(k). *See* Am. Psychiatric Ass'n, *Gender Dysphoria Fact Sheet* (2013), https://www
.psychiatry.org/File%20Library/Psychiatrists/Practice/DSM/APA_DSM-5-Gender-Dysphoria.pdf.

The condition must continue and be treated for at least six months. By requiring documentation, employers and landlords received an important safeguard against fraudulent claims. Transgender renters and employees gained valuable protections against discrimination in employment and housing.

Some might dismiss the definition as an unwarranted burden, having to provide a doctor's note. We sought consciously to benefit from the experience of legislators across the country to allow a variety of evidence; we also understood that many in the transgender community receive care or treatment, making evidence of this kind readily available.

E *Preserve the Autonomy of Faith Communities*

Before the Utah Compromise, Utah's nondiscrimination statute never reached certain religious organizations – this structural feature is less an exemption than a set-aside, separating society into secular and sectarian spheres. SB 296 and 297 carried forward that separate-spheres model.[72] We also retained discretion in hiring when an employer needs workers with specific characteristics, called *bona fide* occupational qualifications.[73]

Utah's previous protections omitted Utah's freestanding religious schools. Numbering in the dozens, these schools include those in Catholic, Baptist, and evangelical traditions.[74] Such religious schools receive insulation even if not owned or directed by a specific church.

As a lay church, religious figures in The Church of Jesus Christ of Latter-day Saints as well as members of other religious traditions often are business people who also hold religious office, that dual identity opens the possibility for punishment by secular authorities for disfavored positions through, for example, loss of one's professional license. We protected speech in a nonreligious setting and forestalled such results.[75]

The division of secular and sectarian occurred in housing, too. As Professor Wilson observed at the time: "SB296 accomplishes a balancing act between non-discrimination protections and religious liberties by placing faith groups outside the bounds of state dictates. Thus, existing law simply exempts religious sole corporations, like the LDS Church, giving them much-needed autonomy [and also] leaves aside wholly-owned corporations, the classic example of which is Brigham Young University."[76]

---

[72] Utah Code § 34A–5–102(i)(ii).
[73] § 34A–5–106(3)(a)(i).
[74] Robin Fretwell Wilson, *SB296 Comes in the American Tradition of Live and Let Live*, Salt Lake Trib. (Mar. 9, 2017), https://perma.cc/2NLC-HFVH; Utah Code §34A–5–106(3)(a)(ii).
[75] 2015 Utah S.B. 297, Gen. Sess. (Utah 2015), https://perma.cc/6Y84-7NNT.
[76] Wilson, *supra* note 74.

F *Recognize the Dual Nature of Marriage as Civil and Religious*

SB 297, Protections For Religious Expression And Beliefs About Marriage, Family Or Sexuality, protects specific practices related to marriage, borrowing from the states that voluntarily enacted same-sex marriage by statute or initiative.[77] Like those states, we protected the decision not to solemnize, host, or facilitate a marriage on religious grounds, gave step-offs for the clergy, allowed religious counselors to decide whom they would counsel, and protected those covered from lawsuits and government coercion.[78] We assured religious groups that government could not strip their ability to perform recognized marriages if a group or official declined to perform same-sex marriages.[79]

We gave absolutely essential assurance to religious groups that avail themselves of protections that their tax-exempt status would not be disturbed.[80] While Professor William N. Eskridge, Jr. in this volume urges that tax exemption would not be at risk even in the absence of specific protections, statutes have a calming and norming effect. Explicit protections both signal to disappointed parties that moving against a religious entity's tax exemption will serve no purpose and avoids the chilling effect that might follow silence in the law on such a central question.

We avoided the unseemliness of clerks turning away gay couples, too.[81] SB 297 creates, for the first time in Utah, a legal duty for someone to provide solemnization services for every couple with the legal right to marry.[82] But we provided a mechanism that avoids needless clashes over conscience. The innovation: the county clerk's office can designate any willing celebrant, whether a worker in the office or someone in the community authorized and willing to perform marriages for all who ask. Offices might select someone in the community for a variety of reasons, including scheduling and a staff working at capacity. Should no one be willing, the county clerk is required to perform marriages.

---

[77] S.B. 297, Gen. Sess. (Utah 2015); *supra* note 9 [Marriage statutes like HB 438 (Md. 2012)].

[78] S.B. 297, Gen. Sess. (Utah 2015).

[79] § 63G-20-201(2).

[80] Utah Code § 63G-20-102(1)(b)(i) (2016). Government retaliation includes "impos[ition of] a formal penalty on, fines, disciplines, discriminat[ion] against, deni[al of] the rights of den[ial of] benefits to, or deni[al of] tax-exempt status of a person." *Id.* § 63G-20-102(1)(b)(i).

[81] Rowan County, Kentucky clerk Kim Davis refused to issue any marriage licenses after the legalization of same-sex marriage and blocked others from doing so, too. The ACLU sued in federal court, which ruled all couples must be provided licenses. Davis refused, was held in contempt of court, jailed, and then released under order not to interfere with others issuing marriage licenses. Davis appealed, but dismissed her appeal after Kentucky enacted a law removing the names and signatures of county clerks from marriage licenses. *Miller v. Davis*, ACLU (Sept. 19, 2016), https://perma.cc/UVP8-7GLM. Kentucky has since paid $225,000 in fees in that litigation. John Cheves, *State of Kentucky Must Pay Nearly $225,000 in Legal Fees for Kim Davis Case*, Lexington Herald Leader (July 21, 2017), https://perma.cc/BW3A-AG5G.

[82] Utah Code §17-20-4 (1)-(2).

Whatever method used, every clerk's office must provide immediate service to all couples.[83] There can be no retaliation from the government if an employee other than the elected clerk chooses not to solemnize a marriage – and no one need know of that choice, avoiding the humiliation experienced by gay couples elsewhere.[84] This means government workers are not forced to violate their consciences *and* LGBT people are treated like everyone else, receiving seamless access to marriage – a win-win. This common sense solution – removing religious persons from choke points on the path to constitutional rights – has saved Utah and its citizens from destructive litigation.

Consider the North Carolina magistrate who asked not to perform marriages before North Carolina enacted a law allowing magistrates to recuse themselves;[85] she was given no recourse other than quitting or being fired, despite protections for religious exercise under the federal employment nondiscrimination law, Title VII of the Civil Rights Act of 1964.[86] Title VII permits reasonable accommodation for a religious belief or practice where it does not cause an undue burden on the employer or coworkers. Receiving no accommodation, the magistrate left her job and went for years without wages or benefits amounting to $210,000.00.[87] To recoup, she had to file a complaint with the federal authorities, attend hearings and arguments, wait on the decision, navigate a settlement, and face the harsh light of national media. Like Kentucky in Kim Davis's case, North Carolina paid $325,000 to settle the case. It was a loss for everyone involved. Far better to avoid these considerable human costs by taking citizens out of positions of conflict, avoiding the need to pick winners and losers.

G Give Everyone as Much Liberty as Possible Without Infringing Other Values

A hallmark of the Utah Compromise was its emphasis on individual liberties. At a time of great fear about the place of traditional values in our culture, we were especially concerned to permit Utahns space to speak about their religious and moral commitments. To honor the principle of fairness for all, protections for speech needed to extend to all, whether the speaker held a traditional view or not.

SB 296 protects employees from discrimination based on their nondisruptive expression within the workplace about marriage, family, and sexuality where

---

[83] *Id.*

[84] § 63G-20–102 (1).

[85] S.B. 2, Gen. Assem. (N.C. 2015).

[86] Myrick v. Warren, 16-EEOC-0001 (2017), https://perma.cc/TX67-JCHB (holding that under Title VII, 42 U.S.C. §§ 2000e to 2000e-17, the North Carolina Administrative Office of Courts discriminated against the former magistrate by failing to accommodate her religious belief against participating in same-sex marriages).

[87] Settlement Agreement and Release, BECKET (Jan. 23, 2018), https://perma.cc/N9HR-PYC2.

employers permit such speech by anyone and it is not "in direct conflict with the essential business-related interests of the employer."[88] This protection extends outside the workplace, too. Employers may not take action against an otherwise qualified person for lawful expression outside the workplace regarding the person's religious, political, or personal convictions, including convictions about marriage, family, or sexuality.[89] So, whether an employee attends a pro-life rally or a gay-pride parade on the weekend, they cannot be reprimanded for that at work.

Disagreement on these matters will not disappear overnight, if ever. In our democratic society, people must remain free to believe and speak on those topics, whatever view they hold, without fear of government retaliation or censure.

H *End Divisiveness with an Enduring Compact*

SB 296 reflected "the Legislature's balancing of competing interests."[90] We pre-empted local law that was inconsistent to give employers uniformity across the state.[91] We tied the fate of protections for both sides to one another through a non-severability clause. Thus, if any part of the bill is invalided by a court, the remainder will be "rendered without effect and void."[92]

This measure keeps both sides honest – no one is incentivized to undo concessions through litigation. Though unusual, adding a non-severability provision assured stakeholders that the arrived-at bargain would not be revisited, permitting everyone to move forward.

III UTAH'S UNPLOWED GROUND

True, we did not provide answers for every question sparked by *Kitchen*, as this volume illustrates.[93] The Utah Compromise did not extend to public accommodations, to the chagrin of some.[94] We lacked the benefit of local laws to guide our decision-making. The Utah Legislature is inherently cautious about regulating to questions that have not been tested on a smaller field.

Still, we are proud to have enacted protections that outstrip those in many "blue" states. Indeed, nondiscrimination norms established in the Utah

---

[88] UTAH CODE § 34A–5–112.

[89] *Id.*

[90] UTAH CODE § 34A–5–102.7.

[91] §57–21-2.5.

[92] § 57–21-2.7.

[93] For a discussion of special concerns raised by public accommodations, see e.g., Laycock, Chapter 3; Krotoszynski, Chapter 7; Melling, Chapter 19; Eskridge, Chapter 22; Hollman, Chapter 23; McConnell, Chapter 28; and Pizer, Chapter 29.

[94] UTAH CODE § 13–7-1 et seq; Nelson Tebbe, et al., *Utah "Compromise" to Protect LGBT Citizens from Discrimination Is No Model for the Nation*, SLATE (Mar. 18, 2015), https://perma.cc/E9SX-H5WV.

Compromise shape Utah's culture to be a more inclusive, tolerant one – even in public places.

Other unplowed ground: how to ensure faith-guided child welfare agencies can make placements of children that are consistent with their faith tenets – a pressing concern in states where religious adoption agencies are shouldering much of the load. As the CEO of the National Council for Adoption has observed, "the whole [adoption] system would collapse on itself" if religious adoption agencies closed.[95] Many close when faced with violating their faith tenets.[96]

In Utah, LDS Family Services long placed between 300 and 600 children annually.[97] But this "titan in the domestic adoption field" closed its adoption placement services in Utah before the Utah Compromise.[98] Faith-guided adoption agencies are "especially effective in placing special needs children who usually are hard to place."[99] The protection that SB 297 might have afforded for such agencies to reopen ultimately proved too much to achieve consensus on.[100]

As Figure 32.2 shows, the United States is a mix of laws working in different directions on the question of whether adoption agencies can serve only those families that are consonant with their faith. Ten states explicitly say social services agencies can follow their faith in placement.[101]

Some provide specific exemptions for adoption agencies to make the same kinds of placements after same-sex marriage that the agencies made before.[102] Newer stand-alone laws allow agencies to decline to provide services, while making

---

[95] Stephen V. Monsma & Stanley W. Carlson-Thies, Free to Serve: Protecting the Religious Freedom of Faith-Based Organizations (2015) (quoting Nicholas D. Kristof, *Learning from the Sins of Sodom*, N.Y. Times (Feb. 28, 2010).

[96] See Berg, Chapter 24, for examples; Laurie Goodstein, *Illinois Bishops Drop Program Over Bias Rule*, N.Y. Times (Dec. 29, 2011); Patricia Wen, *Catholic Charities Stuns State, Ends Adoptions*, Bos. Globe (Mar. 11, 2006).

[97] See Ryan Morgenegg, *LDS Family Services No Longer Operating as Adoption Agency*, The Church of Jesus Christ of Latter-day Saints, https://perma.cc/HZ9T-JTFJ.

[98] Kathryn Joyce, *Why Is the Mormon Church Getting Out of the Adoption Business?*, Daily Beast, https://perma.cc/V9JB-HFLF.
  LDS Family Services provides counseling about adoption, but stopped making placements in 2014. *Licensing Search*, Utah Dep't of Human Servs., Office of Licensing, https://perma.cc/UW74-5GTV.

[99] Monsma &Thies, *supra* note 95 at 31, 39 (quoting Issues of Faith, Justice, and Forgiveness: Working with Faith-Based Organizations to Foster Diversity of Mission 2 (Sept. 2008)).

[100] Utah Code § 63G-20–201(1) (leaving discretion "for ecclesiastical purposes only").

[101] These states are Alabama, Connecticut, Maryland, Michigan, Minnesota, North Dakota, South Dakota, Rhode Island, Texas, and Virginia. *See* Appendix, Chapter 35, at Col. 6.

[102] These states are Connecticut, Maryland, Minnesota, and Rhode Island. *See* Appendix, Chapter 35, at Col. 6.

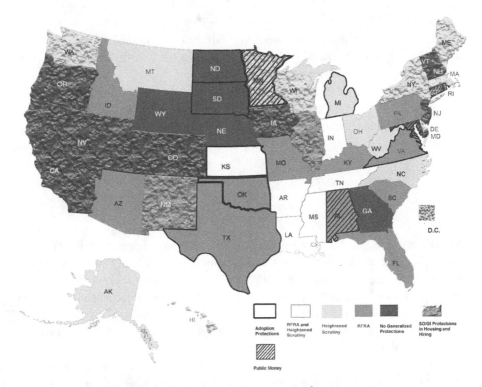

FIGURE 32.2 Religious exemptions in adoption context

referrals.[103] But no one should doubt the pain and humiliation of being turned away when seeking to give children a permanent loving home.

As Professor B. Jessie Hill explains elsewhere, when taxpayer money becomes involved, matters get especially thorny. That shoe has quietly fallen. In the closing hours of the Obama administration, a regulation was finalized, effective January 11, 2017, that all recipients of federal grants cannot "discriminate" against "beneficiaries" or participants on the "basis of age, disability, sex, race, color, national origin, religion, sexual orientation, or gender identity."[104]

In South Carolina, a religious foster-care agency, one of the state's largest agencies, is currently at risk of forced closure by the state's Department of Social Service, which interpreted this regulation as barring that agency from recruiting only families that practice the agency's religion – *e.g.*, Christians.[105] South Carolina's governor has asked the federal government for a waiver.

---

[103] These states are Alabama, Michigan, North Dakota, South Dakota, Texas, and Virginia. *See* Appendix, Chapter 35, at Col. 7.
[104] Health and Human Services Grants Regulation, 81 FR 89393–01; 45 C.F.R. § 75.300.
[105] Tim Smith, *Sumter Group Home Director Responds to Governor Siding with Faith-Based Foster Care Approach*, SUMTER ITEM (Feb. 23, 2018), https://perma.cc/Z4KK-XHAQ.

Declaring either side the winner sends a bad message: "close up shop" is as bad as allowing prospective adoptive families to be told "we don't serve you here." What is most important is the needs of the children. They need homes.

One solution may be taking government money out of adoption agencies' hands and placing it in potential parents' pockets. In that way, all potential parents will be served equally, and all would have the resources to make this profound commitment to children.[106] This would allow all adoption agencies to continue their vital work while preserving respect for all families.

IV A TRANSFORMATION IN VIEW

As humans, our natural impulse is to assume that one person's rights come at another's expense. We can be selfish; we sometimes reflexively desire to restrict the ability for anyone to disagree with us. When I voted with colleagues to limit marriage to one man and one woman, I thought I was protecting my ability to practice my faith. With *Goodridge* just handed down, challenging our views of marriage as a heterosexual institution, I thought it was best to restrict other people's actions in order to protect my own beliefs.

During SB 296 and 297's legislative process, a light went on. I thought to myself, "I am a Christian and I believe in the New Testament, in loving your neighbor, and in trying to be compassionate and tolerant." I realized that by looking out for those who may not agree with me, I was living my religion. These good, Christian principles are ones that we ought to not just talk about, we ought to actually live them. Utah's landmark law does just that.

As I have become more compassionate and tolerant, I am getting respect back from others. Far better, I have learned, is to do the hard work Utah did: to ask how we can secure rights for everyone.

This transformation in views can be hard to make. The label *Utah Compromise* does not help. Like most Utahns, I have deep-seated religious beliefs. And like many of my colleagues in the Utah Legislature, I am a very conservative legislator. Some in my state rankle at the term "Utah Compromise" which the media attached to the law. Like them, my religious principles are not in any way, shape, or form compromisable. But nothing in this landmark legislation forces anyone to change doctrine or beliefs. Quite the contrary, we protected religious organizations and people of faith in the ability to maintain their doctrines and beliefs.

---

[106] Kelsey Dallas, *How Children Get Caught in the Clash Over LGBT and Religious Rights*, DESERET NEWS (Mar. 1, 2018), https://perma.cc/DZF2-NW6T.

V CONCLUSION

If there is one lesson from Utah's experience around marriage and LGBT rights, it is this: find a statutory solution before judicial rulings are made. In a pluralistic society with differing views about the great questions facing us, there is a better way than litigation. Legislating, rather than litigating, gives us the ability to find common ground.

When *Kitchen* and *Obergefell* declared marriage to be a fundamental right for same-sex couples, they left unresolved important questions about discrimination and the scope of civil rights laws. They left unresolved core questions about religion's role in civil society. Striving for fairness for all offered Utah a way to protect the LGBT community while cementing protections for the religious community.

In the end, none of the stakeholders got everything they wanted, but everyone gained specific and very significant statutory protections that a court could not deliver, and all without the rancor experienced elsewhere. The result is a less costly, more enforceable, and *more decent* legal regime in which all can coexist, true to who we are while respecting others for who they are – a true win-win.

33

Shared Spaces and Brave Gambles

Governor Michael O. Leavitt

I am a Westerner. In my part of the world, mountains are high, mesas are long, and debates over the use of publicly owned land are elevated to questions of ultimate truth. One side believes God created the earth for mankind's uses: wise stewardship is required, but the resources should bless God's children. The other side believes the lands themselves are sacred and seeks to protect them as wilderness "untrammeled by man."[1] Both sides profess to love the land, but both hold very different views of how to express their reverence.

This debate was crisply captured by bumper stickers I saw on two cars side-by-side in an intersection. One bumper sticker said, "Earth first. We'll mine the other planets later."[2] The other bumper sticker read, "Save the Earth. Kill yourself."[3]

I was not sure if those two extreme statements were intended as arguments or as parody. Either way, these two bumper stickers illustrate the way public policy debates are conducted in our adversarial system of democracy. Both sides present a binary choice between good and evil. This chapter argues that where faith and sexuality intersect in public policy, such binary choices are not only unnecessary but destructive. It discusses five conditions that together can yield shared-space solutions to the seemingly intractable conflict between religious freedom and LGBT rights.

I SHARED SPACES

The ongoing debate between LGBT advocates and those who defend religious freedom is too often conducted in the same binary fashion as those bumper stickers. LGBT-rights advocates argue that religious freedom is simply an excuse to

[1] Kevin Proescholdt, *Untrammeled Wilderness*, 61 MINN. HISTORY 114 (Fall 2008), https://perma.cc/7AMG-NWMC.
[2] Marc D. Goldfinger, *Earth First!: A Brief History*, https://perma.cc/7AMG-NWMC.
[3] Grant Potts, *Church of Euthanasia*, in THE ENCYCLOPEDIA OF RELIGION AND NATURE 384 (Bron Taylor ed., 2005).

discriminate against LGBT people. At the extreme, those who defend religious freedom declare that sexual identity deserves no legal protection whereas the exercise of religion deserves maximal protection.

This pattern is not unique to debates over public lands or LGBT rights. Debating issues at the extremes is characteristic of American democracy. Pick any set of controversial issues related to what we value, protect, or prioritize and this proves to be true. For example, in the immigration debate, discussions of reproductive freedom, and even matters related to science like climate change, the discussion starts at ideological extremes.[4] In time, the messy, contentious, and sometimes inefficient process we know and love as democracy results in finding a shared space that accommodates diverse opinions and needs.

These tensions are part of the human experience. As Americans, we have learned to deal with these situations. We have been doing it – sometimes more successfully than others – but in the end always striving to find a way to live together peaceably. This is one of the core characteristics of America. We find workable solutions to accommodate people of extremely diverse backgrounds, beliefs, and needs. Had we not succeeded, the United States would no longer exist. Indeed, that is the unique genius of America.

Much of the solution to these tensions lies in the American notion of pluralism. Fundamental disagreements can exist among intelligent, informed people of good will. Whether the issue involves our use of land or finding the balance between LGBT rights and religious freedom, America needs an approach that to the maximum extent possible allows space for all people to live according to their fundamental beliefs and needs. America needs an approach that finds the shared spaces, resolving conflicts that may arise with win-win solutions that are not dependent on demands for ideological purity.

Such solutions come from taking tangible first steps. In September 1993, I was in Washington DC with a morning meeting at the White House. The night before, I received a call notifying me that the meeting had been cancelled. Secret negotiations between the government of Israel and the Palestine Liberation Organization (PLO) had concluded and a signing ceremony had preempted the meeting. Because I had flown from Utah to DC, the caller invited my wife and me to attend.

The event took place on the South Lawn of the White House. A large audience had assembled, including several hundred members of the media from around the world. A lone table and a simple podium stood on a small platform with the White House as its backdrop. This was a profound moment in history. The Jews and Palestinians had for centuries fought over land they both occupied and both viewed as holy, but for different reasons. Finally, they had agreed to what would be known as the Oslo Accords. This was not a full solution, but it was a step toward a long-term

---

[4] For descriptions of polarization today, see Brownstein, Chapter 2; Greenawalt, Chapter 8; DiGirolami, Chapter 21; Berg, Chapter 24.

solution. A group of Israeli and Palestinian children sat together. The children wore matching tee shirts that read "Planting Seeds of Peace."[5]

Despite the pageantry of the moment, the sound of chanting protestors on both sides of the agreement could be heard from across the street in Lafayette Park. Helicopters hovered overhead as part of the unprecedented security arrangements required when world leaders assemble.

Finally, the door to the South Portico of the White House opened and three men with serious faces emerged. It was a surreal moment. There they were, Yitzhak Rabin, prime minister of Israel on the left; Bill Clinton, president of the United States in the middle; and Yasser Arafat, chairman of the PLO, on the right.

Prime Minister Rabin spoke deliberately and soberly: "We are soldiers who have returned from battle stained with blood," he said. "We who have fought against you, the Palestinians, we say to you today, in a loud and clear voice: Enough of blood and tears. Enough!" Then, dressed in his familiar Arab head scarf, Chairman Arafat spoke in Arabic. He referenced the hopefulness of people on both sides that this conflict would end and concluded by saying, "It is time to give peace a chance."

Documents were signed and the world held its breath, waiting to see if these men, bitter enemies for decades, would shake hands. In great symbolism, President Clinton stood with arms outstretched as if to nudge them closer. They paused, looked one another in the eye, and shook hands. It was a magical moment.[6]

While the moment was magical, the process of getting to this modest step forward was not magic. Endurance, long suffering, and the sobering reality that brute force was not producing the result either side desired brought them to the moment. Both knew a perpetual continuation of the hostilities came at great cost, in both blood and treasure. Their agreement represented a small step but it produced hope. Since then, hope has ebbed and flowed. Still, history must admire Rabin and Arafat for what Clinton called their "brave gamble."

II A BRAVE GAMBLE

A brave gamble took place in 2015 when the LGBT and faith communities mutually worked for passage of what is now known as the Utah Compromise. Representatives of both groups met repeatedly, honestly seeking to understand one another. Though the discussions involved tension and disagreement, the two sides were held together by strong conveners and a commonly defined objective. They sought fairness, not unilateral advantage. All the traditional points of view were present. There were

---

[5] Thomas L. Friedman, *Rabin and Arafat Seal Their Accord as Clinton Applauds "Brave Gamble*," N.Y. TIMES (Sept. 13, 1993), http://www.nytimes.com/learning/general/onthisday/big/0913.html.

[6] Aaron David Miller, *Oslo Stakeholders Reflect on Peace Process After 20 Years*, AL JAZEERA AM. (Sept. 12, 2013), https://perma.cc/7E8J-RWHH.

naysayers on both sides who worried about giving an inch in their traditional battle of extreme points of view.

In the end, legislation passed in a deeply red state that extended protection against discrimination in housing and employment for LGBT people while also protecting the capacity of churches and critical auxiliary organizations to carry out their essential missions and doctrines.[7] Predictably, the outcome was praised by a large majority of people and criticized by advocates at both extremes who thought the Utah Compromise gave up too much ground. The doubting extremes on both sides said it was not replicable elsewhere.

A few weeks later I participated in a thoughtful discussion at the Brookings Institution in Washington DC, which was organized to analyze the Utah Compromise.[8] Afterward, I joined a small group for dinner at a Georgetown restaurant. The dinner group included a national LGBT rights leader and one of the religious leaders who had played a significant role in brokering the Utah compromise. During the after-dinner discussion, I asked whether successful passage of the Utah Compromise could be used as a template for action elsewhere in the United States. Various opinions were expressed. The religious leader offered an observation and a pivotal question. The observation was that Utah is a conservative state with a strong religious community.[9] He spoke of the resistance the bill had from the faith community and that the bill passed because leaders of the faith community moved forward in the face of that criticism. He said, "The bill passed because leaders of the faith community fought hard for LGBT rights." He then turned to the LGBT advocate and asked, "The real question now is whether in a different setting you would fight for our rights?"

The LGBT advocate is a lawyer, a senior officer of a well-known national LGBT group. The advocate paused thoughtfully before speaking. "Under the right circumstances, I think we could."

What are the circumstances where advocates for religious freedom and LGBT rights could advocate for a shared-space solution? What needs to occur for those conditions to exist? The years I have worked in public policy making cause me to believe there are five conditions that must exist for a shared-space solution to emerge in politics: common pain, a shared belief, political equilibrium, skilled conveners, and, finally, simultaneous benefit.

---

[7] For details, see Adams, Chapter 32.

[8] *See Gays, Mormons, and the Constitution: Are There Win-Win Answers for LGBT Rights and Religious Conscience?*, BROOKINGS INST. (Mar. 16, 2015), https://perma.cc/SXM5-MU87.

[9] At the time of passage, Utah was the single most conservative state in the nation, measured by voting in the prior presidential election, and the second most religious, measured by self-identified religiosity. *See* Robin Fretwell Wilson, *Marriage of Necessity: Same-Sex Marriage and Religious Liberty Protections*, 64 CASE W. RES. L. REV. 1161 (2014).

A Condition 1: Common Pain

The treaty I witnessed on the South Lawn of the White House came about when Israel and the PLO, each for its own reasons, became motivated to find a solution. Each, for different reasons, felt the pain of generations of bitterness and bloodshed. They used different, but complementary, words to express their pain. Rabin used the words "Enough of blood and tears. Enough!" Arafat's expression, "It's time to give peace a chance," made clear he and his people were ready for a solution. While both undoubtedly had strategic reasons to engage and neither was ready to give up, they both concluded that their attempts to use brute force to get their way were not working and their people were suffering as a result.

In Utah, the LGBT community had tried unsuccessfully for years to pass non-discrimination legislation. At the same time, the protectors of religious freedom in Utah could see threats on the horizon and wanted clarity in the law to provide the protections required to ensure they could exercise their faith freely. As talks matured, it became apparent that the protectors of religious freedom were also interested in eliminating discrimination, and that LGBT rights advocates really did not want to eliminate religious freedom.

In both these cases, while their pain was different, both sides felt the anxiety of uncertainty. Both sides had other priorities requiring attention. Each side independently concluded that "under the right conditions" they could benefit from a shared-space solution. This opened a window of opportunity in which both sides were willing to consider making a brave gamble that could meet most of their individual objectives.[10]

B Condition 2: A Shared Belief

Resolution between factions always starts with a human connection – some component of commonality. Make no mistake, this does not have to include friendship or trust, rather it can be just a glimpse, a whiff, a faint taste of common thought. Judging from their body language that day on the South Lawn of the White House, Rabin and Arafat hated each other, but the common thought was that only bad things were coming from their centuries' old battle. It was the smallest of threads, but enough that skilled conveners could use it to slowly knit the fabric of agreement.

The Utah Compromise did not resolve all the issues between the LGBT community and religious freedom advocates. Not even close.[11] However, in contrast to the Palestinian-Israeli conflict, over time real respect and friendships developed. Most importantly, the two groups came to understand that both sides supported basic

---

[10] For an argument that this is possible in all but the hardest cases, see Laycock, Chapter 3.
[11] As one example, it did not reach public accommodations. See Laycock, Chapter 3; Pizer, Chapter 29; Adams, Chapter 32.

fairness – fairness for all. The realization of that common view provided conveners the ability to slowly build a small platform of agreement.

C Condition 3: Political Equilibrium

It would be naïve to believe that conflicts as complex as those mentioned in this chapter could be solved by persuasion alone. Struggles over rights – especially those connected to identity – are fierce political and cultural battles that often cause people in other settings to resort to violence and war. Here, people on both sides of the issue view the outcome as vital to their survival and well-being and to the shape of our culture in the future.

It was General Carl von Clausewitz, a nineteenth-century military theorist, who said, *"War is a mere continuation of policy (politics) by other means."*[12] My experience in politics causes me to believe one can reverse von Clausewitz's observation and it remains true. Politics is war by other means.

Von Clausewitz taught that war is fought not just to prevail in one's objectives, but also to render the adversary incapable of resisting. *"War therefore is an act of violence intended to compel our opponent to fulfil our will,* "he said.[13] In other words, if either side believes that it has a sustainable advantage, there is no incentive to settling for less than everything. Shared-space solutions are rarely achieved on the strength of goodwill alone. If either Arafat or Rabin had been convinced that continued use of brute force would have produced a unilateral victory, the Oslo Accord ceremony I watched would have never occurred. It was the sustained existence of unacceptable, painful equilibrium that made the deal possible. This is true in nearly all negotiations and disputes and so it is in politics.

Von Clausewitz's theories of war describe well the political objectives of each warring party in the LGBT rights and religious freedom conflict. Both sides hire professionals and build organizations with a singular mission – to mold the culture and shape government statutes that best protect their interest and limit their adversary's. Hundreds of millions of dollars are spent each year as both sides seek unilateral victory.[14] This is a political struggle and, like war, it will stop only if one side succeeds in eliminating the capacity of the other to resist, unless there is a moment when both sides feel roughly equivalent levels of risk and potential reward. Those are moments when shared-space solutions can emerge.

---

[12] CARL VON CLAUSEWITZ, VOM KRIEG (J. Graham trans., 1832), https://perma.cc/QUB7-SMGR.

[13] *Id.*

[14] For an estimate of spending by LGBT advocates, see Ryan Anderson, Chapter 27 (estimating $500 million by a single donor alone). By contrast, Alliance Defending Freedom received a tenth of that amount in annual contributions, or about $50 million. *See* Form 990 for 2015, https://perma.cc/3T2G-FAX6.

D *Condition 4: Skilled Conveners*

It is worth remembering that the United States of America is the product of a brave gamble facilitated by great conveners. In the early 1780s, our country was made up of thirteen very separate and independent colonies operating as a group of loosely aligned states.[15] This arrangement was memorialized under an agreement known as the Articles of Confederation.[16] It was a mess. However, finding a resolution to the problem was extraordinarily difficult because the colonies were deeply divided about the nature and role of government.

Many of the leaders and their constituents believed a central national government was required to maintain order and other necessary components of a successful society. Others, having just extricated themselves though a costly revolutionary war from the king of England, wanted nothing to do with a strong national government. The two parties were loath to speak with each other.

James Madison went to the only person in the Americas capable of convening the two sides, General George Washington, who had led the fledgling nation in gaining its independence.[17] He told Washington his attendance would attract political leaders from other states, who would join a constitutional convention out of respect for him.[18] He was right. Though the story is more complicated, it was Washington's convening power that set the stage for the Constitutional Convention in Philadelphia that produced the shared-space solution between those who supported and those who opposed a national government.

Leaders of Norway and other world powers convened the parties required to produce the Oslo Accords. The tenacity of a group of insightful community leaders and legislators lead to the Utah Compromise.

Shared-space solutions start with skilled conveners who do far more than issue invitations based on their stature. They bring the judgment to know when windows of opportunity present themselves. The conveners must have sufficient stature that the parties will listen to and have some degree of trust in them. Once discussions start, the conveners act as diplomats, counselors, problem-solvers, and healers. Warring parties always need help finding a shared solution. Conveners are peacemakers.

E *Condition 5: Simultaneous Benefit*

Both the Utah Compromise and the Oslo Accords recognized the need for both sides to receive definable benefits under the agreement simultaneously. The Oslo

---

[15] Robert Middlekauff, The Glorious Cause: The American Revolution, 1763–1789, 640–41 (2005).

[16] *Id.*

[17] Ron Chernow, Washington: A Life 457–58 (2010).

[18] *Id.* at 520–27.

Accords detailed a series of activities each side committed to accomplish, contingent on the successful completion of the other parties' tasks.[19]

The Utah Compromise came during a period when religious freedom bills were being considered in other states. One year before, in 2014, Arizona's governor vetoed a bill to amend its state Religious Freedom Restoration Act (RFRA),[20] which attracted fierce criticism despite close similarities with the federal RFRA Congress passed with overwhelming bipartisan support in 1993.[21] Arizona's legislature enacted the bill on party line votes with virtually no public debate.[22] The legislators who voted for the bill and the governor who ultimately vetoed it were vigorously attacked, and out-of-state businesses threatened economic boycotts.[23]

Equally controversial was Indiana's RFRA, enacted only two weeks after the Utah Compromise.[24] It attracted numerous boycotts, beginning with Salesforce, which announced an end to its business expansion in Indiana.[25] Soon after, Arkansas enacted a RFRA of its own that closely mirrored the federal RFRA.[26] These state laws and those who passed them were accused of hostility and hatred toward LGBT people.[27]

By contrast, the Utah Compromise extended important new protections simultaneously for both the faith community and the LGBT community. The protections for religious freedom were far more consequential than those in the failed legislation in Arizona, as Professor Douglas Laycock explains elsewhere in this volume.[28] Likewise, the LGBT community was granted important new protections it had sought unsuccessfully for years.[29] Because protections were secured through negotiation among the parties and emerged from a process that simultaneously yielded significant new legislative projections for both groups, the bill was embraced and

---

[19] *See generally* Israel-Palestine Liberation Organization Agreement: 1993, https://perma.cc/ 95YN-QFCC.

[20] S.B. 1026 (Ariz. 2014).

[21] 42 U.S.C. § 2000bb-2000bb-4.

[22] *See* S.B. 1026, 51st Leg., 2d Reg. Sess. (Ariz. 2014) (legislative history), https://perma.cc/7BWJ-RZK3.

[23] *See* Fernanda Santos, *Arizona Governor Vetoes Bill on Refusal of Service to Gays*, N.Y. TIMES (Feb. 26, 2014).

[24] *See* Senate Enrolled Act No. 101, 119th Gen. Assembly, 1st Reg. Sess. (Ind. 2015).

[25] Claire Zillman, *Salesforce Boycotts Indiana Over Fear of LGBT Discrimination*, FORTUNE (Mar. 26, 2015), https://perma.cc/G7DJ-27RS.

[26] S.B. 975, 90th Gen. Assembly, 1st Reg. Sess. (Ark. 2015).

[27] *See* Jessica Glenza, *Arkansas Passes Indiana-Style "Religious Freedom" Bill Criticized as Anti-Gay*, GUARDIAN (Mar. 31, 2015).

[28] *See* Laycock, Chapter 3 (reviewing RFRA's track record when invoked against nondiscrimination laws).

[29] For that history, see Adams, Chapter 32.

celebrated as progress for both parties.[30] Brave gambles require the potential of simultaneous benefits for both parties.

III FINDING A BRAVE GAMBLE

The musical *Hamilton* chronicles the life of Alexander Hamilton in toe-tapping rap cadence.[31] This includes a depiction of Hamilton's famous pistol duel with then vice president of the United States, Aaron Burr, with whom Hamilton had had a long-running personal rivalry. It was their own private war, elegantly illustrating von Clausewitz's point that the primary objective of war (and, by extension, politics) is not only to impose one's will on an adversary, but to eliminate the capacity to rebound.[32]

Despite the rhythm and clever rhyme of the rap, as the fateful moment approaches, the insanity of this moment blares more loudly than the music or clever lyrics. A man sitting next to me uttered, to himself, "Somebody should have stopped this." Yet Hamilton's and Burr's friends not only stood by while this happened, they participated by facilitating it.

One can only imagine the after-the-fact guilt and remorse. Hamilton was dead. Burr's career was ruined.[33] There were no winners and it did not need to happen. No one was willing to walk into that shared space to make the brave gamble of saying "Stop!"

Nationally, the religious freedom and LGBT rights clash resembles hundreds of individual duels. Bills are filed in state legislatures, ordinances are proposed before local governments, and litigation specialists on both sides file lawsuits with one thing in common, promoting their side's purposes and silencing the other side.[34] Each is a standoff – a duel not unlike the one between Hamilton and Burr. In the same way that battles combine into wars, political duels form a national culture. In aggregate and over time, if either religious freedom or LGBT rights are silenced, advocates will claim victory, but the United States will have lost.

Here is the common ground: to build their cases, both groups depend on a fundamental freedom referred to as moral agency – the ability to choose right from

---

[30] Laurie Goodstein, *Utah Passes Antidiscrimination Bill Backed by Mormon Leaders*, N.Y. TIMES (Mar. 12, 2015); *Utah's LGBT Anti-Discrimination Bill Passes with Blessing of Mormon Church*, GUARDIAN (Mar. 12, 2015).

[31] *See* Rebecca Mead, *All About the Hamiltons*, NEW YORKER (Feb. 9, 2015), https://perma.cc/W9BT-9FH2.

[32] *Clausewitz: War as Politics by other Means*, ONLINE LIBRARY OF LIBERTY, https://perma.cc/D9HU-W33L.

[33] *See* RON CHERNOW, ALEXANDER HAMILTON 716 (2004).

[34] For a review of bills and lawsuits, see Melling, Chapter 19; Hollman, Chapter 23; Ryan Anderson, Chapter 27; Pizer, Chapter 29.

wrong and to act for ourselves.[35] A fundamental doctrine of The Church of Jesus Christ of Latter-day Saints, often referred to as the Mormon Church, of which I am a member, is that moral agency is the inalienable human right to follow one's own conscience. Moral agency does not create an entitlement to steal or murder or lie because one's conscience tolerates it. We create governments to restrain crime and even punish guilt when that occurs. However, neither governments nor the people that form them have the right to suppress the conscience of another human being.[36] Our world includes such a wide diversity of human needs and experience that a peaceful world could not exist otherwise.

Whether taught by philosopher or prophet, moral agency is the foundation of a civil society. Simply stated, the shared space between LGBT rights and religious freedoms does not reside at either extreme, but rather at the center.

When an LGBT person asks to be protected from discrimination because of who they love, or the gender they identify with, that claim is based on moral agency. Their plea is for fairness. Likewise, when people expect the right to exercise their faith, or the right *not* to be religious, they too are acting from their moral agency and petitioning for fairness. As Elder Von G. Keetch noted during the conference that preceded this book, moral agency also includes the right of all people – including LGBT persons – to live according to their core beliefs to the greatest extent reasonably possible.[37]

In the struggles between LGBT rights and religious freedom, the shared space is to be found in a robust pluralism that ensures fairness – fairness for all.

To a person who is gay, lesbian, bisexual, or transgender, fairness for all includes protection from being denied a livelihood, a place to live, or basic services just because of who they are. To the religious adherent, fairness for all means the free exercise of religion, including the right to freely associate with fellow believers. That right cannot be absolute everywhere, to be sure, but there are many important spheres where it must be vigorously protected or religious freedom becomes meaningless.

This latter point deserves careful reflection, for it is often misunderstood. While some conceive of religion as merely a private belief system, most experience faith and God in the company and communion of fellow believers, as Michael A. Helfand explains elsewhere in this volume (Chapter 11). The right of religious

---

[35] *Agency*, THE CHURCH OF JESUS CHRIST OF LATTER-DAY SAINTS (Apr. 24, 2017), https://perma .cc/W2PF-QBJ3.

[36] THE CHURCH OF JESUS CHRIST OF LATTER-DAY SAINTS: DOCTRINE AND COVENANTS 134:4 ("[W]e do not believe that human law has a right to interfere in prescribing rules of worship to bind the consciences of men, nor dictate forms for public or private devotion; that the civil magistrate should restrain crime, but never control conscience; should punish guilt, but never suppress the freedom of the soul."). For a similar argument from the Roman Catholic tradition, see Lori, Chapter 13.

[37] Elder Von G. Keetch, Executive Director of the Public Affairs Department, The Church of Jesus Christ of Latter-Day Saints, Yale University (Jan. 20, 2017). *See* Chapter 14.

people to gather and associate with fellow believers who live the same faith is essential to religious freedom. Without that, for most religious communities, there is no meaningful religious freedom. Faith communities must have wide autonomy to order their religious affairs, not only with respect to core worshipping activities but also with respect to employment, religious schools, religious charities, and other areas vital to their ability to perpetuate their faith and carry out their religious missions.[38] The unencumbered process of religious self-definition lies at the heart of religion itself and religious freedom. To label the fundamental need and right of religious people to gather and build institutions of community and meaning as merely "discrimination" does a serious injustice to people of faith, as Elder Von Keetch emphasized at the conference whose presentations became this book.[39]

As we interact with each other in shared spaces, there must, of necessity, be more give and take, more willingness to compromise, more searching for ways to accommodate diverse needs in a pluralistic society. That accommodation must run both ways, benefiting LGBT and religious freedom.

Can LGBT advocates and religious freedom defenders find alignment in their view of fairness? Can legislative bodies, courts, and administrative policy makers find the right words to achieve fairness to all? The answer is yes, so long as the objective is to find the shared space proceeding from the foundational principle of moral agency – the protection of conscience.

Elections are won using simple, big, ideologically crisp themes. However, once in the legislative process, compromises generally have to be made to actually get something done. An unwillingness to engage in legislative compromise usually means that nothing happens.

Close observers of political power know that among the most commonly repeated mistakes in politics is overreach. When a party or group gains power, after having been out of power for a time, they feel compelled to take advantage of the moment to deliver their mandate.

Overreach inevitably comes at the expense of the minority that was defeated in the recent election or that ends up in the losing position in a specific struggle for an objective. Resentment results and a backlash creates an appetite for retaliation. Ultimately, the aggrieved achieve power and restart the cycle of overreach. True, in some cases, each iteration of power gets closer to a shared-space solution, but other times it results in prolonged conflict, discrimination, pain, and sometimes outright war.

---

[38] For elaboration in these spheres, see Helfand, Chapter 11; Leith Anderson, Chapter 12; Lori, Chapter 13; Berg, Chapter 24; Hoogstra et al., Chapter 25; Hill, Chapter 26.

[39] Keetch, *supra* note 37 (critiquing statements made in connection with the release of U.S. COMM'N ON CIVIL RIGHTS, PEACEFUL COEXISTENCE: RECONCILING NONDISCRIMINATION PRINCIPLES WITH CIVIL LIBERTIES (2016), https://perma.cc/XLV6-63ET (statement of Chairman Martin Castro)).

Those who seek to decide the debate between LGBT rights and religious freedom by silencing the other side will not only fail but do a terrible disservice to America's culture and the fabric of civility and good will that still binds us despite deep differences. Just as the duel between Hamilton and Burr ranks among the most pointless episodes in US history, it would be equally pointless to resolve the conflict between religious freedom and LGBT rights through socially enforced censorship.

In the world of politics and public policy, clarity occasionally replaces chaos, statesmanship overcomes selfishness, compromise displaces gridlock. The reality is, such moments occur when brute force has failed and everyone involved senses that defeat is a real possibility; fatigue and fear give birth to decency and the mutual respect needed to give as well as get. Despite shrill voices, I sense we are getting closer to that point in the LGBT rights and religious-liberty standoff, for it is clear neither side can simply impose its will at an acceptable cost. When that moment comes, those who seek a just peace – those who seek fairness for all – should be ready to take the following concrete steps.

First, solution seekers on both sides must start by finding a common rhetorical platform or shared language upon which agreement can be built. Second, they must seize the collaborative moment when it arrives. Third, they must find conveners of stature to bring the sides together. Fourth, they must find incremental avenues of progress to build momentum and trust. Finally, they must undertake simultaneous action to protect both sides.

A *Shared Language*

Shared space requires shared language. In the 1980s, after decades of hardline communist thinking, Mikail Gorbachev led the Soviet Union in a new direction and described his economic and political reform using one word, "Perestroika."[40] It meant "to open up." While such an endeavor involves endless complexity and nuance, the use of a simple word allowed him to gain widespread buy-in for a historic change.

While most people believe in LGBT equality and the importance of religious freedom,[41] there is not yet the language to express a shared space where both communities are protected. This is where the phase "fairness for all" serves an important purpose. It speaks clearly and unambiguously of a shared objective that both the LGBT and faith community want – to be treated fairly.

---

[40] *See generally* Mikhail S. Gorbachev, Perestroika: New Thinking for Our Country and the World (1987).

[41] For polls on both sets of views, see Brownstein, Chapter 2; Laycock, Chapter 3; Greenawalt, Chapter 8.

B The Collaborative Moment

The creation of shared space for religious freedom and LGBT rights requires peace-makers to seize the collaborative moment – the moment when the opportunity for cooperation and compromise among these often divided communities appears. The recipe for success in the bone-on-bone world of democratic advocacy involves both self-interest and goodwill, but not in equal parts. When victory seems certain, goodwill among advocates is scarce. However, the risks of uncertainty generate the goodwill required for a collaborative solution. Storied diplomat Henry Kissinger once remarked that "the absence of alternatives clears the mind marvelously."[42] Like courtroom litigants, advocates become open to a collaborative solution when they sense the possibility of defeat. It is uncertainty that often produces a transformative moment when agreement can be reached. When uncertainty for both sides around an issue becomes high enough, realism gels and both sides feel sufficiently vulnerable to allow for a collaborative moment. The shared space is found and a permanent, sustainable solution unfolds. When moments like this occur, they must be embraced.

In the LGBT and religious liberty standoff, those moments open and close in different ways and at different times depending on the context. It takes a discerning eye to recognize such a moment. Congress is different than state legislatures, and each state is unique. In Utah, the moment came in early 2015 after years of relationship- and trust-building efforts between the religious and LGBT communi-ties – combined with the uncertainty of the Supreme Court's impending gay-marriage decision. This atmosphere produced a mutual desire to reach a sustainable compromise despite the certainty that it would not be perfect for either side.

Similar discussions are being held, often quietly below the radar, in many other states. They are most productive when they are organic and arise from a shared interest in building a community that works for everyone, rather than the product of national advocacy groups seeking ideological purity. It is also vital that prominent legislative leaders from both sides of aisle become personally invested in the process and over time educate their colleagues.

Congress is more difficult, but the process is similar: shared need, strong relation-ships and trust built over time, prominent legislative stakeholders from both political parties, and ideological flexibility. At this writing, it is less clear when the moment in Congress will open, but I am certain it eventually will. Both sides have too much to lose and uncertainty is growing.

C Conveners of Stature

When the collaborative moment comes, it will take astute conveners to recognize it and seize it. In Utah, those conveners included Equality Utah and the LDS Church.

---

[42] *Henry Kissinger, Man of the Year: They Are Fated to Succeed*, TIME (Jan. 2, 1978).

Equality Utah had worked for years to lay the groundwork for a common-ground solution but could not overcome the inherent resistance of a religiously conservative state. Church representatives had been meeting privately for years with members of the LGBT community to better understand their needs and explore ways to address them while preserving the freedom of religious organizations and individuals to live out their traditional religious beliefs regarding marriage, family, gender, and sexuality. Both sides recognized in the uncertainty before *Obergefell* a moment to act for good of all.

Then the Church took the unprecedented step of holding a press conference with some of its most senior religious leaders to announce Church support for legislation that would take a balanced approach to the issue.[43] That act transformed the possibility of a collaborative moment into a reality, altering both cultural and legislative realities in Utah. On its side, Equality Utah courageously urged often-skeptical local and national groups to embrace the process, work for the best outcome, avoid explosive denunciations, and not let the perfect be the enemy of the good. The result changed Utah for the better.

Other states and Congress must find their conveners of stature – their senior statesmen and trusted institutions willing to risk reputation, support, friendships, and funding to seize the best moment to make a good enough, sustainable peace. Those who seek fairness for all have an urgent need to find their General Washingtons who are willing to take personal risks and lead the community to a higher good.

D *Avenues for Incremental Progress*

In deciding how to approach the multidimensional conflicts between religious freedom and LGBT rights, experience teaches the value of moving in small steps. While there are certainly exceptions, sound public policy is rarely implemented through large-scale enactments, but rather through incremental progress, slowly building momentum until there is directional clarity. A single law, a single court decision, a single election will not resolve the controversy between religious freedom and LGBT rights. But the combined effect of many small steps toward mutual understanding and meaningful compromise can result in a change of direction that makes overall resolution possible.

Fairness for all invites policy makers to identify new venues for progress. Rather than belaboring the problem of wedding vendors, for instance, both sides might explore other venues of progress that hold the promise of cultivating closer working relationships among the contending parties as well as a healthier, more tolerant civic culture. Hospital visitation rights for same-sex couples might be one area of easy

---

[43] See Adams, Chapter 32, for details.

agreement.[44] Another might be enhancing public services for at-risk LGBT youth.[45] Even small areas of agreement like these can build momentum for progress. Cooperation that leads to success in small areas lays the foundation for further cooperation that may lead to success in more significant areas. This diplomatic approach for resolving tensions between nations has value for resolving conflicts between competing social factions.

In looking for venues for incremental progress, it is helpful to remember that people – including policy makers – are motivated by greed, fear and the desire to touch the hand of greatness. Greed is exemplified by a desire to advance one's ideological agenda even when there is no real benefit to one's own group, but only harm to the other party. We see this in ferocious efforts by some advocacy groups to crush dissenters from the current orthodoxy regarding sexuality, often individuals of no real consequence whose dissent threatens little or nothing of the groups' broader agenda.[46]

Fear, especially fear of failure or domination, may have the salutary effect of pushing otherwise implacable adversaries toward compromise, or it may – as in the case of some religious conservatives – drive them to hold out against clearly justified measures to help LGBT persons, fearing that any concession will trigger an avalanche of major defeats. The Oslo Accords happened because both Israel and the Palestinians feared the costs of continued war more than they feared the loss of their current entrenched positions.

What I call "touching the hand of greatness" consists of an appeal to our highest impulses and to historic opportunities – the chance to do something of lasting importance, to be known as a peacemaker in a time of turmoil. A wise and respected convener can tap these motivations to win the adoption of incremental and progressive measures, assuring the parties that such efforts are part of forging a larger, historic compact to reconcile meaningful protections for LGBT Americans with security for religious freedom and thus establish peace.

E *Simultaneous Action to Protect Both Sides*

Each side in the standoff between religious freedom and LGBT rights is too powerful and deeply entrenched to accept unilateral measures. Measures that benefit one side must be fairly matched with measures that favor the other. Protecting LGBT employees from discrimination, for instance, must come with protections for religious employers to select employees who live by the employer's religious commitments. Like the Utah Compromise, any effort to reconcile these interests

---

[44] See Pizer, Chapter 29, for the importance of decision-making for one's partner.

[45] See Minter, Chapter 4, for the public health crisis facing LGBT youth.

[46] For discussion of nondiscrimination law being used as a sword, rather than a shield, see Ryan Anderson, Chapter 27.

must offer a meaningful win for both sides. The Utah experience showed that erstwhile adversaries can work together when there is the potential of mutual advantage. Not only is this win-win approach deeply principled, and therefore maximally defensible, it lays the groundwork for further compromise and agreement. Trust grows as each side gains more from cooperation than from remaining fixed in opposition. Ideally, this principle of mutually beneficial action is the standard to judge any serious effort at resolving the conflicts between religious freedom and LGBT rights.

IV CONCLUSION

The conflict between LGBT rights and religious freedom has been mired too long in the politics of extremes. The country needs a different path forward – a path that begins with the recognition that each side has legitimate claims to legal protection and social recognition. The conference that Professors William N. Eskridge, Jr. and Robin Fretwell Wilson organized, and that I am proud to have participated in, is a hopeful sign that dialogue and ultimately progress are possible, with meaningful engagement among people of good will.

But the conditions must be ripe for that "brave gamble" I have described. We must continue developing shared language for describing the pain and vulnerability experienced by LGBT Americans and religious people and institutions, as well as language to express hope for reconciliation and workable solutions. We must look for collaborative moments as they make their sudden, and at times unexpected, appearance. We must find conveners of stature – those rare statesmen with the capacity for bringing contentious parties together. We must find issues where incremental achievements can build trust and momentum toward further progress. And finally, we must be prepared to insist that solutions benefit both sides – that each side is made more secure in its ability to live according to its deepest convictions and needs. Fairness for all, to be more than a slogan, must be a guiding principle for resolving the manifold conflicts between religious freedom and LGBT rights.

Resolving those conflicts will likely require patient and sustained progress for years to come. The depth and complexity of the conflicts are unlikely to be decided in a single moment. Our federal system offers many opportunities to experiment with different legal frameworks on a state level, to refine them based on experience, and to extend those solutions elsewhere with appropriate adjustments to account for local conditions. The conflicts that divide LGBT Americans from religious Americans are shaped by local politics and culture no less than any other important conflicts in our society.

Most importantly, we should begin not with our grievances in mind but with our commitment to each other and our common humanity. Despite differences, we share a world of similar experiences, aspirations, and hopes. We are sons and daughters, fathers and mothers, brothers and sisters; we love and worry about our children and grandchildren; we want to live in dignity in communities that are safe and friendly; and we all need places and spaces where we can associate with those who share our deepest convictions. And we are Americans, stewards of a noble constitutional heritage of freedom and equality and heirs of a great, if imperfect, tradition of reconciling profound differences so people can live together in peace. That is a lot for community leaders, elected officials, scholars, lawyers, activists and negotiators – people of good will – to work with. It is the stuff of which durable settlements can be forged. The conditions for peaceful coexistence already exist. Will we have the decency and courage to seize the opportunity that is before us?

"We are not enemies, but friends," Abraham Lincoln reminded – pleaded – in his First Inaugural. "We must not be enemies. Though passion may have strained, it must not break our bonds of affection."[47] It is "the better angels of our nature" that must inspire us. That advice went unheeded prior to the Civil War. We must heed it now as we reject bumper-sticker extremes on religious freedom and LGBT rights and instead seek a lasting resolution in a genuine pluralism that fosters mutual respect and peace.

---

[47] ABRAHAM LINCOLN, GREAT SPEECHES WITH HISTORICAL NOTES BY JOHN GRAFTON (Stanley Appelbaum ed., 1991).

PART IX

Afterword

34

Masterpiece Cakeshop

Impact on the Search for Common Ground

Rabbi David N. Saperstein

I have spent my entire career championing civil rights – including women's rights and LGBTQ rights – as an expression of my most fundamental religious values. I have spent those same years championing religious freedom rights as an expression of my core civil rights commitments. What links those endeavors together is my firm belief that the protections of fundamental rights are indivisible. If any group is persecuted or oppressed or discriminated against, it endangers everyone's protections of civil rights and civil liberties. Yet too often today, advocates for religious freedom and for civil rights find themselves squaring off. The vision is etched in my mind after the Supreme Court's decision in *Masterpiece Cakeshop, Ltd.* v. *Colorado Civil Rights Commission* of dueling press messaging on the steps of the Court espousing clashing views in sound bites, leaving little room for nuance. Yet having worked personally with leaders of many organizations that submitted briefs on the various sides of this case, I know that many would accept the validity of the principles being asserted by the opposing side, while differing sharply on what the Court should do. There are all too few places, however, for such leaders to engage in constructive efforts to find common ground and to explore if compromise is both possible and wise.

That dearth makes this volume a vital, incisive, and timely contribution to the national conversation on how our nation, our society, and our legal system should balance the tension between different sets of fundamental rights. These tensions represent a clash of legal principles, cultural values, and attitudes. This volume identifies and probes potential areas of common ground and compromise that balance the free exercise of religion and the freedom of expression with civil rights protections barring discrimination against a range of protected categories. Some chapters seek common ground where advocates on different sides of the debate can agree; others try to map out sensible compromises with enough "wins" for each side that both would be willing to give up or postpone less essential claims.

These chapters were written before the United States Supreme Court's decision in *Masterpiece Cakeshop*.[1] I was asked to hold my contribution until *Masterpiece Cakeshop* was issued in order to reflect on what the decision means for the urgent moral and legal issues this volume addresses and for the proposals made by its contributors searching for common ground, compromise, and enhanced civility in our discourse.

By confining its decision in *Masterpiece Cakeshop* to how Colorado applied its law to Jack Phillips's refusal to bake a cake for a same-sex wedding celebration, the Court disturbed little of the background law. But it affirmed the validity of religious liberty and civil rights principles that would be embodied in balanced legislation that seeks to embrace fundamental rights that too often are seen as in tension.

The Court might have decided *Masterpiece Cakeshop* a number of ways. It might have come down with a clear decision that religious free exercise protections include the right to be free from being forced by the government to participate in activities that violate core beliefs, even if doing so results in harm to members of groups protected by civil rights laws. Relatedly, the Court might have held, as Justice Thomas articulated in his concurrence, that preparing a cake for a same-sex marriage is expression that cannot be compelled without exceedingly good reasons.[2] Under this analysis, the Court might have concluded that the state, having failed to present such a reason, needed to provide an exemption from nondiscrimination legislation in similar situations to *Masterpiece Cakeshop*. Or conversely, the Court might have held that an exemption was neither mandated nor justified on two linked grounds: first, that state or local civil rights protections clearly pass muster under the standard set forth in *Employment Division v. Smith*,[3] which applies rational basis review to facially neutral and generally applicable laws; and second, even if strict scrutiny was required, the state's compelling interests in ensuring civil rights coverage would bar a precedent that could result in so many businesses claiming exemptions that exemptions would swallow the rule, gravely undercutting the entire structure of civil rights protections in America.[4]

Any of those holdings by the Court would have, on the one hand, resolved many of the arguments between those holding different views about which claims or interests should prevail – those of the baker or those of the couple. On the other hand, a constitutional mandate from the Court, whatever its legal merits and long-term social gains, might well, for better or for worse, have derailed efforts to find common ground and exacerbated fraught cultural battles by taking issues out of the

---

[1] No. 16–111, slip op. (U.S. June 4, 2018).
[2] *Masterpiece Cakeshop*, slip op., at 11 (Thomas, J., concurring). Justice Thomas did not reach the issue of whether civil rights laws would satisfy strict scrutiny review.
[3] 494 U.S. 872 (1990).
[4] *See* Koppelman, Chapter 9; *Masterpiece Cakeshop*, slip op., at 10.

realm of political deliberation, as the dissenting justices warned in *Obergefell v. Hodges*.[5] Whichever way the Court might have resolved the balance between the competing rights claims, millions very likely would have applauded such a decision, while millions would have condemned it. Instead, what seems clear is that the *Masterpiece Cakeshop* decision, in not resolving the underlying core issues, makes this book's effort to find common ground and compromise more timely and more valuable than ever.

I THE *MASTERPIECE CAKESHOP* DECISION

Instead of addressing the core religious freedom / free speech and civil rights claims, the seven-judge majority in *Masterpiece Cakeshop* focused on the Colorado Civil Rights Commission's denial of fair treatment to the baker, Phillips, and the religious claims he made. An earlier religious liberty case decided by the Supreme Court, *Lukumi Babalu Aye v. City of Hialeah*,[6] considered the constitutionality of laws and regulations that, on their face or in their intent (as evidenced by the history of the laws), targeted religious groups or reflected animus toward religion or specific religions.[7] In *Lukumi*, the Court unanimously, with various opinions, struck down a Florida city's law prohibiting ritual animal sacrifices conducted by adherents of the Santeria religion on the grounds that the "ordinances had as their object the suppression of religion."[8] Justice Kennedy, writing for the Court, was joined only by Justice Stevens in grounding the decision on statements made by city officials. In *Masterpiece Cakeshop*, the laws and regulations in question were not hostile to religion and were neutral on their face. However, Justice Kennedy broadened the analytical lens he used in *Lukumi*[9] to bar hostility in the *implementation* of non-discrimination law – in this case by an adjudicatory entity. During the Commission's meetings, one of the commissioners stated, "Freedom of religion and religion has been used to justify all kinds of discrimination throughout history, whether it be slavery, whether it be the holocaust ... And to me is one of the most despicable pieces of rhetoric that people can use to – to use their religion to hurt others."[10]

---

[5] 135 S. Ct. 2584, 2611–12 (2015) (Roberts, C.J., dissenting) ("Supporters of same-sex marriage have achieved considerable success persuading their fellow citizens – through the democratic process – to adopt their view. That ends today. Five lawyers have closed the debate and enacted their own vision of marriage as a matter of constitutional law. Stealing this issue from the people will for many cast a cloud over same-sex marriage, making a dramatic social change that much more difficult to accept.").

[6] 508 U.S. 520 (1993).

[7] *Id.* at 540–542. Only Justice Stevens joined Justice Kennedy in this portion, II-A-2, of the decision.

[8] *Id.* at 542.

[9] *Id.* at 534.

[10] Masterpiece Cakeshop, Ltd. v. Colorado Civil Rights Commission, No. 16-111, slip op. at 13 (U.S. June 4, 2018).

None of the other commissioners took issue with these comments, leading the majority on the Court to conclude that this reflected hostility to the religious claims that Phillips was making. I am confident that the contributors to this volume would differ sharply on whether or not these comments actually constituted a level of "hostility to religion"[11] that was constitutionally disqualifying.[12] But the principle of neutral treatment of religious claims, both in the law *and* the implementation of the law, was the standard affirmed in this decision.[13]

Some supporters of the baker's point of view argued this was a victory for their side.[14] They pointed out that the baker won the case; the Commission's decision and the penalties imposed on Phillips were nullified; Phillips's religious freedom claims were clearly held to be constitutionally protected claims; and the Court expanded the scope of religious freedom protections to require not only lack of facial neutrality but also neutral implementation.[15]

---

[11] *Id. at* 18.

[12] *See id.*, slip op. at 2–3 (Ginsburg, J., dissenting); see *also infra*, note 15.

[13] Ironically, just a few weeks later, many of the justices in the majority of *Masterpiece Cakeshop* comprised the five-justice majority upholding the travel ban, finding the law to be facially neutral. Trump v. Hawaii, No. 17–965, slip op., at 29 (U.S. June 26, 2018). Despite finding facial neutrality, the Court mentioned it would consider extrinsic evidence – the President's expressions of hostility to a religious group – but would uphold the ban "so long as it can reasonably be understood to result from a justification independent of unconstitutional grounds." *Id.* at 32. In finding a number of rational policy bases justified the law, the Court made little mention of the hostile statements. *Id.* at 33–39.

This is surprising given the Court's approach in *Masterpiece Cakeshop*. In contrast to the one civil rights commissioner whose comments the Court highlighted in *Masterpiece Cakeshop*, the President was the principle promulgator and implementer of the so-called "Muslim ban." His statements were far more explicitly aimed at the target of the government action; he consistently expressed hostility to Muslims both before and after enacting the travel ban decrees; and the statements were far more extensive in number. *Id.* at 27–28. Yet, the Court did not take these together to be disqualifying hostility, unlawful religious discrimination, or establishment of religion.

[14] *See, e.g.*, Marissa Mayer, What People Are Saying About Jack Phillips' Win at the Supreme Court, ALLIANCE DEFENDING FREEDOM (June 8, 2018), https://perma.cc/Q82T-Y7G6. Emilie Kao, *Why the Supreme Court's Ruling for a Christian Baker Was Not "Narrow,"* THE HERITAGE FOUNDATION (June 12, 2018), https://perma.cc/WL5K-GTKJ.

[15] For a more extensive discussion of facial neutrality, see David Saperstein, *Public Accountability and Faith-Based Organizations: A Problem Best Avoided*, 116 Harv. L. Rev. 1353 (2003). Critics of the *Masterpiece Cakeshop* decision will likely argue that the Court's standard of no hostility to religion is an overly broad and vague standard for judging whether a religious freedom claim has been treated fairly. Questions about the propriety of and methodology for considering legislative intent in constitutional cases have long perplexed the Court. See WILLIAM N. ESKRIDGE, JR., DYNAMIC STATUTORY INTERPRETATION 207–39 (1994). Moreover, "if the government defendant can prove by way of rebuttal that it would have reached the same decision even if the invidious motive had not been present, then the challenged decision will be upheld." Vikram David Amar & Alan Brownstein, *Attitudinal and Doctrinal Takeaways from the Masterpiece Cakeshop Case*, VERDICT (June 15, 2018), https://perma.cc/4W36-ADBG (citing *Arlington Heights v. Metropolitan Housing Development Corp.*, 429 U.S. 252 (1977).

Comments by government officials or members of government entities, such as a state civil rights commission, often contain critical, even derogatory language where there may be no evidence of prejudice in an official's decision. *Masterpiece Cakeshop's* focus on hostility

Advocates of LGBTQ rights likewise found much to take comfort from the decision.[16] Despite having found for the baker, the Court eschewed holding that free exercise and/or free speech claims generally trump civil rights protections. Justice Kagan, in her concurrence to *Masterpiece Cakeshop*, suggested that absent the religious hostility involved, the Court might have found the civil rights claims should prevail:

> Colorado law, the Court says, "can protect gay persons, just as it can protect other classes of individuals, in acquiring whatever products and services they choose on the same terms and conditions as are offered to other members of the public." For that reason, Colorado can treat a baker who discriminates based on sexual orientation differently from a baker who does not discriminate on that or any other prohibited ground. But only, as the Court rightly says, if the State's decisions are not infected by religious hostility or bias.[17]

And even Justice Kennedy's majority opinion articulated the significant interests the government has in protecting LGBTQ rights. He strongly emphasized the dignitary harms imposed on victims of discrimination:

> Our society has come to the recognition that gay persons and gay couples cannot be treated as social outcasts or as inferior in dignity and worth. For that reason the laws and the Constitution can, and in some instances must, protect them in the exercise

---

expressed by a single decision-maker among many could result in endless disputes over what is and is not hostility, with lawyers combing through comments made not just in formal proceedings but in speeches, articles, and interviews to try to show a pattern of hostility.

One should expect advocates to comb the record for indications of hostility in corners far beyond what was seen as relevant in the past. Already this is shaping the way that similar cases are being litigated. Shortly following the Court's decision in *Masterpiece Cakeshop*, the Alliance Defending Freedom (ADF) – which represented Phillips in *Masterpiece Cakeshop* – filed a petition for the Court to grant, vacate, and remand *Arlene's Flowers, Inc. v. Washington*, a case involving a florist who similarly refused to serve a same-sex couple seeking floral arrangements for their wedding. *See* Smith, this volume, for details of the case. In its petition, ADF urged that sending the case back to Washington state "would allow the state courts to consider the evidence of government hostility toward the faith of Barronelle Stutzman, owner of Arlene's Flowers." *See* Supplemental brief of petitioners Arlene's Flowers, Inc., et al., June 6, 2018, https://perma.cc/UG8B-ZMDR.

Justice Ginsburg would likely view most of these record searches as unnecessary. In her view, the record in *Masterpiece Cakeshop* did not set forth constitutionally hostile statements: "The different outcomes the Court features do not evidence hostility to a religion of the kind we have previously held to signal a free-exercise violation, nor do the comments by one or two members of one of the four decision-making entities considering this case justify reversing the judgment below." *Masterpiece Cakeshop*, slip op. at 2–3 (Ginsburg, J., dissenting).

[16] Lauren Gray, *NCLR Statement on the Supreme Court Decision in* Masterpiece Cakeshop v. Colorado Civil Rights Commission, NAT'L CTR. FOR LESBIAN RIGHTS (June 4, 2018), https://perma.cc/JT28-FPNB; Garrett Epps, *Justice Kennedy's* Masterpiece *Ruling*, THE ATLANTIC (June 4, 2018), https://perma.cc/UUH6-ZUS9.

[17] *Masterpiece Cakeshop*, slip op. at 3–4 (Kagan, J., concurring).

of their civil rights. The exercise of their freedom on terms equal to others must be given great weight and respect by the courts.[18]

Dignitary harms are not just something to be avoided – they play a role in weighing competing claims. Thus, freedom of religion ensures:

> ... that a member of the clergy who objects to gay marriage on moral and religious grounds could not be compelled to perform the ceremony without denial of his or her right to the free exercise of religion. This refusal would be well understood in our constitutional order as an exercise of religion, an exercise that gay persons could recognize and accept without serious diminishment to their own dignity and worth.[19]

Justice Kennedy follows the suggestion that clergy should be exempted from nondiscrimination laws with a strong affirmation of arguments that LGBTQ rights advocates often make more generally – concerns about exceptions swallowing the rule:

> Yet if that exception were not confined, then a long list of persons who provide goods and services for marriages and weddings might refuse to do so for gay persons, thus resulting in a community-wide stigma inconsistent with the history and dynamics of civil rights laws that ensure equal access to goods, services, and public accommodations.[20]

And later:

> Any decision in favor of the baker would have to be sufficiently constrained, lest all purveyors of goods and services who object to gay marriages for moral and religious reasons in effect be allowed to put up signs saying "no goods or services will be sold if they will be used for gay marriages," something that would impose a serious stigma on gay persons.[21]

Regardless of one's view of the specific holding in this case, Justice Kennedy's serious treatment and embrace of both the religious liberty and civil rights claims in this case is encouraging for the pursuit of common ground and compromise. While other justices joined him in this decision, it is unknown how strongly the others in the majority shared these views. Justice Kennedy's attempt to balance these claims clearly reflects his evolving views on LGBTQ rights.[22] On the last day of the term, Justice Kennedy announced his retirement.[23] There is, of course, no

---

[18] *Id.* at 9.

[19] *Id.* at 10.

[20] *Id.*

[21] *Id.* at 12.

[22] Scott Bomboy, *Justice Kennedy's Legacy in the Gay Rights Decisions*, CONSTITUTION DAILY, NAT'L CONST. CTR. (June 27, 2018), https://perma.cc/Z4VC-5ULV.

[23] READ: *Justice Kennedy's Retirement Letter*, CNN (June 27, 2018), https://perma.cc/U83Z-DF26.

guarantee that his successor will follow course, and many civil rights advocates worry that whoever is confirmed will be more disinclined toward protecting LGBTQ interests.[24]

What is clear is that the high court, in basing its decision on narrow technical grounds, has left the decision of how to resolve the competing claims for another time. In the last week of its 2017 term, the Court sent back to the Washington Supreme Court for reconsideration in light of the *Masterpiece Cakeshop* a decision, *Arlene's Flowers Inc. v. Washington*, involving the refusal by a florist to make a flower arrangement for the same-sex wedding of her longtime client.[25] As a result, it may be some time before a case raising the same issues reaches the Supreme Court, leaving it to the state courts and legislatures, Congress, and/or the federal executive branch to shape policies. This could lead to contradictory results in which some states and localities advance religious freedom at the expense of LGBTQ, women's, and other civil rights, while other states and localities tilt this balance in the opposite direction. For such an evolving checkerboard of laws, one need look no further than the Appendix to this volume. Still other states and localities may seek compromise along the lines of what some states and localities, like Utah, have done.

Indeed, some have pointed out that legislative approaches offer more opportunities for compromise than do judicial decisions. As Utah State Senator J. Stuart Adams observes in his chapter on the laws popularly known as the "Utah Compromise,"[26] "in times of great social change, people look to legislators to take colliding trains off a collision course ... when legislatures do not act, courts are left to decide competing rights without the advantages of the legislative process."[27] And Chief Justice Roberts makes a similar argument in his dissent in *Obergefell*.[28] Whether one would prefer an expeditious judicial resolution of the religious freedom and civil rights balance or not, the Court's narrow decision in *Masterpiece Cakeshop* leaves open the opportunity to robustly explore common ground and compromise efforts, including those proposed in this volume.

II HOW *MASTERPIECE CAKESHOP* AFFECTS VARIOUS COMMON GROUND PROPOSALS ADVANCED IN THIS VOLUME

Since none of the compromise or common ground proposals made in this volume involve hostility toward religion, and all recognize the importance of both the

---

[24] Kent Greenfield & Adam Winkler, *Without Kennedy, the Future of Gay Rights Is Fragile*, N.Y. Times (June 28, 2018), https://perma.cc/6WKG-CQCE; Tim Fitzsimons and Brooke Sopelsa, *LGBTQ Advocates Celebrate Kennedy's Legacy But Fear What's Next*, NBC News (June 27, 2018), https://perma.cc/XS4P-4YR5.

[25] Order List, 585 U.S. __ (June 25, 2018), https://perma.cc/3X9Z-ADQQ.

[26] S.B. 296, Gen. Sess. (Utah 2015); Utah S.B. 297, Gen. Sess. (Utah 2015).

[27] *See* Adams, Chapter 32.

[28] *See supra* note 5.

religious freedom and civil rights claims involved, the *Masterpiece Cakeshop* decision does not, at a macro level, constrain any of the proposals. But the implications of the decision may raise some challenges over specific elements of certain proposals.

One of the most frequently proposed common ground efforts in this volume involves a procedural rather than a substantive approach. A significant majority of the chapters call for a more civil discourse, a willingness to listen openly and fully consider the competing claims.[29] They address the human costs – the dignitary, psychological, and functional damage – both to those forced to participate in activities to which they have sincere and deeply held religious objections as well as to those who face discrimination in employment, housing, or public establishments that provide goods, services, or accommodations because of their race, religion, national origin, gender identity, or sexual orientation.[30]

One chapter that digs deeply into this issue is Linda McClain's "The Rhetoric of Bigotry and Conscience in Battles over 'Religious Liberty v. LGBT Rights.'" On the one hand, she explains, calling someone a bigot has inherent aspects of incivility, yet when referring to specific positions and to rhetoric targeting minorities, such a term may be accurate. How do we distinguish between when using the word "bigotry" is a valid use of the term and when it is not? McClain concludes:

> Charges of "branding as a bigot" often stem from analogies between past and present forms of exclusion and injustice. These charges are often needless and provocative. The mere step of drawing analogies between past and present forms of discrimination to point out how, over time, new insights and understandings lead to recognition that such treatment lacks justification is not a charge of bigotry. Nor should a charge of bigotry be inferred simply from explanations about the constitutional limits of using religious and moral beliefs as a basis for (1) excluding others from a constitutional right (such as the fundamental right to marry) or (2) denying them the protection of civil rights laws. On the other hand, it is needlessly provocative to indict religious beliefs as a "pretext" or "code word" for discrimination in order to explain that there must be limits to acting on such beliefs – however sincere – in the marketplace. The better path, modeled by Justice Bosson's concurring opinion in *Elane Photography*, is to speak in terms of the requirements of civility or tolerance, or the 'price of citizenship' in a pluralistic society.[31]

---

[29] *See, e.g.,* Minter, Chapter 4; Gramick, Chapter 10; Leith Anderson, Chapter 12.

[30] *See* Leavitt, Chapter 33 ("To a person who is gay, lesbian, bi-sexual, or transgender, fairness for all includes protection from being denied a livelihood, a place to live, or basic services just because of who they are. To the religious adherent, fairness for all means the free exercise of religion, including the right to freely associate with fellow believers. That right cannot be absolute everywhere, to be sure, but there are many important spheres where it must be vigorously protected or religious freedom becomes meaningless.").

[31] *See* McClain, Chapter 17. What to make of charges of bigotry and whether refusal amounts to bigotry are addressed by numerous contributors. Ronald Krotoszynski examines theories of

Other proposals would deploy this call for more civil discourse and greater respect for opposing claims as a means of clarifying common ground or shaping compromise. Alan Brownstein observes:

> [C]ompromises can be negotiated. Daunting difficulties exist but they can be confronted and resolved. Indeed, for people who are committed to both the liberty and equality rights of the LGBT community and to religious liberty for people of all faiths, there really is no choice but to pursue negotiated compromises, even if doing so sometimes appears to be futile.[32]

Shannon Minter argues that neither side wins if the other side totally loses:

> Conservative religious communities cannot count themselves successful in protecting religious freedom if it comes at the cost of causing grievous harm to vulnerable young people and their families. And the LGBT movement cannot effectively protect LGBT youth until it acknowledges that the LGBT children in those communities need their families and their faiths.[33]

Archbishop William Lori lays out a clear exposition of the Catholic Church's commitment to freedom of religion even while affirming the Church's commitment to human dignity of all (regardless of sexual orientation) and the importance of protecting against discrimination. Although he concludes, "not all will agree on what constitutes unjust discrimination," Lori urges:

> Most, if not all faith communities have resources and tools to help navigate through cultural complexity, whatever its sources. Perhaps the experience of engaging in robust ecumenical and interreligious dialogue can teach us how to go about improving the dialogue between faith and culture. Other resources and tools include the principles for moral cooperation, rules for discernment, the natural law tradition and the respect of faith for reason. Most of all, it requires a willingness on the part of all to come together in search of common ground, rooted in objective truth.[34]

Indeed, Justice Kennedy in his majority opinion urges a similar approach: "[T]hese disputes must be resolved with tolerance, without undue disrespect to sincere

---

third-party harm, *see* Krotoszynski, Chapter 7; Steven Smith shows how painting others as bigots has clouded public dialogue and even litigation, *see* Smith, Chapter 18; Marc DeGirolami traces the rise of anti-Christian identity politics, *see* DeGirolami, Chapter 21; and Sarah Warbelow lays out the sources and impact of discrimination against LGBT individuals, *see* Warbelow, Chapter 31.

[32] *See* Brownstein, Chapter 2.

[33] *See* Minter, Chapter 4. Dennis Hollinger echoes Minter's point, arguing that frameworks within Christian ethics affirm robust protections of freedom for both religious and LGBTQ communities. *See* Hollinger, Chapter 5. Sister Jeannine Gramick discusses the establishment of similar frameworks within the Catholic tradition. *See* Gramick, Chapter 10.

[34] *See* Lori, Chapter 13.

religious beliefs, and without subjecting gay persons to indignities when they seek goods and services in an open market."[35]

It should be noted that some very strong chapters in this volume sought principally, and quite effectively, to give the most compelling argument for the rights claims they feel should prevail, rather than developing common ground or compromise.[36] In the context of the broader volume, these chapters play an essential role in posing with clarity exactly what are the rights and harms involved on the differing sides of this debate – rights and harms that must be addressed by proposals seeking common ground or compromise discussed in this book.

Perhaps the most well-known legislative compromise is a pair of laws popularly known as the Utah Compromise,[37] which reached only housing and hiring discrimination, as discussed in the chapters by former Utah Governor Mike Leavitt, an experienced statesman and policymaker; the late Elder Von Keetch of The Church of Jesus Christ of Latter-day Saints ("LDS Church"), then the outside general counsel to the LDS Church; and Utah State Senator J. Stuart Adams, who played a central role in passing the pieces of legislation at the core of the compromise.[38] The compromise added sexual orientation and gender identity to Utah's existing laws banning discrimination in housing and employment based on religion, race, sex, pregnancy, age, national origin, and disability,[39] laws with which Utah employers and housing providers were long familiar. The agreement to extend nondiscrimination protections to include not just lesbian, gay, and bisexual people, but also the transgender community,[40] was foundational to the compromise. At the same time, the compromise maintained the existing fifteen-employee threshold[41] for coverage under the employment nondiscrimination law and the small landlord exemption[42] under the housing nondiscrimination law, thereby protecting small businesses' right to hire and fire on whatever grounds they might want, including religious objections to hiring employees. That categorical set-aside means smaller employers can continue to preference family members or make decisions on any ground, even grounds barred to larger employers by civil rights protections. The compromise also exempted from coverage of the law houses of worship, religious primary and secondary schools, and religious corporations and their wholly owned subsidiaries, the classic examples of which are the LDS Church itself and its subsidiary, Brigham Young University.[43] Nothing in the *Masterpiece Cakeshop*

---

[35] Masterpiece Cakeshop, Ltd. v. Colorado Civil Rights Commission, No. 16–111, slip op. at 18 (U.S. June 4, 2018).

[36] *See, e.g.*, Melling, Chapter 19; Ryan Anderson, Chapter 27.

[37] S.B. 296, Gen. Sess. (Utah 2015); Utah S.B. 297, Gen. Sess. (Utah 2015).

[38] *See* Adams, Chapter 32; Leavitt, Chapter 33; Keetch, Chapter 14.

[39] Utah Code §§ 34A–5–106, 57–21–5.

[40] §§ 34A–5–102(1)(k), 57–21-2(16).

[41] § 34A–5–102(1)(i)(D).

[42] § 57–21–5(1).

[43] §§ 34A–5–102(1)(i)(ii), 57–21–5(2), 57–21–5(4), 57–21–5(7).

decision constrains compromises like the one Utah fashioned, as the laws involved did not include public accommodations. Much like the *Masterpiece Cakeshop* decision – which paints a vision of laws giving protections for both religious liberty and civil rights – the Utah Compromise left the complex issue of the delicate braiding of rights in the public accommodations sphere to be resolved in the future.

This volume picks up where the Utah Compromise left off, at public accommodations, and squarely grapples with whether sexual orientation and gender identity (SOGI) nondiscrimination laws should contain religious exemptions. Such a substantive compromise is offered by one of the editors of this volume, Robin Fretwell Wilson. In her chapter, "Bathrooms and Bakers: How Sharing the Public Square Is the Key to a Truce in the Culture Wars," Wilson suggests that businesses regulated as public accommodations should have to obey neutral civil rights laws without prevailing on an exemption claim. But the business owner need not personally engage in the activity that either an employee or subcontractor can provide, thereby mitigating violations of the owner's religious beliefs.

Douglas Laycock focuses on the distinction between small businesses and large corporations, writing:

> I would not grant exemptions for refusing to serve gays and lesbians in contexts not directly related to the wedding or the marriage. Exemptions should not be extended to large and impersonal businesses even in the wedding context. But for very small businesses, where the owner is likely to be personally involved in providing any services, we should exempt wedding vendors so long as another vendor is available without hardship to the same-sex couple.[44]

Laycock is importing a device – a size threshold that exists in the employment discrimination provisions of Title VII of the 1964 Civil Rights Act and in parallel state laws like Utah's – into the related body of public accommodation law.[45] Neither the federal law banning discrimination in public accommodations (Title II of the Civil Rights Act of 1964) nor any statewide public accommodations law to date, has used a size threshold, presumably (among other reasons) because the size of the business providing goods or services does not mute or otherwise not affect the impact on the customer.[46] When the business has five

---

[44] *See* Laycock, Chapter 3. Elsewhere, Laycock elaborates, indicating a "very small business" would be one with five employees or less, which only a subset of "closely-held corporations" like the one at issue in *Hobby Lobby*, would satisfy. *See* Thomas Berg, *Response from Scholars Supporting "Marriage Conscience" Religious Liberty Protection*, MIRROR OF JUSTICE (Nov. 7, 2013), https://perma.cc/3QW3-9AQE. (Note, however, that Laycock is discussing exemptions from civil rights nondiscrimination laws, whereas *Hobby Lobby* considered exemptions from an insurance requirement.) Since Laycock suggests the exemption is not available to "large, impersonal businesses," it will be necessary for those trying to implement this approach to clarify exactly where the line between small and large corporations would be drawn. *See* Laycock, Chapter 3.

[45] 42 U.S.C. § 2000e-2 (1964).

[46] Title II of the Civil Rights Act of 1964, 42 U.S.C. §2000a; *see* Appendix.

employees or fewer, and when other businesses can be found by a couple to perform the requested wedding-related service without substantial hardship, then the couple would have to seek the service elsewhere.[47]

Laycock's proposal is a bit different than Wilson's. Wilson, too, limits her proposal to businesses closely identified with the owner, where, absent an accommodation, the owner would be required to personally perform the service. But in her view, the owner must play the responsible role in ensuring that everyone is served. If the owner cannot find another employee or subcontractor to perform the service, the owner must do it personally. This structure of requiring the business, not the owner, to serve all customers attempts to mitigate the dignitary harms to the customers by seamlessly providing access. Obviously, ensuring that the provision of services would be seamlessly provided is a central challenge. And for the owners of the business, if there were no employee or subcontractor willing to provide the services, it would put them in exactly the dilemma Phillips faced in *Masterpiece Cakeshop*. Nothing in the holding of *Masterpiece Cakeshop* would restrict either Wilson's or Laycock's proposal. Neither involves hostility to religion; both acknowledge the religious freedom and civil rights claims embraced by Justice Kennedy's majority opinion. The only caution would be how broad the impact of Laycock's size requirement would be in terms of Kennedy's concern about the real-life dignitary and functional harms of exemptions too often invoked.

Laycock, however, would exempt a business small enough that the objecting owner would be in a position of personally providing the service, when other businesses would willingly serve the couple. This is because the balance of hardships – conscientious objectors forced to close businesses (because they refuse to be complicit in providing services that the state and the courts say are required regardless of religious objections) versus offended couples referred to other professionals who "get to live their own lives by their own values" – favors protecting the owner.[48] Owners in this instance would be in exactly the dilemma faced by Phillips when no other businesses are easily available to same-sex couples.

There will be advocates for the civil rights claims who would argue that in public accommodations, the small versus large distinction should not hold or that couples must always be served by the business they desire.[49] If Justice Kennedy's views were

---

[47] *See* Laycock, Chapter 3; Thomas Berg, *Response from Scholars Supporting "Marriage Conscience" Religious Liberty Protection*, MIRROR OF JUSTICE (Nov. 7, 2013), https://perma.cc/3QW3-9AQE.

[48] *See* Laycock, Chapter 3.

[49] Indeed, contributors to this volume would draw different lines of distinction. Ronald J. Krotoszynski, Jr. highlights the commercial nature of businesses, giving more discretion to religious schools and churches because they are truly private, *see* Krotoszynski, Chapter 7; Thomas C. Berg points to non-profit status, *see* Berg, Chapter 24; while Jennifer C. Pizer cautions against "altering" the marketplace with different rules for purveyors guided by faith, *see* Pizer, Chapter 29.

held by at least one of the four conservatives who signed his majority opinion,[50] either in whole or in part, or his successor, then the issues of dignitary harms and concerns about granting large number of exemptions to business owners would give heavier weight to protecting LGBTQ rights in the balance of accommodating religious freedom.[51]

Laycock's proposal does, however, include devices to mute harm to same-sex couples, such as the size limit itself and the restriction of that exemption "so long as another vendor is available without hardship to the same-sex couple," while Wilson's proposal includes devices to mute harm to purveyors like Phillips, such as explicitly authorizing the use of other employees and prearranged subcontractors.

Kent Greenawalt proposes a similar distinction to Laycock's and Wilson's, suggesting that in the context of public accommodations, exemptions from civil rights laws should depend on how directly (deserving greater protection) or indirectly an owner is involved with an activity to which they object.[52] In this view, persons being asked to be physically present at the wedding – say, by catering the event or taking photographs – deserve accommodation, while those more distant from the wedding itself (presumably like the baker or florist) would have less claim on an accommodation.

These proposals assume we can distinguish between the business and the principals running the business using a variety of factors. Certainly some religious liberty advocates, however, emphasize that businesses have the same right to religious liberty and other constitutional protections, like free speech protections, as do other "persons" protected by the Constitution, citing the Court's ruling in *Burwell v. Hobby Lobby Stores, Inc.*[53] But there is a key difference between *Hobby Lobby* and the status of the religious liberty claims in *Masterpiece Cakeshop*. In *Hobby Lobby*, the Court interpreted a crucial term in the federal Religious Freedom

---

[50] Masterpiece Cakeshop, Ltd. v. Colorado Civil Rights Commission, No. 16–111, slip op. at 12 (U.S. June 4, 2018).

> Justice Thomas's concurrence does not contain the affirmation of the rights on each side, found in the majority decision. Justice Thomas basically concludes that the outcome should be resolved in favor of Phillips and other objecting owners since "States cannot punish protected speech because some group finds it offensive, hurtful, stigmatic, unreasonable, or undignified." *Masterpiece Cakeshop*, slip op. at 12 (Thomas, J., dissenting).

[51] Douglas NeJaime and Reva Siegel lay out a helpful analysis of what might happen if dignitary harm is part of the Court's analysis. *See* NeJaime and Siegel, Chapter 6. Considerations of third-party harms, they write, should be relevant not only to whether to grant or deny religious accommodation but to shaping those accommodations as well:

> Accommodations should be designed in ways that mitigate the impact on third parties. Here, both material and dignitary harms are relevant. Citizens should be protected not only from deprivation of goods and services, but also from the stigma that refusals and denials can produce. Put differently, accommodations should be structured in ways that (1) ensure access to goods and services, and (2) shield citizens from stigmatizing encounters.

[52] *See* Greenawalt, Chapter 8.

[53] 134 S. Ct. 2751 (2014).

Restoration Act ("RFRA")[54] speaking to who counts as a "person" able to bring RFRA challenges to federal laws burdening religious practice or belief. The *Hobby Lobby* Court used statutory language to inform its holding that Congress meant "person" to encompass closely held businesses, bolstering its reading of RFRA with older free exercise cases extending constitutional protections to kosher delis and retail establishments.[55] The *Hobby Lobby* Court then found that the government failed to establish that its policy passed RFRA's "least restrictive means"[56] for sustaining federal laws burdening religion.

Crucial to the *Hobby Lobby* Court's analysis and holding was the Obama administration's exemption of churches and certain religious organizations from the Patient Protection and Affordable Care Act requirement that covered employers provide essential health benefits, which the administration had extended to requiring contraceptive coverage for employees free of charge in any health plan offered.[57] In successive regulations, the Obama administration widened an exemption from this duty given originally only to churches to also encompass religious nonprofits.[58] The accommodation required insurance companies to provide directly the mandated coverage when the nonprofits opted out.[59] The accommodation was structured in such a way that it did not cost insurance companies offering group coverage anything and succeeded in ensuring that all employees received the coverage free of charge.[60] If the government could make this exemption and work-around available to any religious nonprofit that objected to providing reproductive health care, the *Hobby Lobby* Court reasoned, then such an option should be available as well to

---

[54] 42 U.S.C. § 2000bb-1 (1993).

[55] *Burwell*, 134 S.Ct. at 2767.

[56] *Id.* at 2783–85.

[57] 'Group Health Plans and Health Insurance Issuers Relating to Coverage of Preventive Services Under the Patient Protection and Affordable Care Act' 76 FR 46621 (3 August 2011).

[58] 'Coverage of Certain Preventive Services Under the Affordable Care Act', 78 FR 8456–01, 8461, 8462, 8465 (6 February 2013).

[59] 'Coverage of Certain Preventive Services Under the Affordable Care Act', 78 FR 8456–01, 8461, 8462, 8465 (6 February 2013).

[60] Burwell v. Hobby Lobby Stores, Inc., 134 S. Ct. 2751, 2782 (2014) ("HHS has concluded that insurers that insure eligible employers opting out of the contraceptive mandate and that are required to pay for contraceptive coverage under the accommodation will not experience an increase in costs because the 'costs of providing contraceptive coverage are balanced by cost savings from lower pregnancy-related costs and from improvements in women's health.' 78 Fed.Reg. 39877. With respect to self-insured plans, the regulations establish a mechanism for the eligible employers' third-party administrators to obtain a compensating reduction in the fee paid by insurers to participate in the federally facilitated exchanges. HHS believes that this system will not have a material effect on the funding of the exchanges because the 'payments for contraceptive services will represent only a small portion of total [federally facilitated exchange] user fees.' Id., at 39882; see 26 CFR § 54.9815–2713A(b)(3).").

For self-funded plans, the administrator for the federal health plan exchange provided the objected-to coverage to women free of charge and were reimbursed dollar for dollar by a discounted fee for running the exchange. 45 CFR § 147.131.

closely held corporations with similar religious objections.[61] This was the least restrictive means of furthering what the Court seemed to have assumed was a compelling interest ensuring its scheme of comprehensive health coverage for women as well as men.[62] In short, the decision still ensured that all women would be provided contraceptive coverage and no harm would follow when religious entities (business or non-profit) choose the accommodation.[63] In contrast, in *Masterpiece Cakeshop*, an exemption based on religious objections, made by a business bound by public accommodation law, would create not only dignitary harm but also the denial of important services. Justice Kennedy's opinion suggests that such harms might run afoul of the protections to which the LGBTQ community is entitled.[64]

Nor have legislators squarely grappled with writing nondiscrimination laws that provide accommodations for wedding vendors. The underlying nondiscrimination law in Colorado and similar laws in other states that bar SOGI discrimination in public accommodation were written before same-sex marriage was recognized in the jurisdiction, and in many instances anywhere in the world.[65]

An intriguing part of this volume is devoted to competing claims in the context of religious institutions. Several discuss claims of discrimination in the context of what Michael Helfand calls "implied consent."[66] This approach is not a clear example of compromise, since it asks what happens when a business or religious institution is allowed to make distinctions that the law otherwise would treat as discrimination, either because the civil rights law leaves them to the side of its literal scope or expressly exempts the religious institution in certain instances (for example, the Title VII's religious exemption) or because the institution prevails in a free exercise claim for an exemption.

Advocates on both sides might well differ on whether an accommodation should have been granted but be far more likely to agree that devices to mute harm, such as providing information beforehand, should be included as an element of common ground. Moreover, they do seek to advance legal and societal civility around these issues by minimizing the potential harm to those who might be affected by a religiously motivated decision. Since *Masterpiece Cakeshop* focuses on whether an exemption is required for business owners (and does not evaluate the permissibility of accommodations for religious institutions that have been granted them), it is not broadly relevant here. However, these proposals echo the concerns expressed in

---

[61]   *Burwell*, 134 S.Ct. at 2763.

[62]   *Id.* at 2780.

[63]   It should be remembered that employees of houses of worship were not guaranteed contraceptive coverage. Press Release, *Reform Movement Decries Supreme Court Ruling in Hobby Lobby, Conestoga Wood*, RELIGIOUS ACTION CENTER OF REFORMED JUDAISM (June 30, 2014), https://perma.cc/F3AA-CWCE (noting that houses of worship were "totally exempt under the ACA").

[64]   *Masterpiece Cakeshop, Ltd.*, No. 16-111, slip op. at 10.

[65]   Wilson, Chapter 30; Appendix.

[66]   *See* Helfand, Chapter 11.

the opinions by Justices Kennedy, Kagan, and Ginsburg, that potential harms to members of the protected groups should be minimized.

Helfand asserts a robust notion of the autonomy of religious institutions to make their own decisions as to their internal affairs, including whom they hire. Helfand's theory of implied consent requires that an employer communicate its religious character to a prospective employee so the employee knows who and what the religious entity is and stands for when seeking a job – he or she accepts the position with an implied agreement to adhere to the employer's restrictions. In this scheme the further one moves away from an inherently religious institution as the employer toward a commercial business operated by a religious owner, the weaker the implied consent is and the greater the protections accorded to employees. The implied consent is weakest when one moves beyond the context of employees to customers of public establishments (as in *Masterpiece Cakeshop*): "[I]t seems unlikely that an implied consent approach would conceptualize entering a store as a form of joining the business in a pursuit of collective religious objectives."[67]

Like Helfand, B. Jessie Hill drills down on the potential for harm when civil rights laws stop at the front gates of religious universities. She begins with the difficult question of how to assess whether an institution is religious enough to justify receiving an exemption from various federal requirements.[68] Some might use the standards she cites – "formal religious affiliation," "pervasiveness of the religious mission," "willingness to educate and employ those who do not share its mission," "the visibility of the school's religious commitment," and its "nonprofit status"[69] – as guideposts for whether religious institutions other than just religious universities deserve special accommodations. For Hill, in assessing exemption requests, the balance one should strike is between institutional autonomy and third-party harm that arises from students not being aware of the religious nature of a university. Hill offers a solution similar to the implied consent framework Helfand proposes. She suggests that universities could be required – as they are for Title IX exemptions – to "identify the conflict" between their religious character and Title VII, RFRA, or the ministerial exception.[70] With explicit disclosure, administrators can show explicit consent. This offers the benefit to students (or employees) of forewarning if a school received an exemption allowing it to impose religious restrictions on their students. The school receives security, too, that its religious restrictions will be honored.

Shannon Minter describes another way that some advocates have sought to make the exemption status more explicit, an approach "supported by the Human Rights Campaign, GLSEN and several other groups."[71] This approach asks "the

---

[67] *Id.*
[68] *See* Hill, Chapter 26.
[69] *Id.*
[70] *Id.*
[71] *See* Minter, Chapter 4.

Department of Education to list schools claiming a religious exemption [from Title IX] in a prominent place on its website, so that at least students can know whether a particular school would protect them or not."[72] Some religious freedom advocates have labeled such lists a tool for shaming religious institutions, although it is difficult to argue against transparency and factual information.[73] Such information-forcing rules have long been used to mitigate third-party harm.[74] Civil rights advocates would argue notice of discrimination is not sufficient; it should be barred.

Holly Hollman also addresses the impact of nondiscrimination laws on religious entities. She asserts that in such situations, an authentic understanding of America's long traditions of religious liberty and church–state separation can make compromise and accommodation more likely. In evaluating competing claims for religious exemptions and civil rights law regarding religious entities, she argues that the impact of government funding of religious entities should and does have a significant impact in evaluating the balance between competing claims.[75] Similarly, other religious entities like religious colleges and other government-funded or government-contracted agencies, such as adoption programs or social service entities, are addressed in chapters by Shirley Hoogstra and colleagues at the Council for Christian Colleges and Universities, by Leith Anderson of the National Association of Evangelicals, by Jennifer Pizer of Lambda Legal, and by Thomas Berg of University of St. Thomas.[76]

As to religious agencies providing government-funded services, President Obama signed an executive order that maintains protections for the ability of social service providers to retain their religious character while receiving government aid (so long as religious activities like worship, education and proselytization are separated by time or location from programs funded by direct government aid). At the same time, the order embraced common-ground recommendations to provide augmented religious liberty protections for social service beneficiaries. In domestic direct aid programs, when such beneficiaries object to the religious provider, the providers must make

---

[72] *Id.*

[73] Anugrah Kumar, *Education Dept. Releases "Shame List" of Faith-Based Colleges Seeking Title IX Exemption from Transgender Rules*, THE CHRISTIAN POST (Apr. 30, 2016), https://perma.cc/HQR8-BAHH.

[74] *See* Robin Fretwell Wilson, *Unpacking the Relationship Between Conscience and Access*, in LAW, RELIGION, AND HEALTH IN THE UNITED STATES (Holly Fernandez Lynch, I. Glenn Cohen, Elizabeth Sepper, eds. Cambridge University Press 2017).

[75] *See* Hollman, Chapter 23.

[76] *See* Hoogstra et al., Chapter 25; Leith Anderson, Chapter 12; Pizer, Chapter 29; Berg, Chapter 24. As to religious agencies providing government funded services, President Obama passed an executive order that, while protecting the right of social service providers to maintain their religious character (so long as religious worship, education, and proselytization were separated by time and place from the government funded programs), required that when any recipient objected to being served by a religious provider, the provider had to find a secular alternative. (This approach, placing responsibility on the provider, is akin to what Prof. Wilson is suggesting the *Masterpiece Cakeshop* situation.) That latter requirement was overturned by a subsequent executive order by President Trump. *See* Melissa Rogers, *President Trump Just Unveiled a New White House "Faith" Office. It Actually Weakens Religious Freedom*, WASH. POST (May 14, 2018).

reasonable efforts to identify an alternative provider that is acceptable to the beneficiary and of comparable value and accessibility, whether that was a secular provider or
another religious provider that was not objectionable to the beneficiary. (This
approach, placing responsibility on the provider, is akin to what Wilson is suggesting
in the *Masterpiece Cakeshop* situation.)   The order also required religious providers
to give such beneficiaries written notice of this "alternative provider" requirement and
other protections for their religious liberty.   Unfortunately, President Trump struck
these religious freedom protections in an executive order he signed in May 2018. [77]

In the view of civil rights advocates in this volume, and elsewhere,[78] tax dollars
should never be used to discriminate, which requires that nondiscrimination rules
follow the expenditure of tax dollars. In many areas of civil rights laws, any government funding of any part of an institution triggers institution-wide coverage by civil
rights laws.[79] Some religious freedom advocates have suggested that compromise
can be struck in which the nondiscrimination principle applies only to funded
programs and not the entire institution.[80] We have seen an example of this in one
arena, adoption and foster care, in which a number of states have specified that the
receipt of government funds dictates only what happens in the supported program,
not across all of the organization's operations. For instance, Maryland provided in its
same-sex marriage law that adoption agencies may continue to make the kinds of
placements they made before Maryland recognized same-sex marriage so long as
they do not accept government funds in that specific program.[81] Last year, Alabama
enacted a law to protect religious adoption agencies from adverse action by the state
if they make placement decisions based on religious criteria, but only in privately
funded programs.[82]

Where does this overview of the many constructive proposals in this book leave us
after the *Masterpiece Cakeshop* decision in terms of contemporary and future
political realities? The polls show growing support in America for protecting the
rights of people on the grounds of sexual orientation and gender identity. Among the

---

[77] *See* Melissa Rogers, *President Trump Just Unveiled a New White House "Faith" Office. It
Actually Weakens Religious Freedom*, Wash. Post (May 14, 2018), https://www.washingtonpost
.com/news/acts-of-faith/wp/2018/05/14/president-trump-just-unveiled-a-new-white-house-faith-
office-it-actually-weakens-religious-freedom/?noredirect=on&utm_term=.c5886a689c20.

[78] *See* Eskridge, Chapter 22; Hollman, Chapter 23; Berg, Chapter 24. *See also* Saperstein, *supra*
note 15.

[79] *See* Civil Rights Restoration Act of 1987, codified at 20 U.S.C. § 1687, 29 U.S.C. § 794, 42
U.S.C. § 2000d–4a, and 42 U.S.C. § 6101 et seq. (requiring recipients of government funding to
comply with civil rights laws in all programs, rather than only those to which the funding is
applied, overturning Grove City College v. Bell, 465 U.S. 555 (1984), which had held that a
student receipt of federal financial aid triggered Title IX sex discrimination requirements only
for the financial aid office and not all university programs).

[80] While this approach might embody the principle that tax dollars cannot be used to discriminate, this would be a reversal of a long-standing civil rights movement goal – to wipe out all
discrimination beginning with any entities receiving government funding.

[81] 2012 Maryland Session Laws ch. 2. *See also* Minn. Stat. § 517.201. Rhode Island gave an
absolute exemption. R.I. Gen. Laws § 15–3–6.1.

[82] Alabama Act 2017–213.

younger generation, such protections are favored by significant majorities. According to the Public Religion Research Institute, "[Y]oung people are solidly opposed [to allowing businesses that provide wedding services to refuse services on religious grounds to same-sex couples,] while older Americans are divided. Nearly two-thirds (64%) of young people (age 18–29) say wedding-based businesses should not be allowed to refuse services to same-sex couples on religious grounds."[83] A 2018 survey asking a similar question found that 77% of millennial women and 59% of millennial men agreed businesses should not be able to discriminate against customers based on their beliefs.[84] For those concerned about protecting religious liberty, or remaining relevant and vibrant as faith communities, now is the time, while sizable differences in opinion still exist, to come together, find common ground, and secure peaceful coexistence.

On the question of the urgency to act, a lesson from the past is germane. For twenty years, the proposed federal Employment Non-Discrimination Act barring discrimination on the grounds of sexual orientation and gender identity contained a broad exemption for religious institutions.[85] In 2007, the U.S. Conference of Catholic Bishops, the General Conference of Seventh Day Adventists, and the Union of Orthodox Jewish Congregations of America signed a public letter to Congress indicating that, while neutral on the bill, the exemption protected their interests.[86] When, finally, the bill passed the Senate in 2013 with even a slightly broader religious exemption, a reissue of that letter – or, better yet, a little encouragement for passage on the House side by those entities – might well have helped the bill become law. Yet, they decided not to reissue the letter.[87]

After trying for twenty years to enact a law including this compromise, some key supporters in the LGBTQ rights community, on the heels of *Hobby Lobby*, withdrew their support for the broad exemption and refocused on a more comprehensive piece of legislation, the Equality Act.[88] What was in reach for the religious

---

[83] Daniel Cox & Robert P. Jones, *Most Americans Oppose Restricting Rights for LGBT People*, Pub. Religion Res. Inst., (Sept. 14, 2017), http://perma.cc/GC7X-DZF9.

[84] Brenden Pingle, *Survey: Millennials Still Value Religious Freedom*, Wash. Examiner (July 3, 2018), https://perma.cc/3S38-KBWS.

[85] *See* Employment Non-Discrimination Act of 2013, S. 815, 113th Cong. § 4 (as passed by Senate, Nov. 7, 2013), available at https://perma.cc/57BE-43P4. (passing the Senate by a vote of 64–32).

[86] *See* Joint letter to Hon. George Miller (chairman) and Howard "Buck" McKeon (ranking member), House Committee on Education and Labor, U.S. House of Representatives, Oct. 18, 2007.

[87] *See* USCCB *Chairmen Explain Opposition to ENDA*, United States Conference of Catholic Bishops (Nov. 4, 2013), https://perma.cc/FQM8-3JV2; Lanae Erickson Hatalsky, *Questions and Answers about the Employment Non-Discrimination Act*, Third Way (June 28, 2013), https://perma.cc/2DCT-JW26.

[88] Press Release, Am. Civil Liberties Union, Gay & Lesbian Advocates & Defenders, Lambda Legal, Nat'l Ctr. for Lesbian Rights & Transgender Law Ctr., Joint Statement on Withdrawal of Support for ENDA and Call for Equal Workplace Protections for LGBT People (July 8, 2014), https://perma.cc/FN4X-HQMN; Equality Act, H.R. 2282, https://www.congress.gov/bill/115th-congress/house-bill/2282.

communities for two decades may now end with broader legislation, a narrower exemption, or, as is currently the case with the bill, no exemption at all.

Regardless of what the courts do, presumably, someday, control of Congress will change hands, with progressives, who are more often supportive of LGBTQ rights, in power. For those who prioritize protecting religious freedom, what may be achievable today may not be in the future.

For those who prioritize civil rights, the likely configuration of the Supreme Court in the post-Kennedy era does not bode well for tilting the balance between civil rights and religious liberty claims towards civil rights. Further, a robust reading of the compelling interest of the government in protecting civil rights, necessary to securing such rights through the courts, may be less frequently affirmed by the federal courts.

Many Americans fall between these two polls. Many share my belief that, as a constitutional matter, the protection of civil rights is a compelling governmental interest that can justify restricting religious exemptions. Many also genuinely believe, as I do, that religious freedom and civil rights are both representative of America's vision of fundamental rights. For Americans who see the need for common ground as self-evident, now is the time to seek a constructive compromise.

Most of the proposals in this book involve some degree of compromise on each side. The fundamental foundation of our constitutionally protected rights is that they are not subject to majoritarian decisions or political trade-offs. In contrast, in those situations where rights are not directly protected, and the Constitution does not preclude legislative balancing, political compromise means each side will need to accept bearing some costs they do not want to incur, at least while society reaches a clearer consensus on how to balance religious freedom and civil rights interests. This will include rights-related interests to which they feel entitled but which the Court does not directly or sufficiently protect.

No matter how passionately some Americans may wish to see the Supreme Court resolve these issues on their side, if we accept that the culture wars tear at the strained threads of American comity and civility that bind us together – and that litigation may in the short run exacerbate those strains – Justice Kennedy's decision in *Masterpiece Cakeshop* gives us the opportunity to find societal and legislative paths to shore up common ground where it exists – and the space and conditions to work for compromise where common ground may not yet exist. The time to see if this is possible is before us.

ACKNOWLEDGMENTS

I want to express my appreciation to Noah Fitzgerel and Nathan Bennett of the Religious Action Center of Reform Judaism for their invaluable assistance. Professors Alan Brownstein and Robin Fretwell Wilson also provided significant assistance.

Appendix of Laws

Robin Fretwell Wilson

State	State Review of Neutral Laws (Col. 1)	LGBT Employment & Housing Protections (Col. 2)	Scope of Public Accommodation Laws (Col. 3)	SOGI Public Accommodation Laws (Col. 4)	Specific (Surgical) Protections for Marriage (Col. 5)	Adoption Protections Passed Together with Other Legislation (Col. 6)	Stand-Alone Adoption Protections (Col. 7)
Alabama	RFRA Only: ALA. CONST. art. I, § 3.01 (constitutional amendment).						ALA. CODE § 26–10D-1 et seq. (2017).
Alaska	Heightened Scrutiny Only: Larson v. Cooper, 90 P.3d 125, 131–32, n.31 (Alaska 2004); Swanner v. Anchorage Equal Rights Comm'n, 868 P.2d 274 (Alaska 1994).		BROAD: ALASKA STAT. 18.80.300.				
Arizona	RFRA Only: ARIZ. REV. STAT. ANN. § 41-1493.01, et seq. (2016).		BROAD: ARIZ. REV. STAT. ANN. §§ 41-1441, 41-1461, 41-1462, 41-1491.				

(continued)

Arkansas	RFRA & Heightened Scrutiny: ARK. CODE ANN. § 16-123-401, et seq. (2015); Gipson v. Brown, 749 S.W.2d 297 (Ark. 1988).	INTERMEDIATE: ARK. CODE ANN. §§ 11-4-607, 16-123-102.			
California	No RFRA or Heightened Scrutiny	CAL. GOV'T CODE § 11135, 12920, 12940, 12949 (West 2016); see also Assemb. 2601, 1991–1992 Cal. Leg. Reg. Sess. (Feb. 11, 1992); Assemb. 196, 2003–2004 Leg., Reg. Sess. (Cal. 2003) (enacted 2003, became effective January 1, 2004).	BROAD: CAL. GOVT. CODE § 12926; CAL. CIVIL CODE § 51.	CAL. CIVIL CODE § 51(b) (West 2016).	Passed after judicial decisions required same-sex marriage, In re Marriage Cases, 183 P.3d 384 (Cal. 2008); Hollingsworth v. Perry, 133 S. Ct. 2652 (2013); CAL. FAM. CODE § 400(a) (West 2013).
Colorado	No RFRA or Heightened Scrutiny	COLO. REV. STAT. §§ 24-34-402, 24-34-501 (2014). See also Colorado	BROAD: COLO. REV. STAT. §§ 24-34-401,	COLO. REV. STAT. § 24-34-601 (2014).	

(continued)

State	State Review of Neutral Laws (Col. 1)	LGBT Employment & Housing Protections (Col. 2)	Scope of Public Accommodation Laws (Col. 3)	SOGI Public Accommodation Laws (Col. 4)	Specific (Surgical) Protections for Marriage (Col. 5)	Adoption Protections Passed Together with Other Legislation (Col. 6)	Stand-Alone Adoption Protections (Col. 7)
		Anti-Discrimination Act, S. 08-200, 2008 Leg., (Colo. 2008).	24-34-402, 24-34-601.				
Connecticut	RFRA Only: CONN. GEN. STAT. § 52-57lb (West 2013).	CONN. GEN. STAT. §§ 46a-60, 46a-46c (West 2009). *See also* An Act Concerning Discrimination on the Basis of Sexual Orientation, Pub. Acts No. 91-58 (Reg. Sess.) (codified as amended at CONN. GEN. STAT.	BROAD: CONN. GEN. STAT. §§ 46a-51, 46a-63, 46a-64, 46a-81p.	CONN. GEN. STAT. § 46a-63 (1) (2016).	Passed just after judicial decision requiring same-sex marriage, Kerrigan v. Comm'r of Pub. Health, 289 Conn. 135, 140-41 (2008): 2009 Conn. Legis. Serv. § 19 (West); Conn. Gen. Stat. §	CONN. GEN. STAT. § 46b-35b (2009).	

(continued)

		§ 46a-64c (West 2009)); An Act Concerning Discrimination, H.R. 6599, 2011 Leg, Reg. Sess. (Conn. 2011).			§ 46a-60 (West 2009); Conn. Gen. Stat. § 46b-35b, 46b-150d, 52–57b1 (2013); Conn. Gen. Stat. §§ 46a-63(1), 46a-64c (2016).
Delaware	No RFRA or Heightened Scrutiny	Del. Code Ann. tit. 19, § 711 (2014). See also An Act to Amend Titles 6, 9, 18, 19, 25, and 29 of the Delaware Code Relating to Discrimination in Employment, Public Works Contracting, Housing, Equal Accommodations and the Insurance Business, ch. 90, sec. 4, 77 Del. Laws 264 (2009) (codified as Del. Code Ann.	Broad: Del. Code Ann. tit. 19 § 710; Del. Code Ann. tit. 6 §§ 4502, 4504	Del. Code Ann. tit. 6, § 4502(14) (2014).	Del. Code Ann. tit. 13 § 106 (West 2013);

(continued)

State	State Review of Neutral Laws (Col. 1)	LGBT Employment & Housing Protections (Col. 2)	Scope of Public Accommodation Laws (Col. 3)	SOGI Public Accommodation Laws (Col. 4)	Specific (Surgical) Protections for Marriage (Col. 5)	Adoption Protections Passed Together with Other Legislation (Col. 6)	Stand-Alone Adoption Protections (Col. 7)
		Tit. 6, §§ 4603, 4604 (West 2014)); Gender Identity Nondiscrimination Act, S. 97, 147th Gen. Assemb. (Del. 2013).					
District of Columbia	No RFRA or Heightened Scrutiny	D.C. Code § 2–1402.11, (LexisNexis 2012); D.C. Code § 2–1402.21 (2015). *See also* Human Rights Act of 1977, D.C. Law 2–38, title II, 24 D.C. Reg. 6038 (Dec. 13, 1977) (codified at D.C. Code § 2–1402.21 (LexisNexis	INTERMEDIATE: D.C. Code § 2–1401.03, 2–1402.02.	D.C. Code § 2–1402.02(24) (2015).	D.C. Code § 2–1402.21 § 46–406(e) (2013).		

(continued)

State					
		2012)); Human Rights Clarifications Amendment Act of 2005, Council Bill 16–389 (D.C. 2005).			
Florida	RFRA Only: FLA. STAT. § 761.01, et seq. (2016).		NARROW: FLA. STAT. §§ 760.02, 760.10.		
Georgia	No RFRA or Heightened Scrutiny				
Hawaii	Heightened Scrutiny Only: Dedman v. Board, 740 P.2d 28 (Haw. 1987).	HAW. REV. STAT. §§ 378–2, 515–3 (2015). Hawaii did enact a law in 2011 to clarify existing law with regard to sex discrimination on the basis of gender identity in employment. See A Bill for an Act Relating to Civil Rights, Act 76,	Intermediate: HAW. REV. STAT. §§ 378–1, 378–3, 489–2.	HAW. REV. STAT. § 489–2 (2015).	S. 1, 27th Leg, 2nd Special Sess. 2, 6 (Haw. 2013).

(continued)

State	State Review of Neutral Laws (Col. 1)	LGBT Employment & Housing Protections (Col. 2)	Scope of Public Accommodation Laws (Col. 3)	SOGI Public Accommodation Laws (Col. 4)	Specific (Surgical) Protections for Marriage (Col. 5)	Adoption Protections Passed Together with Other Legislation (Col. 6)	Stand-Alone Adoption Protections (Col. 7)
		sec. 3, 2006 Haw. Sess. Laws 214, 215 (codified as Haw. Rev. Stat. § 489–3 (2015)); H.R. 546, 26th Leg. (Haw. 2011).					
Idaho	RFRA Only: Idaho Code § 73–402, et seq. (2016).		Broad: Idaho Stat. §§ 67–5902, 67–5910.				
Illinois	RFRA Only: 775 Ill. Comp. Stat. 35/1, et seq. (2010).	775 Ill. Comp. Stat. 5/3–101 (2010). See also An Act Concerning Human Rights, Pub. Act No. 93–1078, art. 1, 2004 Ill. Laws 4837, 4838 (codified as 775 Ill. Comp. Stat. 5/1oz(A) (2010)).	Intermediate: 775 Ill. Comp. Stat. §§ 5/1oz, 5/2–101, 5/5–101, 5/5–102.1.	Ill. Comp. Stat. 5/5–101(A) (2010).	S. 10 § 209(a-10), 98th Gen. Assemb., Reg. Sess. (Ill. 2013); 775 Ill. Comp. Stat. 5/3–101, 5/5–102.1 (2010).		

		BROAD:
Indiana	RFRA & Heightened Scrutiny: IND. CODE § 34-13-9-1, et seq. (2016); City Chapel Evangelical Free Inc. v. City of South Bend, 744 N.E.2d 443, 445-51 (Ind. 2001); Church of Christ v. Metropolitan Board of Zoning Appeals, 371 N.E.2d 1331 (Ind. Ct. App. 1978).	IND. CODE § 22-9-1-3.
Iowa	No RFRA or Heightened Scrutiny	IOWA CODE §§ 216.2, 216.8 (2016). *See also* An Act Relating to the Iowa Civil Rights Act and Discrimination Based Upon a Person's Sexual Orientation or Gender Identity, S. 427, 82d Gen. Assemb., Reg. Sess. § 1 (Iowa 2007).	**BROAD:** IOWA CODE §§ 216.2, 216.6, 216.7.	IOWA CODE § 216.2(13) (2016).

(continued)

State	State Review of Neutral Laws (Col. 1)	LGBT Employment & Housing Protections (Col. 2)	Scope of Public Accommodation Laws (Col. 3)	SOGI Public Accommodation Laws (Col. 4)	Specific (Surgical) Protections for Marriage (Col. 5)	Adoption Protections Passed Together with Other Legislation (Col. 6)	Stand-Alone Adoption Protections (Col. 7)
Kansas	RFRA & Heightened Scrutiny: KAN. STAT. ANN. § 60–5301, et seq. (2015); Lower v. Bd. of Dirs. of the Haskell Cnty. Cemetery Dist., 56 P.3d 235, 244–46 (Kan. 2002); State v. Evans, 796 P.2d 178 (Kan. Ct. App. 1990).		INTERMEDIATE: KAN. STAT. ANN. § 44–1002.				
Kentucky	RFRA Only: KY. REV. STAT. ANN. § 446.350 (West 2015); Gingerich v. Commonwealth, 382 S.W.3d 835, 844 (Ky. 2012).		BROAD: KY. REV. STAT. §§ 344.030, 344.090, 344.130.				

(continued)

State						
Louisiana	RFRA & Heightened Scrutiny: LA. REV. STAT. ANN. § 13:5231, et seq. (2015); State v. Victor, 15–339 (La. App. 5 Cir. 5/26/16), 195 So. 3d 128.		BROAD: LA. REV. STAT. § 51:2232.			
Maine	Heightened Scrutiny Only: Foltin v. Roman Catholic Bishop, 871 A.2d 1208, 1227–30 (Me. 2005); Rupert v. Portland, 605 A.2d 63 (Me. 1992).	ME. REV. STAT. tit. 5, § 4582 (2015); 2005 Bill Text ME S.B. 413, PL1993, c. 327 (effective June 29, 2005). See also P.L. 2005, c. 7, § 1 (Me. 2005).	INTERMEDIATE: ME. REV. STAT. tit. 5 § 4553.	ME. REV. STAT. tit. 5, § 4553(8) (2015).	ME. REV. STAT. TIT. 19-A, § 655 (2013).	
Maryland	No RFRA or Heightened Scrutiny: Montrose Christian Sch. Corp. v. Walsh, 770 A.2d 111, 123 (Md. 2001).	MD. CODE ANN., State Gov't §§ 20–606, 20–705 (West 2015). See also H.R. 51, ch. 120, sec. 3 2009 Md. Laws 540, 554 (codified at MD.	INTERMEDIATE: MD. CODE ANN., State Gov't §§ 20–301, 20–303, 20–601, 20–605.	MD. CODE ANN., STATE GOV'T § 20–301 (West 2015).	MD. CODE ANN., FAM. LAW §§ 2–201, 2–202 (West 2013) (lacking amendments present in 2012 Md. Laws § 3);	MD. CODE FAM. LAW § 2–202 (2012).

(continued)

State	State Review of Neutral Laws (Col. 1)	LGBT Employment & Housing Protections (Col. 2)	Scope of Public Accommodation Laws (Col. 3)	SOGI Public Accommodation Laws (Col. 4)	Specific (Surgical) Protections for Marriage (Col. 5)	Adoption Protections Passed Together with Other Legislation (Col. 6)	Stand-Alone Adoption Protections (Col. 7)
		CODE ANN., State Gov't § 20–304 (West 2015)); Fairness for All Marylanders Act of 2014, 2014 Md. Legis. Serv. ch. 474 (West) (codified at MD. CODE ANN., State Gov't § 20–101(e)).			2012 Md. Laws §§ 2–3; MD. CODE ANN., INS. § 8–402 (2013) (defining "fraternal organization").		
Massachusetts	Heightened Scrutiny Only: Rasheed v. Comm'r of Corr, 845 N.E.2d 296, 302–03, 308 (Mass. 2006); Attorney General v. Desilets, 636	MASS. GEN. LAWS, chap. 151B§ 4 (2016). See also An Act Making It Unlawful to Discriminate on the Basis of Sexual Orientation,	BROAD: MASS. GEN. LAWS, ch. 151B §§ 1, 4	MASS. GEN. LAWS, ch. 151B, § 4(18) (2016).			

(continued)

	N.E.2d 233 (Mass. 1994).	1989 Mass. Acts 516; An Act Relative to Transgender Anti-Discrimination, S.735, 189th Gen. Ct. (Mass. 2016).			
Michigan	Heightened Scrutiny Only: McCready v. Hoffius, 586 N.W.2d 723, 729 (Mich. 1998), vacated on other grounds, 593 N.W. 2d 545 (Mich. 1999); Porth v Roman Catholic Diocese, 532 N.W.2d 195 (Mich. Ct. App. 1995).	BROAD: MICH. COMP. STAT. §§ 37.2201, 37.2301.			MICH. COMP. LAWS §§ 400.5a, 710.23g, 722.124e (2015).
Minnesota	Heightened Scrutiny Only: Hill-Murray Federation of Teachers v. Hill-Murray High School, 487 N.W.2d	MINN. STAT. ANN. §§ 363.08 subd. 2, 363.09 (2015). See also H.R. 585, 2015 Sess., 89th Leg. (Minn. 2015).	BROAD: MINN. STAT. ANN. §§ 363A.03, 363A.20, 363A.23, 363A.26.	MINN. STAT. ANN. § 363A.03 (34) (2015).	MINN. STAT. ANN. §§ 363A.26, 517.09, 517.201 (West 2013).	MINN. STAT. ANN. § 517.201 (West 2013).

(continued)

State	State Review of Neutral Laws (Col. 1)	LGBT Employment & Housing Protections (Col. 2)	Scope of Public Accommodation Laws (Col. 3)	SOGI Public Accommodation Laws (Col. 4)	Specific (Surgical) Protections for Marriage (Col. 5)	Adoption Protections Passed Together with Other Legislation (Col. 6)	Stand-Alone Adoption Protections (Col. 7)
	857 (Minn. 1992); State v. Hershberger, 462 N.W.2d 393, 396–99 (Minn. 1990).						
Mississippi	RFRA & Heightened Scrutiny: MISS. CODE. ANN. § 11-61-1 (West 2015); In re Brown, 478 So. 2d 1033 (Miss. 1985).						
Missouri	RFRA Only: MO. REV. STAT. § 1.302, et seq. (2015).		BROAD: MO. REV. STAT. 213.010.1, 213.065.1				
Montana	Heightened Scrutiny Only:		BROAD: MONT. CODE ANN.				

512

State				
	Davis v. The Church of Jesus Christ of Latter-day Saints, 852 P.2d 640 (Mont. 1993); St. John's Lutheran Church v. State Comp. Ins. Fund, 830 P.2d 1271, 1276–77 (Mont. 1992).	§§ 49-2-101, 49-1-102.		
Nebraska	No RFRA or Heightened Scrutiny: In re Interest of Anaya, 758 N.W.2d 10, 19 (Neb. 2008).		BROAD: NEB. REV. STAT. §§ 48-1102, 48-1103, 48-1108; NEB. REV. STAT. §§ 20-133; 20-137.	
Nevada	No RFRA or Heightened Scrutiny	NEV. REV. STAT. § 118.100, 613.340 (2015). See also Assemb. 311, 1999 Sess., 70th Leg. (Nev. 1999); Assemb. 211, 2011 Sess., 76th Leg. (Nev. 2011).	NARROW: NEV. REV. STAT. §§ 613.310, 613.320, 613.350, 651.050.	NEV. REV. STAT. § 651.050(3) (2015).

(continued)

State	State Review of Neutral Laws (Col. 1)	LGBT Employment & Housing Protections (Col. 2)	Scope of Public Accommodation Laws (Col. 3)	SOGI Public Accommodation Laws (Col. 4)	Specific (Surgical) Protections for Marriage (Col. 5)	Adoption Protections Passed Together with Other Legislation (Col. 6)	Stand-Alone Adoption Protections (Col. 7)
New Hampshire	No RFRA or Heightened Scrutiny: Appeal of Trotzer, 719 A.2d 584, 589 (N.H. 1998).	N.H. Rev. Stat. § 354-A:6 (2018). *See also* An Act Amending the Law Against Discrimination to Prohibit Discrimination on Account of a Person's Sexual Orientation, ch. 108, 1997 N.H. Laws 88, 92 (codified as N.H. Rev. Stat. § 354-A:10 (2018)) ; *See also* An act prohibiting discrimination based on gender identity, H.B. 1319 (N.H. 2018).	Intermediate: N.H. Rev. Stat. §§ 354-A:2, 354-A:18.	N.H. Rev. Stat. § 354-A:16-17 (XIV) (2018); *See also* An act prohibiting discrimination based on gender identity, H.B. 1319 (N.H. 2018).	N.H. Rev. Stat. § 457:37 (III) (2013).		

(continued)

New Jersey	No RFRA or Heightened Scrutiny	N.J. Stat. §§ 10:5–9.1 (2015).	INTERMEDIATE: N.J. STAT. §§ 10:5–5, 10:5–12.	N.J. STAT. § 10:5–5(l) (2015).	
New Mexico	RFRA Only: N.M. STAT. ANN. § 28–22–1, et seq. (2015).	N.M. STAT. ANN. § 28–1–7 (2015). *See also* An Act Relating to Human Rights, S. 28, 46th Leg., 1st Sess. (N.M. 2003).	BROAD: N.M. STAT. ANN. §§ 28-1-2, 28-1-9.	N.M. STAT. ANN. § 28–1–2(H) (2015).	N.M. STAT. ANN. §§ 28–1–2 (H), 28–1–7 (2015).
New York	Heightened Scrutiny Only: Catholic Charities v. Serio, 859 N.E.2d 459, 465–68 (N.Y. 2006).	Only sexual orientation protection: N.Y. EXEC. LAW §§ 290, 291, 296(1)–(1-a) (McKinney 2016). *See also* Secs. 2, 7, §§ 291, 296(2) 2002 N.Y. Laws at 46, 48 (codified as amended at N.Y. EXEC. LAW §§ 291, 296(2) (McKinney 2016)). Courts have interpreted provisions of the Human Rights Laws to cover transgender	NARROW: N.Y. EXEC. LAW, art. 15 §292; N.Y. EDUC. LAW § 313.	Only sexual orientation protection: N.Y. EXEC. LAW § 292 & 296 (McKinney 2016). Courts have interpreted provisions of the Human Rights Laws to cover transgender persons.	N.Y. DOM. REL. LAW §§ 10-b(1), 10-b(2) (McKinney 2013).

(continued)

State	State Review of Neutral Laws (Col. 1)	LGBT Employment & Housing Protections (Col. 2)	Scope of Public Accommodation Laws (Col. 3)	SOGI Public Accommodation Laws (Col. 4)	Specific (Surgical) Protections for Marriage (Col. 5)	Adoption Protections Passed Together with Other Legislation (Col. 6)	Stand-Alone Adoption Protections (Col. 7)
		people. *See also* Sexual Orientation Non-Discrimination Act of 2002, ch. 2, § 5, 2002 N.Y. Sess. Laws 48–56 (McKinney 2016).					
North Carolina	Heightened Scrutiny Only: Matter of Browning, 476 S.E.2d 465 (N.C. Ct. App. 1996).						
North Dakota	No RFRA or Heightened Scrutiny		BROAD: N.D. CENT. CODE § 14–02.4–02, § 14–02.4–08				N.D. CENT. CODE § 50–12–03 (2009).

(continued)

State						
Ohio	Heightened Scrutiny Only; Humphrey v. Lane, 728 N.E.2d 1039 (Ohio 2000).		Narrow: Ohio Code §§ 4112.01, 4112.02.			
Oklahoma	RFRA Only: Okla. Stat. tit., 51 § 251, et seq. (2015).		Broad: Okla. Stat. Ann. tit. xxv §§ 1301, 1307, 1401.			
Oregon	No RFRA or Heightened Scrutiny: Meltebeke v. Bureau of Labor & Indus., 903 P.2d 351, 359–62 (Or. 1995).	Or. Rev. Stat. §§ 659A.403, 659A.421 (2015). See also The Oregon Equality Act of 2007, S. 2, 74th Leg, Reg. Sess. (Or. 2007).	Broad: Or. Rev. Stat. § 659A.001, 659A.400, 659A.006.	Or. Rev. Stat. § 659A.400 (2015).		
Pennsylvania	RFRA Only: Pa. Stat. tit. 71, § 2403, et seq. (2016).		Intermediate: 43 Pa. Stat. §§ 954, 955.			
Rhode Island	RFRA Only: R.I. Gen. Laws § 42–80.1-1, et seq. (West 2006).	R.I. Gen. Laws §§ 28–5-7, 34–37–2.2, 34–37–2.2 (2015). See also An Act Relating to Civil Rights, ch. 32, sec. 7, 1995 R.I. Pub. Laws 83	Narrow: R.I. Gen. Laws §§ 11–24-3, 28–5-6.	R.I. Gen. Laws § 11–24-3 (2015).	R.I. Gen. Laws Ann. § 15–3-6.1 (West 2013); R.I. Gen. Laws § 28–5-7 (2015).	R.I. Gen. Laws § 15–3-6.1 (2013).

State	State Review of Neutral Laws (Col. 1)	LGBT Employment & Housing Protections (Col. 2)	Scope of Public Accommodation Laws (Col. 3)	SOGI Public Accommodation Laws (Col. 4)	Specific (Surgical) Protections for Marriage (Col. 5)	Adoption Protections Passed Together with Other Legislation (Col. 6)	Stand-Alone Adoption Protections (Col. 7)
		(codified as R.I. GEN. LAWS Ann. § 11–24–2 (Supp. 2013)); An Act Relating to Civil Rights, H. 5920A, Gen. Assemb. (R.I. 2001).					
South Carolina	RFRA Only: S.C. CODE. ANN. § 1–32–10, et seq. (2015).		NARROW: S.C. CODE. ANN. §§ 1–13–30, 1–13–80, 45–9–10.				
South Dakota	No RFRA or Heightened Scrutiny		BROAD: S.D. CODIFIED LAWS § 20–13–1, 20–13–18, 20–13–22.				S.D. CODIFIED LAWS §§ 26-6-36 – 26-6-41 (2017).
Tennessee	RFRA & Heightened Scrutiny: TENN. CODE ANN. § 4-1-407 (West		BROAD: TENN. CODE ANN. §§ 4–21-102, 4-21-405.				

(continued)

	2015); State ex rel. Swann v. Pack, 527 S.W.2d 99, 107 (Tenn. 1975); Wolf v. Sundquist, 955 S.W.2d 626 (Tenn. App. 1997); State v. Loudon, 857 S.W.2d 878 (Tenn. Crim. App. 1993).				
Texas	RFRA Only: Tex. Civ. Prac. & Rem. Code Ann. § 110.001, et seq. (2016).				TEX. HUM. RES. CODE § 45.001 et seq. (2017).
Utah	No RFRA or Heightened Scrutiny	2015 Utah Laws Ch. 13. UTAH CODE §§ 34A-5-102 to -112; 57-21-2 to -7; 57-21-12 (2015).	BROAD: UTAH CODE §§ 13-7-2, 34A-5-102.		UTAH CODE §§ 17-20-4; 30-1-6; 34A-5-102 to -112; 57-21-2 to -7; 57-21-12; 63G-20-102 to -303 (2015).
Vermont	No RFRA or Heightened Scrutiny	VT. STAT. ANN. tit. 21, § 495(a) (2014); VT. STAT. ANN. tit. 9, § 4503 (2015). *See also* An Act Relating to Discrimination on	BROAD: VT. STAT. ANN. tit. 21, § 495d; VT. STAT. ANN. tit. 9, §§ 4501, 4502.	VT. STAT. ANN. tit. 9, § 4501(1) (2015).	VT. STAT. ANN. tit. 8 §§ 4501(b), tit. 9 § 4502(l), tit. 18, § 5144(b) (2013).

519

(continued)

State	State Review of Neutral Laws (Col. 1)	LGBT Employment & Housing Protections (Col. 2)	Scope of Public Accommodation Laws (Col. 3)	SOGI Public Accommodation Laws (Col. 4)	Specific (Surgical) Protections for Marriage (Col. 5)	Adoption Protections Passed Together with Other Legislation (Col. 6)	Stand-Alone Adoption Protections (Col. 7)
		the Basis of Sexual Orientation, No. 135, 1992 Vt. Acts & Resolves 26, 30–31 (codified as Vt. Stat. Ann. tit. 9, § 4502(a) (Supp. 2013)); S. 0051, 2007–2008 Leg., Reg. Sess. (Vt. 2007). *See also* 1 V.S.A § 144; S. 51, 2007 Vt. Laws 41 (legislative history).					
Virginia	RFRA Only: Va. Code Ann. § 57–2.02 (2015).						Va. Code Ann. § 63.2–1709.3 (2012).

Washington	Heightened Scrutiny Only: City of Woodinville v. Northshore United Church of Christ, 211 P.3d 406, 410 (Wash. 2009); Munns v. Martin, 930 P.2d 318 (Wash. 1997).	WASH. REV. CODE §§ 49.60.180, 49.60.222 (2015). *See also* An Act Relating to the Jurisdiction of the Washington Human Rights Commission, ch. 4, 2006 Wash. Sess. Laws 12 (codified as WASH. REV. CODE § 49.60.215 (2012)).	BROAD: WASH. REV. CODE § 49.60.040.	WASH. REV. CODE § 49.60.040(2) (2015).	WASH. REV. CODE § 26.04.010 (2013).
West Virginia	Heightened Scrutiny Only: *State v. Everly*, 146 S.E.2d 705 (W.Va. 1966) (applying a standard of review that is unclear, but inconsistent with *Employment Division v. Smith*).		BROAD: W. VA. CODE § 5-11-3.		

(continued)

(continued)

State	State Review of Neutral Laws (Col. 1)	LGBT Employment & Housing Protections (Col. 2)	Scope of Public Accommodation Laws (Col. 3)	SOGI Public Accommodation Laws (Col. 4)	Specific (Surgical) Protections for Marriage (Col. 5)	Adoption Protections Passed Together with Other Legislation (Col. 6)	Stand-Alone Adoption Protections (Col. 7)
Wisconsin	Heightened Scrutiny Only: Coulee Catholic Schs. v. Labor & Indus. Review Comm'n, 768 N.W.2d 868, 884–87 (Wis. 2009); State v. Miller, 549 N.W.2d 235 (Wis. 1996).	Only sexual orientation protection: WIS. STAT. §§ 106.50, 111.36 (2015). *See also* An Act to Amend 15.04 (1) (G), 16.765 (1) and (2) (a), 21.35, 66.39 (13), 66.395 (2m), 66.40 (2m), 66.405 (2m), 66.43 (2m), 66.431 (3) (E) 2, 66.432 (1) and (2), 66.433 (3) (a) and (C) 1. B and (9), 101.22 (1), (1m) (B), (2m) and (4m), 101.221 (1), 111.31 (1) to (3), 111.32 (5) (a), 111.70 (2), 111.81 (9)	INTERMEDIATE: WIS. STAT. §§ 106.52, 111.32, 111.337.	Only sexual orientation protection: WIS. STAT. § 106.52(1)(e)(1) (2015).			

(B), 111.85 (1),
227.033 (1), 230.01
(2), 230.18, 234.29
and 942.04 (1) (a) to
(C) and (3); And to
Create 111.32 (4s)
and (5) (I) of the
Statutes,
Relating to
Prohibiting
Discrimination
Based Upon Sexual
Orientation,
Assemb. 70, 1981
Assemb.
(Wis. 1982).

Wyoming

No RFRA or
Heightened
Scrutiny

NARROW:
WYO. STAT.
ANN. § 6-9-101,
27-9-105.

Subject Index

Laws Index

Cases Index

CPSIA information can be obtained
at www.ICGtesting.com
Printed in the USA
LVHW021642311219
642209LV00016B/347